The Old Firm's Proud Past

A Season By Season Account
Of
Mountain Ash Rugby Football Club's
Memorable Era of Rugby

1875 – 1940

Martyn Ham

Grosvenor House
Publishing Limited

All rights reserved
Copyright © Martyn Ham, 2024

The right of Martyn Ham to be identified as the author of this
work has been asserted in accordance with Section 78
of the Copyright, Designs and Patents Act 1988

The book cover picture is copyright to Martyn Ham

This book is published by
Grosvenor House Publishing Ltd
28-30 High Street, Guildford, Surrey, GU1 3EL.
www.grosvenorhousepublishing.co.uk

This book is sold subject to the conditions that it shall not, by way of
trade or otherwise, be lent, resold, hired out or otherwise circulated
without the author's or publisher's prior consent in any form of
binding or cover other than that in which it is published and
without a similar condition including this condition being
imposed on the subsequent purchaser.

A CIP record for this book
is available from the British Library

ISBN 978-1-80381-262-5

Contents

	Page
Acknowledgements	v
Forewords	vii
Things to Remember When Reading This Book	xi
In Memory	xiii
The Early Years: 1875-1890	1
The 1890s	14
The 1900s	81
A Summary Of The Seasons 1894-1910: The Old Firm's "First Golden Era"	177
The 1910s	179
The 1920s	232
A Summary Of The Seasons 1921-1925: The Old Firm's "Second Golden Era"	234
The 1930s	311
Club Records 1875 to 1940	398
Reflections On The Era 1875 to 1940	406

Acknowledgements

I would like to thank the following for helping me compile the information in this book:

- The Officers and committee of Mountain Ash Rugby Football Club for use of the team photographs included;
- Mr Tony Woolway of Media Wales Ltd for readily agreeing to the reproduction of the original match reports published in the Aberdare Leader, South Wales Daily News and Western Mail. These have greatly enhanced this historical account and helped put Mountain Ash RFC's history in a greater context;
- Anna Sander, Archivist of Balliol College, Oxford, Hills and Saunders Photography, of Maidenhead, and Gillman and Soame Photography of Kidlington, Oxford, for allowing the reproduction of the photograph of William Napier Bruce;
- Julia Ziomek, Helen Kerslake and the late Alan Edwards in Mountain Ash Library for their help with my various queries;
- Steven Graham and Judith George in Aberdare Library and Tony Davidson, Katrina Coopey and Stephen Cole in Cardiff Library for their retrieval of countless fiche reels of old Western Mail, South Wales Daily News and Aberdare Leader newspapers;
- Ruth Barclay, I.T. tutor, for her help in broadening my knowledge which helped me put this book together;
- The Welsh Rugby Union, in particular Peter Owens, for allowing the reproduction of the WRU Minutes contained in this book;
- Gareth Burridge, for his translation from English to French and vice versa when writing to the French Clubs mentioned in this account;
- Gwyn Prescott, author, for enlightening me to the South Wales Daily News and the information it contained about Mountain Ash RFC in the 1890s;
- Wayne Hankins, photographer and the proprietor of Mountain Ash Studio, who helped me reproduce some of the photographs in this book, and last but certainly not least,
- Wayne Pearson, for his skill in designing the book cover.
- All the staff at Grosvenor House Publishing – especially Becky Banning who has been my main point of contact – for doing such a superb job producing the three books I have written.

I am truly thankful to you all,

Martyn Ham,
Author

Forewords

I felt compelled to write this book after discovering Mountain Ash RFC's pre-World War II history. I had heard numerous stories about "The Old Firm's" past exploits and been told by many people how good the Club was back then. The only details I knew were picked up from various published articles from the Aberdare Leader and in the Centenary Season book titled, "The First 100 Years". About 20 plus years ago, I decided to take a look at some old editions of the Aberdare Leader of the early 1920s, which had been labelled a "golden era" for Mount. I soon discovered the reports of some great matches and victories for "The Old Firm", and it went on from there.

Over the last few years, I have made a concerted effort to conclude my research and have now "hit a wall" and feel I must now share this great past with you. In many ways, it is an unknown history, which is another reason why I just had to get it published. It is far too good a story not to be told. What surprised me about all this was the detail that I found in the seasons from 1894/95 on. My problem compiling this book was deciding what not to include rather than the other way round!

When you read it, please think of the people that contributed to the era – the players, the Club officials, the ancillaries, and those that helped fund the Club. This book is dedicated in many ways to them and it is also a contribution to the history of Mountain Ash RFC and to the town of Mountain Ash. I also hope it acts as an inspiration to the Club's future players to go out there and write their own chapter in this great Club's history.

As a proud Mountain Ash RFC supporter, it gives me great pleasure to take up no more of your time and let you get on with the book. I hope you enjoy touching the past as much as I did,

Martyn Ham,
Author & Lifelong Mount Fan,
July 2015

Additional Foreword: August 2022

This book was the first one I wrote about the history of Mountain Ash Rugby Club, but it was published on a smaller page. Since then, two further books have been published – "The Old Firm's Proud Past, Volume 2, 1940-1990", and "The Old Firm's Proud Past, Volume 3, 1990-2020", both on an A4 size page. I decided on the bigger page to display the greater number of photographs as well as I could.

After Volume 3 was released in December 2021, I decided that the trilogy of books about the great history of the Club should be given the same priority and published on the same size page, so I decided to go ahead and republish. These books put the Club's history on the record and will be with us forever, so it was important to me to bring the first book into line with the other two and put it on an A4 page.

The other thing that has happened since publication in 2015 is that a small amount of new information has come to light, and I have included this in this book. There are photographs of the 1906/07 Mount team, forward Tom Shepherd's Welsh Trial cap and Glamorgan League medals, the Glamorgan League Knock Cup won by the Old Firm in 1913/14, and of the unluckiest of players, Sid Congdon, who came so close to a coveted Welsh cap in the 1920s.

The era 1875-1940 is a special one for Mountain Ash RFC, with so many triumphs, great matches, and top players, including Internationals, playing for the Club. Hopefully, the bigger page in this book will help illustrate it in a better way. Hope you enjoy it,

Martyn Ham,
Author & Lifelong Mount Fan,
August 2022

On Behalf of Mountain Ash RFC

What a privilege! When I was asked by the author to write a foreword for this eagerly-anticipated and meticulously-written chronicle of our Club's very proud history, my initial thoughts were that I had to get this pitched absolutely perfect for it would be forever in the public domain. A difficult job…for a Miskin Boy!

The author, Martyn Ham, is a lifelong friend, indeed, another Miskin Boy! Under the scholarly tutelage of Peter Fahey, himself a former Mountain Ash player, Martyn became a fine outside half in his formative years, but sadly, illness cruelly curtailed his on-field endeavours before his teenage years set in. Nonetheless, throughout his life he has contributed so very richly to this Club of ours that he stands proudly alongside many of those mentioned in his book as a true ambassador, or should it be, a Black and Ambassador!

Every club has legends and every club has its characters; they are the people that help define a club's history. Players are the true currency, but all players will recognise the efforts of non-playing personnel who tirelessly, and often without so much as a grateful pat on the back, toil away to ensure a club thrives. Mountain Ash Rugby Football Club has had its fair share since its formation in 1875, and it's doubtless that many more will follow in the years to come. What is important to all who count themselves as Mount fans is that successive legacies are created for the history to grow richer by the year.

This volume – there are two more planned – serves to give the reader a flavour of the early years, up to the onset of the Second World War. There are match reports hailing the exploits of rugby heroes of a bygone age; heroes who are now being written about in a way they probably never knew was possible. It is, essentially, a book which will serve to expertly record and preserve our history, and, more poignantly, one which will reinforce our love for our Club,

Mark Bennett,
Honorary Secretary,
July 2015

Things to Remember When Reading This Book

Welsh Rugby Pre-World War II

For younger readers, and those reading this book in years to come, please bear in mind that until regional rugby was introduced into Wales at the start of the 2003/04 season, the players which formed the Welsh team for an International match were picked from the Clubs of Wales. From the game starting in Wales in the 1870s when the first Clubs were formed, up until the end of the 1989/90 season, Clubs were referred to as "first class" or "second class". Usually, International players were selected from "first class" Clubs. It was a term used by the media, as the Welsh Rugby Union officially saw all Clubs as equal. The strongest Clubs were referred to as "first class" and well deserved that label, but there were also other "first class" Clubs that were no better than the stronger so-called "second class" Clubs. Being described as a "first class" Club was much sought after during these years although there was never any criteria a Club had to meet to get it. However, the labels stuck with most Clubs for over 100 years until the start of the 1990/91 season when National League rugby was introduced to Wales.

Points Awarded

The following values have been used in this book :

Season	Try Points	Conversion	Penalty	Drop Goal
1890/91	1	2	2	3
1891/92	2	3	2	3
1892/93	2	3	3	4
1893/94 on	3	2	3	4

It was not entirely clear from certain match reports of the points each team scored. It was clear enough as to which team won the match or whether it was drawn, but the total points for each Club may be slightly out in some cases.

Fixtures Listed

All fixtures listed are known games played and come from published records, not hearsay. In all games, the Mountain Ash score is first, whether home, away or playing on a neutral ground.

Abbreviations Used

Within a season's fixtures, the following abbreviations have been used:

Try = T, Penalty = P, Conversion = C, Drop Goal = DG.

These appear after the name of the scorer, e.g. Jim Cummings T, 2P, 3C = one try, two penalties and 3 conversions scored by Jim Cummings.

(L) = Glamorgan League fixture,
(PL) = possible Glamorgan League fixture,
(F) = friendly game,
(PF) = possible friendly game.

Use of + Sign

Try totals will sometimes have a + sign after them. This signifies that more tries might have been scored in the match but it is unproven.

Spellings

There are inconsistencies in some cases in the spelling of names and Clubs which was sometimes the case in the newspapers looked at. For example, the correct spelling of the Mount outside half in the 1900s is Windham Jones, but it was mainly spelt Wyndham Jones; a wing from the 1890s, Llew Deare, was also spelt Llew Deere. There were some Club names that were spelt differently in these years. Examples are Treorky and Treorchy which are synonymous, as is Llanelly and Llanelli. Some newspaper copies were very faint and some spellings were incorrect because of this. My apologies to any family whose ancestor's name has been wrongly spelt.

Date of Matches

The date associated with a match is usually the date of the newspaper report. This means that any game played on a Saturday usually had the date of the game as the Monday following. If a game was played in midweek, the date is usually the day after when the match report was published. Some dates used, however, are the exact dates,

Martyn Ham,
Author

In memory of all those,
both on and off the field of play,
who contributed to this era of rugby
for
Mountain Ash Rugby Football Club,
"the Old Firm"

Mountain Ash Rugby Football Club
"The Old Firm"

The Early Years
1875-1890

The Club's Origins

There have been several articles written about the early years of Mountain Ash Rugby Football Club but the one used in this account is based on the memoirs written by former Secretary Mr Enoch Watkins in the Aberdare Leader in June 1948. Mr Watkins played for the Club from 1916 to 1921 and was a former Secretary at various times from the 1920s until his passing in December 1969.

In the two week historical account which detailed the Club's history from 1876 to 1948, he wrote the following, "For the information concerning the origin and early years of the Club, I am indebted to the late Mr Ben Tiley. In 1921, thinking that this vital information would be lost for all time with the passing of Mr Tiley, I prevailed upon him to write the early history for me, and I have preserved it in my desk for all these years." Ben Tiley played for Mountain Ash RFC in its very early years, captaining the Club for 12 consecutive seasons from 1882 to 1894. In his account of the early years of the Club, he says, "The two gentlemen who first introduced rugby football to Mountain Ash were the Hon. W. Bruce, second son of the first Lord Aberdare, and Mr Ted Williams, son of Mr Roger Williams, Capcoch Inn, and brother of Dr R. Llewellyn Williams, retired Minister of Health, Mountain Ash U.D.C. The former played the game at Oxford University and the latter in the West Mon. Grammar School. When home on holiday, they would practice together on the ground now known as Peace Park, and young men and boys who were taking a walk round the field, joined in the game. Only local sides took part and a very elementary knowledge of the rules was obtained in these games."

William Napier Bruce

William Napier Bruce was born on 18 January 1858 at Duffryn in Aberdare. He was the second son of the first Lord Aberdare, Henry Austin Bruce. He was educated at Harrow, where he played football, and progressed to Balliol College, Oxford, where he shone as a runner, representing Oxford against Cambridge in the ¼ mile in 1877, 1879 and 1880. He read Classics and was called to the Bar in 1883. He was a man of many talents with his career covering law and education, and he was also an academic, having an interest in poetry and producing several pieces of literary work. During his career, he was described as one of the most able men in the Civil Service. In recognition of his work, he was made a member of the Most Honourable Order of the Bath in 1905, and in 1935 was made a member of the Order of the Companions of Honour. He passed away at the age of 78 on 20 March 1936 in Bath.

Ted Williams

Little is known about Ted Williams other than as well as being a prominent player, he was the first ever Mountain Ash RFC captain and he did the job up to 1879.

The Formation of Mountain Ash RFC

Mr Watkins continued, "In 1876, a meeting was called at the Mountain Ash Inn, when all those interested in rugby football were invited to attend. About 30 attended and a Club was formed. That was really the meeting that started the Old Firm on its journey. In the first half of the season, no matches were played, but practice games took place on Saturday afternoons. The captain was Mr Ted Williams, already referred to, and 16 matches were played in the second part of the season, 1876/77. The Clubs played were Cardiff Harlequins, Treherbert, Cross Keys and Aberdare Crusaders, four games being played between each Club." The piece written in the South Wales Echo in January 1958 goes even further than what has just been said and states the "first fixture was against Cardiff Harlequins". Whether this is factually correct is unknown but there must have been grounds for it to be said. In the details below of the 1880s, there are games against all the sides mentioned although the only game against a team from Cross Keys was with Cross Keys Wanderers. At this time, rugby in Wales was a comparatively new sport and in its infancy – Neath and Cardigan, which are the two oldest Clubs, were formed in 1871 – with Clubs having nothing like the profile they had later on.

The Club's Players, Captains & Secretary

Mr Watkins went on to say "The first Secretary was Mr W. Mills and prominent players were Ted Williams, J. Williams, H. Brooks, T. Mortimer and E. Brooks. Ted Williams again captained the side in 1877/78 and 1878/79. The Club played on a field near Newtown Bridge. Teams were now springing up all through the Rhondda with Penygraig and Treherbert most prominent. Pontypridd were met for the first time in 1880/81. The fixtures in those days were generally arranged either a week before being played or during the week in which the game was played. Captain in 1881/82 was a very good all round athlete named W. Harding and prominent players were G. McPherson, H. Meers, I. Jones, A. Sharp. H. Brooks, G. Ponting, J. Curnow, W. Bishop, J. Williams, J. Evans and Ben Tiley. Ben Tiley was elected captain in 1882/83 and for the next 12 seasons remained captain, and became known as the father of the Old Firm. He built up one of the finest sides in Welsh Rugby and the Club really started to climb the ladder of fame under his long captaincy."

<u>Club Captains</u>
<u>1875-1890</u>

1875-1879	Ted Williams
1879-1880	Bill Bishop
1880-1881	Jack Williams
1881-1882	W. Harding
1882-1890	Ben Tiley

Welsh Rugby in General

As new Clubs came into being, the South Wales Football Union was formed in 1878 in an attempt to regulate and better organise the game. This was superseded by the Welsh Football Union at the start of the 1880s – which was the forerunner to today's Welsh Rugby Union – after a meeting was held at the Castle Hotel in Neath. The Clubs that attended this meeting were listed as Swansea, Pontypool, Newport, Merthyr, Llanelli, Bangor, Brecon, Cardiff, Lampeter, Llandovery and Llandeilo RFCs. Why Clubs that were in existence did not attend such as Mountain Ash is unknown. Although the meeting was held in Neath, even Neath RFC did not attend. In 1934, this body became known officially as the Welsh Rugby Union.

As well as Enoch Watkins' written account of these early years, there is limited information available about the 1880s. Below is what was published in the South Wales Daily News, which is a newspaper that no longer exists but covered a lot of rugby in Wales as the game developed in the 1880s and especially in the 1890s.

The Years 1875-1890
Season by Season

Season 1880/81

There were very few rugby reports published in the South Wales Daily News outside a few established teams, but there was one involving Mountain Ash RFC and that is the one shown below. At the time of writing, it is the oldest known game on record.

18 October 1880

<u>Mountain Ash v Dare (Aberdare)</u>

> **FOOTBALL.**
> DARE (ABERDARE) v. MOUNTAIN ASH.—A match was played between the above clubs on Thursday afternoon, on the ground of the latter, and was easily won by the former by three goals, one poster, four tries, and four touches down in self-defence to *nil*.

Season 1881/82

There were not that many rugby reports published by the South Wales Daily News, but of those that were, none were for Mountain Ash RFC.

Season 1882/83

The popularity of rugby was emphasised in the South Wales Daily News' report of this first known Mount v Llwynypia game.

5 March 1883

<u>Llwynypia v Mountain Ash</u>
<u>South Wales Daily News</u>

> LLWYNPIA v. MOUNTAIN ASH. — This match was played on the ground of the former on Thursday last in the presence of some hundreds of spectators, resulting in a decisive victory for the home team by two tries and four touches down to nil. The tries were obtained by R. J. Cook and M. W. Rees. The Llwynpia team were composed of the following men:—T. Hornsby, back; R. J. Cook and M. W. Rees, three-quarter backs; J. Roderick, E. Rees, and T. Jones, half backs; B. Phillips, J. Cox, D. Rees, G. Tobias, J. Treharne, T. Davies, S. Cording, H. Jones, and T. M. Rees, forwards.

Season 1883/84

There was no information about Mountain Ash RFC games in the South Wales Daily News.

Season 1884/85

Treherbert v Mountain Ash

The Old Firm's first known game with Treherbert was published in the South Wales Daily News on 1 December 1884. The text in the newspaper, which was very faint, said, "A match was played between the above teams on Saturday on the ground of the former, ended in a victory for Treherbert by 1 goal (disputed), 2 tries and several touch downs to nil." There is also reference to the 1884/85 season in the Aberdare Leader's match report of the Old Firm's 6-0 win at Penygraig in 1902/03, the report commenting, "We thought that since the Old Firm had suffered defeat on Saturday last at Treherbert, they could not possibly expect to pull it off with a team at whose hands they had suffered defeat from home for the last eighteen years." Eighteen years prior to 1902/03 would have been 1884/85.

Season 1885/86

This season was a season of firsts in reporting terms. There was a first report of a Club Annual General Meeting, there were the first reports of matches against Pontypridd and Penygraig, there were the first named Mount teams and there was a first report of a Mountain Ash 2nd XV game. Below are the details the South Wales Daily News published.

1st XV Fixtures

Opponents	Date	Venue	Scorers/Comments
Pontypridd	26 Oct 1885	Home	Mountain Ash Win. Ben Tiley T.
Cambrian Aberdare	31 Oct 1885	Home	Mountain Ash Win.
Penygraig	9 Nov 1885	Away	Draw.
Aberdare Crusaders	9 Feb 1886	Home	Mountain Ash Win.
Cardiff Harlequins	16 Mar 1886	Home	Mountain Ash Loss.
Aberdare Crusaders	5 Apr 1886	Away	Mountain Ash Win.
Penarth	24 Apr 1886	Away	Mountain Ash Loss.

2nd XV Fixtures

Opponents	Date	Venue	Scorers/Comments
Aberdare Cambrian 2nd XV	27 Nov 1885	Away	Mountain Ash Loss.

Match Reports & Other Publications

21 September 1885

The South Wales Daily News reported the Annual General Meeting of Mountain Ash RFC, naming J. Williams as Captain. Whether this referred to 1st XV captain is unknown as it contradicts the account written by Enoch Watkins in June 1948 which was based on Ben Tiley's written history of the early years of the Club.

> MOUNTAIN ASH CLUB.—The annual meeting of the above club was held on Friday, at the Crosselly Inn, when the following officers were elected for the ensuing year:—Captain, Mr J. Williams; vice-captain, Mr J. Long; treasurer, Mr W. Edwards; secretary, Mr G. Ponting; committee, Messrs W. Hardin, H. Brooks, G. MacPherson, W. Bishop, F. Brooks, C. Manfield, and J. Evans.
> SKEWEN CLUB.—The first meeting of the coming season of the above club was held at the Rock and

26 October 1885

Mountain Ash v Pontypridd

Mount's first recorded game against Pontypridd resulted in a win, legendary player and Old Firm captain, Ben Tiley, scoring a try.

South Wales Daily News

> MOUNTAIN ASH v PONTYPRIDD.— This match was played at Mountain Ash on Saturday, and after a well contested game, ended in a victory for the home team by one try and one touchdown to a try (disputed) and ond touchdown. The try for Mountain Ash was gained by B. Tiley, from a magnificent run from the 25 flag. For Mountain Ash J. Williams played a good game, his running and collaring being splendid.
> ST. MARY'S V. LOUDOUN WESLEYANS.—A match was played in Sophia Gardens between Loudoun

31 October 1885

Mountain Ash v Cambrian Aberdare
South Wales Daily News

> MOUNTAIN ASH v. CAMBRIAN ABERDARE.—A match between the above clubs was played at Mountain Ash, on Thursday, and after a very pleasant game ended in a victory for the home team, althought they put but a very weak team on the field. Score:—Mountain Ash, one try and two touches down; Aberdare, one touch in goal.
> LLANDOVERY SCHOOL v. TOWN.—A match between the above teams was played on the Town ground, on

9 November 1885

Penygraig v Mountain Ash

This game, played at Penygraig, ended in a draw. The South Wales Daily News' report also published the Old Firm's XV that day, which is the earliest reported.

> PENYGRAIG V. MOUNTAIN ASH.—This match was played at Penygraig on Saturday, and resulted in a draw, neither side gaining any definite point. The visitors were much heavier than the home team, who played a good game, considering that this is their first season; their passing also was very good. Teams:— *Penygraig*:—T. Royall, back; R. J. Cooke, R. Cording, D. Llewellyn, and M. W. Rees (captain), three-quarter backs; J. Randall and T. Jones, half backs; William Stubborn, T. Foster, T. Jones, R. Davies, D. Lloyd, D. Williams, J. Evans, and R. Lewis, forwards. *Mountain Ash*:—W. Harding, back; J. Williams (captain), B. Tiley, J. Long, and T. Jenkins, three-quarter backs; G. Ponting and J. Powell, half backs; J. Evans, G. Macpherson, J. Maxworthy, W. Bishop, J. Hays, J. Wheeler, F. Brooks, and H. Brooks, forwards.
>
> OXFORD UNIVERSITY V. R. I. E. C., COOPER'S HILL.—Thousands assembled in the parks to witness this

27 November 1885

Aberdare Cambrian 2nd XV v Mountain Ash 2nd XV
Mountain Ash Loss

The South Wales Daily News reported the Mount XV, which lists 6 backs and 9 forwards, for this game as follows:

Mount Team: Back, C. Hughes; 3/4s, B. Harding, H. Eynon, D. Williams; half backs, J. Bowles, H. Mayors; forwards, P. Hiddy, J. Hayes, Mayors, W. Holly, J. Smith, B. Allen, S. Rees, S. Branch, J. Whitmarsh.

9 February 1886

Mountain Ash v Aberdare Crusaders
South Wales Daily News

> ABERDARE CRUSADERS V. MOUNTAIN ASH.—This match was played at Mountain Ash on Saturday last, before an immense crowd of spectators. The result was a win for the home team by one goal, two tries and one touch-down to three touches down.

16 March 1886

Mountain Ash v Cardiff Harlequins

The South Wales Daily News reported, "Played at Mountain Ash on Saturday in fine weather. A hard game throughout, the home forwards working like horses, but the visitors' backs won the game for them. James ran in and obtained 2 tries in brilliant style, getting behind the posts, from which Erskine kicked goals. The home team obtained 2 tries which were disputed, the ball having been picked out of a scrummage, and the kick for goal was taken under the posts. The game ended in a win for the Harlequins by 2 goals to 1 goal and 1 try (disputed)."

Season 1886/87

There were many local teams playing rugby during this era judging on the amount of results starting to be published. Some of Mountain Ash RFC's results are below.

1st XV Fixtures

Opponents	Date	Venue	Scorers/Comments
Abercarn	11 Oct 1886	Home	Match drawn in favour of Mountain Ash!
Cross Keys Wanderers	8 Nov 1886	Away	Match drawn.
Cardiff United	15 Nov 1886	Home	Mountain Ash Win. Ben Tiley T, W. Bishop T.
Cardiff United	6 Dec 1886	Away	Mountain Ash Win.
Cathays	31 Jan 1887	Home	Mountain Ash Win. J. Evans T, W. Harding C.
Penygraig	14 Feb 1887	Home	Two games played - Mountain Ash Win & Drawn game.

2nd XV Fixtures

Opponents	Date	Venue	Scorers/Comments
Duffryn Rangers	22 Nov 1886	Home	Mountain Ash Win.
Penarth	29 Nov 1886	Away	Mountain Ash Loss.
Ely Rovers 2nds	24 Jan 1887	Away	Mountain Ash Win.

Match Reports & Other Publications

8 November 1886

Cross Keys Wanderers v Mountain Ash
South Wales Daily News

> MOUNTAIN ASH v. CROSS KEYS WANDERERS.—Played on the ground of the latter, and ended in a draw. The superiority of the visitors was shown ten minutes after the start, when they succeeded in scoring two tries, which were disallowed. For the visitors J. Williams, B. Tiley, and C. Hughes played well. Their passing quite baffled the Cross Keys players. The forwards played a good game.
>
> CANTON CRUSADERS v. LONGCROSS.—Played on the Recreation Grounds, and resulted in a victory for Canton by two tries, obtained by Hornblow and Johnson, to three touches down.
>
> ABERTILLERY v. EBBW WANDERERS.—Resulted as follows:—Abertillery, one try and four minors to one disputed try.

15 November 1886

<u>Mountain Ash v Cardiff United</u>
<u>South Wales Daily News</u>

> MOUNTAIN ASH V. CARDIFF UNITED.—Played at Mountain Ash, and ended in a victory for the home team by two tries and four minors to nil. The play of both sides was excellent, and at times the passing was neat. The tries were obtained by B. Tiley and W. Bishop.
> LLWYNYPIA V. YSTRAD.—Played at Ystrad, Llwynypia winning by two tries and one minor to two minors. The tries were obtained by J. Cording and M. Rees.

6 December 1886

<u>Cardiff United v Mountain Ash</u>
<u>South Wales Daily News</u>

> MOUNTAIN ASH V. CARDIFF UNITED. — Played on Saturday, December 4th, in the Sophia Gardens, and ended in a win for Mountain Ash by a goal (from a free kick), a try, and 6 minors to a try and one minor.
> CHRIST COLLEGE, BRECON, V. LLANDOVERY SCHOOL.—This match was played at Brecon on Saturday, and resulted in a draw, each side obtaining a try.

Season 1887/88

Although there were no trophies and League points on offer in the 1880s, games were still competitive as the match with Wattstown turned out to be. The game's popularity was growing locally and this was mentioned in Mount's game at Treforest.

<u>1st XV Fixtures</u>

Opponents	Date	Venue	Scorers/Comments
Treforest	10 Oct 1887	Home	Match Drawn.
Wattstown	24 Oct 1887	Home	Match Drawn or Mountain Ash Loss.

Match Reports & Other Publications

10 October 1887

<u>Mountain Ash v Treforest</u>
<u>South Wales Daily News</u>

> drawn game slightly in favour of the home team, by three minors to two minors.
> TREFOREST V. MOUNTAIN ASH.—Played at Mountain Ash, resulting in a draw. This match was played in the presence of a goodly number of spectators.
> TREFOREST 2ND V. RHYDYFELIN.—Played at Treforest, resulting in a win for the home team by one goal,

24 October 1887

<u>Mountain Ash v Wattstown</u>
<u>South Wales Daily News</u>

> MOUNTAIN ASH V. WATTSTOWN.—Played on the ground of the former, and, after a deal of rough play, ended in a draw. The game finished before time owing to disputes. According to another report furnished us the game was won by Wattstown, who scored 1 try, a disputed try, and 2 minors to 1 minor.
> NEWPORT JUNIORS V. MAINDEE STARS.—Played at Maindee, resulting in a win for Newport Juniors by 4

Season 1888/89

From the limited information, Mount won 6 and drew 1 of the 7 matches reported in the South Wales Daily News. The details are below:

1st XV Fixtures

Opponents	Date	Venue	Scorers/Comments
Aberdare Crusaders	15 Oct 1888	Unknown	Mountain Ash Win.
Treforest	26 Nov 1888	Away	Drawn game.
Pentre	3 Dec 1888	Home	Mountain Ash Win.
Splott Rovers	10 Dec 1888	Away	Mountain Ash Win.
Mardy	21 Jan 1889	Unknown	Mountain Ash Win.
Maritime (Pontypridd)	28 Jan 1889	Home	Mountain Ash Win.
Maritime (Pontypridd)	1 Apr 1889	Away	Mountain Ash Win.

"A" XV Fixtures

Opponents	Date	Venue	Scorers/Comments
Pontypridd Juniors	19 Nov 1888	Home	Mountain Ash Win.

Match Reports & Other Publications

28 January 1889

<u>Mountain Ash v Maritime (Pontypridd)</u>
<u>South Wales Daily News</u>

> 4 minors, to 1 minor.
> MOUNTAIN ASH V. MARITIME (PONTYPRIDD).—A match played between these teams on the Cwmcynon Meadow ended in a win for Mountain Ash by 4 goals, 1 try, 5 minors, to 1 minor.
> TONDU V. TAIBACH HARLEQUINS.—Played on the ground of the latter, and resulted in a win for the

Season 1889/90

This seemed to be a very good season for the Old Firm with both the 1st and 2nd XVs winning all the known games played. The 1st XV had two notable "doubles" over Pontypool and Abercarn.

1st XV Fixtures

Opponents	Date	Venue	Scorers/Comments
Pentre	7 Oct 1889	Home	Mountain Ash Win. Evans T, Mears T, Ponting T.
Pontypool	14 Oct 1889	Away	Mountain Ash Win. T. Bishop T, J. Curnow T, B. Tiley P.
Next XVIII	28 Oct 1889	Home	Mountain Ash Win.
Abercarn	9 Dec 1889	Home	Mountain Ash Win.
Maindy	16 Dec 1889	Home	Mountain Ash Win.
Pontypool	30 Dec 1889	Home	Mountain Ash Win.
Abercarn	17 Feb 1890	Away	Mountain Ash Win.

2nd XV Fixtures

Opponents	Date	Venue	Scorers/Comments
Cilfynydd	14 Oct 1889	Home	Mountain Ash Win.
Miskin Utd	18 Nov 1889	Home	Mountain Ash Win.
Abercarn 2nd XV	24 Mar 1890	Home	Mountain Ash Win.

Match Reports & Other Publications

14 October 1889

<u>Pontypool v Mountain Ash</u>
<u>Mountain Ash 2nd XV v Cilfynydd</u>
<u>South Wales Daily News</u>

...Island, Usk, between the above teams, and ended in a win for Sudbrook by 1 goal and 2 tries to nil.

MOUNTAIN ASH V. PONTYPOOL.—Played on the Polo Grounds, Pontypool, and after a very pleasant game ended in a win for the visitors by 2 goals, 1 try, 1 minor to 1 goal and 2 minors. The try-getters were T. Bishop and J. Curnow. B. Tiley kicked a goal from a free.

MOUNTAIN ASH 2ND V. CILFYNYDD.—A match was played at Mountain Ash between the above teams, and after a very pleasant game ended in a win for the home team by 3 tries to nil.

DOWLAIS V. BLAINA.—Played at Dowlais, and resulted in a victory for the visitors. Result: Dowlais. 1

18 November 1889

Mountain Ash 2nd XV v Miskin United
South Wales Daily News

> **MARITIME (PONTYPRIDD) "A" v. TON RANGERS.**—Played at Pontypridd, and resulted in a win for the home team by 1 goal and 4 minors to 1 try.
>
> **MOUNTAIN ASH 2ND v. MISKIN UNITED.**—Played at Mountain Ash on Saturday, and ended in a win for Mountain Ash by 1 goal, 3 tries, and 2 minors to 1 try and 1 minor.
>
> **MELINGRIFFITH v. RADYR ROVERS.**—Played at Radyr, and, after a fast game, ended in a victory for the visitors by 2 tries, 3 minors to 1 try, 2 minors.

30 December 1889

Mountain Ash v Pontypool

> **MOUNTAIN ASH v. PONTYPOOL.**—Played at Mountain Ash. The game only lasted 30 minutes owing to a late start, the home team scoring 1 goal, 2 tries, and 2 minors to nil.
>
> **MACKINTOSH ROVERS, CARDIFF v. LLANELLY "A" TAAM.**—This match was to have been played at Llanelly

27 January 1890

The following article which appeared in the South Wales Daily News shows even at this very early stage of rugby union's development in Wales, the "big four" had already established themselves as the top Clubs in Wales:

THE SEASON'S MATCHES.

The following will give the positions of the four chief clubs in South Wales up to Saturday last for all the matches played.

	Played	Won	Lost	Drn	For G.	For T.	Agst. G.	Agst. T.
Swansea	20	16	0	4	37	24	4	8
Newport	21	14	4	3	25	41	5	11
Cardiff	23	14	6	3	22	26	14	9
Llanelly	18	7	7	4	7	26	7	10

Summary of All Known 1st XV Games 1875-1889/90

P	W	D	L	Result Unknown	For	Against	Tries Scored	Win Rate %
33	21	6	5	1	Unknown	Unknown	Unknown	75.00

A Selection of the Old Firm's Results

1875 to 1889/90

Matches v Llwynypia

Season	Venue	Result	P	W	D	L
1882/83	Away	MA Loss	1	0	0	1

Matches v Treherbert

Season	Venue	Result	P	W	D	L
1884/85	Away	MA Loss	1	0	0	1

Matches v Pontypridd

Season	Venue	Result	P	W	D	L
1885/86	Home	MA Win	1	1	0	0

Matches v Penygraig

Season	Venue	Result	P	W	D	L
1885/86	Away	Drawn game	1	0	1	0
1886/87	Home	MA Win	2	1	1	0
1886/87	Home	Drawn game	3	1	2	0

Matches v Penarth

Season	Venue	Result	P	W	D	L
1885/86	Away	MA Loss	1	0	0	1

Matches v Pontypool

Season	Venue	Result	P	W	D	L
1889/90	Away	MA Win	1	1	0	0
1889/90	Home	MA Win	2	2	0	0

And so the 1880s ended, with Mountain Ash RFC a local, town team like so many others in Wales. However, by the end of the 1890s, rugby had been transformed and the Club's profile and standing had moved up several levels.

Mountain Ash Rugby Football Club
"The Old Firm"

The 1890s

The Playing Record of the 1890s

Below are the known seasonal playing records of the 1890s:

Season	P	W	D	L	For	Against	Tries Scored	%
1890/91	5	3	0	2	32	30	18	60.00
1891/92	1	1	0	0	2	0	1	100.00
1892/93	14	7	4	3	55+	44+	13+	64.29
1893/94	17	8	4	5	66	59	16	58.82
1894/95	22	17	3	2	226+	39+	58+	84.09
1895/96	31	26	2	3	278+	63+	74+	87.10
1896/97	37	27	5	5	528	84	131+	79.73
1897/98	37	20	1	16	349	216	95	55.41
1898/99	27	13	4	10	197	103	53	55.56
1899/1900	34	24	3	7	351	124	93+	75.00
Total for 1890s	225	146	26	53	2084+	762+	552+	70.67

The Old Firm's Fixtures During the Decade

The strength of the Club's fixtures built as the decade progressed, taking a definite upturn when League rugby started in 1894/95. Prior to this season, fixtures were played against Penarth, which was regarded as a "first class" Club, and local Clubs such as Penygraig, Pontypridd, Llwynypia, Troedyrhiw, Treherbert and Wattstown, all of which were not. Mount also played Clubs from further afield such as Pontardawe, Machen, Morriston, Crumlin, Ebbw Vale and Pontymoile. As well as Glamorgan League fixtures from 1894/95 on, fixtures started to be arranged with such Clubs as Aberavon, Neath, Bridgend, Llanelly, Maesteg and Ebbw Vale. In addition to these, there were regular excursions into England to play Bridgwater & Albion and Plymouth, with games also being played against Cinderford, Portsmouth and Devonport Albion in the south, and Leicester and Northampton in the Midlands.

Welsh Rugby Union Status

Mountain Ash RFC became a member of the Welsh Football Union – the equivalent of the Welsh Rugby Union today – in 1892/93, on Saturday 15 April 1893 to be exact, at a meeting of the Union at the Angel Hotel in Cardiff. Coincidentally or not, the Club's fixtures certainly went up a level after this, although this may also have been due to the introduction of the Rhondda, Merthyr and Aberdare Valley League in 1894/95 – renamed the Glamorgan League in 1895/96 – which was where the Old Firm started making a name for themselves.

Club Captains

The following players captained the Old Firm in the 1890s:

1890-1894	Ben Tiley
1894-1895	Matt Price
1895-1896	E. "Ned" Jenkins
1896-1897	Bert Allen
1897-1898	Fred Millar
1898-1899	Watcyn Phillips
1899-1900	Llew Deare

Ben Tiley, who first captained the Club in 1882, was the stand-out player of this generation, captaining the Club for 12 seasons in succession. Fred Millar was a forward and another significant player, being capped 7 times by Wales between 1896 and 1901. Scrum half Watcyn Phillips and try scoring wing, Llew Deare, were also influential players during this era, scoring plenty of points for the Club. Matt Price and Bert Allen were hard working forwards, and "Ned" Jenkins a talented centre.

The Start of Tournament Rugby

Season 1894/95 was the inaugural year of League rugby for Mountain Ash RFC and the other premier valley Clubs as the Rhondda, Merthyr & Aberdare League was formed. In the first season of the competition, the Old Firm and Llwynypia proved the strongest Clubs, both finishing with the same number of points at the top of the table. A play-off was held in Pontypridd in May 1895, the game ending in controversy after Mount scored a converted try to equal the scores at 8-8, but Llwynypia protesting to the referee that the try had been scored from a throw-in that should have been theirs but had been taken by Mountain Ash. The referee changed his mind and ruled out the try he had awarded the Old Firm, which gave Llwynypia victory – or so they thought. In the off season, the Rhondda, Merthyr & Aberdare League committee decided that the game should be replayed and so it was on 31 October 1895, which was the following season, 1895/96. Another close game took place, Llwynypia scoring in the closing minutes to win the game, 8-7.

The Start of a Golden Era of Rugby

As well as the start of League rugby, the season 1894/95 was also the start of an exceptional era of rugby for the Club – the "First Golden Era" – which also took in the following decade and covered a remarkable 16 seasons overall.

The Glamorgan League

In 1895/96, the Rhondda, Merthyr & Aberdare League was renamed the Glamorgan League and quickly became *the* trophy to win for the premier valley Clubs involved in it. After coming close in 1894/95, the Old Firm made no mistake second time round and finished top of the table to be crowned Glamorgan League champions for a first time in 1895/96.

International Recognition

Forward Frank Mills, who played for Mountain Ash, Swansea and Cardiff at various times during his International career, became Mountain Ash's first player to be capped by Wales when he played against England in 1891/92. He went on to gain 13 Caps between 1892 and 1896, and played in the wins over England, Ireland and Scotland in 1892/93 which gave Wales a first Triple Crown. Another forward, Fred Millar, was the first player to be capped by Wales while playing for the Club when he played against Ireland in 1895/96. He was capped a further 6 times in 1900 and 1901 and was a member of the Wales team that won the Triple Crown for a second time in 1899/1900.

On the Field of Play

The Old Firm's fixture list became far stronger and of a higher profile from 1894/95 on, with some of the strongest Clubs in Wales and England beaten. There were some exceptional seasons in the 1890s such as 1894/95, 1895/96, 1896/97 and 1899/1900, when at least three-quarters of the games played were won. During these seasons, there were wins over Neath, Aberavon, Llwynypia, Pontypridd, Ebbw Vale, Bridgend, Treorky and Tredegar, and also wins over English opposition in the form of Leicester, Bridgwater and Albion, Plymouth and Hartlepool Rovers. The Club also run a 2nd XV with games being played against local Clubs.

Onwards and Upwards

In October 1892, the Club spent £200 – a large sum in the 1890s – on a new ground in Newtown, called the Recreation Ground, and opened it with a game against "first class" Swansea RFC led by former player and Welsh International, Frank Mills.

The Advent of Professional Rugby

In August 1895 there was a split in the rugby fraternity when 21 rugby union Clubs formed the Northern Rugby Football Union which later became known as the Rugby Football League. The break happened due to Clubs in predominantly working-class areas of northern England advocating players should be compensated for time taken off work as a result of playing rugby. With the new organisation allowing payment to players, quite a number of Old Firm players went North from the mid 1890s on.

The Club's Officers

There is not a complete record of the Club's Officers in the 1890s, but what is known is that Mr J.T. Curnow was Club Secretary in 1890/91. Harry Hale did the job in 1892/93 and again from 1895 to 1897. He was succeeded by Mr S. Shipton in 1897/98, with prolific try scoring wing, Llew Deere, doing the job in 1898/99, and Mr Hale returning as Secretary for a third term in 1899/1900. Lord Aberdare was President of the Club in 1892/93.

The 1890s
Season by Season

Season 1890/91

There is little information about this season but what is known is that the Old Firm played 5 games, won 3 and lost 2. Wins were registered against Cwmbran, Pontnewynydd and Phoenix Wanderers, which was a Club based in Pontypool, and the two defeats came at the hands of Crumlin and Welsh Union Club, Penarth. It would appear that the Club also run a 2nd XV due to a reported game being a narrow win over Abercarn "A" and a possible win over Merthyr 2nd XV. There were plenty of teams at all levels of Welsh rugby judging by the number of results reported in the South Wales Daily News. As a matter of interest, there were two results reported for Cefnpennar. The first was a 0-0 draw at home to Bonvilston Stars and the second, versus Crumlin, was another home draw, this time 2 tries all. Penrhiwceiber also had a team, losing by 4 goals and 5 tries to nil to a team called the "Aberdare Young Men's Friendly Society" in a game played at the Ynys Meadow....

Fixtures 1890/91

Opponents	Date	Venue	Score	Tries	Scorers/Comments
Penarth	13 Oct 1890	Away	0-26	0	No scorers.
Cwmbran	20 Oct 1890	Home	4-0	4	Scorers unknown.
Phoenix Wands	27 Oct 1890	Away	15-0	5	Scorers unknown.
Pontnewynydd	1 Dec 1890	Home	12-0	8	J. Sullivan 4T, J. Hoskins 2T, J. Parfitt T, T. Hale T, AN Other 2C.
Crumlin	16 Feb 1891	Away	1-4	1	Scorers unknown.

Summary of Playing Record

P	W	D	L	For	Against	Tries Scored	Win Rate %
5	3	0	2	32	30	18	60.00

Match Reports and Publications

13 October 1890

<u>Penarth 26 Mountain Ash 0</u>

Mount Team: Back, Netherway; 3/4s, Curnow, Parfitt, Mears, Hoskins; half backs, Ponting and Robins; forwards, Grant, Allen Capt, Eddy, Jones, Hill, Edmunds, Watts, Francis.

The Western Mail reported, "The Mountain Ash forwards were pretty nearly as strong as their opponents but they were unable to heel out and thus their halves were placed at a disadvantage."

Season 1891/92

<u>Forward Frank Mills Plays For Wales</u>

Once again, there was limited information available about this season. There was only one match reported in the South Wales Daily News and it was the Old Firm's one try to nil win at Pontypridd. The season also saw former Mount forward, Frank Mills, who had moved on and was playing for Swansea at the time, become the first player who had played for Mountain Ash RFC to play for Wales when he gained the first of his 13 caps against England at Blackheath on 2nd January 1892. Later in the season he gained two more caps against Scotland and Ireland. Cefnpennar also played two known games, winning 6-3 at home against Crumlin, but losing 6-0 at Troedyrhiw.

Fixtures 1891/92

Opponents	Date	Venue	Score	Tries	Scorers/Comments
Pontypridd	23 Nov 1891	Away	2-0	1	Parfitt T.

Match Reports and Publications

23 November 1891

<u>Pontypridd 0 Mountain Ash 2</u>

PONTYPRIDD v. MOUNTAIN ASH.—Played at the Taff Vale Park, the visitors being a team selected for the occasion by Ben Tiley. Several of the best players of the home team were absent. The game was fast throughout. The Mountain Ash men had the advantage in the scrums, and put in some excellent sprinting. In the first half Parfit obtained an excellent try for the visitors, but the attempt to convert by Tiley was a failure, the leather striking the posts. Subsequently Mountain Ash secured two minors, and the homesters one minor, the game ending in a win for Mountain Ash by 1 try, 2 minors to 1 minor for Pontypridd.

Frank Mills
Mountain Ash, Swansea and Cardiff
13 Welsh Caps
1892-1895 v Scotland & Ireland, 1892-1896 v England

Above, forward Frank Mills, who stands in the back row third from the left, and was playing for Swansea at the time, makes his Welsh debut against England at the Rectory Field in Blackheath on 2 January 1892.

Frank Mills was an English-born Welsh forward who played his early rugby for Mountain Ash. Some record books list his Clubs as Mountain Ash, Swansea and Cardiff and others, just Swansea and Cardiff. He gained his first cap on 2 January 1892 against England at Blackheath. During his International career, he was capped 13 times between 1892 and 1896 against England (5 caps), Scotland (4) and Ireland (4). He was a member of the first ever Welsh team that won the Triple Crown in 1892/93, playing in the wins against England at Cardiff Arms Park (12-11), which was a game where tons of coal were burned on the pitch prior to the game in order to soften it after a heavy frost, Scotland (9-0) in Edinburgh – which was Wales' first ever win on Scottish soil, and Ireland (2-0) at Stradey Park, Llanelli. He played for the Old Firm at various times in his International career and was in the Mount team photo of 1892/93. He played for the Old Firm against Llwynypia in the Glamorgan League final replay of 1894/95, which was lost 8-7. He also played for Mount in the exceptional season of 1896/97 when just 5 games were lost from the 37 played. He run an Undertaker's business in Mountain Ash and used to regularly advertise in the Aberdare Leader.

Season 1892/93

WRU Status & New Ground In Newtown
Frank Mills Helps Wales To First Ever Triple Crown

There were two major events in the season. Firstly, in early season 1892, a new ground in Newtown, called the Recreation Ground, on which £200 had been spent, was opened with a game against "first class" Swansea RFC, which was called a "Mills XV" because they were captained by former Mount forward Frank Mills. Following on from this at the end of the season, on Saturday 15 April 1893 at the Angel Hotel in Cardiff, Mountain Ash RFC became a member of the Welsh Football Union, which was the equivalent of the Welsh Rugby Union today. This was just 12 years after the body's official formation in March 1881. The Club run a 1st and 2nd XV during the season and the playing records for each were quite good from the known games played. The 1st XV played 14 games, won 7, drew 4 and lost 3, which gave a win rate of 64.29%. The 2nd XV played 5 known games, winning 4 of these against Aberdare CFC, Aberdare Rovers, Maesycwmmer and Cross Keys Blue Stars, and losing just one to Blackwood Harlequins, which gave a win rate of 80%. There were plenty of local Clubs playing at the time, among them being Penrhiwceiber, Cefnpennar and Mountain Ash Catholics. Former Old Firm forward, Frank Mills, who was still playing for Swansea RFC, was capped in the wins over England, Scotland and Ireland which gave Wales a first ever Triple Crown.

Fixtures 1892/93

Opponents	Date	Venue	Score	Tries	Scorers/Comments
Penygraig	26 Sep 1892	Away	5-10	1	Parfitt T, Tiley C.
Swansea (Mills' XV)	4 Oct 1892	Home	6-13	1	Netheway T, Ben Tiley DG.
Penygraig	10 Oct 1892	Home	0-0	0	No scorers.
Machen	17 Oct 1892	Home	5-0	1	Tiley T, C.
Pontymister	31 Oct 1892	Away	3-2	0	Tiley P.
Mardy	7 Nov 1892	Away	Unknown	Unknown	Match drawn. Scorers unknown.
Pontardawe	14 Nov 1892	Home	12-0	3	Phillips 2T, Ben Tiley T, C, Bishop C.
Morriston	21 Nov 1892	Away	0-8	0	No scorers.
Troedyrhiw	12 Dec 1892	Home	0-0	0	No scorers.
Wattstown	19 Dec 1892	Away	2-0	1	J. Hopkins T.
Grangetown	16 Jan 1893	Away	5-2	1	Match abandoned. J. Carey T, C. Bunny C.
Pontymoile	30 Jan 1893	Home	5-5	1	Murphy T, Bunny C.
Troedyrhiw	6 Feb 1893	Away	12-0	4	J. Netheway T, DG, W. Phillips T, Thomas T, J. Sullivan T.
Pontardawe	10 Apr 1893	Away	0-4	0	No scorers.

Summary of Playing Record

P	W	D	L	For	Against	Tries Scored	Win Rate %
14	7	4	3	55+	44+	13+	64.29

Match Reports and Publications

4 October 1892

<ins>Mountain Ash 6 Swansea (Mills' XV) 13</ins>

Mount Team: Back, T. Bishop; 3/4s, B. Tiley Capt, J. Parfitt, J. Netherway, J. Hoskins; half backs, W. Phillips, D.J.E. Thomas; forwards, S. Francis, A. Allen, D. Thomas, J. Phillips, T. Perrot, W. Beynon, F. Mears, J. Grant.

Former Mount forward, Frank Mills, captained the Swansea XV that officially opened the Old Firm's new ground. The South Wales Daily News reported, "This match proved of considerable interest. It constituted the formal opening on Monday afternoon of the new Recreation Ground which the Mountain Ash Football Club has enclosed at Newtown, which lies in the valley between Mountain Ash and Penrhiwceiber. The ground is a nice tract of flat land which was leased without charge by Messrs Nixon to the Club, and upon it, the Club has expended about £200, many of the members personally assisting to reduce it to a level…. Lord Aberdare is the President of Mountain Ash, and his son, the Hon. H.C. Bruce, one of the Vice Presidents, performed the opening ceremony by kicking off….Bishop made a mark, Tiley landing a goal…. Parfitt made a splendid run but was thrown in touch near the goal line….Tiley's collaring and tackling proved of great service to the home team…."

16 January 1893

<ins>Grangetown 2 Mountain Ash 5</ins>

The South Wales Daily News reported, "The weather was most unfavourable, the field being covered with snow to a depth of several inches….In the scrums, Mountain Ash showed very good form, but the state of the ground made anything like a fast game out of the question….A rush across the visitors' 25 followed and was claimed as a try….the visitors stopped the game and retired from the field contending that Sullivan fell on the ball, while the home team contended that Childs had possession. After a warm altercation, in which allegations of partiality against the referee were made freely by the Mountain Ash men, the match came to a conclusion about a quarter of an hour before the expiration of the second half."

6 March 1893

<ins>Machen v Mountain Ash</ins>

The South Wales Daily News reported, "The visitors arrived and the Machen team were ready for the game, but owing to the 2nd string being unable to proceed to Mountain Ash through the death of the Captain's brother, who was also a player, and to show respect to his memory, the game was abandoned. In spite of these explanations, the Captain of the Mountain Ash team refused to play unless a guarantee of £2 was given. The Machen team offered a return game, but the arbitrary mind of the visitors' Captain prevented the match coming off, and the visitors returned home without going on the field. In fairness to the visitors, it must be said they were anxious to play excepting the Captain, who declined to yield."

15 April 1893

Membership of the Welsh Football Union

On Saturday, 15 April 1893, Mountain Ash RFC became a Welsh Football Union Club. Below is an exert of a report published in the South Wales Daily News on Tuesday, 18 April 1893, of the meeting, and following it is a copy of the original Minutes taken of that meeting, which have come from the Welsh Rugby Union's archives:

> **THE WELSH RUGBY UNION.**
>
> Mr H. S. Lyne (Newport) presided over a general meeting of clubs affiliated to the Welsh Rugby Football Union at the Angel Hotel, Cardiff, on Saturday night.
>
> **FIXTURES FOR NEXT SEASON.**
>
> The Secretary reported the following fixtures for 1893-4:—West trial match, Monday, November 6th; East trial match, Wednesday, November 8th; final trial Saturday, December 2nd; English international in England on January 6th.
>
> **NEW CLUBS.**
>
> The following clubs were admitted into the Union:—Taibach, Pillgwenlly, Abergavenny Press, Mountain Ash, Grangetown, Pontardulais, and Pontymister.

Below are the relevant extracts from the original Minutes....

> *General Meeting*
>
> Held at the Angel Hotel, Cardiff, on Saturday April 15th 1893 under the presidency of Mr HS Lyne.
>
> The minutes of the last General Meeting and two Special Gen: Meetings were read and confirmed.
>
> *New Clubs.*
>
> The Committee having examined the credentials of the following clubs recommended that they be admitted to the Union, and Taibach, Pillgwenlly, Abergavenny Press, Grangetown, Mountain Ash, Pontardulais, and Pontymister were duly elected.

Opposite is the first ever photograph of a Mountain Ash RFC XV which might have been taken to commemorate Welsh Football Union membership. There is no evidence to suggest this but as photographs were new and a rare event in 1892/93, joining Welsh Rugby's governing body might have merited it. Included in the photo is the legendary Ben Tiley, Mount captain from 1882 to 1894. Joining him is Mount's first Welsh International, Frank Mills, who is standing in the back row third from the right as you look, and there is a possibility that Shad Lewis – named as S.C. Lewis below – who became Club Chairman from 1926 to 1937, and who helped keep the Old Firm afloat during some tough economic times during his tenure as Chairman, is also included.

Mountain Ash Rugby Football Club
"The Old Firm"
Season 1892/93

Back Row L-R: Dr E. P. Evans J.P., W. Beynon, T. Perrot, Arthur Allen, D.S. Lewis, J. Phillips, Frank Mills*, W. Eynon, Harry Hale (Secretary),
Middle Row L-R: J. Murphy, T. Bishop, J. Sullivan, Ben Tiley Capt, S.C. Lewis (baby), Joe Hoskins, J.H. Eynon (baby), J. Carey, F. Mears,
Front Row L-R: D.J. Thomas, W. Bradford, Wat Phillips.

* denotes Welsh International

Season 1893/94

The Old Firm played 17 known games during the season, winning 8, drawing 4 and losing 5, scoring 66 points, which included 16 tries, and conceding 59, to give a win rate of 58.82%. The season saw a 6-0 home win over Pontypridd but an 11-0 away loss. There were 0-0 home draws against Ebbw Vale and Swansea's "A" team. As for games against fellow valley Clubs, there was a game against Llwynypia, who were soon to be a power in Welsh rugby and one of the Old Firm's fiercest rivals in the coming years when League rugby started. The season also saw former Mount forward, Frank Mills, gain another 3 Welsh caps in the games against England, Scotland and Ireland.

Fixtures 1893/94

Opponents	Date	Venue	Score	Tries	Scorers/Comments
Pontypridd	2 Oct 1893	Away	0-11	0	No scorers.
Ebbw Vale	9 Oct 1893	Home	0-0	0	No scorers.
Pontnewydd	16 Oct 1893	Home	0-5	0	No scorers.
Llwynypia	23 Oct 1893	Away	13-6	2	Netherway 2T, Bishop P, C, AN Other C.
Troedyrhiw	30 Oct 1893	Home	9-0	3	Jeffries T, Hoskins T, Bradford T.
Taibach	6 Nov 1893	Away	6-3	2	Bradford T, AN Other T.
Treherbert	13 Nov 1893	Home	9-0	2	Tanner T, P, Bradford T.
Risca	27 Nov 1893	Home	8-3	2	Ben Tiley T, C, Jeffries T.
Swansea "A"	26 Dec 1893	Home	0-0	0	No scorers.
Penygraig	1 Jan 1894	Away	0-6	0	No scorers.
Pontymister	15 Jan 1894	Home	5-0	1	Jeffreys T, Tanner C.
Swansea "A"	12 Feb 1894	Away	0-9	0	No scorers.
Llwynypia	5 Mar 1894	Home	0-0	0	No scorers.
Pontypridd	12 Mar 1894	Home	6-0	2	AN Other 2T.
Penygraig	19 Mar 1894	Home	0-0	0	No scorers.
Pontymoile	2 Apr 1894	Home	10-0	2	Tiley T, Bradford T, Tanner 2C.
Ebbw Vale	30 Apr 1894	Away	0-16	0	No scorers.

Summary of Playing Record

P	W	D	L	For	Against	Tries Scored	Win Rate %
17	8	4	5	66	59	16	58.82

Match Reports and Publications

23 October 1893

<u>Llwynypia 6 Mountain Ash 13</u>

The South Wales Daily News summary report of this first known game between the Old Firm and Llwynypia was as follows, "Llwynypia were severely beaten by Mountain Ash and the result really surprised the spectators. Up to breathing time, the play was very uninteresting and it was generally concluded that Mountain Ash would return home beaten by a couple of tries at least. But the Ashites turned the tables completely soon after the interval....It was scarcely to be credited that Mountain Ash were the same team as had lingered through the former half. Their forwards played a most stubborn game, and the tackling and collaring most effective. Llwynypia seemed paralysed during the greater part of the latter half and completely lost their combination. The goal by Bishop from near halfway was a magnificent one and he was very safe as a custodian....in the second half....Mountain Ash rushed the ball to the home 25 where a magnificent bout of passing was displayed and Netherway, the right wing three-quarter, receiving the final pass, scored easily near the uprights. Mountain Ash immediately pressed again and the pressure increased. A free kick was awarded near half way for offside and Bishop placed a magnificent goal...."

30 October 1893

<u>Mountain Ash 9 Troedyrhiw 0</u>

The South Wales Daily News match report commented about one of the Old Firm's tries, "....from a scrum near the visitors' 25, the finest passing on the ground this season was witnessed. Hillman, the home half, passed to Phillips, who gave to Hoskins, the latter doing a fine run crossed over."

8 January 1894

The South Wales Daily News published pen pictures of the Welsh team, amongst which was the Old Firm's former forward, Frank Mills. Here is what they had to say.

"Few forwards in South Wales have achieved quicker distinction in the football field than Frank Mills. He is only 20 years of age, and for two years has represented Wales in her International struggles. He is a native of Mountain Ash, where he commenced his football career, but subsequently went to Swansea and played for the Reserves. This was three years ago, and he then exhibited such good form that he was immediately drafted into the second team, while in the following year, he was given his place amongst the first team forwards. He plays a hard and determined scrummaging game, and in the open has few equals amongst the Welsh pack."

12 March 1894

<u>Mountain Ash 6 Pontypridd 0</u>

The South Wales Daily News reported, "The kick off was timed for 3:30 but owing to the late arrival of the visitors, it was an hour later before the tussle began. Tiley kicked off for the homesters against a strong wind....A scrum was formed....The home pack showed their superiority. In the second half....The home men renewed the attack, and from a scrum near the visitors' 25, Hillman picked up and neatly passed to Phillips, who transferred to Tanner. The latter, drawing the opposition quartette around him, gave to Bradford on the line, who scored amidst applause."

2 April 1894

<u>Mountain Ash 10 Pontymoile 0</u>

In the second half of this game, the South Wales Daily News commented, "....Bradford, from near the home line, received the ball and racing up the field scored behind the posts a really magnificent try...."

Season 1894/95

<u>First Season Of League Rugby For Old Firm</u>
<u>Rhondda, Merthyr & Aberdare League Runners-Up</u>

This was when rugby really got going for the premier Clubs in the Rhondda, Merthyr and Aberdare valleys with the introduction of the Rhondda, Merthyr and Aberdare League. The season was the inaugural one not only for the tournament itself, but for tournament rugby in general for both Mountain Ash RFC and the top Clubs in the Rhondda, Merthyr and Aberdare valleys.

During the season, the Old Firm and Llwynypia proved the strongest Clubs in the competition, Mount beating their Rhondda rivals 6-3 away, but losing the home game 3-0. The match reports in the South Wales Daily News are not clear as to whether there were two semi-finals at the end of the season or whether both Llwynypia and the Old Firm finished at the top of the table on equal points. If there were semi-finals, then Mount beat Ferndale 19-3 and Llwynypia defeated Penygraig 17-5.

The final was held in Pontypridd in May 1895 and ended in controversy after the Old Firm scored a converted try to equal the score at 8-8. Llwynypia protested to the referee that the try had been scored from a throw-in that should have been theirs but had been taken by Mountain Ash. Arthur Gould, the referee, a Welsh International, changed his mind and ruled out the try, which gave Llwynypia victory – or so they thought. In the off season, the Welsh Football Union got involved and eventually it was decided that the game should be replayed, and so it was on 31 October 1895, which was the following season, 1895/96. Another close game ensued, Llwynypia just getting home, without controversy this time, 8-7.

Going back to the 1894/95 season, what a superb one it was for the Old Firm as they beat almost all before them. From the information known, Mount played 22 games, won 17, drew 3 and lost just 2, which gave an impressive win rate of 84.09%. At least 58 tries were scored, which was quite a feat in this era of generally low scoring matches, 226+ points scored and only 39+ conceded. As well as losing 3-0 at home to Llwynypia, the Old Firm suffered their second defeat at the end of the season when they lost 10-8 at home to a Newport XV, which was officially named "J. Hannen's (Newport) team", after leading 8-0 at half time.

Two Mount players, scrum half Wat Phillips and forward Tom Perrot, were picked in the first Welsh trial of the season in November 1894, and former forward Frank Mills, who was playing for Cardiff, gained 3 more Welsh caps, playing against England, Ireland and Scotland.

On the limited information available, it appears that Mountain Ash RFC also run a 2nd XV, with two of the team's known results being a win over Pentre, 6-3, and a loss to Pontypridd "A", 8-0.

Fixtures 1894/95

Opponents	Date	Venue	Score	Tries	Scorers/Comments
Danygraig	24 Sep 1894	Home	6-0	2	Hoskins T, Bradford T.
Merthyr Vale	1 Oct 1894	Home	49-0	12+	J. Hoskins 3T, C, Jeffries 2T, K. Griffiths 2T, W. Phillips T, DG, Taylor T, C, Bradford T, J. Tanner T, Richards T, Allen C, AN Other 3pts.
Argoed	8 Oct 1894	Home	12-0	4	Hillman T, Phillips T, Griffiths T, Hoskins T.
Pontnewydd	22 Oct 1894	Home	11-3	3	Netherway T, C, Bradford T, E. Griffiths T.
Llwynypia (L)	29 Oct 1894	Home	0-3	0	No scorers.
Pontymoile	5 Nov 1894	Home	0-0	0	No scorers.
Pontypridd (L)	12 Nov 1894	Away	9-3	3	J. Carey T, Bill Phillips T, Joe Hoskins T.
Ferndale (PL)	26 Nov 1894	Unsure	13-0	3	Ben Tiley T, Emrys Griffiths T, DG, Fred Millar T.
Barry	3 Dec 1894	Home	8-0	2	Perrot T, AN Other T, Tanner C.
Swansea "A"	Dec 1894	Unsure	Unknown	Unknown	Mount win. Scorers unknown.
Cardiff Northern	10 Dec 1894	Home	3-0	1	Hillman T.
Treorky (PL)	17 Dec 1894	Away	8-3	2	AN Other 2T, C.
Pontymoile	24 Dec 1894	Away	0-0	0	No scorers.
Merthyr (L)	31 Dec 1894	Home	10-3	2	Bradford T, Tiley T, Tanner DG.

Opponents	Date	Venue	Score	Tries	Scorers/Comments
Penygraig (PL)	21 Jan 1895	Home	18-0	4	Tiley T, Phillips T, Hoskins T, Millar T, Tanner 3C.
Cardiff Hornets	25 Feb 1895	Home	11-0	3	Phillips T, Brown C, AN Other 2T.
Merthyr (PL)	4 Mar 1895	Away	7-0	1	K. Griffiths T, W. Phillips DG.
Pontypridd (PL)	11 Mar 1895	Home	20-0	6	Tanner 2T, C, Bradford 2T, Fred Millar T, Hoskins T.
Llwynypia (L)	1 Apr 1895	Away	6-3	1	Bradford T, Ben Tiley P.
Newport XV	29 Apr 1895	Home	8-10	2	J. Hoskins 2T, Ben Tiley C.
Ferndale (L)	6 May 1895	Away	19-3	5	R. Hillman T, Bradford T, Ben Tiley T, Mayers T, AN Other T, J. Tanner C, W. Phillips C.
Llwynypia (L) Merthyr, Aberdare & Rhondda League Play Off.	13 May 1895	Pontypridd	8-8	2	F. Millar T, AN Other T, C.

Summary of Playing Record

P	W	D	L	For	Against	Tries	Win Rate %
22	17	3	2	226+	39+	58+	84.09

Match Reports and Publications

12 November 1894

<u>Pontypridd 3 Mountain Ash 9</u>
<u>Rhondda, Merthyr & Aberdare League</u>

Mount Team: Back, J. Tanner; 3/4s, W. Bradford, J. Hoskins, B. Tiley, W. Taylor; half backs, Phillips Capt, R. Hillman; forwards, T. Perrot, J. Carey, F. Millar, R. Eddy, A. Allen, W.H. Grimshare, J. Jones, F. Morgan.

The South Wales Daily News reported, "Played at Pontypridd, both teams were in admirable condition and evenly matched. For the first 15 minutes, the game was open and exceedingly fast. Two of the players – Beith of Pontypridd and Allen of Mountain Ash – sustained injuries by coming into violent collision with each other. Hoskins put in a clinking kick, which was followed up by the visitors, Carey eventually crossing the line after a magnificent run. The homesters assumed the aggressive….the invasion was stoutly resisted….the homesters were driven back….Tiley, obtaining possession, headed a fine dribble to the home line, where Bill Phillips, the visiting skipper, picked up and crossed. Shortly after, Tiley again obtained possession and passed to Hoskins, who adroitly dodging his opponents and out-running his pursuers, scored."

21 January 1895

<u>Mountain Ash 18 Penygraig 0</u>
<u>Possible Rhondda, Merthyr & Aberdare League Fixture</u>

The South Wales Daily News reported, "Played at Mountain Ash before a large number of spectators….The visitors were very reluctant to turn out as they were a couple of men short. Consequently, the kick off did not take place until 4 o'clock….Hoskins got away with a magnificent run and scored behind the posts. The home forwards rushed the visitors off their feet, Millar following up a magnificent rush, scored. The visitors were fairly outclassed at all points of the game. The homesters played grandly, Hoskins and Tiley at three-quarter being fairly conspicuous. Hoskins gained the try of the match after a magnificent run. Phillips and Hillman outshone the visitors at half back. Carey, Harris, Millar, Francis and Perrot were the pick of the forwards. The chief feature of the game was the grand display of Tanner at back, his play being superb."

1 April 1895

<u>Llwynypia 3 Mountain Ash 6</u>
<u>Rhondda, Merthyr & Aberdare League</u>

Mount Team: Back, J. Tanner; 3/4s, Bradford, Hoskins, Griffiths, Tiley; half backs, Phillips Capt, Hillman; forwards, Carey, Allen, Harris, Sid Moore, Perrot, Millar, Mears, Edey.

The South Wales Daily News reported, "This League match was played at Llwynypia before a large number of spectators….Tiley kicked a splendid goal. Llwynypia, after this, played up, and a scrummage was formed near the visitors' line but rushed back to the centre. Here, Bradford, taking a cross kick, ran clear away and scored in a good position….The homesters pressed but could not pierce the defence….Mountain Ash was now content with collaring, which they did very successfully and Llwynypia were not able to make much headway….Mountain Ash had an anxious time of it, but kept their lines intact, nothing further being scored."

6 May 1895

<u>Ferndale 3 Mountain Ash 19</u>
<u>Rhondda, Merthyr & Aberdare League</u>

Although the South Wales Daily News reported this match as a semi-final, it appears to have been the Old Firm's final Rhondda, Merthyr & Aberdare League match. The newspaper reported, "This, the semi-final League match, took place at Ferndale before a large crowd. Mountain Ash, with this win, tie with Llwynypia, who were leading by 2 points."

13 May 1895

<u>Mountain Ash 8 Llwynypia 8</u>
<u>Rhondda, Merthyr & Aberdare League Play Off</u>
<u>South Wales Daily News</u>

FOOTBALL.

LEAGUE MATCH AT PONTYPRIDD.
MOUNTAIN ASH v. LLWYNYPIA.

The final tie in the league match for the cup offered by the Rhondda and District Football League was played at Pontypridd on Saturday between Mountain Ash and Llwynypia. There was a large gathering of spectators, and the game excited considerable interest. In the first half play was of a scrambling description, relieved occasionally by magnificent runs in which Ben Tiley and Rosser Evans participated. Tom Williams eventually got over for Llwynypia amid deafening plaudits, but the try for goal was abortive. A few seconds afterwards Tom Williams again crossed, and this time a goal was kicked. Half-time score:—Llwynypia, 1 goal 1 try; Mountain Ash, nil. Open play characterised the second half. From a scramble, Miller got away and scored for Mountain Ash, and afterwards a Mountain Ash forward repeated the experiment, the try being converted, thus equalising the score. Llwynypia disputed the goal on the ground that the ball was kicked into touch by a Mountain Ash man, and should have been thrown out by a Llwynypia man and not by the Mountain Ash half-back. Mr A. J. Gould, who refereed, disallowed the goal, and thus the victory remained with Llwynypia.

27 May 1895

<u>South Wales Daily News</u>

WELSH FOOTBALL UNION.

THE MOUNTAIN ASH v. LLWYNYPIA DISPUTE.

At a meeting of the Welsh Football Union at the Queen's Hotel, Cardiff, on Saturday evening, the dispute between the Mountain Ash and Llwynypia teams came up for consideration. The committee, after hearing the arguments, were of opinion that the referee, having given his decision, had no power to alter it, but at the same time they felt that the conduct of the Mountain Ash touch judge was reprehensible. They much regretted that they could not give an award in favour of Llwynypia. There were present at the meeting Mr Lyne (Newport) in the chair, Mr Wilkins (Llanelly), Mr A. J. Davies (Cardiff), and Mr Gwyn (Swansea), secretary.

Season 1895/96

<u>Memorable Season For Old Firm</u>
<u>Glamorgan League Champions & First International Cap</u>

The 1894/95 Rhondda, Merthyr and Aberdare League Championship was eventually resolved at the end of October 1895 when a replay between Llwynypia and Mount took place at Taff Vale Park, Pontypridd, Llwynypia edging home 8-7 in the dying minutes of a close, hard fought, exciting encounter in front of a large crowd. Undeterred by this, the Old Firm went one better at the end of the season, winning the same competition – renamed the Glamorgan League by then – outright, with no need for a play-off this time, which made Mountain Ash RFC the first official champions of the newly named competition. Mount played 14 League games in all, home and away against Penygraig, Llwynypia, Treherbert, Pontypridd, Ferndale, Treorky and Merthyr. The actual record was not published so it is not known if there were any defeats in the League. What is known is that the Old Firm had won all 9 games played in the competition up to the end of February 1896. There was a defeat to Penygraig at the end of the season but as Clubs also played so-called friendly games in addition to League games, it is unclear in the match report what the classification of the game was. A superb season ended with a playing record of played 31, won 26, drawn 2, and lost 3, with 278+ points scored, which included 74+ tries, and just 63+ conceded, which gave one of the highest win rates ever recorded before or since, of 87.10%. The season was predominantly one of win after win except for two draws and three losses. To cap the most memorable season in the 20 year history of the Club, forward Fred Millar was capped by Wales against Ireland in March 1896, which gave him the distinction of being the first player capped while playing for the Club. Former forward, Frank Mills, who had also played for Mount during his International career but was playing for Cardiff at the time, joined him on the International front when he played his last game for Wales, which was his 13th and last cap, against England in January 1896.

Fixtures 1895/96

Opponents	Date	Venue	Score	Tries	Scorers/Comments
Hafod	30 Sep 1895	Home	19-3	5	Phillips 2T, 2C, W. Bradford 2T, Griffiths T.
Pontymoile	7 Oct 1895	Home	0-0	0	No scorers.
Somerset Crusaders	10 Oct 1895	Home	27-0	7	Barnard 2T, Phillips T, C, Owens T, W. Bradford T, R. Hillman T, Hale T, Ben Tiley DG.
Treorky (L)	14 Oct 1895	Home	9-0	3	E. Griffiths T, Ben Tiley T, Phillips T.
Pontypridd (L)	21 Oct 1895	Away	12-8	2	Ben Tiley T, AN Other T, Ben Tiley DG, Phillips C.
Barry	28 Oct 1895	Home	8-0	2	Scorers unknown.

Opponents	Date	Venue	Score	Tries	Scorers/Comments
Llwynypia (L) 1894/95 Merthyr, Aberdare & Rhondda League Play Off replay.	1 Nov 1895	Taff Vale Park, Pontypridd	7-8	1	J. Barnard T, J. Tanner DG.
Merthyr (L)	4 Nov 1895	Home	27-0	7	Wat Phillips 3T, DG, C, Dick Hillman T, Griffiths T, Jim Tanner T, Fred Millar T.
Ferndale (PL)	5 Nov 1895	Away	6-0	2	T. Hale T, AN Other T.
Pontnewydd	11 Nov 1895	Away	3-0	1	Scorer unknown.
Blaina	18 Nov 1895	Home	6-0	2	Fred Millar T, Barnard T.
Treherbert (PL)	25 Nov 1895	Away	12-0	4	Ben Tiley 2T, Jack Tanner 2T.
Llandaff	2 Dec 1895	Home	16-0	4	Scorers unknown.
Cardiff Quins	4 Dec 1895	Home	6-0	2	Griffiths T, AN Other T.
Treorky (PL)	9 Dec 1895	Away	10-0	2	Barnard T, Williams T, Phillips 2C.
Llwynypia (PL)	16 Dec 1895	Away	3-0	1	M. Thomas T.
Cwmbran	23 Dec 1895	Home	3-0	1	Scorer unknown.
Aberavon	6 Jan 1896	Away	0-16	0	No scorers.
Pontymoile	13 Jan 1896	Away	5-3	1	Scorers unknown.
Cardiff Hornets	20 Jan 1896	Home	35-0	9	Scorers unknown.
Llwynypia (PL)	3 Feb 1896	Home	11-8	3	W. Phillips T, C, A. Tucker T, J. Hoskins T.
Aberavon	4 Feb 1896	Home	13-5	3	Ben Tiley T, 2C, Griffiths T, Hoskins T.
Pontypridd (L)	24 Feb 1896	Home	10-0	2	J. Hoskins T, R. Hillman T, W. Phillips DG.
Penygraig (L)	3 Mar 1896	Home	6-0	2	AN Other 2T.
Barry	9 Mar 1896	Away	0-0	0	No scorers.
Barry	Unknown	Home	Unknown	Unknown	Mount win. Scorers unknown.
Pontymister	16 Mar 1896	Home	3-0	1	Scorer unknown.
Ferndale (PL)	23 Mar 1896	Away	9-0	3	Mount win. Scorers unknown.
Treherbert (L)	30 Mar 1896	Home	6-3	2	Fred Millar T, Ben Tiley T.
Pontnewydd	6 Apr 1896	Home	3-0	1	Scorer unknown.
Penygraig (PL)	27 Apr 1896	Away	3-9	1	Phillips T.

Summary of Playing Record

P	W	D	L	For	Against	Tries	Win Rate %
31	26	2	3	278+	63+	74+	87.10

Match Reports and Publications

14 October 1895

<u>Mountain Ash 9 Treorky 0</u>
<u>Glamorgan League</u>

Mount Team: Back, J. Tanner; 3/4s, B. Tiley, W. Bradford, E. Griffiths, J. Barnard; half backs, W. Phillips Capt, R. Hillman; forwards, J.A. Harries, A. Allen, T. Perrot, F. Millar, S. Francis, E. Owens, A. Tucker, T. Hale.

The South Wales Daily News commented, "Some good football was seen at times....The Mountain Ash forwards are a big, heavy lot that can follow up well and should not play such a hard, pushing game. Arthur Allen, T. Hale and Tucker were the best of a good lot. They completely outplayed Treorky and had it not been for the visitors' strong defence, the score would have been much greater. Tiley, Barnard and Tanner played well for Mountain Ash, especially the latter. Bradford and Griffiths should get into a little better form, and if the whole team wish to win the final tie for the League Championship, the sooner they go into hard training, the better for their chances."

21 October 1895

<u>Pontypridd 8 Mountain Ash 12</u>
<u>Glamorgan League</u>

Mount Team: Back, J. Tanner; 3/4s, Ben Tiley, J. Hoskins, E. Griffiths, J. Barnard; half backs, W. Phillips Capt, R. Hillman; forwards, Fred Millar, J.A. Harries, T. Perrot, Evan Owens, A. Tucker, T. Hale, A. Allen, S. Francis.

The South Wales Daily News reported, "Hoskins....dropped a beautiful goal....A sharp game from beginning to end. The Mountain Ash forwards were far superior.... Phillips was the best half on the field....Barnard played well but Tiley has lost his old time brilliancy, although at times he did good work."

The Western Mail reported, "At a general meeting of the Merthyr, Aberdare and Rhondda Valley Rugby Football League on October 9....It was also resolved that the Llwynypia v Mountain Ash match, which was played in Pontypridd in April last, and decided by the Welsh Union to be a drawn game, should be played again on Thursday, 31 October at Taff Vale Park, Pontypridd, kick off 3:15pm, the winners to be presented with the League Cup together with 15 gold medals, and the defeated team to be presented with 15 silver medals. Great interest is being taken in this match, which will, no doubt, draw a large crowd."

1 November 1895

Mountain Ash 7 Llwynypia 8
Rhondda, Merthyr & Aberdare 1894/95 League Play Off Replay

FOOTBALL.

THE RHONDDA CHAMPIONSHIP.
MOUNTAIN ASH V. LLWYNYPIA.

On Thursday Mountain Ash and Llwynypia met on the Taff Vale Park, Pontypridd, to contest for the Glamorgan League Cup. It will be remembered that last season, the teams met on the same ground, to decide the championship of the Rhondda, but, owing to an unfortunate dispute consequent upon the referee altering one of his decisions, the matter was referred to the Welsh Rugby Union, and they ordered the match to be re-played. Keen interest was taken in the encounter, as the wining team, although becoming holders of the cup for the season, will also be presented with gold medals by the league. At mid-day crowds flocked into the town by special trains. Both teams were fully represented, and lined out as follow:—Mountain Ash: Back, J. Tanner; three-quarter backs, B. Tiley, J. Hoskins, E. Griffiths, and J. Barnard; half-backs, W. Phillips and R. Hillman; forwards, Frank Mills, F. Millar, E. Owens, J. A. Harries, A. Tucker, T. Perrott, T. Hale, and S. Francis. Llwynypia: Back, J. Hadridge; three-quarter backs, T. Williams, G. Mills, W. Griffiths, and I. Edmunds; half-backs, A. Powell and I. Thomas; forwards, W. H. Mills, R. Hellings, T. Dobson, B. Phillips, D. Royal, J. Atkins, J. Coombes, and W. Williams. Referee, Mr. H. M. Ingledew, Cardiff.

The game, which was kept up at a terrific pace throughout, was one of the fastest and most exciting ever seen on the ground. Each side made desperate efforts to secure league honours, and the excitement of the huge crowd was sustained at high pitch from start to finish. There was little to choose between the two sides in the first half, but up to the middle of the second half Llwynypia was clearly bested, and a magnificent drop goal which Tanner kicked in the first half, and the really brilliant try of Barnard in the second, simply threw the erstwhile champions of the Rhondda into despair. Just at the middle of the second half, however, their spirits were roused, for George Mills, getting possession in his own territory, made a really fine run, along the touch-line and planted the ball, amid tremendous excitement, right behind the uprights. Griffiths splendidly converted, and thus the points were seven to five. From now on it was nobody's game, and dusk was creeping on apace, and the men put forth redoubled efforts and made matters pretty warm for their opponents. Time after time did they make desperate efforts to cross, and when Tom Williams crossed the Rubicon after a brilliant run the wild scene can better be imagined than described, and the game soon after closed, and Llwynypia won a brilliant game by just one point. Score:—

Llwynypia—1 goal (converted), 1 try.
Mountain Ash—1 goal (dropped), 1 try.

Included in the Mount XV above were forwards Frank Mills, who was a Welsh International, and Fred Millar who gained his first Welsh cap five months later in March 1896.

29 November 1895

The Western Mail's rugby writer, "Welsh Athlete" wrote, "Besides Cardiff and Llanelly, Mountain Ash also basks in the glories of an unbeaten record….25 matches were played last season – 20 won, 3 lost and 2 drawn – whilst 21 goals and 46 tries (235 points) were scored for, and 1 goal and 8 tries (29 points) conceded. Penygraig were the only team that kicked a goal against Mountain Ash. The team just missed winning the Glamorgan League Championship. This season, Mountain Ash has played 11, won 10, lost none and drawn 1. The score for is 9 goals and 30 tries (122 points), whilst 1 goal and 4 tries (17 points) have been recorded against them. So far, they hold top position in the Glamorgan League, having played 5 matches and won them all. The record is certainly one to be proud of, and, in congratulating the Club, I hope I shall be able to extend such congratulations right up to the end of the season."

16 December 1895

<u>Llwynypia 0 Mountain Ash 3</u>
<u>Possible Glamorgan League Fixture</u>

Mount Team: Back, J. Tanner; 3/4s, B. Tiley, J. Hoskins, Griffiths, L. R. Williams;
half backs, W. Phillips Capt, R. Hillman; forwards, Fred Millar, T. Perrot,
Carey, A. Tucker, T. Hale, Allen, F. Mears, J. Davies.

The South Wales Daily News reported, "Played at Llwynypia in wet and foggy weather....The forwards bore the brunt of the work, the backs on both sides failing to hold the wet ball. The homesters rushed over halfway but were stopped by Tanner when looking dangerous....Tanner picked up cleverly and saved a certain try. Mountain Ash relieved to the centre and a scrambling rush took the ball on....one of the forwards fell on the ball and scored. Both teams now played a scrambling game, all the players being covered with mud and hard to recognise, and the game became more a question of luck than anything else....The ground and the ball were quite unfit for play and did not suit the usual game of Llwynypia. Added to this, the home team had a serious defect in the fullback, who gave Mountain Ash the try they obtained. Llwynypia undoubedly had the superior back team and on a dry day would unquestionably have won."

3 February 1896

<u>Mountain Ash 11 Llwynypia 8</u>
<u>Possible Glamorgan League Fixture</u>

Mount Team: Back, J. Netherway; 3/4s, B. Tiley, J. James, D. Griffiths, J. Hoskins; half backs, W. Phillips,
R. Hillman; forwards, Fred Millar, T. Perrot, A. Tucker, E. Owens, Allen, T. Hale,
Davies, Jones.

The South Wales Daily News reported, "Played at Mountain Ash in ideal football weather....From a kick by Hoskins, the ball was secured by Allen who looked all over a scorer when he fell....Hale was knocked out, but soon resumed. Both sides were now playing well, the forwards on both sides showing excellent form. A scrum was formed on the Llwynypia line....Phillips securing the ball, scored in the extreme corner, and the same player, taking the place made a grand kick, the ball striking the post and rebounding into play....Tiley was injured and had to retire. By a rush of the forwards, in which Millar and Perrot were prominent, and from a kick by Netherway, the ball was secured by Hoskins, who passed to Millar, and he to Tucker, who scored between the posts, Phillips converting."

24 February 1896

<u>Mountain Ash 10 Pontypridd 0</u>
<u>Glamorgan League</u>

Mount Team: Back, J. Tanner; 3/4s, B. Tiley, J. Hoskins, Deere, Griffiths; half backs, W. Phillips Capt,
R. Hillman; forwards, Fred Millar, T. Perrot, Owen, A. Tucker, T. Hale, F. Mears, Jones,
J. Davies.

The South Wales Daily News reported, "This League match, in which great interest was taken, was played in fine weather at Mountain Ash before a large crowd. Mountain Ash is at the top of the League, while Pontypridd is well up....From a pass out by Hillman, Hoskins passed to Tiley, who repassing to Hoskins, secured a try....

On resuming, Tanner....a fine run and had Deere not missed the pass, a try must have resulted.... Hillman passed out well from a scrum to Phillips, who ran well and repassed to Hillman, who secured a very fine try....Phillips secured a free and landed a fine goal. The visitors were now completely beaten although they made gallant efforts to score....This was one of the fastest and prettiest games played here this season. For the homesters, Millar, Tucker and Perrot were the most prominent in the forwards, whilst of a good lot of backs, the best were Deere and Hoskins. Tanner, at back, was as usual, excellent."

26 February 1896

The South Wales Daily News published the Glamorgan League table and good news it was for the Old Firm:

GLAMORGAN LEAGUE.
POSITIONS UP TO DATE.

The Mountain Ash team are holding a commanding position at the head of the Glamorgan Football League, and seem likely to retain their position, having won their nine matches decisively, scoring no fewer than 116 points to 16. The table up to date is:—

	Pl'yed.	Won.	Lost.	Drn.	Pts.
1—Mountain Ash	9	9	0	0	18
2—Penygraig	10	7	2	1	15
3—Llwynypia	13	6	6	1	13
4—Treherbert	9	6	3	0	12
5—Pontypridd	10	5	4	1	11
6—Ferndale	10	4	5	1	9
7—Treorky	10	1	9	0	2
8—Merthyr	8	0	8	0	0

W.H. "Fred" Millar
Mountain Ash RFC
7 Welsh Caps
1896 v Ireland, 1900 & 1901 v England, Scotland & Ireland

William Henry Millar, known as "Fred", with a surname that was sometimes spelt Miller, was a forward, and captained the Old Firm in 1897/98, becoming the first player to be capped directly from Mountain Ash RFC. He was a collier in Nixon's Navigation Colliery, Mountain Ash, and was described in one publication as "a stalwart specimen of the Welsh collier". His first cap was against Ireland on 14 March 1896 at Lansdowne Road, Dublin, but he had to wait nearly four years to get another taste of International rugby. In 1900, when he gained his second, third and fourth caps, he was a member of the Welsh team that won the Triple Crown for the second time, playing in the wins against England (13-3) at Kingsholm in Gloucester, Scotland (12-3) at St Helen's, Swansea, and Ireland (3-0) in Belfast. This success was the start of the Golden Era of Welsh rugby, which saw Wales win 6 Triple Crowns before the start of World War I. In his final 3 caps in 1901, he played in the two home wins over England (13-0) and Ireland (10-9) and also in the away defeat to Scotland (18-8), which was a game put back from its original date due to the passing of Queen Victoria. He accumulated 7 Welsh caps in total, all from Mountain Ash RFC, and shortly after his last cap he joined the professional ranks at Hull, one of the first of quite a number of Old Firm players who would make the trek North, making his debut in September 1901.

THE OLD FIRM'S PROUD PAST

Mountain Ash Rugby Football Club
"The Old Firm"
Glamorgan League Champions 1895/96

MOUNTAIN ASH FOOTBALL CLUB.
Glamorgan League Champions. Season, 1895-96.

Back Row L-R: J.P. Curnow (Committee), F. Mears, E. Owen, J. Davies, Fred Millar*, Tom Perrot, Arthur Allen, T. Hale, A. Tucker,
Middle Row L-R: Llew Deere, E. Griffiths, Ben Tiley, Joe Hoskins, Jack Tanner, Dick Hillman, J. Grant (Committee),
Front Row L-R: T.E. Lewis, Wat Phillips (Capt), Harry Hale (Secretary).

* denotes Welsh International

Season 1896/97

<ins>Top Clubs Beaten By Old Firm In Impressive Season</ins>

This was an exceptional season for the Old Firm, following on from the previous two. Out of 37 games played, 27 were won, 5 drawn, and only 5 lost, to give a win rate of 79.73%. In total, 528 points were scored – which included the unprecedented total of at least 131 tries, both of which were massive totals in this era of comparatively low scoring games – and just 84 conceded. Mount won the first 11 games of the season before Llwynypia held them to a draw and remained unbeaten up until 29 December 1896, when they had the little matter of an away game against Leicester at Welford Road. No doubt the Midlands Club had a point to prove, having been beaten 11-0 in Mountain Ash just two months prior to this Christmas fixture. In front of a crowd of 7,000, the Old Firm narrowly lost 3-0. Up until then, they had won 13 and drawn 4. This first defeat of the season didn't have any marked effect on the team's form as 14 wins, one draw and 4 losses followed it in the 19 games played to the end of the season. There were 4 games and 4 wins over local rivals Pontypridd, and 3 games and 3 wins over Aberavon. "The Wizards", as Aberavon were then and still are called, lost only 7 games all season, the South Wales Daily News commenting, "(Aberavon) had the most successful season in its history." There were also "doubles" against Bridgwater and Albion and Bridgend, and wins at Neath, and home to Leicester and Treorky. Two of the five defeats came in the last month of the season, one of them being a narrow 13-11 reverse at Plymouth on an Easter weekend tour; however, the Old Firm made up for it with a 14-4 win over Bridgwater & Albion on the way home. As impressive a season as it was for the Old Firm, they could not retain the Glamorgan League Championship won in 1895/96 and finished 3rd behind champions Llwynypia, who were one of the most powerful Clubs in Welsh rugby at the time. In 2nd place was Treherbert, which the South Wales Daily News reported as "among the leading organisations in the Principality". In the home game with Treherbert in November 1896, the referee so upset the Mount support that he had to have police protection to leave the ground safely, the result being that the Welsh Union stopped home fixtures for a fortnight.

Fixtures 1896/97

Opponents	Date	Venue	Score	Tries	Scorers/Comments
Ferndale (PL)	21 Sep 1896	Home	27-0	7	Deere 2T, Bradford 4T, Hoskins T, W. Phillips 2C, AN Other C.
Canton	26 Sep 1896	Home	34-0	10	AN Other 10T, 2C.
Bridgwater & Albion	5 Oct 1896	Home	23-0	7	Bradford 3T, Deere T, Price T, Hoskins T, Hillman T, AN Other C.
Newport District	5 Oct 1896	Home	11-0	3	AN Other 3T, C.
Pontypridd (L)	12 Oct 1896	Home	31-7	7	R. Hillman 2T, E. Jenkins T, T. Perrot T, W. Bradford T, N. Price T, Llew Deere T, C. Hoskins DG, W. Phillips C, AN Other 2C.

Opponents	Date	Venue	Score	Tries	Scorers/Comments
Bridgend	17 Oct 1896	Away	20-3	4	Bradford 2T, Phillips T, C, Price T, Tanner DG, AN Other C.
Wattstown	19 Oct 1896	Home	8-0	Unknown	Scorers unknown.
Barry	24 Oct 1896	Home	6-5	2	Scorers unknown.
Leicester	28 Oct 1896	Home	11-0	3	W. Bradford T, F. Millar T, F. Mills T, J. Tanner C.
Pontymoile	31 Oct 1896	Home	25-0	6	AN Other 6T, P, 2C.
Aberavon	9 Nov 1896	Away	5-0	1	Jenkins T, Tanner C.
Llwynypia (L)	23 Nov 1896	Home	0-0	0	No scorers.
Treherbert (L)	30 Nov 1896	Home	0-0	0	No scorers.
Morriston	5 Dec 1896	Home	0-0	0	No scorers.
Barry (L)	14 Dec 1896	Away	3-3	1	W. Bradford T.
Pontypridd (L)	21 Dec 1896	Away	19-0	5	E. Jenkins 2T, R. Hillman T, W. Bradford T, J. Hoskins T, W. Phillips C, AN Other C.
Neath	28 Dec 1896	Away	6-0	2	Jenkins T, Morgan T.
Leicester	30 Dec 1896	Away	0-3	0	No scorers.
Treorky (PL)	5 Jan 1897	Home	29-0	5	J. Hoskins 2T, W. Phillips T, DG, 5C, E. Jenkins T, Davies T.
Bridgend	18 Jan 1897	Home	24-3	6	Bert Morgan 2T, J. Hoskins 2T, W. Phillips T, 2C, W. Bradford T, AN Other C.
Merthyr (L)	1 Feb 1897	Home	23-0	7	J. Hoskins 2T, Nat Price 2T, W. Phillips T, C, J.W. Davies T, AN Other T.
Neath	2 Feb 1897	Home	0-0	0	No scorers.
Aberavon	8 Feb 1897	Home	6-0	2	W. Phillips T, Nat Price T.

Opponents	Date	Venue	Score	Tries	Scorers/Comments
Penygraig (L)	15 Feb 1897	Away	3-12	1	W. Morgan T.
Pontypridd (F)	20 Feb 1897	Away	8-0	1	W. Phillips T, P, C.
Llwynypia (L)	1 Mar 1897	Away	0-8	0	No scorers.
Penygraig (L)	8 Mar 1897	Home	12-3	4	J. Davies T, N. Price T, Fred Millar T, AN Other T.
Hibernians	8 Mar 1897	Home	14-0	3	AN Other 3T, P, C.
Pontypridd (F)	15 Mar 1897	Away	25-3	7	Nat Price 3T, Llew Deere 2T, Fred Millar T, Jenkins T, W. Phillips 2C.
Ferndale (L)	22 Mar 1897	Away	21-0	5	Nat Price 2T, Deere 2T, Hoskins T, W. Phillips 3C.
Junior League	29 Mar 1897	Home	31-0	8	AN Other 8T, P, DG.
Aberavon	29 Mar 1897	Home	9-0	Unknown	Scorers unknown.
Cardiff District	5 Apr 1897	Home	43-5	11	AN Other 11T, 5C.
Treherbert (L)	12 Apr 1897	Away	3-12	1	W. Phillips T.
Newport District	16 Apr 1897	Away	23-0	7	AN Other 7T, C.
Plymouth	19 Apr 1897	Away	11-13	2	W. Phillips T, Muxworthy T, Phillips P, Jenkin C.
Bridgwater & Albion	20 Apr 1897	Away	14-4	3	J. Davies T, Deere T, Muxworthy T, Phillips P, C.

Summary of Playing Record

P	W	D	L	For	Against	Tries	Win Rate %
37	27	5	5	528	84	131+	79.73

Match Reports and Publications

5 October 1896

<u>Mountain Ash 23 Bridgwater & Albion 0</u>

The South Wales Daily News commented in its match report, "The kick off was announced to take place at 4 o'clock, but with the visitors missing their train at Newport, it was an hour later when a start could be effected....That Mountain Ash is a coming team was pretty well evidenced on Saturday when they simply made rings around Bridgwater Albions...."

12 October 1896

<u>Mountain Ash 31 Pontypridd 7</u>
<u>Glamorgan League</u>

The South Wales Daily News reported, "Great interest was evidenced in the valleys in this contest between these two old rivals and a large crowd assembled....Mountain Ash....out of the four matches played, have succeeded in winning easily the whole of their matches."

Mount Team: Back, J. Tanner; ¾ backs, C. Hoskins, Ned Jenkins, Llew Deere, W. Bradford; half backs, Dick Hillman, Wat Phillips; forwards, Tucker, Fred Millar*, T. Perrot, Nat Price, F. Mears, Arthur Allen, J. Davies, M. Watkins.

* denotes Welsh International

The South Wales Daily News reported, "The surprise of the valleys on Saturday was undoubtedly the severe thrashing administered to Pontypridd by Mountain Ash. Great Scot! Scarcely anyone would have thought it possible, but nevertheless such was the case. Pontypridd went away with a bang, but gradually Mountain Ash – who, by the way, still have an unbeaten record – wore them out and did almost as they liked with them. It must have been very galling to the visitors' supporters after their team had obtained a lead of 2 goals to nil to see such an utter collapse, but everyone must admit that the fifteen that won were infinitely better than the other lot all round....Again and again the Mountain Ash players came near scoring....The drop out saw the best piece of passing during the afternoon. Phillips at halfway threw to Hoskins and thence the ball was sent along to Jenkins and afterwards to Deere. The latter, finding himself pressed, skilfully gave the ball up again to Jenkins, who scored after a grand round of passing....At one time, some of the Pontypridd players threatened to leave the field, their argument being that the ball was out of bounds, but the officials in the vicinity declared it was not so and the game resumed....Phillips, with an excellent dribble and Bradford, who was in close attendance, picking up, cleared everybody and scored a clinking try....Tanner, who was tried at three-quarter in place of Jenkins, now received an injury to his knee and had to retire. In spite of his absence, however, Mountain Ash still acted on the aggressive, and Deere, picking up on the centre line, sprinted finely and scored another try, which was converted."

28 October 1896

Mountain Ash 11 Leicester 0
South Wales Daily News

FOOTBALL.

LEICESTER v MOUNTAIN ASH.

The Leicester team, continuing their Welsh tour, appeared at Mountain Ash on Tuesday. The weather was cold and miserable, consequently there was not a large number of spectators. The visitors received a good ovation, and did not appear in the least discouraged by their defeats at Swansea and Llanelly. Millar and Phillips appeared fatigued after their tedious journey from Wortley. The teams were:—

POSITION	LEICESTER	MOUNTAIN ASH
Back	Butting	Tanner
Three-quarter	H Wilkinson	Hoskins
Three-quarter	Goddard	Bradford
Three-quarter	A Field	Deere
Three-quarter	W Jagger	Jenkins
Half-back	Jenkins (Neath)	Phillips
Half-back	W J Foreman	Hillman
Forward	E Redmond	Millar
Forward	W Jackson	Price
Forward	S Perry	Tucker
Forward	E Whitehead	Meads
Forward	Page	Allen
Forward	L Garner	Mills
Forward	A Rees	Davies
Forward	Lincoln	Perrott

Referee, Mr T. Williams, Llwynypia.

Mountain Ash kicked off, the ball being well returned. A scrum ensued, from which Jenkins received the ball, and made a smart run, but was collared in the visitors' 25. Leicester were awarded a free kick, and play was subsequently forced into the home 25. The ball was kicked out of a scrum by one of the visitors, and a free kick was awarded Mountain Ash. Tanner kicked for goal, but the ball went wide. Deere picked up and made a good run, but was collared when on the point of scoring. Phillips picked up the ball from a scrum and ran clean away, passing to Bradford, who scored a try, which was not converted. In the home 25 Deere collared the ball, and made a fine run and ultimately passed to Mills, who was collared. Leicester secured a free kick, but nothing was gained. Tanner made a good attempt for goal, but again missed.

HALF-TIME SCORE: G. T. M.
MOUNTAIN ASH 0 1 0
LEICESTER 0 0 0

Leicester restarted, and the Mountain Ash forwards secured the ball, and made a rush to within a yard of the visitors' goal. One of the visitors' forwards picked up and made a good run to the homesters' 25. Play settled down for some time at midway. From a scrum Phillips picked up and passed to Millar, who scored a try, Tanner's kick going wide. Leicester secured the ball from a line-out, and made a fine run. Several fine passes ensued, but were effectually stopped. Jenkins secured from a scrummage and Mills obtained a try, which was converted by Tanner.

FINAL SCORE: G. T. M.
MOUNTAIN ASH 1 2 0
LEICESTER 0 0 0

REMARKS.

The game proved a very exciting one from commencement to finish. The visitors were rather handicapped owing to their long journey and the previous day's match at Llanelly, but nevertheless played an exceedingly fine game. The forwards of both teams were evenly matched, but at half the home team held a great advantage. Phillips for Mountain Ash being the best half on the field. He played a very tricky game. Foreman was the pick of the visitors. Jenkins (whom they brought from Neath as a substitute) was continually playing off-side, and was cautioned by the referee. The three-quarters of the visitors were on the whole a capital lot, but rather slow. Goddard, though, at times showing a rare turn of speed. Field was the pick of their centres. The whole quartette played a grand game, their passing at times being a treat. At full-back Tanner was superior to Battling.

9 November 1896

Aberavon 0 Mountain Ash 5

Mount Team: Back, Tanner; ¾ backs, Bradford, Hoskins, Jenkins, Deere; half backs, Phillips, Hillman; forwards, Mills*, Millar*, Price, Perrot, Davies, Mears, Allen, Tucker.

* denotes Welsh International

The South Wales Daily News reported, "The so far invincible Glamorganshire League team visited the tinplate town and their coming was looked forward to with considerable interest, and conjecture was rife as to how they would shape when pitted against a first rate team….Undoubtedly the better team won….The visitors were the better trained lot and were altogether smarter than the homesters. They caught the Avonites on one of their off days with the inevitable result. The Rhonddaites are certainly a warm lot in every department of the game. Mills, Millar, and Price of the forwards, Phillips of the halves, and Jenkins and Bradford of the backs, played a rattling game…."

23 November 1896

<u>Mountain Ash 0 Llwynypia 0</u>
<u>Glamorgan League</u>

Mount Team: Back, Jack Tanner; ¾ backs, Joe Hoskins, Ned Jenkins, Llew Deere, W. Bradford; half backs, Wat Phillips, Dick Hillman; forwards, Frank Mills* Capt, Fred Millar*, Tucker, Tom Perrot, F. Mears, J. Davies, Arthur Allen, E. Owens.

* denotes Welsh International

The South Wales Daily News' rugby reporter, "Old Stager", reported, "....advance has been made by several of the Clubs in the Glamorgan League at a really phenomenal rate. Halfway through last season, it was evident that some of the Rhondda and North Glamorgan Clubs were rapidly coming to the front, but that Mountain Ash and Llwynypia would attain the high pitch of excellence they have now reached, was not considered probable....Last year, Mountain Ash headed the League, and the records in that competition show that these Clubs came out in this way:

Mountain Ash: P.14, W.13, L.1, 25 Pts ; Llwynypia: P.14, W.7, L.1, 15 Pts

This season, Llwynypia have eclipsed all previous seasons, and in 10 matches have compiled 228 points to 9. Mountain Ash have put up 193 points to 15, but their record is the better, as they have certainly met higher class teams in Leicester and Aberavon, and brought off a veritable triumph by defeating the Avonites down west, too....For a good hour before the match, large crowds were congregating, and, what is significant of the real popularity of the game now in the valleys, the fair sex was strongly represented, there being in attendance more womenfolk than ever previously assembled for a match in North or Mid Glamorgan. Despite the fact that the assemblage at least quadrupled that ever previously gathered on the ground let to the Mountain Ash Club by the Nixon's Navigation Company at a nominal rental, the officials responded to their call, and the arrangements were as good as they could be. A posse of police was present, but the crowd was, during the long wait, most good humoured. Captain Lindsay, the Chief Constable, watched the game from a capital Press box which had been erected for the occasion....It was a keenly contested game of gruelling character, but it was one in which the play of each side disappointed its partisans...."

30 November 1896

<u>Mountain Ash 0 Treherbert 0</u>
<u>Glamorgan League</u>

The South Wales Daily News reported, "....some rough play was indulged in, the referee being repeatedly hooted by the spectators for his awards.

<u>A Rowdy Scene</u>

No sooner was the match over than the indignation which had been expressed by the spectators against the referee culminated in a rush at him as he was leaving the field. Thanks to the energetic action of a number of friends who surrounded him on the way out, Mr S. Shipton (of Mountain Ash) and others got him outside the enclosure, where a couple of Constables took him across the valley to Penrhiwceiber."

21 December 1896

<u>Pontypridd 0 Mountain Ash 19</u>
<u>Glamorgan League</u>

Mount Team: Back, J.E. Jones; ¾ backs, W. Bradford, Joe Hoskins, Ned Jenkins, Llew Deere; half backs, W. Phillips and R. Hillman; forwards, Frank Mills* Capt, Fred Millar*, M. Price, M. Watkins, J. Davies, T. Perrot, T.J. Phillips, A. Tucker.

* denotes Welsh International

The South Wales Daily News reported, "A repetition of the last defeat was hardly expected. Pontypridd were not in it, especially in the second half, when the brilliant display of the visitors simply puzzled them....The combination of the Mountain Ash men could hardly be improved. The visiting quartette played a magnificent game. They appeared to understand one another to a nicety, and the way they passed and repassed and burst through their opponents dazzled Pontypridd and evoked the unstinted admiration of the crowd. Phillips and Hillman were far and away the best halves....Mills, Millar and Nat Price were easily distinguishable for their splendid forward play...."

28 December 1896

Neath 0 Mountain Ash 6

The South Wales Daily News commented in its match report, "Played at Neath before a crowd enthusiastic enough to brave the elements....both teams were practically at full strength....Picking up from a scrummage, the visiting three-quarters put in some pretty passing which baffled the Neath men and Morgans scored. The better team won, no mistake about it. The Mountain Ash team played a downright good game, every man being well in his place. Their full back made no mistakes....The Mountain Ash three-quarters made quite a brilliant show in comparison with the stumbling and blundering of the Neath quartette."

The Old Firm were still unbeaten going into Christmas 1896 when they travelled to play Leicester on 29 December at Welford Road, Leicester.

30 December 1896

Leicester 3 Mountain Ash 0
South Wales Daily News

FOOTBALL.

LEICESTER v MOUNTAIN ASH.
THE HILLMEN'S FIRST DEFEAT.

At Leicester in brilliant weather before a big crowd, Mountain Ash played their full strength, Leicester being short of several players. The Mountain Ash team was Jones, Hoskins, Bradford, Jenkins, Morgans, W Phillips, Hillman, Mills, Millar, Price, Perrott, Phillips, and Mears.

Leicester started against a bright sun, Miller returning into touch. Leicester speedily got possession, W. Phillips returning finely. Even play followed, a free to each side making matters equal. The visitors pressed through Hoskins and Bradford, but Leicester dribbled back, a return effort by Mills relieving. Leicester then rushed down and Braithwaite made a good attempt to drop a goal, the ball going dead. The visitors then came away, but Leicester returning the rush Jones scored a try, which Field failed to convert. Gale then failed to stop a rush; but the ball unluckily went into touch. Mountain Ash dribbled finely into Leicester's quarters, Gale easing the pressure with a fine touch kick. Bradford afterwards ran finely down the wing Jones then made his mark from a weak kick by Phillips, Leicester becoming very dangerous. Mills returned grandly, but after good play by Jones, Field broke away, nearly scoring. Hoskins saved finely, and carried play to the centre.

HALF-TIME SCORE:
	G.	T.	M.
LEICESTER	0	1	0
MOUNTAIN ASH	0	0	0

Mills restarted, Hoskins following with a grand effort, but he unfortunately knocked on, and the Leicester forwards responded by strong rushes. Then Mountain Ash made several openings, but faulty passing and keen tackling spoiled the chances. Jones eventually cleared Leicester's lines by a huge touch kick. Then the visiting forwards came down with a rush, Hoskins shining prominently, and the Leicester quarter was reached, a long spell of fierce scrummage work taking place in Leicester's 25. Jones eventually kicked over his own line. The Leicester pack relieved slightly, but the visitors attacked hotly, Jenkins being held on the line. Mountain Ash had the hardest possible lines, Hoskins sending dead from a free kick. Bryan relieved with a long run, and after exciting work in front of the goal Hoskins stole a Leicester pass and raced down only to be pulled up five yards from the home line. Nothing more was done, Mountain Ash losing their unbeaten record by 3 points.

FINAL SCORE:
	G.	T.	M.
LEICESTER	0	1	0
MOUNTAIN ASH	0	0	0

REMARKS.

It was a really brilliant game. From first to last the visitors exhibited the better football, showing infinitely more resource, and it was only by the keenest tackling and strong touch-kicking that Leicester maintained the advantage gained by A. O. Jones in the first half. Forward Frank Mills was in really brilliant form, and time after time came through the pack in fine style, Millar and Price ably seconding his efforts. At half Leicester were about equal, Foreman and Braithwaite giving W. Phillips and Hillman a rare bustling time of it. Hoskins was by far the best three-quarter on the field, his aggressive movements being good and well-judged. One run of his was the feature of the afternoon. The Mountain Ash third line was not at all at home in the early part of the game, but improved immensely as the game progressed, although Bradford never properly found his feet and lost one or two good openings by failing at easy passes. Leicester, in addition to the halves already mentioned, have to thank A. O. Jones and Field for fine defensive work, while Bryan utilised the only chance he had during the game, to make a strong raid on the visitors' line. At full back Mountain Ash had a good man in Jones, Gale for Leicester completely failing to return. Redman and Gilbert were the best of the home forwards, who, it must be admitted, were very weak, and far below their usual strength. Mountain Ash created a very favourable impression, and were cordially greeted by the 7,000 or 8,000 spectators present.

4 January 1897

<u>Western Mail</u>

Club.	P.	W.	L.	D.	For.	Ag.
Llanelly	16	15	0	1	154	25
Llwynypia	18	17	0	1	312	14
Newport	16	14	1	1	219	22
Mountain Ash	18	13	1	4	232	28
Aberavon	15	13	2	0	170	23
Swansea	18	14	3	1	224	34
Cardiff	15	10	4	1	146	58
Penarth	17	9	5	3	84	61
Neath	20	7	10	3	82	119

The results of the Glamorgan League competition up to date are as follow:—

Club.	W.	L.	D.	F.	A.	L.P.
Treherbert	6	0	1	105	10	13
Mountain Ash	4	0	3	84	15	11
Llwynypia	4	0	1	89	9	9
Pontypridd	4	5	0	30	106	8
Penygraig	3	2	1	15	7	7
Barry	2	5	2	24	32	6
Ferndale	2	4	0	10	65	4
Merthyr	1	4	0	11	84	2
Treorky	1	5	0	12	84	2

18 January 1897

<u>Mountain Ash 24 Bridgend 3</u>
<u>Ashites Improved Form</u>

The South Wales Daily News reported, "Much disappointment was expressed over the absence of Frank Mills (Mount's Welsh International forward), whose suspension by the Welsh Rugby Union was condemned in strong terms. The opinion generally prevailed that the popular forward had been unjustly dealt with and his admirers cannot understand why the committee did not give him an opportunity to defend himself in reference to the charges preferred against him by Mr Butler, Aberavon (a referee). It was erroneously stated in Friday's issue that the ground was suspended earlier in the season for two months. It should have been two weeks."

25 January 1897

The South Wales Daily News reported, "It is rumoured the principal object of the visit of Tanner, Mountain Ash's old full back to the district last week, was to get some promising players for the North, and those who saw Bradford with him on the Pontypridd ground last Thursday considered whether he too was going to desert his comrades at Mountain Ash." Both Jack Tanner and W. Bradford joined the paid ranks of Northern Union Club, Heckmondwike, which was a Yorkshire-based team that played briefly in the latter 1890s until the end of the 1901/02 season.

2 February 1897

<u>Mountain Ash 0 Neath 0</u>

The Western Mail commented, "There was a heavy fall of snow in Mountain Ash and naturally the ground was not very fit for play. At Neath on Boxing Day, the hillmen defeated the homesters easily but on this occasion they were without threequarters Williams and Morgan, and Jones at full back, hence their supporters were not very confident prior to the commencement of the game. Neath had a fairly good team and although they did not anticipate victory, they were not all together without hope....There was a good crowd of spectators, Mabon's Day (a holiday for those working in the coal mines) affording the bulk of the population a holiday. The commencement of the game was delayed for nearly half an hour owing to the lateness of the home team in putting in an appearance....Football would be a dignified title to apply to the game which was nothing more than a scramble....The game ended in a draw and this was just the right sort of finish for it....both packs played finely. Mountain Ash are to be congratulated upon sustaining their record for good play especially in view of the fact that they were without three good men."

15 February 1897

<u>Penygraig 12 Mountain Ash 3</u>
<u>Glamorgan League</u>

Mount's 12-3 loss at Penygraig in the Glamorgan League virtually ended any chance they had of retaining the Championship, "Welsh Athlete" in the Western Mail reporting, "....there was only one really startling reverse in South Wales football on Saturday, that being the defeat of the Mountain Ash team by Penygraig....this, the first defeat in the Glamorgan competition, robs Mountain Ash of much chance of being at the head of the list when the season ends."

22 February 1897

<u>Western Mail</u>

Club.	P.	W.	L.	D	For	Ag.
Llwynypia	25	24	0	1	447	36
Llanelly	22	20	0	2	197	31
Newport	20	17	2	1	263	43
Mountain Ash	25	18	2	5	325	43
Swansea	25	19	4	2	272	55
Aberavon	20	15	5	0	209	42
Cardiff	20	14	5	1	196	71
Penarth	23	12	8	3	133	98
Neath	27	8	15	4	110	185

In the Glamorgan League there was only one game played, that between Llwynypia and Treorky, so that there is no material alteration in the list, which is as follows:—

Club.	W.	L.	D.	F.	A.	L.P.
Llwynypia	9	0	1	197	9	19
Treherbert	6	0	3	113	18	15
Mountain Ash	6	1	3	139	27	15
Pontypridd	5	7	1	53	145	11
Barry	3	6	3	34	41	9
Penygraig	3	5	1	27	44	7
Merthyr	3	5	1	26	141	7
Treorky	3	8	0	62	113	6
Ferndale	1	6	0	7	68	2

1 March 1897

<u>Llwynypia 8 Mountain Ash 0</u>
<u>Glamorgan League</u>

Western Mail rugby writer, "Welsh Athlete", wrote in his Saturday morning review of the afternoon's games, "Up the hills, Llwynypia receive a visit from Mountain Ash. It's sure to be a big fight....on their own ground, Llwynypia, to my way of thinking, are the equal to any team in Wales. Form certainly points towards Llwynypia on their own ground....Llwynypia have won no less than 24 out of their 25 matches they have played. Mountain Ash, on the other hand, have won 18 of their 25, the 7 being accounted for by 2 being lost and 5 drawn. Mountain Ash, I understand, have put in a special preparation. I take it, however, that with so much at stake – that is, with a clean sheet and the record of the Glamorgan League – Llwynypia are not likely to have neglected anything in this respect. It will be a great game but, speaking honestly, I think Llwynypia will just manage to win....Every match in the past has been keenly contested and generally it is thought that there is not much in it."

Mount Team: Back, J. E. Jones; ¾ backs, Joe Hoskins, D.L. Williams, H.W. Morgan, S. Muxworthy; half backs, Wat Phillips Capt, Dick Hillman; forwards, J. Davies, Fred Millar*, Tom Linton, T. J. Phillips, F. Mears, M. Price, J.W. Davies, T. Perrot.

* denotes Welsh International

The South Wales Daily News reported, "The return match between the teams was regarded as the most important League fixture for some time. Llwynypia have been going very strong all through the season....They have so far an unbeaten record, having won 24 out of the 25 matches played, the draw being with Mountain Ash early in the season. The latter on the other hand have, owing greatly to the deprecations of the Northern Union poachers, fallen off slightly from the form displayed a couple of months ago, and of 25 matches played, have lost 2 and drawn 5....they are 4 points behind Llwynypia and it was certain that they would make supreme efforts today to at least make a draw with their brilliant rivals. The gate was a record one, a big contingent having journeyed to Llwynypia from the Aberdare valley and Pontypridd by special train....The game was a battle of giants and a very fine treat, delighting the big crowd....the tremendous roar which resounded through the narrow valley when time was called showed how keen was their delight. Though beaten, Mountain Ash were certainly not disgraced. In the first half they rose to the expectations of their admirers. Their opponents had utterly failed to cross their line, and once at least, the visitors experienced hard lines in not scoring. In the second half, however, although playing with rare dash and pluck, it was clear that unless they met with a stroke of luck, they would be vanquished. Time after time, Llwynypia pressed and their efforts were rewarded by two tries, but these did not fall to their lot without working very hard for them. At forward, the teams were fairly matched, and the result is to a great extent due to the better finish, alertness and the aggressiveness of the home backs...."

Results up to and including February 27th.

	Matches			Points		
	Won.	Lost.	Drn.	For.	Agst.	L.pts.
Llwynypia	10	0	1	205	9	21
Treherbert	6	0	3	113	18	15
Mountain Ash	6	2	3	139	35	15
Pontypridd	5	7	1	55	145	11
Barry	3	6	3	34	41	9
Treorky	4	8	0	71	119	8
Penygraig	3	5	1	27	44	7
Merthyr	3	5	1	26	141	7
Ferndale	1	7	0	13	77	2

15 March 1897

<u>Pontypridd 3 Mountain Ash 25</u>
<u>Friendly Fixture</u>

The South Wales Daily News commented, "Chick of Pontypridd was thrown into touch by Millar when he had got the ball. An unfortunate incident followed, several blows being exchanged between two or three players. This caused some excitement and the episode ended in Millar and Mears of Mountain Ash and McKenzie and Walter Davies being ordered off the field by the referee, who was by no means as firm as he should have been at other stages of the game."

22 March 1897

Ferndale 0 Mountain Ash 21
Glamorgan League

The South Wales Daily News remarked in its match report, "The visitors had to play without four of their best forwards....Millar and Mears are undergoing a period of suspension for irregular conduct at Pontypridd the previous Saturday....The field of play is not enclosed and half of it looks like a ploughed field....A number of spectators were frequently inside the touchline and the committee should make an effort to put a stop to this as such a state of things interfere greatly with the game....The referee, whose decisions on two or three occasions did not please the crowd, was followed and hooted by a number of youngsters on his way to his hotel."

19 April 1897

Plymouth 13 Mountain Ash 11

The South Wales Daily News reported, "Played before a couple of thousand spectators in disagreeable weather at Plymouth....Plymouth started in a sensational manner, scoring two tries within a few minutes of the start....in the second half, the Welshmen more than held their own. The stubborn defence of Plymouth prevented a further score. Mountain Ash time after time swarmed around the home goal and the tries they secured were really meritorious efforts. In the three-quarter line, Muxworthy, Jenkins and Hoskin showed some fine play....Wat Phillips distinguished himself at half and the try he secured was beautifully obtained." "Welsh Athlete" in the Western Mail commented, "Mountain Ash appear to have had a lot of bad luck at Plymouth after having the best of the play."

20 April 1897

Bridgwater & Albion 4 Mountain Ash 14

The South Wales Daily News reported, "At Bridgwater on Monday, the Welshmen finished their tour with a victory....Five minutes from the start, a grand bit of passing between the backs ended in J. Davies scoring an unconverted try....Deere placed Mountain Ash on the attack. The forwards, again developing dashing form and passing, left Deere with the ball, and he ran through the Albion lot in brilliant style and scored behind the posts. Mountain Ash were now going at a great pace, the Albion being outclassed...."

The last known table of the leading Welsh Clubs was also published:

Club	P.	W.	L.	D.	F.	A.
Llwynypia	33	32	0	1	643	54
Llanelly	31	26	1	4	258	45
Newport	27	22	4	1	359	61
Cardiff	28	22	5	1	351	108
Mountain Ash	31	21	5	5	381	85
Aberavon	28	20	7	1	284	75
*Swansea	32	21	8	3	319	101
Penarth	30	14	13	3	186	188
Neath	35	13	18	4	192	206

*Including Saturday's match with Birkenhead, which is counted as a win for Swansea.

24 April 1897

At the end of the season, the South Wales Daily News published reports of the season just ended for a number of Clubs. Mount joined Aberavon, Neath, Treherbert, Morriston, Bridgend and Penygraig in having their season analysed. The report follows:

MOUNTAIN ASH.

Mountain Ash's record for the season, which closed with the match against Bridgwater Albion on Easter Monday, is a fairly satisfactory one, especially when it is considered that the club had to face severe adverse circumstances during the year. The prospects for the season were exceedingly roseate at the start, and so strong was the team, and so excellent the combination both forward and back, that ten victories followed in rapid succession, amongst the defeated teams being Leicester, Aberavon, and Bridgwater Albion. Frank Mills, the old International—who is not likely to again don the jersey, and who has done much to raise the standard of the team—was then at its head, but the first meetings with Llwynypia and Treherbert ended in no score being made by either side. The referee in the Treherbert match was Mr Butler, of Aberavon, and some of his decisions so angered the spectators that a section of them hooted him as he left the ground. The incident was reported to the Welsh Rugby Union, and the ground was suspended for a fortnight. Unfortunately, the affair did not end there, for shortly afterwards Frank Mills was suspended for four Saturdays, in consequence of improper language alleged to have been used by him towards Mr Butler. This decision of the Union caused great dissatisfaction in Mountain Ash, where it was asserted that Mr Mills was not guilty of the accusation brought against him, and that he had been unjustly punished. Mills had played such an important part in football in Wales till then that his suspension naturally annoyed him, and he has not since, if we remember rightly, played. But these were not the only misfortunes that befel the club. After the Llwynypia match on November 21st Tanner, who had done such sterling work for the team as full-back, forsook the club, "poachers" from Heckmondwike having enticed him to cast his lot with that team. His departure was a serious loss to his old comrades, but they soon afterwards found a good substitute in J. E. Jones, of Cardiff, who throughout the remainder of the season proved himself to be one of the best full-backs in the League. The first reverse was sustained at Leicester, the latter just notching a win by a try, and the second, and the worst during the season, followed six weeks later at Penygraig, who won the game by 11 points to 3. In this connection it is a singular fact that up to the present both teams when meeting each other upon their own ground have not been defeated. In the second League match with Llwynypia, on the latter's ground, the visitors lost one of the best games witnessed on the ground by eight points to nil, and a similar reverse met them in the last match with Treherbert. This caused Mountain Ash to take third place in the League, Treherbert jumping to the second position. Bradford, who had wonderfully improved this season, also left for Heckmondwike two or three months ago, but notwithstanding the desertions, the team still had an excellent quartette, Bertie Morgan, a very promising wing, who recently left for Swansea, and Williams, of St. Michael's College, Aberdare, who gave up football after his ordination in Lent, doing splendid service for the club. Hoskins has been a tower of strength throughout the season, and he is justly regarded as one of the smartest three-quarters in the League. Deere and Muxworthy have done fairly well; whilst Jenkins, an old member of the Seaside Stars, Llanelly, a smart, tricky player, has shown promise of a good future. W. Jenkins, who captained the team after Mills, has done yeoman service, and few half-backs there are who can give him points behind the pack. He had an able confrere in Hillman. Of a good pack of forwards Mat Price (who has the distinction of taking top place with Hoskins as a try-getter, both having scored 19 each), Jenkins, and Millar are deserving of special mention. The secretarial duties were efficiently carried out by Mr H. Hall. The record is as follows:—

Season 1897/98

<u>Glamorgan League Runners-Up</u>
<u>Old Firm Lose Players To Northern Union & Take On Strong English Opposition</u>

Mount lost players early on in the season, centre Joe Hoskins joining full back Jack Tanner in the paid ranks of the Northern Union, and scrum half Wat Phillips moving to Pontypridd due to changing his job. The good news for the Old Firm, though, was that Phillips' move didn't last long and he was back in the black and amber jersey by the end of November 1897. The Old Firm's start to the season continued in the same winning vein as the previous season with 6 wins and a draw from the first 7 games played, but that's where it ended. At the end of the season, they had played 37, won 20, drawn 1 and lost 16, scoring 349 points, which included 95 tries, and conceded 216, which equated to a win rate of 55.41%. Although the playing record wasn't as good as in 1896/97, Mount did better in the Glamorgan League, finishing 2nd to Llwynypia, who the Old Firm beat 16-11 at home but lost to away, 4-0. The season saw a "double" over Treorky and Bridgend, 3 wins and a loss to Pontypridd, a convincing win over Maesteg, and close defeats to Aberavon and Neath. In April 1898, the South Wales Daily News reported that Mount had to cancel their game at Morriston because "no players could be procured owing to the coal dispute." The season also saw the Old Firm travel into England on quite a few occasions to play strong opposition. The team travelled to the east Midlands over Christmas 1897, playing Leicester and Northampton on consecutive days, and losing both games, 14-3 and 19-0 respectively. Against Devonport Albion, which was a Club based in Plymouth, and a growing force in English rugby, the game was lost 13-6, and then later in the season, Plymouth RFC overturned their 22-0 loss in Mountain Ash by winning 20-11 in front of 5,000 spectators at their Home Park ground. There was also a win and a loss against Cinderford. The season's top try scorer was wing Llew Deere with 19, followed by International forward Fred Millar with 13 and scrum half Wat Phillips who got 10, and also kicked 14 conversions. The Club also run a 2nd XV, three of the known results being home wins over Treherbert "A", 5-3, and Capcoch, 11-0, and a 3-3 draw with Merthyr Alexandria.

Fixtures 1897/98

Opponents	Date	Venue	Score	Tries	Scorers/Comments
St Paul's, Cardiff	11 Sep 1897	Unknown	27-4	7	Fred Millar 3T, 3C, Llew Deere T, Jack Deere T, E. Griffiths T, Hillman T.
Newport Harriers	20 Sep 1897	Home	27-3	7	Llew Deere T, Jack Deere T, Fred Millar 3T, 3C, Dick Hillman T, E. Griffiths T.
Pontyclun	27 Sep 1897	Home	16-0	4	Jack Deere 2T, Fred Millar T, C, E. Griffiths T, W. Jones C.
Treorky (L)	4 Oct 1897	Away	17-3	5	Deere 2T, W. Jones T, Hillman T, Muxworthy T, Fred Millar C.
Newport District	4 Oct 1897	Unknown	7-7	1	Scorers unknown.
Penygraig (L)	11 Oct 1897	Home	6-4	2	Llew Deere T, Fred Millar T.

Opponents	Date	Venue	Score	Tries	Scorers/Comments
Bridgend	18 Oct 1897	Away	3-0	1	Deere T.
Treherbert (L)	25 Oct 1897	Home	0-11	0	No scorers.
Pontypridd (L)	1 Nov 1897	Away	0-11	0	No scorers.
Cinderford	3 Nov 1897	Unsure	16-7	4	Scorers unknown.
Devonport Albion	8 Nov 1897	Away	6-13	2	Fred Millar T, Inns T.
Penygraig (L)	15 Nov 1897	Away	3-9	1	Tom Linton T.
Aberavon	22 Nov 1897	Home	0-3	0	No scorers.
Pontypridd (F)	29 Nov 1897	Home	3-0	1	Llew Deere T.
Abercarn	4 Dec 1897	Away	0-7	0	No scorers.
Glamorgan Police	6 Dec 1897	Home	22-0	6	Scorers unknown.
Llwynypia (L)	11 Dec 1897	Away	0-4	0	No scorers.
Barry (L)	18 Dec 1897	Away	6-0	2	Fred Millar T, E. Griffiths T.
Leicester	28 Dec 1897	Away	3-14	1	W. Harris T.
Northampton	29 Dec 1897	Away	0-19	0	No scorers.
Bridgend	3 Jan 1898	Home	20-3	6	Llew Deere 2T, Fred Millar T, C, J. Griffiths T, J. Simmonds T, R. Hillman T.
Maesteg	4 Jan 1898	Home	23-4	7	Wat Phillips 3T, C, Llew Deere T, Fred Millar T, L. Parry T, T. Perrot T.
Llanelly	10 Jan 1898	Home	0-17	0	No scorers.
Barry (L)	17 Jan 1898	Home	11-3	3	L. Parry T, Fred Millar T, W. Phillips C, AN Other T.
Pontymoile	24 Jan 1898	Away	0-3	0	No scorers.
Neath	31 Jan 1898	Home	3-5	1	Ben Tiley T.
Llwynypia (L)	7 Feb 1898	Home	16-11	4	AN Other 4T, 2C.
Plymouth	8 Feb 1898	Home	22-0	6	Wat Phillips 3T, C, Llew Deere 2T, M. Watkins T, Fred Millar C.
Pontypridd (F)	14 Feb 1898	Away	13-3	3	AN Other 3T, 2C.
Aberavon	21 Feb 1898	Away	0-6	0	No scorers.
Neath	28 Feb 1898	Away	3-5	1	Griffiths T.
Treherbert (L)	7 Mar 1898	Home	12-0	2	Muxworthy T, Deere T, Harris DG, Phillips C.

Opponents	Date	Venue	Score	Tries	Scorers/Comments
Pontypridd (L)	14 Mar 1898	Home	8-3	2	Scorers unknown.
Plymouth	21 Mar 1898	Away	11-20	3	Deere 2T, Phillips T, C.
Treorky (L)	28 Mar 1898	Home	17-3	5	W. Phillips T, C, J. Davies T, L. Deere T, W. Sage T, AN Other T.
Pontymoile	4 Apr 1898	Home	22-3	6	AN Other 6T, 2C.
Cinderford	11 Apr 1898	Away	6-8	2	AN Other 2T.

Summary of Playing Record

P	W	D	L	For	Against	Tries	Win Rate %
37	20	1	16	349	216	95	55.41

Match Reports and Publications

20 September 1897

<u>Mountain Ash 27 Newport Harriers 3</u>

The South Wales Daily News reported, "Played at Mountain Ash Athletic grounds during fairly good weather. It is almost a misnomer to term the home team as first for 11 out of the 15 were picked from the 2nds....The team is considerably weakened by the loss of scrum half Wat Phillips, who had been unanimously appointed as captain for the season and whose place as captain was filled by Fred Millar, an old International forward (and a future one as it turned out, adding 6 more Welsh caps in 1899/1900 and 1900/1901). It is not too much to say that Mountain Ash has, already, in the opening of this season, suffered more than any other Club in the League by poaching. Ned Jenkins, three-quarter, has been picked to play for Llanelly against Bridgwater, and Phillips is expected to play for Pontypridd against Treherbert."

4 October 1897

<u>Treorky 3 Mountain Ash 17</u>
<u>Glamorgan League</u>

Mount Team: Back, D.E. Lloyd; 3/4s, Llew Deere, Muxworthy, Jack Deere, W. Jones; half backs, Hillman, Emrys Griffiths; forwards, Fred Millar*, Perrot, J. Harries, Arthur Allen, Mann, Deere, Linton, Morgan.

* denotes Welsh International

The South Wales Daily News reported, "Great interest was felt at Treorky and the surrounding district in the contest between these two champion teams of the hills, this being the first appearance of Mountain Ash on the Treorky ground for the last two seasons....There was a large attendance....It is to be regretted that a little roughness was noticeable in the visitors' play, no fewer than 5 of the homesters being laid out, an occurrence which drew forth strong indignation. The Mountain Ash lot were evidently strong. Deere and Jones were the pick of the Mount quartette, especially in defensive tactics."

11 October 1897

<u>Mountain Ash 6 Penygraig 4</u>
<u>Glamorgan League</u>

Mount Team: Back, J.D. Lloyd; 3/4s, J. Tamplin, Llew Deere, W. Jones, Jack Deere; half backs, D.H. Edmunds, R. Hillman; forwards, Fred Millar* Capt, T. Perrot, J. Harris, Arthur Allen, S. Linton, J. Davies, W. Mann, A. Price.

* denotes Welsh International

The South Wales Daily News reported, "….during the second moiety, there was only one team in it – and that was not Penygraig. If Mountain Ash could hold its own against the heavyweights of Penygraig, then it was argued the home backs would do the rest. That forecast was literally fulfilled…."

8 November 1897

<u>Devonport Albion 13 Mountain Ash 6</u>

The South Wales Daily News reported, "….To fill a vacancy, the Albion Club induced Mountain Ash to pay them a visit. The Glamorgan Leaguers, with a desire to make a creditable stand, invited W. Phillips, the Glamorgan County half, their late captain, to accompany them. An application made to the Pontypridd Club, to which Phillips has recently transferred, was met with refusal, but the half back disregarded this and went south."

22 November 1897

<u>Mountain Ash 0 Aberavon 3</u>

Mount Team: Back, J. Netherway; 3/4s, Llew Deere, S. Muxworthy, L. Parry, W. Jones; half backs, D.H. Edmunds, R. Hillman; forwards, Fred Millar* Capt, T. Perrot, H. Beer, A. Inns, J. Davies, W. Cale, T. Linton, E. Owen.

* denotes Welsh International

The South Wales Daily News reported, "The game was fought with grim determination and the pace maintained throughout was the hottest. Up to within 10 minutes of the end, it was practically impossible to see with whom the advantage lay, for play vacillated all over the field. In a word, the game was lost and won during the last 10 minutes when Aberavon went away with a dash that was irresistible."

29 November 1897

<u>Mountain Ash 3 Pontypridd 0</u>
<u>Friendly Fixture</u>

Mount Team: Back, J. Netherway; 3/4s, Llew Deere, S. Muxworthy, D. H. Edmunds, L. J. Parry; half backs, Wat Phillips, R. Hillman; forwards, A. Inns, T. Perrot, H. Beer, T. Linton, H. Evans, A. Allen, Fryer, J. Davies.

The South Wales Daily News reported, "Wat Phillips, who has done splendid service for Pontypridd, opposed, having obtained his transfer to play again for Mountain Ash, where he has returned to work. His inclusion in the home team meant a great gain to it and an equal loss to the visitors, who were by no means confident of the result. The homesters were without the services of Millar (Mount's Welsh International forward)….Before the match commenced, Mr W. Shipton, the Secretary of Mountain Ash, entered a protest against the inclusion of George Evans and Saunders in the visitors' team on the ground that Mr Llewellyn, Secretary of Llwynypia, had informed him that the Club, which had a day off, would not give the necessary sanction to play for Pontypridd….After their splendid victory over Llwynypia last Saturday, it was generally expected that Pontypridd would manage to beat Mountain Ash....The ground was in a terrible state and was dotted here and there with mud and pools of water, rendering anything like a scientific display impossible. It was therefore evident it would be a forward game. This proved to be the case, the encounter throughout being almost entirely confined to the packs. Both were fairly matched in weight, but the home eight made several irresistible rushes and held a slight advantage in the open, Inns being particularly prominent by his dash and capital dribbles....The victory of the homesters was undoubtedly due to their forwards and smart individual work on the part of some of the backs, of whom Llew Deere was the shining light. His first try, after intercepting a pass, was an eye opener, and showed his rare speed. He played throughout, a champion game, and experienced hard lines in not adding a second try when the leather went out of bounds a few inches in front of him."

28 December 1897

<u>Leicester 14 Mountain Ash 3</u>

The South Wales Daily News reported, "In cold, damp weather, these teams met at Leicester in the presence of about 5,000 spectators. The teams were well represented....In the first half, the home team showed much superior combination but after the interval, Mountain Ash warmed to their work and beat the Leicester men in all departments. Considering the long journey which they had undertaken, the form displayed by the Welshmen was very satisfactory. The forwards worked the scrums in skilful fashion and Millar, Davis and Evans were, on several occasions, to the front with excellent dribbling tactics. At half, Harris and Hillman made many good openings, and the three-quarter line showed themselves to great advantage. The forwards, taken on the whole, did some very smart work, and Netherway at back, played a fairly safe game. On the day's form, Mountain Ash should beat Northampton today by some points."

29 December 1897

<u>Northampton 19 Mountain Ash 0</u>

The South Wales Daily News reported, "Played in fine weather on soft ground before about 8,000 spectators, Mountain Ash played the same team, with the exception that E. Griffiths took the place of Andrews in the three-quarter line, which suffered defeat at the hands of Leicester on the previous day....The score fully indicates the nature of play. Never was there seen such a falling off in a team than in Mountain Ash. Compared with their previous day's form in the match against Leicester, the players were decidedly off colour. It is true that in the second half the exhibition given by them was of a fairly good description.... Millar put in some good footwork and Harris, in the three-quarter line, was conspicuous for some smart bits of play."

4 January 1898

<u>Mountain Ash 23 Maesteg 4</u>

Mount Team: Back, T. Davies; 3/4s, J. Simmons, Llew Deere, W. Harris, L. Parry; half backs, Wat Phillips and E. Griffiths; forwards, Fred Millar*, T. Perrot, A. Inns, H. Beer, J. Harris, Alf Fryer, Warren, Osborne.

* denotes Welsh International

The South Wales Daily News reported, "From a scrum, Griffiths picked up and transferred to Deere, who ran three quarters of the length of the field and secured a try....play was rather rough....In a scramble near the visitors' 25, Perrot picked up, and neatly eluding his opponents, crossed over and fell on the ball. In the second half....Phillips made a daring dash and collared the ball from the full back's hands, grounding right under the posts. In the last 3 minutes, Phillips at midway again got possession, and by means of a dodgy, zigzag run, completely outstripped his opponents and secured another try."

7 February 1898

Mountain Ash 16 Llwynypia 11
Glamorgan League

The South Wales Daily News reported, "The return League match was played in the presence of a large crowd....The match excited considerable interest as it was known that if Llwynypia, who now head the League competition, were defeated, their chance of winning the Cup for the third time would be considerably lessened....Llwynypia have won 7 and lost one, while Mountain Ash have won 4 and lost 4....the feeling was that there would be very little difference between the teams.....local feeling ran strong in favour of Mountain Ash, who put out a strong lot. It is a noteworthy fact that Llwynypia have never beaten Mountain Ash on the latter's ground, and that both have held the Cup. Llwynypia tied with Mountain Ash once....The game was one of the finest ever seen on the home ground....The homesters deserved to win for they showed superior combination almost throughout....Mountain Ash have not played such a great game before this season. Their halves and three-quarters were distinctly superior. Phillips and Hillman were cleverer....It was in the back play that Llwynypia were defeated, for forward the teams were evenly matched. The game was of a very fast and exciting character, and the result led to a remarkable demonstration on the part of the home crowd."

8 February 1898

Mountain Ash 22 Plymouth 0

Mount Team: Back, H. Edmunds; 3/4s, Llew Deere, Sam Muxworthy, Griffiths, W. Harris; half backs, W. Phillips, Dick Hillman; forwards, Fred Millar* Capt, J. Davies, A. Inns, Price, T. Linton, Fryer, M. Watkins, J. Osborne.

The South Wales Daily News reported, "....The visitors were badly beaten....From start to finish they scarcely had a look in and the homesters played throughout a remarkably good game. They are improving as the season advances, and their form against Llwynypia clearly shows they will make things hum in forthcoming matches. Wat Phillips was in fine form, and has seldom played a better game, whilst the home backs all round, were far superior to their opponents. It was here that their superiority was chiefly noticeable, Hillman simply making rings round them. Phillips played a magnificent game and was as tricky as ever. The quartette, too, were in fine form....The visiting forwards were a heavy lot, but though able to hold their own well in the tight scrummages, they were not so smart as their opponents once the ball was let loose....The home team is showing marked improvement upon its display earlier in the season and can, on its present form, easily take first place in the League. A few crack teams are to be met during the next few weeks, and if the last two games are to serve as a criterion of what is going to take place, Mountain Ash will certainly make matters lively for their opponents."

14 March 1898

Mountain Ash 8 Pontypridd 3
Glamorgan League

The South Wales Daily News reported, "Of the 3 previous matches, Pontypridd won the first but Mountain Ash won the next two. Pontypridd lead by one point in the League but if their opponent wins today's match, they will take second place to Llwynypia who will this year again be winners....Much interest was centred on the game....Lord Aberdare was amongst the spectators, viewing the match from an enclosure fixed in the Press Box....The game was fast and open and one of the prettiest seen on the ground this season. In the first half, the homesters played a very hard, aggressive game and certainly had the best of matters, but the fact they only crossed the line twice was due to the splendid defence and keen tackling of their opponents."

22 March 1898

GLAMORGAN LEAGUE.

The positions of the clubs in the Glamorgan League up to and including Saturday last are:—

	P.	W.	L.	Dr.	For.	Agst.	Pts.
Llwynypia*	11	9	2	0	80	29	18
Mountain Ash	11	7	4	0	78	59	14
Treherbert	12	7	5	0	97	35	14
Pontypridd	11	6	4	1	61	65	13
Treorky*	9	3	5	1	40	76	7
Penygraig	10	3	6	1	42	68	7
Barry	10	1	9	1	28	94	3

*Treorky failing to fulfil their fixture with Llwynypia on the 19th inst. forfeit two points to the latter. Llwynypia have now won the competition, and are champions of the League for season 1897-98.

5 May 1898

South Wales Daily News

FOOTBALL.

RECORDS OF LOCAL CLUBS.

MOUNTAIN ASH.

The Mountain Ash Club had a lot of ill-luck to contend with at the commencement of the season, but the record as shown below is in every respect one which it can well be proud of under the circumstances. The flitting away of Tanner, the full-back, and Hoskins, one of the finest centres that the club has yet possessed, to the North before the season opened, caused a considerable amount of trepidation as to the team's chances for the year, and the departure of W. Phillips, the captain, to Pontypridd, after a few matches had been played, made matters appear very much worse. A dark cloud, indeed, seemed to be hovering over the club, but the committee and players, although slightly discouraged, went in with a will that deserved the success which, before the close of the year, attended their efforts. The record of the team compares very favourably with that of other Welsh teams when everything is taken into consideration, and especially in view of the difficulties which had to be contended with. It is a source of gratification to the club and its supporters that the team succeeded in reaching the second position in the League competition. The club has once been in possession of the cup, but it was seen as the season advanced that their chances of getting it this year were very remote. For the first half of the season the team was a somewhat indifferent one, as a whole, but it soon improved, and particularly after the return of the veteran half from Pontypridd. The team did fairly well until it met Treherbert from home, and on that occasion they had to play without Phillips, who had for the moment transferred his affections to Pontypridd, although strong efforts were made at the time to allure him to Salford. An amusing tale could be told of the attempts made to capture him, and the way he eluded the tempters at the eleventh hour, when journeying from the Rhondda towards Cardiff, from whence he was supposed to be bound the next morning for Salford. However, "All's well that ends well," and there is no question that Phillips did much by his return to rehabilitate the team, as it were, and to infuse into the players more vigour and confidence in their own powers. After winning six matches the men of the "Mount," as they are known locally, found themselves pitted against Treherbert on the ground of the latter in a League match, which they lost by 11 points to nil, and the following Saturday Pontypridd, who had suffered severely at their hands the year before, piled up an equal number of points against them, Phillips aiding the victors against his old comrades very materially. A victory over Cinderford at home was followed by three defeats in succession, and before the new year was ushered in they were again beaten three times, the old year being finished with a tour to Leicester and Northampton. From now until the close of the season 17 matches were played, and of that number seven were again lost, but the display of the team had greatly improved during the last three months. During that period they piled up a pretty heavy score, Llwynypia, Plymouth, Pontypridd, and Treherbert being rather badly beaten on the home ground. The greatest surprise was the downfall of the League champions, who led at half-time, and looked as if they were going to emerge victors. During the second moiety, however, the homesters woke up in wonderful fashion, and completely turned the tables, their brilliant play before the close resulting in a well-deserved victory by five points. Ben Tiley, the veteran three-quarter, turned out on that occasion, and showed that he could still play a fine game. Mountain Ash has unearthed a number of sterling players, but the most prominent this year, barring W. Phillips, was Ll. Deere, whose fleetness of foot has served his side and himself in good stead on many occasions. He heads the list of scorers, having run in with 19 tries, and the fact that he was chosen for League and county honours shows that he was recognised as a really smart and promising player. In all probability Mountain Ash has lost his services, for just before the close of the season he left for Plymouth, whilst Millar, the captain, who was one of the most prominent of the forwards this year, went to Devonport. Another very promising player is Sam Muxworthy, who is likely to develop into a first-class centre. He played for the League in the inter-League match with Monmouthshire, and his display on that occasion fully justified his selection. Always conspicuous among the forwards was Inns, who also before the close of the season returned to Newport, where his abilities were recognised by the officials of the premier team, for which he has since played more than once. Lord Aberdare has evinced much interest in the club this year, and, together with Lady Aberdare and other members of the family, was frequently a spectator, an enclosure having been fixed up for their convenience below the Press box. This season's secretary was Mr W. Shipton, whose enthusiasm for the game did much to keep the team together when prospects were by no means bright.

Season 1898/99

Old Firm Hold Their Own
Welsh Trial Held In Mountain Ash

This was a similar type of season to 1897/98 with the Old Firm winning just over half their games. There were convincing home wins over Pontypridd and Ebbw Vale, the South Wales Daily News commenting on 16 January 1899 of the latter win, "Mountain Ash must feel somewhat elated after their victory over the Ebbw Valians who, up to Saturday, had not had a goal registered against them this season." The Old Firm played Bridgwater & Albion twice in a matter of days on their Christmas tour, once on the way to playing Plymouth and the other on the way back, the first of which was drawn and the second won. There were also drawn games at home to Aberavon and away at Neath, and narrow losses to Llwynypia, Llanelly, Aberavon, Treorky, Pontypridd and Penygraig. The season's playing record showed 27 games played, 13 won, 4 drawn and 10 lost, with 197 points scored, which included 53 tries, and 103 conceded, to give a win rate of 55.56%. Mountain Ash 2nd XV was also playing regularly and one of their games was a 0-0 draw at home to Abercynon, which was the first known fixture between the Clubs. In some of the other fixtures they played, Ystrad were beaten 17-0, and there were two close defeats to Aberaman, 6-3 at home and 3-0 away. Mountain Ash was also the venue for a Welsh trial match in early December 1898 where two teams of the best players in Wales staked their claim for selection to the national team. Prolific try scoring wing, Llew Deere, also showed his other talents by doubling up as Club Secretary.

Fixtures 1898/99

Opponents	Date	Venue	Score	Tries	Scorers/Comments
Merthyr Vale	26 Sep 1898	Home	14-0	4	Llew Deere T, Fred Millar T, Jack Muxworthy T, J. Davies T, W. Harris C.
Pontypridd (L)	3 Oct 1898	Home	20-3	4	Llew Deere 2T, W. Harris T, Osborne T, Jack Muxworthy DG, 2C.
Aberavon	10 Oct 1898	Away	5-9	1	S. Muxworthy T, AN Other C.
Treorky (L)	17 Oct 1898	Away	8-10	2	Llew Deere T, T. Mears T, Muxworthy C.
Treorky (L)	24 Oct 1898	Home	8-5	2	W. Harris T, Fred Millar T, AN Other C.
Treherbert (PL)	31 Oct 1898	Home	6-3	2	G. Linton T, Jack Deere T.
Pontypridd (L)	7 Nov 1898	Away	0-3	0	No scorers.
Pontymoile	14 Nov 1898	Home	8-0	2	T. Linton T, Muxworthy T, Millar C.

Opponents	Date	Venue	Score	Tries	Scorers/Comments
Morriston	21 Nov 1898	Away	0-6	0	No scorers.
Llanelly	28 Nov 1898	Away	3-8	1	C. Brailey T.
Llwynypia (L)	12 Dec 1898	Home	3-7	1	Tom Linton T.
Barry (L)	19 Dec 1898	Home	32-0	8	Brailey 3T, Ned Jenkins 2T, Llew Deere T, Emrys Griffiths T, E.T. Davies T, Ivor Morgan DG, Fred Millar 2C.
Bridgwater & Albion	26 Dec 1898	Away	0-0	0	No scorers.
Plymouth	27 Dec 1898	Away	6-14	2	Dai Fryer T, Alf Fryer T.
Bridgwater & Albion	28 Dec 1898	Away	5-0	1	Llew Deere T, Fred Millar C.
Chepstow	2 Jan 1899	Home	15-0	5	Scorers unknown.
Ebbw Vale	16 Jan 1899	Home	14-0	4	T. Williams T, Llew Deere T, A. Jenkins T, Fryer T, E. Griffiths C.
Pontymoile	13 Feb 1899	Away	3-9	1	Scorer unknown.
Aberavon	20 Feb 1899	Home	3-3	1	Ivor Morgan T.
Treherbert (L)	27 Feb 1899	Away	11-9	3	Llew Deere 2T, C, Ivor Morgan T.
Glynneath	6 Mar 1899	Home	19-0	5	Scorers unknown.
Penygraig (L)	13 Mar 1899	Home	11-5	3	Llew Deere T, Brailey T, Linton T, AN Other C.
Chepstow	27 Mar 1899	Away	0-0	0	No scorers.
Neath	3 Apr 1899	Away	0-0	0	No scorers.
Pontyclun (PL)	10 Apr 1899	Away	3-0	1	Scorer unknown.
Ebbw Vale	24 Apr 1899	Away	0-6	0	No scorers.
Penygraig (L)	1 May 1899	Away	0-3	0	No scorers.

Summary of Playing Record

P	W	D	L	For	Against	Tries	Win Rate %
27	13	4	10	197	103	53	55.56

Match Reports and Publications

3 October 1898

<u>Mountain Ash 20 Pontypridd 3</u>
<u>Glamorgan League</u>

Mount Team: Back, Jack Muxworthy; 3/4s, Llew Deere, Sam Muxworthy, Brailey, W. Harris; half backs, R. Hillman, T. Mears; forwards, Fred Millar*, E.J. Davies, Osborne, J. Davies, T. Perrot, T. Linton, Beere, Alf Fryer.

* denotes Welsh International

The South Wales Daily News reported, "....there was a good attendance, considerable speculation being rife as to the issue....The homesters, especially the back division keeping up the game at a hot pace, made matters repeatedly ugly for their opponents. Sam Muxworthy and Llew Deere were very aggressive....Jack Muxworthy, picking up, made a random kick, and as the leather sailed over the bar, the crowd cheered lustily....Osborne was conspicuous in initiating the subsequent attack which ended in Harris, after capital play by the brothers Muxworthy, scoring an unconverted try. And a moment later, Deere romped over and Jack Muxworthy improved upon the points."

10 October 1898

<u>Aberavon 9 Mountain Ash 5</u>

Mount Team: Back, Jack Muxworthy; 3/4s, Llew Deere, Sam Muxworthy, Brailey, J. Harris; half backs, Dick Hillman, T. Mears; forwards, Fred Millar*, T. Davies, C. Davies, T. Osborne, Fryer, Linton, Perrot, Beere.

* denotes Welsh International

Although losing this match at Aberavon, the South Wales Daily News referred to Mount's 5-0 win at Aberavon in November 1896, "Aberavon entertained the Mountaineers on Saturday and keen interest was centred on the meeting as the 'Avonites had not forgotten the sensational victory gained by Mountain Ash on the home enclosure at the first meeting of the Clubs in 1896. Both Clubs have started the season well, the visitors having gained a victory over Pontypridd, and Aberavon against Neath. Both teams were strongly represented but the high wind acted somewhat as a deterrent to an open, passing game."

24 October 1898

<u>Mountain Ash 8 Treorky 5</u>
<u>Glamorgan League</u>

Mount Team: Back, Jack Muxworthy; 3/4s, Llew Deere, Sam Muxworthy, W. Brayley, W. J. Harris; half backs, Dick Hillman, T. Phillips; forwards, Fred Millar* Capt, P. Davies, Perrot, Linton, J. Davies, Osborne, A. Fryer, E. Fryer.

* denotes Welsh International

The South Wales Daily News reported, "Treorky, who have hitherto had to content themselves with a back seat in the Glamorgan League, look like providing a veritable surprise package. They have unexpectedly jumped to the front rank of the League teams. Matches have been played with Pontyclun, Barry, Tondu, Whitchurch, Bridgend, Aberavon and Mountain Ash, and each has been won. Last Saturday, Treorky beat Mountain Ash by 2 points (Treorky 10 Mountain Ash 8)....it was natural that the keen fight of the previous week should invest today's match with unusual interest. Mountain Ash held an advantage in the fact that they were playing on their own heath, and it was expected they would spare no effort to clear old scores. The weather unfortunately was very unfavourable and the ground heavy and sodden. It was felt that the facts named would cause the play to be confined to the forwards, and as the homesters were heavier in this respect than their opponents, it was believed they would have the best of matters."

28 November 1898

Llanelly 8 Mountain Ash 3

The South Wales Daily News reported, "The recent rainfall had made the unusually dry soil of Stradey Ground in a sloppy state when the home team met Mountain Ash. A fair crowd gathered....Mountain Ash setting the ball going....an exchange of kicks ensued, which ended in a scrummage in the home territory....relief was temporarily gained....Morgan Williams failed to take the ball (for Llanelli) and the forwards pounced on the ball and set the three-quarters in motion, and Brailey scored a try.... The home spectators did not regard this score with any fear as of late, their opponents have invariably scored first....Half way was the venue of a vigorous tussle....The Mountain Ash forwards were decidedly getting the best of the scrummages at this juncture....The visiting halves were continually off-side and were again penalised by the referee...."

5 December 1898

The South Wales Daily News' esteemed rugby journalist, "Old Stager", reported that Mountain Ash was the venue for a Welsh International trial in which an Old Firm player, the Reverend E.T. Davies, took part.

The Coming Trial at Mountain Ash

"The decision of the Welsh Union committee in altering the title and scope of the old-time East v West trial, which produced nothing but discord between the respective districts, and to substitute it for a trial of the 30 presumably best men in the Clubs of the Principality, without regard to their territorial position, met with cordial appreciation throughout Wales. The trial took place on Saturday at Mountain Ash, but owing to the slippery ground, due to heavy and continuous rain, and the absence of notable half backs, the importance of the match for the purposes designed was exceedingly minimised....Although a convenient excursion service had been arranged, comparatively few people availed themselves of the facilities offered, and when the kick off took place, there was only a thin attendance, and in no place were the spectators more than three or four deep."

26 December 1898

Bridgwater & Albion 0 Mountain Ash 0

The South Wales Daily News reported, "Mountain Ash opened their holiday tour by encountering Bridgwater on the ground of the champions of Somerset. The match aroused great interest and everything being favourable to a fine game, a big crowd lined up....Millar of Mountain Ash was ordered off the field for rough play....half time came with a clean scoresheet, 0-0. Bridgwater lost two forwards injured....Play for the most part was very unscientific....at times play more rough than was at all necessary, Westcott and Morgan, the opposing centres came into collision, referee Beasley of Bristol ordered both off....five men being absent at the finish."

27 December 1898

<u>Plymouth 14 Mountain Ash 6</u>

Mount Team: Back, Linton; 3/4s, Llew Deere, Spiers, Morgan, Jack Deere; half backs, Griffiths, Jenkins; forwards, Fred Millar*, Osborne, Perrot, Davies, A. Fryer, D. Fryer, Lewis, Price.

* denotes Welsh International

The South Wales Daily News reported, "Before about 5,000 spectators in stormy weather, Mountain Ash met Plymouth on Monday. The home team were at full strength but Mountain Ash had to make several alterations to the team at the last moment, Brailey not turning up, whilst Mears was not able to play. Under these circumstances, Spiers, a Devonport Albion forward, was invoked in the three-quarter line....The chief feature of the game was the vigour with which it was contested. At Bridgwater, the Welshmen were told the Plymouthians played a rough game and so they started with more vigorous tackling than was necessary, with the result that the game was very rough before the close....Linton played well at back, and Millar and the two Fryers were the pick of a good pack."

Not content with two games in quick succession over Christmas 1898, the Old Firm returned to Bridgwater and Albion for their third game in 4 days.

28 December 1898

<u>Bridgwater & Albion 0 Mountain Ash 5</u>

The South Wales Daily News reported, "Mountain Ash broke their journey at Bridgwater on Tuesday and with better success than on Saturday....The Somerset men gave a good account of themselves against such strong opponents."

30 January 1899

GLAMORGAN LEAGUE.

The positions of the clubs up to date are:—

Club.	Pl.	W.	Lt.	Dr.	Points For.	Points Agst.	Lge. Pts
Penygraig	6	5	1	0	40	15	10
Treherbert	*8	5	3	0	54	24	10
Mountain Ash	7	4	3	0	77	31	8
Llwynypia	4	3	1	0	58	11	6
Pontyclun	7	3	4	0	50	45	6
Treorky	8	3	5	0	46	45	6
Pontypridd	6	2	4	0	27	75	4
Barry	*8	2	6	0	20	96	4

*Treherbert has protested against the match with Barry on the 21st inst. being considered as a win for the latter club, owing to the game being finished 12 minutes before time.

13 February 1899

The first ever known fixture between Mount and Abercynon took place in February 1899, the South Wales Daily News reporting the 0-0 draw as follows:

> **ABERCYNON v MOUNTAIN ASH RESERVES.**
>
> Played on the latter's ground. The weather has been unfavourable during the whole week, and at the commencement of the match rain was still falling, consequently the ground was in a wretched condition. The match was advertised for 3.30, but the combatants did not enter the arena before 4 o'clock. Abercynon hold a honourable position in the Junior League up to the present, coming second or third. Both teams were fully represented. Mr Ben Lewis, Pontypridd, was appointed referee, but through some unexplained circumstance did not turn up, and Mr W. Giles, Ponting. Union referee, was agreed upon. The homesters won the toss, and kicked off from the Town side, Mears setting the ball in motion, and it was well-returned. Play waged hot and strong in the home 25 for sometime, but from a scrum Joe Lloyd picked up nicely, and had almost a clear course when Bert Thomas, bounding up, pushed him into touch. The homesters received a free, but gained little ground. Griffiths was playing a champion game, and continually had his finger in the pie. Again the visitors prevailed. From a scrum near the home citadel Dai Edwards got possession and tried a drop at goal, but the oval struck the post and rebounded. Again Edwards made his mark in a favourable position, but failed at improving. Abercynon were continually attacking, and experienced hard lines in not scoring.
>
> | Half-time Score— | G. | T. | M. |
> |---|---|---|---|
> | Mountain Ash A. | 0 | 0 | 0 |
> | Abercynon | 0 | 0 | 0 |
>
> Resuming, Paget kicked off, but the kick was mulled. The ball at this stage of the game was travelling rapidly to and fro from side to the other without any decided advantage to either side. The homesters were now pressing fiercely, and war was waged for a considerably long time near the visitors' line.
>
> | Final Score— | G. | T. | M. |
> |---|---|---|---|
> | Abercynon | 0 | 0 | 1 |
> | Mountain Ash Reserves | 0 | 0 | 1 |

20 February 1899

Mountain Ash 3 Aberavon 3

Mount Team: Back, T. Williams; 3/4s, Llew Deere, E. Jenkins, Ivor Morgan, Brailey; half backs, T. Mears and Eynon; forwards, Perrot, E.P. Davies, J. Davies, G.D. Davies, Dai Fryer, Alf Fryer, Osborne, Linton.

The South Wales Daily News reported, "Lord Aberdare occupied a seat in the enclosure below the Press Box….A stiff forward struggle ensued….The home halves, after a severe onslaught, threw out to Deere who ran between the wing and centre and was going well when Dan Jones pulled him down by the leg. Had the veteran half failed to do this, the fleet home wing would have scored from his 25. The visiting pack was playing a hard, aggressive game….Foster of Aberavon just managed to score….The next incident was a splendid dribble by the home forwards from one 25 to the other where Eynon picked up and threw to Ivor Morgan who scored amid cheers. Brailey, amid much excitement, then got to the visitors' 25 and had not Deere's attempt to field been frustrated, a second try would have been inevitable….The game was evenly contested and was one of the most keenly fought yet between the teams."

3 April 1899

Neath 0 Mountain Ash 0

Mount Team: Back, J. Lloyd; 3/4s, Jenkins, Brailey, Llew Deere, Ivor Morgan; half backs, Mears and Griffiths; forwards, Fred Millar*, Osborne, J. Davies, E. Fryer, M. Lewis, D.A. Davies, E. Linton, A. Price.

* denotes Welsh International

The South Wales Daily News report commented, "....owing to a fog of considerable density, the outlook for spectators was decidedly bad....Mountain Ash were without the Reverend E.T. Davies, J. Fryer, Perrot and O'Neill. Neath, although suffering from absenteeism, were strongly represented....To Mountain Ash the highest praise is due for excellent defence....Ned Jenkins' tackling all through had been superb....The character of the display by both teams is indicative of the approaching close of the season, and the comment of a spectator, "anyone would think they were on tour" furnishes a fairly correct criticism and estimate of their form."

17 April 1899

Mountain Ash v Morriston

The South Wales Daily News reported, "Mr Llew Deere, Secretary of Mountain Ash, said that Morriston wired overnight to say they could not find the funds necessary to journey to Mountain Ash. To this, the Mountain Ash Secretary replied that the home Club would meet the expenses. This morning, however, another wire was received stating that Morriston could not get a team together. The matter, we understand, will be reported to the Welsh Union."

28 April 1899

The South Wales Daily News commented, "Feelings of rivalry have run high in many of the League contests of this season, and this keenness has been accentuated by the fact that the champion Club is rewarded by a home fixture with Cardiff, which means a substantial addition in the way of gate money. Far too much roughness has distinguished the contests and squabbling on and off the field has been a regrettable feature.... Certain matters....have caused an increasing popular opinion that these Cup contests should be abandoned even if the continuation of the League should not be stopped by the Welsh Union....During the week, all sorts of rumours had been circulated as to the way in which each Club was going to strengthen its side. The transfers, according to the Secretaries of the Clubs, had been secured, but it is not surprising that the Welsh Union should have determined to hold an investigation into the circumstances. Such an inquiry, if thoroughly conducted, will assuredly result in removing all doubt as to the bona fides of certain Rhondda Clubs and of the strictly amateur status of the 30 odd players who travel from Cardiff to take part in the matches of Clubs affiliated to the Glamorgan League. At present....there is a lot of suspicion that some players do not participate in these particularly rough League matches simply for the love of a game in a better class of company than they could get at home...."

1 May 1899

<u>Penygraig 3 Mountain Ash 0</u>
<u>Glamorgan League</u>

Mount Team: Back, O'Neill; 3/4s, Llew Deere Capt, Jack Deere, E. Jenkins, Ivor Morgan; half backs, Eynon and Mears; forwards, Fred Millar*, E.T. Davies, W.A. Fryer, Dai Fryer, Osborne, D.A. Davies, J. Davies, Linton.

* denotes Welsh International

The South Wales Daily News reported, "The ground was very heavy owing to recent rains….Mr Jenkins, Secretary of the home team, wired to Mountain Ash asking if the visitors would agree to postpone the match. Llewellyn Deere, the Mount Secretary, replied that they would keep the fixture and they made the journey to Penygraig without Brailey at wing, and Emrys Griffiths, half back. The latter's absence was due to a telegram which had been received in the afternoon from his brother-in-law, Wat Phillips, the old Mountain Ash half back, who has played for Salford this season, stating that he had been injured and asking his mother to proceed at once to Salford….Mountain Ash experienced the hardest of lines in failing to make what was a very closely contested game a draw. When they had the wind they failed to score and Hunt's try for Penygraig, after he charged a kick by the full back, was a very lucky one….about 10 minutes until time was called, Mount hovered dangerously about Penygraig's goal. Ivor Morgan once got across and his inability to ground the ball when he was on his back – though many of the spectators near the spot declared he did so – lost the game for his side."

Season 1899/1900

Mount Return To Form & Get Some Big Wins
Fred Millar In Welsh XV That Wins Triple Crown

The Old Firm returned to their best form, playing 34 games, winning 24, drawing 3 and losing just 7, scoring 351 points, which included at least 93 tries, and conceding just 124, to give a win rate of 75%. Several games were high scoring with plenty of tries. One of the biggest home wins in the Club's 24 year history came against Bridgend, when 11 tries were run in and 39 unanswered points scored. There was also a 25-0 home win over the Glamorgan League champions of 1898/99, and one of the Old Firm's fiercest rivals for the trophy, Llwynypia, 7 tries being run in. Other high scoring wins came at Plymouth when 6 tries were scored in a 24-0 win, at Portsmouth where 5 tries were scored in the 15-3 win on Christmas Day 1899, and last, but not least, 5 were scored in the 19-3 home win over Hartlepool Rovers. There were "doubles" over Neath and Ebbw Vale, and two wins over Pontymoile, which was a Club that went on to become Pontypool in 1901/02. In total, there were 3 wins and a draw against Llwynypia, and 2 wins from 3 games against Pontypridd. There were also narrow away losses to Devonport Albion, who were soon to be a power in English rugby, and Bridgwater & Albion. The difficulty of winning the Glamorgan League was underlined in this season because, as good as it was, it was not good enough to finish top, Treorky being crowned champions for the first time. As well as Fred Millar returning to International rugby after a break of 4 years to play a part in Wales' wins over England, Ireland and Scotland, which secured the Triple Crown for the second time, wing and Captain Llew Deere also had a season to remember by being the top try scorer for a second successive season, this time with 24. Once again there was 2nd team rugby, wins being registered over Miskin Harlequins and Troedyrhiw, but a loss to Aberaman.

Fixtures 1899/1900

Opponents	Date	Venue	Score	Tries	Scorers/Comments
Tondu	16 Sep 1899	Unknown	10-0	2	Scorers unknown.
Crumlin	23 Sep 1899	Unknown	3-0	1	Scorer unknown.
Penygraig (PL)	30 Sep 1899	Away	3-6	1	Scorer unknown.
County Police	2 Oct 1899	Home	25-8	7	Scorers unknown.
Treherbert (PL)	7 Oct 1899	Away	0-5	0	No scorers.
Pontymoile	14 Oct 1899	Unknown	17-3	5	Scorers unknown.
Llwynypia (PL)	19 Oct 1899	Away	8-3	2	Scorers unknown.
Devonport Albion	28 Oct 1899	Unknown	3-8	1	Scorer unknown.
Pontypridd (PL)	6 Nov 1899	Away	8-3	2	Llew Deere 2T, Jack Deere C.
Llwynypia (PL)	13 Nov 1899	Home	25-0	7	Jack Deere 2T, C, H. Beer T, Linton T, Ivor Morgan C, AN Other 3T.
Ebbw Vale	18 Nov 1899	Home	13-0	3	Dai Fryer T, Deere T, Mat Price DG, AN Other T.
Neath	27 Nov 1899	Away	5-0	1	Scorers unknown.
Tredegar	4 Dec 1899	Away	15-6	5	Geo Edwards 2T, Jack Deere T, Beere T, AN Other T.
Treorky (L)	11 Dec 1899	Home	3-3	1	Scorer unknown.

Opponents	Date	Venue	Score	Tries	Scorers/Comments
Pontymoile	23 Dec 1899	Unknown	5-3	1	Scorers unknown.
Portsmouth	26 Dec 1899	Unknown	15-3	5	Scorers unknown.
Neath	1 Jan 1900	Home	3-0	0	Jack Deere P.
Pontyclun (L)	13 Jan 1900	Home	16-0	4	Scorers unknown.
Pontypridd (PL)	20 Jan 1900	Home	10-3	2	Llew Deere T, Mat Price DG, AN Other T.
Llwynypia (PL)	5 Feb 1900	Away	8-8	2	Llew Deere 2T, Thomas C.
Aberaman	17 Feb 1900	Home	19-0	4+	Mat Price 2T, Thomas T, 2C, Llew Deere T, AN Other 3pts.
Bridgend	26 Feb 1900	Home	39-0	11	Llew Deere 3T, C, Thomas 2T, 2C, Fryer 2T, Ivor Morgan T, Mat Price T, George Edwards T, Ned Jenkins T.
Pontypridd (L)	3 Mar 1900	Away	3-5	1	Millar T.
Ebbw Vale	10 Mar 1900	Away	5-3	1	Ned Jenkins T, AN Other C.
Treherbert (L)	19 Mar 1900	Home	6-3	2	W. Griffiths T, Ivor Morgan T.
Treorky (L)	24 Mar 1900	Away	0-7	0	No scorers.
Llwynypia (PL)	29 Mar 1900	Unknown	11-0	3	Scorers unknown.
Crumlin	31 Mar 1900	Unknown	13-4	3	Scorers unknown.
Penygraig (PL)	9 Apr 1900	Home	8-8	2	George Edwards T, Llew Deere T, E.H. Thomas C.
Plymouth	14 Apr 1900	Away	24-0	6	Deere 4T, Millar 2T, Thomas 3C.
Bridgwater & Albion	16 Apr 1900	Away	3-8	1	Fryer T.
Glamorgan Lge XV	17 Apr 1900	Home	6-0	2	Ned Jenkins 2T.
Hartlepool Rovers	17 Apr 1900	Home	19-3	5	Ivor Morgan 2T, George Edwards T, Davies T, Loosemore T, AN Other 2C.
W.J. Bancroft's Swansea XV	23 Apr 1900	Home	0-21	0	No scorers.

Summary of Playing Record

P	W	D	L	For	Against	Tries	Win Rate %
34	24	3	7	351	124	93+	75.00

Match Reports and Publications

6 November 1899

<u>Pontypridd 3 Mountain Ash 8</u>

Mount Team: Back, Owen Joseph; 3/4s, Ned Jenkins, Jack Deere, Ivor Morgan, Llew Deere; half backs, Edwards and Thomas; forwards, Fred Millar*, Osborne, Fryer, Perrot, Beere, Linton, Morton, Price.

* denotes Welsh International

The South Wales Daily News reported, "....Llew Deere picked up in the home 25 and ran over with a good try....Soon after the kick off, the Mountain Ash forwards went away with a bang and what looked like a second try ended in a minor. The tactics of the Pontypridd side were often of the kick and rush order....The second half opened somewhat sensationally for the homesters....ran over with a well earned try. Mountain Ash, who were somewhat taken aback by the sudden reverse, then pulled themselves together and removed the venue into the Pontypridd 25. Gradually, by dint of hard forward play, Millar, Fryer and Osborne being prominent, they relegated the homesters to defensive work, and more than once the home line was in imminent danger....Llew Deere again got possession and running at a tremendous rate showed a clean pair of heels and scored under the posts. Jack Deere converted."

13 November 1899

<u>Mountain Ash 25 Llwynypia 0</u>
<u>Possible Glamorgan League Fixture</u>

Mount Team: Back, Jones; 3/4s, Albert Deere, Jack Deere, Ned Jenkins, Ivor Morgan; half backs, Thomas and Edwards; forwards, Fred Millar*, M. Price, Alf Fryer, H. Beer, Osborne, Linton, Albert Price, Morton.

* denotes Welsh International

The South Wales Daily News reported, "It is hard to believe that Llwynypia were so badly defeated, yet so they were, and the heavy score against them gives a fair idea of the general character of the game.....though Mountain Ash led by 13 points at the close of the first half, it was generally felt that Llwynypia would at least hold their own when they had the strong wind behind them. But they failed even to do that, and their punishment during the last 40 minutes was, if anything, even more severe then during the first. Their opponents were in unusually aggressive form....Their forwards more than held their own while the superiority of their backs was strikingly manifest."

4 December 1899

<u>Tredegar 6 Mountain Ash 15</u>

Mount Team: Back, David Fryer; 3/4s, Ned Jenkins, Jack Deere, D. Jenkins, Ivor Morgan; half backs, Thomas and Edwards; forwards, Osborne, Fryer, Mat Price, Morton, Linton, Beere, Alf Price, Perrot.

The South Wales Daily News reported, "Played on Tredegar's Athletic Ground before a fair crowd, a fair amount of interest was manifested in this match for it was the first occasion that these teams faced each other. The kick off was advertised for 3.15 but it was fully 4 o'clock before the teams entered the enclosure of combat. It should be mentioned....were without the services of Fred Millar (Mount's Welsh International forward), Llew Deere and Oscar Williams....Jack Deere covered fully 25 yards in the direction of the enemy's line. When he was on the point of scoring, Ivor Morgan got possession and transferring to Ned Jenkins enabled the latter to gain a lot of ground. The ex-Llanellyite, after dodging a couple of opponents, threw at the proper time to Edwards, who scored in the corner...Dusk now set in and it was absolutely impossible to distinguish the players. Lamps burned on the outskirts of the field and they might also have been employed with advantage on the field, especially in the Press Box....It was Tredegar's first encounter with Mountain Ash and if they don't improve, it might also be their last....They were worsted in every phase of the play, especially the forward department, where the Mountain Ash heavyweights were seen to advantage. In praise of the homesters display....it was not sustained, although at times the attack of the backs was quite brilliant."

11 December 1899

<u>Mountain Ash 3 Treorky 3</u>
<u>Glamorgan League</u>

Mount Team: Back, J. Lloyd; 3/4s, Llew Deere, Jack Deere, E. Jenkins, Ivor Morgan; half backs, Thomas and Edwards; forwards, Fred Millar*, Perrot, Alf Fryer, Dai Fryer, H. Beere, Linton, M. Pryce, J. Jones.

* denotes Welsh International

The South Wales Daily News reported, "The first League game of the season between the above teams was played at Mountain Ash in cold, frosty weather. The contest was anticipated with much interest locally and there was a fair gate. Both teams were strongly represented....The first appearance of the brothers Muxworthy against their old colleagues at Mountain Ash since they severed their connection with the team lent additional interest to the contest....The game was very closely contested throughout and the pace was terrific; indeed, a livelier or faster contest has rarely been seen on the home ground. The visitors played a surprisingly good game and their opponents had all their work cut out to avert a defeat. In the first half.... Mountain Ash's standard of play in no way approached what has been seen in some previous matches. Somehow or other, they could not get into swing. In the second half, however, they showed a vast improvement and the fact that their oft-renewed onslaughts only resulted in one try was due to the splendid defence and keen tackling of the Rhondda men. The home captain made several fine efforts to score and was the best man on his side, whilst Sam Muxworthy was as sharp as a needle and did a lot of useful work. The game was mainly of a forward character but the home pack, on the whole, did not excel. During the closing stages, they warmed up and put in some good work. The home backs were too often neglected, but the offside tactics of the visiting half and the smartness of the forwards contributed very materially to this."

1 January 1900

<u>Mountain Ash 3 Neath 0</u>

Mount Team: Back, J. Barry; 3/4s, Llew Deere, Ivor Morgan, D. Jenkins, J. Davies; half backs, G. Edwards and Thomas; forwards, Fred Millar*, Alf Fryer, Osborne, Beere, M. Price, T. Perrot, D. Morton, T. Linton.

* denotes Welsh International

The South Wales Daily News reported, "The rivalry between the Clubs has been very keen, Mountain Ash having beaten Neath in the last match. After the recent defeat of Llanelly by the Neathites, the homesters anticipated a hard tussle but were determined to make a bold bid for the leading position....The home forwards played with more dash and had possession of the ball a great deal oftener than the visiting eight....

the greasy state of the ball prevented good combined play....The forwards on both sides played a hard game....Millar played a splendid game, his smart following up and sure tackling bringing him constantly to the front. At three-quarter, the homesters appeared to have the advantage, the two Deeres going strongly and on two occasions ill luck alone prevented them from scoring."

5 February 1900

<u>Llwynypia 8 Mountain Ash 8</u>
<u>Possible Glamorgan League Fixture</u>

Mount Team: Back, Hiles; 3/4s, Llew Deere, Ivor Morgan, Thomas, D. Jenkins;
half backs, Edwards and Thomas; forwards, Fred Millar*, M. Price, Osborne, Beere, Alf Fryer, Dai Fryer, T. Linton, Morton.

* denotes Welsh International

The South Wales Daily News reported, "The two previous matches resulted in wins for Mountain Ash, 8-3 at Llwynypia and 25-0 at Mountain Ash, the latter being the heaviest experienced by the ex-champions. Several players were absent on both sides....Jack Deere, the three-quarter, left last Tuesday for Hull, having accepted a good offer to join that team....The pace was very hot and fast throughout, and the game teemed with stirring incidents. The excitement was sustained to the end, the issue remaining in doubt until a minute to the call of time....a race for possession and just as Deere was about to kick the ball dead, he collided violently with one of the uprights and fell – a piece of ill luck which ended in W.R. Williams scoring for Llwynypia....the conversion struck the bar. In less than three minutes, the visitors were attacking strongly and a splendid round of passing ended in Deere showing a clean pair of heels and scoring a fine try, which Thomas converted. The homesters then led by 3 points, but a brilliantly got try scored by Deere equalised matters. The game was well worth witnessing and it was evident from the start that the homesters were resolved to do their utmost to make up for the last two defeats. Their opponents, on the other hand, were equally as determined, and the result was a really fine game, although a few times, the display was marred by an undesirable amount of feeling. The teams were evenly matched as could possibly be. The forwards had a hard, gruelling game and both packs brought off some fine rushes and footwork. The halves watched each other very closely but the display behind was not up to either team's usual standard...for Mountain Ash, Deere and Ivor Morgan were continually conspicuous, the former's rare pace enabling him to turn what looked like a defeat into a draw." On 17 April 1900, Llwynypia drew 6-6 with Cardiff at the Arms Park, which gave a good indication of the strength of some of the valley Clubs in 1899/1900.

26 February 1900

<u>Mountain Ash 39 Bridgend 0</u>

Mount Team: Back, W. Jones; 3/4s, Llew Deere, W. Thomas, Ned Jenkins, Ivor Morgan;
half backs, T. Edwards and T. Linton; forwards, Fred Millar*, M. Price, H. Beere, Will Osborne, Alf Fryer, T. Morton, Perrot, Dai Fryer.

* denotes Welsh International

The South Wales Daily News commented in the first half, "The game was rather monotonous....In a struggle to obtain possession, Millar was thrown against the posts and knocked out. Fryer picked up and scored. Nothing now could stop the continual bursts of the home backs and some very pretty and effective bits of play were seen."

19 March 1900

Mountain Ash 6 Treherbert 3

Glamorgan League

The South Wales Daily News reported, "....great disappointment was caused at Mountain Ash when the visitors failed to appear with the ordinary train. A telegram was received to the effect that the Rhonddaites would come down by the workmen's train to Abercynon, and thence by brake to Mountain Ash. Consequently the kick off was delayed for a considerable time....With the sun and wind against them, Mat Price kicked off at 4:25 for the homesters...."

9 April 1900

Mountain Ash 8 Penygraig 8

Possible Glamorgan League Fixture

There are some old Club caps in the Mountain Ash Clubhouse that date back 100 years or so. These may be the ones that were presented to each player that had represented the Old Firm during the season. In this report, the South Wales Daily News commented, "Although advertised for 4 o'clock, the kick off did not take place until after 5 owing to the late arrival of the Penygraig team. Advantage was taken of the time to present the home team with the season's caps, the interesting duty being performed by Mr Evan Jenkins, stationer, Mountain Ash, who also spoke a few words of encouragement to the players."

14 April 1900

Plymouth 0 Mountain Ash 24

Mount Team: Back, Barry; 3/4s, Llew Deere, Thomas, Ned Jenkins, Ivor Morgan; half backs, Edwards and Thomas; forwards, Fred Millar*, Price, Beere, Fryer, Morton, Perrot, Osborne, Fryer.

* denotes Welsh International

The South Wales Daily News reported, "At South Devon place, Plymouth, these teams met before 8,000 spectators in glorious weather....The game was contested at a rare pace. In the first half, the Welshmen were the better lot and kept the ball travelling....Millar played a very fine game and led his pack in almost every movement. Deere was also in grand form and the halves and backs, as a whole, played a pretty and effective game. Plymouth only became dangerous once or twice during the whole game."

24 April 1900

Local Club Records

Mountain Ash

The South Wales Daily News summed up the Old Firm's season as follows, "Though this has not been the best season the Club has had, Mountain Ash deserve all credit for their record and Mr Llew Deere is to be congratulated upon the way in which he has kept his men together. He has been the biggest scorer, having no fewer than 24 tries to his credit. The Club possesses a number of youngsters who give every promise of developing into class players next season. During the year, 351 points have been scored, which includes 93 tries, with only 99 conceded.

Top Try Scorers: Llew Deere 24, Jack Deere 11, Fred Millar 7, George Edwards 7, Ivor Morgan 6, E. Jenkins 6, Alf Fryer 5, Mat Price 5, Tom Linton 4, Wm Thomas 3, D. Moreton 3, H. Beere 3, T. Perrot 2, Dai Fryer 2.

Goal Kickers: Jack Deere 12 conversions and a penalty, D.J. Thomas 11 conversions."

The try count and points conceded given here are both slightly less than the figures in the "Summary of Playing Record" shown at the end of the list of fixtures played above.

A Selection of the Old Firm's Results 1890/91 to 1899/1900

Matches v Llwynypia

Pre-Rhondda, Merthyr & Aberdare League/Glamorgan League

Opponents	Season	Venue	Score	P	W	D	L
Llwynypia	1893/94	Away	13-6	1	1	0	0
Llwynypia	1893/94	Home	0-0	2	1	1	0

From Start of Rhondda, Merthyr & Aberdare League/Glamorgan League

Opponents	Season	Venue	Score	P	W	D	L
Llwynypia (L)	1894/95	Home	0-3	1	0	0	1
Llwynypia (L)	1894/95	Away	6-3	2	1	0	1
Llwynypia (L) Merthyr, Aberdare & Rhondda League Play Off.	1894/95	Pontypridd	8-8	3	1	1	1
Llwynypia (L) 1894/95 Merthyr, Aberdare & Rhondda League Play Off replay.	1895/96	Pontypridd	7-8	4	1	1	2
Llwynypia (PL)	1895/96	Away	3-0	5	2	1	2
Llwynypia (PL)	1895/96	Home	11-8	6	3	1	2
Llwynypia (L)	1896/97	Home	0-0	7	3	2	2
Llwynypia (L)	1896/97	Away	0-8	8	3	2	3
Llwynypia (L)	1897/98	Away	0-4	9	3	2	4
Llwynypia (L)	1897/98	Home	16-11	10	4	2	4
Llwynypia (L)	1898/99	Home	3-7	11	4	2	5
Llwynypia (PL)	1899/1900	Away	8-3	12	5	2	5
Llwynypia (PL)	1899/1900	Home	25-0	13	6	2	5
Llwynypia (PL)	1899/1900	Away	8-8	14	6	3	5
Llwynypia (PL)	1899/1900	Unknown	11-0	15	7	3	5

Total Games Played v Llwynypia in the 1890s

P	W	D	L
17	8	4	5

Matches v Pontypridd

Pre-Rhondda, Merthyr & Aberdare League/Glamorgan League

Opponents	Season	Venue	Score	P	W	D	L
Pontypridd	1891/92	Away	2-0	1	1	0	0
Pontypridd	1893/94	Away	0-11	2	1	0	1
Pontypridd	1893/94	Home	6-0	3	2	0	1

From Start of Rhondda, Merthyr & Aberdare League/Glamorgan League

Opponents	Season	Venue	Score	P	W	D	L
Pontypridd (L)	1894/95	Away	9-3	1	1	0	0
Pontypridd (PL)	1894/95	Home	20-0	2	2	0	0
Pontypridd (L)	1895/96	Away	12-8	3	3	0	0
Pontypridd (L)	1895/96	Home	10-0	4	4	0	0
Pontypridd (L)	1896/97	Home	31-7	5	5	0	0
Pontypridd (L)	1896/97	Away	19-0	6	6	0	0
Pontypridd (F)	1896/97	Away	8-0	7	7	0	0
Pontypridd (F)	1896/97	Away	25-3	8	8	0	0
Pontypridd (L)	1897/98	Away	0-11	9	8	0	1
Pontypridd (F)	1897/98	Home	3-0	10	9	0	1
Pontypridd (F)	1897/98	Away	13-3	11	10	0	1
Pontypridd (L)	1897/98	Home	8-3	12	11	0	1
Pontypridd (L)	1898/99	Home	20-3	13	12	0	1
Pontypridd (L)	1898/99	Away	0-3	14	12	0	2
Pontypridd (PL)	1899/1900	Away	8-3	15	13	0	2
Pontypridd (PL)	1899/1900	Home	10-3	16	14	0	2
Pontypridd (L)	1899/1900	Away	3-5	17	14	0	3

Total Games Played v Pontypridd in the 1890s

P	W	D	L
20	16	0	4

Matches v Treorky

Opponents	Season	Venue	Score	P	W	D	L
Treorky (PL)	1894/95	Away	8-3	1	1	0	0
Treorky (L)	1895/96	Home	9-0	2	2	0	0
Treorky (PL)	1895/96	Away	10-0	3	3	0	0
Treorky (PL)	1896/97	Home	29-0	4	4	0	0
Treorky (L)	1897/98	Away	17-3	5	5	0	0
Treorky (L)	1897/98	Home	17-3	6	6	0	0
Treorky (L)	1898/99	Away	8-10	7	6	0	1
Treorky (L)	1898/99	Home	8-5	8	7	0	1
Treorky (L)	1899/1900	Home	3-3	9	7	1	1
Treorky (L)	1899/1900	Away	0-7	10	7	1	2

Matches v Penygraig

Pre-Rhondda, Merthyr & Aberdare League/Glamorgan League

Opponents	Season	Venue	Score	P	W	D	L
Penygraig	1892/93	Away	5-10	1	0	0	1
Penygraig	1892/93	Home	0-0	2	0	1	1
Penygraig	1893/94	Away	0-6	3	0	1	2
Penygraig	1893/94	Home	0-0	4	0	2	2

From Start of Rhondda, Merthyr & Aberdare League/Glamorgan League

Opponents	Season	Venue	Score	P	W	D	L
Penygraig (PL)	1894/95	Home	18-0	1	1	0	0
Penygraig (L)	1895/96	Home	6-0	2	2	0	0
Penygraig (PL)	1895/96	Away	3-9	3	2	0	1
Penygraig (L)	1896/97	Away	3-12	4	2	0	2
Penygraig (L)	1896/97	Home	12-3	5	3	0	2
Penygraig (L)	1897/98	Home	6-4	6	4	0	2
Penygraig (L)	1897/98	Away	3-9	7	4	0	3
Penygraig (L)	1898/99	Home	11-5	8	5	0	3
Penygraig (L)	1898/99	Away	0-3	9	5	0	4
Penygraig (PL)	1899/1900	Away	3-6	10	5	0	5
Penygraig (PL)	1899/1900	Home	8-8	11	5	1	5

Total Games Played v Penygraig in the 1890s

P	W	D	L
15	5	3	7

Matches v Ferndale

Opponents	Season	Venue	Score	P	W	D	L
Ferndale (PL)	1894/95	Unsure	13-0	1	1	0	0
Ferndale (L)	1894/95	Away	19-3	2	2	0	0
Ferndale (PL)	1895/96	Away	6-0	3	3	0	0
Ferndale (PL)	1895/96	Away	9-0	4	4	0	0
Ferndale (PL)	1896/97	Home	27-0	5	5	0	0
Ferndale (L)	1896/97	Away	21-0	6	6	0	0

Matches v Merthyr

Opponents	Season	Venue	Score	P	W	D	L
Merthyr (L)	1894/95	Home	10-3	1	1	0	0
Merthyr (PL)	1894/95	Away	7-0	2	2	0	0
Merthyr (L)	1895/96	Home	27-0	3	3	0	0
Merthyr (L)	1896/97	Home	23-0	4	4	0	0

Matches v Treherbert

Pre-Rhondda, Merthyr & Aberdare League/Glamorgan League

Opponents	Season	Venue	Score	P	W	D	L
Treherbert	1893/94	Home	9-0	1	1	0	0

From Start of Rhondda, Merthyr & Aberdare League/Glamorgan League

Opponents	Season	Venue	Score	P	W	D	L
Treherbert (PL)	1895/96	Away	12-0	1	1	0	0
Treherbert (L)	1895/96	Home	6-3	2	2	0	0
Treherbert (L)	1896/97	Home	0-0	3	2	1	0
Treherbert (L)	1896/97	Away	3-12	4	2	1	1
Treherbert (L)	1897/98	Home	0-11	5	2	1	2
Treherbert (L)	1897/98	Home	12-0	6	3	1	2
Treherbert (PL)	1898/99	Home	6-3	7	4	1	2
Treherbert (L)	1898/99	Away	11-9	8	5	1	2
Treherbert (PL)	1899/1900	Away	0-5	9	5	1	3
Treherbert (L)	1899/1900	Home	6-3	10	6	1	3

Total Games Played v Treherbert in the 1890s

P	W	D	L
11	7	1	3

Although winning the Glamorgan League on only one occasion in the 1890s after the competition's start in 1894/95, the above record shows that the Old Firm was as consistent and as hard a team to beat as any other in the tournament. Even Llwynypia, who were Glamorgan League champions in 1894/95, 1896/97 and 1897/98, and had built a reputation as one of the leading sides in Wales, failed to come out on top in the head to heads.

A Selection of the Old Firm's Non League Fixtures in the 1890s

Matches v Bridgend

Opponents	Season	Venue	Score	P	W	D	L
Bridgend	1896/97	Away	20-3	1	1	0	0
Bridgend	1896/97	Home	24-3	2	2	0	0
Bridgend	1897/98	Away	3-0	3	3	0	0
Bridgend	1897/98	Home	20-3	4	4	0	0
Bridgend	1899/1900	Home	39-0	5	5	0	0

Matches v Maesteg

Opponents	Season	Venue	Score	P	W	D	L
Maesteg	1897/98	Home	23-4	1	1	0	0

Matches v Ebbw Vale

Opponents	Season	Venue	Score	P	W	D	L
Ebbw Vale	1893/94	Home	0-0	1	0	1	0
Ebbw Vale	1893/94	Away	0-16	2	0	1	1
Ebbw Vale	1898/99	Home	14-0	3	1	1	1
Ebbw Vale	1898/99	Away	0-6	4	1	1	2
Ebbw Vale	1899/1900	Home	13-0	5	2	1	2
Ebbw Vale	1899/1900	Away	5-3	6	3	1	2

Matches v Aberavon

Opponents	Season	Venue	Score	P	W	D	L
Aberavon	1895/96	Away	0-16	1	0	0	1
Aberavon	1895/96	Home	13-5	2	1	0	1
Aberavon	1896/97	Away	5-0	3	2	0	1
Aberavon	1896/97	Home	6-0	4	3	0	1
Aberavon	1896/97	Home	9-0	5	4	0	1
Aberavon	1897/98	Home	0-3	6	4	0	2
Aberavon	1897/98	Away	0-6	7	4	0	3
Aberavon	1898/99	Away	5-9	8	4	0	4
Aberavon	1898/99	Home	3-3	9	4	1	4

Matches v Llanelly

Llanelly were Welsh Club Champions in 1896/97

Opponents	Season	Venue	Score	P	W	D	L
Llanelly	1897/98	Home	0-17	1	0	0	1
Llanelly	1898/99	Away	3-8	2	0	0	2

Matches v Newport

Newport were Welsh Club Champions in 1894/95 & 1895/96

Opponents	Season	Venue	Score	P	W	D	L
Newport XV	1894/95	Home	8-10	1	0	0	1

Matches v Neath

Opponents	Season	Venue	Score	P	W	D	L
Neath	1896/97	Away	6-0	1	1	0	0
Neath	1896/97	Home	0-0	2	1	1	0
Neath	1897/98	Home	3-5	3	1	1	1
Neath	1897/98	Away	3-5	4	1	1	2
Neath	1898/99	Away	0-0	5	1	2	2
Neath	1899/1900	Away	5-0	6	2	2	2
Neath	1899/1900	Home	3-0	7	3	2	2

Matches v Pontymoile
(associated with Pontypool RFC at this time)

Opponents	Season	Venue	Score	P	W	D	L
Pontymoile	1892/93	Home	5-5	1	0	1	0
Pontymoile	1893/94	Home	10-0	2	1	1	0
Pontymoile	1894/95	Home	0-0	3	1	2	0
Pontymoile	1894/95	Away	0-0	4	1	3	0
Pontymoile	1895/96	Home	0-0	5	1	4	0
Pontymoile	1895/96	Away	5-3	6	2	4	0
Pontymoile	1896/97	Home	25-0	7	3	4	0
Pontymoile	1897/98	Away	0-3	8	3	4	1
Pontymoile	1897/98	Home	22-3	9	4	4	1
Pontymoile	1898/99	Home	8-0	10	5	4	1
Pontymoile	1898/99	Away	3-9	11	5	4	2
Pontymoile	1899/1900	Unknown	17-3	12	6	4	2
Pontymoile	1899/1900	Unknown	5-3	13	7	4	2

Matches v Penarth

Opponents	Season	Venue	Score	P	W	D	L
Penarth	1890/91	Away	0-26	1	0	0	1

Matches v Swansea

Swansea were Welsh Club Champions in 1898/99 & 1899/1900

Opponents	Season	Venue	Score	P	W	D	L
Swansea	1892/93	Home	6-13	1	0	0	1
Swansea	1899/1900	Home	0-21	2	0	0	2

Matches v Tredegar

Opponents	Season	Venue	Score	P	W	D	L
Tredegar	1899/1900	Away	15-6	1	1	0	0

Matches v Leicester

Opponents	Season	Venue	Score	P	W	D	L
Leicester	1896/97	Home	11-0	1	1	0	0
Leicester	1896/97	Away	0-3	2	1	0	1
Leicester	1897/98	Away	3-14	3	1	0	2

Matches v Cinderford

Opponents	Season	Venue	Score	P	W	D	L
Cinderford	1897/98	Unsure	16-7	1	1	0	0
Cinderford	1897/98	Away	6-8	2	1	0	1

Matches v Bridgwater & Albion

Opponents	Season	Venue	Score	P	W	D	L
Bridgwater & Albion	1896/97	Home	23-0	1	1	0	0
Bridgwater & Albion	1896/97	Away	14-4	2	2	0	0
Bridgwater & Albion	1898/99	Away	0-0	3	2	1	0
Bridgwater & Albion	1898/99	Away	5-0	4	3	1	0
Bridgwater & Albion	1899/1900	Away	3-8	5	3	1	1

Matches v Plymouth

Opponents	Season	Venue	Score	P	W	D	L
Plymouth	1896/97	Away	11-13	1	0	0	1
Plymouth	1897/98	Home	22-0	2	1	0	1
Plymouth	1897/98	Away	11-20	3	1	0	2
Plymouth	1898/99	Away	6-14	4	1	0	3
Plymouth	1899/1900	Away	24-0	5	2	0	3

Matches v Devonport Albion

Opponents	Season	Venue	Score	P	W	D	L
Devonport Albion	1897/98	Away	6-13	1	0	0	1
Devonport Albion	1899/1900	Unknown	3-8	2	0	0	2

There were no known games played against Abertillery, London Welsh, Cardiff, Cross Keys, Glamorgan Wanderers, Bath, Coventry and Nuneaton in the 1890s.

Mountain Ash RFC Players That Went North 1890/91 to 1899/1900

JOE HOSKINS, who was a member of the first "Old Firm" team that became Glamorgan League champions in 1895/96, was one of the first Mountain Ash RFC players to "go north". He signed for Salford, making his debut on 4 September 1897 against St Helen's. He became a prolific try scorer, crossing the line for 30 tries during the 1897/98 season, which made him the Northern Union's and Salford's top try scorer that season. He played 51 games in total for Salford, scoring 37 tries and kicked one goal, a total of 113 points overall. He also played twice for Lancashire.

JACK TANNER, was a full back and played for Mountain Ash in the 1890s. He moved North in 1896/97, joining a Northern Union Club called Heckmondwike, which was based in Yorkshire, and played briefly in the Northern Union from the latter 1890s until the end of the 1901/02 season.

W. BRADFORD, was a centre and played for the Old Firm in the 1890s. He followed full back Jack Tanner in 1896/97 and moved from Mountain Ash RFC to Yorkshire to play for Northern Union Club, Heckmondwike.

JACK DEARE, a three-quarter, who played for Mount from 1897/98 on and was the brother of Llew Deare, joined Hull at the start of February 1900.

Mountain Ash Rugby Football Club
"The Old Firm"
Circa 1893/94-1900/1901

Other than the Old Firm's Welsh International forward, Fred Millar, who is in the back row of the above photograph third from the left as you look, with his arms folded, none of the other players' names are known for certain. The first mention of Millar in an Old Firm XV was in 1893/94 and his last season was in 1900/1901 when he went North, joining the professional ranks at Hull Northern Union Club (Rugby League as it became known). With this in mind, the season the photograph covers is somewhere between 1893/94 and 1900/1901.

Mountain Ash Rugby Football Club
"The Old Firm"

The 1900s

Welsh Rugby's Golden Era

The decade 1900 to 1910 was a big part of Welsh rugby's "Golden Era", which lasted from 1900 to 1914. During this decade, Wales won the Triple Crown 5 times, the Grand Slam twice, and defeated New Zealand 3-0 in 1905, which was the All Blacks' only defeat on their 32 match tour of Great Britain. Between 1900 and 1914 Wales won 43 games and drew one from 56 played.

The Old Firm's Playing Record In The 1900s

In this, one of the strongest decades in the history of Welsh rugby, the Old Firm had an impressive record, taking on some of the strongest Clubs in Wales and England. Below are the known seasonal playing records of the 1900s:

Season	P	W	D	L	For	Against	Tries Scored	%
1900/01	25	14	5	6	182	91	51	66.00
1901/02	26	16	1	9	287	142	77	63.46
1902/03	28	22	3	3	353+	59+	88+	83.93
1903/04	24	14	3	7	127+	70+	32+	64.58
1904/05	27	20	1	6	242	80	68	75.93
1905/06	30	16	4	10	211	137	60	60.00
1906/07	33	18	3	12	196+	106+	52+	59.09
1907/08	26	13	0	13	188	140	52	50.00
1908/09	33	19	3	11	125+	138+	33+	62.12
1909/10	36	18	7	11	200	160	27+	59.72
Total for 1900s	288	170	30	88	2111+	1123+	540+	64.24

A Golden Era For The Old Firm

The seasons 1900 to 1910 were a continuation of the "First Golden Era" for Mountain Ash RFC which started in 1894/95, as well as part of the "Golden Era" of Welsh rugby. The Old Firm took on and beat some of the strongest Clubs in Wales such as Llanelly, Abertillery, Neath, Aberavon, Newport, Penarth and Pontypool, and tough "second class" Clubs such as Llwynypia, Maesteg, Penygraig, Pontypridd and Treorky. There were also games against London Welsh, Bath, Devonport Albion – a power in England around 1901 – Plymouth, Bristol, Taunton, Bridgwater & Albion and Irish tourists, Belfast Collegians and Dublin Old Wesley. During the decade, Mount won the majority of their games in each season bar one – and even then they broke even, won the ultra competitive Glamorgan League in 1908/09, came close to lifting the trophy again on several other occasions, beat the Canadian national touring team, had 4 players capped during the era, and had the joint highest try scorer in a season in Wales in their ranks. It was an impressive record which was as good as any other Club, even though Mountain Ash RFC was regarded as "second class" by the media.

The Glamorgan League

This was *the* competition to win for a valleys Club, being much sought after with the games played in the tournament not being for the faint hearted. The Old Firm were well up for the challenge throughout the decade and were always in the hunt for the trophy, coming close on several occasions before winning it for the second time in the Club's history in 1908/09. They came close to winning the competition earlier in the decade in 1904/05, coming joint top of the League but losing the play-off, and there was another second place finish in 1909/10.

Club Captains

The following players captained the Old Firm between 1900 and 1910:

1900-1901	Tom Walton
1901-1902	Jack Muxworthy
1902-1903	Reuben Carpenter
1903-1904	George Edwards
1904-1905	Dick Thomas
1905-1909	Wyndham Jones
1909-1910	Seth Francis

Mount had some talented backs as captains during this decade. Tom Walton was a full back, Jack Muxworthy a centre, and George Edwards a scrum half. Reuben Carpenter was a try scoring wing of note and outside half Wyndham Jones was a player who would have been capped more than once in a different era. With Mount forward Dick Thomas also getting capped, the Club was captained by two Welsh Internationals for five seasons during the decade.

2nd XV Triumph

The Club's reserve XV made 1908/09 a season to remember as they also finished a successful season by winning the Aberdare and Merthyr District League Championship.

International Touring Side Beaten

The stand-out season in the 1900s was 1902/03. Included in an impressive playing record of 22 wins and 3 draws from 28 known games played was a 28-0 home win over the first touring Canadian national team.

Mount Player Sets New Welsh Try Scoring Record in Season

Along with Fred Jowett of Swansea, Mount wing Reuben Carpenter set a new Welsh try scoring record in 1902/03 when he ran in 42 tries.

Mount Players Gain Representative Honours

During the decade, 4 players from the Club were capped by Wales. In 1900 and 1901, forward Fred Millar was capped 6 times and was a member of the Welsh XV that beat England, Scotland and Ireland in

1899/1900 to win the Triple Crown. Shortly after, another Mount forward, Will Osborne, was also capped 6 times in 1902 and 1903, also being a member of a Welsh team that won the Triple Crown again in 1902. Following him in 1905 was mercurial outside half Wyndham Jones, who would probably have been capped more than once in a different era, who got his one and only Welsh cap in 1905, making the most of his chance by scoring a try and making another, to play a big part in Wales' 10-3 win at Swansea over Ireland, which clinched a third Triple Crown in six years. And last, but certainly not least, was another forward, Dick Thomas, who was capped 4 times between 1906 and 1909, and made his debut against South Africa on their first tour of Britain, Ireland and France in 1906, and was a member of two triumphant Welsh teams that won the Triple Crown and Grand Slam in 1908 and 1909.

Quite a number of players were picked to play for various representative teams during the decade. In 1908/09, 4 Mount players, namely Jim Donovan, a centre three-quarter, Welsh Internationals Wyndham Jones and Dick Thomas, and forward George Caple, were chosen for Glamorgan in their match against Australia, Caple getting his team's only try that day in the 11-3 defeat.

No Permanent Match Venue

Throughout this decade, the Club never really had a permanent match venue but played most home games at the Mountain Ash Athletic Grounds.

The Trail North

During these years, there were frequent movements to the professional ranks of the Northern Union, later to be called Rugby League. Of the Old Firm's more prominent players, Welsh Internationals Fred Millar and Will Osborne joined Hull and Huddersfield respectively, and Welsh try scoring record holder, wing Reuben Carpenter, moved to Oldham. By 1908/09, there were professional Clubs close-by playing Northern Union rugby in Aberdare, Merthyr, Mid Rhondda and Treherbert. All provided a challenge for the Old Firm.

The Club's Administration And Finances

Come what may, Mountain Ash RFC always kept its head above water but frequently struggled financially. The Cresselly Inn was used as the Club's headquarters during the decade. With regard to the Club's administration, Harry Hale was Secretary in the very early years of the 1900s. Short term replacements followed in Bert James and former captain Ben Tiley. Jack Jasper did the job from 1907 on. In the Glamorgan League winning season of 1908/09, Mr H. J. Carpenter was Chairman and Mr J.T. Wheeler the Club Treasurer. They were succeeded in 1909 by Mr Herbert George and David Harris, who took over as Chairman and Treasurer respectively. Mr H.E. Gray was Club President from 1908 to 1910.

The 1900s
Season by Season

Season 1900/01

<u>Excellent Season For Old Firm</u>
<u>Llanelli Beaten At Stradey Park</u>

After four straight defeats at the start of the season, one of these being in Plymouth against Devonport Albion which was one of the strongest teams in England at the time – and a Club which was referred to in the match report of Mountain Ash v London Welsh in 1902/03 as English champions – the Old Firm won 7 and drew 2 of their next 9 games against strong opposition. Starting with an away draw at Treorky, Mount got home wins against Bridgend, Llwynypia, Neath, London Welsh and Tredegar, and gained a famous 11-3 win over Llanelly at Stradey Park on Boxing Day 1900, with the Western Mail commenting in its match report, "Mountain Ash proved their class by handsomely defeating Llanelly." The winning run came to an end at Swansea who ended the season as Welsh champions. In the second half of the season, there were further wins against Ebbw Vale, Tredegar, Pontymoile – which was synonymous with Pontypool in these early days – Maesteg, Penygraig, Pontypridd and Treorky. There was also a home draw with Llanelly. It completed a fine season for the Old Firm with the known playing record showing 25 games played, 14 won, 5 drawn and 6 lost, with 182 points, including 51 tries scored, and 91 conceded, to give a win rate of 66%. Forward Fred Millar made it a memorable season for the Club by being capped against England, Scotland and Ireland, to take his cap tally to 7. The season proved to be his last as he joined the professional ranks at Hull in September 1901. The season also saw a reserve XV playing, with wins recorded over Grangetown, Mountain Ash Crusaders and Ynyshir.

Fixtures 1900/01

Opponents	Date	Venue	Score	Tries	Scorers/Comments
Devonport Albion	24 Sep 1900	Away	0-16	0	No scorers.
Crumlin	8 Oct 1900	Away	0-8	0	No scorers.
Neath	15 Oct 1900	Away	0-4	0	No scorers.
Maesteg	22 Oct 1900	Away	6-7	2	Francis T, Warren T.
Penygraig (PL)	5 Nov 1900	Home	12-3	4	George Edwards T, D.L. Davies T, Warren T, Beere T.
Treorky (L)	12 Nov 1900	Away	3-3	0	Wyndham Jones P.
Pontymoile	26 Nov 1900	Away	0-0	0	No scorers.
Bridgend	3 Dec 1900	Home	14-0	4	Wyndham Jones T, Fryer T, Williams T, AN Other T, Jones C.

Opponents	Date	Venue	Score	Tries	Scorers/Comments
Llwynypia (L)	10 Dec 1900	Home	6-3	2	George Edwards T, Fryer T.
Neath	17 Dec 1900	Home	9-4	3	Scorers unknown.
Tredegar	24 Dec 1900	Home	9-6	3	George Edwards T, Wyndham Jones T, Will Osborne T.
London Welsh	26 Dec 1900	Home	16-0	4	Dai Fryer T, George Edwards T, Ivor Morgan T, Warren T, Lucimore C, Muxworthy C.
Llanelly	27 Dec 1900	Away	11-3	3	Wayne Morgan 2T, C, Wyndham Jones T.
Swansea	31 Dec 1900	Away	0-14	0	No scorers.
Ebbw Vale	14 Jan 1901	Home	13-0	3	Scorers unknown.
Tredegar	21 Jan 1901	Home	21-0	5	Scorers unknown.
Plymouth	28 Jan 1901	Away	3-10	1	Scorer unknown.
Ebbw Vale	11 Feb 1901	Away	0-0	0	No scorers.
Pontymoile	18 Feb 1901	Home	29-0	7	Scorers unknown.
Maesteg	25 Feb 1901	Away	3-0	1	Scorer unknown.
Penygraig (PL)	4 Mar 1901	Home	6-4	2	Williams T, AN Other T.
Llwynypia (PL)	11 Mar 1901	Away	3-3	1	Scorer unknown.
Pontypridd (PL)	8 Apr 1901	Home	6-0	2	Williams 2T.
Llanelly	15 Apr 1901	Home	0-0	0	No scorers.
Treorky (L)	22 Apr 1901	Home	12-3	4	Sage T, Fred Millar T, AN Other 2T.

Summary of Playing Record

P	W	D	L	For	Against	Tries Scored	Win Rate %
25	14	5	6	182	91	51	66.00

Match Reports and Publications

15 October 1900

Neath 4 Mountain Ash 0

The Western Mail reported, "....Play was mainly confined to the forwards and, certainly, the Neath eight had none the best of matters. The fact is, the Mountain Ash eight combined better and really proved themselves cleverer than the home pack. Millar, Osborne and Beere struck me as the pick...."

22 October 1900

Maesteg 7 Mountain Ash 6

The Western Mail commented, "....the Mountain Ash men seemed to amble up and down the field in very listless style. Time after time excellent chances were lost either through the slovenliness of play or the sluggardliness of a player. Lucimore and O'Neill were the saving quantities on their side. The former is fast developing into an ideal three-quarter and should more than compensate for the loss of Deere." This, no doubt, was a reference to Llew Deere, who was the Old Firm's captain in 1899/1900, who played for Neath versus Mount the week before. The report ended thus, "If Mountain Ash hope to make anything like a record this season, there will need to be some serious pruning in the team as at present constituted."

5 November 1900

Mountain Ash 12 Penygraig 3
Possible Glamorgan League Game

The Western Mail commented, "Ivor Morgan and Ned Jenkins reappeared in the home quartette....the ball went across to the other touchline, and inside the 25, Fryer, getting possession, used excellent judgement at the right moment, sent on to Edwards, who got over with a try three minutes from the start....It was only the slippery state of the ground and the greasiness of the ball that stopped the home side from putting on a score....Warren at last added to the score in an unexpected manner by crossing over the line with a visiting forward hugging him....The ball was sent out to the Mountain Ash three-quarters, and each in turn handling, Williams looked all over a scorer, but was collared a yard from the line. From some loose scrambling work, D.L. Davies literally forced his way over the line in the corner...."

12 November 1900

Treorky 3 Mountain Ash 3
Glamorgan League

Mount Team: Back, W. Thomas; 3/4s, W.L. Williams, Ned Jenkins, Ivor Morgan, F. Lucimore; half backs, Geo Edwards, Wyndham Jones; forwards, F. Millar* Capt, W.T. Osborne, H. Beer, C. Warren, Alf Fryer, A. Price, Dai Fryer, D.L. Davies.

* denotes Welsh International

The Western Mail reported, "....Ned Jenkins was injured and carried off the field....A little unpleasantness took place just before half time. The referee ordered Tom Jones, the Treorky half back, off the field. This appeared quite uncalled for and if Mr Davies, the referee, had been subjected to rough treatment, he would have no one to blame but himself. The offence complained of, as seen from the Press Box, was really nothing. Heavy rain fell in the second half, and the state of the ball was such as to prevent passing....Williams, the Mount wing, was given the ball and had passed all except Walton, but the latter saved by pushing him into touch....One of the Mountain Ash centres was given the ball and had a clear field, but Sam Muxworthy smartly captured him and saved what appeared to be a certain try. The homesters were kept inside their own half for 10 minutes and effected some brilliant saves...."

3 December 1900

Mountain Ash 14 Bridgend 0

The Western Mail reported, "Played before a fair crowd in ideal football weather....Mountain Ash were without Millar and Osborne, who had journeyed to Neath to take part in the trial match, and Beere and Davies, who were unable to turn out. Great difficulty was experienced in obtaining substitutes as the reserve team refused to help the premiers. Bridgend included W. Jones, the Cardiff centre."

8 December 1900

The rugby reporter, "Welsh Athlete", wrote in the Western Mail on the Saturday morning of Mount's Glamorgan League match against Llwynypia, "In the hills, the most interesting contests will be those between Mountain Ash and Llwynypia and Treorky and Pontypridd....Treorky will win comfortably, but there is room for considerable doubt as to the other game. Both teams have very in-and-out form....Mountain Ash have been the more consistent certainly, but against this, one has to put the fact that Llwynypia have made wonderful strides of improvement of late. That it will be a close fight, I am convinced."

10 December 1900

<u>Mountain Ash 6 Llwynypia 3</u>
<u>Glamorgan League</u>

Mount Team: Back, O'Neill; 3/4s, W. Williams, F. Lucimore, W. Thomas, I. Morgan; half backs, George Edwards, Wyndham Jones; forwards, Fred Millar*, C. Warren, W.T. Osborne, Beere, Alf Fryer, Dai Fryer, A. Price, A. Coles.

* denotes Welsh International

The Western Mail's rugby reporter "Welsh Athlete" reported, "The first match of the season between Llwynypia and Mountain Ash would, in the ordinary way, engage considerable attention, but, in addition to this, the engagement was under the auspices of the Glamorgan League, and, accordingly this made the match still more attractive. Mountain Ash were able to put their strongest team on the field but Llwynypia were without Alexander, who was laid up after the trial match at Neath and Hellings, who is captain of Llwynypia, failed his Club in this important League engagement, preferring to assist Devonshire in a County competition match. Heavy rain was falling and the ground was very soft....A smart follow-up and tackle by Alf Fryer upset Bob Jones and rushed play to the Llywnypia 25. Then there was some smart passing between Williams and Lucimore, which caused the Llwynypia defence considerable trouble....only a determined bit of defence by Llwynypia kept Mountain Ash out....For the next 10 minutes, it was a series of scrums right on the Llwynypia line. A dozen or more chances were given to the three-quarters, but on each occasion the Mountain Ash backs experienced considerable difficulty in handling and each of the chances was lost....fine kicking by Ivor Morgan kept Llwynypia on their own ground. Time after time, Mountain Ash took up the attack after this and eventually some grand following up by their two or three forwards coming up was rewarded....Fryer scored a try." In the second half...."the ball came out to W. Thomas. He had only the full back to beat and had Morgan been on this wing, it was a certainty for a score. He foolishly held on....he was pulled down. The Mountain Ash forwards were not to be denied and immediately rushed play to the Llwynypia goal line....At the finish....a scramble on the line saw George Edwards score a try." "Welsh Athlete" summed up the day by saying,"....a game of importance and the result, I should say, has a great bearing on the Glamorgan League competition, for which Mountain Ash now seem to have a rosy chance."

Next up for the Old Firm was Neath who, just a week before this game, were 3rd in the Western Mail's unofficial Welsh Club Championship table, having played 11, won 8, drawn 2, and lost 1.

17 December 1900

<u>Mountain Ash 9 Neath 4</u>

The Western Mail's reporter, "Welsh Athlete", commented, "Either Neath is very much "down the course" just now or Mountain Ash are even better than I made them out to be after their victory over Llwynypia. I hope the latter is the case....Mountain Ash played one of the best games of the season. Every man was in the pink of condition, and, despite the hard going, they kept up the pace to the end. Millar, Deere and Ivor Morgan were in their happiest vein and initiated some capital bits of play. O'Neil at full back never played a finer game and with his well judged kicks, saved his side a lot of work....Up to date, the records of some of the principal Welsh teams are as follows:

<u>Western Mail Welsh Club Table</u>

Club	P	W	L	D	%
Newport	10	9	0	1	95.00
Swansea	14	13	1	0	92.85
Aberavon	14	10	3	1	75.00
Neath	12	8	3	1	70.83
Cardiff	12	6	5	1	54.16
Llanelly	13	6	7	0	46.15

I should be glad if Mountain Ash would send in their record to date."

26 December 1900

<u>Mountain Ash 16 London Welsh 0</u>

Mount Team: Back, Lucimore; 3/4s, Parry, Muxworthy, Sage, Morgan; half backs, Wyndham Jones, George Edwards; forwards, Fred Millar* Capt, Will Osborne, Beere, Fryer, Dai Fryer, Alf Price, Perrot, Warren.

* denotes Welsh International

The Western Mail reported, "Before a good crowd, Mountain Ash were without several players but succeeded in finding useful substitutes. The turf was in good condition considering the recent weather....A delay was caused by Edwards, the home half, being injured and carried off the field....Dai Fryer scored under the posts....George Edwards now returned to the field and from a scrum, he and Wyndham Jones interpassed and Edwards scored under the posts. The Welsh backs started passing but could make no ground." In the second half...."Millar got the ball from a lineout and was conspicuous for some good work. Mountain Ash continued to press and Sage showed splendid form. From a dribble Ivor Morgan scored a try wide out...."

27 December 1900

Llanelly 3 Mountain Ash 11
Western Mail

LLANELLY V. MOUNTAIN ASH.

There was a large holiday crowd at Stradey on Wednesday afternoon for this match, which was played under favourable conditions. Before the game was ten minutes old it was made quite clear that the visitors meant strict business. They infused into their play an element of dash and "devil" that was conspicuously absent from the display of their opponents. There was some passing in the Llanelly half, and Wayne Morgan on the right wing went over with a smart try. The same player with a good kick added the two extra points. Nettled by this reverse the home team now put more energy into their work, but they were met with a stubborn determination on the other side. At the interval the score read: Mountain Ash, 1 goal; Llanelly, nil. The second half was opened by Ben Davies, and, following up his kick, D. L. Bowen, the Cardiff forward who was included in the Llanelly team, made a fine run which seemed likely to end in a score. A series of scrums was waged in the Llanelly 25, and ultimately Wyndham Jones ran in with a second try for the visitors, which remained unconverted. Not long after Wayne Morgan, who played a fine game for Mountain Ash, went over with a third try, the place kick again failing. It was quite evident that the scarlets were now a badly-beaten team, but they played up with commendable pluck, and Gabe, with a brilliant effort, scored a try, which was not converted.

Final score:

	G.	T.	M.
Mountain Ash	1	2	0
Llanelly	0	1	0

REMARKS.

On the day's form there can be no question as to which was the better team. The visitors played a splendid game all through, and caught the scarlets napping. Their forwards are a fine lot of men, who can make things warm for any pack. They quite overpowered the scarlet eight, and dribbled and rushed with great effect. The display of the home team was most disappointing. If we except Gabe, Walters, and T. Samuel, the rest of the team played miles below their usual form. The forwards were stale, and the backs were no better, Ben Davies and Evan Lloyd being frosts of the most wintry character. Gabe was in brilliant form, and it was pitiful to see the little support he received from the other backs.

29 December 1900

The Western Mail's rugby journalist, "Welsh Athlete", commented in his pre-match report between the Old Firm and Swansea, "....Swansea ought to win their match with Mountain Ash, although I anticipate the All Whites will have a tough battle, for Mountain Ash are exceptionally strong forward. Where Mountain Ash will lose, I should think, would be at three-quarter. Forward, I feel confident they will hold their own with the Westerners; indeed, I fancy three forwards out of the Mountain Ash team will gain their caps this year." He wasn't quite right – Fred Millar was capped later in the season and Will Osborne a year later in 1902. The South Wales Daily News previewed the game as follows, "Swansea today meet Mountain Ash and it is quite clear the engagement is not quite of the usual character. Swansea....against the scotch forwards during the Christmas holidays, appeared to have nothing to spare....Now, Mountain Ash prides herself, justifiably, on her pack of forwards, who did what they liked with the Llanelly lot. They are visiting Swansea in the pink of condition, fresh from a convincing victory over Llanelly at Stradey. Can it be that they have the ambition and the ability to imperil the home record of the powerful All Whites? One never knows what may happen when a hills team plays in its very best form....I venture to say Swansea will do as well against them as they (Mountain Ash) did against Llanelly."

31 December 1900

<u>Swansea 14 Mountain Ash 0</u>

"Welsh Athlete" in the Western Mail commented, "It becomes more and more clear every Saturday that the struggle for the South Wales Championship is to be confined to Newport and Swansea. We can gauge Swansea's strength....from their match with Mountain Ash on Saturday. To defeat Mountain Ash by a goal and four tries....is much to Swansea's credit, for it will be remembered that Mountain Ash proved their class by handsomely defeating Llanelly the other day." On 15 April 1901, the Western Mail published Swansea's playing record for the season which showed 33 games played, 29 won, 2 drawn and 2 lost. It was also mentioned that Swansea was one of the Clubs to defeat Mount during the season.

11 March 1901

<u>Llwynypia 3 Mountain Ash 3</u>
<u>Glamorgan League</u>

> The encounter between Llwynypia and Mountain Ash (my correspondent writes) provided excitement galore for the biggest gate seen in the Llwynypia enclosure this season. The visitors were wired to and requested to be on hand in good time, but they ignored this, with the result that the game did not commence until 5.15, and was finished in semi-darkness. It was, perhaps, the most even game ever seen on the ground, for the result hung in the balance until the very last moment, and neither side was able to turn the scale. Mountain Ash were certainly the more powerful team. They had more weight in the scrums, and, despite the fact that their eight included two or three shirkers, they heeled out frequently. Save on one occasion, however, the backs were unable to score. The Llwynypia men made up in cleverness what they lacked otherwise, and the effort by which Bob Parry scored was an excellent bit of footwork. Just on the finish Richards (an ex-Cardiffian) made a big run, and, after beating the defence, nearly won the game for his side, but he was not quite fast enough. The Mountain Ash team would have done better to have made it a forward game. If they had they would probably have won, despite the strenuous efforts of Alexander, Dobson, and J. Hellings.

8 April 1901

<u>Glamorgan League Table</u>
<u>Western Mail</u>

	P.	W.	L.	D.	Pts.
Pontypridd	6	4	1	1	9
Treherbert	6	4	1	1	9
Mountain Ash	7	3	2	2	8
Llwynypia	7	1	2	4	6
Treorky	5	0	2	3	3
Penygraig	5	0	4	1	1

13 April 1901

In this Saturday edition of the Western Mail, the Old Firm v Llanelly match was previewed as follows, "Llanelly will play at Mountain Ash and will have to improve upon their previous performances this season to return home winners."

15 April 1901

<u>Mountain Ash 0 Llanelly 0</u>

In summing up this and other matches that were played on Saturday, 13 April, "Welsh Athlete" commented in the Western Mail, "Llanelly, defeated on their own ground earlier in the season, did very well in playing Mountain Ash to a draw." The match seemed to be an unspectacular affair. The Western Mail report was as follows:

LLANELLY V. MOUNTAIN ASH.

Played at Mountain Ash in showery weather before a fair crowd.

The Mountain Ash Brass Band played a selection of music on the ground previous to the match. Thomas kicked off for Llanelly, Edwards returning. Llanelly took a dribble down field. Mountain Ash relieved to half-way, Edwards kicked, and Williams prevented a return. Edwards was held near the line after a good attempt to score. Llanelly kicked to half-way, but, getting off-side, were penalised. Mountain Ash had hard lines in not scoring, Williams and Morgan failing to get over. Scrum after scrum was fought out just on the Llanelly line, but only a minor resulted. Llanelly dribbled well to half-way, Williams saving. Llanelly were penalised, and Millar's kick took play close to the line, where Edwards was injured, having to go off. Ivor Morgan, receiving from Jenkins, made a good attempt to score.

Half-time score.	G.	T.	M.
Mountain Ash	0	0	0
Llanelly	0	0	0

Millar re-started, and Llanelly kicked to half-way. Mountain Ash took play to the visitors' line. Poor passing by the homesters let Llanelly down-field. The home forwards wheeled continually, never giving their backs a chance. Friar and Osborne dribbled towards the visitors' line, but kicked too hard. The ball rolled to touch. Llanelly relieved, taking play back to half-way, where Lucimore misfielded, and Llanelly got down to the home line, where the next few scrums were fought out. Ivor Morgan, with a strong run, removed play to half-way. Wyndham Jones, Jenkins, and Harris put in good work, Harris's pass to Williams being forward, about a yard from the line. Time was now called.

Final score:	G.	T.	M.
Mountain Ash	0	0	0
Llanelly	0	0	0

22 April 1901

<u>Mountain Ash 12 Treorky 3
Glamorgan League
Western Mail</u>

TREORKY V. MOUNTAIN ASH.

This league match was played on the latter's athletic ground before an immense and enthusiastic crowd of spectators. The rivalry between these two teams awakened the keenest interest, and speculations were rife as to the ultimate result of the match, which was the last of the season between these teams. It will be recollected that when the Ashites visited Treorky the game ended in a draw. The ground was in the pink of condition, and a fast and open game was anticipated.

In the first half, after a nice bout of passing, Sage scored for Mountain Ash in the corner. The kick at goal failed. Just before the interval Millar scored the second try, which was also left unconverted. Two more tries were scored for Mountain Ash in the second half, while Treorky failed to cross more than once.

Final score.	G.	T.	M.
Mountain Ash	0	4	0
Treorky	0	1	0

THE GLAMORGAN LEAGUE.

Other than the match between Mountain Ash and Treorky, there was little interest in Glamorgan League circles on Saturday. Mountain Ash's victory puts them up another two points, but on a ratio of matches played they are still behind Pontypridd and Treherbert. To-day Penygraig, who recently defeated Treherbert and Mountain Ash, will meet Pontypridd at Penygraig, and a keen contest is expected. The position up to date is thus:—

	P.	W.	L.	D.	Pts.
Mountain Ash	9	4	3	2	10
Pontypridd	6	4	1	1	9
Treherbert	7	4	2	1	9
Llwynypia	7	1	2	4	6
Treorky	5	0	3	3	3
Penygraig	6	2	4	1	5

Pontypridd eventually won the Glamorgan League for the first time at the end of the season.

Season 1901/02

2nd Impressive Season In Succession For Old Firm
Mount Forward Will Osborne Plays For Wales

This was another good season for the Old Firm with an end of season playing record of played 26, won 16, drawn 1, and lost 9, with 287 points scored, which included 77 tries, and 142 conceded, which gave a win rate of 63.46%. Mount played a strong fixture list with the win of the season probably being the 10-3 home victory over Llanelly. There was also a "double" over Pontypool and wins against Neath, Maesteg, Treorky, Llwynypia and the season's Glamorgan League champions, Treherbert. There were four wins in the season over Pontypridd, the 40-0 home rout in April 1902 being described in the South Wales Daily News as "A League Record Score". There were some close defeats as well against strong opposition such as away to Bristol, in Plymouth in front of 9,000 spectators against Devonport Albion, which was one of the strongest Clubs in England at the time, at Treorky, and at home to Aberavon. It seems that the Old Firm were a match for any Club in Wales or England, especially on home soil, with the handful of games played against Devonport Albion in this and nearby seasons, always taking place in Plymouth. Will Osborne became the latest of the Club's Welsh Internationals when he was capped against England at Blackheath and scored a try on his debut to help Wales to a 9-8 win. He added another two caps to his tally before the end of the season in the victories over Scotland and Ireland which gave Wales their third Triple Crown. However, controversy courted his selection, the Scottish XV initially refusing to play claiming he had signed professional forms. The game went ahead, Osborne having to sign a statement denying the allegation. An amateur game rugby union might officially have been, but suspicions of Clubs making inducements to players were rife, and probably true, with "Old Stager" reporting in the South Wales Daily News that the Welsh Rugby Union were to meet to discuss the "rumours as to professional practices by several Clubs", and no doubt the dispute between Mount and Treorky over the transfer of Sam and Jack Muxworthy centred around this. Passions run high in some games, the game at Swansea being hard fought on and off the field, with fights among the spectators causing the police to get involved and restore order. As in previous seasons, the Club run a reserve XV.

Fixtures 1901/02

Opponents	Date	Venue	Score	Tries	Scorers/Comments
Whitchurch	23 Sep 1901	Home	19-3	5	Scorers unknown.
Blaina	30 Sep 1901	Home	11-0	3	Scorers unknown.
Swansea	7 Oct 1901	Away	0-22	0	No scorers.
Crumlin	14 Oct 1901	Home	28-0	8	Scorers unknown.
Devonport Albion	21 Oct 1901	Away	3-10	1	Jones T.
Neath	4 Nov 1901	Home	15-0	3	Dai Fryer T, Willie Harris T, W. L. Williams T, Tom Walton DG, C.
Pontypool	11 Nov 1901	Home	8-7	2	Sam Muxworthy T, P. O'Neill T, Tom Walton C.
Aberavon (L)	18 Nov 1901	Away	0-11	0	No scorers.
Llanelly	25 Nov 1901	Home	10-3	2	Jack Muxworthy T, Fryer T, Tom Walton 2C.
Treherbert (PL)	2 Dec 1901	Away	0-10	0	No scorers.

Opponents	Date	Venue	Score	Tries	Scorers/Comments
Pontypridd (F)	16 Dec 1901	Away	6-3	2	Willie Harris T, Nicholls T.
Maesteg (L)	30 Dec 1901	Away	6-6	2	W.L. Williams 2T.
Bristol	6 Jan 1902	Away	0-3	0	No scorers.
Pontypridd (PL)	13 Jan 1902	Home	15-0	5	Scorers unknown.
Pontypool	18 Jan 1902	Away	8-0	2	Jones & Morgan 8pts.
Llwynypia (L)	27 Jan 1902	Home	16-6	4	Jack Muxworthy 2T, Ivor Morgan T, Willie Harris T, Tom Walton 2C.
Treorky (L)	10 Feb 1902	Home	19-3	5	W.L. Williams 3T, AN Other 2T, Tom Walton 2C.
Cwmcarn	17 Feb 1902	Home	21-3	5	Scorers unknown.
Treorky (L)	24 Feb 1902	Away	0-3	0	No scorers.
Pontypridd (PL)	3 Mar 1902	Away	17-3	3	Scorers unknown.
Treherbert (L)	17 Mar 1902	Home	11-0	3	Hugh Jones T, Willie Harris T, W. L. Williams T, Tom Walton C.
Aberavon (L)	24 Mar 1902	Home	0-6	0	No scorers.
Maesteg (L)	7 Apr 1902	Home	25-0	7	Scorers unknown.
Llanelly	14 Apr 1902	Away	0-29	0	No scorers.
Pontypridd (L)	21 Apr 1902	Home	40-0	12	W.L. Williams 4T, Wyndham Jones 2T, Syd Francis 2T, Willie Harris T, C, Jack Lloyd T, Hugh Jones T, Tom Perrot T, Tom Walton C.
Penygraig (PL)	28 Apr 1902	Away	9-11	3	Scorers unknown.

Summary of Playing Record

P	W	D	L	For	Against	Tries Scored	Win Rate %
26	16	1	9	287	142	77	63.46

Match Reports and Publications

16 September 1901

<u>Glamorgan League</u>
<u>Improving Standard of Play</u>

The South Wales Daily News reported, "The Rhondda Clubs will soon be in the midst of the contests....under the Glamorgan League, the main purpose of which was to improve the game in the hills. It certainly has not failed in its object....Several crack Welsh and English Clubs have fallen before some of the League teams but still there is much room for improvement....In past seasons much has been said and written about alleged roughness owing to the keen rivalry existing between some of the contesting teams, and there is no doubt that in some quarters the condemnation was not altogether without justification....The more sportsmanlike the spirit....the more popular the Clubs will become and they will secure the goodwill....of the teams from a distance that are to meet them on their own ground. The contests for the Cup and title of the Championship this season are likely to be as keen and exciting as in past years."

23 September 1901

<u>The Rhondda Clubs</u>
<u>The League and Transfers</u>

The South Wales Daily News reported, "....Players of prominence appear to have promised to join two and sometimes three Clubs. Poaching has been carried on in the most glaring fashion and some Club officials have been particularly busy. The result has been that defections are reported from some Clubs....and "ructions" have started over the transfers....Most of the migrations of this year are surrounded with suspicious circumstances....The Muxworthys, Sam and Jack, have not always been content to play for the love of the game...."

7 October 1901

<u>Swansea 22 Mountain Ash 0</u>
<u>Rough Play – Free Fights Among Spectators</u>

The South Wales Daily News reported, "Swansea found Mountain Ash a much harder nut to crack than their opponents of the previous three weeks and the game was only won after Swansea strained every nerve and played up to their best form....The game, writes my Swansea correspondent, was far too rough as the forwards stood up to each other with an astonishing amount of vigour....Muxworthy at three-quarter was very active; he put in some really good sprints and tackled well on a few occasions....The game continued at a great pace, the ball being rushed up and down the field till two men were wounded and the contest was suspended for a few minutes. The excitement waxed high among the spectators, free fights taking place, and the police had to intervene...."

26 October 1901

The following article was written in the Aberdare Times by its reporter, "Focus", "The football season is well upon us again and the numerous fields and hillsides bear unmistakable evidence of it. A football and a field, wherein to play, is almost becoming indispensable in every town and village in Glamorganshire....if there is a football field there will also be found many a merry heart, and a dull existence converted into an interesting and happy one. Given a place to play in, there remains very little difficulty in getting a team. It is no use denying it, let the men who hold up their hands in holy horror of the game say what they will, there is no game in England and Wales so fascinating to the people and so attracts their attention as football. No newspaper can afford to ignore it, while indeed at very important matches, they can afford to set up temporary telephonic communication between a newspaper office and a scene of the contest, and find that it pays after all."

4 November 1901

Mountain Ash 15 Neath 0

Mount Team: Back, Tom Walton; ¾ backs, W.L. Williams, Sam Muxworthy, Ivor Morgan, W. Harries; half backs, George Edwards, Wyndham Jones; forwards, Will Osborne, Deere, Perrot, Dai Fryer, Warren, Sylvester, A. Price (only 14 players named).

Easy Win for Homesters

The South Wales Daily News reported, "....as a rule between the two, the contest is generally fought between the forwards. The visitors in this department have always been able to muster a strong lot, and against such a powerful eight as the homesters, a hard, gruelling game was looked forward to." The Aberdare Times commented, "There was general dissatisfaction on Saturday night among those persons who had travelled a few miles to witness this game at Mountain Ash. Spectators invariably like a tight game, with only a win by a hair's breadth when the final time is called. It was not so between Mountain Ash and Neath. The result was an easy win for the home team. With the exception of one or two of the visiting forwards, there was no redeeming feature in Neath's play."

11 November 1901

Mountain Ash 8 Pontypool 7

Mount Team: Back, T. Walton; ¾ backs, W.L. Williams, Sam Muxworthy, Jack Muxworthy, P. O'Neill; half backs, George Edwards Capt, W. Harris; forwards, Will Osborne, Perrot, R. Price, Alf Fryer, Dai Fryer, R. Coles, C. Warren, D. Davies.

The South Wales Daily News reported, "....a fair crowd lined the ropes. The match was timed for 3:30 but owing to the late arrival of the visitors, it was 4 o'clock before the teams entered the field. Pontypool, formerly known as Pontymoile, brought over their strongest team. The home team was considerably weakened by the absence of several players. Wyndham Jones was absent playing for Cardiff, Beere has been honoured in playing for Somerset against Devon at Taunton, his place being taken by Davies from the 2nds. Ivor Morgan and Billy Sage are on the sick list....scrambling play followed around the Pontypool citadel. O'Neill, through sheer strength, forced himself through a bunch of forwards and scored in the corner. Walton converted...."

18 November 1901

Mountain Ash Reserves 9 Abercynon 5
South Wales Daily News

ABERCYNON v MOUNTAIN ASH RESERVES.

A Junior League match was played on the latter's ground, before a fair crowd. There were several absentees owing to the fact of the senior teams encroaching upon the reserves.

Final Score—	G.	T.	M.
Mountain Ash Reserves	0	3	0
Abercynon	1	0	0

25 November 1901

Mountain Ash 10 Llanelly 3
South Wales Daily News

MOUNTAIN ASH v LLANELLY.

An ideal day favoured the meeting of these old rivals. The result of the match was a foregone conclusion, the Scarlets going very strong this season. W. Arnold, of Neath, accompanied the Llanelly team and intended playing centre, but a wire was sent from his old club informing the officials that he was not entitled to play, as he had not secured his transfer. A rearrangement of the team was therefore necessary. Mountain Ash turned out a strong fifteen. Another player unable to don the jersey was Beere. When the teams met last, at Llanelly, Mountain Ash secured a victory. To-day they were made up as follow:—

Mountain Ash—Back, T Walton; three-quarter backs, W L Williams, S Muxworthy, Ivor Morgan, and J Muxworthy; half-backs, G W Edwards (captain) and W J Harris; forwards, A Osborne, A Fryer, D Fryer, T Perrott, A Price, A Cole, T Horsman, and H Jones.

Llanelly—Back, Bob Richards; three-quarter backs, M Williams, E Lloyd, D M Davies, and J Auckland; half-backs, Tom Samuel and Ben Davies; forwards, D Walters (captain), J Watts, I Lewis, W J Thomas, Bob Thomas, Keenan, P C Stacey, and Tom Davies.

Ben Davies started for Llanelly, and from a line out the Llanelly forwards got away and carried play to the home 25. Getting possession from the halves, Morgan Williams put in a short punt and Walton failing to hold, W. J. Thomas scored for Llanelly. Lloyd failed to negotiate and Mountain Ash woke up after this reverse, and a bout of passing nearly ended in Williams scoring in the right hand corner. The same player made another good attempt to get over, and Morgan Williams only floored him in the nick of time. A free granted to Llanelly relieved the pressure.

Sam Muxworthy was Injured,

and had to retire from the field. A long series of scrummages ensued after this near the halfway mark. The Mountain Ash forwards heeled out splendidly, but their backs utterly failed to do anything with the chances that came their way. Mountain Ash continued to have the best of the argument, and Morgan Williams mulling the ball J. Muxworthy scored. Walton converted amid cheers. Two Llanelly men a minute later made for the ball at the same moment, and both failing the home forwards were let in, and were stopped only a few yards from the line. Half-time was then called.

Half-time Score—
	G.	T.	M.
Mountain Ash	1	0	0
Llanelly	0	1	0

Within a few minutes of the kick-off Mountain Ash were able by a fine kick by Walton to take up the aggressive. It was only a momentary advantage, however, as the Llanelly forwards by some fine play changed the venue to the other end of the field. Auckland was next responsible for a capital burst, but the wing man failed to take and a glorious chance was thrown away. Soon after Morgan Williams again made a bad mistake, and Fryer picking up scored in a favourable position. Walton had no difficulty in converting. Llanelly now woke up and gave Mountain Ash a warm time of it. The Llanelly backs were continually handling, but something went wrong at the crucial moment. It was decidedly hard lines. Mountain Ash played up pluckily, their forwards in particular showing good form. Llanelly were prevented from scoring.

Final score—
	G.	T.	M.
Mountain Ash	2	0	1
Llanelly	0	1	0

16 December 1901

Pontypridd 3 Mountain Ash 6
Friendly Fixture

The South Wales Daily News reported, "....though it was not a League fixture, a good deal of interest was centred on it, the visitors being accompanied by a strong contingent of their supporters. The weather was very wintry, a cold wind sweeping across the field, which was a bit heavy in places owing to the recent heavy rains. Both teams were strongly represented, but the visitors' forwards were without Beere, one of their heaviest men....Ivor Morgan, picking up, went off with one of his dodgy runs, and having trickily doubled one of the opposing backs, gave a nice opening to Nicholls, and the old Llanellyite went across with another unconverted try, which was largely as a result of two or three of the home backs being caught napping.... the homesters attacked time and again in real earnest. A stubborn defence was presented, the tackling being very effective, and after a good deal of pressure, the Cup holders (Pontypridd) were driven to midfield.... Inch by inch the homesters, by hard, dogged play, got nearer to the line, but do what they would, their opponents would not let them score, and ultimately Walton removed the venue with a useful kick....the home forwards covered half the field with a vigorous rush, Walton being laid low for a time in a plucky effort to stop them...."

6 January 1902

Bristol 3 Mountain Ash 0

Mount Team: Back, T. Walton; ¾ backs, J. Morgan, J. Lloyd, Muxworthy, Thomas; half backs, Harries and Edwards; forwards, Bell, Fryer, Jones, Perrot, Price, Horsman, Coles, Mears.

Mountain Ash Captain Injured

The South Wales Daily News reported, "This match was played at Bristol in dreadfully wet weather. Bristol had several absentees, and on the visitors' side, Williams, Dai Fryer and Osborne were away, the latter standing down in view of the International match next Saturday at Blackheath." The game being referred to here was the Wales v England match, which was Mount forward Will Osborne's first cap. The report went on, "Jarman, Bristol's former captain, who has retired from regular play, turned out and had a great reception. Harries and Edwards for Mountain Ash opened out, but passing with a greasy ball was difficult....a clever dribble took the ball half the length of the field, Walton kicking to touch just in time to save a try. A brilliant round of passing by the home backs ensued but Muxworthy, by tackling Desprez, saved the situation. Bristol were attacking with great vigour but Muxworthy, intercepting a pass, very skilfully went off with only Oates in front. His punt lacked direction, however, and Bristol easily recovered. There was some exciting play, Courtenay, after an interception, but Walton tackled him and again the attack was staved off. Considering the state of the ground, play was up to a high standard....the visitors....for the first time encroached on their rivals' ground....Ivor Morgan had a capital chance but missed a good opening. Edwards, the Mountain Ash captain, was injured at this point, and had to leave the field. Just before the interval, Bristol scored. The Mountain Ash side went off at a great pace at the opening of the second half....the Bristol line was in great danger. Desprez saved but a minute later....Walton kicked at goal but the shot failed. Edwards returned....A fine forward rush by the Welshmen altered the aspect of play and Bristol's defence was severely foxed for a time....Ivor Morgan intercepted, but in dribbling, kicked over the line and out of play. Bristol again tried passing....In quick succession, the Mountain Ash backs retaliated, and Lloyd and Jones put in a rattling good run....the Bristol forwards did some very fine work but were opposed to a resolute defence and each attack was frustrated, the visiting backs going down on the ball in the most fearless manner."

13 January 1902

Mountain Ash 15 Pontypridd 0
Glamorgan League
South Wales Daily News

MOUNTAIN ASH v PONTYPRIDD.

This League match was played on the Mountain Ash Ground. Great interest was centred in th contest between the old rivals, with the result that a fairly decent gate was attracted. It is well known that Pontypridd have never beaten the home team on Mountain Ash ground, and it is a pity that they were greatly handicapped this time by several absentees. The homesters turned out the best possible team, the only absentee being Osborne, who had journeyed to Blackheath to do duty for Wales. D. Thomas, from the three-quarter line, was substituted by Jack Lloyd, and at forward George Mears replaced R. Coles. Mr J. H. Webb, Newport, had charge of the teams, which lined out as follow—

Pontypridd—Back, Francis; three-quarter backs, A Lewis, A Morgan, B Warlow, and L Phillips; half-backs, C Usher and T Stokes; forwards, D Roberts (captain), Rowley Thomas, F Burn, Whitehead, F Kellard, T Kehoe, T Jones, and E Vaughan.

Mountain Ash—Back, T Walton; three-quarter backs, W L Williams, J Muxworthy, J Morgan, and D Thomas; half-backs, G W Edwards (captain) and W J Harries; forwards, H Beer, A Fryer, T Perrott, H Jones, G Mears, D Fryer, A Price, and T Horsman.

An uneven contest from start to finish. Play was marred to a great extent by the offside irregularities of Stokes, with the result that he was continually penalising his own team. There was no comparison between the full-backs, Walton invariably finding touch with long kicks. The home three-quarter line was greatly superior to that of the visitors, Muxworthy, Williams, and Morgan completely out-classing Alun Morgan, Warlow, and Lewis, and not on one occasion throughout the game did the Pontypridd men initiate a round of passing, and only once did they invade the home territory during the second half. Harries and Edwards made rings round the opposing halves, and nine times out of ten they got possession of the ball. At forward there was not much to choose, both backs doing their utmost for their own side.

Final Score—   G. T. M.

Mountain Ash 0 5 0
Pontypridd 0   0

18 January 1902

Pontypool 0 Mountain Ash 8

The Western Mail reported, "....this match was anticipated with much interest in view of the good show made at Mountain Ash by Pontypool, who were beaten....The game proved exceedingly interesting, though the visitors missed two good chances of scoring from penalty kicks. About the middle of the first half, Jones and Morgan scored in rapid succession for Mountain Ash...."

Western Mail

GLAMORGAN LEAGUE COMPETITION.
Up to and including Saturday, January 18, 1902:—

Club.	P.	W.	D.	L.	Points. F.	Points. A.	Lg. Pts.
Treherbert	7	6	1	0	51	9	13
Maesteg	7	4	1	2	38	29	9
Aberavon	8	4	1	3	49	16	9
Llwynypia	6	2	1	3	17	42	5
Mountain Ash	4	1	1	2	21	21	3
Pontypridd	5	1	1	3	14	33	3
Treorky	4	1	0	3	6	24	2
Penygraig	3	0	0	3	3	27	0

27 January 1902

Mountain Ash 16 Llwynypia 6
Glamorgan League

Mount Team: Back, T. Walton; ¾ backs, W.L. Williams, Jack Muxworthy, Sam Muxworthy, Ivor Morgan; half backs, W.J. Harris and Bevan; forwards, W.T. Osborne*, Alf Fryer, H. Jones, Dai Fryer, T. Perrot, A. Price, T. Horsman, Mears.

* denotes Welsh International

The South Wales Daily News reported, "....A good deal of interest centred in the meeting and a good crowd lined the ropes....Osborne, the International forward, picked up and made a brave effort to score. He was collared but passed the ball back....it bounced off Harris and Jack Muxworthy, picking up, had no difficulty in scoring an unconverted try....Llwynypia were well beaten and the score by no means indicates the difference between the teams. In the first half the homesters lost numerous chances due mainly to indifferent passing at critical moments. At the interval, the Rhondda men led by a try but the second half had not been long in progress before the homesters got into their stride. From then until the end, Llwynypia were fairly outclassed....Their halves were beaten, the home couple continually getting the ball, Harris being very conspicuous. Jack Muxworthy was the best of the home three-quarters and played a champion game throughout. Walton was in brilliant form...."

Will Osborne
Mountain Ash RFC
6 Welsh Caps
1901/02 & 1902/03 v England, Scotland & Ireland

William Thomas Osborne became Mountain Ash RFC's third player to be capped by Wales. He made his debut on 11 January 1902 against England at Blackheath in the Four Nations Championship and made it a game to remember by scoring a try in Wales' 9-8 victory. Controversy courted him in Wales' next game when Scotland initially refused to play, alleging that he had signed professional forms with a Northern Union Club. Osborne denied this and signed a statement denying the allegation, eventually playing in Wales' 14-5 win. A triumphant season ended for Osborne personally and Wales at Lansdowne Road in Dublin with a 15-0 win securing the Championship and the Triple Crown. All in all, he played in five victories for Wales in his six appearances. His links with the Northern Union, later called Rugby League, were officially confirmed when he joined Huddersfield at the start of the 1903/04 season at the height of his International career, transferring to Hull in October 1906. He also gained a Yorkshire County cap during his time playing Northern Union rugby.

10 February 1902

<u>Mountain Ash 19 Treorky 3</u>
<u>Glamorgan League</u>
<u>Western Mail</u>

MOUNTAIN ASH v TREORKY.

A great deal of interest was centred in this League match, which was played at Mountain Ash. Treorky having been going very strong of late their supporters fondly hoped that they would be able to lower the colours of the home team. A fortnight ago the visitors brought off an unexpected victory against Treherbert, who top the League table, and it was admitted on all hands that they were far and away the best team. Mountain Ash, however, are exceptionally strong on their own ground, and having this advantage in their favour, coupled with their recent performances, there was great confidence among their friends prior to the match. It was a hard task for an outsider to weigh the chances of the teams, but there was a consensus of opinion that the game would be a close one, and that the margin of points on either side would be very small. The day was beautifully fine, there being scarcely a breath of wind. A large number of the partisans of Treorky made the journey, and the crowd lining the ropes when the teams took the field was one of the largest seen locally this season. The teams were—

Mountain Ash—Back, T Walton; three-quarter backs, J Muxworthy, J Lloyd, S Muxworthy, and W L Williams; half-backs, G W Edwards (captain) and W J Harries; forwards, W T Osborne, H Beer, A Fryer, H Jones, D Fryer, T Perrott, A Price, and T Horsman.

Treorky—Back, J Schofield; three-quarter backs, Lewis Lewis, J Bebb, A Evans, and E White; half-backs, D J Thomas and J Davies; forwards, W Falcon, Bob Jones, F Ramsay, J Thomas, W Davies, D Jones, I B Davies, and G J Attwood.

Referee, Mr R. Pollock, Newport.

"At the last moment two changes were made in the home team, Edwards and Fryer being replaced by Bevan and Mears. There were three changes also in the Treorky team....Mountain Ash gained several yards from the lineout and the first scrum was formed within a few yards of the visitors' line. Getting possession, Muxworthy transferred to Bevan, and the latter doubling his man nicely, scored amid great cheering.... Harries, the home centre, had some teeth knocked out, and retired. On resuming, the Mountain Ash three-quarters participated in a dribble which culminated in Williams scoring an unconverted try....There was not a little unnecessary roughness introduced into the play at this juncture, and the referee had to caution one of the Treorky men. Treorky played with great vigour during the initial stages of the second moiety....A dispute between the spectators led to blows and a most disorderly scene ensued, which resulted in the interference of the police and players, and play was suspended for some time....Treorky scored....The next incident of note was the charging of the ball by one of the Treorky men which resulted in the ball bursting. There was another at hand and no delay was caused. Mountain Ash attacked vigorously shortly after.... Lewis scored from a cross kick, Walton converted. Within two minutes Williams added another unconverted try from a bout of passing...."

<u>Western Mail</u>

POSITIONS OF CLUBS.
RUGBY.

	P.	W.	D.	L.	Points.
Cardiff	19	17	1	1	92.10
Swansea	21	17	3	1	88.09
Newport	19	13	4	2	78.94
Aberavon	21	14	3	5	73.80
Treherbert	21	14	2	5	71.42
Maesteg	22	13	2	7	63.63
Mountain Ash	18	11	1	6	63.88
Llanelly	18	10	1	7	58.33
Treorky	18	9	0	9	50.00
Penygraig	18	8	2	8	50.00
Bridgend	18	7	1	10	41.66
Llwynypia	16	5	2	9	37.50
Neath	20	6	1	13	32.50
Pontypridd	24	5	5	14	31.25

3 March 1902

<u>Pontypridd 3 Mountain Ash 17</u>
<u>Glamorgan League</u>

Mount Team: Back, T. Walton; ¾ backs, Jack Muxworthy, Sam Muxworthy, W.L. Williams, J. Lloyd; half backs, George Edwards Capt, W.J. Harries; forwards, Will Osborne*, H. Beere, Dai Fryer, H.P. Jones, A. Price, T. Horsman, G. Mears, T. Perrot.

* denotes Welsh International

The South Wales Daily News reported, "More than usual interest was displayed in this return League engagement, the Cup holders and their supporters regarding it as the toughest of the season. They were by no means confident of victory and there prevailed almost a consensus of opinion that the boys of the Mount, who have been going much stronger than their opponents of late, would have the better of the struggle. This they certainly had when the teams met a few weeks ago at Mountain Ash, the Pontypriddians on that occasion, being outclassed and defeated by five tries to nil....There was a good gate and the visitors were accompanied by a strong contingent of supporters. Mountain Ash were strongly represented, the only absentee being Alf Fryer, who was on the injured list....The game was unquestionably the best seen on the home ground this season. It bristled with stirring incidents, was fast and fairly open and both sides strove hard for supremacy....The home defence was superb in the first half but it broke down completely during the later stages of the second half when the visitors played with dash, and this accounts for the big score made against Pontypridd."

17 March 1902

<u>Mountain Ash 11 Treherbert 0</u>
<u>Glamorgan League</u>

The South Wales Daily News reported, "....A great deal of interest was centred on the game and upon the final issue, as a defeat to Treherbert might jeopardise the chances of heading the League list for the season. In the last match at Treherbert, the Rhonddaites were victorious but the Mountain Ash men, even then, ought to have won. A determined effort was now to be made by the Old Firm to avenge their defeat and a hard game was anticipated. It was almost 5 o'clock when Perrot for Mountain Ash kicked off against a strong wind. They were further handicapped by the non appearance of Walton, who failed to turn up. They decided to play with 14 men in the hope that their back would join them later on....Walton now came on the field and both sets of scrummagers became even in numbers....The game was very keenly contested at this point and a brilliant burst by the home forwards took play beyond half....Fryer and Osborne headed the forwards and changed the venue to near the Rhondda 25 line....kick across the field, where

W.L. Williams fielded cleverly and raced behind with a well earned try....the home backs allowed the ball to go into touch a few yards from the goal-line. A hard and gruelling game was played for the next few minutes with no advantage being gained by either side....a scrum was ordered. Several attempts to cross were made by the visitors, but each time the keen tackling of the home quartette prevented any damage being done. Eventually relief came through Fryer kicking down....Now the superiority of the home forwards became apparent, and with clever dribbling, they carried all before them, ending in Hugh Jones scoring among a bunch of forwards....The best piece of work in the match....the home forwards had dropped down to the 25 where Willie Harris, with great cleverness, scored under the posts. Walton was next to contribute a fine bit of play. Following his own kick, he reobtained and was only tackled a yard or two off the line....The pick of the home front rank were Osborne, Dai Fryer and Perrot, followed closely by the others....The victory was well earned and reflects great credit on the homesters."

24 March 1902

Mountain Ash 0 Aberavon 6
Glamorgan League

The South Wales Daily News commented, "The visit of Aberavon to Mountain Ash was long and eagerly anticipated. Both teams are about equally matched, and singularly both organisations have about the most powerful set of forwards in the League. A large and enthusiastic crowd assembled....great excitement prevailed.... Prior to fielding, it was feared that the homesters would have to play one man short as Hillman failed to put in an appearance. A change was ultimately made and Fryer went out from the pack, he being replaced by Mayers....A hard tussle was waged between the forwards for some minutes in the home 25. Ultimately, relief came to the hillites by a fine kick by Walton to touch at halfway....Following a knock-on, a scrum was formed about five yards out, and Will Harris, by a pass from Edwards, came within an ace of scoring....the home forwards distinguished themselves and again Alf Fryer and Deere got near the line with a good dribble....A good pass was given by Edwards to Fryer who gave to Muxworthy. The left centre went away and looked all over a scorer, but a fine tackle brought him down.....The excitement was now intense especially when the home forwards dribbled in masterly style over the line....A few hard scrums followed....Walton misjudged the wind although his kick was a fine one....The tit-bit of the match was now seen. A magnificent burst by the whole of the Aberavon backs.... try....The game came fully up to expectations, especially when it transpired the back division of the homesters was disorganised and that a sterling forward like Fryer had to be called upon to play in the centre....The really strong point in the visitors' play was in this department....Fryer's loss from the front rank was keenly felt....Jack Muxworthy was the best of the home three-quarters...."

7 April 1902

Mountain Ash 25 Maesteg 0
Glamorgan League

After leading 13-0 at half time, the South Wales Daily News reporter commented, "In the second half, four of the Maesteg men left the field to catch a train....Some of the spectators were annoyed at the conduct of the players and the matter will probably be reported to the Union."

21 April 1902

Mountain Ash 40 Pontypridd 0
Glamorgan League

Mount Team: Back, Tom Walton; ¾ backs, W.L. Williams, W. Harris, J. Lloyd, J. Francis; half backs, George Edwards Capt, Wyndham Jones; forwards, Will Osborne*, Perrot, Dai Fryer, H. Jones, Alf Price, G. Mears, G. Hughes, D. Davies.

* denotes Welsh International

A League Record Score

The South Wales Daily News reported, "The last match of the season at Mountain Ash....The visitors have shown anything but good form lately and the team has been disorganised in almost all positions. The Old Firm had several reserves playing....The three-quarters have ever been a source of trouble for the hillites, although they are fortunate that W. Harris is available at centre. Injuries caused the retirement of Sam and Jack Muxworthy....Although the homesters put on a record score, their victory was not due to any cracking of the visitors but through really clever back play and combination. Seldom have the home backs been seen to better advantage, and with very few exceptions, their passes were well given and equally well taken. One of the surprising features was the smartness displayed by Francis and Lloyd, the two reserve men. The visiting forwards were well whacked, and Wyndham Jones and George Edwards were in their element."

THE OLD FIRM'S PROUD PAST

Mountain Ash Rugby Football Club
"The Old Firm"
Season 1901/02

Back Row L-R: J. Grant, H. Hughes, Jack Muxworthy, Alf Price, Sam Muxworthy, Will Osborne*, Alf Fryer, G. Mears, Jack Deere, Harry Hale (Secretary),

Front Row L-R: Tom Perrot, Dai Fryer, Reuben Carpenter***, Matt Price, George Edwards, Tom Walton, Wyndham Jones**, Llew Deere (holding ball).

* denotes Welsh International in 1901/02 & 1902/03;   ** denotes Welsh International in 1904/05;
*** denotes the scorer of a Welsh record of 42 tries in 1902/03 along with Fred Jowett of Swansea RFC.

Season 1902/03

One Of The Best For Old Firm
Canadian National XV Beaten
Wing Reuben Carpenter Sets New Welsh Try Scoring Record

This was an exceptional season for the Old Firm with the team being unbeaten at home, and only losing one game up to mid February 1903 and three in the whole season, which were all away from home. The end of season playing record showed 28 games played, 22 won, 3 drawn and 3 lost, which was a win rate of 83.93%, with 353+ points scored, which included 88+ tries, and a measly 59+ points conceded, which included 18 clean sheets. Perhaps the most high profile win, but maybe not thought of as such back then, was the Old Firm's 28-0 victory over the first touring Canadian national XV. Mount, along with Swansea and Cardiff beat the tourists convincingly, Llanelly just about won 11-9, but Ulster, Bristol and London Scottish all lost. All in all, Canada played 21 matches, won 7, drew 2 and lost 12. The season saw "doubles" over London Welsh, Pontypridd, Penygraig, Penarth, Llwynypia and Wellington of Somerset. There were also wins against Maesteg, Plymouth, Aberavon and Treherbert. When the Old Firm won 6-3 at London Welsh, the Exiles had just lost by the same score to Devonport Albion, which was a strong Club of the time and referred to in the Aberdare Leader's report as English champions. The Leader also reported that Mount recorded a first win at Penygraig in 18 years. There were three 0-0 draws – at home to Llanelly and Treorky, and away at Maesteg. There was a first known game against an Irish Club when, on Boxing Day 1902, the Old Firm welcomed and beat Dublin Old Wesley, 11-0. The three Clubs that defeated the Old Firm – Plymouth, Aberavon and Glamorgan League champions for the season, Treherbert – were all beaten in Mountain Ash. The fact that Treherbert won the Glamorgan League despite a magnificent season for the Old Firm showed the strength and competitiveness of the competition and how hard it was to win. Try scoring wing Reuben Carpenter scored 42 tries in the season, which the 1975/76 Centenary Season historical publication, "The First 100 Years", stated set a new Welsh Club try scoring record jointly with Fred Jowett of Swansea RFC, who also scored the same number during the season. Forward Will Osborne made it a special season by gaining 3 more Welsh Caps when he played against England, Scotland and Ireland, in what turned out to be his last International appearances.

Fixtures 1902/03

Opponents	Date	Venue	Score	Tries	Scorers/Comments
Pontnewydd	29 Sep 1902	Home	30-0	8	Jack Muxworthy 2T, C, Sam Muxworthy T, George Edwards T, W.L. Williams T, D. Davies T, Walton 2C, AN Other 2T.
Maesteg (L)	18 Oct 1902	Home	18-0	4	Williams T, AN Other 3T, 3C.
Treherbert (PL)	15 Nov 1902	Home	14-5	4	Scorers unknown.
Penygraig (PL)	22 Nov 1902	Home	22-0	6	Handford T, R. Carpenter T, AN Other 16pts.
Plymouth	29 Nov 1902	Away	0-13	0	No scorers.
Roath	1 Nov 1902	Home	13-7	3	Scorers unknown.
Pontnewydd	8 Nov 1902	Home	Unknown	Unknown	Mount win. Scorers unknown.

Opponents	Date	Venue	Score	Tries	Scorers/Comments
Wellington (Somerset)	6 Dec 1902	Home	23-0	7	Scorers unknown.
Penarth	20 Dec 1902	Away	20-0	4	Scorers unknown.
Grangetown	27 Dec 1902	Unknown	39-0	10	Scorers unknown.
Plymouth	27 Dec 1902	Home	30-0	8	Scorers unknown.
Dublin Old Wesley	27 Dec 1902	Home	11-0	3	R. Carpenter 2T, C, Hugh Jones T.
Penarth	29 Dec 1902	Home	13-9	1	R. Carpenter T, 2DG, C.
Wellington (Somerset)	5 Jan 1903	Away	4-0	0	Walton DG.
Canada	13 Jan 1903	Home	28-0	8	Wyndham Jones 3T, R. Carpenter 2T, C, George Edwards 2T, Handford T, Muxworthy C.
Llanelly	2 Feb 1903	Home	0-0	0	No scorers.
Maesteg (L)	14 Feb 1903	Away	0-0	0	No scorers.
Pontypridd (L)	16 Feb 1903	Home	8-0	2	Jack Muxworthy T, Tom Linton T, R. Carpenter C.
Treherbert (L)	28 Feb 1903	Away	0-5	0	No scorers.
Penygraig (PL)	7 Mar 1903	Away	6-0	2	Carpenter 2T.
London Welsh	14 Mar 1903	Away	6-3	2	R. Carpenter 2T.
Treorky (PL)	28 Mar 1903	Home	0-0	0	No scorers.
Pontypridd (PL)	4 Apr 1903	Away	12-3	4	Carpenter 3T, Price T.
Aberavon (L)	6 Apr 1903	Away	0-6	0	No scorers.
Llwynypia (L)	11 Apr 1903	Home	18-3	3+	Muxworthy T, Handford T, Carpenter T, AN Other 9pts.
London Welsh	13 Apr 1903	Home	26-5	5	Reuben Carpenter 2T, P, 2C, Handford 2T, DG, Jack Muxworthy T.
Llwynypia (L)	14 Apr 1903	Away	3-0	1	R. Carpenter T.
Aberavon (L)	20 Apr 1903	Home	9-0	3	Hanford T, Mears T, J. Muxworthy T.

Summary of Playing Record

P	W	D	L	For	Against	Tries Scored	Win Rate %
28	22	3	3	353+	59+	88+	83.93

Match Reports and Publications

15 November 1902

<u>Mountain Ash 14 Treherbert 5</u>
<u>Possible Glamorgan League Fixture</u>

The Aberdare Leader reported, "These teams met at Mountain Ash in wretched weather before a good crowd. During the last 35 minutes the homesters proved themselves head and shoulders above their opponents. Great preparations are being made for Saturday next, when the two undefeated teams in South Wales, Penygraig and Mountain Ash, will meet. The Old Firm have played 9, won 9, and scored 136 points against 9."

22 November 1902

<u>Mountain Ash 22 Penygraig 0</u>
<u>Possible Glamorgan League Fixture</u>

The Aberdare Leader reported, "Played at Mountain Ash in glorious weather, the crowd was not what would be expected in what has been termed a "Battle Royal". Both teams were undefeated up to Saturday. Penygraig had won all with the exception of one which ended in a draw, but their scoring powers were not equal to the home team. Both teams entered the arena confident of victory and the excitement among the crowd ran high when the Mountaineers set the oval in motion. It was not long before the homesters displayed their scoring powers....up came Wyndham like a deer and in the twinkling of an eye left the Penygraig player minus the ball and transferred to Handford, who initiated the first try....Muxworthy got possession and smartly gave to Carpenter, who scored the second try. The whistle blew for half time. The game was not very old before the referee found it necessary to order a Penygraig forward off the field. After this the visitors lost heart and Mount once again did the needful easily. Penygraig were handicapped playing with six forwards, but even if they had all remained on the field, there was no doubt in the mind of anyone present who would have been victorious. For when you think of the Old Firm leaving the field with 22 points to nil, there is little doubt. To me the best back on the field was Wyndham Jones, who did some of the smartest bits of work that one wished to see on a football field. He was followed by Handford and Walton. In the forwards, Osborne, Fryer and Beere shone. The game played was equal to that of any premier Welsh team."

29 November 1902

<u>Plymouth 13 Mountain Ash 0</u>

The Aberdare Leader had a short report which was as follows, "The two teams were strongly represented, and the game was a very hard one, but no doubt prevails as to the better side. It was a pity to see the ruin of such a record, and by an English team....I shall expect to see retaliation soon. It is to be regretted that the Mountaineers had to be reported as indulging in very rough play which necessitated a forward being ordered off the field."

27 December 1902

<u>Mountain Ash 30 Plymouth 0</u>

The Aberdare Leader reported, "....on Monday, the Mountaineers had a chance to retaliate and they did so with vengeance. There were many distinguished personages present, including members of the W.F.U., Lord Aberdare, the Right Hon. Lyndhurst Bruce and other members of the family. Apparently they all thoroughly enjoyed themselves in witnessing a grand game of football. Doubtless there is a football treat in store for Mountain Ash and district during the holidays, especially if the Old Firm keep in the form they are at present. On Christmas Day they have the Belfast Collegians, on Boxing Day, Dublin Old Wesley and on Saturday, Penarth."

27 December 1902

Mountain Ash 11 Dublin Old Wesley 0
Western Mail

MOUNTAIN ASH V. DUBLIN OLD WESLEY.

This match was played at Mountain Ash in the presence of a good holiday crowd. Referee, Mr. John (Pontypridd).

In the first five minutes the game opened out splendidly, play being confined to the visitors' quarters. From a forward rush Hugh Jones registered the first try for the homesters, which was not improved upon. Through good footwork the Belfast forwards changed the venue, and Harris almost dropped a goal. Play in midfield followed.

Half-time score.	G.	T.	M.
Mountain Ash	0	1	0
Dublin Old Wesley	0	0	0

Hamlet re-started, and exchange kicking amongst the backs ensued, from which play settled in the Irishmen's quarters. On two occasions the ball was sent out cleanly to the "Mount" backs, but knocking on impeded their progress. Moffat next made a fine burst, but Harris grassed him splendidly. From a scrum George Edwards picked up and passed to Jones, who gave to Muxworthy, and Carpenter, travelling at top speed, received and rounded Hinton and scored. The last-named player goaled. Shortly afterwards Wyndham Jones picked up and slung across to Carpenter, who went for the line in tip-top fashion, finishing up a good run by placing a try. The attempt at goal proved abortive. The visitors now "bucked up," and no further scoring occurred.

Final score.	G.	T.	M.
Mountain Ash	1	2	0
Dublin Old Wesley	0	0	0

5 January 1903

Wellington (Somerset) 0 Mountain Ash 4
Western Mail

WELLINGTON V. MOUNTAIN ASH.

Played at Wellington.

The game commenced with very even play, but Wellington quickly pressed severely until Walton relieved, play settling down in midfield. Then the home forwards rushed magnificently down to the visitors' line, but the defence was too good. Mountain Ash retaliated well, and, from clever outside work, Carpenter dashed over, but was called back for going into touch. After this Mountain Ash came away well. Time after time they were within an ace of scoring, but the defence of the Wellington men was invulnerable. At intervals the Wellington men got away to half-way, but were driven back to their line. The visitors, however, failed to get through by half time.

Half-time score.	G.	T.	M.
Wellington	0	0	0
Mountain Ash	0	0	0

In the second half the visitors at once commenced attacking, Walton dropping a magnificent goal from the 25 flag. Then Marks was knocked out and retired. Wellington, however, continued to attack splendidly with their fourteen men, and play became very fast, both sides attacking alternately with the greatest vigour. Again Wellington attacked through the three-quarters with superb play, Walton saving just in time. Play of a most interesting character followed, the men straining every effort to equalise, but the defence was too good. Nothing further was scored. The game throughout was splendidly contested, notwithstanding that Wellington played with fourteen men during the greater part of the game. Walton did an immense amount of work, whilst Rowsell, the Wellington captain, was, undoubtedly, the best man on the field, although the game was of such an even character that it was difficult to individualise.

Final score.	G.	T.	M.
Mountain Ash	*1	0	0
Wellington	0	0	0

*Dropped goal.

13 January 1903

Mountain Ash 28 Canada 0
South Wales Daily News

THE CANADIANS' TOUR.
Match at Mountain Ash.

The Canadians played their second match in the Principality on the Mountain Ash ground. The visitors had the assistance of Freear, the Irish International, who played in the centre. The teams were:—

Mountain Ash—Back, T. Walton; three-quarter backs, Handford, Sage, Muxworthy, and Carpenter; half-backs, W Jones (captain) and Geo. Edwards; forwards, Osborne, Beere, Jones, Price, Fryer, Linton, Caple, and Davies.

Canadians—Back, Farroll; three-quarter backs, Darling, Bould, Freear, and Creig; half-backs, Gillespie and Jack; forwards, McClure, Phillips, Macdonald, Purvis, Du Moulin, Stanway, and Button.

McClure started for the visitors, and Gillespie failing to field Fryer's return kick the first scrummage took place in the visitors' 25. For a time the game was waged between the forwards. It was not long before it became apparent that the visitors knew little of the Welsh game, for when all their men were on the left side of the field close to a scrummage Carpenter had no difficulty in racing over and gaining the first try. The attempt to convert was futile. Wyndham Jones was the next to score, but again the additional two points were not gained. After a good bout of passing Carpenter scored, and the same player converted. Gillespie then cleverly got away from a scrummage and gained a lot of ground, but Walton was safe, and the homesters again attacked. Handford and Edwards scored unconverted tries before the interval.

Half-time Score—
	G.	T.	M.
Mountain Ash	1	4	0
Canadians	0	0	0

Faverty replied to Osborne's restarting kick and placed nicely to touch at halfway. The home forwards, with the International and Beere in the van, travelled close to their opponents' line, and Edwards nonplussed both Gillespie and Jack by skirting the scrummage and scoring behind the posts. Muxworthy converted. McDonald became prominent, and twice ran down the centre of the field, but was stopped by Walton. The forwards, however, kept at it with dogged pertinacity, and although a lot of liberty was allowed them in handling the ball, the backs failed to break clean away. Bould and Freear nearly scoring, and Walton touched down in defence. W. Jones scored, and repeated the same thing shortly afterwards, both tries being unconverted. The Canadians then exhibited fine defence, and Handford was twice stopped on the line.

Final Score—
	G.	T.	M.
Mountain Ash	2	5	0
Canadians	0	0	0

Remarks.

The game was fairly interesting. The visitors were unable to cope with the passing of the Mountain Ash backs, and at half Wyndham Jones and Edwards proved too smart for Gillespie and his partner, who were time after time beaten. Osborne, Hugh Jones, and Fryer were the most prominent of the home forwards, and Macdonald and McClure of the Canadians. Darling, the visiting custodian, shaped well in the second half, kicking to touch as a rule. Walton was in fine fettle, and never made a mistake.

21 January 1903

<u>The Canadians' Tour</u>
<u>Welsh Teams a "Bitter Pill"</u>

The South Wales Daily News reported, "Speaking at a dinner given to the Canadians by the Bristol Rugby Football Club, Mr McClure, the captain of the Canadians said that their success against Bristol was an emergence from darkness into light....They were told by some before they left Canada that they would not win a game. They had done better than that, for until they went to Wales to play, they had won the majority of their matches, but Wales was a bitter pill for them, and in some ways they were not sorry to leave the Principality (laughter)...."

2 February 1903

<u>Mountain Ash 0 Llanelly 0</u>
<u>Western Mail</u>

MOUNTAIN ASH V. LLANELLY.

A great game was witnessed at Mountain Ash, the visitors being Llanelly. The men of the "Mount," it may be mentioned, have only been beaten once this season, viz., at Plymouth, and they have scored over 300 points to something under 50 points by their opponents. The Llanelly team, too, have an excellent record, the principal scalps they have taken being that of Cardiff, and it was felt that the wearers of the black and amber would have to go all the way to retain their ground record, although Llanelly were minus the services of Newton and Alcwyn Jones. It was a very favourable day for football, although the weather looked a little threatening, and some slight showers rendered the turf slippery. The attendance was above the average, and amongst those present were a couple of Welsh Union officials, who had come up to see Arnold play, in view of Monday's selection of three-quarters to represent Wales at Inverleith. Those were Mr. Ack Llewellyn and Mr. A. J. Gould, of Newport; the latter acting in the capacity of referee. The teams were:—
Llanelly: Back, Strand Jones; three-quarter backs, R. T. Gabe, Arnold, Bob Richards, and E. M. Davies; half-backs, White and Ben Davies; forwards, Dan Walters, Bob Thomas, W. J. Thomas, Watts, H. Watkins, P.C. Stacey, P.C. Davies, and D. Davies. Mountain Ash: Back, Walton; three-quarter backs, E. Carpenter, J. Muxworthy, S. Muxworthy, and E. Handford; half-backs, G. Thomas and W. Jones; forwards, Osborne, A. Fryer, D. Fryer, D. Davies, T. Linton, G. Mears, Caple, and H. Edgar.

"The opening stages were of an exciting nature....A good deal of keenness was infused into the play and the referee had to caution one of the players for undoubted brutality....Play dragged for a while until Gabe made a fine run, but in trying to dodge Walton near the line, Carpenter came across at full speed and brought off a fine tackle which saved a try....Soon after the restart, Wyndham Jones, in being tackled, had his leg hurt, and afterwards was of little use to his side....The rain continued and reduced the ground to a quagmire. Mountain Ash were heavier in front and were having most of the game, but the conditions were against pretty or accurate play. Strand Jones had a kick charged down by Jack Muxworthy, and Carpenter, running well, almost scored, but W. Davies got it to touch in-goal just in time."

The Aberdare Leader commented in its report of this game, "Keen interest was manifested in the visit of the "Tinplaters" to Mountain Ash on Saturday last. The interest was aroused in that Llanelly brought their strongest available fifteen. The visitors included the Welsh International custodian Strand Jones, R.T. Gabe, the International centre, and Willie Arnold, who was also a likely candidate for the "Red Cap"....It was fully 3:30 when the teams entered the field. It was soon evident that it was to be a keenly contested game. Scrummage after scrummage was the order for a considerable time....At last Mountain Ash came within an ace of scoring by clever intercepting by Carpenter....Immediately after the restart Mountain Ash pressed, which resulted in Carpenter and Muxworthy coming again within an ace of scoring....Mountain Ash pressed and it was odds on Beere scoring. A splendid chance was lost owing to Beere holding too long. Both sides pressed in turns from now to the finish, the standing feature being Walton's superb back play....The game was keenly fought from beginning to end. Those who expected to see a brilliant display of football were disappointed. The game was so keen that neither side allowed the ball to go far enough to give a display of that style of back play which is so characteristic of Welsh teams. Of the visitors, R. T. Gabe was the only outstanding figure. The hero of the homesters was Carpenter, while Walton was also a tower of strength." The South Wales Daily News summed up the game as follows, "Mountain Ash have retained their ground record and this was not obtained by a mere fluke. A pointless game was a fitting result to a hard, dogged match, fought with grim determination from beginning to end....It was essentially a forward game....For possession of the ball and good packing, the visitors took the palm, although outweighed. On the other hand, the Old Firm's rushing tactics and all round loose play counteracted their opponents superiority in other departments. There was not a shirker amongst the whole of the forwards; every man did his quota....Beere, Fryer and Osborne were conspicuous in the home front rank though the others were not far behind....Wyndham Jones and George Edwards (the Mount half backs) shone up well considering the chances they had. It was in defence that the Old Firm captain (Wyndham Jones) shone more particularly. He picked up at the forwards' feet and saved repeatedly....The defensive powers of the Mountain Ash quartette came into evidence on several occasions....Muxworthy and Handford were the pick. The joy of the homesters knew no bounds after the magnificent manner in which Walton played at full back. Never has he been in better form. His kicking and fielding left nothing to be desired and, in comparison with Strand Jones, passed better than the International....". In the Llanelly XV above, Strand Jones was capped by Wales 5 times in 1902 and 1903, R.T. Gabe played for Llanelli and Cardiff and was capped 21 times by Wales between 1901 and 1908, Willie Arnold was capped once by Wales in 1903, and Mount's very own outside half, Wyndham Jones, played for Wales on one occasion in 1905, and forward Will Osborne was capped 6 times in 1902 and 1903 to complete quite an array of talent on show in this match.

7 March 1903

<u>Penygraig 0 Mountain Ash 6</u>
<u>Possible Glamorgan League Fixture</u>

The Aberdare Leader reported, "About 800 supporters of the "Old Firm" journeyed to the Rhondda on Saturday last. They were wild with enthusiasm, as well as a release, to see them leave the T.V.R. platform. The weather on the whole was favourable....Many at home as well as abroad were making grave mental speculations as to the result....The Rhonddaites thought to retaliate on Saturday for the defeat they suffered at the hands of the Mountaineers earlier in the season. But the anticipations were not realised and instead of being "more than conquerors" were again brought a cropper. We thought that since the "Old Firm" had suffered defeat on Saturday last at Treherbert, they could not possibly expect to pull it off with a team at whose hands they had suffered defeat from home for the last eighteen years. But they did, and had a margin of six points. It was a hard fought game and contained very little brilliant football. Carpenter, who scored the two tries, was easily the best man on the field. In the front rank of the visitors, Osborne, Beere and Dai Fryer were the pick…. Now my lads you did well, keep this up and you'll make things hum in the Glamorgan League. Don't rest on your oars as you are so liable to do, but play not only at home, but from home, and the cup is yours."

14 March 1903

<u>London Welsh 3 Mountain Ash 6</u>

The Aberdare Leader reported, "Mountain Ash encountered London Welsh at the Metropolis on Saturday last….They beat the citizens by the same number of points as did the English champions, Devonport Albion, 6-3. Not bad for the "Old Firm" from home too. Continue to keep it up my lads. Aberavon are making a bold bid for that cup. You cannot afford to lose a peg or let your form go down the least. It is an acknowledged fact in the football world that George Edwards, the Mountaineers' half back, is the renowned Dicky Jones' rival."

4 April 1903

<u>Pontypridd 3 Mountain Ash 12</u>
<u>Possible Glamorgan League Fixture</u>

The Aberdare Leader reported, "Notwithstanding the great counter attraction at Mountain Ash of the South Wales Final Cup tie, many of the staunch supporters of the Old Firm journeyed with them to Pontypridd. The rain fell in torrents. After a keen struggle in the rain and mud and wind, the Mountaineers returned victors with a margin of nine points. Out of the four tries, Carpenter, who was the hero of the game, initiated three, and Price the other. Mount are going strong for the Cup and medals. If they keep it up things will be alright, otherwise they can say farewell."

6 April 1903

<u>Aberavon 6 Mountain Ash 0</u>
<u>Glamorgan League</u>

The Western Mail commented, "….the defeat of the Old Firm leaves the Championship in a state of delightful uncertainty. Treherbert have completed their League engagements, and their position is such a favourable one that the defeat of Aberavon at Mountain Ash will probably mean they, Treherbert, will retain the cup."

13 April 1903

<u>Mountain Ash 29 London Welsh 12</u>

Mount Team: Back, Tom Walton; ¾ backs, Sam Muxworthy, Jack Muxworthy, Reuben Carpenter, E. Handford; half backs, Wyndham Jones, George Edwards; forwards, Will Osborne*, Fryer, Alf Price, D. Davies, E. Morgan, George Caple, G. Mears, Beere.

* denotes Welsh International

The Aberdare Leader reported, "Mountain Ash encountered London Welsh at home on Saturday. Keen interest was manifested in that London Welsh had a strong team, captained by Willie Llewellyn. A fine display was witnessed. Carpenter was easily the best back on the field. His second try was simply marvellous." The Western Mail commented in its match report, "Ideal weather favoured the visit of the London Welshmen to Mountain Ash…. Carpenter receiving from Muxworthy, made off….Not to be denied, picking up the oval in the loose and near the centre, made a really brilliant, dodgy run, which ended in him scoring his 40th try, thus tying with Jowett of Swansea for tries during the season….From the restart, Fryer went away with a dribble and Carpenter finished the movement by scoring (his 41st try of the season)."

20 April 1903

<u>Mountain Ash 9 Aberavon 0</u>
<u>Glamorgan League</u>

The Western Mail reported, "The centre of interest as far as Glamorgan League football was concerned, was to be found on the Mountain Ash enclosure. Both teams were confident of success, and as victory for either side would probably mean the ultimate possession of the League trophy for the ensuing twelve months, intense excitement prevailed. The weather was all that could be desired and when the teams took the field, a large crowd had assembled."

The Aberdare Leader reported, "It was a hard forward game. The play was characterised throughout with a lot of unnecessary roughness and brutality. Somehow, the visitors have become victims to this kind of play this season and their game on Saturday was no exception. Fortunately, a good man in the person of Mr Douglas of Cardiff, had charge of the teams and easily managed the situation."

Season 1903/04

Good Season For Mount Despite Five Players Going North

Early season, the Old Firm lost 5 players to the paid ranks of the Northern Union. Welsh International forward, Will Osborne, full back Tom Walton, and centre three-quarters Jack Muxworthy and Llew Deere, all joined Huddersfield, and record try scoring wing from 1902/03, Rueben Carpenter, joined Oldham. Even though losing these players, it was another good season for Mount with only 7 games lost from the 24 known games played, with wins against Maesteg, Treorky and Pontypridd, and "doubles" over Penarth, Penygraig and Cilfynydd, the latter game being the first time both Clubs had played each other. There were also draws with Aberavon and Llwynypia. The playing record for the season showed 24 games played, 14 won, 3 drawn and 7 lost, with 127+ points, including 32+ tries scored, and 70+ points conceded. All this converted to a win rate of 64.58%, which was a good return considering the quality of player lost to the Northern Union early in the season. The Aberdare Leader's rugby reporter, Muddled Oaf, asked in September 1903, "Why, or why cannot they have a field to themselves like other teams? Alas, the Land of Pennar is not superabundant in fields, and the few it has will soon be converted into sites for habitations." This was a reference to the fact that the Old Firm had no regular home pitch – a situation which continued until after the First World War, when the Rec was used.

Fixtures 1903/04

Opponents	Date	Venue	Score	Tries	Scorers/Comments
Chepstow	3 Oct 1903	Home	15-3	3	Scorers unknown.
Roath	10 Oct 1903	Home	Unknown	Unknown	Mount win. Scorers unknown.
Llwynypia (PL)	17 Oct 1903	Home	0-0	0	No scorers.
Treorky (PL)	24 Oct 1903	Home	5-0	1	Caple T, Francis C.
Penygraig (PL)	31 Oct 1903	Away	11-6	Unknown	Bevan & Edwards 11pts.
Aberavon (L)	9 Nov 1903	Away	0-8	0	No scorers.
Pontardulais	16 Nov 1903	Unknown	12-0	4	AN Other 4T.
Penarth	28 Nov 1903	Home	12-0	4	Mog Bevan T, E. Handford T, Bevan T, Caple T.
Plymouth	30 Nov 1903	Away	0-6	0	No scorers.
Cilfynydd (L)	7 Dec 1903	Home	6-0	2	Mog Bevan T, George Edwards T.
Pontypridd (L)	21 Dec 1903	Away	0-3	0	No scorers.
Penygraig (L)	28 Dec 1903	Home	9-0	3	Mog Bevan T, W. Ware T, Williams T.
Aberdare (L)	11 Jan 1904	Away	5-13	1	AN Other T, C.
Maesteg (L)	18 Jan 1904	Away	3-8	1	Morgan T.
Cilfynydd (PL)	25 Jan 1904	Away	9-0	3	George Edwards T, E. Handford T, Williams T.
Treorky (PL)	15 Feb 1904	Away	0-8	Unknown	No scorers.
Maesteg (L)	22 Feb 1904	Home	4-0	0	George Evans DG.

Opponents	Date	Venue	Score	Tries	Scorers/Comments
Penarth	29 Feb 1904	Away	6-0	2	Mog Bevan T, D. Davies T.
Treherbert (L)	12 Mar 1904	Home	3-3	1	AN Other T.
Pontypridd (PL)	12 Mar 1904	Home	14-0	4	W. Ware T, AN Other 3T, C.
Cwmbran	19 Mar 1904	Home	3-0	1	AN Other T.
Aberavon (L)	2 Apr 1904	Home	3-3	1	Wyndham Jones T.
Aberdare (PL)	16 Apr 1904	Home	7-0	1	Morgan T, Williams DG.
Cwmbran	23 Apr 1904	Away	0-9	0	No scorers.

Summary of Playing Record

P	W	D	L	For	Against	Tries Scored	Win Rate %
24	14	3	7	127+	70+	32+	64.58

Match Reports and Publications

12 September 1903

The Aberdare Leader's reporter, "Muddled Oaf", reported, "The Mountain Ash premier team undoubtedly had a severe blow in the losing of three of their prominent players – Reuben Carpenter, the wing three-quarter has joined the Oldham team; Osborne, the forward, has departed to Huddersfield, and Walton, the full back, has also gone to Huddersfield, all through the Northern Union poaching. But there's life in the old team yet. They still have some influential supporters and expert players such as Beere, Fryer and several others. At their annual meeting last week, it was decided that a second team shall be run. By their doing so, the first team will never suffer from lack of funds or supporters."

17 October 1903

<u>Mountain Ash 0 Llwynypia 0</u>
<u>Possible Glamorgan League Fixture</u>

"Muddled Oaf" reported in the Aberdare Leader, "Although the Old Firm were minus Osborne, Walton, Carpenter and Muxworthy – who have left them to seek the coveted dollar – the team contrived to play throughout with brilliancy….their successors played up well."

28 November 1903

<u>Mountain Ash 12 Penarth 0</u>

The Aberdare Leader reported, "….the home team were minus the services of Geo. Evans, Beere, Fryer, Wyndham Jones, Ware and Williams…..Penarth were expected to just about win, but the Mount reserves played a dashing game and turned the tables on their opponents and beat them to the tune of four tries to nil."

25 January 1904

<u>Cilfynydd 0 Mountain Ash 9</u>
<u>Possible Glamorgan League Fixture</u>

The Western Mail commented in its match report, "….it being the first visit of the Old Firm to Cilfynydd, great interest was taken in the game…."

22 February 1904

<u>Western Mail</u>

GLAMORGAN LEAGUE COMPETITION.
Positions up to and including Saturday, February 20:—

	P.	W.	D.	L.	Pts.
*Treherbert	11	7	2	2	18
Maesteg	10	7	1	2	15
*Aberavon	12	6	1	5	15
Treorky	12	6	2	4	14
Mountain Ash	12	6	1	5	13
Pontypridd	13	5	2	6	12
Aberdare	10	5	0	5	10
†Llwynypia	10	4	1	5	7
†Penygraig	10	4	0	6	6
Cilfynydd	11	0	0	11	0

* Two points added, † two points deducted—infringement of rules.

<u>Mountain Ash 4 Maesteg 0</u>
<u>Glamorgan League</u>

The Western Mail reported, "The weather was wretched. The Mount have been doing none too well and it was felt that they would have to play a very strong game to revenge the reverse sustained in the previous match with the Llynfi Valley men. The visitors were well represented but the same could not be said of the home Club....George Edwards dropped a goal....A delightful round of passing, in which the home backs handled, looked like terminating in a score. The last pass, however, went astray, and a chance was lost....A beautiful dribble from half way by the home forwards took the oval over the Maesteg line, and Morgan showed splendid pace on the heavy turf, just failed to score. Things were looking rosy for the Mount, whose forwards were playing a grand game...."

12 March 1904

<u>Mountain Ash 3 Treherbert 3</u>
<u>Glamorgan League</u>

"En Avant" reported in the Aberdare Leader, "This important League match was played on Monday last in wretched weather. After a long hesitation, owing to the state of the ground, it was decided to make the best of it, and with very few supporters, both teams took the field. Rain fell continually, and the thirty players, wallowing in mud, looked anything like rugby players....they decided after about 15 minutes of the second half to love and leave it."

<u>Mountain Ash 14 Pontypridd 0</u>
<u>Possible Glamorgan League Fixture</u>

"En Avant" reported, "Owing to Pontypridd's late arrival, the oval was not set in motion until 4:30. The game was of a rough and scramble nature, and contained very little brilliant scientific football....Ware's try was the feature of the match. Possibly, the Old Firm is only polishing another star for the Northern Union. Many complain about the non success of the Old Firm, but few really support them. Ah! I forgot. Perhaps they occupy the grandstand on Penrhiwceiber on Saturdays."

2 April 1904

<u>Mountain Ash 3 Aberavon 3</u>
<u>Glamorgan League</u>

"En Avant" reported in the Aberdare Leader, "The question of the Glamorgan League is such an undecided one at present, and both teams are in the running. Consequently, great interest was manifested in the contest.....Wyndham Jones intercepting, and going at top speed looked a scorer all over, but was tackled in the nick of time...from a scrum near the line, Jones, the homesters Captain, slipped round their blind side and scored a smart, but unconverted try....Time after time, the homesters and the visitors took their turn in attack, but neither could break their line of defence. A hard fought game was declared a draw. The score is no criterion of the game. Several times the Old Firm failed at the critical moment through sheer bad luck. The homesters try was smartly got, as so was the visitors. Williams was greatly missed as centre, and undoubtedly if he had been present, he would have prevented the Avonites sharing the spoils."

Season 1904/05

Wyndham Jones Has Welsh Debut To Remember
Old Firm Tie At Top Of Glamorgan League

The prestige and consequent difficulty of being crowned Glamorgan League champions was again emphasised when a very good season for the Old Firm wasn't enough to lift the trophy, Mount finishing joint top of the table with local rivals Aberdare on 22 points. It showed the Glamorgan League was *the* competition to win and what a hard fought one it was in the Golden Era of Welsh rugby. The play-off final with Aberdare eventually took place in October of the following season, 1905/06. This was due to Aberdare's win over Treorky being gained on the last official day of the season – a win that brought them equal with Mount on points – no extension to the season being allowed by the Welsh Football Union. There were some good wins for the Old Firm during the season. There were "doubles" over Pontypridd, Treorky and Penarth, and wins against Maesteg, Penygraig, Aberavon, Treherbert and Cilfynydd. The end of season playing record saw 27 games played, 20 won, 1 drawn and 6 lost, with 242 points and 68 tries scored, and just 80 conceded, which gave an impressive win rate of 75.93%. One of the Old Firm's best players in this era was Wyndham Jones, who was a running outside half who lit up many a game. He crowned a fine season for the Club and for himself personally when he got his sole Welsh cap against Ireland at Swansea, and made the most of it as well, scoring a try and making another to guide Wales to a famous 10-3 win that secured the Triple Crown for a fourth time. The favourable comments made about Jones in various match reports suggested he would have gained more than one cap if he had played at a different time to the so called "Golden Era" of Welsh rugby.

Fixtures 1904/05

Opponents	Date	Venue	Score	Tries	Scorers/Comments
Roath	19 Sep 1904	Home	14-0	4	Scorers unknown.
Dinas Powis	26 Sep 1904	Home	12-0	4	Scorers unknown.
Pontardulais	3 Oct 1904	Home	18-0	6	Scorers unknown.
Pontardulais	10 Oct 1904	Away	9-0	3	Scorers unknown.
Maesteg (L)	17 Oct 1904	Home	10-0	2	Scorers unknown.
Treorky (L)	24 Oct 1904	Away	5-0	1	Williams T, C.
Maesteg (F)	31 Oct 1904	Away	0-20	0	No scorers.
Pill Harriers	7 Nov 1904	Home	0-0	0	No scorers.
Cilfynydd (L)	21 Nov 1904	Away	5-0	1	Williams T, Wyndham Jones C.
Treherbert (L)	28 Nov 1904	Away	3-6	1	Jenkins T.
Grange Stars	5 Dec 1904	Home	29-0	9	Scorers unknown.
Penygraig (L)	12 Dec 1904	Home	6-0	2	Williams 2T.
Aberdare (F)	19 Dec 1904	Away	3-8	1	Williams T.
Penarth	2 Jan 1905	Unsure	19-0	5	Scorers unknown.
Pontypridd (L)	9 Jan 1905	Home	18-8	6	P. C. Williams 3T, George Mears T, George Edwards T, Peter O'Neill T.
Glamorgan Police	30 Jan 1905	Home	3-8	1	AN Other T.
Treorky (L)	6 Feb 1905	Home	11-0	3	Williams T, C, Wyndham Jones T, Hughes T.
Ystrad Stars	13 Feb 1905	Home	8-0	2	AN Other 2T, C.
Pontypridd (L)	20 Feb 1905	Away	5-0	1	Wyndham Jones T, Jack Thomas C.
Penygraig (L)	6 Mar 1905	Away	3-6	1	L. Morgan T.
Aberavon	20 Mar 1905	Away	3-6	1	Williams T.

Opponents	Date	Venue	Score	Tries	Scorers/Comments
Penarth	27 Mar 1905	Home	7-0	1	Weare T, AN Other DG.
Aberavon	27 Mar 1905	Home	8-3	2	L. Morgan T, AN Other T, J. Thomas C.
Treherbert (L)	10 Apr 1905	Home	13-5	3	Penalty Try, AN Other 10pts.
Glamorgan Police	17 Apr 1905	Home	8-0	2	AN Other 2T, C.
Cwmbran	24 Apr 1905	Home	14-3	4	Scorers unknown.
Aberdare (L)	29 Apr 1905	Away	8-7	2	Wyndham Jones 2T, Jack Thomas C.

Summary of Playing Record

P	W	D	L	For	Against	Tries Scored	Win Rate %
27	20	1	6	242	80	68	75.93

Match Reports and Publications

17 October 1904

<u>Mountain Ash 10 Maesteg 0</u>
<u>Glamorgan League</u>

The South Wales Daily News reported, "Contrary to expectations, the League match at Mountain Ash was rendered specially attractive and exciting through the policy adopted to play an open game. Indeed, there were occasions when the display became sensational and there was not a single dull moment during the game. The first 10 minutes was brimful of excitement, the home team infusing such dash and determination into their play that the Maesteg line was placed in imminent danger, and it might be added it was only tough luck that robbed Mount of a score....By common consent, it was one of the best League encounters seen at Mount for a long time....Mountain Ash forwards made up for the lack of weight in their dashing play when the ball came loose, and in dribbling and rushing, they were slightly ahead of their opponents. Three-quarter play reached a higher state of perfection on the winners' side, and it was the smartness of the back division in snapping up their chances that gave the team victory. They understood each other's play better than the Llynfi men....At half, Wyndham Jones was in as good fettle as ever, and his nippiness and cleverness in making openings were the features of the afternoon....Fryer, Caple and Price shone in the home rank. The victory, which was well deserved, ought to go a long way towards securing a better measure of public support for Mountain Ash."

24 October 1904

<u>Treorky 0 Mountain Ash 5</u>
<u>Glamorgan League</u>

The South Wales Daily News reported, "The most important match under the auspices of the Glamorgan League was played at Griffin Park, Pentre....Today's match excited more than ordinary interest. The display of Treorky this season has so far been very consistent, while Mountain Ash had only taken part in one severe engagement – against Maesteg, when they agreeably surprised their supporters by their capital performance.... The first successful bout of passing was brought off by Mountain Ash. Wyndham Jones running smartly, made a good opening, which almost ended in Jenkins scoring, the half back being tackled five yards out....A sensational bit of play followed. Williams, the Mountain Ash right wing, getting possession in his own 25, ran strongly, and put in a high kick. Regaining possession, he scored under the posts and converted...."

12 December 1904

<u>Mountain Ash 6 Penygraig 0</u>
<u>Glamorgan League</u>

The South Wales Daily News reported, "Always one of the most interesting in the home programme....the home team, having shown consistent form throughout the season, and the visitors having of late played in great style, a keen game was anticipated. As Jenkins, the home centre had gone North, W. Sage was prevailed upon to take his place....It was a tough fight between both packs, each playing good football....Penygraig have to thank their pack for the lowness of the score against them...."

28 December 1904

MAESTEG v. MOUNTAIN ASH.
A Disappointment.

Great disappointment was caused at Maesteg Tuesday when it became known that the Mountain Ash team had not arrived at the appointed time. A large crowd of spectators assembled near the home headquarters eagerly awaiting the expected visitors. The referee, Mr H. J. Taylor, of Cardiff, was in attendance, but at 3 o'clock a telegram was received stating that the Mountain Ash team had missed their train connection at Pontypridd, and could not possibly arrive in time to play the match.

6 February 1905

<u>Mountain Ash 11 Treorky 0</u>
<u>Glamorgan League</u>

Mount Team: Back, J. Thomas; ¾ backs, Williams, Hughes, Peter O'Neill, Sage; half backs, George Edwards, Wyndham Jones Capt; forwards, Dai Fryer, D. Davies, H. Beere, J. Mears, Alf Price, T. Linton, Wilkins, George Caple.

The South Wales Daily News reported, "The homesters are bent upon making a great effort to secure League honours, and fully realised the importance of winning every home match. The ground was in bad condition on the cheap side when the visitors kicked off. Soon after, O'Neill cut out an excellent opening for Williams who scored and converted....Edwards served his partner capitally and Wyndham Jones rushed over....Seeing the Old Firm forwards were playing such a fine game, it was distinctly hard for the visiting eight to be let down after having won a foothold close in....From a scrum, Wyndham Jones cut out an old-time opening and Hughes, being the last to receive, swerved through three or four opponents and scored cleverly....The state of the ground let one to predict a strictly forward game, but the subsequent handling of the home team was quite first class....O'Neill's opening which led to the first try made that player give one of his best exhibitions throughout the first half....It would be invidious to name any home forward after their excellent display. The home halves were too smart and clever for their vis-à-vis...."

6 March 1905

Penygraig 6 Mountain Ash 3
Glamorgan League
South Wales Daily News

PENYGRAIG v. MOUNTAIN ASH.
"DICK" THOMAS AND WYN JONES.
Probable Caps Do Well.

A most important match under the auspices of the Glamorgan League was played between the above teams at Penygraig on Saturday. The chances of Mountain Ash securing chief honours in the league are exceptionally rosy, the Old Firm having only lost one match out of nine played, thus placing them at present in the leading position. Penygraig, on their own ground, have always proved doughty opponents, and only on two occasions since the existence of the teams have Mountain Ash gained victory on the Belle Vue. The interest in this encounter was greater than usual, and an excursion was run from Mountain Ash in connection with the game, a large contingent of the visitors' supporters availing themselves of the cheap fare. The team were well represented, and the supporters of the respective sides were confident of the issue culminating in a win for their pets. The previous engagement at Mountain Ash ended in a victory for the home team by two tries. A thick drizzling rain fell during the day, which made the ground very sloppy. The teams were as follow:—

Penygraig—Back, Gordon Thomas; three-quarter backs, Simmonds, Loates, Clissold, and Davies; half-backs, Williams and Ridley; forwards, H Jones, G Matthews, R Thomas, D Bowen, W Owens, T Evans, E Evans and Flynn.

Mountain Ash—Back, J Thomas; three-quarter backs, O'Neill, Weare, L Morgan, and J Hughes; half-backs, Wyndham Jones and Edwards; forwards, D Fryer, G Mears, A Price, Linton, P.C. Wilkins, A Fryer, Caple, and D Davies.

Referee, Mr Phelps, Barry.

The South Wales Daily News reported, "There was a sensational opening to the game. Harry Jones, kicked off for Penygraig, the ball fell into the hands of Fryer. He hesitated and Willie Owen, dashing up, charged down his kick, bowled over the full back, who dropped the ball, and scored in about fifteen seconds. This probably creates a record for an early score….Mountain Ash again got into the home ground….Wyndham made good attempts to score. Ultimately during a temporarily poor defence, Morgan got over….Resuming, Mountain Ash gave the homesters an anxious ten minutes, the forwards beating the Penygraig pack, whose play had somewhat deteriorated. The visitors' backs got going several times and nearly got over, Wyndham Jones and Edwards making good openings….the home backs brought off a good bout of passing which resulted in Davies scoring in the extreme corner….A keen struggle in which no quarter was given by either side….Penygraig owe their victory to the robust play of their forwards, and after the first 10 minutes of the second half, had the full measure of their opponents. Behind the scrum, Mountain Ash were superior, their halves in particular being far ahead of the Penygraig pair….Mountain Ash were well served by Fryer, Weare, Caple and Wyndham Jones."

15 March 1905

The Aberdare Leader reported, "The Aberdare Club is gradually gaining a strong position in the fight for the Cup. They have three stiff matches in Penygraig and Mountain Ash away and Mountain Ash home. On Good Friday they journey to Mountain Ash, Saturday Penygraig, on Easter Monday they play Mountain Ash, and on the 29th they wind up the season with a League match at Treorky."

20 March 1905

<u>Aberavon 6 Mountain Ash 3</u>
<u>Players Ordered Off</u>

The South Wales Daily News reported, "....The visitors....gave the 'Avonites an anxious time in front of their goal. Here the ball was smartly heeled out by the visitors, and a capital round of passing ended in Williams scoring an easy try....Price, Mountain Ash, and Leyshon, the Aberavon forward, were ordered off for striking each other....Mountain Ash were best served by the two Fryers in the forwards....The result fairly represents the character of the play, and for the first time this year, Aberavon met with a well deserved victory."

27 March 1905

<u>Mountain Ash 8 Aberavon 3</u>

Mount Team: Back, J. Thomas; ¾ backs, Hughes, L. Morgan, Ware, O'Neil; half backs, Wyndham Jones*, George Edwards; forwards, Dai Fryer, George Caple, H. Beere, Dai Davies, Mears, Alf Price, T. Linton, P.C. Wilkins.

* denotes Welsh International

The South Wales Daily News reported, "The Old Firm, free from League worries, were at home to Aberavon, the weather turning out fine, and this coupled with the fact that Aberavon was the visiting team caused more than the average number to muster round the touchline....Wyndham Jones kicked high, and smart following up saw the visiting back tackled on his line. George Edwards fed Wyndham Jones. The captain, working to the left, gave to Ware, who was pushed into touch only a yard out....A most unusual thing now occurred. A high kick sent to James saw the Aberavon back tear away. He dribbled about 20 yards and kicked but L. Morgan came on at full tilt and charged down, receiving the ball from the kick. He kept his head cool, dribbled over, and scored...."

10 April 1905

<u>Mountain Ash 13 Treherbert 5</u>
<u>Glamorgan League</u>
<u>A Regrettable Incident: Beere Kicked in the Head</u>

The South Wales Daily News reported, "The interesting triangular duel between Penygraig, Aberdare and Mountain Ash for the Glamorgan League Championship made this match at Mountain Ash of much importance. In the last three matches, Treherbert annexed five points and the Old Firm one, and since the latter had to win this match to keep among this season's leaders, it was not surprising that a much larger crowd than usual lined the ropes....A regrettable incident occurred near to half time. A visiting forward, who was named – according to the crowd – kicked Beere in the head. Beere was taken off bleeding. The referee could not see what a section of the crowd claim to be a deliberate foul....A general caution was administered....The visiting pack were superior to the home pack in the tight but both were equally matched in the loose. For the homesters, Caple, Linton, Fryer and Williams were good...."

The South Wales Daily News also published the following article on this date which gives an indication of some of the rugby played in South Wales at the time:

Rough Football.

SCENES AT ABERAVON.—UNSPORTING SPECTATORS.

'Bravon Player Ordered Off.

REFEREE ENLISTS POLICE AID.

Is football degenerating in South Wales? The recent games played at Aberavon seem to point to it in no uncertain manner. The Llanelly v. Aberavon game on Saturday started in friendly spirit enough: in fact, it was well into the second half that anything in the nature of roughness occurred. Lewis Thomas was first laid out—the 'Bravon outside half. He received a nasty smack on the head. Then Cole, the Llanelly forward, was led off the field, and a few minutes afterwards the referee (Mr Harry, of Swansea) had occasion to lecture two of the forwards, one on either side, and this culminated in the referee complaining to the police of the conduct of a section of the crowd, some of the spectators hooting and threatening, and one of them going so far as to aim a missile at Mr Harry, who fortunately escaped injury. From the Press box the game did not appear to be unduly rough, but as one of the players said to our representative, "You can't see there what happens when a player is on the ground in a scrummage or in a close rush." Roughness apart the game was an extremely interesting one to watch.

PLAYER KICKED AT MOUNTAIN ASH.

In the Treherbert v. Mountain Ash match on the ground of the latter club Beere, the old Somerset forward, was kicked on the head and taken off the field bleeding freely. Mr D. H. Bowen was the referee, and though he cautioned the players generally he did not order anyone off, probably owing to the offender being screened from his observation at the time of the incident. The crowd near the spot unhesitatingly named and naturally condemned the offender.

Three Players "Named" at Cardiff.

At Cardiff the crowd on three occasions named players for unnecessary charges, exhorting them "to play the game."

29 April 1905

Aberdare 7 Mountain Ash 8
Glamorgan League

The Aberdare Leader reported, "The most important match of the season was fought out at the New Athletic Grounds, Aberdare, on Monday afternoon. The gate was the largest seen on the grounds with the exception of the Aberdare v Aberaman match two seasons ago. Both teams turned out at full strength. Mountain Ash started against the wind....Mount were penalised....the ball rose beautifully, the home linesman raised his flag for a goal but the referee decided that the leather went just outside the upright. On crossing over, the advantage lay with the Old Firm, but they could not manage to break through....first try for Aberdare amidst great enthusiasm. From a huge punt, Wyndham Jones followed up smartly, beat Geo. Reddick for possession and scored the equalising try. Jack Thomas converted to put Mount 5-3 in front. The Mountaineers, encouraged by this success, played with renewed vigour but the homesters offered a stubborn defence. Aberdare dropped a goal through Arnold to make it 7-5....Loose play on the part of the home defence again let in Wyndham Jones and he beat all opposition to score an unconverted try. A few minutes later time was called with Mountain Ash leading by one point."

1 May 1905

Glamorgan League
Undecided Championship: Aberdare Ties With Mountain Ash

The South Wales Daily News reported after Aberdare's home win over Treorky, "By their victory, Aberdare have tied with Mountain Ash for the Glamorgan League trophy, each having notched 22 points. In the ordinary course of things, another match on neutral ground between the champions should have been played to decide the issue. As it is, however, this was the last match of the season and it appears to be unlikely the Welsh Football Union, now that the season is over, will sanction a final combat, so that owing to this peculiar predicament, the Cup will have to be withheld and its resting place will not be decided until next season."

Wyndham Jones
Mountain Ash RFC
1 Welsh Cap v Ireland 1904/05

Below is a photograph of Wyndham Jones and the rest of the Welsh XV that beat Ireland 10-3 to win the Triple Crown decider at St Helen's, Swansea on 11 March 1905:

Back Row L-R: A.J. Davies (touchjudge), W. O'Neill (Cardiff), D. Jones (Treherbert), A.F. Harding (London Welsh), H.W. Watkins (Llanelli), G. Travers (Pill Harriers), W. Joseph (Swansea), W. Williams (referee),

Middle Row L-R: J.F. Williams (London Welsh), J.J. Hodges (Newport), R.T. Gabe (Cardiff), W.M. Llewellyn Capt (Newport), E.G. Nicholls (Cardiff), E.T. Morgan (London Welsh),

Front Row L-R: R.M. Owen (Swansea), G. Davies (Swansea), W. Jones (Mountain Ash).

The events of this match, in which the Old Firm's outside half, Wyndham Jones, gained his one and only Welsh Cap is summed up superbly below in an article written by the Western Mail's esteemed rugby journalist, J.B.G. Thomas, in February 1976:

The Great Day Wyndham Was Crowned Hero

"When the legendary W.J. "Billy" Trew, of Swansea, was unable to play for Wales against Ireland in the Triple Crown decider at St Helen's, Swansea, on March 11, 1905, he made his reserve a very happy man. It provided Wyndham Jones of Mountain Ash with a treasured cap in an era when it was almost impossible to break into the Welsh side.

In those days, as now, there were many outstanding players in the side and the young and promising players had to wait for their turn, hoping that the "great ones" would either retire or withdraw now and again through injury.

As 1905 remains one of the greatest years in Welsh rugby history, it is easy to recall why, when one realises that the national XV contained such remarkable players as Willie Llewellyn, Gwyn Nicholls, Rhys Gabe and Teddy Morgan at three-quarter; Trew and Owen at half back, and such hardy forwards as Will Joseph, George Travers, Billy Neill, A.F. Harding, David Jones, J.F. Williams, Jehoida Hodges and Harry Watkins.

Mountain Ash were a splendid Club side in those days and this season the Club, still extremely active, celebrates its Centenary Year. Wyndham Jones remains one of the hallowed players in the Club's records.

Pelted

The reason is that the new cap played an important part in the Wales victory by 10-3 over a strong Irish side, while Gwyn Nicholls was recalled to the side in place of the injured Dan Rees of Swansea and pelted with mud as he took the field. Swansea supporters believed that Frank Gordon should have played as the official reserve.

Nicholls played an outstanding match, although in later years he said, "I regretted playing in this match." He marked a famous Irish centre, Basil Maclear, who always wore white mittens, and tackled him superbly and, more important, Nicholls went on to lead Wales to victory later in the year against the then unbeaten first All Blacks, and played in four additional matches for Wales despite the fact that supporters in the West called him a "veteran." In those far off days the rivalry between East and West was truly intense.

In the match against Ireland, it was the Irishmen who took the lead with a try through their outside half, T.H. Robinson, and as both sides for the first time in their history were battling against each other for the Triple Crown, it was a vital match, hard and uncompromising.

Mobbed

First, he (Wyndham Jones) was sent away by Dickie Owen and sold an enormous "dummy" to the Irish defence before darting over at the posts for a splendid try. The crowd roared with delight. George Davies kicked the goal and Wales were in the lead. Next, the daring Jones whipped the ball from the feet of the Irish forwards as they rushed, dodged through them, and sent Dr Teddy Morgan racing in for another try. Davies again converted and Wales led 10-3 at the interval. There was no score in the second half and the Welsh team, winners of the Triple Crown for the fourth time, were mobbed as they left the field and Wyndham Jones was the hero of the day.

Later, the Triple Crown winners were each presented with a replica of a miner's lamp. It is roughly half size of the lamps then used by Jones himself and many others in the side at their daily work. Made by Thomas and Williams Ltd of Aberdare, it carries the official WRU badge of the Prince of Wales feathers, and the souvenir of a famous day is much treasured by one of the players' grandchildren, Gareth Jones of the Western Mail Sports staff.

In those glorious days of the first "Golden Era", the WRU were generous to their heroes with gifts to commemorate successful seasons. Nowadays the professional laws prevent such presentations other than caps, jerseys and badges for blazers, and players are limited to a momento not exceeding £20 in value.

Wyndham A. Jones was born in Loughor and lived most of his life in Mountain Ash. On his retirement from the field he represented the Mid District on the rugby union in the 1920s and 30s, during which time he served many years as a selector. He was one of the "Big Five" who selected another valley outside half named Jones who became the outstanding player in his position in the 1930s, Clifford Jones, who is now a member of the "Big Five" selecting the present Welsh XV.

Maybe, if the present Welsh side wins the Triple Crown this year, the South Wales area of the National Union of Mineworkers will present the players with souvenir lamps as they did the return of the Welsh Lions in 1971. It would be a happy gesture, but first the Welsh XV has to win on Saturday. If they remember the dash and daring of Wyndham Jones, they will do so."

Season 1905/06

<u>Glamorgan League Championship Dominates Season</u>

The Glamorgan League dominated this season with the Old Firm in contention for the Championship at the start and end of it. In October 1905, the play-off for the 1904/05 Championship took place at Pontypridd against Aberdare. The game was hard fought but lost 10-0 and was not without controversy. In the build up to the game, 3 players applied to transfer to Aberdare from Swansea and Llanelli. After investigation, the Welsh Football Union concluded that inducements had been offered by Aberdare and postponed all transfers to the Club. Prior to the game, Aberdare considered pulling out due to the W.F.U.'s actions. There were also accusations that the Aberdare Club had paid Treorky £15 to "throw" the last game of the 1904/05 season, which allowed Aberdare to draw level on points with Mount at the top of the Glamorgan League. It was all unsavoury stuff. Later in the season, the Old Firm were again involved at the top of the Glamorgan League and were unbeaten along with Penygraig in February 1906, but an away loss to the Rhondda Club dashed their hopes of a first Championship since 1895/96. Although the season wasn't as good as the previous ones in the decade, all of which were quite exceptional, it was still a good one. There were notable "doubles" over Treorky and Bath, and wins over Pontypridd, Llanelly and Bridgend. The 16-13 win at Bath was on Boxing Day 1905, and in the away 11-6 loss at Llanelly, the Scarlets scored in the dying minutes of a hard fought game to clinch victory. There were also home draws against Aberavon and Penygraig. Mount had a backline full of talented players such as scrum half Harry Thomas, outside half Wyndham Jones and centre Sam Muxworthy. Dick Thomas, a future Welsh International forward, also made his mark. The end of season playing record showed 30 games played, 16 won, 4 drawn and 10 lost, with 211 points scored, which included 60 tries, and 137 conceded, which gave a creditable win rate of 60%. The Club also run a reserve XV which played in a Junior League competition. Some of the team's results during the season were a 0-0 draw with Tirphil, a 6-5 win over Cwmbran Boys, a 13-0 win over Trealaw, and a 3-0 win away to Treherbert Stars.

Fixtures 1905/06

Opponents	Date	Venue	Score	Tries	Scorers/Comments
Dinas Powis	2 Oct 1905	Home	29-0	7	Scorers unknown.
Penarth United	9 Oct 1905	Home	6-0	2	AN Other 2T.
Aberdare Glamorgan League Play Off 1904/05	10 Oct 1905	Pontypridd	0-10	0	No scorers.
Bridgend	16 Oct 1905	Away	0-9	0	No scorers.
Treorky (L)	23 Oct 1905	Home	3-0	1	P. Shaw T.
Merthyr (PL)	6 Nov 1905	Home	3-0	1	Scorer unknown.
Treherbert (PL)	13 Nov 1905	Home	16-0	4	Scorers unknown.
Troedyrhiw (PL)	20 Nov 1905	Home	0-0	0	No scorers.
Pill Harriers	27 Nov 1905	Home	0-3	0	No scorers.
Llanelly	4 Dec 1905	Away	6-11	2	Hirst T, Shaw T.
Roath	11 Dec 1905	Home	11-0	3	Scorers unknown.
Troedyrhiw (L)	25 Dec 1905	Home	20-0	6	Ainsworth 2T, Sam Muxworthy T, Wyndham Jones T, Harry Thomas T, Ireland T, Dick Thomas C.

Opponents	Date	Venue	Score	Tries	Scorers/Comments
Caerphilly (PL)	26 Dec 1905	Home	14-0	4	Scorers unknown.
Bath	27 Dec 1905	Away	16-13	3	Pullen T, Thomas T, Caple T, Muxworthy P, 2C.
Penarth	1 Jan 1906	Away	6-14	2	Scorers unknown.
Pontnewydd	8 Jan 1906	Away	3-3	1	AN Other T.
Merthyr (L)	15 Jan 1906	Home	9-0	3	Harry Thomas 2T, Wyndham Jones T.
Pontypridd (PL)	22 Jan 1906	Home	6-0	2	Wyndham Jones T, Shaw T.
Pill Harriers	29 Jan 1906	Away	0-11	0	No scorers.
Aberavon	12 Feb 1906	Away	0-11	0	No scorers.
Llanelly	19 Feb 1906	Home	9-6	3	Taylor T, Shaw T, Ainsworth T.
Penygraig (L)	26 Feb 1906	Away	0-9	0	No scorers.
Penarth	5 Mar 1906	Home	9-10	3	Muxworthy 2T, Taylor T.
Caerphilly (L)	12 Mar 1906	Home	11-3	3	AN Other 3T, C.
Treorky (L)	19 Mar 1906	Away	3-0	1	Sam Muxworthy T.
Penygraig (L)	26 Mar 1906	Home	0-0	0	No scorers.
Bridgend	2 Apr 1906	Home	8-7	2	Sam Muxworthy T, C, Ainsworth T.
Bath	9 Apr 1906	Home	20-8	6	Dick Thomas 2T, Harry Thomas T, C, Muxworthy T, Shaw T, AN Other T.
Treherbert (L)	16 Apr 1906	Away	3-9	1	AN Other T.
Aberavon	23 Apr 1906	Home	0-0	0	No scorers.

Summary of Playing Record

P	W	D	L	For	Against	Tries Scored	Win Rate %
30	16	4	10	211	137	60	60.00

Match Reports and Publications

10 October 1905

<u>Mountain Ash 0 Aberdare 10</u>
<u>1904/05 Glamorgan League Play-Off Final</u>

Mount Team: Back, Jack Thomas; ¾ backs, Eddy Ainsworth, Arthur Ireland, Ivor Bevan, Shaw; half backs, Wyndham Jones* Capt & Harry Thomas; forwards, George Caple, Wilkins, Mears, Dick Thomas, Davies, Price, Stone, Linton.

* denotes Welsh International

The South Wales Daily News reported, "The match between Mountain Ash and Aberdare to decide last year's Championship of the Glamorgan League was played at Pontypridd on Monday. Both teams secured the same number of points in the League last season but the teams had finished their arrangements at the close of the season. It was feared at one time that Aberdare would scratch owing to the decision of the Welsh Football Union in postponing the confirmation of Peter Lockman, Downing and Rhys Rees, and this would certainly tell against their chances of winning. What influenced the Aberdare committee in turning out was their desire that League finances should not suffer. The contestants had been in strict training for the match….a keen, tough struggle was anticipated." The Aberdare Leader reported the match as follows, "Mountain Ash had a splendid opportunity of drawing first blood. From a high kick, the ball dropped close to the posts, but a score went begging owing to two men going for the ball. Mount were having as much, if not more of the game than Aberdare, their backs handling oftener than their opponents, but bad passing at the last moment lost them one or two chances. The interval arrived with no score. The restart promised some exciting football. Wyndham Jones picked up cleverly, and passing to Ireland, the latter fumbled badly and lost a splendid chance. Aberdare three-quarter, Flooks, got possession and raced away at top speed, and amidst tremendous enthusiasm, scored a pretty try which was converted. Mount renewed their efforts after this reverse, but the keen tackling of the Aberdare backs prevented a score. A fine dribble by the Aberdare forwards saw the opposing quartette flurried. Mog Bevan, picking up, feinted to pass and dodging a few opponents, scored a try under the posts which Arnold converted. From now until the end, Mount pressed hard but failed to break through the Aberdare defence. The Mount's best forward was undoubtedly Dick Thomas. Caple and Linton also played well. In the three-quarters, Ireland, with one or two exceptions, played a good game, while Paddy Shaw on the other wing, although playing fairly, was not up to his normal standard." The South Wales Daily News commented, "Wyndham Jones was the most polished back…."

4 December 1905

<u>Llanelly 11 Mountain Ash 6</u>

Mount Team: Back, Jack Thomas; ¾ backs, Hirst, Haines, Ireland, Shaw; half backs, Thomas, Wyndham Jones*; forwards, Caple, Wilkins, Fryer, Herbert, Sullivan, Stone, Tirely, Thomas.

* denotes Welsh International

The South Wales Daily News reported, "In their match at Stradey….Shaw, after making a fine run, kicked across field, and the visitors all but scored….A minute or two later, the visitors made an unsuccessful attempt to drop a goal….The ball came out on the visitors' side of the scrummage and Shaw was the last to receive the oval. He made a fine burst, and Mason failed to hold him, but he was grounded within a yard or so of the line….a number of the visiting forwards brought about a fine dribble and placed their side once more in a favourable position to score, but only a minor resulted. The Scarlets gradually worked their way to the visitors' 25, where Ben Davies attempted to drop a goal, the ball striking the post….Thomas scored….On resuming play (in the second half), Wyndham Jones made a fine opening and when confronted by the Llanelly custodian, he passed to Hirst, who scored a well merited try. A few moments later, a visitor kicked up the field and Mason attempted to make a mark but lost the ball, and Shaw raced over with the visitors' second unconverted try. These reverses infused more vigour into the homesters….The game was now fought out in semi-darkness and Llanelly were making repeated attacks upon the visitors' line without success….The spectators at Stradey almost despaired of Llanelly winning the match against Mountain Ash. For a considerable time the visitors were leading by a single point, and despite Llanelly's repeated attacks, no points were registered. Darkness set in, and the final was fast approaching, the spectators meanwhile being in an excited state. The tension was relieved when D. J. Rees forced his way through with the winning points and it was concluded that the game was won and lost. No sooner had Mountain Ash kicked off than Griff Rowe scored another try for Llanelly and then time was declared. It will thus be seen that the Scarlets only managed to convert a defeat into one of victory in the last couple of minutes of the game….Mountain Ash must be complimented on the relentless fashion in which they resisted the onslaughts of the Scarlets in the second half…."

25 December 1905

<u>Mountain Ash 20 Troedyrhiw 0</u>
<u>Wyndham Jones Badly Hurt</u>
<u>Glamorgan League</u>

The South Wales Daily News reported, "This Glamorgan League match was played at Mountain Ash before a large crowd….the home spectators were curious to see the New Zealand tactics as demonstrated by the visitors….Wyndham Jones initiated a fine round of passing which culminated in Sam Muxworthy, after deceiving the defence with a feint, crossing the line…..from the following play, Wyndham Jones diddled the opposition by a feint and went over easily. The home passing, which was bang up to Welsh traditions, saw Muxworthy give a bullet-like pass to Ainsworth, who crossed wide out….Jenkins restarted for the Whites but within a few seconds, the Black and Ambers were attacking very severely. The referee displeased the crowd by his interpretation of the new rules and he had to speak to the unruly ones among the spectators…. Wyndham Jones was now helpless, having sustained a nasty injury to his collar bone in a tackle and had to retire from the field….The home team were in irresistible form. All the forwards and backs played as one man. Troedyrhiw are to be commiserated with in meeting the homesters at the top of their form…."

27 December 1905

<u>Bath 13 Mountain Ash 16</u>
<u>South Wales Daily News</u>

Bath v. Mountain Ash.

At Bath in delightful weather. There was plenty of scoring in the first half. West crossed for Bath after nice dribbling, Prosser goaling. Pullen scored for the visitors, Muxworthy converting. Prosser scored for Bath, no goal resulting, but Muxworthy converted another try for the Welshmen by Thomas. Caple scored for the visitors, and Muxworthy kicked a penalty goal. West scored and converted for Bath.

Final Score—   Points.
Mountain Ash………………………………… 16
Bath………………………………………………… 13

Remarks.

Mountain Ash were too strong for Bath forward, their pack being far heavier than the citizens, and it was this advantage which gave them a decided pull. However, Bath showed prettier combination. The Welsh full back was very safe, and Muxworthy's goal kicking was of immense value to them. The game was decidedly vigorous, and there were several stoppages for injuries, but happily none were serious. Mountain Ash just deserved their win.

22 January 1906

Mountain Ash 6 Pontypridd 0
Glamorgan League

Mount Team: Back, J. Williams; ¾ backs, Ireland, Muxworthy, Shaw, Ainsworth; half backs, Wyndham Jones* Capt, Harry Thomas; forwards, C. Stone, I. Taylor, Macquire, Alf Price, C. Herbert, D. Davies, H. Beer, Alf Fryer.

* denotes Welsh International

The South Wales Daily News reported, "The improved form of Pontypridd made their visit to Mountain Ash more interesting than has been any of their visits for the past two seasons.... Wyndham Jones received and cross kicking, put his men on-side. Shaw, keeping the ball at his toe, raced away at top speed and scored. It was an exceptional piece of work on the part of Shaw...."

Remarks

"The game opened fast but the heavy state of the ground made the players slow up long before the finish. Pontypridd had a good 15 out while the home pack was handicapped by the absence of three first teamers. The visitors as a consequence more than held their own in the tight but the homesters were superior in the open....Ireland and Ainsworth were the best of the home threes. Stone, Herbert, Alf Fryer and Davies were the best of the home pack."

19 February 1906

Mountain Ash 9 Llanelly 6

Mount Team: Back, Jack Thomas; ¾ backs, Ainsworth, Muxworthy, Ireland, Shaw; half backs, G. Edwards, Tom Linton; forwards, Caple, P.C. Wilkins, Alf Fryer, C. Stone, Alf Price, Taylor, Sullivan, McGuire.

The South Wales Daily News reported, "The famous Scarlets visited Mountain Ash to play the return fixture. Great enthusiasm prevailed locally and a huge crowd was anticipated. The previous match between the teams at Stradey was well fought, the Old Firm only lost during the last ten minutes. The County match robbed the homesters of Wyndham Jones (a Welsh International) and P.C. Dick Thomas (who was capped against South Africa later in 1906, in the first half of the 1906/07 season). Llanelly were well represented. Both teams were loudly cheered as they filed out of the players' pavilion, and it was seen that George Edwards and Linton took the places of the regular home halves. Edwards kicked off from the Newtown end....The game opened fast and continued so throughout. The homesters had to field an unrepresentative team and also lost two men through injuries. These were not due to roughness but were the outcome of keenness. Both packs were well matched and the irresistible rushes of each eight were delightful to watch....D. J. Rees of Llanelly was a host at half and his quick turn deceived the home pair, but Ireland and Muxworthy were too difficult to negotiate. For the homesters, Jack Thomas, a back, deserves praise both for play and pluck. The two centres, Muxworthy and Ireland, were ubiquitous, whilst Shaw and Ainsworth were not one whit behind. Geo Edwards and Linton were by no means overplayed and the former stopped rushes galore. In the forwards, Wilkins was the best, closely followed by Fryer, Taylor, Caple and Price. The score about represents the play. The spectators were delighted at the open game."

26 February 1906

<u>Penygraig 9 Mountain Ash 0</u>
<u>Glamorgan League</u>

The South Wales Daily News reported, "What was regarded as a decisive contest in the Glamorgan League competition during the present season took place at the Bellevue Ground, Penygraig. Intense interest was therefore manifested in the encounter and a large crowd congregated. Mountain Ash had chartered a special train and numbers of their supporters accompanied the team. The Dinas band played selections prior to the match and during the interval. Both teams had not lost a single match in the League competition but Penygraig had played one more match than their opponents." The report ended by saying, "The Mountain Ash committee were very much hurt by the paragraph which appeared in a contemporary suggesting that the Scarlets contracted ringworm at the Mountain Ash ground on Saturday last. The players very emphatically deny the implied assertion and the committee are determined to have their players medically examined."

26 March 1906

<u>Mountain Ash 0 Penygraig 0</u>
<u>Glamorgan League</u>

The South Wales Daily News reported, "The great race between these teams for premier League honours is causing excitement akin to that of former years, and the game had been looked forward to by both sides with quiet confidence....The day's result practically decides the chances of Penygraig for the top position in the Glamorgan League. The Old Firm had lost one match and drawn one, whilst the Rhondda men had only drawn one...."

2 April 1906

<u>Mountain Ash 8 Bridgend 7</u>

Mount Team: Back, J. Thomas; ¾ backs, Shaw, Ireland, Muxworthy, Ainsworth; half backs, Wyndham Jones*, Harry Thomas; forwards, T.C. Wilkins, Alf Fryer, George Caple, Alf Price, Taylor, McGuire, G. Mears, Deere.

* denotes Welsh International

The South Wales Daily News reported, "....The Penybont team played the return match at Mountain Ash. The former match ended in victory for Bridgend but the homesters were determined to win on Saturday.... Matthews dropped a superb goal, placing the visitors 4 points ahead....From halfway, Wyndham Jones, fielding cleverly from a wheel, made a great opening, and every man handled, but Shaw was tackled a yard out. The game was now a beautiful spectacular treat, and enthusiasm ran high when Muxworthy, seeing a chance, beat Nekrews and Pennell and scored a clever try in a favourable position....Right from the restart, the home team got close in, and after an attempt on the right had been frustrated, Harry Thomas drew away to the left and several transfers were given and taken until Ainsworth received and scored a beautiful try. Sam Muxworthy secured the additional points with a wonderful kick....

<u>Remarks</u>

The game reached a high standard and the excellence of the play and spirit was in marked contrast to that of last week (when Mount played Penygraig)....both sides played the true Welsh game....For the homesters, Harry Thomas, at inside half, was the outstanding player, and Wyndham Jones opened up after a slow start. Muxworthy, Ainsworth and Ireland gave of their best, and Thomas, the back, was again in top form. Of the forwards, Fryer, Stone and McGuire were best."

9 April 1906

<u>Mountain Ash 20 Bath 8</u>

Mount Team: Back, J. Thomas; ¾ backs, Shaw, Ireland, Muxworthy, Ainsworth; half backs, Wyndham Jones*, Harry Thomas; forwards, C. Wilkins, McGuire, George Caple, P.C. Dick Thomas, Alf Fryer, Alf Price, Taylor, G. Mears.

* denotes Welsh International

The South Wales Daily News reported, "Bath visited Mountain Ash to play a return fixture. The Christmas match proved a great attraction in the cathedral town and the match was anticipated to produce a good game. The ground was in perfect condition when Bath kicked off from the Newtown end....The inside half of Bath stopped Harry Thomas three times when the latter tried to break through....the open play of both teams was much appreciated and solo bits by Shaw and Goodin (of Bath) received well merited applause.... Dainton and Lewis were extremely active on Bath's right wing and frequently tackled their men in possession, but West, failing to gather, let Caple away, and passing enabled Harry Thomas to score. Immediately afterwards, Muxworthy, taking the ball on the line, fed Dick Thomas, and the ball travelled from Caple to Ireland, and finally to Shaw, who scored a well obtained try. The kick again failed....The visitors' right wing, Dainton, came in for great applause for a great save when confronted by three opponents....Dainton and Mesiter scored for Bath, Hodges converting one. For Mountain Ash, Muxworthy and P.C. Dick Thomas (2) scored tries in the second half, Harry Thomas converting."

30 April 1906

The South Wales Daily News reported, "A meeting of the Glamorgan Football League was held at the Park Hotel, Pontypridd. Two protests were made by Mountain Ash – one against Treherbert for playing Gwilym Walters and P.C. Neyland without their transfers, and against Aberdare for playing Reddick of Caerphilly. The grounds for both objections having been substantiated....four points were added to the Old Firm's total. A technical point was then raised on one of the rules, which stipulated that a Championship must be decided on or before the 15th of April of each year. This was brought forward in view of the fact that Penygraig played a match after the date mentioned, and if the points were counted up to the 15th of April only, this would make Penygraig and Mountain Ash tie. A discussion upon this matter was adjourned to a special meeting to be held on May 16th. The Cup, therefore, will not be handed over to Penygraig today, as was anticipated by the team's supporters. It was understood that the match played between Penygraig and Treherbert after the 15th happened because of a misunderstanding in arrangements between the teams, which necessitated the postponement of the game."

Season 1906/07

Dick Thomas Capped Against South Africa

This season is best summed up by the report written of it by the Aberdare Leader's reporter, "Muddled Oaf", in May 1907: "During the last few weeks, I have often felt sorry for the splendid players who represented Mountain Ash Rugby XV because they deserved a better fate than that which was allotted to them. The League's trophy should have gone to the Mount XV, its true home. I remember that at the commencement of the season, there were grave doubts that the team would continue or not. However, a wise counsel prevailed and a thorough overhauling of the machinery of the Club led to a modest start and throughout the entire season, they exceeded the expectations of their most sanguine supporters. But a cruel fate ordained that Treorky should become possessors of the Cup. In that memorable meeting, the Old Firm were distinctly head and shoulders above their opponents. The Club has also suffered a great deal from lack of funds and the remoteness of the field from the headquarters. Again, certain people, who profess to be "loyal" supporters, begrudged parting with their sixpences, hence the smallness of the gates. But a number of the team's followers, including local tradesmen, have liberally subscribed to the funds. In years gone by, several giants of the "handling code" were turned out to represent the national XV. During this season, the team were honoured by having P.C. Dick Thomas created an International, whilst Wyndham Jones was always selected for the County matches. The former was conspicuous by his raw bursts and dribbling abilities in the forwards....Wyndham Jones saw openings when his co-workers saw none and he has been of inestimable service to many of the recruits who were given a trial. Johnny Thomas, the full back, was always a thorn in the progress of his opponents and his fine judgement in touch finding, coupled with his rare abilities in tackling, stamps him as being one of the best backs in the League. At half back, Wyndham Jones played with both Harry Thomas and George Edwards in turn. Among the forwards, sterling service was given by Dick Thomas and George Caple, whose displays always set an example to the rest of the forwards of whom Taylor, Stone, Shepherd and Macguire were always well in front. No Club could accuse the Mountain Ash XV of failing to fulfil their away matches, and they played the same open game away, as they did at home. The team has had a very successful season as far as victories are concerned, having at the commencement of the season, defeated Merthyr. They twice defeated the Darians, obtained a 10-4 victory over Taunton, beat Bath 3-0, beat Belfast Collegians 9-3, Pontypridd 6-5, Llwynypia 6-3, Bridgend 9-0, Newport by a try to nil, and Aberavon by the grand score of 2 goals and a try to love. They have also defeated Treherbert, Ebbw Vale, County Police, Cefnpennar, Cardiff Mackintosh and Caerphilly, the latter team being beaten by the record score of 24 points to nil. The Old Firm also played drawn games with Pontypridd, Penarth and Pontardawe. Their record read as follows: For – 18 goals, 51 tries and 217 points; against – 14 goals, 19 tries, 121 points, leaving the margin of 96 points to the good. The Club has not fared badly on the whole, but their fine record only adds to the irony of their misfortune in losing the Glamorgan League. Secretary Ben Tiley had his heart and soul in the team, and no Club had a better worker than he. I wish the team adieu until next September and better luck next time."

Some of the other facts not included in the above report were as follows. There were 10 tries scored in the home win against local rivals Aberdare. At this time, there were also quite a number of junior sides in the Mountain Ash area, one being Cefnpennar, who were referred to in the match report of their game with Mount as the "Pennar All Blacks"! In the Old Firm's home 10-5 win over Merthyr, 2 players from Mount and 3 from Merthyr were sent off in a rough encounter. The end of season playing record from known games played was played 33, won 18, drawn 3, and lost 12, with 196+ points scored, which included 52+ tries, and 106+ conceded, which gave a win rate of 59.09%. Forward Dick Thomas became the Club's 5th Welsh International when he was capped against South Africa in December 1906 which was the Springboks' inaugural tour of Great Britain and Ireland. Throughout its history up to this point, Mountain Ash RFC had no fixed match venue. However, there was good news during the season as there was mention of a 999 year lease on land near the town centre.

Fixtures 1906/07

Opponents	Date	Venue	Score	Tries	Scorers/Comments
Aberavon	29 Sep 1906	Away	0-7	0	No scorers.
Pontardawe	6 Oct 1906	Away	0-8	0	No scorers.
Merthyr (L)	13 Oct 1906	Home	10-5	2	Wyndham Jones T, Arthur Ireland T, Johnny Thomas DG.
Treherbert (L)	20 Oct 1906	Away	6-5	2	Peter Ring T, Wyndham Jones T.
Pontypool	22 Oct 1906	Away	0-5	0	No scorers.
Pontypridd (F)	27 Oct 1906	Away	0-0	0	No scorers.
Penygraig (L)	10 Nov 1906	Home	3-4	1	Lloyd-Jones T.
Bridgend	17 Nov 1906	Away	6-8	2	Paddy Shaw T, Wyndham Jones T.
Aberdare	24 Nov 1906	Away	3-7	1	Scorer unknown.
Merthyr (PL)	15 Dec 1906	Away	0-8	0	No scorers.
Aberdare	26 Dec 1906	Home	34-0	10	Danny England 2T, Arthur Ireland 2T, Lloyd-Jones 2T, George Edwards T, 2C, Harry Thomas T, R. Thomas T, Ainsworth T.
Ebbw Vale	29 Dec 1906	Home	11-0	3	Dick Thomas 2T, Arthur Ireland T, Johnny Thomas C.
Glamorgan Police	12 Jan 1907	Home	4-0	0	AN Other DG.
Cefnpennar	19 Jan 1907	Home	6-0	2	Dick Thomas T, Harry Thomas T.
Caerphilly (L)	26 Jan 1907	Home	24-0	6	Lloyd-Jones 2T, Harvey Thomas 2T, Arthur Ireland T, Paddy Shaw T, Johnny Thomas C, AN Other 2C.
Caerphilly (L)	16 Feb 1907	Away	12-3	3	AN Other 3T, George Caple P.
Cardiff Mackintosh	23 Feb 1907	Home	3-0	1	George Edwards T.
Treorky (L)	2 Mar 1907	Away	0-6	0	No scorers.
Penygraig (L)	9 Mar 1907	Away	0-7	1	No scorers.
Pontypool	11 Mar 1907	Home	0-3	0	No scorers.
Pontardawe	16 Mar 1907	Home	3-3	Unknown	Scorer unknown.
Bath	23 Mar 1907	Home	3-0	0	Jack Thomas P.
Penarth	30 Mar 1907	Away	0-5	0	No scorers.

Opponents	Date	Venue	Score	Tries	Scorers/Comments
Belfast Collegians	1 Apr 1907	Home	9-3	3	Paddy Shaw 2T, Lloyd-Jones T.
Aberdare (L)	6 Apr 1907	Away	6-0	2	AN Other 2T.
Treorky (L)	20 Apr 1907	Home	6-7	2	Paddy Shaw T, AN Other T.
Newport	23 Apr 1907	Home	3-0	1	Lloyd-Jones T.
Bridgend	27 Apr 1907	Home	9-0	3	George Edwards T, Danny England T, Dick Thomas T.
Aberavon	4 May 1907	Home	13-0	3	Wyndham Jones T, AN Other 2T, 2C.
Taunton	Unknown	Unknown	10-4	Unknown	Scorers unknown.
Pontypridd (PL)	Unknown	Unknown	6-5	2	AN Other 2T.
Llwynypia (PL)	Unknown	Unknown	6-3	2	AN Other 2T.
Penarth	Unknown	Unknown	Unknown	Unknown	Drawn game. Scorers unknown.

Summary of Playing Record

P	W	D	L	For	Against	Tries Scored	Win Rate %
33	18	3	12	196+	106+	52+	59.09

Match Reports and Publications

13 October 1906

<u>Mountain Ash 10 Merthyr 5</u>
<u>Glamorgan League</u>

"Muddled Oaf" reported in the Aberdare Leader, "This Glamorgan League fixture created unusual interest, inasmuch as Merthyr, being a strong team this season, brought over a large crowd of supporters to the Mountain Ash Athletic Grounds. From the very kick off, the homesters were the aggressors....in the twinkling of an eye, the ball was secured by Johnny Thomas, the home full back, who with his usual left kick, dropped a beautiful goal for Mountain Ash amidst applause....Harry Thomas, the Old Firm's clever inside half, was conspicuous by some smart play, and in charging down a kick by Cross, Thomas secured and sent to Wyndham Jones, who got over the line with a pretty try for Mountain Ash....the concluding portions of the game in the initial moiety were marred by a regrettable incident which arose out of a dispute between some of the forwards. Mr Evan John of Pontypridd, who officiated, had reason to caution the players and stop the game. He continually appealed to them to indulge in less unnecessary roughness, but as his words were disregarded, he was forced to send A. Fryer of Mountain Ash and P.C. Jones of Merthyr off the field to the accompaniment of the vigorous hooting of the crowd. As matters cooled down a bit in the opening stages of the second moiety, the Old Firm got away nicely and Arthur Ireland succeeded in scoring a nice try for Mountain Ash. Scarcely a minute elapsed....McGregor got over for a grand try for Merthyr which was converted. Things were beginning to hum, and there was plenty of feeling displayed, as was evidenced in the number of free fights that took place on the ground. Disgraceful tactics were enacted by some of the Merthyr players, which were resented by some of the Aberpennarites. So, the referee, Evan John, had no alternative but to send Burgess, the Merthyr full back and George Caple, the home captain, off the field. Afterwards, another of the Merthyr men was sent off the field. That no fewer than five players should be sent off the field in a Glamorgan League fixture indicated a very disgraceful state of affairs, and from what I can gather, the matter will be brought before the authorities of the W.F.U."

20 October 1906

<u>Treherbert 5 Mountain Ash 6</u>
<u>Glamorgan League</u>

"Muddled Oaf" reported in the Aberdare Leader, "Wyndham Jones was the hero of his side during the second half. He was as ubiquitous that day as in his old days and by means of some skilful work added a second try for his side. Try as they would, Treherbert could not penetrate the Pennar defence, where Johnny Thomas was seen playing a great game. His touch finding was superb."

27 October 1906

Aberdare Leader reporter, "Muddled Oaf", commented, "I understand that the Mountain Ash Club have been able to secure a very suitable piece of ground near to the town on a 999 years lease. The local tradesmen had set a splendid example to other towns in putting their shoulder to the Club's wheel."

8 December 1906

<u>"A Fine Forward"</u>

The Aberdare Leader published the following, "The above is the heading to an article in Monday's "Sporting Chronicle" on last Saturday's game, Wales v South Africa, at Swansea, in reference to P.C. R. "Dick" Thomas. "There was one good man in the pack, he was R. Thomas.....he and the local man, Joseph, were splendid. Some of the others were poor and will have to give to younger and more dashing men." Without doubt, this is unbiased criticism, coming as it does from a Mancunian journalist. No representative Welsh team will be complete unless the latest International recruit from Mountain Ash figures in it. More power to your elbow Dick, my boy, and many more caps to come!"

15 December 1906

<u>Merthyr 8 Mountain Ash 0</u>
<u>Possible Glamorgan League Fixture</u>

"Muddled Oaf" reported in the Aberdare Leader, "This match was played at Penydarren Park, Merthyr, before a record crowd. With a view of preventing a recurrence of the Mountain Ash scenes, the Clubs had arranged to drop those men responsible for the mischief, so Mount were minus the services of a few of their most prominent players. However, P.C. Dick Thomas, the International forward, partnered Wyndham Jones at half back, whilst several local young bloods were included in the pack. Merthyr were at full strength.... unfortunate that the Old Firm were minus the services of the best of their players, consequently, nothing short of a defeat was expected. The forwards were equally matched but the Mount backs were weaker. Mountain Ash also felt the loss that day of Harry Thomas, their versatile half back."

26 December 1906

<u>Mountain Ash 34 Aberdare 0</u>
<u>Crossed Ten Times-Heavy Scoring By The Old Firm</u>

The Western Mail reported, "....It soon became evident that the homesters were having a "day out" for within 15 minutes, they crossed the line no less than four times...."

29 December 1906

<u>Mountain Ash 11 Ebbw Vale 0</u>

"Muddled Oaf" reported in the Aberdare Leader, "In this match, which was played at the Mountain Ash Athletic Grounds before a good crowd, the Aberpennarites succeeded in doing what the Dare XV failed to do, viz. defeating the smart Valian team by a score of 11 points to love! The game was the best played on these grounds. From the outset, it was evident that the home forwards were in fine fettle....In the second moiety....Dick Thomas, the local International, got possession, and, like a shot from a gun, made for his opponents' line. He was obstructed by the Ebbw Vale wing and full back but with some good headwork, he doubled cleverly to the left and raced home amidst a scene of intense enthusiasm, it was a truly meritorious try....The key to the Old Firm's success was the steadfast resolution of the forwards and this materially helped the halves and three-quarters to combine effectively."

19 January 1907

Mountain Ash 6 Cefnpennar 0

"Muddled Oaf" reported in the Aberdare Leader, "The first meeting of the season between the Pennar "All Blacks" and the Mount premier XV took place at the Mountain Ash Athletic Grounds on Saturday before a good attendance. The game in the first half was extremely fast and exciting. Dick Thomas scored a fine try for Mountain Ash after gaining a good slice of ground and scrum half Harry Thomas added another after a bout of passing by the backs. After the interval, the "All Blacks" succeeded in keeping their opponents strictly on the defensive. Dick Thomas tried to add another try or two, but he was too well watched...."

23 February 1907

Mountain Ash 3 Cardiff Mackintosh 0

The Aberdare Leader reported, "....the citizens brought a powerful XV which had already earned a reputation for themselves in the Cardiff and District Senior League....The game was a spectacular treat and was very evenly contested...."Paddy" Shaw (of Mountain Ash), the Irish International (checked out and not an Irish rugby union International), made a splendid run, which would have ended in a score had not a good tackle been effected near the line....the game was contested in good spirit and the Old Firm kept up its reputation."

23 March 1907

Mountain Ash 3 Bath 0

"Muddled Oaf" reported in the Aberdare Leader, "The return visit on Saturday last of the West of England team to Mountain Ash Athletic Grounds produced much interest. True, the climatic conditions were not of the best. The visitors were fairly well represented, whilst the Pennarites were minus the services of Wyndham Jones, Arthur Ireland and Harry John. The state of the ground, coupled with the disadvantage of playing in the face of a cross wind, mitigated against anything like a scientific display. The visitors were penalised and the resulting kick by Jack Thomas, the home full back, left the Pennarites leading 3-0....The Pennarites, who had been defeated last week by only a solitary try at the hands of Pontypool, gave the visitors a warm time and had rough luck in not scoring. I understand that the Pennarites are looking forward eagerly to the "annual" with the Darians (Aberdare RFC) during the holidays."

1 April 1907

Mountain Ash 9 Belfast Collegians 3

The Western Mail reported, "The game was not many minutes old before Thompson was carried off the field. This reverse somewhat unnerved the visitors....Wyndham Jones....was playing a wonderful game....was brought down only a few yards out. Mount were not to be denied, a splendid bout of passing ended in Paddy Shaw grounding....From a round of passing initiated by Wyndham Jones, in which every man in the three-quarter line participated, Paddy Shaw got over in the corner...."

Mountain Ash Rugby Football Club
"The Old Firm"
Season 1906/07

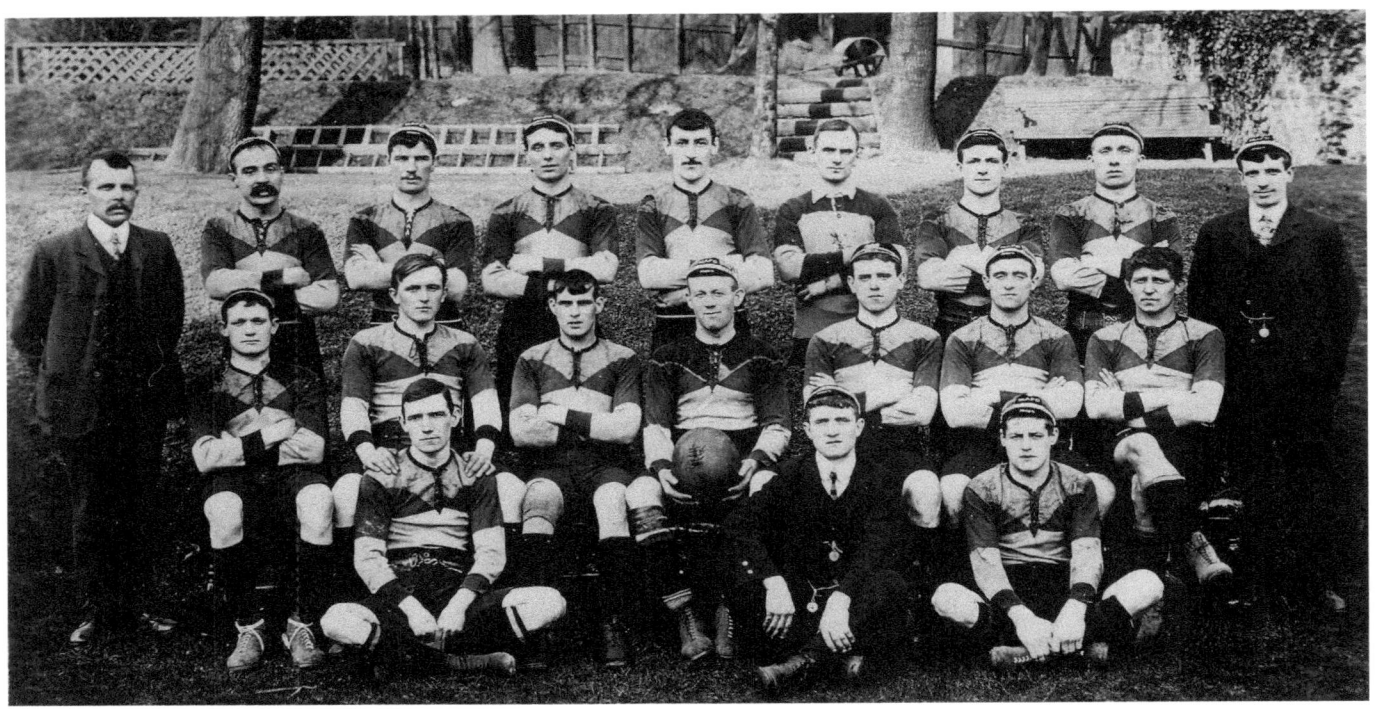

Only a few names are known in the above photograph. In the back row on the far left is Secretary Harry Hale. Next to him is Alf Fryer. The player holding the ball is George Caple, and in the bottom row, on the left with his legs crossed, is the Old Firm's Welsh International outside half, Wyndham Jones.

6 April 1907

Aberdare 0 Mountain Ash 6

The Aberdare Leader's reporter, "Spectator", reported, "....this fixture took place before the largest crowd of the season....the battle had been a grim one, the tackling of both sides being a little too keen, with the result that players were injured. The home team were the unfortunate ones....with only twelve men remaining on the field, it was surprising the Mountaineers did not pile on a huge score."

27 April 1907

Mountain Ash 9 Bridgend 0

The Aberdare Leader reporter, "Muddled Oaf", reported, "The homesters were minus several notable players including Harry Thomas, Stone and Wyndham Jones, who stood down in view of the following Monday's match with Newport (see match below, this Aberdare Leader date is later than the Western Mail date below). Horsman played at full back in the absence of Johnny Thomas whilst Danny England represented Ainsworth at three-quarter back. The Bridgend forwards found in the home defensive line, men who knew the game well. The visiting forwards were on the aggressive and the Old Firm narrowly escaped being trodden upon. By dint of some footwork, the Aberpennarites penned the Bridgend men well within their own territory. At last George Edwards, the home inside half, got the ball away on the blindside, and after tricking a few opponents, scored a good but unconverted try. After some more passing by the home backs, Danny England added the second try, and in doing, injured his collar bone. After half time, the defence of the Old Firm warded off attack after attack. The venue was soon changed, Alf Fryer heading a forward rush for Mount. Shaw scored a "try" which was disallowed. Then Taylor picked up and initiated a bout of passing amongst the home forwards which culminated in P.C. Dick Thomas scoring the third try."

23 April 1907

<u>Mountain Ash 3 Newport 0</u>

Mount Team: Back, Johnny Thomas; ¾ backs, Paddy Shaw, Lloyd-Jones, Arthur Ireland, Eddy Ainsworth; half backs, George Edwards, Wyndham Jones*; forwards, George Caple, Alf Fryer, Taylor, R. Thomas, Shepherd, Dai Davies, Dick Thomas*, Macquire.

* denotes Welsh International

<u>Western Mail</u>

MOUNTAIN ASH V. NEWPORT.

To-day (Monday) the premier Newport team visit Mountain Ash to play the "Old Firm." The match has been brought about by the influence of Mr. T. Millar (Mountain Ash), the well-known referee, who is very friendly with the Newport players. The full team is expected, with the exception of Francis at half, but Chris. Williams, of Merthyr, has promised to fill the vacancy. Newport will meet Devonport Albion on Saturday next, and as they had no match on Saturday they intend to-day's game to be part of their training to meet the champions of the west. The finances of the "Old Firm" are not in such a satisfactory condition as is desirable, and the committee appeal strongly to all friends and lovers of the game to show their sympathy by turning up to welcome the Newport boys. As Mountain Ash are at present playing a splendid game, they should make the Usksiders go all the way.

LORD ABERDARE KICKS OFF.

Newport took a strong team to Mountain Ash on Monday, and a large crowd witnessed the match. Lord Aberdare kicked off. There was no score in the first half, but in the second Lloyd Jones scored a try, which remained unconverted. There was no further scoring.

4 May 1907

<u>Mountain Ash 13 Aberavon 0</u>

The Aberdare Leader's reporter, "Muddled Oaf", commented, "Congratulations to the Mountain Ash Rugby Fifteen! They have succeeded in doing what even the Abertawe All Whites had failed to do, viz. defeat Aberavon by the score of 2 goals and a try to love. This was the Pennarites' last match of the season….the Old Firm have had their own back and have wound up their season's fixtures nicely….Despite the efforts of the Aberavonites, they could not beat the defence of the homesters, who, on the day's form, were in great trim. The Aberpennarites played, one and all, a sound game, Aberavon being beaten in every department. But when I look back, I think of the chances the Old Firm have missed this season of winning the Glamorgan League. I adhere to my former assertion that the Mountain Ash XV was the most consistent team in the League."

Dick Thomas
Mountain Ash RFC
4 Welsh Caps v South Africa, France, Ireland & Scotland
1906-1909

Above, Mount forward Dick Thomas, sitting far right as you look in the middle row with his arms folded, wins his first Welsh cap against South Africa at Swansea on 1 December 1906, which was the first ever game between Wales and the Springboks.

Dick Thomas played for Mountain Ash between 1904 and 1912. After starting his working life as a miner, he joined the police force and was transferred to the Aberdare Division of the Glamorgan Constabulary when he transferred to Mountain Ash RFC. During his time in the police force, he won the Glamorgan Police Heavyweight Boxing Championship. He was very well regarded and a bit of a hero in Mountain Ash. When he left for Bridgend RFC at the end of the 1911/12 season, he was described in an Aberdare Leader report as the "idol of the Gods locally, and will be greatly missed." During his playing career, he represented Glamorgan on up to 20 occasions, including games the county played against New Zealand, South Africa and Australia. He was an athletic, tough, uncompromising forward who also played, when called upon, at outside half and in the three-quarters. After impressing against the Springboks in Glamorgan's 6-3 defeat in front of 40,000 at Cardiff Arms Park in October 1906, he won his first Welsh cap just over a month later. The 11-0 defeat by South Africa was Wales' first in 11 years in Swansea but Thomas came out of it as one of the few with an enhanced reputation. Shortly after this game he contracted appendicitis, which was a life threatening condition in the early 1900s. This put him out of rugby for a season or so and ultimately led to him only being capped 4 times in total. After he recovered, he gained his second and third caps in season 1907/08, playing in the first ever game between Wales and France, which Wales won comfortably 36-4. He followed this up by keeping his place for the game in Belfast against Ireland, Wales' 11-5 win clinching their 5th Triple Crown and first ever Grand Slam, the South Wales Daily News' legendary rugby reporter, "Old

Stager", commenting that Thomas was the game's stand-out forward. In December 1908, he played for Glamorgan against the touring Australians and got involved in some fisticuffs many think led to his non selection against England in early 1909. It wasn't long before he returned to the Welsh team, though, playing in the 5-3 win against Scotland in February 1909, which turned out to be his 4th and final International appearance. Although he was picked to play against France in the following game, illness stopped him playing and he also missed the final game of the Championship against Ireland. Both games were won which gave Wales a second successive Triple Crown and Grand Slam.

In early 1915, with the First World War underway, he joined the 16th Battalion Welsh Regiment and was soon promoted to Company Sergeant Major. He was killed in action at Mametz Wood in France on 7 July 1916 during the Battle of the Somme, aged 32. In the letter Thomas' wife and two children received about his passing, the writing officer who happened to be a former team-mate of Thomas at Bridgend RFC wrote, "I am deeply grieved to tell you my old friend Dick was killed while attacking the wood....I had already recommended him for an MC for his gallantry and splendid example to his men." Thomas never received the Military Cross as, at that time, they were not awarded posthumously. He was one of 13 Welsh Internationals who lost their lives fighting in the so-called Great War and is one of 72,195 men commemorated at the Thiepval Memorial to the Missing of the Somme in France.

<u>Dick Thomas' Resting Place</u>

<u>Thiepval Memorial to the Missing of the Somme</u>

Season 1907/08

Old Firm Keeps Flag Flying In Face Of Adversity

Once again, an article written by Aberdare Leader reporter, "Muddled Oaf", at the end of the season is the starting point for giving information on the Old Firm's fortunes. The following article appeared in May 1908: "Mountain Ash Rugby Football Club has had a rather varied season in that it has been fortunate and unfortunate....the Club has met with many successes, but its financial position has been anything but enviable, which is a great pity, it being one of the oldest in South Wales. The team have given some splendid performances and have succeeded in defeating some of the smartest combinations in South Wales. Yet, there were times when the committee had difficulty bringing the players together. The empty coffers of the Club are due greatly to their playing ground, which is mounted in such a position that hundreds have witnessed the game from Penrhiwceiber Road without payment. The counter attraction at Aberdare and Merthyr (this probably refers to the Northern Union/Rugby League Clubs in these towns, although Aberdare Northern Union Club as it was called, did not officially start until 1908/09), has also greatly drained the "gates" of the Club. The position of full back was occupied by Johnny Thomas and on some occasions by T. Horsman....splendid work was contributed by the three-quarter line which included Eddy Ainsworth, Paddy Shaw, Lloyd Jones, Ireland, Evan Jones and earlier in the season, D.B. Davies. At half back, Wyndham Jones was always the most accomplished player and a more consistent man never played in the Glamorgan League at outside half. Wyndham Jones was ably served by Harry Thomas, who has also shown some clever form, while George Edwards occasionally deputised for Thomas at inside back. Throughout the season, the team's forwards have shown wonderful form. Several from the local junior sides were given a place in the team. P.C. Dick Thomas....the shining light of the pack and his burst, coupled with his abilities as an attacker, were always irresistible. George Caple displayed sound judgement and has often led his side out of dangerous positions. R. Thomas, Alf Fryer, Joe Ellery, Macquire, Jarman, Shepherd, Stone, P.C. Hill, D. Davies and others have also contributed their share to the team's success. There has been some talk of professionalism in this district, but I understand that the men of Pennar will stand true to the flag of amateurism. Some talk that a soccer Club, to be started next season, is also doing the rounds in sporting circles, but there is no definite information on the matter. I wish the Mountain Ash Rugby Club every success." Some other facts about the 1907/08 season are as follows. The Old Firm gained "doubles" over Maesteg and Bridgend, and gained victories over Aberavon, Pontypool, Bath, Pontypridd and Penarth. There were close defeats to Abertillery, Pontypool and Pontypridd. Forward Dick Thomas got his second and third Welsh caps when he played against Ireland and France, which helped Wales to the Triple Crown, a first ever Grand Slam, and the Championship. The season's known playing record read played 26, won 13, lost 13, with 188 points scored, which included 52 tries, and 140 conceded, which gave a win rate of exactly 50% – which was good, but not as good as the previous seasons of the decade.

Fixtures 1907/08

Opponents	Date	Venue	Score	Tries	Scorers/Comments
Maesteg (L)	28 Sep 1907	Home	13-0	3	David B. Davies 2T, Dick Thomas T, Johnny Thomas C, AN Other C.
Abertillery	5 Oct 1907	Home	3-10	1	Harry Thomas T.
Aberavon	12 Oct 1907	Home	6-0	2	Taylor T, P.C. Dick Thomas T.
Merthyr (L)	19 Oct 1907	Away	5-3	1	Macquire T, Harry Thomas C.

Opponents	Date	Venue	Score	Tries	Scorers/Comments
Treherbert (PL)	26 Oct 1907	Home	13-3	3	Paddy Shaw T, Ainsworth T, Taylor T, Evan Jones C, AN Other C.
Penygraig (F)	9 Nov 1907	Away	0-3	0	No scorers.
Pontypool	23 Nov 1907	Home	8-3	2	Ainsworth 2T, Evan Jones C.
Pontardawe	30 Nov 1907	Away	3-5	1	Taylor T.
Abertillery	7 Dec 1907	Away	6-9	2	Evan Jones T, Dick Thomas T.
Treorky (PL)	14 Dec 1907	Home	6-11	2	Ainsworth T, Mcguire T.
Pontypool	21 Dec 1907	Away	0-3	0	No scorers.
Llwynypia (L)	21 Dec 1907	Away	5-7	1	Dick Thomas T, Johnny Thomas C.
Llwynypia United	26 Dec 1907	Home	3-5	1	Jarman T.
Bath	27 Dec 1907	Away	8-5	2	Harry Thomas T, Evan Jones T, Johnny Thomas C.
Plymouth	30 Dec 1907	Away	6-14	2	AN Other 2T.
Paignton	4 Jan 1908	Away	6-11	2	Ainsworth 2T.
Pontypridd (F)	1 Feb 1908	Home	17-0	5	Ainsworth 2T, P.C. R. Thomas T, Wyndham Jones T, Harry Thomas T, Evan Jones C.
Bridgend	15 Feb 1908	Away	9-4	3	Pat Shaw T, P.C. R. Thomas T, Harry Thomas T.
Llwynypia (L)	22 Feb 1908	Home	21-0	5	Arthur Ireland T, DG, Paddy Shaw T, Wyndham Jones T, Shepherd T, Ainsworth T, Johnny Thomas C.
Maesteg (PL)	7 Mar 1908	Away	6-0	2	Mcguire T, George Caple T.
Penygraig (F)	14 Mar 1908	Home	0-6	0	No scorers.
Pontypridd (F)	21 Mar 1908	Away	3-9	1	Paddy Shaw T.
Bridgend	28 Mar 1908	Home	16-0	4	Lloyd-Jones 2T, Harry Thomas T, C, Paddy Shaw T, George Caple C.

Opponents	Date	Venue	Score	Tries	Scorers/Comments
Penarth	6 Apr 1908	Away	8-0	2	Dick Thomas T, Lloyd-Jones T, Harry Thomas C.
Llanelly	25 Apr 1908	Away	0-26	0	No scorers.
Penarth	27 Apr 1908	Home	17-3	5	Wyndham Jones 2T, Dick Thomas T, Ainsworth T, George T, AN Other C.

Summary of Playing Record

P	W	D	L	For	Against	Tries Scored	Win Rate %
26	13	0	13	188	140	52	50.00

Match Reports and Publications

14 September 1907

The Aberdare Leader reporter, "Muddled Oaf", commented, "....Important changes have taken place which have aroused the football world. In professional rugby, the Northern Union bombshell has exploded, it is true, but it has not left its trace in the Aberdare valley....the Mountain Ash premier Rugger will again enter the Glamorgan League this season, and from what I understand, they intend leaving their cards there. They have been fortunate in obtaining the use of the grounds again this year, and with the number of supporters they already have, the team should be successful, financially and otherwise. At their annual general meeting held recently, Mr Wheeler of the Cresselly Inn has been appointed Treasurer, with Messrs Bert James and J.J. Jasper as joint Secretaries. They have an excellent list of fixtures and their prospects, in spite of the strenuous opposition to the professional team nearby, are as rosy as ever." (The professional team referred to may have been one of the Northern Union Clubs nearby in Treherbert or Merthyr. Aberdare Rugby League Club played its first official season in 1908/09).

21 September 1907

"Muddled Oaf" commented in the Aberdare Leader, "It is rumoured that the popular half back, Wyndham Jones, has once more declined an invitation to go "up North". This is encouraging news to Old Firm supporters. The team's chances for the possession of the Glamorgan League seem to be as rosy as ever. As the only senior rugger XV in the Aberdare valley, the team ought to command support."

28 September 1907

<u>Mountain Ash 13 Maesteg 0</u>
<u>Glamorgan League</u>

"Muddled Oaf" reported in the Aberdare Leader, "....the visitors brought over a strong combination. The opening exchanges saw the forwards fighting hard for possession....With the skill that has characterised the work of the Old Firm forwards in the past, they turned defence into attack, where the heroic Dick Thomas raised a great cheer in crossing over for the first try of the season....the Old Firm succeeded in winning their first League match by a decent margin. Surely, the team will make a good bid for the Cup this year."

12 October 1907

Mountain Ash 6 Aberavon 0

"Muddled Oaf" reported in the Aberdare Leader, "These old rivals met at the Mountain Ash Athletic Grounds. The Seasiders brought a team which included Alby Davies and Willie Thomas, both prominent three-quarter backs. Aberpennar were minus Johnny Thomas, their able full back, who has been injured.... The game was a forward one....the battle between the respective eights was immense....keen tackling ensued. The home forwards were so persistent in timing their rushes that they succeeded in scoring a clever try by Taylor. Try as they would, Aberavon could get no further than the half way line. Before the interval, Dick Thomas increased the score...."

2 November 1907

"Muddled Oaf" commented in the Aberdare Leader, "....good performances in the Inter-League match between Glamorgan and Monmouthshire last Saturday....Again, the Old Firm has more representatives than any other Club and they were D. Lloyd-Jones and Shaw at three-quarter back; Harry Thomas and Wyndham Jones at half; and P.C. Dick Thomas and R. Thomas in the forward pack. We congratulate P.C. Dick Thomas on scoring all the points for the Glamorgan side. He was always to the forefront and his bursts were simply irresistible. The Welsh Union officials ought not to hesitate in again selecting Dick for national honours. Harry Thomas and Wyndham Jones played finely together, but they missed a few good scoring chances for their side....Up to date, the Mountaineers have an untarnished League record....their meeting with Penygraig next Saturday ought to attract quite a crowd at the Tonypandy grounds. Johnny Thomas, the team's full back, hopes to turn out after his injury of a few weeks back. The Aberpennarites are determined to "have a bit of their own back" from the erstwhile Rhondda champions."

9 November 1907

Penygraig 3 Mountain Ash 0
Friendly Fixture

The Aberdare Leader reported, "This season, Penygraig have backed out of the Glamorgan League but nevertheless they have given a good show against all their opposing teams so far and their greatest opponents in the past were the Mountain Ash XV....The Mountain Ash men played up brilliantly and some magnificent tackling was made by backs Shaw and Ainsworth....The Mountain Ash backs showed some fine handling in which Lloyd-Jones, Shaw and Ainsworth were always prominent. Penygraig appeared to be beaten in every department yet the Old Firm failed to cross their line owing to good defence. Wyndham Jones, who was about the finest half back on the field, initiated another bout of passing which ended in Ainsworth being the last to receive. This clever Mount three-quarter eluded quite a number of his opponents and dashed over for a capital try. However, Mr Smith the referee disallowed the points on the plea that it accrued from a pass that was slightly forward."

23 November 1907

Mountain Ash 8 Pontypool 3

Mount Team: Back, Johnny Thomas; ¾ backs, Shaw, Taylor, Evan Jones, Ainsworth; half backs, Wyndham Jones* and Harry Thomas; forwards, Dick Thomas*, George Caple, R. Thomas, Fryer, Macquire, Sheppard, D. Davies, Jarman.

* denotes Welsh International

"Muddled Oaf" reported in the Aberdare Leader, "The visit of Pontypool, that crack Monmouthshire organisation, attracted a large crowd. In the previous meeting last season at the Pontypool Enclosure, the Old Firm were defeated by only a try to nil. Since then, Ponty has worked wonders....their victory over Devonport Albion will not be easily forgotten....Pontypool team included a few International men....Initial advantage came to Pontypool....unconverted try. Morris of Pontypool was making a beeline for the home goal when Ainsworth, the home wing dashed across at full pelt and tackled him just as he was going to drop over the line....Ainsworth succeeded in scoring a beauty of a try for the Old Firm which was improved by Evan Jones....After a few scrummages, Harry Thomas, the home half, got the ball away to Wyndham Jones who passed to Evan Jones, who opened up finely, out distancing Pritchard and Evans, sent across to Ainsworth who dashed up and scored his second try. The best of the home three-quarter line, who were all in fine fettle, were Shaw and Ainsworth, while Wyndham Jones and Harry Thomas enhanced their reputation at half back. Of the home forwards, P.C. Dick Thomas and R. Thomas – the "Dancing Dicks of Aberpennar" – Fryer and Caple, were always prominent."

30 November 1907

The Aberdare Leader's reporter, "Muddled Oaf", commented, "Aberpennar will be entertained by Abertillery, the Monmouthshire League champions next Saturday....By the way, it has become public property that the Old Firm is in heavy financial straits and that the gate receipts in the past few matches are not enough to meet expenses. Of course, the committee put it down to the counter attractions at Aberdare and Merthyr (maybe referring to football or Northern Union rugby), but the free view which the public have of the games from Penrhiwceiber Road is, I believe, the cause. Something must be done now. Could not the Welsh Union give a helping hand?"

27 December 1907

Bath 5 Mountain Ash 8

"Muddled Oaf" reported in the Aberdare Leader, "The Mountain Ash XV paid their annual visit to Bath on Boxing Day, when both sides were well represented. In the first half, the Bath forwards got well away with the ball at their feet but some fine tackling by the Aberpennar backs kept the homesters out of their territory. Afterwards, the Old Firm capitally worked the scrums, and their three-quarters got well away with a fine bout of combination, which gained them much territory. A pass to Harry Thomas saw him romp over for a pretty but unconverted try for the Old Firm. From the restart, Bath got away and their forwards made some magnificent dribbling movements which were neutralised by the daring defensive work of Johnny Thomas, the plucky Pennar full back. The homesters continued to attack from all sides but Johnny Thomas was equal to the occasion and warded off the attacking tactics of the Bath men. The Old Firm next turned defence into attack, but failed to score owing to some fine tackling by the homesters....In the second half, Bath came away with some fine forward work once more, but the defence of the Old Firm was sound and the Gloucester men were continually driven out of the Mountaineers' quarter. Afterwards, the Mount got away but the home custodian had to touch down to save a powerful forward rush on the part of the visitors. From a lineout, the ball came to Evan Jones, the Old Firm's centre. Dodging a couple of opponents, he rushed over with another beautiful try, which this time was improved upon with a grand kick by Johnny Thomas. Bath retaliated hotly, and forward Tom West found a loophole in the Old Firm's defence and succeeded in scoring a try, which was converted. Mount bucked up once more, but failed to add to the score."

<u>Western Mail</u>

BATH V. MOUNTAIN ASH.

Bath played Mountain Ash at Bath in splendid weather, before a big crowd. R. Thomas scored for the visitors in the first five minutes, this being all the scoring in the first portion of the game. Bath had plenty of the game in the second half, but Jones got in for the Welshmen. Then Tom West scored for Bath, A. Hatherill converting. Bath were thus beaten by three points.

Final score:

	G.	T.	P'ts.
Mountain Ash	1	1	8
Bath	1	0	5

1 February 1908

<u>Mountain Ash 17 Pontypridd 0</u>
<u>Friendly Fixture</u>

Mount Team: Back, Johnny Thomas; ¾ backs, Shaw, E. Jones, Ainsworth, A. Bridgman; half backs, Wyndham Jones*, Harry Thomas; forwards, P.C. R. Thomas*, Geo. Caple, G. Stone, German, Shepherd, Macquire, Joe Ellery, P.C. Hill.

* denotes Welsh International

<u>Western Mail</u>

PONTYPRIDD OUTPLAYED.

AN EASY VICTORY ACHIEVED BY MOUNTAIN ASH.

"Muddled Oaf" reported in the Aberdare Leader, "Some fine passing was witnessed in which Caple, Macquire and P.C. R. Thomas were prominent….Dick Thomas romped over with a clever unconverted try. Harry Thomas deceived his opponents with a dummy pass, after which he passed to Wyndham Jones who zigzagged his way into the Pontypridd 25 and registered another try. Harry Thomas and Wyndham Jones made another "scalping expedition"….another unconverted try….Wyndham Jones won another try for the Land of Pennar. Ainsworth added another….game ended in a great victory for Mountain Ash by the score of 17 points to love." The Western Mail commented, "It was a friendly as Pontypridd is not in the League."

15 February 1908

<u>Bridgend 4 Mountain Ash 9</u>

Mount Team: Back, Jack Thomas; ¾ backs, E. Jones, Eddy Ainsworth, Lloyd-Jones, Pat Shaw; half backs, Harry Thomas and Wyndham Jones*; forwards, P.C. R. Thomas*, Geo. Caple, J. Taylor, T. Shepherd, P.C. Hill, T. Stone, R. Jarman, Macquire.

* denotes Welsh International

"Muddled Oaf" reported, "….After the change of ends….The Aberpennar forwards were the clever pack in all round play, whilst Wyndham Jones and Harry Thomas were much better adapted to the game in all its bearings than were the home half backs. Clever as the Bridgend backs were, the Aberpennar quartette were a great deal more brainy on the day's form."

14 March 1908

Mountain Ash 0 Penygraig 6
Friendly Fixture

"Muddled Oaf" reported in the Aberdare Leader, "The homesters were again minus the services of Police Constable R. Thomas, who stood down in view of next Saturday's International match." This referred to Dick Thomas' 3rd cap in the Ireland v Wales match in Belfast which Wales won 11-5.

28 March 1908

Mountain Ash 16 Bridgend 0

Mount Team: Back, Horseman; ¾ backs, Paddy Shaw, Lloyd-Jones, Evan Jones, Eddy Ainsworth; half backs, Harry Thomas and Wyndham Jones*; forwards, P.C. Dick Thomas*, George Caple, Joe Ellery, Jarman, Macguire, Taylor, Shepherd, Stone.

* denotes Welsh International

"Muddled Oaf" reported in the Aberdare Leader, "....the Pennarites continued to attack. From a scrum in neutral territory, Wyndham Jones gave a well directed pass to Lloyd-Jones who completely deceived the defence with a corkscrew run to score a capital try, converted by Harry Thomas. A magnificent piece of work was next contributed by Wyndham Jones who got away nicely from a scrum and got the homesters well into the Bridgend quarter, where Jones transferred the ball to Paddy Shaw, who romped over for another good try....In the second half, by dint of some hard play, Lloyd-Jones added another try for his side...."

25 April 1908

Llanelly 26 Mountain Ash 0

"Muddled Oaf" commented in the Aberdare Leader, "On Good Friday last, the Mountain Ash Club took a very poorly represented XV to Stradey Grounds where they were entertained by the Llanelly team. Only four of the regular players in the Pennar team were present, and the result....was a foregone conclusion...."

27 April 1908

Mountain Ash 17 Penarth 3
Western Mail

"OLD FIRM" IN FORM.

PENARTH BADLY BEATEN AT MOUNTAIN ASH.

The Western Mail reported, "....Police Constable Dick Thomas got the ball, and, racing beautifully along the touchline scored, with nearly half a dozen of the visitors hanging on to him...."

Season 1908/09

"Double" For Mount
Old Firm Win Glamorgan League
Mountain Ash Reserves Win Aberdare & Merthyr District League

After coming close in previous seasons, the Old Firm at last won the Glamorgan League Championship, which was the second time the Club had lifted the trophy since the competition started in the mid 1890s. The team lost just one game, and finished with a League playing record of played 16, won 12, drawn 3 and lost 1, the only defeat being a close one at Treorky. As well as being unbeaten at home in the League, Mount also recorded home wins against Plymouth, Penarth, Bath and Bridgend. However, one of the downsides of the season was a record defeat at Plymouth – 44-0. Overall, the playing record showed 33 games played, 19 won, 3 drawn and 11 lost. There were 125+ points scored, which included 33+ tries, and 138+ conceded (higher than the points scored due to the heavy defeat in Plymouth), which converted to a win rate of 62.12%. The Aberdare Leader's rugby reporter, "Muddled Oaf", commented in November 1908 that "Wyndham Jones, the brilliant Mountain Ash outside half, was included in the Cardiff team that played the Stade Francais XV on Monday last in Paris." This was the only known game Jones played for any other Club as he was mentioned on numerous occasions in various Old Firm matches over the years, being one of the lynchpins of the Mount XV, playing for the Club for a dozen seasons overall. Four Mount players, namely Jim Donovan, the centre three-quarter, Wyndham Jones, at outside half, Dick Thomas, the Welsh International forward, and forward George Caple, were chosen for the Glamorgan team that played Australia – which was the first time the Wallabies had visited Wales – Caple getting Glamorgan's only try in the 11-3 defeat. There was a first mention of Shad Lewis, who later became Club Chairman between 1926 and 1937 and a benefactor. He was mentioned as part of the Mountain Ash RFC Reserves that won the Aberdare and Merthyr District League Championship which was for junior teams. Mount lost players to the Northern Union, Arthur Hill, Ike Taylor, Dai Fryer and Macquire (Christian name unknown) joining the newly formed Aberdare Northern Union Club, and talented scrum half, Harry Thomas, joining Batley. Former Mount captain in the 1899/1900 season, Llew Deare, was instrumental in setting up the Aberdare Club, but it was not a success and was short lived, closing at the end of the 1908/09 season, which was its first and only one. There were also International honours for Mount forward, Dick Thomas, who gained his 4th and final Welsh Union cap in the victory against Scotland in Inverleith, helping Wales to win the Triple Crown, the Grand Slam and the Championship for a second consecutive season. He officially "went North" just after the Scotland game, but if the records available are correct, they show he moved back and fore between rugby union and Northern Union rugby. Somehow the Welsh Football Union never found out about this otherwise he would have been banned from rugby union for life such was the animosity to the professional code. During his Northern Union career, it was reported he played for Aberdare, Warrington and a Welsh League XIII which beat Australia 14-13 in 1908/09 – although he played for the Old Firm in 1910/11! Away from the rugby, the Club struggled financially, starting the season in deficit, which was nothing new, and once again showed great resolve to "keep the flag flying", come what may.

Fixtures 1908/09

Opponents	Date	Venue	Score	Tries	Scorers/Comments
Pontardawe	26 Sep 1908	Away	5-6	1	Hill T, C.
Cardiff Mackintosh	3 Oct 1908	Home	9-3	3	AN Other 2T, Wyndham Jones T.
Plymouth	3 Oct 1908	Home	10-8	2	Alf Price T, Eddy Ainsworth T, DG.
Pontnewydd	10 Oct 1908	Home	16-0	4	Arthur Ireland T, Eddy Ainsworth T, Dick Thomas T, George Edwards T, Jim Donovan 2C.

Opponents	Date	Venue	Score	Tries	Scorers/Comments
Caerphilly (L)	17 Oct 1908	Home	16-0	4	Dick Thomas T, D. Lloyd Jones T, Stone T, Eddy Ainsworth T, Jim Donovan 2C.
Pontypridd (PL)	19 Oct 1908	Home	3-0	0	Johnny Thomas P.
Penygraig (PL)	31 Oct 1908	Away	0-3	0	No scorers.
Maesteg (PF)	7 Nov 1908	Away	0-12	0	No scorers.
Penarth	14 Nov 1908	Home	3-0	1	Eddy Ainsworth T.
Aberavon	21 Nov 1908	Away	0-3	0	No scorers.
Abertillery	28 Nov 1908	Away	0-10	0	No scorers.
Bath	5 Dec 1908	Home	8-0	2	Jim Donovan T, C, Dick Thomas T.
Treorky (L)	12 Dec 1908	Home	6-0	2	Dai Arthur Davies T, Harry John T.
Pontnewydd	19 Dec 1908	Away	3-0	1	George Caple T.
Bath	28 Dec 1908	Away	3-17	1	Jenkins T.
Llwynypia (L)	11 Jan 1909	Home	0-0	0	No scorers.
Penygraig (PL)	6 Feb 1909	Home	18-0	6	Harry John 2T, George Caple 2T, Dai Arthur Davies T, Dick Thomas T.
Llwynypia (L)	8 Feb 1909	Away	3-3	1	W. John T.
Bridgend	20 Feb 1909	Home	3-0	1	Eddy Ainsworth T.
Treorky (L)	27 Feb 1909	Away	3-9	1	W. John T.
Pontypridd (L)	6 Mar 1909	Away	10-3	2	Wyndham Jones T, Eddy Ainsworth T, Jim Donovan 2C.
Llwynypia Utd (L)	6 Mar 1909	Away	3-0	0+	Harry John 3pts.
Penygraig (L)	20 Mar 1909	Away	Unknown	Unknown	Drawn game. Scorers unknown.
Maesteg Glamorgan League Cup Semi-Final	20 Mar 1909	Llwynypia	0-6	0	No scorers.
Penarth	27 Mar 1909	Away	0-3	0	No scorers.
Plymouth	10 Apr 1909	Away	0-44	0	No scorers.
Pontardawe	17 Apr 1909	Home	3-0	1	Beere T.
Bridgend	1 May 1909	Away	0-8	0	No scorers.
Merthyr (L)	Unknown	Home	Unknown	Unknown	Mount win. Scorers unknown.
Merthyr (L)	Unknown	Away	Unknown	Unknown	Mount win. Scorers unknown.
Llwynypia United (L)	Unknown	Home	Unknown	Unknown	Mount win. Scorers unknown.
Maesteg (L)	Unknown	Home	Unknown	Unknown	Mount win. Scorers unknown.
Maesteg (L)	Unknown	Away	Unknown	Unknown	Mount win. Scorers unknown.

Summary of Playing Record

P	W	D	L	For	Against	Tries Scored	Win Rate %
33	19	3	11	125+	138+	33+	62.12

Match Reports and Publications

8 August 1908

The Aberdare Leader reported, "In spite of the fact that followers of the soccer code have tried to foster the game at Mountain Ash, the Rugger Club will continue to run their team as in days gone by. The Club have had a hard struggle to keep the ship clear of the shallows of insolvency, but through the assiduous efforts of the Secretary, coupled with the support of several who have the interests of the game at heart in this district, the team will doubtless continue to flourish. The Annual General Meeting....was held last Wednesday at the Cresselly Inn, Mr H.E. Gray, J.P., Merthyr Vale, was re-elected President; Mr Wheeler, Cresselly Inn, Treasurer; and Captain, Mr Wyndham Jones. Mr Bert James, a former Secretary presented the accounts, which showed that outstanding liabilities of the Club were something like £86. The total receipts at the "gate" were £126, 16s, 2d, whilst the Vice Presidents contributed £12, 10s, 6d and the guarantors £69. The statement of accounts was accepted as satisfactory. The secretarial work is being done by Mr J. Jasper."

5 September 1908

The Aberdare Leader asked, "How will Mountain Ash Club fare this season? The team is being slowly drained of some of its most notable players. Dick Thomas, one of the best of their forwards, has now cast in his lot with the Aberdare professional Club. Harry Thomas, the team's clever inside half back, has also signed for Batley, and had his trial on Tuesday afternoon last. Other players who have gone to Aberdare are Ike Taylor, Macquire, Dai Fryer, Arthur Hill, etc."

19 September 1908

"Muddled Oaf" reported in the Aberdare Leader, "The trial match in connection with the Mountain Ash Football Club, held on Saturday at the Mountain Ash Athletic Grounds, resulted in a complete success. The match was not only a spectacular treat, but served to show to the sporting fraternity in the "Land of Pennar" that the team will be well supplied this season with good players, in spite of the fact that the team has already lost some of its prominent men of the past season, who have cast their lots with the Aberdare Northern Union thirteen and Batley. I understand that there are plenty of players of grit who are fighting for their places in the team and this ought to give the Club's selection committee plenty of scope to choose from. Thus Secretary Jasper and his committee are sanguine that the season will be a very promising one, and they hope, with the material they have in hand, to build up a team which will uphold the grand reputation of the Old Firm. It would be well if the Club were better supported financially. I regret to learn that spectators often avail themselves to a free view of the match from several positions in the town! Hence the smallness of the "gates". By the way, the Club are truly indebted to Mr Wheeler, "mine host", at the Cresselly Inn, for his kindness. He is a true-hearted sportsman."

26 September 1908

Pontardawe 6 Mountain Ash 5

The Aberdare Leader reported, "...the Pennarites had to rearrange their team owing to the migration of several of their players to the ranks of the Aberdare N.U. Club....Mountain Ash are to be congratulated on doing so well. At full back, Johnny Thomas was as nimble as ever, whilst Ainsworth acted as a leader of the younger blood in the three-quarter line. Wyndham Jones and Donovan hit it off nicely at half back, whilst the forwards are coming to understand each other better. I wish the team every success."

3 October 1908

<u>Mountain Ash 10 Plymouth 8</u>

Mount Team: Back, Johnny Thomas; ¾ backs, D. Nekrews, D. Lloyd Jones, A. Ireland, E. Ainsworth; half backs, Wyndham Jones*, George Edwards; forwards, George Caple, P.C. R. Thomas*, T. Shepherd, Bevan, C. Stone, P.C. Hill, D. Davies, Alf Price.

* denotes Welsh International

"Muddled Oaf" reported in the Aberdare Leader, "The Pennarites opened the game through their International forward, Police Constable Dick Thomas....Peters, the visiting outside half, drew first blood for his side with a remarkable try, which he also improved upon. From the restart, the home centre got on the aggressive once more, and Arthur Ireland and Lloyd Jones severely tested Hoskins, the visiting custodian. Alf Price, the home reserve forward, scored a try which was not improved upon. In the second half, the Plymouth forwards played together in a grand manner and Caple succeeded in saving his lines at the cost of an injury to his head....Ainsworth added to the score with a beautiful dropped goal."

10 October 1908

<u>Mountain Ash 16 Pontnewydd 0</u>

The Aberdare Leader commented, "The Pontnewydd forwards were not quite up to the standard of the Mount eight, which is among the finest packs in the county."

21 November 1908

<u>Aberavon 3 Mountain Ash 0</u>

Mount Team: Back, Johnny Thomas; ¾ backs, Eddy Ainsworth, Dai Arthur Davies, Payne, Farrow; half backs, George Edwards, J. Donovan; forwards, P.C. Bevan, C. Stone, Geo. Caple, A. Jenkins, Joe Ellery, Tom Shepherd, Dai Davies, Alf Price.

The Aberdare Leader reported, "Played at the Athletic Grounds, Port Talbot, these teams have always been great rivals and Aberavon's performances during the past few weeks have stamped them as one of the finest Clubs in South Wales. With a considerably weakened team, the supporters of the Old Firm feared defeat. Mountain Ash were without the services of D. Lloyd Jones, Ireland, Wyndham Jones, whilst the Seasiders were at full strength. So, the Pennarites were represented by practically a junior side, while Aberavon played their League fighting giants. It was refreshing to witness the manner in which the Mountain Ash recruit three-quarters defended their lines, time after time, and the good individual work done by Johnny Thomas, the full back, and Ainsworth....Ainsworth, the Pennarites' brilliant wing three-quarter, sustained a nasty kick to his knee and had to be carried off the field. Nothing was registered up to the interval. The game was afterwards more exciting than ever, and a smart movement by the Aberavon outside half-back would have resulted in a score had not the backs been reliable in their tackling. Caple, Shepherd and Bevan were always conspicuous in the forward department. They came near scoring on several occasions. They were very unfortunate in losing Johnny Thomas, their clever full back, who was carried off owing to an injury. Only thirteen in number, and pitted against a more formidable side of fifteen, the Mount continued to play up pluckily. Willie Thomas scored the only try of the match for Aberavon....To run a team of the standard of Aberavon to only a single try on the Aberavon territory is no mean feat. For the Old Firm, Jack Thomas and Ainsworth did very well up to the time of their injuries. Donovan and Edwards were powerful at half, whilst the pick of the forwards were Caple, Bevan, Shepherd, Stone and Ellery."

5 December 1908

Mountain Ash 8 Bath 0

Mount Team: Back, Farrow; ¾ backs, Stubbings, Donovan, Payne, Dai Arthur Davies; half backs, Wyndham Jones*, George Edwards; forwards, Dick Thomas*, Bevan, Hill, Dai Davies, Joe Ellery, Jarman, A. Jenkins, A. Corn.

* denotes Welsh International

The Aberdare Leader reported, "Wyndham Jones, the homesters' clever outside half, broke his way through and swung the ball out to Dai Arthur Davies....who cleverly drew the defence to transfer the ball to Donovan, who beat Meister, the Bath centre, and scored a capital try for his side, after having run from the half way line....George Edwards, the home half back, sustained a severe injury to his head as the result of a pure accident. In the second moiety....The oval came to Dai Arthur Davies, who sent across to Payne, and the latter to Donovan. He swung across to P.C. Dick Thomas, who romped over with a neat try, which was converted by Donovan. The Old Firm played a brilliant game all through. Bath too, needed a deal of watching."

Glamorgan League Table

Club	P	W	L	D	Points
Mountain Ash	4	4	0	0	8
Llwynypia	4	4	0	0	8
Merthyr	8	3	4	1	7
Treorky	4	3	0	1	7
Maesteg	4	2	2	0	4
Pontypridd	3	0	2	1	1
Penygraig	1	0	1	0	0
Llwynypia United	1	0	1	0	0

12 December 1908

Mountain Ash 6 Treorky 0
Glamorgan League

Mount Team: Back, Johnny Thomas; ¾ backs, Harry John, Donovan, D. Arthur Davies, Payne; half backs, Wyndham Jones*, George Edwards; forwards, George Caple, Harry Beere, Alf Price, A. Jenkins, Tom Shepherd, Dai Hill, Dai Davies, Joe Ellery.

* denotes Welsh International

The Aberdare Leader reported, "Played at the Mountain Ash Athletic Grounds on Saturday....as Treorky have held the Championship recently, the interest taken was intense, especially as Treorky and Mountain Ash are undefeated this season in the League. The Old Firm were without the services of the three constables who figure in the forward pack, and who were doing duty that day for the County Police at Penarth. Johnny Thomas made a welcome reappearance at full back, whilst Harry Beer and Dai Hill were included in the pack. The League champions fielded a powerful side....A few sensational bursts were made by Wyndham Jones, the home outside half, who sorely taxed the defence of the League champions. Afterwards, Wyndham Jones smartly snapped up the ball and romped over the line with what appeared to be a try, but the point was disallowed by the referee....Dai Arthur Davies ran over with a beautiful try for the Old Firm, which was unconverted....Dai Arthur Davies again got the ball, and sent across to Donovan, after having gained ground, and the latter neatly put Harry John over with a try in the corner. Thus Mountain Ash succeeded in defeating the famous Rhondda XV. For the homesters, Dai Arthur Davies was in magnificent form. Donovan and Payne were also good. The home halves were clever, whilst Jack Thomas at back was as safe as ever."

11 January 1909

<u>Mountain Ash 0 Llwynypia 0</u>
<u>Glamorgan League</u>

The Western Mail reported, "The visit of Llwynypia to Mountain Ash created a good deal of interest inasmuch as both teams are unbeaten in the League….The game was even until Wyndham Jones and Albert Jenkins got away and rushed play right on the visitors' line….Johns, the home wing, twice, as the result of excellent passing, made tracks for the line, and was only brought down a few yards out. In the second half Mountain Ash held the advantage all the way through and Wyndham Jones and Caple both crossed, but were recalled owing to some infringement. These decisions by the referee seemed to have exasperated the home supporters and he was subjected to a hostile demonstration at the close of the game, but there was no untoward incident. Undoubtedly, Mountain Ash had most of the game and deserved to have won by at least 6 points, but luck seemed to be against them."

30 January 1909

"Muddled Oaf" reported in the Aberdare Leader, "By the way, supporters of the Old Firm were greatly disappointed with the decision of the Welsh Union, who failed to include P.C. Dick Thomas in the International game at Cardiff the other day. Wales sadly needed forwards of Dick's stamp and the Union could do worse than include him in the pack against Scotland."

6 February 1909

<u>Mountain Ash 18 Penygraig 0</u>
<u>Possible Glamorgan League Fixture</u>

The Aberdare Leader reported, "In the first moiety, the "Old Firm" assumed the aggressive….Playing with unusual vigour, the Pennarites heeled prettily and Benjamin, the new inside half back, got the ball away to Wyndham Jones, who in turn, transferred the oval to Dai Arthur Davies who scored a beautiful try for the homesters. A smart kick by Ainsworth enabled Harry John to increase the score with another try. It was pleasant to witness the way in which the home backs and forwards handled the greasy ball. After the resumption, Penygraig were outclassed in every department….The home forwards were in prime form and George Caple, the veteran scrummager and dribbler, showed that he is not yet a spent force in scoring two magnificent tries."

8 February 1909

<u>Llwynypia 3 Mountain Ash 3</u>
<u>Possible Glamorgan League</u>

The Western Mail reported, "….Saturday's match with Mountain Ash secured a large crowd….The Llwynypia Drum and Fife Band marched before the players took the field….Llwynypia were decidedly unfortunate….a smart passing bout ended in Hellings scoring a seemingly fair try, which was disallowed, the visiting toughjudge holding up his flag for an infringement on the line. This incident aroused much dissatisfaction amongst players and spectators, and the referee, Mr Lewis, used splendid tact in keeping the game under control….Llwynypia had their work cut out to watch Wyndham Jones. Donovan, at centre, was brilliant…."

6 March 1909

<u>Pontypridd 3 Mountain Ash 10</u>
<u>Glamorgan League</u>
<u>Western Mail</u>

A SPIRITED CONTEST.
MOUNTAIN ASH FIGHT HARD FOR LEAGUE POINTS.

"The Old Firm received a severe shaking at Pontypridd on Saturday, when they faced the team which is still at the bottom of the Glamorgan League. On paper form, the game should have been a foregone conclusion for the visitors seeing that they tie with Llwynypia at the head of the table, but it proved to be one of the most stubbornly contested fights witnessed on the Ynysangharad ground this season. Both teams were well represented and each had much at stake. The homesters were anxious to still further retrieve their reputation, while an adverse result would seriously affect Mountain Ash's chances of winning the League Championship. A large number of supporters came with the visitors and the partisan spirit taken up by them and imitated by the home contingent seemed to infect the players, for the game soon became strenuous to a degree, and this vigour was maintained throughout….It was in the three-quarter line that the superiority of the visitors showed itself, their attack being far more convincing. Whenever they got the ball, there was the moral certainty of a good bout of passing, and only the good defence of the home backs kept the score down in the first half. Wyndham Jones' try was a beauty and was the result of a fine sprint in which Jones doubled three of the defence and planted the ball almost behind the posts….In the second half, Pontypridd did rather more than a full share of the attacking and there was a warm scene near the visitors' line. Pontypridd were attacking for more than five minutes, scrum following scrum, the tackling being most deadly, and no one given time to kick. Eventually, Critchett essayed to drop but the ball skidded off his foot, went to the opposite wing, where Pugh picked up and got over….Play of an exciting character continued and eventually Ainsworth increased the visitors' lead, this try being the result of a fine bout of passing….Mountain Ash quite deserved to win….the game, apart from too much spirit, was well worth witnessing."

10 April 1909

<u>Plymouth 44 Mountain Ash 0</u>

The Aberdare Leader commented, "To fulfil their annual match with Plymouth, the Mountain Ash Club sent a very poorly represented team to the southern shipping place on Saturday last. Johnny Thomas, the clever full back, had to be deputised by George Caple, the forward, whilst P.C.s Bevan and Thomas, two other forwards, and Geo. Edwards, the half back, also helped to complete the three-quarter back line."

8 May 1909

The Mountain Ash Rugby Football Club
Winners of the Glamorgan League

The Aberdare Leader reported, "The Mountain Ash Rugby Football Club has succeeded in doing just what I predicted some time back, viz. winning the Glamorgan League trophy for this season. The Pennarites fully deserve their victory. They fought hard and long for their laurels in the face of great drawbacks. Out of sixteen matches played, the team won twelve, and have only lost one, and drawn three. Thus, they headed the League with 27 points. During the season, some excellent displays were given at half by Messrs Wyndham Jones, the Captain, who officiated at outside half. Benjamin, the "feeder", has been an acquisition to the team. Then Johnny Thomas was seen to immense advantage at full back. In the backline, rattling good work has been contributed by Eddy Ainsworth the wing man, Jim Donovan at centre, young Dai Arthur Davies, formerly of the Aberdare County School, Harry John, Arthur Ireland, Evan Jones, Mog Ashford and others. P.C. Dick Thomas, the Welsh International and County man, has also proven his ability as a three-quarter. Grand work was also contributed by the veteran George Caple, together with P.C. Bevan, P.C. Hill, Joe Ellery, Tom Shepherd, Dick Jarman, A. Jenkins, Dai Davies, A. Price, Williams and others. The majority of players stood true to pure amateurism in the face of tempting offers to become professionals."

Mountain Ash Reserves RFC

"Muddled Oaf" reported in the Aberdare Leader, "This junior organisation, which boasts of several players of sound ability, now claim to have secured the Championship of the Aberdare and Merthyr District League. They have had the best of matters over the Merthyr Reserves, their greatest opponents throughout the whole of the season. The team was composed of some players who have done duty for the now defunct Cefnpennar United, Mountain Ash Stars and Newtown Clubs. They have played bustling football throughout, and prominent amongst his colleagues every Saturday was Bradford, whose displays at three-quarter and full back left little room for criticism. Mog Ashford and Bevan were also clever. The forward pack was well trained and Shadrach Lewis, formerly of the Aberdare County School, was also prominent." Shadrach Lewis may well be "Shad" Lewis who went on to become Club Chairman and benefactor in the 1920s and 30s.

THE OLD FIRM'S PROUD PAST

Mountain Ash Rugby Football Club
"The Old Firm"
Glamorgan League Champions 1908/09

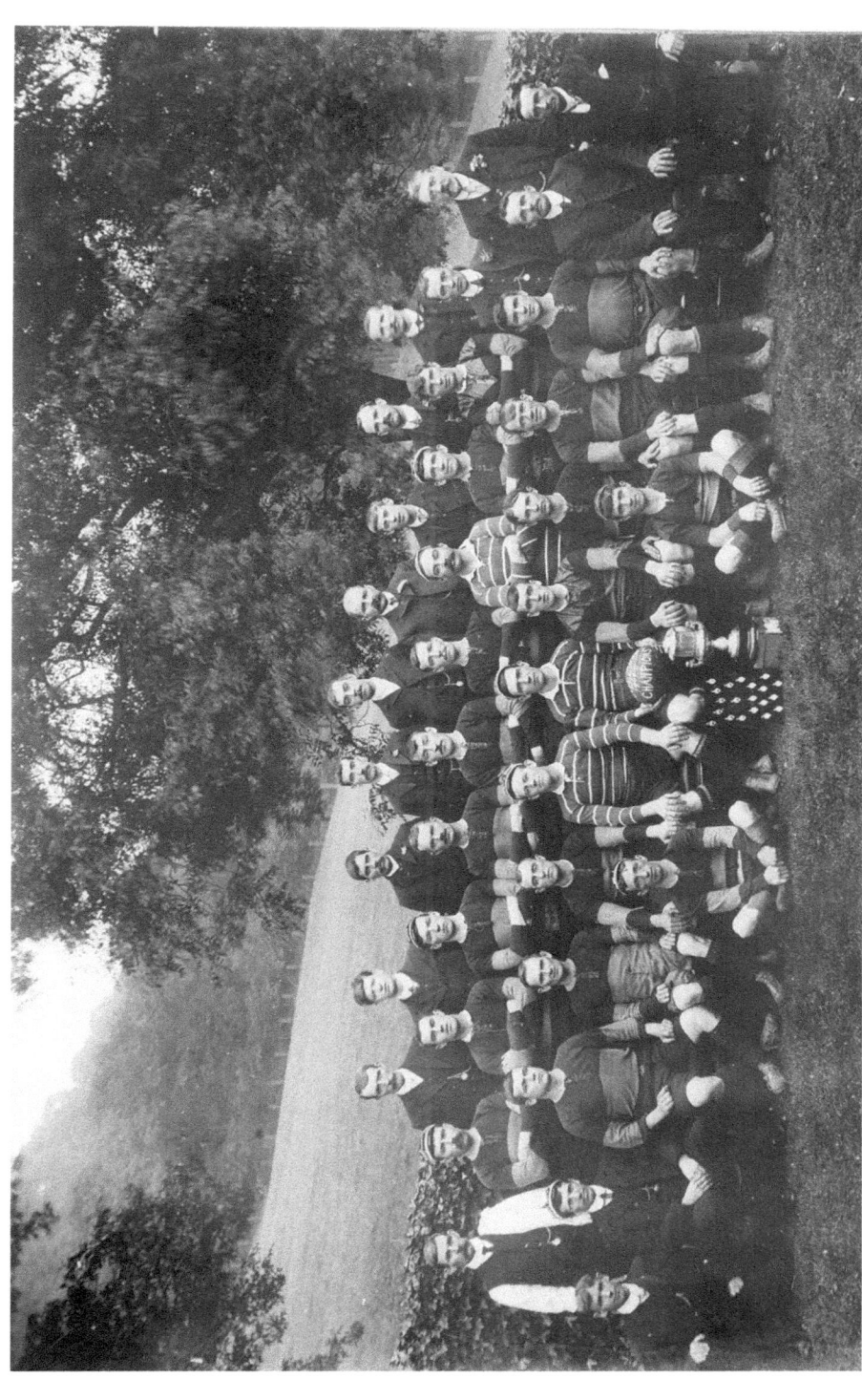

Back Row L-R: J. Gregory, J. Kynan, D. Davies, J. Perkins, D. Griffiths, E. Clode, W. Morgan, D.E. Lewis, W. Cresswell,
Middle Row L-R: A. Parry (Trainer), A. Price, P.C. John, D.A. Davies, P.C. Hill, C. Stone, P.C. Bevan, A. Fryer, J. Ellery, D. Davies, W. Scott, J.T. Wheeler (Treasurer),
Front Row L-R: J. Jones (Asst Trainer), J. Jasper (Secretary), A. Jenkins, G. Edwards, E. Ainsworth, G. Caple, A.W. Jones* Capt, J. Benjamin, H. John, R. Jarman, T. Shepperd, H. Hale, H.J. Carpenter (Chairman),
Sitting on Grass L-R: J. Donovan, J. Thomas.

* denotes Welsh International

Season 1909/10

Season Sees Some Good Wins For Old Firm
Wyndham Jones Announces His Retirement

At the start of the season a celebratory dinner was held to commemorate the winning of the Glamorgan League Championship the previous season which Ben Tiley, the Old Firm's legendary captain between 1882 and 1894 attended. There was also a decision made by the Club committee not to play at Maesteg in the Glamorgan League because of "the regrettable scenes in the match between Maesteg and Mountain Ash last season….but, in the event of the Glamorgan League being agreeable, to their playing Maesteg upon a neutral ground for the points, the Secretary shall have power to arrange to play these." Whether any of this actually happened is not known but no games with Maesteg for the season were reported. The Old Firm were unbeaten on their Christmas tour, beating Bridgwater & Albion on Boxing Day, and drawing at Bath the day after. The season also saw Pontardawe's two year home record and Treorky's unbeaten run in the Glamorgan League and home record taken. There were also wins over Bridgend, Pontypridd, Abertillery and Bath. There was a home draw against Aberavon and a close loss to Cross Keys. The Old Firm finished runners-up in the Glamorgan League and had an actual overall playing record of played 36, won 18, drawn 7 and lost 11, scoring 200 points, which included at least 27 tries, and conceding 160, which equated to a win rate of 59.72%. At the end of the season, the Old Firm suffered a big loss as mercurial outside half, Wyndham Jones, who had been the lynchpin in the Old Firm XV for a dozen years and was capped against Ireland in 1905, announced his retirement.

Fixtures 1909/10

Opponents	Date	Venue	Score	Tries	Scorers/Comments
Cardiff Mackintosh	18 Sep 1909	Home	16-0	4	Harry John T, Johnny Thomas C, AN Other 3T, C.
Penylan	25 Sep 1909	Home	3-0	1	AN Other T.
Bridgend	2 Oct 1909	Away	6-5	2	Fryer T, Wyndham Jones T.
Grangetown	9 Oct 1909	Home	29-0	5+	Harry John T, George Caple T, Stubbings T, Eddy Ainsworth T, Ivor Bevan T, Johnny Thomas 2C, AN Other 10pts.
Cross Keys	16 Oct 1909	Home	3-4	1	Jimmy Donovan T.
Aberavon	1 Nov 1909	Away	0-3	0	No scorers.
Treorky (F)	20 Nov 1909	Home	6-8	2	D.F. Davies T, George Caple T.
Swansea	22 Nov 1909	Away	6-35	2	Benjamin T, Loveluck T.
Rhymney	4 Dec 1909	Away	3-6	1	Trevor Flooks T.
Pontardawe	6 Dec 1909	Away	6-5	2	Trevor Flooks T, Bradford T.
Penarth	18 Dec 1909	Away	0-8	0	No scorers.
Bridgwater & Albion	27 Dec 1909	Away	4-0	0	Thomas DG.
Bath	28 Dec 1909	Away	0-0	0	No scorers.

Opponents	Date	Venue	Score	Tries	Scorers/Comments
Pontypridd (L)	8 Jan 1910	Home	8-0	2	Loveluck T, Hopkins T, Johnny Thomas C.
Canton	15 Jan 1910	Home	9-0	2	Ainsworth T, Hopkins T, Johnny Thomas P.
Pontardawe	29 Jan 1910	Home	3-3	1	Trevor Flooks T.
Penylan	14 Feb 1910	Away	3-3	Unknown	Scorer unknown.
Rhymney	21 Feb 1910	Home	0-0	0	No scorers.
Treorky (L)	7 Mar 1910	Away	5-3	1	Trevor Flooks T, AN Other C.
Treorky (F)	14 Mar 1910	Away	0-9	0	No scorers.
Bath	21 Mar 1910	Home	14-0	Unknown	Scorers unknown.
Aberavon	16 Apr 1910	Home	3-3	1	AN Other T.
Abertillery	Unknown	Unknown	Unknown	Unknown	Mount win. Scorers unknown.

Summary of Above Playing Record

P	W	D	L	For	Against	Tries Scored	Win Rate %
23	11	5	7	127+	95+	27+	58.70

Summary of Actual Playing Record

P	W	D	L	For	Against	Tries Scored	Win Rate %
36	18	7	11	200	160	Unknown	59.72

Match Reports and Publications

4 September 1909

The "Old Firm" Banquet
Presentation of the Glamorgan League Cup and Medals

"Muddled Oaf" reported in the Aberdare Leader, "On Monday evening at the Drill Hall, Mountain Ash, a grand banquet was given in honour of Mountain Ash Rugby Football team. About 150 supporters sat down to an excellent dinner. The Chairman opened proceedings by proposing a toast to the King. The toast was drunk with great enthusiasm and with musical honours. Mr Gray, who presided, then announced that he had to perform the event of the evening and that was the presentation of the Glamorgan League Cup to the Captain of the Mountain Ash Football Club. In the course of a happy speech, he alluded to the fact that it was as far back as 1895 that the Cup came to Mountain Ash last, and he sincerely hoped that now it had come again, it would be a long time before it left. They were all aware that for the past few years the team had been working under some disadvantage, mainly on account of the unsuitability of the ground. But still, after the hard work and in spite of many difficulties, they had attained their object in bringing the Cup to Mountain Ash. No small amount of their success was due to the hard work of their very excellent Captain, Mr Wyndham Jones. He had played for them for a period of twelve years, and he had been their skipper for many seasons. Mr Gray, amidst great cheering, called Mr Wyndham Jones to receive the Cup on behalf of his team. It was handed round the room, each one drinking and wishing prosperity to the Old Firm. The Chairman then presented each of the players, the Secretary and trainer with a medal. Mr Wyndham Jones in acknowledging the Cup and medals on behalf of himself and fellow players, said he had always received the greatest support from the players and supporters of the team. It had always been an ambition to bring the Cup back to Mountain Ash, and his objective had been attained. He was not likely to receive another medal, but that would not prevent him doing his level best for the Club....Numerous toasts were made and the evening ended with the singing of "God Save the King."

2 October 1909

<u>Bridgend 5 Mountain Ash 6</u>

Mount Team: Back, Stubbings; ¾ backs, Eddy Ainsworth, Jim Donovan, Bowen, Harry John; half backs, Wyndham Jones*, Benjamin; forwards, Jarman, Tom Shepperd, George Caple, Brown, Will Douse, Phillips, Jenkins, Fryer.

* denotes Welsh International

The Aberdare Leader reported, "Intense interest was centred in the meeting between these two well known Clubs at Bridgend on Saturday last. A new man, in the person of Phillips of Bridgwater, was included in the Aberpennar forward pack, whilst Stubbings, a local junior player, deputised Johnny Thomas at full back. Bowen, a new man, was also given a trial in the three-quarter line. The Old Firm had the upper hand and from a lineout Fryer got the ball away and romped over for a neat try for his side....In the second moiety the home forwards found their feet, but could make very little headway near the Mountain Ash quarter.... The Mountain Ash men got a scrummage near the Bridgend line, where Wyndham Jones secured the ball and got over the line with a well merited try....Thus the Old Firm won their first prominent away match by a point."

22 November 1909

<u>Swansea 35 Mountain Ash 6</u>

The Western Mail reported, "Swansea received an amazing shock on Saturday when, after fifteen minutes, they found themselves two tries behind a team they were expected to rout from the start....The Old Firm went off with a dash....they were desirous of creating a good impression, but so great was their onslaught that no footballers, even from the hills, could be expected to keep up such pressure for any length of time. It was certainly a great performance by the "Mountaineers" to put on two tries, only one other team having scored as much against Swansea this season....Benjamin, skirting the blindside of the scrum, scored in the corner. The ball had scarcely been dropped out when Loveluck, snapping up in the open, made off and scored a very well deserved try....Loveluck, the left centre for the Old Firm, is a very fine player. His try was particularly good and he is bound to be heard of much more. Wyndham Jones and Benjamin are a very decent pair of halves. Johnny Thomas, at back, did very creditably, whilst Jarman, Shepherd and Caple did well in the pack."

6 December 1909

<u>Pontardawe 5 Mountain Ash 6</u>

The Western Mail commented, "....Mountain Ash has the honour of being the only second class team to defeat Pontardawe on their own ground for two seasons...."

27 December 1909

<u>Bridgwater & Albion 0 Mountain Ash 4</u>

The Western Mail reported, "Mountain Ash opened their Christmas tour with a match at Bridgwater against the Albion Club.....a good crowd assembled, but the ground was in a very heavy condition. The game.... was largely controlled by the forwards, the Mountain Ash pack showing to best advantage and frequently getting the ball from the scrums....from a free to Mountain Ash, the ball struck the cross bar and rebounded into play....Thomas dropped a goal....Griffiths was nearly over for Mountain Ash....the defence of the visitors was very sound...."

28 December 1909

<ins>Bath 0 Mountain Ash 0</ins>
<ins>Western Mail</ins>

A KEEN GAME AT BATH.

CLEVER TACKLING BY MOUNTAIN ASH.

	G.	T.	P'ts.
Bath	0	0	0
Mountain Ash	0	0	0

There was a keen forward game between these teams at Bath. The home backs secured the ball more frequently than the Welshmen, but the visitors tackled splendidly. The Mountain Ash forwards used their feet cleverly, but nothing was scored at half-time. Play was all in Bath's favour in the second half, Mountain Ash not being able to get out of their own half, but a keen game ended in a draw.

8 January 1910

<ins>Mountain Ash 8 Pontypridd 0</ins>
<ins>Glamorgan League</ins>

Mount Team: Full back, Jack Thomas; ¾ backs, Hopkins, Loveluck, Farrow, Ainsworth; half backs, Wyndham Jones*, Benjamin; forwards, Tom Shepherd, George Caple, Dallimore, Alf Williams, Dick Jarman, Dai Watts, P.C. John, Joe Ellery.

* denotes Welsh International

"Muddled Oaf" reported in the Aberdare Leader, "This Glamorgan League match took place on Saturday last at the Mountain Ash Athletic Grounds....Loveluck romped over in brilliant style. In the second half Benjamin got the ball away and nearly got over....Hopkins, in getting possession, beat both an opponent and the full back in a race, and dodged over with a neat try which Johnny Thomas converted....The match ended in another brace of League points for the Old Firm. The Pennarites are improving in every match. On Saturday's form the home forwards played a remarkably fine game. Wyndham Jones and Benjamin were very sharp at half back. Of the three-quarters, Loveluck once more held the top place, whilst Hopkins and Ainsworth were good in attack and defence."

29 January 1910

"Muddled Oaf" reported, "If it were possible for the Welsh Rugby Union to reinstate Northern Union players, the rugby game, which is fast dying in the hill districts, would again become what it was five or six years back, and Wales would still hold topmost position in the rugby world. What a rush home there would be if the Welsh Rugby Union saw their way clear to reinstate these players!"

7 March 1910

Treorky 3 Mountain Ash 5
Glamorgan League

Mount Team: Back, Johnny Thomas; ¾ backs, Trevor Flooks, Arthur Loveluck, W. Hopkins, Eddy Ainsworth; half backs, Wyndham Jones* and Benjamin; forwards, Tom Shepherd, George Caple, P.C. Bevan, Alf Fryer, Dai Watts, Dick Jarman, W. Phillips, T. Griffiths.

* denotes Welsh International

The Western Mail reported, "This important League encounter attracted a large crowd to the Treorky Athletic Ground on Saturday and they were rewarded by witnessing what was undoubtedly the hardest struggle of the season. The home team had a cherished ground record to maintain, and furthermore, they had won all their League matches to date, whilst Mountain Ash had only been defeated by Penygraig....Flook scored a magnificent try for Mountain Ash after fifteen minutes play, sprinting in grand style from his own 25...."

21 March 1910

Mountain Ash 14 Bath 0

There was no match report in the Western Mail but the following was published:

LOCAL RUGBY RESULTS.

	Pts		Pts
Swansea	11	Cardiff	0
Newport	3	Gloucester	3
London Welsh	8	Neath	6
Aberavon	0	Maesteg	8
Pontypool	3	Llanelly	0
Mountain Ash	14	Bath	0
Cinderford	44	Clifton	0
Lydney	23	Stroud	10
Bristol	14	Cheltenham	0

21 May 1910

Mountain Ash Rugby Football Club
Review of 1909/10

The Aberdare Leader's reporter, "Muddled Oaf" wrote, "This has been a most trying season for the Club, but they secured the runners-up medals in the Glamorgan League against Treorky, their perennial rivals. Mr A. Hill acted as Vice Chairman and Mr David Harris became the Treasurer of the Club. Mr Jack J. Jasper made a most capable Secretary. Jack Thomas earned the distinction of scoring the largest number of points. Thomas kicked 5 penalties, dropped 2 goals and converted 8 tries, thus making a total of 39 points. Ainsworth, on the right wing, eventually became the top scorer with 7 tries. Arthur Loveluck, the new centre, registered 5 tries, whilst the same number of tries was secured by Trevor Flooks of Aberdare, the flying winger. Hopkins of Llantwit Major, D.W. Francis, Harry John and the trio of clever reserves, viz. Farrow, Ted Griffiths and Dai Arthur Davies were good. Wyndham Jones, the veteran, was as good as ever, whilst delightful displays were given by Benjamin, who registered 6 tries. Mellish often acted as a good forward reserve. There were good men in the persons of Shepherd, Caple, P.C. Bevan (Aberdare), Fryer, Jarman, Ellery, Brown (Cheltenham), Alf Williams, Charlie Stone, Will Douse (late of Aberavon), Bowen, Dai Watts and Dai Williams. Altogether, the Club has played 36 matches, won 18, lost 11 and drawn 7. They have scored over 200 points in total, with 160 against."

A Selection of the Old Firm's Results 1900/01 to 1909/10

To put the information below into some sort of context, the Western Mail listed "the principal Welsh teams" as Newport, Swansea, Aberavon, Neath, Cardiff and Llanelly in 1900/01. In 1901/02, the Clubs listed in a table of playing records were Swansea, Cardiff, Newport, Treherbert, Aberavon, Maesteg, Llanelly, Treorky, Bridgend, Penygraig, Llwynypia, Neath, Pontypridd and Mountain Ash. Later on in the decade, in 1908/09, the leading Clubs were listed as Swansea, Cardiff, Llanelly, Neath, Newport, Aberavon and Bridgend.

Matches v Treorky

Opponents	Season	Venue	Score	P	W	D	L
Treorky (L)	1900/01	Away	3-3	1	0	1	0
Treorky (L)	1900/01	Home	12-3	2	1	1	0
Treorky (L)	1901/02	Home	19-3	3	2	1	0
Treorky (L)	1901/02	Away	0-3	4	2	1	1
Treorky (PL)	1902/03	Home	0-0	5	2	2	1
Treorky (PL)	1903/04	Home	5-0	6	3	2	1
Treorky (PL)	1903/04	Away	0-8	7	3	2	2
Treorky (L)	1904/05	Away	5-0	8	4	2	2
Treorky (L)	1904/05	Home	11-0	9	5	2	2
Treorky (L)	1905/06	Home	3-0	10	6	2	2
Treorky (L)	1905/06	Away	3-0	11	7	2	2
Treorky (L)	1906/07	Away	0-6	12	7	2	3
Treorky (L)	1906/07	Home	6-7	13	7	2	4
Treorky (PL)	1907/08	Home	6-11	14	7	2	5
Treorky (L)	1908/09	Home	6-0	15	8	2	5
Treorky (L)	1908/09	Away	3-9	16	8	2	6
Treorky (F)	1909/10	Home	6-8	17	8	2	7
Treorky (L)	1909/10	Away	5-3	18	9	2	7
Treorky (F)	1909/10	Away	0-9	19	9	2	8

Matches v Llwynypia

Opponents	Season	Venue	Score	P	W	D	L
Llwynypia (L)	1900/01	Home	6-3	1	1	0	0
Llwynypia (PL)	1900/01	Away	3-3	2	1	1	0
Llwynypia (L)	1901/02	Home	16-6	3	2	1	0
Llwynypia (L)	1902/03	Home	18-3	4	3	1	0
Llwynypia (L)	1902/03	Away	3-0	5	4	1	0
Llwynypia (PL)	1903/04	Home	0-0	6	4	2	0
Llwynypia (PL)	1906/07	Unknown	6-3	7	5	2	0
Llwynypia (L)	1907/08	Away	5-7	8	5	2	1
Llwynypia (L)	1907/08	Home	21-0	9	6	2	1
Llwynypia (L)	1908/09	Home	0-0	10	6	3	1
Llwynypia (L)	1908/09	Away	3-3	11	6	4	1

Matches v Pontypridd

Opponents	Season	Venue	Score	P	W	D	L
Pontypridd (PL)	1900/01	Home	6-0	1	1	0	0
Pontypridd (F)	1901/02	Away	6-3	2	2	0	0
Pontypridd (PL)	1901/02	Home	15-0	3	3	0	0
Pontypridd (PL)	1901/02	Away	17-3	4	4	0	0
Pontypridd (L)	1901/02	Home	40-0	5	5	0	0
Pontypridd (L)	1902/03	Home	8-0	6	6	0	0
Pontypridd (PL)	1902/03	Away	12-3	7	7	0	0
Pontypridd (L)	1903/04	Away	0-3	8	7	0	1
Pontypridd (PL)	1903/04	Home	14-0	9	8	0	1
Pontypridd (L)	1904/05	Home	18-8	10	9	0	1
Pontypridd (L)	1904/05	Away	5-0	11	10	0	1
Pontypridd (PL)	1905/06	Home	6-0	12	11	0	1
Pontypridd (F)	1906/07	Away	0-0	13	11	1	1
Pontypridd (PL)	1906/07	Unknown	6-5	14	12	1	1
Pontypridd (F)	1907/08	Home	17-0	15	13	1	1
Pontypridd (F)	1907/08	Away	3-9	16	13	1	2
Pontypridd (PL)	1908/09	Home	3-0	17	14	1	2
Pontypridd (L)	1908/09	Away	10-3	18	15	1	2
Pontypridd (L)	1909/10	Home	8-0	19	16	1	2

Matches v Treherbert

Opponents	Season	Venue	Score	P	W	D	L
Treherbert (PL)	1901/02	Away	0-10	1	0	0	1
Treherbert (L)	1901/02	Home	11-0	2	1	0	1
Treherbert (PL)	1902/03	Home	14-5	3	2	0	1
Treherbert (L)	1902/03	Away	0-5	4	2	0	2
Treherbert (L)	1903/04	Home	3-3	5	2	1	2
Treherbert (L)	1904/05	Away	3-6	6	2	1	3
Treherbert (L)	1904/05	Home	13-5	7	3	1	3
Treherbert (PL)	1905/06	Home	16-0	8	4	1	3
Treherbert (L)	1905/06	Away	3-9	9	4	1	4
Treherbert (L)	1906/07	Away	6-5	10	5	1	4
Treherbert (PL)	1907/08	Home	13-3	11	6	1	4

Matches v Abertillery

Opponents	Season	Venue	Score	P	W	D	L
Abertillery	1907/08	Home	3-10	1	0	0	1
Abertillery	1907/08	Away	6-9	2	0	0	2
Abertillery	1908/09	Away	0-10	3	0	0	3
Abertillery	1909/10	Unknown	Score unknown. Mount win.	4	1	0	3

Matches v Penygraig

Opponents	Season	Venue	Score	P	W	D	L
Penygraig (PL)	1900/01	Home	12-3	1	1	0	0
Penygraig (PL)	1900/01	Home	6-4	2	2	0	0
Penygraig (PL)	1901/02	Away	9-11	3	2	0	1
Penygraig (PL)	1902/03	Home	22-0	4	3	0	1
Penygraig (PL)	1902/03	Away	6-0	5	4	0	1
Penygraig (PL)	1903/04	Away	11-6	6	5	0	1
Penygraig (L)	1903/04	Home	9-0	7	6	0	1
Penygraig (L)	1904/05	Home	6-0	8	7	0	1
Penygraig (L)	1904/05	Away	3-6	9	7	0	2
Penygraig (L)	1905/06	Away	0-9	10	7	0	3
Penygraig (L)	1905/06	Home	0-0	11	7	1	3
Penygraig (L)	1906/07	Home	3-4	12	7	1	4
Penygraig (L)	1906/07	Away	0-7	13	7	1	5
Penygraig (F)	1907/08	Away	0-3	14	7	1	6
Penygraig (F)	1907/08	Home	0-6	15	7	1	7
Penygraig (PL)	1908/09	Away	0-3	16	7	1	8
Penygraig (PL)	1908/09	Home	18-0	17	8	1	8
Penygraig (L)	1908/09	Away	Score unknown. Drawn game.	18	8	2	8

Matches v Neath

Opponents	Season	Venue	Score	P	W	D	L
Neath	1900/01	Away	0-4	1	0	0	1
Neath	1900/01	Home	9-4	2	1	0	1
Neath	1901/02	Home	15-0	3	2	0	1

Matches v Llanelly

Opponents	Season	Venue	Score	P	W	D	L
Llanelly	1900/01	Away	11-3	1	1	0	0
Llanelly	1900/01	Home	0-0	2	1	1	0
Llanelly	1901/02	Home	10-3	3	2	1	0
Llanelly	1901/02	Away	0-29	4	2	1	1
Llanelly	1902/03	Home	0-0	5	2	2	1
Llanelly	1905/06	Away	6-11	6	2	2	2
Llanelly	1905/06	Home	9-6	7	3	2	2
Llanelly	1907/08	Away	0-26	8	3	2	3

Matches v London Welsh

Opponents	Season	Venue	Score	P	W	D	L
London Welsh	1900/01	Home	16-0	1	1	0	0
London Welsh	1902/03	Away	6-3	2	2	0	0
London Welsh	1902/03	Home	26-5	3	3	0	0

Matches v Maesteg

Opponents	Season	Venue	Score	P	W	D	L
Maesteg	1900/01	Away	6-7	1	0	0	1
Maesteg	1900/01	Away	3-0	2	1	0	1
Maesteg (L)	1901/02	Away	6-6	3	1	1	1
Maesteg (L)	1901/02	Home	25-0	4	2	1	1
Maesteg (L)	1902/03	Home	18-0	5	3	1	1
Maesteg (L)	1902/03	Away	0-0	6	3	2	1
Maesteg (L)	1903/04	Away	3-8	7	3	2	2
Maesteg (L)	1903/04	Home	4-0	8	4	2	2
Maesteg (L)	1904/05	Home	10-0	9	5	2	2
Maesteg (F)	1904/05	Away	0-20	10	5	2	3
Maesteg (L)	1907/08	Home	13-0	11	6	2	3
Maesteg (PL)	1907/08	Away	6-0	12	7	2	3
Maesteg (PF)	1908/09	Away	0-12	13	7	2	4
Maesteg Glamorgan League Cup Semi-Final	1908/09	Llwynypia	0-6	14	7	2	5
Maesteg (L)	1908/09	Home	Score unknown. Mount win.	15	8	2	5
Maesteg (L)	1908/09	Away	Score unknown. Mount win.	16	9	2	5

Matches v Bridgend

Opponents	Season	Venue	Score	P	W	D	L
Bridgend	1900/01	Home	14-0	1	1	0	0
Bridgend	1905/06	Away	0-9	2	1	0	1
Bridgend	1905/06	Home	8-7	3	2	0	1
Bridgend	1906/07	Away	6-8	4	2	0	2
Bridgend	1906/07	Home	9-0	5	3	0	2
Bridgend	1907/08	Away	9-4	6	4	0	2
Bridgend	1907/08	Home	16-0	7	5	0	2
Bridgend	1908/09	Home	3-0	8	6	0	2
Bridgend	1908/09	Away	0-8	9	6	0	3
Bridgend	1909/10	Away	6-5	10	7	0	3

Matches v Newport

Newport were Welsh Champions in 1902/03 and 1909/10

Opponents	Season	Venue	Score	P	W	D	L
Newport	1906/07	Home	3-0	1	1	0	0

Matches v Cross Keys

Opponents	Season	Venue	Score	P	W	D	L
Cross Keys	1909/10	Home	3-4	1	0	0	1

Matches v Ebbw Vale

Opponents	Season	Venue	Score	P	W	D	L
Ebbw Vale	1900/01	Home	13-0	1	1	0	0
Ebbw Vale	1900/01	Away	0-0	2	1	1	0
Ebbw Vale	1906/07	Home	11-0	3	2	1	0

Matches v Swansea

Swansea were Welsh Champions in 1900/01, 1901/02, 1903/04, 1904/05 and 1907/08

Opponents	Season	Venue	Score	P	W	D	L
Swansea	1900/01	Away	0-14	1	0	0	1
Swansea	1901/02	Away	0-22	2	0	0	2
Swansea	1909/10	Away	6-35	3	0	0	3

Matches v Penarth

Opponents	Season	Venue	Score	P	W	D	L
Penarth	1902/03	Away	20-0	1	1	0	0
Penarth	1902/03	Home	13-9	2	2	0	0
Penarth	1903/04	Home	12-0	3	3	0	0
Penarth	1903/04	Away	6-0	4	4	0	0
Penarth	1904/05	Unsure	19-0	5	5	0	0
Penarth	1904/05	Home	7-0	6	6	0	0
Penarth	1905/06	Away	6-14	7	6	0	1
Penarth	1905/06	Home	9-10	8	6	0	2
Penarth	1906/07	Away	0-5	9	6	0	3
Penarth	1906/07	Unknown	Score unknown. Drawn game.	10	6	1	3
Penarth	1907/08	Away	8-0	11	7	1	3
Penarth	1907/08	Home	17-3	12	8	1	3
Penarth	1908/09	Home	3-0	13	9	1	3
Penarth	1908/09	Away	0-3	14	9	1	4
Penarth	1909/10	Away	0-8	15	9	1	5

Matches v Pontypool/Pontymoile

Opponents	Season	Venue	Score	P	W	D	L
Pontymoile	1900/01	Away	0-0	1	0	1	0
Pontymoile	1900/01	Home	29-0	2	1	1	0
Pontypool	1901/02	Home	8-7	3	2	1	0
Pontypool	1901/02	Away	8-0	4	3	1	0
Pontypool	1906/07	Away	0-5	5	3	1	1
Pontypool	1906/07	Home	0-3	6	3	1	2
Pontypool	1907/08	Home	8-3	7	4	1	2
Pontypool	1907/08	Away	0-3	8	4	1	3

Matches v Aberavon

Opponents	Season	Venue	Score	P	W	D	L
Aberavon (L)	1901/02	Away	0-11	1	0	0	1
Aberavon (L)	1901/02	Home	0-6	2	0	0	2
Aberavon (L)	1902/03	Away	0-6	3	0	0	3
Aberavon (L)	1902/03	Home	9-0	4	1	0	3
Aberavon (L)	1903/04	Away	0-8	5	1	0	4
Aberavon (L)	1903/04	Home	3-3	6	1	1	4
Aberavon	1904/05	Away	3-6	7	2	1	5
Aberavon	1904/05	Home	8-3	8	2	1	5
Aberavon	1905/06	Away	0-11	9	2	1	6
Aberavon	1905/06	Home	0-0	10	2	2	6
Aberavon	1906/07	Away	0-7	11	2	2	7
Aberavon	1906/07	Home	13-0	12	3	2	7
Aberavon	1907/08	Home	6-0	13	4	2	7
Aberavon	1908/09	Away	0-3	14	4	2	8
Aberavon	1909/10	Away	0-3	15	4	2	9
Aberavon	1909/10	Home	3-3	16	4	3	9

Matches v Tredegar

Opponents	Season	Venue	Score	P	W	D	L
Tredegar	1900/01	Home	9-6	1	1	0	0
Tredegar	1900/01	Home	21-0	2	2	0	0

Matches v Devonport Albion

Opponents	Season	Venue	Score	P	W	D	L
Devonport Albion	1900/01	Away	0-16	1	0	0	1
Devonport Albion	1901/02	Away	3-10	2	0	0	2

Matches v Bath

Opponents	Season	Venue	Score	P	W	D	L
Bath	1905/06	Away	16-13	1	1	0	0
Bath	1905/06	Home	20-8	2	2	0	0
Bath	1906/07	Home	3-0	3	3	0	0
Bath	1907/08	Away	8-5	4	4	0	0
Bath	1908/09	Home	8-0	5	5	0	0
Bath	1908/09	Away	3-17	6	5	0	1
Bath	1909/10	Away	0-0	7	5	1	1
Bath	1909/10	Home	14-0	8	6	1	1

Matches v Bridgwater & Albion

Opponents	Season	Venue	Score	P	W	D	L
Bridgwater & Albion	1909/10	Away	4-0	1	1	0	0

Matches v Plymouth

Opponents	Season	Venue	Score	P	W	D	L
Plymouth	1900/01	Away	3-10	1	0	0	1
Plymouth	1902/03	Away	0-13	2	0	0	2
Plymouth	1902/03	Home	30-0	3	1	0	2
Plymouth	1903/04	Away	0-6	4	1	0	3
Plymouth	1907/08	Away	6-14	5	1	0	4
Plymouth	1908/09	Home	10-8	6	2	0	4
Plymouth	1908/09	Away	0-44	7	2	0	5

There were no known games played against Cardiff, Glamorgan Wanderers, Leicester, Coventry and Nuneaton in the 1900s.

Mountain Ash RFC Players That Went North 1900/01 to 1909/10

W.H. "FRED" MILLAR, who gained 7 Welsh rugby union caps between 1896 & 1901 whilst playing for Mountain Ash RFC, joined Hull, making his debut on 7 September 1901. Millar made 43 appearances for the Humberside club but only managed 2 tries.

LLEW DEARE, who captained Mountain Ash RFC in 1899/1900, was one of 4 Mount players who joined Huddersfield prior to the 1903/04 season starting. He captained the Northern Union Club during the season, which turned out to be one of poorest it had experienced, Deare and the other Welsh players in the Huddersfield team taking the brunt of the blame. There were accusations they were not worth their place and their services be dispensed with immediately. Deare also played twice for Yorkshire and went on to play a leading role in the formation of Aberdare Northern Union Club in 1908/09.

W.T. "WILL" OSBORNE, a forward, was capped 6 times by Wales in 1902 and 1903 before joining the professional ranks at Huddersfield, making his debut on 5 September 1903. He later transferred to Hull, making his debut on 20 October 1906. In November 1908, Hull put him on the transfer list for the princely sum of £16. However, he was still playing for Hull in 1909/10 when Aberdare Leader reporter, "Muddled Oaf", reported on 22 January 1910, "The most popular forward at present in the Hull N.U. Club is Osborne, the old Mountain Ash and Welsh International forward, who left his native heath many years ago. Osborne's display is much talked about, especially his performances against such a redoubtable side as Hunslet." During his time up North, he also gained a Yorkshire county cap.

TOM WALTON, a full back, joined Huddersfield before the start of the 1903/04 season. He was still playing League in 1908/09, the Aberdare Leader reporting, "....the Aberdare Northern Union Club have secured the services of Walton, who is available at full back."

JACK MUXWORTHY, a centre three-quarter, joined Huddersfield at the start of the 1903/04 season but little else is known about his Northern Union career.

REUBEN CARPENTER, who played wing for the Old Firm and was the joint top Welsh try scorer with Fred Jowett of Swansea in 1902/03, joined Oldham before the start of the 1903/04 season.

BERT JENKINS, a centre three-quarter, joined Wigan in 1904 and played there until 1920, where he became one of the finest players of his generation. His career took in 451 games in which he scored 218 tries. He played in the Welsh Rugby League team's first ever match on 1st January 1908 at The New Athletic Grounds in Aberdare against New Zealand, a game Wales won 9-8. He was the only man to play in all Wales' Rugby League Internationals from 1908-1914, and was captain of the first Northern Union Test team which played Australia in December 1908 in London, which was a game that ended 22-22. In total, he was capped by Great Britain 12 times and went on the 1910 and 1914 tours to Australia and New Zealand, being top try scorer on the 1910 trip.

HARRY THOMAS, who played scrum half for Mount, signed for Batley in 1908/09.

IKE TAYLOR, a Mount forward, signed for Aberdare Northern Union Club when it was formed in 1908/09.

DAI FRYER, who was a forward for the Old Firm between 1897/98 and 1904/05, joined Batley in 1905/06, and played there for 3 seasons, where he played a total of 77 games, scoring 7 tries. He returned to South Wales in 1908/09 and joined the newly formed Aberdare Northern Union Club.

ARTHUR HILL, who was a forward for the Old Firm, signed for the Aberdare Northern Union Club when it was formed in 1908/09. However he was named as the Vice Chairman of Mountain Ash RFC at the start of the 1909/10 season, so his venture into the professional ranks appeared to be short lived.

CHRISTIAN NAME UNKNOWN, SURNAME MACQUIRE, was a forward who signed for the Aberdare Northern Union Club when it was formed in 1908/09.

DICK THOMAS, who gained 4 Welsh caps and was Old Firm Captain in 1904/05, officially "went North" just after his last Welsh appearance against Scotland in 1909. Prior to this, it appears he had been going back and fore between the two codes. The Welsh Football Union could not have known about this otherwise they would have banned him for life. The Aberdare Leader reported on 5 September 1908 that "Mountain Ash is being slowly drained of some of its notable players. Dick Thomas, one of the best of their forwards, has now cast in his lot with the Aberdare professional Club." Following on from this, on 26 September 1908, the Aberdare Leader named a Dick Thomas in the Aberdare Northern Union team that played its first ever away match, against St Helen's, as one of its three-quarters. On 10 October 1908, a P.C. Dick Thomas played for the Old Firm versus Pontnewydd. However, in the Aberdare Leader dated 16 January 1909, which was published 3 weeks before his last Welsh Cap against Scotland on 6 February 1909, it was reported, "Dick Thomas, the clever forward in the ranks of the Aberdare Northern Union team, has been selected to take part in the Welsh League XIII that will play against Australia, the Kangaroos, at Merthyr next Saturday. Dick played a great game in the trial match at Ebbw Vale recently." At the end of 1911/12, the Leader reported that Thomas was moving to Bridgend RFC and also mentioned the following season he was playing well. In 1913/14, Thomas was reported to be playing for Warrington in early November 1913 and a few weeks later, for Bridgend Rugby Union Club in South Wales. It seems that unless there were several men of the same name, then Dick Thomas defied the odds before officially turning professional.

A Summary Of The Seasons 1894-1910
The Old Firm's "First Golden Era"

The 16 seasons starting in 1894/95 and ending at the conclusion of the 1909/10 season were a mighty impressive time for Mountain Ash RFC. All that was said and done in these seasons has already been written but below is a brief summary of the Club's "First Golden Era" (the second being from 1921 to 1925):

The Old Firm's Playing Record

Below are the playing records that comprised these years:

Season	P	W	D	L	For	Against	Tries Scored	Win Rate %
1894/95	22	17	3	2	226+	39+	58+	84.09
1895/96	31	26	2	3	278+	63+	74+	87.10
1896/97	37	27	5	5	528	84	131+	79.73
1897/98	37	20	1	16	349	216	95	55.41
1898/99	27	13	4	10	197	103	53	55.56
1899/1900	34	24	3	7	351	124	93+	75.00
1900/01	25	14	5	6	182	91	51	66.00
1901/02	26	16	1	9	287	142	77	63.46
1902/03	28	22	3	3	353+	59+	88+	83.93
1903/04	24	14	3	7	127+	70+	32+	64.58
1904/05	27	20	1	6	242	80	68	75.93
1905/06	30	16	4	10	211	137	60	60.00
1906/07	33	18	3	12	196+	106+	52+	59.09
1907/08	26	13	0	13	188	140	52	50.00
1908/09	33	19	3	11	125+	138+	33+	62.12
1909/10	36	18	7	11	200	160	27+	59.72
Total	476	297	48	131	4040+	1752+	1044+	67.44

Three seasons had win rates of over 80%, three over 70%, four over 60% and five over 50%, with the poorest season being one with a win rate of 50% where as many games were won as lost. The average win rate over the 16 seasons was 67.44% which was a high percentage over such a long time against strong opposition.

The Golden Era Of Welsh Rugby
The Golden Era of Welsh Rugby took in the years 1900 to 1910. During these years, Wales were extremely successful on the International front, winning five Triple Crowns and two Grand Slams, and beating the All Blacks in 1905. The era saw plenty of talented players in Wales and some strong Club sides which Mount took on, and beat.

The Club's Fixtures
The Old Firm took on and beat some of the strongest Clubs in Wales, England and Ireland such as Llanelly, Abertillery, Neath, Aberavon, Newport, Penarth, Pontypool, Llwynypia, Maesteg, Penygraig, Pontypridd, Treorky, Ebbw Vale, Bridgend and London Welsh. There were also wins over English opposition in the form of Leicester, Bridgwater and Albion, Plymouth, Hartlepool Rovers, Bath, Plymouth and Taunton, and Irish Clubs, Belfast Collegians and Dublin Old Wesley.

International Recognition
Five players in total from Mountain Ash RFC were capped by Wales during this era. Four of these represented Wales on a total of 18 occasions while playing for the Club. Fred Millar (1896-1901, 7 caps) played in the Welsh Triple Crown winning season of 1900, Will Osborne (1902-1903, 6 caps) in the Triple Crown winning team of 1902, Wyndham Jones (1905, 1 cap) scored one try and made a second in Wales' 10-3 win over Ireland in 1905 which won the Triple Crown for a third time, and Dick Thomas (1906-1909, 4 caps) played in the 1908 and 1909 Welsh teams that won the Triple Crown and Grand Slam in successive seasons, the Grand Slam being the first ever won by Wales as France joined the competition, the Four Nations becoming the Five Nations. And of course there was also forward Frank Mills, whose International career was well underway when the Club's "First Golden Era" started. Although he played for the Club at various times between 1892 and 1896 when his 13 Welsh caps were awarded, these are usually attributed to Swansea and Cardiff RFCs, although some historical books list Mountain Ash as one of his Clubs due to the fact that he played for the Old Firm during his International career. All in all, these 5 Mount players amassed 31 Welsh International caps in the "Golden Era" of Welsh rugby, which was an impressive total for a so-called "second class" Club.

Glamorgan League Championships
This was *the* competition to win for the strongest of the valley Clubs. The Old Firm won the Glamorgan League on two occasions during this era, in 1895/96 and 1908/09. On two other occasions, the Club finished joint top of the table but lost the play-off in 1894/95, when the competition was known as the Rhondda, Merthyr & Aberdare League, and in 1904/05. Year in, year out, Mount was one of the teams a Club had to beat if it was to have any chance of winning this prestigious tournament.

Canadian National XV Beaten
In 1902/03, the Old Firm beat the first touring Canadian national XV on their tour of Great Britain, winning 28-0.

Mount Player Sets New Welsh Try Scoring Record
Along with Fred Jowett of Swansea, Mount wing Reuben Carpenter set a new Welsh try scoring record for a season when he ran in 42 tries in 1902/03.

Mountain Ash Rugby Football Club
"The Old Firm"

The 1910s

The Playing Record Of The 1910s

Only 5 seasons were played between 1910 and 1920 due to the First World War putting rugby well and truly in the background from 1914-18. In the playing years, the Club also run a reserve team and junior teams. Below are the known seasonal playing records of the 1910s:

Season	P	W	D	L	For	Against	Tries Scored	%
1910/11	39	21	3	15	179+	124+	18+	57.69
1911/12	36	20	6	10	188	137	19+	63.89
1912/13	28	10	4	14	131	159	26+	42.86
1913/14	40	21	6	13	179+	229+	31+	60.00
1919/20	24	5	4	15	49	147	10+	29.17
Total for 1910s	167	77	23	67	726+	796+	104+	52.99

The seasons leading up to 1913/14 were rebuilding ones, with the reward coming in the last season before the outbreak of war.

The Old Firm's Fixtures During The Decade

The years up to 1914 were a continuation of the "Golden Era" of Welsh rugby, which spanned from 1900 to 1914. Although regarded as a "second class" Club, Mount frequently took on and beat what the media regarded as "first class" Clubs. The decade saw the first known fixtures with Cardiff and occasional games against Swansea and Llanelly. There were regular fixtures against Bridgend, Abertillery, Neath, Cross Keys, Penarth, Pontypridd, Maesteg and Ebbw Vale, amongst others. The Old Firm made frequent trips into England, usually going on tour at Christmas and Easter, and played Bath, Bridgwater and Albion, Cinderford, Coventry and Nuneaton on their travels. There was also a match against Yorkshire Club, Headingley, when they visited South Wales on tour.

The Glamorgan League

As had been the case since its formation in the mid 1890s, the Glamorgan League continued to be *the* competition to win for a valley Club. The Old Firm's regular opposition in the tournament were Treorky, Penygraig, Treherbert, Maesteg, Pontypridd, Ferndale and Llwynypia. The start of the 1910s saw the Old Firm rebuilding and introducing new players. They were runners-up in 1911/12 and lost in the semi-final of the Glamorgan League Cup competition in 1912/13 before achieving success.

Season 1913/14 – "The Double"
The Mount team came of age in this last season before the outbreak of war, being crowned Glamorgan League champions and winning the Glamorgan Times Cup, which was the Glamorgan League's cup competition, beating Maesteg 4-3 in the final at Treherbert, courtesy of a drop goal five minutes from time.

Club Captains
The following players captained the Old Firm between 1910 and 1920:

1910-1911	Jack Hopkins
1911-1912	Arthur H. Loveluck
1912-1913	W. Welch
1913-1914	Tom Sheppard
1914-1916	First World War
1916-1918	W. Mellish
1918-1919	Vic Potter
1919-1920	Tom Sheppard

No rugby was played for two years from 1914 due to the First World War, but some games were played from 1916 on with the Mount team being made up mostly of miners, who were exempt from service. The only full season played in the second half of the decade was 1919/20, veteran forward Tom Sheppard, who had first played for the Old Firm in 1906/07, captaining the Club, which meant he had the distinction of leading the team either side of the War. He was one of the most respected Mount forwards of his generation and played in several Welsh trials, representing the Old Firm for at least eighteen years overall, finishing at the end of the 1924/25 season.

Ground Breaking Tour To France
In March 1912, the Old Firm travelled for the first time outside the U.K. They were among the first Welsh Clubs to travel across the Channel to France, playing games against Bayonne and Pau.

International Recognition Put On Hold
Although forwards Tom Sheppard and Wilfred Perryman were prominent for the Old Firm and fancied for a Welsh cap, there were no further additions to the Club's Internationals, although they and several other Mount players represented Glamorgan County, which was quite an honour during this era of rugby.

The Great War
After winning the "double" in 1913/14 the future was looking bright, but the outbreak of war saw that potential never realised. There is no list of the playing and Club members that lost their lives during the carnage of the War, but the one fatality that is known about is that of the Club's former Welsh International, Dick Thomas, who was capped 4 times between 1906 and 1909. He was killed in action while serving in the Welch Regiment at Mametz Wood in France in the Battle of the Somme on 7 July 1916. He was one of 13 Welsh International players that lost their lives during the First World War.

The End Of The War
The Centenary Season's historical account titled, "The First 100 Years", stated a first General Meeting of the Club was held in December 1918 at the Duffryn Hotel, which only 22 people attended. They were told the Club had an overdraft of £180 – a substantial sum in 1918 – which had to be cleared before a start could be made. The pre-War Chairman, Secretary and Treasurer, Messrs Herbert George, Ted McGregor and David Harris respectively, settled the debt from their own pockets. This very generous gesture saved the Club from extinction and signalled the start of the inter-War era.

Rugby Returns To The Town
The season 1919/20 saw the Old Firm re-emerge after a five year break and start playing regularly once again. It was a tough season against strong opposition but Mountain Ash RFC was up and running again, and it also had its plus points as a future Welsh cap, Tom Collins, made his debut for the Club.

The Trail North
The temptations of being paid to play rugby continued to attract players to the Northern Union, and yet again a handful of players left.

The Club's Ground And Headquarters
The Duffryn Hotel became the Club's new headquarters in 1913/14, replacing the Cresselly Arms. The Old Firm had no regular home pitch and played at a number of locations in or near the town. The team played at the Mountain Ash Athletic Grounds until the end of 1910/11. In 1911/12, they used Mountain Ash Cricket Ground/Duffryn Grove, and after 1913/14 and before 1920/21, the Club started its long use of the Rec and remained there until the end of the 1993/94 season.

The Club's Officers
Jack Jasper was Secretary in 1910/11 and handed over to Ted McGregor, who did the job either side of the First World War until 1920. Mr Herbert George was Chairman for the five seasons played in the decade and David Harris the Club Treasurer. Mr H. Bonham Carter of London was President in 1910/11 and 1912/13, with Lord Aberdare filling the post in 1911/12. It was during the War years that Enoch Watkins, who was associated with some of the Old Firm's greatest moments in the 1920s and 30s, started his 50 year association with the Club, serving as Secretary on several occasions over the years.

Onwards And Upwards
The problem of financing the Club reared its head during the decade. However, come hell or high water, the Old Firm continued playing week by week, season after season, against all opposition whatever their "class".

The 1910s
Season by Season

Season 1910/11

<u>Mount Included In Western Mail Welsh Club Championship</u>

This was the first season in which the "Welsh Club Championship" was mentioned, the Old Firm's playing record being listed in the second tier of the competition in the Western Mail newspaper. There was no official Welsh Championship until the National League started in 1990/91 but the Western Mail published its own table in 1910/11 of what it saw as the leading Clubs. The two Divisions listed in the newspaper at the end of April 1911 showed Clubs with varying differences in the games they had played during the season. How the playing records of the Western Mail divisions were comprised is unknown but it varies markedly from the known playing record of the Old Firm below. The Western Mail table showed 11 more wins and 5 more losses than the known playing record meaning that at least another 16 games took place which are not known about. The Welsh Championship win rate is also far better than the known playing record and is probably a better indication of the Old Firm's season. On the other hand, the Aberdare Leader's reporter, "Muddled Oaf", said in his end of season review in May 1911, "This season has been a very trying one for Mountain Ash Rugby Club", which suggests the season could have been better. From the known records, Mount were unbeaten in the Glamorgan League at the end of November 1910 and inflicted Pontypridd's first loss in the competition with a 7-3 home win. The season also saw wins over Bridgend, Penarth, Penygraig, Blaenavon and Llwynypia. There were some close losses during the season such as the ones against Cross Keys, who were still undefeated in January 1911, Neath, who ended the season as Welsh champions, Penygraig and Treorky. The Irish Club, Garryowen, was on the Mount fixture list for a match in early December 1910, but unfortunately there is no trace of a match report, even in the Garryowen Club when it was queried in 2013. It was also reported that Welsh International forward, Dick Thomas, and centre Jack Hopkins played for the Glamorgan County XV and centre Dai Arthur Davies, who was studying at Goldsmith's College, London, played for Kent. Overall, Mount's record from known games was played 28, won 10, drawn 3 and lost 15, with 110 points scored, which included 18+ tries, and 124 conceded, which gave a win rate of 41.07%. This compared with a "Welsh Championship" playing record of played 34, won 21, drawn 3 and lost 10, with points scored equalling 179, tries scored not being reported, and 113 conceded, which equated to a win rate of 64.70%.

Fixtures 1910/11

Opponents	Date	Venue	Score	Tries	Scorers/Comments
Canton	17 Sep 1910	Home	21-0	Unknown	Mellish 3pts, AN Other 18pts.
Bridgend	15 Oct 1910	Away	8-0	2	Dick Thomas T, Johnny Thomas T, Phillips C.

Opponents	Date	Venue	Score	Tries	Scorers/Comments
Llwynypia (PF)	22 Oct 1910	Away	0-4	0	No scorers.
Penarth	24 Oct 1910	Home	3-0	Unknown	Scorer unknown.
Penygraig (L)	5 Nov 1910	Away	9-8	3	W. Tiley T, Johnny Thomas T, W. Mellish T.
Abertillery	12 Nov 1910	Away	0-10	0	No scorers.
Blaenavon	19 Nov 1910	Home	11-0	3	Jack Hopkins 2T, Jack Thomas C, AN Other T.
Cross Keys	21 Nov 1910	Away	0-5	0	No scorers.
Pontypridd (PL)	3 Dec 1910	Home	7-3	0	Johnny Thomas P, Ivor Bevan DG.
Bargoed (L)	5 Dec 1910	Away	3-4	1	T. Phillips T.
Bath	27 Dec 1910	Away	0-3	0	No scorers.
Bridgwater & Albion	28 Dec 1910	Away	5-10	1	W. Mellish T, Brennan C.
Pontardawe	31 Dec 1910	Home	0-0	0	No scorers.
Penygraig (PL)	7 Jan 1911	Home	5-3	1	Ivor Bevan T, Johnny Thomas C.
Cross Keys	14 Jan 1911	Home	0-3	0	No scorers.
Pontardawe	21 Jan 1911	Away	0-3	0	No scorers.
Penarth	30 Jan 1911	Away	0-9	0	No scorers.
Neath	11 Feb 1911	Away	0-6	0	No scorers.
Llanhilleth	13 Feb 1911	Home	3-6	1	W. Mellish T.
Maesteg (L)	14 Feb 1911	Away	0-23	0	No scorers.
Treorky (L)	4 Mar 1911	Away	0-3	0	No scorers.
Llwynypia (L)	11 Mar 1911	Home	9-3	1	Jack Hopkins DG, George Edwards T, C.
Ferndale (L)	25 Mar 1911	Away	5-6	1	Ivor Bevan T, Johnny Thomas C.
Treorky (L)	1 Apr 1911	Home	0-0	0	No scorers.
Penygraig (Cup)	1 Apr 1911	Home	3-6	1	Griffiths T.
Leicester League	18 Apr 1911	Home	5-3	Unknown	Scorers unknown.
Ferndale (PL)	22 Apr 1911	Home	13-3	3	Ivor Bevan T, Johnny Thomas DG, AN Other 2T.
Bridgend	24 Apr 1911	Home	0-0	0	No scorers.

Summary of Above Playing Record

P	W	D	L	For	Against	Tries Scored	Win Rate %
28	10	3	15	110	124	18+	41.07

Western Mail "Welsh Championship" Playing Record

P	W	D	L	For	Against	Tries Scored	Win Rate %
34	21	3	10	179	113	Unknown	64.70

The playing record shown at the start of the account of this decade under the heading, "The Playing Record of the 1910s", is not the same as any of the two above. This is because both the above contradict each other. For example, the Old Firm lost 15 from the 28 known fixtures listed above but lost only 10 of 34 Western Mail "Welsh Championship" games. What is known about this season is that Mount won at least 21 games, drew at least 3 and lost at least 15. These three add up to 39 games. Therefore the known playing record is recorded as played 39, won 21, drawn 3 and lost 15, which gave a win rate of 57.69%. The same principle has been applied to points and tries, making the totals 179+ for points scored, 124+ conceded, and 18+ tries scored.

Match Reports and Publications

15 October 1910

<u>Bridgend 0 Mountain Ash 8</u>

Mount Team: Full back, Johnny Thomas; ¾ backs, Bevan, J. Hopkins, Jimmy Donovan, Rogers; half backs, George & Phillips; forwards, P.C. Dick Thomas*, Geo. Llewellyn, Tom Shepherd, Alf Jenkins, G. Bowen, T. Griffiths, Alf Williams, A. Lewis.

* denotes Welsh International

"Muddled Oaf" reported in the Aberdare Leader, "No score was registered at the interval. After the change of ends, Dick Thomas romped over with a brilliant unconverted try. Later, Johnny Thomas scored a try, which was majorised by Phillips, the half-back."

5 November 1910

The Aberdare Leader reported, "Police Constable Dick Thomas (4 Welsh caps in 1906, 1908 and 1909 while playing for the Old Firm) of Mountain Ash captained the Glamorgan County XV in their Inter-League match against Monmouthshire at Brynmawr on Saturday. J. Hopkins, the Mountain Ash centre three-quarter was also honoured. He opened the score for Glamorgan with a clever try. The critics present considered Hopkins the finest centre on the field."

3 December 1910

<u>Mountain Ash 7 Pontypridd 3</u>
<u>Possible Glamorgan League Fixture</u>

Mount Team: Full back, C. Davies; ¾ backs, Jack Hopkins, W.A. Tiley, Mellish, Ivor Bevan; half backs, Tom Phillips and Johnny Thomas; forwards, P.C. Dick Thomas*, Tom Shepherd, Alf Williams, George Caple, A. Jenkins, G. Llewellyn, Dick Jarman, Alf Fryer.

* denotes Welsh International

"Muddled Oaf" reported in the Aberdare Leader, "Played at Mountain Ash last Saturday, both teams were previously undefeated in the Glamorgan League competition....an infringement secured a penalty, which Johnny Thomas kicked for a half time lead of 3-0 to Mount. Play in the second moiety became very exciting and Ponty failed from several free kicks. Jenkins, in fielding the ball from a cross-kick, fed Bevan, who dropped a pretty goal amongst a bunch of his Ponty opponents....So the homesters succeeded in smashing Ponty's League record at last! For Mount, P.C. Dick Thomas played a becoming game throughout. Splendid work was also contributed amongst the forwards by Tom Shepherd, George Caple and Dick Jarman. At half back, Phillips was quite nippy, whilst Johnny Thomas was clever and effective. The pick of the third line were Jack Hopkins and Mellish."

5 December 1910

Bargoed 4 Mountain Ash 3
Glamorgan League
Western Mail

SENSATIONAL FINISH.

GAME AT BARGOED TERMINATES IN DISORDER.

	G.	T.	P'ts.
BARGOED	1	0	4
Mountain Ash	0	1	3

Perhaps the most sensational finish to an important football match in the Rhymney Valley was that of Bargoed v. Mountain Ash on Saturday. The fixture was played at Bargoed, and the first half ended with the homesters leading by a dropped goal, kicked by E. J. Rees, their centre.

Play in the second half was not vigorous, but curious at times, and it was evident that the "Old Firm" were bent on winning. It was a Glamorgan League match, and the men of "Mount" had not yet been whacked this season. Fully twenty minutes of the second half had passed and no points had been registered by the visitors. They were the aggressors now, however, and the argument was in the home territory.

Play was loose and rough, and, following on a scramble, Phillips, for Mountain Ash, dribbled the ball over the line. He did not touch the ball down, but was knocked out. The ball was kicked out of bounds. The referee awarded Mountain Ash a try. Then there was a row. Spectators rushed into the field of play, and between them and certain players who protested against the try the referee was in quite an uncomfortable situation for some time. Mountain Ash missed with the kick at goal. Mr. Gamlin (Pontypridd), the referee, stopped the game before time, stating that he did this in consequence of the conduct of the home spectators and players. The affair will be reported to the Welsh Union.

27 December 1910

Bath 3 Mountain Ash 0
Western Mail

MOUNTAIN ASH DEFEATED BY A PENALTY TRY.

	G.	T.	P'ts.
BATH	0	1	3
Mountain Ash	0	0	0

Mountain Ash fielded at Bath on Boxing Day the best forward team they have played, and were rather unfortunate to lose. In the first five minutes the ball got among the Bath three-quarters near the Welshmen's line, and Russell dribbled across. He was fouled, and the referee awarded a penalty try, which was not converted. Caple led the visiting forwards grandly. Vincent Coates, of Cambridge, was of great assistance to Bath, his tackling being immense.

28 December 1910

<u>Bridgwater & Albion 10 Mountain Ash 5</u>
<u>Western Mail</u>

A FORWARD GAME.

MOUNTAIN ASH UNFORTUNATE IN SOMERSET.

The game was largely of a forward character, occasionally brightened by good outside play. The visiting backs lost some capital chances by dropping passes, but were unfortunate in not scoring more, a curious decision of the referee in the first half robbing them of one try. Bridgwater were superior in the first half, but Mountain Ash were much the better side in the second, and their try was very smartly obtained.

7 January 1911

<u>Mountain Ash 5 Penygraig 3</u>
<u>Possible Glamorgan League Fixture</u>

Mount Team: Full back, Johnny Thomas; ¾ backs, Ivor Bevan, Dai Arthur Davies, Jack Hopkins, Mellish; half backs, Tom Phillips, P.C. Dick Thomas*; forwards, Tom Shepherd, Alf Fryer, D. Bowen, A. Jenkins, Joe Ellery, Dick Jarman, Dai Davies, Warren.

* denotes Welsh International

"Muddled Oaf" wrote in the Aberdare Leader, "This important Glamorgan League match took place at Mountain Ash last Saturday. The Mount team have not lost a point in the League tourney this season." He also continued to say, "In the Welsh Football Union Club Championship, the Mountain Ash Club are topmost, having played 14 matches, won 11, lost 3 and drawn 0, and have a record of 78.50 Championship points."

14 January 1911

<u>Mountain Ash 0 Cross Keys 3</u>

Mount Team: Full back, Johnny Thomas; ¾ backs, Jack Hopkins, Dai Arthur Davies, Ivor Bevan, Mellish; half backs, Tom Phillips, P.C. Bevan; forwards, P.C. Dick Thomas*, Owen, Alf Fryer, Dai Davies, George Caple, Merry, Joe Ellery and Dick Jarman.

* denotes Welsh International

The Aberdare Leader reported, "The undefeated Monmouthshire League team were entertained by the Mount team in the return match at Mountain Ash....the Mountaineers failed to score having been awarded two penalty kicks. In the second moiety, Cross Keys succeeded in registering a try. The visitors were afterwards so severely penned within their own territory that they withdrew three forwards for defence. Yet the homesters failed to score and had to submit to a defeat by 3-0."

13 February 1911

Western Mail

WELSH CLUB CHAMPIONSHIP.

	P.	W.	D.	L.	Points For	Points Agst.	Percentage of Wins.
Cardiff	24	21	0	3	335	69	87.50
Swansea	25	21	1	3	382	64	86.00
Neath	25	19	2	4	278	49	80.00
Abertillery	26	18	4	4	219	79	76.92
Newport	26	18	1	7	274	105	71.15
Pontypool	28	15	6	7	179	79	64.28
Llanelly	21	12	2	7	191	136	61.90
Aberavon	24	10	3	11	131	92	47.91

	P.	W.	D.	L.	Points For	Points Agst.	Percentage of Wins.
Pontardawe	16	14	1	3	129	45	80.55
Brynmawr	24	17	2	5	214	45	75.00
Treorky	26	17	2	7	184	105	69.23
Pontypridd	23	12	5	6	123	98	63.04
Mountain Ash	19	11	0	8	120	86	57.80
Penygraig	22	10	2	10	123	95	50.00
Bridgend	22	7	1	14	97	244	34.09

A draw counts as half a win.

24 April 1911

Mountain Ash 0 Bridgend 0
South Wales Daily News

MOUNTAIN ASH v. BRIDGEND.

Mountain Ash, 0; Bridgend, 0.

The home team were all round superior to the visitors, but score they could not either by forward dribbles or passing by the backs. Bridgend deserve praise for their defence, which never wavered, but still they were lucky to avoid defeat. The home halves and forwards were easily better than the visitors' halves and threes, and Shepherd should be singled out for special mention. Jones, the visiting back, although not as good as J. Thomas, got through a tremendous amount of work.

24 April 1911

Western Mail

Welsh Rugby Club Championship.

NEATH TOP FOR SECOND YEAR.

	P.	W.	L.	D.	Points F.	Points A.	P'age.
Neath	38	31	4	3	436	72	85.52
Cardiff	36	29	6	1	479	131	81.94
Swansea	37	28	6	3	449	115	79.72
Abertillery	38	25	6	7	286	123	75.00
Newport	38	25	9	4	386	156	71.05
Pontypool	43	25	10	8	254	108	67.44
Llanelly	34	18	12	4	211	213	58.82
Pontardawe	30	24	5	1	233	89	81.66
Treorky	35	26	7	3	272	128	78.57
Pontypridd	36	22	8	6	270	166	69.44
Brynmawr	32	21	9	2	246	68	68.75
Mo'tain Ash	34	21	10	3	179	113	64.70
Aberavon	35	17	13	4	212	118	54.28
Penygraig	28	12	14	2	137	167	46.42
Bridgend	34	9	23	2	131	334	29.41

13 May 1911

Review of the Clubs

"Muddled Oaf" gave a very brief report of the season in the Aberdare Leader as follows: "This season has been a very trying one for Mountain Ash Rugby Club. However, several juniors of real merit have been unearthed, especially Ivor Bevan, who has become quite a versatile wing three-quarter. Mr Jack Jasper, the team's plucky Secretary, has worked very hard indeed to keep the team above water and Mr Herbert George, solicitor, has given great assistance to the team."

Season 1911/12

Old Firm Break New Ground With French Tour
New Look Team Finish Runners-Up In Glamorgan League

In March 1912, Mountain Ash RFC became one of the first Welsh Clubs to cross the Channel to play French opposition. In Mount's case, the Clubs concerned were Pau and Bayonne and in two accounts of the Club's history, firstly in a Welsh rugby magazine called "Rugger Sport" in November 1964, and secondly in the 1975/76 Centenary publication, "The First 100 Years", it was stated both these French Clubs were beaten on this very first overseas tour. Unfortunately, there were no match reports in the Aberdare Leader although there was reference to the trip, and, despite contacting both French Clubs in 2014, no information was forthcoming. The tour was ground breaking stuff back in 1912 and was the first of several tours the Club went on to make, with the others being in the first half of the 1920s. The Old Firm started the season late due to a decision to postpone fixtures in September 1911 owing to "quite a number of members of the "Old Firm"....on active service....and have joined Kitchener's Army." When the season did get underway, there was a convincing home win over Cross Keys plus other wins over Maesteg, Penarth, Pontypridd and Abertillery, the latter being described as "the Monmouthshire Champions." There was also a home draw with Treorky which resulted in a visiting player being escorted, for his own safety, from the ground by a selection of Mount players and the police! There were other, less exciting draws, such as the one at Bath on Boxing Day 1911, at home to Bridgend, and away at Pontypridd. There were also close defeats at Penarth, Aberavon and Llwynypia. For a second season, the Old Firm were included in the Western Mail's Welsh Club Championship and once again had a better playing record than that compiled from known games played. The Aberdare Leader's rugby reporter, "Muddled Oaf", wrote on 27 April 1912, "In the Welsh Championship Tourney, the Mountain Ash team have now played 36 matches, won 20, lost 10 and drawn 6. They have secured 188 points for and 137 against and have a total of 63.89%. They are now fourth on the list." There was also a complimentary comment made in the match report of the home win over Cross Keys in September 1911, the Western Mail's reporter commenting, "....the Welsh Rugby Union will find in the Old Firm's ranks a couple worthy to don the scarlet before the season is over." The Club finished the season as runners-up in the Glamorgan League and it was also reported in the Aberdare Leader that, "Dai Bowen, the clever forward of the Mount XV, has been selected to represent Glamorgan County in their inter-league match against Monmouthshire at Pontypridd", and, "Mr Herbert George, solicitor, the Vice President of Mountain Ash RFC, has obtained a seat on the Glamorgan County Committee." All these facts and comments suggest it was one of the most eventful seasons in the Club's 36 year history. The only downside was the departure at the end of the season of Mount's Welsh International forward, Dick Thomas, to Bridgend, due to him being posted there as a police constable. Thomas had played for the Club since 1904/05 and was described in the Aberdare Leader as the "idol of the Gods".

Fixtures 1911/12

Opponents	Date	Venue	Score	Tries	Scorers/Comments
Cross Keys	25 Sep 1911	Home	17-6	Unknown	Scorers unknown.
Resolven	7 Oct 1911	Home	3-0	1	AN Other T.
Abertillery	14 Oct 1911	Away	3-16	0	Scorer unknown.
Treorky (F)	16 Oct 1911	Away	0-8	0	No scorers.
Penarth	28 Oct 1911	Away	6-8	2	Ivor Bevan T, Fryer T.
Aberavon	30 Oct 1911	Away	0-6	0	No scorers.
Bridgend	6 Nov 1911	Home	3-3	1	Ivor Bevan T.
Ferndale (PL)	18 Nov 1911	Away	3-0	1	C. Merry T.
Treherbert (PL)	2 Dec 1911	Home	12-0	4	Ivor Bevan T, Jack Hopkins T, Mansfield T, AN Other T.

Opponents	Date	Venue	Score	Tries	Scorers/Comments
Maesteg (PL)	9 Dec 1911	Home	6-0	2	Tich Thomas T, Owen Jones T.
Bath	27 Dec 1911	Away	3-3	1	Owen Jones T.
Penarth	30 Dec 1911	Home	3-0	1	Owen Jones T.
Pontardawe	27 Jan 1912	Home	6-0	2	Thomas T, Ted Bradford T.
Abertillery	3 Feb 1912	Home	6-4	0	Bowen T, Bradford T.
Aberavon	17 Feb 1912	Home	0-4	0	No scorers.
Pau (France)	9 Mar 1912	Away	Unknown	Unknown	Scorers unknown.
Bayonne (France)	9 Mar 1912	Away	Unknown	Unknown	Scorers unknown.
Llwynypia (PL)	9 Mar 1912	Home	0-3	0	No scorers.
Treherbert (PL)	16 Mar 1912	Away	5-3	1	Breacher T, Dick Jarman C.
Treorky (L)	30 Mar 1912	Home	0-0	0	No scorers.
Pontypridd (L)	6 Apr 1912	Home	3-3	1	Owen Jones T.
Pontypridd (L)	13 Apr 1912	Away	6-3	2	Shepherd T, Ivor Bevan T.
Maesteg (L)	27 Apr 1912	Away	0-8	0	No scorers.
Newbridge	30 Apr 1912	Away	0-6	0	No scorers.

Summary of Above Playing Record

P	W	D	L	Results Unknown	For	Against	Tries Scored	Win Rate %
24	10	4	8	2	85+	84+	19+	54.55

Western Mail "Welsh Championship" Playing Record

P	W	D	L	For	Against	Tries Scored	Win Rate %
36	20	6	10	188	137	Unknown	63.89

The Western Mail "Welsh Championship" playing record above, other than tries scored which were not published, has been used at the start of the account of this decade under the heading, "The Playing Record of the 1910s". It shows more games played, more wins, more draws, more losses, and more points scored and conceded, and is a fairer reflection of the season based on known games played.

Match Reports and Publications

5 August 1911

<u>The Mountain Ash Rugby Football Club</u>

The Aberdare Leader reported, "The annual general meeting of the above Club was held on Saturday evening last at the Glancynon Hotel. The chair was occupied by Mr Herbert George, solicitor, who was supported by Messrs David Harris, Treasurer of the Club, and E.R. McGregor. Mr. J.J. Jasper, the Secretary, presented the balance sheet of the Club, which was adopted. The election of Officers took place as follows: President, Lord Aberdare; Vice President, Mr. H. Bonham Carter, London; Captain, Mr Jack Hopkins; Treasurer, Mr David Harris; Hon. Secretary, Mr J.J. Jasper, 42 Aberpennar Road, Mountain Ash. Committee: Messrs Herbert George (Chairman), J.T. Wheeler, E.R. McGregor, W. Cresswell, D. Griffiths, W. Payne, D. Davies, D. Horrigan, J. Morgan, W. Gregory, C. Wilkins, D. Bevan, J. Jones, H. Rees, E. Bradwick, D. Rees, B. Davies, E. James, R. Evans and J. Price.

All the old players will be available with the exception of Wyndham Jones (Mount's Welsh International) and George Edwards, who will be substituted by Llewellyn Morgan and Blythe of Penygraig. The team will play all their matches on the Mountain Ash Cricket Ground, which is situated near the Duffryn Grove. They will also run a reserve team and two junior Clubs, who will play their matches on Mondays."

10 September 1911

<u>Old Firm's Patriotic Move</u>

The Aberdare Leader reported the following, "The members of the Mountain Ash Rugby Football Club have decided not to proceed with their fixture list for the present, at any rate. The season was to have commenced on Saturday last with a trial match. The keen recruiting during the week, however, had taken away all interest in football and the Club decided to suspend operations. Quite a number of members of the "Old Firm" are on active service and have joined Kitchener's Army. Mr E.R. McGregor, the Old Firm's Secretary, did good work as recruiting officer of Mountain Ash during the week."

25 September 1911

<u>Mountain Ash 17 Cross Keys 6</u>
<u>Western Mail</u>

STILL ALIVE.

THE "OLD FIRM" GIVE A SPLENDID EXHIBITION.

	G.	T.	P'ts.
MOUNTAIN ASH	3	1	17
Cross Keys	0	2	6

The "Old Firm" are not yet dead, for on Saturday they showed their followers and the visiting team, Cross Keys, that they are yet worthy exponents of the Rugby code in the Aberdare Valley. The Mount forwards worked like Trojans, and, headed by P.C. Perryman and Shepherd, were continually on the leather, and if they maintain their present form the Welsh Rugby Union will find in the "Old Firm's" ranks a couple worthy to don the scarlet ere the season is over. The game was played in good spirit, and, despite the greasy state of the turf, some splendid bouts of passing were witnessed on both sides. Mention must be made of Lloyd Jones (late of Pontypridd), whose attack was fine, and Bacon (Cross Keys), who continually saved his side from disaster.

6 November 1911

<u>Mountain Ash 3 Bridgend 3</u>

FORTUNATE BRIDGEND.

OVEREAGER "OLD FIRM" PLAYERS LOSE SCORES.

The Western Mail reported, "The Bridgenders were decidedly fortunate in dividing the honours at Mountain Ash for the Old Firm were infinitely the better team, and it was only over-eagerness of the forwards that prevented scores. The little passing witnessed during a pleasantly contested game was contributed by the Old Firm's backs, of whom Ivor Bevan played brilliantly on the left wing….Bridgend opened the scoring. The Old Firm soon equalised, Thomas initiating a fine passing movement which resulted in Bevan scoring a really fine try. For Mountain Ash, Johnny Thomas, Ivor Bevan, Mock, Shepherd and Bowen were the pick…."

9 December 1911

Glamorgan League Table

Club	P	W	D	L	Points
Mountain Ash	4	4	0	0	8
Ferndale	6	3	2	1	8
Pontypridd	3	2	1	0	5
Penygraig	5	1	2	2	4
Treorky	4	2	0	2	4
Llwynypia	3	1	1	1	3
Maesteg	3	0	2	1	2
Treherbert	5	0	0	5	0

27 December 1911

Bath 3 Mountain Ash 3
Western Mail

MUD SCRAMBLE AT BATH.

MOUNTAIN ASH PLAYER GETS LEG BROKEN.

	G.	T.	P'ts.
Mountain Ash	0	1	3
Bath	1	0	3

In pouring rain. The ground was like a quagmire, and football was of the poorest description in consequence. Bath invaded the Welshmen's quarter directly, and Norman Coates landed a penalty goal.

Mountain Ash speedily equalised. Their three-quarters brought off quite a clever round of passing. They were playing five three-quarters, and Owen Jones dived over in the corner. Level play was witnessed till the interval.

Bath were hard pressed on resuming. Jones kicking well for them. In a tackle O'Leary, one of the Mountain Ash forwards, broke his leg, and was removed on an ambulance. A veritable mud scramble ended in a draw of three points each.

3 February 1912

<u>Mountain Ash 6 Abertillery 4</u>

Mount Team: Back, A. Mock; ¾ backs, Bradford, Jack Hopkins, M. Mansfield, Ivor Bevan; half backs, Owen Jones and Thomas; forwards, Tom Shepherd, C. Merry, Dai Bowen, P.C. Perryman, Dick Jarman, Breacher, Joe Ellery, Hendy.

"Muddled Oaf" reported in the Aberdare Leader, "The previous encounter at Abertillery ended in a win for the Monmouthshire team. Mountain Ash were minus Jack Thomas at full back, one of the Mansfield brothers at three-quarter, and Caple and Fryer in the forward line….In the first few minutes, Abertillery secured from a scrummage and Richardson dropped a goal….Bevan of Mountain Ash nearly scored…. Mock, from a free kick, almost dropped a goal….Bowen scored, but the referee disallowed the point…. Bevan was held on the line. From the following scrummage, Bowen succeeded in scoring near the uprights, and Jones failed with the resulting kick. After the restart, a round of passing by the homesters resulted in Bradford scoring, but Mr Morgan, the referee, again disallowed the point….Bradford succeeded in scoring the winning points, he, however, failed to convert. For the Mount, the pick were Mock at full back, Mansfield, Bevan and Bradford amongst the backs and Shepherd, Breacher and Bowen of the forwards."

17 February 1912

<u>Mountain Ash 0 Aberavon 4</u>

Mount Team: Back, Johnny Thomas; ¾ backs, Ivor Bevan, Jack Hopkins, Ike Mansfield, Ted Bradford; half backs, Owen Jones, Tich Thomas; forwards, Tom Shepherd, George Caple, P.C. Perryman, Dick Jarman, Joe Ellery, D. Bowen, W. Williams and Ballinger.

"Muddled Oaf" reported in the Aberdare Leader, "Mr John, the referee, had cause to send one of the visiting players off the field for striking one of the home forwards. Mansfield carried the ball over the line and claimed a try which the referee, however, disallowed. No score was registered up till the interval. In the second half, Hopkins, the visiting outside half received the ball and dropped a clever goal. So, Aberavon won the match by a dropped goal, 4 points to nil."

The Old Firm's French Tour
March 1912

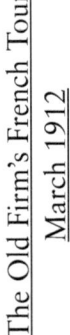

Back Row L-R: A.N. Other, A.N. Other (both in suits), Caple, Bowden, Merry, A.N. Other (in suit), Perryman, Shepherd, Jarman, Breacher, Williams, Cresswell (Linesman),

Middle Row L-R: Mansfield, West, Hopkins Capt, Bevan, Bradford,

Front Row L-R: Morgan (Trainer, kneeling), Thomas (sitting), Beer (sitting), Jones (Trainer, kneeling).

9 March 1912

The following is an exact duplicate of what was published in the Aberdare Leader:

<u>The "Old Firm" in France</u>
<u>A Few Quotes by "Drank"</u>

"One of the forwards thought he was going to die going over in the boat.

The customs authorities came down on a famous box of cigarettes, and not getting the duty, the officer shared the lot amongst the team.

The Parisian food was not to the liking of Dai, skipper Jack and Braddy. They didn't half beef about the house, and oh – the worm soup.

Who lost his bag? A bad shot and 8 miles from nowhere, shaveless and shirtless for the rest of the journey.

The luncheon basket at Pau was like Mother Hubbard's cupboard, at any rate only enough for one individual, and so the others had none, poor things.

What a raid on the picture postcard shops. Naughty, naughty; they wouldn't pass through the English post.

That's not an aeroplane", said Boniface. "It's one of Lord Aberdare's pigeons. But it was the sort of pigeon they don't make pie of.

Do you confetti? One of the team, a forward, left his heart in charge of a dainty mademoiselle. He's going back."

30 March 1912

<u>Mountain Ash 0 Treorky 0</u>
<u>Glamorgan League</u>

Mount Team: Back, Ted Bradford; 3/4s, Ivor Bevan, Owen Jones, Bert Morgan, M. Mansfield; half-backs, Ike Mansfield and Tich Thomas; forwards, Dai Bowen, P.C. Perryman, Hubert Fortt, Dick Jarman, Breacher, Alf Fryer, Williams and Dick Fryer.

<u>Keen Game at the Mount</u>

"Muddled Oaf" reported in the Aberdare Leader, "An important meeting between the old League rivals took place at the Mount on Saturday. The previous match had resulted in a win for the Rhondda men….After the interval, the match became very vigorous and the referee had occasion to caution several players. Eventually he sent Hayward, one of the Treorky forwards, off the field for deliberately fouling Tich Thomas, the home half back. This greatly incensed the crowd, and Hayward was escorted from the field by the police, assisted by the Mountain Ash players. The result was a pointless draw. It was one of the keenest games of the season, and although the Old Firm played a good game, they were handicapped in being without a few of their best men. The most prominent player on the home side was, without doubt, Tich Thomas the half back, M. Mansfield, Ted Bradford at full back, and Bert Morgan also performed admirably. The pick of the forwards were Dai Bowen, P.C. Perryman and Dick Jarman. In the Glamorgan League matches, the Mount has now played 11 matches, won 7, lost 3 and drawn 1, and have a total of 15 League points."

Western Mail

AN ANGRY CROWD.
SCENE AT THE MATCH AT MOUNTAINS ASH.

	G.	T.	P'ts.
Mountain Ash	0	0	0
Treorky	0	0	0

There was an unpleasant incident in the pointless match at Mountain Ash on Saturday. The game was rough, and Haywood was given marching orders for fouling Tich Thomas. When Haywood was sent off the field the crowd rushed on, but he was guarded by the police and Mountain Ash players, who escorted him to the street with no hurt.

Mr. G. Walters, the referee, in an interview, said:—"Haywood deliverately fouled Thomas, and I did not hesitate to order him off the field."

6 April 1912

Mountain Ash 3 Pontypridd 3
Glamorgan League

"Muddled Oaf" reported in the Aberdare Leader, "….The Mount has now gradually ascended the League ladder, and, by virtue of the draw, have become the runners-up to Treorky for the Championship. I understand that the Mount fifteen have been invited to play a home and away engagement with the famous Swansea Club during next season. This will give a great fillip to the rugger code down the Mount."

13 April 1912

Pontypridd 3 Mountain Ash 6
Glamorgan League
Grand Achievement by the Old Firm

The Aberdare Leader reported, "….the Mountain Ash Club have not only secured two valuable points, but have smashed Pontypridd's ground record. Now the Mount team will play Treorky in the final for the Championship of the trophy." This comment contradicted the comment made in the Aberdare Leader above, on 6 April 1912, when it was stated that Treorky had won the Glamorgan League. There is no record of any so-called final or play-off being played and so it has been assumed Treorky were outright winners of the Glamorgan League in 1911/12. The report went on to say, "At a special meeting of the Welsh Union held at Cardiff….the matter of the Mountain Ash v Treorky match was brought for consideration. The Union decided to suspend Hayward, the Treorky forward, till the end of April, for striking Thomas, the Mountain Ash half-back."

20 April 1912

The Aberdare Leader reported, "….the mascot of the Mountain Ash Club is a brown retriever dog, who parades the field every Saturday clothed in black and amber. It is stated that he came out of the Treorky match without a scratch!

The "Mount Nugget", Tich Thomas, the team's diminutive inside half-back, has been making wonderful progress of late. Having played for the Juniors in November last, he is now the star artiste of the Old Firm and a first reserve for Glamorgan County honours.

I understand that P.C. Dick Thomas, our local International, has gone over to the Bridgend Club, for whom he plays a grand game. Dick was the "idol of the Gods" locally, and will be greatly missed."

18 May 1912

Review of Season 1911/12

"Muddled Oaf" reported in the Aberdare Leader, "Never in the history of Mountain Ash Rugby Football Club were so many juniors played as during the past season. The experiment proved a great success. The team named "the Old Firm" could be called "the New Firm" instead. They have played some very interesting and exciting matches and have defeated some of the leading Clubs in Glamorgan. Yet the team was hardly as powerful as the one that won the Glamorgan League in days gone by. Those were the balmy days of Miller (namely Fred Millar, Mount's Welsh International of the late 1890s), Ben Tiley, Wyndham Jones (Welsh International in 1905), Osborne (Will Osborne, Welsh International in 1902 & 1903) and P.C. Dick Thomas (Welsh International in 1906, 1908 & 1909), men who created surprises and who achieved great feats. The full back position this season was at first occupied by the popular Johnny Thomas. In the three-quarters were Ivor Bevan, a brilliant scoring wing, Mansfield, Owen Jones, Ted Bradford, the erstwhile Newtown player, Bert Morgan, the other Mansfield, Jack Hopkins and a few others. At half back, "Tich" Thomas proved himself a veritable Dicky Owen. Of the forwards, Tom Shepherd was, as usual, the shining light, and was grandly supported by Dai Bowen, P.C. Perryman, Dick Jarman, Fryer and several others. The Club's little trip to France was a successful innovation...."

Season 1912/13

Old Firm Take On Strong Opposition In Wales and England

This season saw quite a number of fixtures against English opposition. The Old Firm undertook an arduous Christmas tour when, after travelling all night, they took on Coventry followed by Nuneaton, both in torrential rain and on heavy pitches. Not satisfied with these two games, a third followed on the way home, against Bath. The return of a draw, a win and a narrow loss respectively was quite a good return from 3 games in 3 days against strong opposition! A "double" was achieved over Nuneaton later in the season with a home win, and the defeats at Bath and Cinderford were also overturned on home soil. There were other home wins over Maesteg, who finished the season as Glamorgan League champions, Penarth and Llwynypia, and there was a draw against Pontypridd. There were no details available about where Mount finished in the Glamorgan League, but in the Glamorgan League's Cup competition, known as the Glamorgan Times Cup, the Old Firm lost in the semi-final to Treorky. At Swansea, the season's Welsh champions inflicted one of the biggest ever defeats on the Old Firm – 39-0 – although in the return at Duffryn Grounds, some respect was restored, Swansea only getting home 11-3. There was also a home game against Cardiff which was hard fought but lost 14-0, and there were also close defeats against Neath twice, Bridgend, Abertillery, Penarth and Llanelly. For a third season running, Mount was listed in the Western Mail's so-called Welsh Club Championship 2nd tier, finishing around 11th place with a playing record similar to that compiled from known games played. This showed 28 played, 10 won, 4 drawn and 14 lost, in which 131 points were scored, with the number of tries not reported, and 159 conceded, to give a win rate of 42.86%. This compared to one game less and one less defeat from known games played and 26+ tries scored, which gave a win rate of 44.44%.

Fixtures 1912/13

Opponents	Date	Venue	Score	Tries	Scorers/Comments
Cinderford	21 Sep 1912	Away	0-7	0	No scorers.
Glynneath	28 Sep 1912	Home	5-3	1	Ivor Bevan T, Johnny Thomas C.
Maesteg (PL)	28 Oct 1912	Away	3-11	Unknown	Scorer unknown.
Penygraig (PL)	19 Oct 1912	Away	0-0	0	No scorers.
Cardiff University	26 Oct 1912	Home	17-0	5	Ivor Bevan 2T, Wilkins T, Dick Fryer T, AN Other T, Davies C.
Penarth	9 Nov 1912	Home	7-0	1	Jarman T, DG.
Brynmawr	16 Nov 1912	Home	11-0	3	Blacker T, Lodwick T, Ivor Bevan T, Johnny Thomas C.
Bridgend	23 Nov 1912	Away	3-6	0	Johnny Thomas P.
Pontardawe	7 Dec 1912	Home	3-3	1	Dai Arthur Davies T.
Cardiff	9 Dec 1912	Home	0-14	0	No scorers.
Llwynypia (L)	21 Dec 1912	Home	8-3	2	Dai Arthur Davies T, C, Tom Shepherd T.

Opponents	Date	Venue	Score	Tries	Scorers/Comments
Coventry	27 Dec 1912	Away	3-3	1	Lodwig T.
Nuneaton	28 Dec 1912	Away	12-0	4	Hubert Fortt T, Dai Davies T, Perryman T, Hendy T.
Bath	30 Dec 1912	Away	0-6	0	No scorers.
Abertillery	11 Jan 1913	Home	0-3	0	No scorers.
Neath	18 Jan 1913	Away	3-6	1	Tom Shepherd T.
Cinderford	1 Feb 1913	Home	6-5	2	Josh Davies T, Will Owen T.
Swansea	8 Feb 1913	Away	0-39	0	No scorers.
Penarth	1 Mar 1913	Away	5-6	1	J. Stegman T, Josh Davies C.
Swansea	8 Mar 1913	Home	3-11	1	Ivor Bevan T.
Pontypridd (L)	15 Mar 1913	Home	9-9	1	D.A. Davies T, Perryman DG, Ginger Davies C.
Nuneaton	25 Mar 1913	Home	11-3	Unknown	Scorers unknown.
Bath	26 Mar 1913	Home	8-0	2	Ernie Hill T, C, Warren T.
Llanelly	14 Apr 1913	Away	4-5	0	Ernie Hill DG.
Maesteg (PL)	26 Apr 1913	Home	4-0	0	Ernie Hill DG.
Neath	3 May 1913	Home	0-3	0	No scorers.
Treorky Glamorgan League Cup Semi-Final	3 May 1913	Away	0-8	0	No scorers.

Summary of Above Playing Record

P	W	D	L	For	Against	Tries Scored	Win Rate %
27	10	4	13	125	154	26+	44.44

Western Mail "Welsh Championship" Playing Record

P	W	D	L	For	Against	Tries Scored	Win Rate %
28	10	4	14	131	159	Unknown	42.86

The Western Mail "Welsh Championship" playing record above, other than tries scored which were not published, has been used at the start of the account of this decade under the heading, "The Playing Record of the 1910s". It shows one more game played, the same number of wins and draws, one more loss, and more points scored and conceded, and is a fairer reflection of the season based on known games played.

Match Reports and Publications

9 November 1912

<u>Mountain Ash 7 Penarth 0</u>

Mount Team: Back, Jack Thomas; ¾ backs, Jarman, Joshua Davies, Owen Jones, Ivor Bevan; half backs, Weeks, Lodwig; forwards, Alf Fryer, George Caple, Tom Shepherd, Dick Fryer, P.C. Perryman, Blacker, Fortt, Davies.

The Aberdare Leader's rugby writer, "Muddled Oaf", reported, "This was the best pack of forwards the Old Firm had turned out this season. Penarth's side....was the same team that defeated Cardiff earlier in the season. In the first moiety, Owen Jones, the home centre, got the backs in motion. The ball came to Jarman, the clever wing, who scored a beautiful try for Mount. After half time, Penarth drove to equalise matters but in vain. On the day's form, the Mount men played brilliantly and got the better of their doughty opponents. Eventually, Jarman placed the issue beyond all doubt in dropping a fine goal."

9 December 1912

<u>Mountain Ash 0 Cardiff 14</u>
<u>Western Mail</u>

> Rugby football seems to have fallen on evil days in the Mountain Ash district, and I am quite satisfied from my visit to the Mount on Saturday that but for the self-sacrifice of a few enthusiastic supporters of Rugby in the district the code would be as extinct as the dodo. Their "gates" have dwindled down to practically nothing, and those who have so loyally kept the flag flying are in the unhappy position of being guarantors for a substantial debt to the bank. While I have never been an advocate of systematic grants by the Welsh Union to constituent clubs, I cannot help feeling that this is one of the cases in which the Union ought to come to the assistance of men who have shown a real interest in fostering and preserving Rugby in a district which was up to a few years ago one of the minor strongholds of the game, but which today is almost completely in the hands of our Soccer friends. What is appreciated by these struggling clubs more than Welsh Union grants is the granting of fixtures to them by the leading clubs, and but for the heavy rain and the general wretchedness of the weather on Saturday there would have been an attendance on the Mountain Ash ground which would have yielded considerable financial assistance to the club. One can only hope that the example of Newport and Cardiff, though somewhat belated, will be emulated by Swansea, Llanelly, Neath, and Pontypool, so that the waning interest in Rugby in the Hills districts may be revived. There was a time when Wales found it necessary to go to those districts for the flower of their strong, vigorous manhood, and I have an idea that the day is not far distant when that necessity will arise again, and the Welsh Union, as the controlling authority, are placed under a deep sense of responsibility to realise this with as little delay as possible and before it is too late.

Some of the other comments later on in this report were as follows: "Mountain Ash are to be congratulated upon putting up an exceptionally good fight against Cardiff....The feature of the match was the robust, bustling play of the Mountain Ash forwards....the Cardiff eight had to go all out to give their backs the necessary opportunities....of the Mountain Ash three-quarters....the man to distinguish himself was Ivor Bevan....in the front line, Shepherd and Perryman were the two outstanding players....It was a clean, keen game, in which the Mountain Ash forwards bore the brunt of the battle for their side."

21 December 1912

<u>Mountain Ash 8 Llwynypia 3</u>
<u>Glamorgan League</u>

The Aberdare Leader's rugby reporter, "Muddled Oaf", reported, "Both teams occupy favourable positions in the League. The sides were always keen rivals for the Glamorgan Cup, and in the 90s they fought out two desperate finals on the Taff Vale Park, Pontypridd. The Rhonddaites secured the trophy first, but in the following season, Mountain Ash secured both the Cup and the gold medals (this refers to Llwynypia's Glamorgan League win in 1894/95 after a replay and the Old Firm's Glamorgan League Championship in 1895/96). Tom Shepherd and P.C. Perryman were again the pick of the home forwards, whilst the shining lights of the backs were Mansfield, Ivor Bevan, Josh Davies and Dai Arthur Davies...."

On tour over Christmas 1912, the Old Firm played the following 3 games:

27 December 1912

<u>Coventry 3 Mountain Ash 3</u>
<u>Western Mail</u>

"OLD FIRM" IN COVENTRY.

	G.	T.	P'ts.
Mountain Ash	0	1	3
Coventry	0	1	3

Mountain Ash, after an all night journey, met Coventry in pouring rain and on a soddened turf. The Coventry forwards were scarcely equal to those on the other side, and in the first half an opening was made for Lowerdick, who went through. D. Davies's kick failed. Coventry gave their opponents a lot of trouble in the second half, and a minute before the whistle blew equalised. The visitors played a better game on the whole.

28 December 1912

<u>Nuneaton 0 Mountain Ash 12</u>
<u>Western Mail</u>

GOOD FORWARD PLAY.

	G.	T.	P'ts.
MOUNTAIN ASH	0	4	12
Nuneaton	0	0	0

Nuneaton entertained Mountain Ash on Friday. The game was played in a deluge, with the ground almost a quagmire. Good forward play was witnessed by both sides. Fortte at length scored for the visitors, and just before the interval D. Davies again scored from a cross-kick.

Nuneaton tried desperately in the second half, and the visitors saved luckily several times. Prettyman and Hendy again scored for the visitors after forward work.

30 December 1912

<u>Bath 6 Mountain Ash 0</u>

Mount Team: Full back, S. Weeks; ¾ backs, Jarman, Josh Davies, Dai Arthur Davies, Ivor Bevan; half backs, Lodwig and Morgan; forwards, Tom Shepherd Capt, Bowen, Gibbon, P.C. Perryman, H. Fortt, D. Davies, Jenkins, P.C. John.

The Aberdare Leader reported, "This was the last match of the tour for the Mountaineers and was played at Bath on Saturday last in stormy weather....one of the home forwards scored a try for his side. Even play followed and the Mount were very successful with their kicking, yet the defence of the Bath men was sound. After the change of ends, Bath added another try and emerged victors by 6-0."

11 January 1913

<u>Mountain Ash 0 Abertillery 3</u>

The Aberdare Leader reported, "....Mountain Ash have themselves to blame for this narrow defeat. The homesters, throughout the game, missed many glorious chances – they were poor opportunists.... Tom Shepherd proved himself the finest forward on the field. Shepherd is a magnificent leader...."

18 January 1913

<u>Neath 6 Mountain Ash 3</u>

Mount team: Full back, R. Fryer; ¾ backs, Ivor Bevan, Dai Arthur Davies, S. Weeks, R. Jarman; half backs, Lodwick and the Rev. T.J. Morgan; forwards, Tom Shepherd, P.C. Perryman, D. Bowen, Hubert Fortt, A. Davies, J. Gibbon, J. Jenkins, G. Vigors.

The Aberdare Leader reported, "....The Mountain Ash men again raised the siege and a brilliant burst ended in Tom Shepherd scoring a grand unconverted try....After the change of ends, matters were more even but Neath infused new life into their play. However, Mountain Ash dashed away once more and just missed scoring. The All Blacks had anticipated an easy win. From the start to the finish, the Mount players gave a hard and plucky show, and on the day's play, the Old Firm should have won. The Mount forwards played the best game under the wretched conditions. The most conspicuous on the Mount side were Shepherd, P.C. Perryman, Davies, the Rev. T.J. Morgan, Fryer and D.A. Davies."

8 February 1913

<u>Swansea 39 Mountain Ash 0</u>

At the time of this game, Swansea had lost just one game all season and were on their way to being the season's Welsh Club champions. The Aberdare Leader commented about the game as follows, "....Thus the Old Firm was beaten by the biggest score ever registered against them. The form of the Mount players was below expectation. This match should serve as a great lesson to the Mount players. They can learn a great deal from the methods of the All Whites. Mountain Ash people are ready to give the Swansea Club a hearty welcome on their return visit – the first in their history – to the Duffryn Grounds."

8 March 1913

<u>Mountain Ash 3 Swansea 11</u>

The Aberdare Leader reported, "On Saturday last, the visit of the Welsh champions to the Duffryn Grounds....large crowd present....The Old Firm showed they could still manage to give those teams in the forefront a good game and there were times on Saturday when, with a little more luck, the Mount would have won. The score does not gauge the merits of the sides exactly, for during the most part of the game, the home lot were well up to their opponents and the opinion of the Swansea men was that the Old Firm had given them a very good game. The star artiste on the Swansea side was undoubtedly Jack Bancroft (Bancroft won 18 Welsh caps from 1909 to 1914). His wonderful kicking hampered the Mount forwards and turned an advantage gained by the home men into a loss. Once, however, he made a mistake, and he was clean beaten by Ivor Bevan who scored a try for Mount. The same Ivor Bevan was the best man on the Mount side." The Western Mail commented that "Ivor Bevan crossed....beating Bancroft in the easiest possible fashion....It was a nice sporting game and it is hoped that it will lift the drooping spirits of rugby in the valley."

24 March 1913

Western Mail

WELSH CLUB CHAMPIONSHIP.

	P.	W.	L.	D.	Points For	Points Agst.	Per cent.
Swansea	29	23	1	6	367	66	89.65
Newport	31	22	5	4	385	106	77.41
Abertillery	24	15	4	5	205	59	72.91
Aberavon	27	15	4	8	210	54	70.37
Pontypool	31	18	7	6	175	67	67.74
Neath	29	15	7	7	205	89	63.10
Cardiff	30	17	9	4	378	96	63.33
Llanelly	30	14	10	6	158	104	56.66

	P.	W.	L.	D.	Points For	Points Agst.	Per cent.
Cross Keys	26	23	1	2	388	25	92.30
Maesteg	32	21	3	8	223	57	78.12
Pill Harriers	23	14	5	4	150	37	69.56
Llwynypia	24	13	4	7	140	33	68.75
Pontypridd	26	15	7	6	200	77	61.53
Ferndale	23	11	8	4	101	58	56.52
Penygraig	15	6	6	3	67	87	50.00
Merthyr	27	8	9	11	77	155	50.00
Mountain Ash	25	10	11	4	127	142	48.00
Penarth	23	9	10	4	103	142	47.82
Pontardawe	16	4	5	7	29	35	46.87
Bridgend	24	7	15	3	95	216	33.41

25 March 1913

Mountain Ash 11 Nuneaton 3
Western Mail

A DECISIVE VICTORY.

	G.	T.	P'ts.
MOUNTAIN ASH	1	2	11
Nuneaton	0	1	3

Mountain Ash defeated Nuneaton rather decisively on Monday at Mountain Ash, and were more superior to the visitors than the score would suggest. The home forwards were much stronger, whilst the backs possessed pace and cleverness. Their victory, however, was chiefly due to their forwards.

26 March 1913

Mountain Ash 8 Bath 0
Western Mail

BATH SUFFER DEFEAT.

INTERESTING GAME AT MOUNTAIN ASH.

	G.	T.	P'ts
MOUNTAIN ASH	1	1	8
Bath	0	0	0

The visit of Bath to Mountain Ash on Tuesday brought a fine crowd to the Dyffryn Field. The "Old Firm" was well represented, although Perryman was on the injured list, while Bath brought over a strong team, which included Vincent Coates, the English international.

Shepherd commenced operations for Mountain Ash, who played up the field. From a kick by Ernie Hill an exciting moment ensued. Coates (not the international) failed to hold the ball, and Bethell ran up. A scrum was ordered. The ball came to Ernie Hill and F. Keane, who passed to Ivor Bevan. The home nippy wing sprinted for the line, and a score was only denied him through being held up on the line by the visiting full-back. From a scramble Warren, one of the home forwards, followed up smartly and scored right under the bar. Ernie Hill converted easily. In the course of this play P. P. Hope, the visitors' half-back, was injured, and had to be carried off the field.

In the second half Hope returned, and Bath soon made efforts to equalise. They forged their way up, and several scrums were formed near the Mount line. Relief was at last brought by Ivor Bevan. Hope brought off a really fine run, but was brought down by Josh Davies. The home forwards were putting plenty of energy into their play, and they forced the visitors on the defensive. From a scrum near the line the ball was passed from Lodwick to Ernie Hill, and the latter scored in the corner. F. Keane failed with the kick. Vincent Coates, the international, and his brother Norman brought off some excellent play, but a few minutes later Josh Davies tackled the international in possession. Jarman, one of the home wings, received a gash on the forehead, which compelled him to retire. Coates and his brother worked hard for their team, but they were too closely watched by the home three-quarters.

14 April 1913

Llanelly 5 Mountain Ash 4

The Western Mail commented on this game at Stradey Park, "....The Llanelly players....had anticipated a holiday and felt disappointed that they did not get it.....The visitors are to be complimented upon the dogged fight which they put up, and to Ernie Hill goes not a little of the credit for this. His drop goal was a smart bit of opportunism, and he was distinctly unlucky in failing to win the game for his side when towards the end they were awarded two penalty kicks which were entrusted to him...."

Western Mail

WELSH CLUB CHAMPIONSHIP.

	P.	W.	L.	D.	Points For.	Points Agst.	Per cent.
Swansea	35	27	2	6	416	79	85.71
Newport	36	27	5	4	430	116	80.55
Abertillery	28	17	5	6	217	65	75.00
Aberavon	30	17	5	8	230	59	70.00
Pontypool	36	22	8	6	226	78	69.44
Neath	33	18	8	7	269	119	65.15
Cardiff	36	21	10	5	430	112	62.50
Llanelly	33	15	12	6	163	120	54.54

	P.	W.	L.	D.	Points For.	Points Agst.	Per cent.
Cross Keys	30	26	2	2	433	47	90.00
Maesteg	36	24	4	8	254	62	77.77
Pill Harriers	25	15	5	5	159	43	70.00
Pontypridd	30	16	7	7	220	87	65.00
Llwynypia	27	14	5	7	153	64	64.81
Ferndale	25	12	9	4	118	68	56.00
Merthyr	29	9	10	11	80	163	50.00
Penarth	28	10	13	7	118	159	48.21
Pontardawe	18	5	6	7	32	38	47.22
Penygraig	17	6	7	4	72	108	47.05
Mountain Ash	28	10	14	2	131	159	39.28
Bridgend	27	7	17	4	95	232	33.33

26 April 1913

Mountain Ash 4 Maesteg 0
Possible Glamorgan League Fixture

Mount team: Back, D. Duglan; ¾ backs, Tom Nutt, Josh Davies Capt, Keane, Tom Thomas; half backs, Lodwig and Hill; forwards, Tom Shepherd, Davies, Woolridge, T. Nott, H. Frothy, R. Jarman, J. Gibbon, J. Allen.

The Aberdare Leader reported, "Considerable interest was taken in this important fixture owing to the splendid position which Maesteg occupies in the Glamorgan League. The visitors were powerfully represented whilst the Old Firm were minus Ivor Bevan, the clever wing three-quarter, P.C. Perryman and Jack Thomas, the full back....Mountain Ash were all over their opponents, who showed nothing like the form of League champions....just before the final whistle, Ernie Hill dropped a beautiful goal and thus defeated the League champions. On the day's play, the Old Firm fully justified their win. The forwards were well balanced, whilst the backs left nothing to chance and were almost as good as the original quartette."

Season 1913/14

<u>Old Firm Win "Double"</u>
<u>Glamorgan League Champions & Cup Winners</u>

This was a memorable season for the Old Firm, achieving the holy grail of being crowned Glamorgan League champions through finishing top of the League table and winning the Glamorgan League's cup competition, called the Glamorgan Times Challenge Cup. The winning of the League Championship was the third time the Old Firm had been crowned champions since the competition started in the mid 1890s. The achievement of winning the Cup and League was the ultimate for a Rhondda, Merthyr or Aberdare valley Club as the Glamorgan League was *the* competition to win in this era of rugby. From its inception, it was hard fought-for and was a physically tough tournament to win, with most games close, hard fought affairs that were no place for the faint hearted, and played in front of some large, hostile crowds. Any Club winning the League Championship was a resilient one, but to come out on top in both the Cup and League was special and as good as it got for a valley Club.

Both triumphs did not come easily. From the 9 known League games played, 6 were won – Ferndale H and A, Maesteg H, Treorky H, Pontypridd H and Merthyr H, 2 drawn – Pontypridd A and Llwynypia A, and 1 lost – Maesteg A. The home win over Treorky was described in the Aberdare Leader as the "talk of South Wales". In the Cup competition, there was a first round win over Ferndale and then two typically close, hard fought games in the semi-final against Treherbert, which the Old Firm eventually won 3-0 in the replay, after the first game was drawn 3-3. The final itself, played at Treherbert, was against a fancied Maesteg team which was the previous season's Glamorgan League champions and were one of the Clubs to have lowered the Old Firm's colours in this season's campaign, although Mount had also beaten them as well. The game was hard fought and went down to the wire, a drop goal 5 minutes from time putting the Old Firm in front for the first time in the game, which was a lead they were not to lose. After the final whistle had sounded, Mount captain Hubert Fortt was carried off the field with the Cup amid scenes of great celebration. And the celebrations did not end there either, as the players received a "most hearty welcome" when they returned to Mountain Ash. In a game against old rivals Llwynypia during the season, the Aberdare Leader's rugby reporter, "Muddled Oaf", commented, "Matches between Mountain Ash and Llwynypia have been looked upon as derby meetings. It was at a match with Llwynypia 18 years ago that Mountain Ash took a record gate of £129." The match he was referring to is the one that took place in 1895/96 when Mount won the Glamorgan League for the first time.

The season also saw other notable wins over Penarth and Neath with games also played against two of the "big four" of Welsh rugby in Cardiff at the Arms Park, which was lost 12-6, and Llanelli at Stradey Park, which was lost 21-0 at the start of the season. There was a Christmas tour to the Midlands where two games were played in quick succession, one on Christmas Day 1913 against Nuneaton – lost 22-12 – and a second, probably on Boxing Day, against Coventry – which was also lost, this time 13-6. The Old Firm were a proud, resilient bunch and returned to Nuneaton later in the season, in April 1914, and overturned their Christmas defeat with a 6-5 win.

The known playing record for the season was played 40, won 21, drawn 6, lost 13, with points scored 179+, which included at least 31 tries, and 229+ points conceded, which gave a win rate of 60%. One of the last comments made by "Muddled Oaf" in the Aberdare Leader in his match report of the Cup final win over Maesteg was as follows, "They (Mount) have won the Glamorgan League, the Glamorgan Times Cup and defeated the famous Neath Club. This betokens a new lease of life for the Club and augurs well for next year." As things turned out, he couldn't have been more wrong as the Great War put rugby well and truly in the background for the next 4 years.

Fixtures 1913/14

Opponents	Date	Venue	Score	Tries	Scorers/Comments
Merthyr (L)	15 Sep 1913	Home	4-0	0	Keene DG.
Llanelly	27 Sep 1913	Away	0-21	0	No scorers.
Abertillery	29 Sep 1913	Home	3-8	0+	Scorer unknown.
Cardiff Centrals	11 Oct 1913	Home	14-4	4	Bethel T, Idwal Williams T, Tom Shepherd T, Tich Thomas T, AN Other C.
Treorky (PL)	13 Oct 1913	Away	3-4	1	Tom Shepherd T.
Ferndale (L)	20 Oct 1913	Away	6-3	2	Tich Thomas 2T.
Cwmbran	1 Nov 1913	Home	20-0	Unknown	Scorers unknown.
Glynneath	8 Nov 1913	Away	7-3	0	Davies P, Sid Thomas DG.
Maesteg (L)	10 Nov 1913	Home	6-0	2	Wakely T, W. Welsh T.
Treorky (L)	22 Nov 1913	Home	5-0	1	Wakely T, Weaver C.
Penarth	1 Dec 1913	Away	0-14	0	No scorers.
University College, Cardiff	13 Dec 1913	Home	5-0	1	Mansfield T, Ben Evans C.
Resolven	20 Dec 1913	Home	7-3	1	Hubert Fortt T, Owen Jones DG.
Nuneaton	25 Dec 1913	Away	12-22	Unknown	Scorers unknown.
Coventry	27 Dec 1913	Away	6-13	2	Mansfield T, Warren T.
Llwynypia (PF)	27 Dec 1913	Away	0-16	0	No scorers.
Abertillery	29 Dec 1913	Away	0-5	0	No scorers.
Treherbert (PL)	5 Jan 1914	Home	5-0	1	Sheppard T, England C.
Ferndale (L)	17 Jan 1914	Home	3-0	1	Hubert Fortt T.
Cardiff	19 Jan 1914	Away	6-12	2	Ike Mansfield T, Dick Fryer T.
Llwynypia (PL)	2 Feb 1914	Home	0-3	0	No scorers.
Glynneath	14 Feb 1914	Home	8-8	2	Gibbon T, Welch T, Owen Jones C.
Penarth	21 Feb 1914	Home	9-3	3	Welch T, Hubert Fortt T, Wakely T.
Ferndale Glamorgan Times Cup	21 Feb 1914	Home	5-0	1	Scorers unknown.
Pontypridd (L)	28 Feb 1914	Away	3-3	1	W. Welch T.
Neath	7 Mar 1914	Away	3-3	1	Lodwick T.
Llwynypia (PL)	9 Mar 1914	Home	0-0	0	No scorers.
Treherbert (PL)	21 Mar 1914	Away	3-0	1	Bethel T.

Opponents	Date	Venue	Score	Tries	Scorers/Comments
Resolven	21 Mar 1914	Home	Unknown	Unknown	Mount win. Scorers unknown.
Maesteg (L)	28 Mar 1914	Away	0-9	0	No scorers.
Pontypridd (L)	30 Mar 1914	Home	9-0	2	Welsh T, Weaver P, AN Other T.
Treherbert Glamorgan Times Cup Semi-Final	4 Apr 1914	Pontypridd	3-3	0	Alby Davies P.
Llwynypia (L)	6 Apr 1914	Away	0-0	0	No scorers.
Nuneaton	12 Apr 1914	Away	6-5	0+	Scorers unknown.
Treherbert Glamorgan Times Cup Semi-Final Replay	15 Apr 1914	Pontypridd	3-0	0	Danny England P.
Ferndale (PL)	18 Apr 1914	Away	3-23	1	Ike Mansfield T.
Merthyr (L)	18 Apr 1914	Home	3-0	0	Danny England P.
Pontypool	20 Apr 1914	Away	0-35	0	No scorers.
Neath	2 May 1914	Home	5-3	1	Danny England T, Dai Arthur Davies C.
Maesteg Glamorgan Times Cup Final	9 May 1914	Treherbert	4-3	0	Welsh DG.

Summary of Playing Record

P	W	D	L	For	Against	Tries Scored	Win Rate %
40	21	6	13	179+	229+	31+	60.00

Match Reports and Publications

30 August 1913

The Aberdare Leader reported, "I note that the Mountain Ash Rugby Club is running a grand professional sports meeting with the object of strengthening its funds. I hope their efforts will prove successful for no Club deserves better support than the Old Firm, which has had to surmount so many obstacles during the past few years."

6 September 1913

The Aberdare Leader reported, "Mountain Ash Rugby Football Club – Mr Herbert George, solicitor, has again been appointed Chairman of this Club, whilst Mr D. Harris will once more act as Treasurer. Mr E.R. McGregor has been re-elected Secretary. A strong committee has been formed, which will include new members....The new headquarters will be the Duffryn Hotel, where suitable baths and other facilities have been provided. The Club will again have the use of the Duffryn Grounds. It is the intention of the Club to participate in the Challenge Cup competition that is being arranged by the Welsh Rugby Union."

1 November 1913

"Muddled Oaf" reported in the Aberdare Leader, "Followers of Mountain Ash are strongly of the opinion that Tom Shepherd and P.C. Perryman should gain their International Caps this season. Providing Shepherd maintains his present form, his chances this year are certainly great." The report continued, "I came across Dick Thomas, that great Northern Union forward, in Aberdare on Saturday last. Dick, who is a prominent playing member of the Warrington Club, has been on the sick list during the past few weeks."

8 November 1913

Aberdare Leader reporter, "Muddled Oaf", commented, "Owing to a number of the most prominent members of last season's junior Clubs having become members of the Old Firm this season, the district of Mountain Ash is now without a junior rugger Club. Last year there were three. The officials of the premier organisation would do well were they to form a few Clubs in the district. The Old Firm this season includes the pick of the junior Clubs of the past year. What a pity the Harlequins and Mount Juniors have thrown up the sponge. Surely there is plenty of talent in the town. And what about Penrhiwceiber? Is soccer proving too attractive to some?"

10 November 1913

<u>Mountain Ash 6 Maesteg 0</u>
<u>Glamorgan League</u>
<u>Mountain Ash in Form</u>

The Western Mail reported, "Acting upon a promise made some time ago to a couple of enthusiastic officials who have stood loyally by the Old Firm for some years and saved the Club from extinction, I paid a visit to Mountain Ash on Saturday and saw Maesteg beaten by two tries to nil in the Glamorgan League. The weather was in pleasing contrast to that experienced when Cardiff played at the Mount last season. The sun shone with good grace, and one could see and admire the beauty of the ground's surroundings, and feel quite happy in that little sheltered hollow among the everlasting hills....enhanced one's feelings of satisfaction and content was the spectacle of a record attendance for the season. Let me say at this point that it was the merest fraction of many I have seen at Mountain Ash in the heyday of the Club....Mr Herbert George, the Chairman, and Mr Ted McGregor, the indefatigable Secretary, were simply jubilant in their joyousness and confessed to seeing visions of a reawakened interest in the affairs and doings of the Mountain Ash Club. It fitted in with the circumstances of the day that Mountain Ash should have won the match, and won it purely on merit. They were a better side than Maesteg on the day's form, and if they can cultivate a little more method and finish in their back play, they will go far in the League Championship. But one preliminary essential is that Thomas, the outside half, should remember that there are four three-quarters playing behind him....Prettier play would have been seen if Thomas had passed to centres Welsh and Josh Davies, both of whom were in good fettle. Welsh....gives every promise of developing into a first class centre and I wonder why he has not been given a trial in the Cardiff Reserves. In saying this, I am not suggesting that he should now be taken away from Mountain Ash....but what I do say is that he is a player worth having. The way he made his burst for the line and scored the second try was worthy of a Gwyn Nicholls....It was a grim, strenuous battle between the two packs, and the two men who stood out as being superior to the other fourteen were Shepherd of Mountain Ash and P.C. Williams of Maesteg. The former played his usual honest, resourceful game, and his work in the lineout was particularly good. He was also one of the first down in the scrum and kept his men well together....although the game was disappointing as a spectacle, it was typical of hard, robust, league football. It would have been more enjoyable to all concerned if the backs had been given more of the ball....The Old Firm have now won 3 of 4 League matches and their next merry meeting with Treorky at the Mount next Saturday ought to be another big drawing card."

22 November 1913

<u>Mountain Ash 5 Treorky 0</u>
<u>Glamorgan League</u>

Mount Team: Back, Weaver; ¾ backs, Rhys Evans, Welsh, Flo Keene, Owen Jones; half backs, Tich Thomas and Lodwig; forwards, Tom Shepherd Capt, Warren, P.C. Perryman, Wakely, Dick Fryer, Hubert Fortt, Woolridge, Gibbon.

"Muddled Oaf" reported in the Aberdare Leader, "The leadership of the Glamorgan League depended on the result of this match. Amongst the spectators was Lord Aberdare, who appeared to be keenly interested in the proceedings....Mountain Ash opened the game and immediately assumed the aggressive. Shepherd and Perryman soon headed a brilliant forward rush, and play settled in the Treorky quarters....Tich Thomas broke away from a scrum, crossed the line, but the point was not allowed. A striking feature of the match was the great duel between Daly James and Weaver, the respective custodians. In this end, Weaver appeared to obtain the mastery, and some clever passing on the part of the home backs nearly resulted in a score. From the ensuing lineout, P.C. Perryman initiated a well conceived bout of passing. The home forwards obtained possession, and a brilliant burst enabled Wakely to romp over with a try, which was converted by Weaver.... Although Treorky had brought over their strongest side, they were clearly outclassed in every department by the Old Firm, whose great victory was the talk of South Wales."

29 November 1913

The Aberdare Leader reported, "Police Constable Dick Thomas, the veteran ex-Welsh International, and the doyen of the sporting fraternity at Mountain Ash, is at present a prominent member of the Bridgend Rugby F.C. He combines more than the average strength of a forward with the speed of a three-quarter, and his work in the open is most effective. However, his recent indisposition has kept him out of the team for a while. Ruggerites at Mountain Ash greatly deplore his absence. Nevertheless, the Old Firm is served admirably by another sterling member of the Force in P.C. Perryman, who, together with Tom Shepherd, is a power to contend with."

13 December 1913

Aberdare Leader reporter, "Muddled Oaf", commented, "Tom Shepherd, the ever popular skipper of the Mountain Ash Club has been selected for the Welsh International Trial Match. I hope he will gain his cap this season."

20 December 1913

"Muddled Oaf" reported in the Aberdare Leader, "Tich Thomas, the clever inside halfback, who so ably partnered Lodwig in working the scrummage for the Mount team, has now accepted an invitation to play for some Northern Union Club, greatly to the regret of the home supporters and to the team in general."

27 December 1913

<u>Coventry 13 Mountain Ash 6</u>
<u>Western Mail</u>

MOUNTAIN ASH BEATEN AT COVENTRY.

	G.	T.	P'ts.
COVENTRY	2	1	13
Mountain Ash	0	2	6

The weather was dull for the Coventry and Mountain Ash contest at Coventry. Coventry kicked off with the advantage of the ground, but the visitors soon pressed, and England was kept off the home line by the backs. Coventry soon afterwards managed to drive their opponents down the field, and Hall, beating Jones, scored an unconverted try. Mountain Ash, generally getting the ball out of the scrum and keeping Coventry on the defensive, had much the better of the game, and Mansfield got over the home line. Weaver failed to convert.

The second half opened badly for the visitors, whose forward play fell off, and Coventry scored a couple of converted tries in the first few minutes. The home team kept Mountain Ash close to the line for the next quarter of an hour, but then the visitors drove them down the field and had a scrimmage on the line, from which Warren got over. Davies's kick took the ball below the cross-bar. The game became rather rough in the last stages, and ended with the visitors making a desperate struggle to score.

17 January 1914

<u>Mountain Ash 3 Ferndale 0</u>
<u>Glamorgan League</u>

"Muddled Oaf" reported in the Aberdare Leader, "The Old Firm had reached the top of the Glamorgan League table as a result of beating Treherbert the previous Saturday. Mountain Ash thoroughly deserved their victory, and the home forwards to a man, distinguished themselves. Tom Shepherd, without doubt, was the finest forward on the field. Amongst the backs, Danny England and Ike Mansfield were always in the picture. Weaver at full back was good. The Mount have now played seven matches, won six and only lost one. Surely they deserve every effort the public could give them." The report went on, "When it became known in Mountain Ash and district last Friday evening that the Old Firm's brilliant forward, Tom Shepherd, had once again been overlooked by the Welsh Union selection committee, there was intense indignation, because he is a most brilliant forward, and one of the finest of sportsmen throughout South Wales. Shepherd has always shown great speed and fine opportunism."

19 January 1914

Cardiff 12 Mountain Ash 6

Mount Team: Back, F. Weaver; ¾ backs, Josh Davies, W. Welsh, Owen Jones, Danny England; half backs, W. Lodwig & Ike Mansfield; forwards, Tom Shepherd, Dick Fryer, Woolridge, P.C. John, A. Gibbon, Hubert Fortt, Warren, F. Wakely.

Western Mail

SIX TRIES AT CARDIFF.

OLD FIRM GIVE BLUE AND BLACKS HARD GAME.

	C.	T.	P'ts.
CARDIFF	0	4	12
Mountain Ash	0	2	6

Mountain Ash are to be congratulated on putting up such a great fight on the Cardiff Arms Park on Saturday. On the run of the play Cardiff hardly deserved victory by six points. In the first half Mountain Ash were the superior side, and fully deserved the two tries that they gained.

There was only a small attendance, and early play was all in favour of the visitors, their forwards playing finely and keeping Cardiff penned in their own 25. However, Cardiff were not long in finding their form, and rushed play to the visitors' 25, where, from a line-out, Tom Jones gave to Tudor Williams, who ran over with a splendid try. Play became of an exciting nature, and from the kick out the "Old Firm" went down the field, and from a scrum George Jones threw to Tom Jones, but his pass was intercepted by Mansfield, who dashed over with a try. A few minutes afterwards R. Fryer scored the visitors' second try. Play for the next few minutes was fairly even. Cardiff had hard lines in not scoring, their "threes" handling in fine style. Just before the interval Callan registered Cardiff's second try, and the teams crossed over on level terms.

On the re-start the Cardiff forwards were seen to better advantage, and carried play to the visitors' goal line, where Goff gathered the leather in fine style and crossed, but was called back for a knock-on, and a scrum was formed five yards out. The home eight made several determined rushes, but Weaver, the visiting full-back, stopped nearly every rush. At last Green got away nicely for Cardiff, and throwing out a long slinging pass to C. B. Davies, the latter crossed with the homesters' third try. Just before the end W. P. Thomas scored a fourth try for Cardiff.

The outstanding players for the visitors were Sheppard, Wakeley, and Fryer among the forwards, while their "three's" were better than the home four right along the line. Weaver, the visitors' full-back, gave a great exhibition.

21 February 1914

Mountain Ash 9 Penarth 3

Mount Team: Back, Bob Hill; ¾ backs, M. Mansfield, Welch, Owen Jones, Rhys Evans; half backs, Ike Mansfield & Lodwig; forwards, Tom Shepherd Capt, A. Davies, T. Warren, Wakely, Dick Fryer, H. Fortt, Dick Jarman, P.C. Johns.

Old Firm's Magnificent Victory

"Muddled Oaf" reported in the Aberdare Leader, "....a large number braved the elements in order to witness a battle royal between the all conquering Seasiders and the homesters. Rain fell in torrents....Welch, the homesters' brilliant centre three-quarter, opened the score with an unconverted try....the oval was secured by Hubert Fortt who romped over for the homesters' second try. After the change of ends, the Penarth forwards made a determined dash....the homesters lead was reduced....Tom Shepherd, the Mount skipper, scored a try. Afterwards, a little scene occurred when a Penarth forward threatened the touchjudge, stating that Shepherd had gone into touch. A number of spectators rushed into the field of play but eventually the home officials smoothed matters over. This victory for the Old Firm will do the Club a tremendous amount of good. To head the Glamorgan League and conquer a side of conquerors is no little achievement for a Club of youngsters."

28 February 1914

Pontypridd 3 Mountain Ash 3
Glamorgan League

A comment in the very brief Aberdare Leader match report by "Muddled Oaf" was as follows, "The Mountain Ash Club is treated very badly, not only by the weather, but by the sportsmen who view the game from the line. During the last four home matches, the gate has totalled only about £5. Although the gates are discouraging, the standard of local rugby is good, as is evidenced by the fine achievements made by the players of late, especially defeating the all powerful Penarth team. It is to be hoped that better luck is in store for them."

7 March 1914

Neath 3 Mountain Ash 3

Mount Team: Back, F. Weaver; ¾ backs, Sid Thomas, W. Welch, H. Farrow, M. Mansfield; half backs, Lodwick and Ike Mansfield; forwards, Hubert Fortt, P.C. Johns, A. Bethel, A. Davies, W. Woolridge, H. David, F. Llewellyn, David Thomas.

The Aberdare Leader reported, "The team had some prominent absentees in the persons of Tom Shepherd the captain, Owen Jones, Wakely, P.C. Perryman, Warren and Fryer. Lodwick, the Mount half back, scored a beautiful try for his side....Dai Morgan, one of the home centres, scored the equalising try in the last minute of the game – a narrow escape for Neath, who otherwise would have had their reputation besmirched....Individually and collectively, the members of the Mount team were in great form. Mountain Ash are recovering their old prestige day by day." The report also added, "Police Constable W. Perryman, one of the Mount forwards, is verily a giant among the players, standing 6ft 2in. in height and weighing 13st. 10lbs. He is speedy and shines in open play and has also gained County honours."

21 March 1914

Glamorgan League Table

Club	P	W	L	D	Points
Mountain Ash	10	7	0	3	17
Treorky	10	6	1	3	15
Maesteg	9	6	3	0	12
Treherbert	10	4	2	4	11
Llwynypia	7	5	1	1	11
Ferndale	11	4	5	2	10
Pontypridd	7	1	4	2	4
Merthyr	9	0	7	2	2

28 March 1914

Maesteg 9 Mountain Ash 0
Glamorgan League

The Aberdare Leader's reporter, "Muddled Oaf", commented, "....the character of play was anything but of a drawing room nature....". A week later, he reported, "The bad treatment received at Maesteg on the previous Saturday when no fewer than eight of the Mountain Ash players were severely injured, has greatly handicapped the team for coming matches. I understand that the committee feel like cancelling the fixtures arranged with Maesteg for next season."

4 April 1914

Mountain Ash 3 Treherbert 3
Glamorgan Times Cup Semi-Final

"Muddled Oaf" reported in the Aberdare Leader, "Early in the game the Old Firm were exceedingly unfortunate in losing Owen Jones, their brilliant centre three-quarter, who was carried off suffering from an injured knee. Treherbert were the first to score when they landed a penalty goal....After the interval, the Old Firm played up in better spirit and equalised from a penalty goal scored by Alby Davies, one of the Mount forwards. The scores being even at the final, the referee ordered the teams to play extra time but nothing resulted, and the match culminated in a draw of three points each. The match will, therefore, have to be replayed."

6 April 1914

Llwynypia 0 Mountain Ash 0
Old Firm Champions?

The Western Mail reported, "By running Llwynypia to a pointless draw and by the failure of Maesteg to defeat Treherbert, the Old Firm are practically certain of being the Glamorgan League champions."

15 April 1914

Mountain Ash 3 Treherbert 0
<u>Glamorgan Times Cup Semi-Final Replay</u>

The Western Mail reported, "The semi-final of the Glamorgan League Cup competition was replayed at Ynysangharad Park, Pontypridd, and resulted in a win for Mountain Ash. The previous match ended in a draw. Mountain Ash will now meet Maesteg in the final. Both Clubs brought down a large number of supporters....There was no mistake about the tackling which was keen at times, and injuries were numerous....The Mountain Ash forwards forced their way up to the Treherbert 25 and would have scored, but for one of their forwards knocking on. Well on in the second half, a Mountain Ash man was tripped, the referee awarding a penalty, England kicked a goal."

2 May 1914

"Muddled Oaf" reported in the Aberdare Leader, "At a meeting of the Glamorgan League held last week, the Mountain Ash Club were declared the champions of the Glamorgan League. The team fully deserved the honour, for they had worked hard for the trophy. The Old Firm are also the team to meet Maesteg in the "Glamorgan Times" Cup Final. Here's luck to Messrs Tom Shepherd and Co."

Mountain Ash 5 Neath 3

Mount Team: Back, Weaver; ¾ backs, Dai Arthur Davies, Josh Davies, Flo Keane, Danny England; half backs, Lodwick and Mansfield; forwards, Hubert Fortt, Alby Davies, Gibbon, Warren, P.C. John, Dick Fryer, P.C. Perryman, Williams.

"Muddled Oaf" reported in the Aberdare Leader, "Tremendous interest was centred in the meeting of the Glamorgan League champions and the famous Neath All Blacks at the Duffryn Grounds on Saturday....The homesters continued to press....from a scrummage Danny England intercepted a pass by the Neath halves and scored a beautiful try, which was converted by Dai Arthur Davies....After the change of ends, the home halves were brilliant, whilst the forwards fairly excelled themselves. In the end the All Blacks were bound to acknowledge a defeat at the hands of a superior team on the day's play. The result caused a sensation in the prominent rugger circles throughout South Wales, and the Mount team received the heartiest congratulations. They have obtained a trio of triumphs this season, viz. 1) winning the Glamorgan League, 2) defeating Neath, 3) being the finalists of the Glamorgan Times Cup."

9 May 1914

<u>Mountain Ash 4 Maesteg 3</u>
<u>Glamorgan Times Cup Final</u>

Unfortunately, the Mount XV for this game was not named. The Aberdare Leader reported, "The Mountain Ash XV journeyed to Treherbert on Saturday last to meet the famous Maesteg XV in the final of the Glamorgan Times Challenge Cup competition. A smart movement....resulted in an unconverted try for Maesteg....Five minutes from the end the Old Firm were rewarded for their persistence, when Welsh, their clever centre three-quarter, secured the ball just outside the Maesteg 25 and dropped a magnificent goal. The Old Firm were unquestionably the superior side and thoroughly merited the honours of the game. Weaver, at full back, fairly excelled himself. The quartette did a great deal of useful tackling. They beat the Maesteg defence on several occasions, but lost many golden opportunities of scoring through over excitement. At the conclusion of the match, Mr D. Rees, M.E., President of the Treherbert F.C., presented the Cup to Hubert Fortt, the acting Captain of the Mountain Ash team. The player and the Cup were hoisted on high and carried to the headquarters of the local Club. When the players reached Mountain Ash, they received a most hearty welcome. Thus, the Old Firm, despite heavy drawbacks at the commencement, have had their most successful season for many years. They have won the Glamorgan League, the Glamorgan Times Cup and defeated the famous Neath Club. This betokens a new lease of life for the Club and augurs well for next year."

Above is the Glamorgan League Knockout Cup won by the Old Firm after beating Maesteg 4-3. It gave Mountain Ash RFC a prestigious double of League and Cup for the 1913/14 season.

Tom Sheppard
A True Old Firm Warrior

Mount forward Tom Sheppard was born in 1888 and played for the Old Firm for 19 seasons, starting in 1906/07 and finishing after the 1924/25 season. He was a very well thought-of forward due to his prowess on the field and is referred to numerous times in this book, always being in the thick of the action. Many observers of the time thought he was good enough to get a coveted Welsh cap, but the nearest he got was a Welsh trial. At the end of his playing days, he emigrated to the United States where he worked in the automotive industry and stayed for the rest of his life. He passed away in Michigan on 28 March 1960. His grandson, Matthew Hurley, who lives in the States, has provided the photographs below of Tom's Welsh Trial cap and Glamorgan League medals.

Tom Sheppard's Welsh Trial Cap: 1911

Tom Sheppard's Glamorgan League Medals

Photographs Of The Front Of The Medals

Photographs Of The Back of The Medals

Medal On The Left:	This is the 1909/10 season medal Tom received when the Old Firm finished runners-up in the Glamorgan League.
Middle Medal:	This is the 1913/14 season medal Tom was presented with by the Glamorgan League when the Mount XV won the double of Glamorgan League championship and the Glamorgan League Cup.
Medal On The Right:	This is the 1908/09 season medal Tom received when Mount won the Glamorgan League.

In this era of rugby, the Glamorgan League championship was much sought after, and each season the competition saw hard-fought matches, some of which were no place for the faint-hearted. The middle and right-hand side medals above are the most prestigious because they are a winner's medals and were presented to Tom as part of the Mount XV which won the Glamorgan League twice and the Cup once.

Seasons 1914/15-1918/19

Following on from the last comments of the 1913/14 season, there was not a "next year" in rugby terms because of the outbreak of World War I. There was no rugby played until 1916 when, according to an historical account of the Club published in the "Welsh Rugby" magazine in March 1970, some games were played, with the Old Firm team being comprised mostly of miners, who were exempt from service. People connected to the Club lost their lives in the conflict. Probably the best known of these was former forward, Dick Thomas, who gained four Welsh caps between 1906 and 1909 while playing for Mount. He lost his life at Mametz Wood in France on 7 July 1916 in the Battle of the Somme, which was one of the bloodiest conflicts of the War. Once hostilities had ceased, the Club reformed but this had its problems. According to the Centenary Season's historical account titled, "The First 100 Years", there was a General Meeting of the Club in December 1918 at the Duffryn Hotel which was attended by only 22 people. In that meeting, the bank wanted repayment of an overdraft of £180. In a very magnanimous gesture, Messrs Herbert George, Ted McGregor and David Harris, who were Chairman, Secretary and Treasurer respectively before the War, wiped out the debt from their own pockets so that the Club could continue. This very generous act enabled the Old Firm to return to the field of play for the 1919/20 season.

Season 1919/20

<u>Tough First Season Back For Old Firm</u>

This was the first season after the end of the Great War and the first one since the "double" winning season of 1913/14, and it saw the Old Firm play some strong sides. The further back the history of any rugby Club is looked at, the lower the scoring generally. Whether this accounted for some of the extremely low scoring of the Mount team during the season is unclear, but consider these facts. The Old Firm didn't score a single point in 13 of the 24 known games played, and scored, in total for the season, just 49 points, which included just over 10 tries! This was an average of just over 2 points and not even one try per game! Maybe this was because the teams they were up against were just too good, but consider the Old Firm's defence. Not more than 8 points were conceded in 19 of the 24 known games played and, in total for the season, only 147 was conceded, which works out at just over 6 per game – which was a very good defensive record for a side that won only 5 games. It suggests that the Old Firm were a dogged outfit, competitive and hard to beat, with few frills. The season was the first for centre Tom Collins, who went on to be capped by Wales in 1923, so there was some talent in the Mount attack. The low scoring nature of Mount's games was even emphasised in 10 of the 15 defeats, with the losing margin being 7 points or less. The end of season known playing record showed 24 games played, 5 won, 4 drawn and 15 lost, with a lowly 49 points scored, which included just 10+ tries, and 147 conceded, 71 of which was conceded in the four games against Abertillery, Neath, Ebbw Vale and Llanelly; and even in two of these, the losing margin was just 11 and 12 points. Of the 5 known games won, all were at home, the best being against Maesteg, Pontypridd and Yorkshire visitors, Headingley. There was also another win according to the Centenary season's historical account, "The First 100 Years". In that publication, it was stated that "the beating of Neath at the Gnoll in 1920 by a try gave Mountain Ash the cherished "Evening Express Award of Merit"." However, details of that game were never found in either this season or the one following, 1920/21. The season also saw two hard fought games against the 1918/19 Welsh champions, Pill Harriers, one a home draw and the other a narrow away loss. There were a number of narrow defeats, the highest profile one being 6-3 at home to Cardiff. As a matter of interest, both scrum half Sid Congdon and full back Fred Samuel were in the Llanelly team that won 11-0 at Mountain Ash at the end of the season. At the start of the 1921/22 season, both had transferred to the Old Firm, Samuel being capped three times later that season, and Congdon getting oh so close to a Welsh cap and playing for the Club until he retired at the end of the 1928/29 season. In the last minute defeat at Pontypridd, the Western Mail commented, "This was one of the most attractive fixtures on the Pontypridd list." All this resulted in a win rate of 29.17% for the season, as tough a season it appears, as Mountain Ash RFC had endured in its 44 year history.

Fixtures 1919/20

Opponents	Date	Venue	Score	Tries	Scorers/Comments
Abertillery	13 Oct 1919	Away	0-24	0	No scorers.
Penarth	20 Oct 1919	Unknown	3-8	1	Wat Phillips T.
Abertillery	27 Oct 1919	Home	0-6	0	No scorers.
Neath	3 Nov 1919	Away	0-12	0	No scorers.
Crumlin	10 Nov 1919	Home	11-5	3	Tom Collins T, A. Ward T, Thomas T, F. Keane C.
Pontypridd	17 Nov 1919	Home	6-3	2	Tom Shepherd T, W. Thomas T.
Treherbert	1 Dec 1919	Home	0-7	0	No scorers.
Pill Harriers	8 Dec 1919	Home	0-0	0	No scorers.
Pontypridd	15 Dec 1919	Away	0-3	0	No scorers.
Cardiff	22 Dec 1919	Home	3-6	1	Wat Phillips T.
Pill Harriers	27 Dec 1919	Away	0-4	0	No scorers.
Newbridge	5 Jan 1920	Away	4-7	0	AN Other DG.
Barry	12 Jan 1920	Home	0-0	0	No scorers.
Resolven	26 Jan 1920	Home	7-0	0+	H. Farrow DG, AN Other 3pts.
Crumlin	2 Feb 1920	Away	3-3	1	AN Other T.
Ebbw Vale	16 Feb 1920	Away	3-24	1	Biddiscombe T.
Aberavon	23 Feb 1920	Home	0-0	0	No scorers.
Maesteg	1 Mar 1920	Away	0-6	0	No scorers.
Treherbert	8 Mar 1920	Away	0-3	0	No scorers.
Cross Keys	22 Mar 1920	Away	3-7	0+	Scorer unknown.
Aberavon	29 Mar 1920	Away	0-8	0	No scorers.
Headingley	3 Apr 1920	Home	3-0	1	Charlie Sage T.
Maesteg	5 Apr 1920	Home	3-0	0+	Scorer unknown.
Llanelly	26 Apr 1920	Home	0-11	0	No scorers.

Summary of Playing Record

P	W	D	L	For	Against	Tries Scored	Win Rate %
24	5	4	15	49	147	10+	29.17

27 October 1919

Mountain Ash 0 Abertillery 6

ABERTILLERY WIN.
BRILLIANT FOOTBALL IN GAME AT MOUNTAIN ASH.

Mount Team: F. Keane; A. Ware, R.H. Pugh, Tom Collins, Wat Phillips; Josh Davies, J. Donovan; Tom Sheppard, A. Gibbon, H. Fortt, Duncan, W. Perryman, P. Warren, J. Beynon, R. Fryer.

The Western Mail reported, "The game at Mountain Ash on Saturday was the best of the season and produced a high standard of excellence....Both sets of forwards played finely and it was encouraging to the home supporters to see a great improvement. They got the ball away on several occasions to the backs, who must have scored had there been any weakness in the Abertillery defence. Both teams made every effort to play the best football and it was a great game. Abertillery's backs were the smarter and made the best use of their opportunities.

Josh Davies, who played outside half (for Mount), should be given another trial. His defence was the feature of his play, and when he has had more practice with Donovan, Mountain Ash will be well served at half back. Tom Sheppard led the home pack splendidly."

3 November 1919

Neath 12 Mountain Ash 0

The Western Mail reported, "Robust forward play, which several times endangered the safety of the Neath line, was the characteristic of the display of Mountain Ash at the Gnoll on Saturday. Behind, the combination of the visitors was faulty, hence their failure. Mountain Ash went off with a bang. Their forwards bustled the Neath men considerably, and had the backs been able to rise to the occasion, the defence would have been broken in the first 10 minutes....For the visitors, Sheppard, Gibbon and Fryer showed great dash in front; Mellish was the better of the halves and Ward of the wings. Keane also did well for Mountain Ash."

17 November 1919

Mountain Ash 6 Pontypridd 3

Mount Team: F. Keane; F. Ward, R.H. Pugh, Tom Collins, Rev. T. Christopher, J. Legge, W. Thomas, Tom Shepherd, A. Gibbon, R. Fryer, J. Jenkins, D. Harrison, P.C. W. Perryman, E. George, J. Beynon.

The Western Mail reported, "....there was little to choose between the packs, neither of which gave the ball as they should. It was at three-quarter that Mountain Ash held the advantage and they should have scored three or four more tries. Ward and the Rev. T. Christopher were both smart wings and in Collins, Mountain Ash have a most promising centre. He was easily the best three-quarter on the ground."

7 December 1919

Pill Harriers 4 Mountain Ash 0

The size and weight of the ball was emphasised by the Western Mail report of this match when it was mentioned, "Towards the end of the first half, two Mountain Ash players – W. Thomas and Jim Fryer – were both knocked out and had to leave the field, in each case through being struck by the ball...."

22 December 1919

Mountain Ash 3 Cardiff 6

Western Mail

STRENUOUS RUGBY GAMES.

CARDIFF'S HARD FIGHT AT MOUNTAIN ASH.

By "OBSERVER."

The anticipation that Cardiff would by no means have an easy passage at Mountain Ash on Saturday was fully realised. Playing the characteristic Rhondda game, the "Old Firm" fully extended their opponents, and their tactics succeeded admirably in keeping in check the speedier and more resourceful Taffside backs. Like a pack of greyhounds, the Mountain Ash forwards followed the ball relentlessly, and got in amongst the Cardiff halves and three-quarters with a rapidity which prevented them from developing offensive movements. From the home team's point of view it was the correct game to play under the circumstances, for had the visitors' backs been allowed room to work in, the adverse score would have been large. Probably, the "Old Firm" were playing above form for this special occasion. At all events, their determination and thoroughness gave their visitors a fright, and the issue was in doubt until the whistle had gone. Two distinct styles were in opposition, and while the more classic methods of the Cardiff men makes play a prettier spectacle, the sweeping rushes of the Mountain Ash team provided abundant thrills and exciting situations. These rushes gave the visitors immense trouble to keep in check, and but for a really brilliant defence the football world would have had a great surprise.

Playing with the wind in the first half, the Taffsiders did most of the attacking, but Dodd and Pepperall were marked to such an extent that they could not get the ball away quick enough to the centres to enable the latter to open up the game in the way they desired. Then, again, the struggle for possession in the scrums was not altogether in Cardiff's favour, and, therefore, Bryant and Powell's partnership were few and far between. With the wind behind them in the second half, Mountain Ash made a special effort, and developed the tactics so successfully employed in the first half to such an extent that the forwards practically took matters into their own hands. For the most part, Cardiff were on the defensive in this moiety, and their tackling and gathering was superb, and time after time they earned the ungrudged applause of the spectators for the manner in which they repelled the most dangerous Mountain Ash rushes. Curiously enough the "Old Firm's" try was gained in typical Welsh fashion, and I believe that the visitors were taken by surprise, when, instead of taking the ball at their toes, the home men essayed passing. By the time the ball was in the hands of Wat Phillips the defence was beaten and the winger sprinted over with a clever try, about which there was not the slightest doubt.

The report finished by saying, "Farrow and Legge, the Old Firm's halves were the "live wires" of the home team's attack....Pugh, the full back did exceedingly well, and Phillips and Gibson were frequently prominent. As a final word, the Cardiff Club is to be commended in giving a fixture to a Club like Mountain Ash. A Club with such traditions is worthy of a "leg up" and Cardiff's visit attracted a large crowd. Mr Ben Lewis, the referee, took a firm attitude....and insisted on the forwards packing with no more than three in the front rank."

2 February 1920

Crumlin 3 Mountain Ash 3

The Western Mail commented, "Despite the heavy nature of the ground, a fine, open game resulted at Crumlin, both sides playing splendid football. The pace was also exceptional and there was not a dull moment. Mountain Ash played well together, especially the rear rank, and it is certainly gratifying to see that the famous old team is on the upgrade. They possess a lusty pack who scrummage well and do good work in the open. Their skipper, Tom Sheppard, is always in the thick of the fray and sets a splendid example. The Mount scored in the first half after a brilliant round of passing....After about 15 minutes play in the second half, the game was stopped, both balls going into the river...."

16 February 1920

Ebbw Vale 24 Mountain Ash 3
A Lovely Black Eye!

The Aberdare Leader's reporter, "The Watchman", made the following comment on 2 April 1938, some 18 years after the above game, "....the writer, a youngster of 17 played at Ebbw Vale, in season 1919-20, in his first game for the Old Firm. To be quite frank it should also have been the last, but there was a survival for a few more games, mostly away from home – a difficulty always being experienced in those days to get players to go away....a solitary try scored by P.C. Charlie Sage, who eventually went North. The Old Firm side included Jesse Legge and Harry Farrow at half, with Bobby Pugh at full back....In getting the Old Firm's solitary try, P.C. Sage got the finest black eye I remember seeing."

23 February 1920

Mountain Ash 0 Aberavon 0
Western Mail

"OLD FIRM" STAND FIRM

STRENUOUS GAME ENDS IN A POINTLESS DRAW.

By "FORWARD."

	G.	T.	Pts.
Mountain Ash	0	0	0
Aberavon	0	0	0

It was pleasing to renew acquaintance with Mountain Ash once again on Saturday after a lapse of six years, and to find that those who were fighting hard before the war to keep the Rugger flag flying are still carrying on with the good work, and are in the happy position of being on good terms with the bank. Saturday's "gate" meant a substantial accession to their credit balance, in spite of a counter-attraction at the Pavilion in the form of a brass band competition. After their victories over Swansea, Llanelly, Neath, and other Welsh clubs, Aberavon were expected to add the scalp of the "Old Firm" to their wigwam, especially as they turned out a full and representative side. There was some uncertainty about Jim Jones, the Welsh international forward, taking his place in the pack, but although he was suffering from the effects of the kick he received on his knee in the Scottish match at Inverleith, he pluckily turned out, but could not show anything approaching his best form. Capt. A. S. Burge, who refereed the match, kept the game going at a terrific pace in the first half, play travelling from goal to goal with delightful rapidity. Forwards and backs mixed it up without restraint on either side, and several times scores seemed imminent. But something went wrong with the works every time an attacking movement was developed, and when the interval was announced the scoring sheet was blank.

In the second half the general standard of play was not so good, and it was plain to see that the hot pace of the first half had left a good many bellows to mend on both sides. Realising the superiority of the Aberavon back division, the Mountain Ash men bent all their efforts on making it a forward game, and in the circumstances this was their correct and safest policy.

There was very little between the two packs in the tight, but in the open the home forwards were distinctly better than the Aberavon eight, notwithstanding the fact that they carried one very distinct passenger in khaki knicks, whose chief interest in the game seemed to be that of watching his comrades doing all the hard graft. And the irony of it all was that this particular individual was the heftiest man in the home pack. However, the other seven Mountain Ash forwards strove manfully to keep their opponents outside the danger zone, and in this they succeeded right up to the very end. Con Evans, the Aberavon scrum half, tried hard several times to set his backs going, but Biddiscombe carried too many guns for him, and on the day's form was the cleverer of the two. All the other backs on both side, with the exception of the two custodians, were only moderate, the outside halves and centres being deficient in the essential quality of breaking through and making openings for their wing men. That seems to be the weak spot in nearly every Welsh team this season. Still, it was a clean, strenuous sporting game, and the "Old Firm" are to be congratulated upon having done so well against such formidable opponents. Teams:—

Mountain Ash: R. H. Pugh; W. Phillips, W. Welch, H. West, and A. N. Other; F. Biddiscombe and H. Farrow; T. Sheppard, A. Gibbon, H. Footte, E. George, H. Brown, R. Fryer, P.C. Sage, and J. Jenkins.

3 April 1920

Mountain Ash 3 Headingley 0
Western Mail

HEADINGLEY FAIL AT MOUNTAIN ASH.

	G.	T.	Pts.
Mountain Ash	0	1	3
Headingley	0	0	0

The visiting team was given a splendid reception at Mountain Ash on Good Friday, where they met the "Old Firm." The visitors are a capable side, and included a number of outstanding players. Netherwood, the right centre, and Cairns, on the left wing, were the outstanding players among the visiting backs. Mountain Ash rose to the occasion and played their best game of the season. For the homesters Collins played a great game at full-back, and Skym and Potter played well at centre. Ward and West were too well marked. Biddiscombe and Cotter had a great tussle with their opponents. Fortt, Sage, Cherrymen, and Fryer were most prominent amongst the home backs. Sage scored the only try from a great burst near the line.

26 April 1920

Mountain Ash 0 Llanelly 11
Western Mail

LLANELLY'S FINE BACK PLAY.

	G.	T.	Pts.
Llanelly	1	2	11
Mountain Ash	0	0	0

Mountain Ash spectators at Saturday's match were provided with some thrills. The visiting backs have a great reputation, and they more than upheld their fame. Bryn Williams was the outstanding three-quarter, and apart from his wonderful pace, he contributed many smart bits of play. Idwal Thomas was also prominent. Glan. Thomas was somewhat handicapped, as Condon was too closely watched by Biddiscombe. Fred Samuel played a fine game at full-back. The "Old Firm" were unfortunate in having many players away. The home forwards played a great game, and held the advantage both in the scrum and loose. Morgan was injured quite early in the game, and Mountain Ash played seven forwards, Dick Fryer going full-back. The secret of the Scarlets' success was the wonderful display of their backs. The last score by Bryn Williams was one of the finest tries of the season. Teams:—

Mountain Ash: D. W. Griffiths; D. Skym, T. Collins, W. Phillips, and W. Morgan; F. Biddiscombe, and Vic Potter; H. Fortte, T. Sheppard, P.C. Sage, P.C. Perryman, J. Allen, J. Fryer, R. Fryer, and T. Grant.

Llanelly: Fred Samuel; Bryn Evans, M.C., Hendy Evans, Idwal Thomas, and Bryn Williams; S. Condon and G. Thomas; T. J. Bowen (capt.), Bobby Evans, Alfred Davies, Aneurin Thomas, Rev. J. Stephens, Jack Jones, Joe Evans, and T. J. Phillips. Referee: Mr. A. Vines.

A Selection of the Old Firm's Results 1910/11 to 1919/20

Matches v Maesteg

Opponents	Season	Venue	Score	P	W	D	L
Maesteg (L)	1910/11	Away	0-23	1	0	0	1
Maesteg (PL)	1911/12	Home	6-0	2	1	0	1
Maesteg (L)	1911/12	Away	0-8	3	1	0	2
Maesteg (PL)	1912/13	Away	3-11	4	1	0	3
Maesteg (PL)	1912/13	Home	4-0	5	2	0	3
Maesteg (L)	1913/14	Home	6-0	6	3	0	3
Maesteg (L)	1913/14	Away	0-9	7	3	0	4
Maesteg Glamorgan Times Cup Final	1913/14	Treherbert	4-3	8	4	0	4
Maesteg	1919/20	Away	0-6	9	4	0	5
Maesteg	1919/20	Home	3-0	10	5	0	5

Matches v Pontypridd

Opponents	Season	Venue	Score	P	W	D	L
Pontypridd (PL)	1910/11	Home	7-3	1	1	0	0
Pontypridd (L)	1911/12	Home	3-3	2	1	1	0
Pontypridd (L)	1911/12	Away	6-3	3	2	1	0
Pontypridd (L)	1912/13	Home	9-9	4	2	2	0
Pontypridd (L)	1913/14	Away	3-3	5	2	3	0
Pontypridd (L)	1913/14	Home	9-0	6	3	3	0
Pontypridd	1919/20	Home	6-3	7	4	3	0
Pontypridd	1919/20	Away	0-3	8	4	3	1

Matches v Bridgend

Opponents	Season	Venue	Score	P	W	D	L
Bridgend	1910/11	Away	8-0	1	1	0	0
Bridgend	1910/11	Home	0-0	2	1	1	0
Bridgend	1911/12	Home	3-3	3	1	2	0
Bridgend	1912/13	Away	3-6	4	1	2	1

Matches v Penygraig

Opponents	Season	Venue	Score	P	W	D	L
Penygraig (L)	1910/11	Away	9-8	1	1	0	0
Penygraig (PL)	1910/11	Home	5-3	2	2	0	0
Penygraig (Cup)	1910/11	Home	3-6	3	2	0	1
Penygraig (PL)	1912/13	Away	0-0	4	2	1	1

Matches v Llwynypia

Opponents	Season	Venue	Score	P	W	D	L
Llwynypia (PF)	1910/11	Away	0-4	1	0	0	1
Llwynypia (L)	1910/11	Home	9-3	2	1	0	1
Llwynypia (PL)	1911/12	Home	0-3	3	1	0	2
Llwynypia (L)	1912/13	Home	8-3	4	2	0	2
Llwynypia (PF)	1913/14	Away	0-16	5	2	0	3
Llwynypia (PL)	1913/14	Home	0-3	6	2	0	4
Llwynypia (PL)	1913/14	Home	0-0	7	2	1	4
Llwynypia (L)	1913/14	Away	0-0	8	2	2	4

Matches v Penarth

Opponents	Season	Venue	Score	P	W	D	L
Penarth	1910/11	Home	3-0	1	1	0	0
Penarth	1910/11	Away	0-9	2	1	0	1
Penarth	1911/12	Away	6-8	3	1	0	2
Penarth	1911/12	Home	3-0	4	2	0	2
Penarth	1912/13	Home	7-0	5	3	0	2
Penarth	1912/13	Away	5-6	6	3	0	3
Penarth	1913/14	Away	0-14	7	3	0	4
Penarth	1913/14	Home	9-3	8	4	0	4
Penarth	1919/20	Unknown	3-8	9	4	0	5

Matches v Cardiff

Opponents	Season	Venue	Score	P	W	D	L
Cardiff	1912/13	Home	0-14	1	0	0	1
Cardiff	1913/14	Away	6-12	2	0	0	2
Cardiff	1919/20	Home	3-6	3	0	0	3

Matches v Cross Keys

Opponents	Season	Venue	Score	P	W	D	L
Cross Keys	1910/11	Away	0-5	1	0	0	1
Cross Keys	1910/11	Home	0-3	2	0	0	2
Cross Keys	1911/12	Home	17-6	3	1	0	2
Cross Keys	1919/20	Away	3-7	4	1	0	3

Matches v Llanelly

Opponents	Season	Venue	Score	P	W	D	L
Llanelly	1912/13	Away	4-5	1	0	0	1
Llanelly	1913/14	Away	0-21	2	0	0	2
Llanelly	1919/20	Home	0-11	3	0	0	3

Matches v Neath

Neath were Welsh Champions in 1910/11

Opponents	Season	Venue	Score	P	W	D	L
Neath	1910/11	Away	0-6	1	0	0	1
Neath	1912/13	Away	3-6	2	0	0	2
Neath	1912/13	Home	0-3	3	0	0	3
Neath	1913/14	Away	3-3	4	0	1	3
Neath	1913/14	Home	5-3	5	1	1	3
Neath	1919/20	Away	0-12	6	1	1	4

Matches v Abertillery

Opponents	Season	Venue	Score	P	W	D	L
Abertillery	1910/11	Away	0-10	1	0	0	1
Abertillery	1911/12	Away	3-16	2	0	0	2
Abertillery	1911/12	Home	6-4	3	1	0	2
Abertillery	1912/13	Home	0-3	4	1	0	3
Abertillery	1913/14	Home	3-8	5	1	0	4
Abertillery	1913/14	Away	0-5	6	1	0	5
Abertillery	1919/20	Away	0-24	7	1	0	6
Abertillery	1919/20	Home	0-6	8	1	0	7

Matches v Treorky

Opponents	Season	Venue	Score	P	W	D	L
Treorky (L)	1910/11	Away	0-3	1	0	0	1
Treorky (L)	1910/11	Home	0-0	2	0	1	1
Treorky (F)	1911/12	Away	0-8	3	0	1	2
Treorky (L)	1911/12	Home	0-0	4	0	2	2
Treorky Glamorgan League Cup Semi-Final	1912/13	Away	0-8	5	0	2	3
Treorky (PL)	1913/14	Away	3-4	6	0	2	4
Treorky (L)	1913/14	Home	5-0	7	1	2	4

Matches v Swansea
Swansea were Welsh Champions in 1912/13

Opponents	Season	Venue	Score	P	W	D	L
Swansea	1912/13	Away	0-39	1	0	0	1
Swansea	1912/13	Home	3-11	2	0	0	2

Matches v Pontypool

Opponents	Season	Venue	Score	P	W	D	L
Pontypool	1913/14	Away	0-35	1	0	0	1

Matches v Ebbw Vale

Opponents	Season	Venue	Score	P	W	D	L
Ebbw Vale	1919/20	Away	3-24	1	0	0	1

Matches v Aberavon

Opponents	Season	Venue	Score	P	W	D	L
Aberavon	1911/12	Away	0-6	1	0	0	1
Aberavon	1911/12	Home	0-4	2	0	0	2
Aberavon	1919/20	Home	0-0	3	0	1	2
Aberavon	1919/20	Away	0-8	4	0	1	3

Matches v Treherbert

Opponents	Season	Venue	Score	P	W	D	L
Treherbert (PL)	1911/12	Home	12-0	1	1	0	0
Treherbert (PL)	1911/12	Away	5-3	2	2	0	0
Treherbert (PL)	1913/14	Home	5-0	3	3	0	0
Treherbert (PL)	1913/14	Away	3-0	4	4	0	0
Treherbert Glamorgan Times Cup Semi-Final	1913/14	Pontypridd	3-3	5	4	1	0
Treherbert Glamorgan Times Cup Semi-Final Replay	1913/14	Pontypridd	3-0	6	5	1	0
Treherbert	1919/20	Home	0-7	7	5	1	1
Treherbert	1919/20	Away	0-3	8	5	1	2

Matches v Bath

Opponents	Season	Venue	Score	P	W	D	L
Bath	1910/11	Away	0-3	1	0	0	1
Bath	1911/12	Away	3-3	2	0	1	1
Bath	1912/13	Away	0-6	3	0	1	2
Bath	1912/13	Home	8-0	4	1	1	2

Matches v Nuneaton

Opponents	Season	Venue	Score	P	W	D	L
Nuneaton	1912/13	Away	12-0	1	1	0	0
Nuneaton	1912/13	Home	11-3	2	2	0	0
Nuneaton	1913/14	Away	12-22	3	2	0	1
Nuneaton	1913/14	Away	6-5	4	3	0	1

Matches v Coventry

Opponents	Season	Venue	Score	P	W	D	L
Coventry	1912/13	Away	3-3	1	0	1	0
Coventry	1913/14	Away	6-13	2	0	1	1

Matches v Bridgwater & Albion

Opponents	Season	Venue	Score	P	W	D	L
Bridgwater & Albion	1910/11	Away	5-10	1	0	0	1

Matches v Cinderford

Opponents	Season	Venue	Score	P	W	D	L
Cinderford	1912/13	Away	0-7	1	0	0	1
Cinderford	1912/13	Home	6-5	2	1	0	1

Matches On Tour In France

Opponents	Season	Venue	Score	P	W	D	L	Result Unknown
Pau	1911/12	Away	Result & score unknown	1	0	0	0	1
Bayonne	1911/12	Away	Result & score unknown	2	0	0	0	2

There were no known games played against Glamorgan Wanderers, Tredegar, Newport, London Welsh, Leicester and Plymouth in the 1910s.

Mountain Ash RFC Players That Went North 1910/11 to 1919/20

J. BENJAMIN, who joined the Old Firm in 1908/09, played scrum half for Mountain Ash RFC and moved North prior to the 1910/11 season starting. It is not known which Northern Union Club he played for or anything else about his Northern Union career.

ARTHUR LOVELUCK, who captained the "Old Firm" in 1911/12, joined Salford. He played centre in the 1913/14 team that beat Huddersfield 5-3 in the Championship Final played at Headingley on 25 April 1914. His brothers Ned, Gwilym and "Buller" also played for the Old Firm in the 1920s,"Buller" following him into the paid ranks.

"TICH" THOMAS, who played scrum half for Mountain Ash RFC in 1913/14, was a young player "on the up" when he went North in December 1913. Other than the Aberdare Leader reporting his departure to the professional ranks as follows, "Tich Thomas....has accepted an invitation to play for some Northern Union Club, greatly to the regret of Mountain Ash supporters...", nothing else is known about his career.

IVOR BEVAN, was a centre/wing for Mount and was another who was reported to have gone North in February 1914, but the Club he joined was not mentioned and nothing else is known about his Northern Union career.

Mountain Ash Rugby Football Club
"The Old Firm"

The 1920s

The Playing Record

The Old Firm had two five year spells of contrasting fortunes in the 1920s. The first five seasons of the decade saw the Club rise and hit the heights of success whereas the closing five saw more games lost than won in each season, with two of these being particularly poor by previous standards. Below are the known seasonal playing records of the 1920s which show quite graphically this rise and fall:

Season	P	W	D	L	Results Unknown	For	Against	Tries Scored	%
1920/21	27	9	5	13	0	124+	93+	26+	42.59
1921/22	52	37	5	10	0	591	198	26+	75.96
1922/23	41	22	5	12	2	325+	192+	69+	62.82
1923/24	36	18	4	14	0	270+	157+	57+	55.56
1924/25	29	17	3	8	1	122+	110+	29+	66.07
1925/26	26	9	3	14	0	175	215	38+	40.39
1926/27	22	4	1	17	0	86+	239+	14+	20.46
1927/28	23	6	5	12	0	133+	177+	33+	36.96
1928/29	30	11	2	17	0	179	277	34+	40.00
1929/30	22	5	3	14	0	118	163	25	29.55
Total for 1920s	308	138	36	131	3	2123+	1821+	351+	51.15

Club Captains

1920-1921	Gwilym R. Loveluck
1921-1922	Jim Beynon
1922-1924	Sid Congdon
1924-1925	P.J. Skym
1925-1926	George Morgan
1926-1927	Dr. E.B. Rees
1927-1929	Jim Coughlin
1929-1930	Haydn Williams

Other than forward Jim Beynon in 1921/22, who led Mount in one of the Club's most successful seasons, all the Mount captains in the 1920s were talented backs. Gwilym Loveluck was a centre and one of three brothers who joined the Old Firm in the early 1920s. Scrum half Sid Congdon, who joined from Llanelly in 1921/22 and captained the side for two seasons from 1922 to 1924, was one of the unluckiest of players, coming tantalisingly close to a Welsh cap after being Welsh reserve on a dozen or so occasions. P.J. Skym, George Morgan, Dr E.B. Rees, Jim Coughlin and Haydn Williams were all talented backs who captained Mount between 1924 and 1930.

Seasons 1921/22 To 1924/25
The Old Firm's "Second Golden Era"

The period 1920 to 1927 was described in the Centenary Season's historical publication, "The First 100 Years", as the "Golden Era". This was not quite true and if the term "Golden Era" is to be used, then it has to apply to the seasons 1921 to 1925 only, as they were head and shoulders above the others when looking at what was achieved during this era of rugby. These years should also be regarded as the "Second Golden Era" as the years 1894 to 1910 were well worthy of being called the Club's "First Golden Era" (see pages 177 and 178).

The Playing Record

Season	P	W	D	L	Results Unknown	For	Against	Tries Scored	%
1921/22	52	37	5	10	0	591	198	26+	75.96
1922/23	41	22	5	12	2	325+	192+	69+	62.82
1923/24	36	18	4	14	0	270+	157+	57+	55.56
1924/25	29	17	3	8	1	122+	110+	29+	66.07
Total	158	94	17	44	3	1308+	657+	181+	66.13

During this era, the Old Firm took on and beat quite a number of Clubs the media termed "first class" such as Neath, Llanelli, Aberavon, Cardiff, Abertillery, Swansea, Pontypool, Cross Keys and Penarth, with Newport the only "first class" Club not played during these seasons. There were also wins against a selection of English Clubs such as Bath, Bridgwater & Albion, Headingley, Otley, Nuneaton, Weston-super-Mare, Newton Abbot and Falmouth. There was also a win against Irish tourists, Belfast Collegians, at the Rec.

Record Number Of Games Won

The season 1921/22 was impressive with the Old Firm playing a remarkable 52 games, winning 37, drawing 5 and losing just 10. Not a point was conceded in 34 of these games, wing "Buller" Loveluck scoring 39 tries in the season.

As Good A Season As Any

The following season, 1922/23, was even better and probably ranks, even to this day, as the greatest ever. Wins were recorded over Cardiff - in a game that opened the newly built grandstand at the Rec - Llanelli, Bath, reigning Welsh champions Cross Keys, and Neath, amongst others.

Two Big Wins On The Road

In 1923/24, the Old Firm took Pontypool's ground record and also won at Swansea. This latter win gave the Club wins at some time in its history over the "big four" Clubs of Welsh rugby - Cardiff, Llanelli, Newport and Swansea.

Tragic End To Season
Although another good season followed in 1924/25, it was overshadowed by the accidental death of Mount wing, Percy Hoskins, at Aberavon.

Mount Players Achieve International Recognition
Full back Fred Samuel completed a superb 1921/22 season for the Club by being capped 3 times by Wales against Scotland, Ireland and France. The following season, 1922/23, centre Tom Collins was capped at Lansdowne Road, Dublin, against Ireland. During these "glory years", Mount had several players who made the Welsh Trials but just missed out. Two players that came close were scrum half Sid Congdon and wing "Buller" Loveluck, who were Welsh reserves on a dozen and eight occasions respectively, but never managed to get a coveted Welsh cap.

The French Connection
Mountain Ash RFC had been one of the first Welsh Club's to cross the Channel and visit France back in 1912. Three more trips took place in the 1920s. The first, in 1921/22, saw the Old Firm play Brive and Périgueux. A year later, in 1922/23, there were two games against Clermont Ferrand, and lastly in 1924/25, Stade Francais was the opposition.

New Grandstand At The Rec
A new grandstand with changing rooms was opened by Cardiff RFC at the Rec on 4 December 1922. It was a proud day for Mountain Ash RFC and it was made all the more memorable with an 11-5 win over the "blue and blacks".

The Glamorgan League
During the "Second Golden Era", the Old Firm never won the Glamorgan League, and the lack of comment made in match reports about it, and the fact that Mount would have at least challenged for the title during these seasons, suggests the Club did not enter the competition after the end of the First World War until 1927/28.

In Summary
With the four seasons of the "Second Golden Era" incorporating wins over famous Clubs, two players being capped by Wales, three tours being made to France, and the building of a new grandstand at the Rec, it truly was a great era of rugby for Mountain Ash RFC.

The Seasons 1925/26 To 1929/30
The last five years of the decade were tough seasons. Although the Old Firm beat Cross Keys, Ebbw Vale, Glamorgan Wanderers, Maesteg, Pontypridd and Treorky, the wins against these Clubs and others were far fewer than previously experienced.

The Attraction Of Rugby League
The Old Firm continued losing players to the Northern Union – which was renamed Rugby League in 1922. Both Mount's two Welsh Internationals of the decade, full back Fred Samuel and centre Tom Collins, along with try scoring wing "Buller" Loveluck, all went North, joining Hull Rugby League Club.

Former Mount Player Becomes Welsh Selector
In 1925/26, Mount's former Welsh International outside half, Wyndham Jones, who was capped in 1905 and scored a try to help Wales win the Triple Crown in his only International appearance, became a Welsh selector and continued in the post into the 1930s.

First Game Against Welsh Academicals
Boxing Day 1927 saw the official formation in the town of another Club called the Welsh Academicals. On Boxing Day 1926 a game had been played between Mount and a Mountain Ash County School Old Boys XV, which was the forerunner to the Welsh Academicals being formed. Both the school caretaker, Jimmy Austin, and Mount's former Secretary, Enoch Watkins, were instrumental in running the Academicals for many years, and the Club is still functioning now in 2015, 88 years after its formation.

The Club's Administration
The following is known about the 1920s. Jack Jarvis was Club Chairman in 1921/22, but there is no information about which individuals held the post up to 1926/27 when Shad Lewis became Chairman and held the post for the rest of the decade. With economic conditions getting ever harder as the 1920s progressed due to the decline of the South Wales coal industry, it seems certain that Lewis' financial help kept Mount up and running at a time when a number of established Clubs were in dire straits, with some asking the Welsh Union for financial assistance or ceasing to exist. The 1975/76 Centenary Season historical account, "The First 100 Years", has Enoch Watkins as Secretary from 1920 to 1927, but although he was certainly Secretary in 1922/23 and 1923/24, Edward D. Richards was mentioned as such in 1924/25, with Ted – known as "Ned" – Bradwick taking over in 1925/26 and doing the job for the rest of the decade. As for the Treasurer's job, Clem Austin held the post in 1924/25 and W.E. Gough – Christian name unknown – took over in 1926/27, finishing at the end of 1929/30. The decade also saw the Club start using the Glancynon Hotel – the current Clubhouse – as its headquarters, where Club Chairman, Shad Lewis, was the publican.

The 1920s
Season by Season

Season 1920/21

<u>Old Firm Show Promise</u>

From the 27 known games played, the Old Firm won 9, drew 5 and lost 13, scoring 124+ points, which included 26+ tries, and conceded 93+, to give a win rate of 42.59%. From the information available, it seems that Mount may have had a better record than this from the comments made in the Aberdare Leader. For instance, the team might have either drawn with or beat a Newport XV, the Aberdare Leader's reporter, "Woodlander", writing on 30 October 1920 said, "Phew! Five matches in ten days! The Old Firm have always been out for capturing records, and if that isn't a test of the calibre of the team, especially when one of the matches was with the celebrated Newport lot, well I should like to know what is. Moreover, the Mount boys emerged from this great test without a single loss." As there is no more information about playing Newport, who were the reigning Welsh champions from 1919/20 at the time, the game has not been included in the fixtures listed below. On 1 January 1921, "Woodlander" reported, "The boys of the Rec have nothing to be ashamed of at the close of the half season. They have played 23 matches, an average of nearly 6 matches per month, and have won 9, drawn 4 and lost 10. When it is taken into consideration that some of the finest teams in Wales have been met and that 5 of the lost matches were only lost by 1 point, it is a record of which the team may well be proud. It is interesting to place on record those 1 point defeats – Abertillery away, Penarth home, the invincible Cross Keys home, Ynysybwl home and Resolven home. The gate is improving and the second moiety of the Old Firm's season promises to be more successful than the first." During the season, Mount registered home wins over Blaina, Aberaman, Pontypridd and Bridgend, lost two close games against Ebbw Vale, and drew at home against Treherbert, who were the season's Glamorgan League champions. There was also a Christmas Day loss at Bridgend and a 0-0 draw at Skewen on Boxing Day 1920. It was at this time that new players started to join the Club, the Aberdare Leader's reporter, "Woodlander", commenting that "the trio of Lovelucks are a tremendous acquisition to the Old Firm....". The best known of these because of their try scoring exploits were wing "Buller" Loveluck and his brother, Gwilym, who played centre, and, according to the Centenary Season's historical account, "The First 100 Years", were signed from Aberavon and Pyle respectively. Things were on their way up for the Old Firm, with more new signings following for the 1921/22 season.

Fixtures 1920/21

Opponents	Date	Venue	Score	Tries	Scorers/Comments
Aberaman	11 Sep 1920	Away	0-6	0	No scorers.
Taffs Well	18 Sep 1920	Home	23-0	7	Skym 3T, C, Tommy Grant 2T, Harry West T, Tom Collins T.
Resolven	25 Sep 1920	Home	0-7	0	No scorers.
Glynneath	25 Sep 1920	Home	8-15	2	Loveluck T, Harry West T, Edgar George C.
Blaina	9 Oct 1920	Home	6-0	2	Skym T, Buller Loveluck T.
Ynysybwl	9 Oct 1920	Away	3-4	1	Loveluck T.
Abercarn	16 Oct 1920	Away	8-5	2	Loveluck T, Thomas T, Feltham C.
Crumlin	18 Oct 1920	Home	3-3	1	Loveluck T.
Risca	30 Oct 1920	Away	9-6	1	Buller Loveluck T, Feltham DG, AN Other C.
Pontycymmer	30 Oct 1920	Home	27-0	3+	Buller Loveluck 3T, AN Other 18pts.
Glynneath	30 Oct 1920	Away	0-0	0	No scorers.
Ebbw Vale	6 Nov 1920	Away	0-3	0	No scorers.
Bridgend	1 Jan 1921	Away	0-15	0	No scorers.
Skewen	1 Jan 1921	Home	0-0	0	No scorers.
Abertillery	1 Jan 1921	Away	Unknown	Unknown	Abertillery win by 1pt. Scorers unknown.
Penarth	1 Jan 1921	Home	Unknown	Unknown	Penarth win by 1pt. Scorers unknown.
Cross Keys	1 Jan 1921	Home	Unknown	Unknown	Cross Keys win by 1pt. Scorers unknown.
Ynysybwl	1 Jan 1921	Home	Unknown	Unknown	Ynysybwl win by 1pt. Scorers unknown.
Resolven	1 Jan 1921	Away	Unknown	Unknown	Resolven win by 1pt. Scorers unknown.
Llanhilleth	8 Jan 1921	Away	0-9	0	No scorers.
Llanhilleth	22 Jan 1921	Home	3-0	1	Buller Loveluck T.
Pontypridd	5 Feb 1921	Home	8-3	1+	Gwilym Loveluck T, Mellish C, AN Other 3pts.
Bridgend	12 Mar 1921	Home	6-5	1	George Allen T, P.
Ebbw Vale	16 Apr 1921	Home	3-6	0+	Scorer unknown.
Aberaman	16 Apr 1921	Home	14-3	3+	Ike Grant T, Tom Collins T, West T, AN Other 5pts.

Opponents	Date	Venue	Score	Tries	Scorers/Comments
Talywain	23 Apr 1921	Home	0-0	0	No scorers.
Treherbert	7 May 1921	Home	3-3	1	George Allen T.

Summary of Playing Record

P	W	D	L	For	Against	Tries Scored	Win Rate %
27	9	5	13	124+	93+	26+	42.59

Match Reports & Publications

9 October 1920

<u>Mountain Ash 6 Blaina 0</u>

Mount Team: Williams, B. Loveluck, T. Collins, G. Loveluck, I. Skym, Shon Thomas, E. Loveluck, H. Fortt, C. Sage, R. Fryer, J. Allen, T. Grant, P. C. Perryman, Ben Teague, J. Fryer.

The Aberdare Leader's rugby reporter, "Woodlander", reported, "the trio of Lovelucks are a tremendous acquisition to the Old Firm for they show splendid resource on every occasion......but when B. Loveluck ran half the field and got over, the crowd showed frenzied delight."

30 October 1920

<u>Risca 6 Mountain Ash 9</u>

"Woodlander" reported in the Aberdare Leader, "....On Thursday, the boys visited Risca and ideal football weather favoured them. The supporters rolled up like a pay day. Charabancs, cars, trains, in fact any old thing would do as long as they got there. Risca folk swear that the whole of the Mount came, for they were heard from miles around. Their cheers were most impartial, and any good movement on either side obtained due reward. The game was one of the season's best. When the Old Firm's backs got a chance, there was only one team in it. Buller's try and Feltham's drop goal will be remembered for many a day....Spectators were given a real treat."

<u>Mountain Ash 27 Pontycymmer 0</u>

"Woodlander" reported in the Aberdare Leader, "....The weather was great and the way the ball was thrown about reminded one of the famous London Harlequins. It was only Buller's extra speed that got him 3 tries."

<u>Glynneath 0 Mountain Ash 0</u>

"....the match attracted a great crowd but value for money was lacking. Dirty tactics were frequent, and on no occasion has the Mount team returned with more bumps, bruises and black eyes. The watchword was evidently, "play the man and not the ball". In the first half, the Mount looked like going under, no doubt the strenuous games of the week had told its tale and left them stale – but oh what a difference when they turned round. The forwards gave one of their best displays of the season and with a little more steadiness at the psychological moments (these kind of moments come in every footballer's life), a score must have resulted. As it was, like a smile, it didn't come off and the game ended in a pointless draw. Fixtures between Glynneath and Mount in my opinion are not productive of best football, and perhaps the dropping of this engagement for at least a season might alter things. Next Saturday, Ebbw Vale is the rendezvous for the Old Firm. They are a tough nut to crack, but a crack team can do lots of things."

6 November 1920

Ebbw Vale 3 Mountain Ash 0

"Woodlander" reported in the Aberdare Leader, "....no doubt the gruelling the Old Firm partook of at Glynneath was responsible for the lowering of their colours by the Ebbw Valians on Saturday. A large crowd greeted the Old Firm and the game was really fine and open. The Vale forwards controlled the scrums so well that the Mount backs had few chances to attack....it was only a few minutes to whistle time before the Mount citadel fell. The spectators at the Monmouthshire ground were enthusiastic over the sporting tactics displayed by the Mount, many declaring it was the best game of the season."

22 January 1921

"Woodlander" commented in the Aberdare Leader in his match report, "The latest problem. Feltham has gone North. If a man tries to become a professional and fails and then comes back again, is he pro or amateur?"

5 February 1921

Mountain Ash 8 Pontypridd 3

Mount Team: Mellish, Buller Loveluck, Collins, Gwilym Loveluck, I. Grant, McPherson, W. L. Jones, Perryman, Beynon, Fred Morgan, T. Grant, J. Allen, Stan Morgan, G. Allen, Ted Griffiths.

"Woodlander" reported in the Aberdare Leader, "The visitors to the Rec on Saturday afternoon were the famous Pontypridd players. Although not the players of twenty years ago, when they put up some of the stiffest fights that the Old Firm ever took part in, they play a fine game. Perryman, Fred Morgan and T. Grant were the pick of a fine pack."

12 March 1921

Mountain Ash 6 Bridgend 5

Mount Team: H. West, B. Loveluck, W. Phillips, G. Loveluck, J. Thomas, Ted Griffiths, Trevor Davies, R. Fryer, H. Brown, Stan Morgan, J. Fryer, J. Allen, G. Allen, L. Fryer, L. Beynon.

The Aberdare Leader reported, "The visit of Bridgend had been looked forward to with considerable interest for had not Bridgend become famous for defeating Swansea and Cardiff? The Old Firm were rather unlucky to have to take the field without Collins, their brilliant centre, otherwise the two teams were equally matched. The ground was in a wretched condition and the Mountain Ash committee should seriously consider whether some of the matches could not be played elsewhere, for the turf has no chance of recovery." The "brilliant centre" Collins, referred to in this report, is Tom Collins who went on to play for Wales in 1923.

16 April 1921

Mountain Ash 14 Aberaman 3

The Aberdare Leader reported, "The local rugger derby between the above teams was completely spoiled by rough play. The Mount men were overwhelmingly superior to the Amanites. The Old Firm put out a strong team, Ike Grant taking the place of Loveluck, the team thus being practically the same as was fielded for Ebbw Vale. A huge crowd assembled around the Rec enclosure and watched the play and fouls, frequent, especially on the visitors' side....Collins was crocked on two occasions and other players were badly hurt. Aberaman scored a try but failed to majorise it despite the claims of players and touch judge. Actually, the ball went outside the goal posts by five or six yards. The game, a tiresome one, ended in victory."

7 May 1921

<u>Mountain Ash 3 Treherbert 3</u>

Mount Team: Harry West, Buller Loveluck, Tom Collins, Gwilym Loveluck, W. Phillips, Teddy Griffiths, Trevor Davies, R. Fryer, Jim Fryer, Beynon, G. Allen, L. Fryer, J. Allen, Ben Teague, Ike Grant.

"Woodlander" reported in the Aberdare Leader, "At the end of a comparatively good season, one feels almost compelled to write nice things about our local young "Old Firm". It must not be thought they are absolutely "it" – very far from it, but with every intention to be kind and yet critical, they have a lot to learn. On Saturday, the champions of the Glamorgan League were entertained at the Rec and like the majority of teams that have visited the stony enclosure, came, saw and did not conquer. Seven seasons have passed since the Old Firm walked away with the trophy put up by the W.R.U. Many things have happened and yet lots of feeling, not antagonistic, entered into the game. Recollections of past players and severe reminders of present ones sought to blot out the long period of war. Both sides respected each other much more than they did in the old days, especially considering the fact that the proceeds were to go to the local distress fund....£21 was handed over to the fund."

<u>Mountain Ash Rugby Football Club</u>
<u>"The Old Firm"</u>
<u>Season 1920/21</u>

Back Row L-R: Dan Horrigan (Trainer), Tom Collins, George Allen, Wilfred Perryman, T. Grant, J. Thomas, Enoch Watkins (Secretary),
Middle Row L-R: Stan Morgan, W.R. Loveluck, Dick Fryer, J. Allen, Fred Morgan,
Front Row L-R: Jim Beynon, T. Llewellyn, Gwilym Loveluck Capt, Ted Griffiths, T. Davies, L. Morgan (Trainer).

Season 1921/22

Memorable Season For Old Firm
37 Wins, A French Tour & Fred Samuel's Welsh Cap

What a superb season this was for the Old Firm under the captaincy of Jim Beynon. Several new players were signed to increase the strength of the team which included scrum half Sid Congdon, full back Fred Samuel and forward Oliver Davies, all from Llanelly RFC. There was also a tour to France – the Club's second following the inaugural trip in 1911/12 – a South Wales Echo article published in January 1958 and the Club's Centenary publication, "The First 100 Years", both stating Périgueux and Brive were the opponents. Unfortunately, although both Clubs were contacted in 2014 asking for match details, none were forthcoming. Full back Fred Samuel impressed throughout the season and got his reward when he was capped 3 times by Wales in the second half of the season, playing against Scotland, France and Ireland. In the South Wales Echo's historical account of January 1958, it was stated that Samuel was joined by seven other Mount players in the Welsh trials during the season, namely, centre Tom Collins, scrum half Sid Congdon, wing "Buller" Loveluck, three-quarter Gwilym Loveluck, and forwards Tom Brown, Oliver Davies and Tom Shepherd. It completed Mount's best post World War I season to date.

The Aberdare Leader's rugby reporter, "Woodlander", summed up the season in an article published on 13 May 1922 in which he said, "The Old Firm played 52, won 37, drew 5, lost 10, with points for 591 and points against 198. Buller Loveluck scored 39 tries, Tom Collins scored 128 points and Fred Samuel scored 106 points. Scrum half Sid Congdon has had a magnificent season. There are rumours that he will be made Captain next season. If so, he will fully deserve it and uphold the best traditions of the Old Firm. There are rumours that Jim Beynon (Messrs Nixon's popular draughtsman) is retiring. He has been a power to his side in the most successful season for twenty years. The Old Firm have a remarkable record, playing 34 matches without a point scored against them. A Grandstand is to be built at the Rec. Prospects for next season are excellent and there are already matches arranged against Headingley, Belfast Collegians, Llanelli, Pontypool, Cross Keys, Neath, Bridgwater, Bath, Maesteg and Swansea (to open the new Stand). The Old Firm made an impression in France for they have received a flattering nine invitations for next season, both in Paris and the south. The team will probably go over twice! The same backs will play next season. What a team it would have been had the forwards been anything like the backs. Never mind, pluck up, buck up and good luck to next season." Of the 52 games listed in his report, details of 41 of them are below. The season's actual playing record, played 52, etc. varies from the played 47, won 40, drawn 2, lost 5, points for 506 and points against of 128, which was in the Centenary Season's historical account, "The First 100 Years". Where exactly this playing record came from is unknown and it seems incorrect. The other apparent mistake in "The First 100 Years" is the statement that "Buller Loveluck, playing on the wing, was able to score 43 tries and broke the 20 year old record of Reuben Carpenter." The Leader's reporter, "Woodlander", states he scored 39 tries, and surprisingly there was no mention in his summary of full back Fred Samuel's 3 Welsh Caps or any of the other players who had Welsh trials.

During the season, there were notable wins over Treorky, Pontypridd, Bridgend and Aberavon. The season also included games against English, French and Irish opposition. There was a "double" over Yorkshire Club, Otley, a convincing away win over Weston and a 5-0 home win over Belfast Collegians. On the Old Firm's Christmas tour, there was a 10-10 draw at Bath on Boxing Day 1921 and a 15-0 win at Cheltenham the day after. There were narrow home and away losses against the season's eventual Welsh champions, Cross Keys, 5-3 at the Rec and 6-4 in the dying minutes away from home. The Club also had other teams. In January 1922, the South Wales Daily News reported a 0-0 draw for Mountain Ash Reserves away at Pontypool and a 6-0 win for Mountain Ash Boys at home to Pontypool Boys.

Fixtures 1921/22

Opponents	Date	Venue	Score	Tries	Scorers/Comments
Taffs Well	5 Sep 1921	Home	27-3	Unknown	Scorers unknown.
Abertillery	12 Sep 1921	Home	3-9	0+	Scorers unknown.
Weston-super-Mare	24 Sep 1921	Away	21-0	6	Scorers unknown.
Abercarn	24 Sep 1921	Home	4-0	0	Fred Samuel DG.
Ebbw Vale	26 Sep 1921	Away	4-5	0	R. Fryer DG.
Talywain	3 Oct 1921	Home	16-0	Unknown	Scorers unknown.
Glamorgan Wanderers	10 Oct 1921	Home	9-0	3	Watty Phillips T, AN Other 2T.
Aberaman	15 Oct 1921	Away	7-0	1	Oliver Davies T, Tom Collins DG.
Penarth	17 Oct 1921	Away	7-0	1	Loveluck T, Fred Samuel DG.
Briton Ferry	31 Oct 1921	Home	12-0	2	Ben Teague T, Jack Allen T, Tom Collins DG, Fred Samuel C.
Abertillery	7 Nov 1921	Home	0-0	0	No scorers.
Crumlin	14 Nov 1921	Away	3-0	0	Fred Samuel P.
Penarth	21 Nov 1921	Home	9-0	Unknown	Scorers unknown.
Abercarn	28 Nov 1921	Away	0-0	0	No scorers.
Treorky	5 Dec 1921	Home	10-3	Unknown	Scorers unknown.
Barry	12 Dec 1921	Home	23-3	Unknown	Scorers unknown.
Cardiff	17 Dec 1921	Home	6-7	1	Sid Congdon T, Fred Samuel P.
Cross Keys	19 Dec 1921	Away	4-6	0	Harry DG.
Otley	24 Dec 1921	Away	11-0	Unknown	Per Otley RFC. Scorers unknown.
Bath	26 Dec 1921	Away	10-10	2	W. Loveluck T, Phillip T, Phil Hughes DG.
Cheltenham	27 Dec 1921	Away	15-0	3	Tom Collins T, DG, Loveluck T, Phillips T, Fred Samuel C.
Cardiff & District	2 Jan 1922	Home	25-0	Unknown	Scorers unknown.
Ogmore Vale	9 Jan 1922	Away	0-0	0	No scorers.
Pontypridd	16 Jan 1922	Away	5-3	0+	Scorers unknown.
Bridgend	30 Jan 1922	Home	3-0	0	Fred Samuel P.
Ogmore Vale	6 Feb 1922	Home	12-3	Unknown	Scorers unknown.
Briton Ferry	13 Feb 1922	Away	3-14	0+	Scorer unknown.
Aberavon	20 Feb 1922	Away	0-9	0	No scorers.
Cross Keys	27 Feb 1922	Home	3-5	1	Tom Collins T.
Barry	13 Mar 1922	Home	22-3	Unknown	Scorers unknown.
Aberavon	14 Mar 1922	Home	7-3	0	Fred Samuel P, H. Farrow DG.
Pontardawe	20 Mar 1922	Home	15-0	Unknown	Scorers unknown.
Crumlin	27 Mar 1922	Home	12-0	Unknown	Scorers unknown.

Opponents	Date	Venue	Score	Tries	Scorers/Comments
Ebbw Vale	10 Apr 1922	Away	3-10	0+	Scorer unknown.
Otley	15 Apr 1922	Home	11-0	3	Tom Collins 2T, Jack Allen T, AN Other C.
Belfast Collegians	17 Apr 1922	Home	5-0	1	Sid Congdon T, C.
Aberaman	22 Apr 1922	Away	3-3	1	Griffiths T.
Bridgend	24 Apr 1922	Away	9-11	1	Buller Loveluck T, Fred Samuel 2P.
Penylan	1 May 1922	Home	6-0	Unknown	Scorers unknown.
Périgueux (France)	Unknown	Away	Unknown	Unknown	Scorers unknown.
Brive (France)	Unknown	Away	Unknown	Unknown	Scorers unknown.

Summary of Above Playing Record

P	W	D	L	Results Unknown	For	Against	Tries Scored	Win Rate %
41	25	5	9	2	345+	110+	26+	70.51

Summary of Actual Playing Record

P	W	D	L	For	Against	Tries Scored	Win Rate %
52	37	5	10	591	198	Unknown	75.96

Match Reports & Publications

Mountain Ash RFC was encouraging Junior rugby as far back as the post WWI years. An article that appeared in the Aberdare Leader in September 1921 follows:

<ins>Mountain Ash Schools' Rugby League</ins>
"Yet another season – the third in the history of the above League – is about to commence. In contrast to the two last seasons, there is no trepidation and pessimism this time. The League has been safely steered through the troubled waters of uncertainty and is now entering a smooth calm harbour. The splendid backing of the public towards the end of last season has done much to give a tremendous fillip to the "old code" for the youngsters. The standard of play by the boys is such that they are an attraction in themselves and there is every prospect that last season's fine record will be eclipsed. The premier Club have dealt magnificently with the League and have granted the use of the Rec for Saturday afternoon matches with the following town teams: Swansea, Cardiff, Newport, Pontypool, Aberavon, Maesteg, Llanelly and Rhondda. It is certain that the local enthusiasts will turn up in huge numbers to witness these interesting games." The article went on to name the local teams that underpinned the town team. These were Duffryn, Caegarw, Darrenlas, the County School, the Higher Standard, Newtown, Miskin, Ynysboeth, Carnetown and Ynysybwl.

10 October 1921

<ins>Mountain Ash 9 Glamorgan Wanderers 0</ins>
The South Wales Daily News reported, "The first half was played under most trying conditions owing to the blazing sun. The second half was a great improvement upon the first, the Old Firm treating the large crowd to a brilliant display. Three tries were scored from beautiful handling. Particularly clever was the score by Watty Phillips, his pace serving him well."

17 October 1921

Penarth 0 Mountain Ash 7

The South Wales Daily News reported, "A good crowd assembled at Penarth. Immediately after kick off, it was obvious the visiting forwards were much too good for Penarth. They gave a very clever display in the open, and in the scrums, heeling the ball with monotonous regularity. In consequence, their backs had far more opportunities than Penarth, who were continually defending. Eventually a fine movement was initiated by Prior, and the ball, travelling along the backs, saw Loveluck score a try wide out...."

17 December 1921

Mountain Ash 6 Cardiff XV 7

The Aberdare Leader reported, "A splendid fillip was given to rugby in the 'Darian valley by the visit of a Cardiff XV to Mountain Ash. The Old Firm, as they are universally known, put up an excellent exhibition of the handling code, and Fred Samuel, who is in the running for his Welsh cap despite injuries, enhanced the great reputation he has built up. Congdon, who hails from Llanelly, the Club that Samuel left to join the Hill team, also did remarkably well despite the clever opposition of Podd, the Cardiff reserve centre, who deputised with distinction at Leicester a fortnight ago. The Old Firm put up a wonderful fight and they were, on the run of play, unfortunate in not being able to declare the scores even. Cardiff won the toss and played with a stiff breeze. Pretty play in the opening stages led to a Cardiff attack but the Mountain Ash defence was good....Congdon and Parry broke away cleverly around the blindside and inter-passing took the Old Firm to the visitors' line....Samuel sent play back to the Cardiff line with a great touch finder. Jim Fryer was hurt and had to leave the field for "repairs"....After good passing, Charlie Bryant crossed for Cardiff in the corner. After this Mountain Ash were most persistent in their efforts and Congdon was prominent in a scrummage on the Cardiff line. Just before the interval, the Taffsiders (Cardiff) were penalised and Fred Samuel dropped a lovely goal (to make it 3-3). Following the restart, Johnson received from a scrum and dropped a magnificent goal from 30 yards against a stiff breeze. Mountain Ash set up a series of attacks and the Cardiff line narrowly escaped from being crossed. Fred Samuel hit the posts when dropping a goal....Geo. Allen made a grand burst but was well tackled on the line....Congdon crossed in the corner but Samuel failed to convert. The Old Firm were decidedly unlucky in not winning for they played by far the better game."

19 December 1921

Cross Keys 6 Mountain Ash 4

The South Wales Daily News reported, "This match at Pandy Park was robbed of much of its interest through the absence of Fred Samuels, the visiting custodian, whose brilliant display on Thursday in the Welsh trials considerably enhanced his reputation....Samuels unfortunately damaged his ankle." In the second half, the report went on to say, "From a loose rush, Harry dropped a neat goal, putting the visitors ahead. The visitors' kicking was good and it was only splendid defensive work which kept them out. In the last few moments, Mountain Ash were penalised and Ossie Hicks kicked a splendid goal." Cross Keys were Welsh Club champions at the end of the season.

26 December 1921

Bath 10 Mountain Ash 10
South Wales Daily News

BATH 2-0-10, MOUNTAIN ASH 1-2-10.

The visitors by vigorous and powerful play started to attack at once, and at half time were 2 tries ahead. W. LOVELUCK scored first and a mistake by Bath's full back let through PHILLIP. PHIL HUGHES dropped a fine goal early in the second half. Bath made a splendid recovery and VOWLES and J. RICHARDSON obtained tries, Woodward adding the extra points in each case. The visiting full back played a wonderful game.

27 December 1921

Cheltenham 0 Mountain Ash 15
South Wales Daily News

At Cheltenham. Mountain Ash had the better of the opening play, and LOVELUCK scored near the posts. Samuel failed at goal. The Welshmen continued to have the best of matters, and following a fine round of passing, PHILLIPS got possession near the Cheltenham 25, and with a fine turn of speed he raced past Eden and Watson and scored in the corner.

The second half was well contested, with Cheltenham slightly superior in the forward line. The Welshmen, however, continued to play a better game at back, and COLLINS scored a try for Samuel to add the extra points.

Cheltenham were frequently dangerous, but could not finish, and the Welshmen came again, and COLLINS dropped a goal.

30 January 1922

Mountain Ash 3 Bridgend 0

The South Wales Daily News reported, "Keen scrummaging followed the kick off, both sides pressing in turn, Samuel (of Mountain Ash) being prominent on more than one occasion with good defensive work and touch finding. Play was right on the visitors' line when Mountain Ash were awarded a penalty and Fred Samuel kicked a fine goal. This proved to be the only score of the game, Bridgend finding Samuel too strong in defence."

20 February 1922

Aberavon 9 Mountain Ash 0
South Wales Daily News

Player Ordered Off.

ABERAVON 1-2-9, MOUNTAIN ASH 0-0-0.

Mountain Ash visited Aberavon for the first time this season. The visitors were heavily handicapped owing to the absence of six of their regular forwards.

There was a nasty scene near the end, when Allan, a visiting forward, tackled W. J. Hopkins and the referee promptly ordered him off. There was a great outcry against the offending player and some of the spectators almost showed a tendency to rush the field.

27 February 1922

Mountain Ash 3 Cross Keys 5
South Wales Daily News

MOUNTAIN ASH 0-1-3, CROSS KEYS 1-0-5.

Keen, without being over-vigorous, the game was a closely contested one and attracted a record crowd at the Mountain Ash Recreation Ground. The visitors' heavier pack exerted a pressure in the early stages of the game, but the backs were not able to carry home the attack. COLLINS' try in the first half was a brilliant performance and finished a full round of passing from the scrum near the half-way line.

Cross Keys were more in the picture in the second half and exploited back play to a larger extent. Although less spectacular than Collins' try, MORRIS' score was well made and was attributable to persistent and resourceful play on the part of Winmill, the outstanding figure on the visiting side. Hicks did equally well in majorising from a by no means easy angle.

14 March 1922

Mountain Ash 7 Aberavon 3
South Wales Daily News

Surprising Results.

MOUNTAIN ASH 2-0-7, ABERAVON 0-1-3

(By "Old Stager.")

It is a generally accepted rule in Rugby football that a side which wins solely as a result of kicks from the field of play, especially if their own defence has been penetrated, should sympathise with their opponents and give thanks for their good fortune. Of course, there are exceptions to such a rule; and there has been no more notable exception this season than that which occurred at Mountain Ash yesterday. The "Old Firm," more by reason of ill-luck and inexperience than anything else, failed to break down Aberavon's defence on any single occasion, but had they not obtained a sufficient margin of points to give them victory they would have been one of the most unfortunate sides I have seen. They had far away the better of the game, and especially so in the second half when they overcame troubles and trials which would have broken any but the stoutest hearts.

Aberavon did not do themselves justice. I have seen them in half-a-dozen contests this season, and on neither of those occasions have they shown such indifferent form, and allowed their energies to be so ill-directed.

Won with Thirteen Men.

Opening the second half with whatever advantage might be gained from Mountain Ash's misfortune in having to bring Geo. Allen out of the pack to take the place of Ivor Davies (a youthful right wing of promise, who had badly twisted his ankle), they quickly found themselves in a position of greater numerical superiority by reason of Collins, the "Old Firm's" left centre, meeting with an injury which caused concussion, and necessitated his retirement from the game. Yet Mountain Ash continued to hold the upper hand; indeed, their superiority was more marked as far as mere aggressiveness was concerned when they only had six men in the pack instead of eight. For some inexplicable reason Aberavon seemed to be nervous and over-anxious; they tried their hardest, but in the second period their endeavours were so obvious that they were frustrated almost before they were put into operation. Their backs, it is true, were not as clever or elusive as they usually are, and cannot be let off without a share of the blame, though it was the surprising failure of the forwards that was the main cause of the defeat. The "Old Firm's" pack is far from being an ideally selected octette; indeed, they seemed to be the weakest section of the side, but they obtained a mastery which was in itself sufficient to warrant success for their side. Jim Jones, for once in a way, failed to inspire his men, who were beaten in the scrummages, and who were far below their high average form in the loose.

With the advantages and chances which came his way owing to the success of his forwards Congdon naturally had an enjoyable afternoon. He was fortunate, too, in that Dan Jones, who was directly opposed to him, was lacking in experience, and all that comes with experience. For a youth, however, the Aberavon scrum-worker did well; he has ability (as his fitting for a son of Dan Jones, who played at inside half for Wales in 1897) and should be worth perservering with.

The "Old Firm's" quartette enjoyed more opportunities than their opponents, whose most valuable work was of a defensive character. Collins, for Mountain Ash, was the most classic player of the bunch, his deceptive running frequently bringing him into prominence, and if it was not for a physical handicap which he can never overcome, he would train on to be a great centre. Farrow, too, is alert and useful, and the fact that his style contrasts with that of Collins makes him all the more effective, and the quartette the prettier to watch. Loveluck, who made the best run of the day, following a clever interception when Aberavon were moving dangerously, is worth a place in the best company, and shone (perhaps by reason of his extra chances) more than Ring, who is playing better than ever at the moment.

Williams, Aberavon's custodian, gave a splendid display, the value of which should not be minimised because he compared unfavourably with Fred Samuel, who showed that his form in internationals is all wrong, and who would not have held any advantage had he not improved upon that.

The Scores.

The whole of the scoring came in the first half, and most of it in the first five minutes. SAMUEL kicked a lovely penalty goal from the touchline after two minutes play, and three minutes later Hunt Davies made a perfect opening for RING to score a try which was as pretty as one could wish for. Then, shortly before the interval, Congdon won an attacking position, and everything worked like clockwork for FARROW to obtain the desired position to drop a goal. Mountain Ash ought to have gone further ahead, for they had the better of a bright game, but they did not.

Referee Knocked Out.

One remarkable incident occurred during the game. Mountain Ash were attacking when Congdon dropped at goal but failed to rise the ball, which cannoned into the referee, and knocked him clean out. Before he collapsed he managed to sound his whistle to stop the game, and a considerable interval elapsed before he was able to resume. Teams:—

Aberavon.—Back, E. Williams; three-quarters, J. Ring, D. Hunt Davies, T. Parker, and W. Ould; half-backs, Dan Jones and W. J. Hopkins; forwards, Jim Jones, L. Jenkins, R. Randall, D. Tobin, J. H. Davies, T. Tobin, W. Hopkins, and W. Jenkins.

Mountain Ash.—Back, Fred Samuel; three-quarters, Buller Loveluck, T. Collins, H. Farrow, and Ivor Davies; half-backs, T. Parry and S. Congdon; forwards, J. Beynon, R. Fryer, J. Fryer, G. Allen, F. Morgan, Buller Evans, O. Davies, and G. Chamberlain.

Referee—Mr. R. W. Barry, Cardiff.

The Old Firm v Club Athlétique Périgueux
French Tour 1921/22

The above photograph of the Old Firm was taken on tour in Périgueux in France. Only some of the names in it are known. In the back row, from left to right as you look, is the Old Firm's Trainer, Dan Horrigan, wearing a hat. The player wearing what looks like a Welsh cap on the right is likely to be full back Fred Samuel, who was capped 3 times in the second half of the 1921/22 season. To Samuel's right is Club Secretary Enoch Watkins. In the middle row, kneeling, from left to right, is centre Tom Collins. The two players to his right as you look are backs Gwilym and "Buller" Loveluck followed by forward George Allen. In the front row, from left to right, the first three players are forwards Dick Fryer and Jim Beynon – who was the season's captain – and scrum half Sid Congdon.

With the help of Club supporter, Mr Gareth Burridge, the two boards behind the team were translated into English. The board on the left is a World War I memorial in memory of those who died in the conflict, with the letters C.A.P. heading it representing Club Athlétique Périgueux. The board to the right is a warning to those spectators who make excessive, abusive noise, to keep quiet!

17 April 1922

Mountain Ash 5 Belfast Collegians 0
South Wales Daily News

> **MOUNTAIN ASH 1-0-5, BELFAST COLLEGIANS 0-0-0.**
>
> Mountain Ash adapted their play to the conditions with better success than the visitors, who were expected to show up well in front. S. Larmour, McKoe, and Marput were prominent, and played a hard game for the visitors. Campbell (full-back) and Gillespie were the most prominent among their backs and saved their side repeatedly. Mountain Ash forwards excelled in the loose, and contributed sweeping rushes which deserved scores. Mountain Ash were without Oliver Davies, who injured his knee, for the greater part of the game. It was a most enjoyable game and played in excellent spirits. CONGDON scored and converted his try.

Fred Samuel
Mountain Ash RFC & Wales
3 Welsh Caps
1921/22 v Scotland, Ireland & France

Unfortunately, very little is known about Thomas Frederick Samuel. He was born on 8 January 1897 in Llanelli and played for Llanelli RFC before joining Mountain Ash RFC for the 1921/22 season. He was capped 3 times by Wales, all in the second half of the 1921/22 season, and played in two Welsh wins and a draw, kicking two conversions. At the end of this season, he followed several former Mount players by signing for Hull Northern Union (Rugby League) Club. He later emigrated to Australia for a brief period. He was last seen in Coventry during the Blitz of 1941, where it is believed he died.

Mountain Ash Rugby Football Club
"The Old Firm"
Season 1921/22

Back Row L-R: J. Collins, Oliver Davies, Ted McGregor, H. Farrow, Jim Fryer, Fred Morgan, I. Davies, Dick Fryer, W. Evans, Jack Allen, C. Brown, Ben Teague, Dan Horrigan (Trainer),

Middle Row L-R: Enoch Watkins (Secretary), W. Phillips, Gwilym Loveluck, Jim Beynon Capt, Tom Collins, W.R."Buller" Loveluck, Jack Jarvis (Chairman),

Front Row L-R: J. Legg, Tom Parry, Fred Samuel*, Sid Congdon, W. Llewellyn (Baggage Man).

* denotes Welsh International

Season 1922/23

<u>A Season To Savour As Mount Hit Heady Heights</u>
<u>Tom Collins Plays For Wales</u>

This was a second superb season in succession for the Old Firm. As good as 1921/22 had been, this one turned out to be even better and remains one of the greatest seasons in the Club's long and proud history. It didn't get off to a great start though. At the start of October 1922, Mount's Welsh International full back, Fred Samuel, went North, joining Hull, but although losing a fine player, a great season followed for the Old Firm with wins over Cross Keys, who were the reigning Welsh champions from 1921/22, Cardiff, Llanelli, Neath, Bridgend, Penarth, Glamorgan Wanderers – which the Aberdare Leader reported was the "first visit to the Cardiff Suburbians" – and English opposition in the form of Bath, Bridgwater & Albion, and Headingley. It was highly impressive stuff.

The 11-5 win over Cardiff on 4 December 1922 was the official opening of the new grandstand at the Rec and crowned a very prestigious day for the Club. There were draws against Abertillery twice and Pontypool, and close defeats at Llanelli and Pontypool, the latter two games being played over three days, the Aberdare Leader's reporter, "Woodlander", commenting, "The Old Firm's weekend tour has been disastrous for both games were signal defeats." It showed how much was expected from this Mount side and they certainly delivered.

The season's record showed 41 games played, 22 won, 5 drawn, 12 lost, and 2 games on tour against Clermont in France where the result was unknown. In total, at least 325 points were scored – which was a lot back then considering the low scoring nature of most of the games played by all Clubs – which included at least 69 tries, with 192+ points conceded. All this converted to a win rate of 62.82% – which wasn't bad for a valleys Club against high quality opposition.

On the International front, "Woodlander" reported in the Aberdare Leader in January 1923, "The Probable Welsh XV will include Tom Brown of Mountain Ash in the forward line and in The Rest, Sid Congdon and Tom Collins at inside and right centre respectively. The reserves for The Rest will include Buller Loveluck of Mountain Ash at left wing." As it turned out, centre Tom Collins was the sole Mount player to be capped by Wales, becoming the Old Firm's 7th Welsh cap when he played against Ireland at Lansdowne Road, Dublin. It was stated in the South Wales Echo's historical account of January 1958 and the Centenary season's publication, "The First 100 Years", that there was also a third tour to France, where the Old Firm played two games against Clermont Ferrand. Although Clermont was contacted in 2014 asking for match details, there was no response. Whatever the score in France was, this was a second superb season for the Old Firm.

Fixtures 1922/23

Opponents	Date	Venue	Score	Tries	Scorers/Comments
Risca	Sep 1922	Home	17-0	Unknown	Scorers unknown.
Penylan	16 Sep 1922	Home	12-3	3	Harry Corsi T, AN Other T, Penalty Try, Fred Samuel P.
Ynysybwl	16 Sep 1922	Home	11-0	3	AN Other 2T, Tom Parry T, Fred Samuel C.
Crumlin	30 Sep 1922	Home	9-3	Unknown	Scorers unknown.
Pontypool	2 Oct 1922	Away	3-8	0	Fred Samuel P.
Llanelly	3 Oct 1922	Away	3-6	1	Loveluck T.
Penarth	9 Oct 1922	Home	18-5	3	Gwilym Loveluck 2T, Harry Corsi T, R.G. Beynon P, 3C.
Neath	14 Oct 1922	Home	12-4	4	Gwilym Loveluck 3T, Tom Parry T.
Abertillery	21 Oct 1922	Away	0-0	0	No scorers.
Aberaman	21 Oct 1922	Home	3-0	1	AN Other T.
Maesteg	28 Oct 1922	Home	6-10	2	Gwilym Loveluck T, Dick Fryer T.
Risca	4 Nov 1922	Away	3-7	0+	Scorers unknown.
Bridgwater & Albion	11 Nov 1922	Home	24-0	8	Buller Loveluck 4T, Tom Collins 2T, Sid Congdon T, Harry Corsi T.
Ebbw Vale	18 Nov 1922	Away	3-3	1	Buller Loveluck T.
Bargoed	25 Nov 1922	Away	11-0	3	Buller Loveluck T, Gwilym Loveluck T, Tom Collins T, Simmonds C.
Abertillery	2 Dec 1922	Home	3-3	1	Loveluck T.
Briton Ferry	9 Dec 1922	Away	6-5	1	Harry Corsi T, Tom Brown P.
Cardiff Official opening of the Grandstand at the Rec.	4 Dec 1922	Home	11-5	3	P.J. Skym T, Buller Loveluck T, Tom Collins T, Hugh Jones C.
Cross Keys	16 Dec 1922	Away	0-8	0	No scorers.
Glamorgan Wanderers	23 Dec 1922	Away	17-5	3	Tom Collins 2T, DG, Harry Corsi T, Brown 2C.
Treorky	6 Jan 1923	Home	3-3	1	Buller Loveluck T.
Pontypool	13 Jan 1923	Home	0-0	0	No scorers.
Crumlin	20 Jan 1923	Away	0-4	0	No scorers.
Talywain	27 Jan 1923	Away	0-11	0	No scorers.

Opponents	Date	Venue	Score	Tries	Scorers/Comments
Bath	3 Feb 1923	Home	13-3	3	Buller Loveluck 2T, Sid Congdon T, Oliver Davies 2C.
Ebbw Vale	17 Feb 1923	Home	0-10	0	No scorers.
Penarth	24 Feb 1923	Home	19-3	5	Tom Collins 2T, 2C, Dyke Jones T, Gwilym Loveluck T, Buller Loveluck T.
Briton Ferry	10 Mar 1923	Home	6-0	1	Sid Congdon T, P.
Llanelly	10 Mar 1923	Home	6-3	2	Buller Loveluck T, J. Williams T.
Maesteg	12 Mar 1923	Away	0-24	0	No scorers.
Glamorgan Wanderers	21 Mar 1923	Home	22-12	4	L. Lewis T, J. Simmonds T, Buller Loveluck T, Tom Collins T, Oliver Davies P, AN Other P, 2C.
Bridgend	31 Mar 1923	Home	29-0	7	Tom Collins 2T, Oliver Davies 2T, Emrys Davies T, Buller Loveluck T, Tom Parry T, Dick Fryer DG, Tom Brown 2C.
Neath	31 Mar 1923	Away	4-19	0	Tom Collins DG.
Headingley	31 Mar 1923	Home	16-3	4	Buller Loveluck 2T, Jim Fryer T, Emrys Davies T, W. Thomas 2C.
Bargoed	7 Apr 1923	Home	17-7	1+	Buller Loveluck T, AN Other 14pts.
Cross Keys	9 Apr 1923	Home	3-0	1	Haydn Coopey T.
Glynneath	21 Apr 1923	Home	12-3	2	Dick Fryer T, Buller Loveluck T, Sid Congdon DG, Thomas C.
Aberaman	28 Apr 1923	Away	0-3	0	No scorers.
Glynneath	5 May 1923	Away	3-9	1	Ben Teague T.
Clermont Ferrand (France)	Unknown	Away	Unknown	Unknown	Scorers unknown.
Clermont Ferrand (France)	Unknown	Away	Unknown	Unknown	Scorers unknown.

Summary of Playing Record

P	W	D	L	Results Unknown	For	Against	Tries Scored	Win Rate %
41	22	5	12	2	325+	192+	69+	62.82

Match Reports & Publications

9 September 1922

"Woodlander" reported in the Aberdare Leader, "At the commencement of the 1922/23 season, one can only express a hope that the season's doings will at least equal that of last. It seems but yesterday since I was holding forth on the mighty prowess of the Mountaineers, still the months intervening are only four, a mere handful. Much has been done for the new season and much remains to be accomplished. The new stand, not finished, is becoming an outstanding feature for passers-by, but my merry gentlemen of great wit and snaring sarcasm, wait ye, it is coming along and will be a fait accompli before the electric juice of the Council pours forth its light on the dark corners of the Mount....There is no gain saying the fact that out of the thirty men, there is an outstanding, victorious team. The talent is there, and if not hidden in the ground, will surely play a great part in the coming season of rugby. The Old Firm is stronger than ever, and has budding talent just bursting for the opportunity to come into full bloom. On Saturday's form, Tom Parry may be chosen as the shining light, and, of course, Samuel, sure as ever. Collins and also Corsi....were very noticeable, Sid Congdon is absolutely safe, and Teague also shone on many occasions. Much improvement is needed forward and then, well, everything is possible."

2 October 1922

<u>Pontypool 8 Mountain Ash 3</u>

The Western Mail reported, "After a lapse of many years, the fixtures have been renewed between Pontypool and the Old Firm." This game was the last known game before Fred Samuel turned professional, joining Hull, the Western Mail commenting, "Samuel, the star man of the visiting fifteen took a drop from a penalty and the ball fell well below the cross-bar. Pontypool were preparing to drop out from the 25 line when everybody was amazed to see the referee motioning them to the centre of the field, signifying that he had allowed a goal."

3 October 1922

<u>Llanelly 6 Mountain Ash 3</u>
<u>Refreshing Rugby: Fine Game In Ideal Weather at Stradey</u>

The Western Mail reported, "In ideal weather, Llanelly were visited for the first time this season at Stradey Park on Monday night by the Old Firm....Mountain Ash fielded a representative side which included Sid Congdon and Fred Samuel, ex-members of the Scarlets' team....The opening stages of the game were fast and open, and it was obvious, as was afterwards proved, that a refreshing variety of rugby would be seen.... With the forwards sharing the honours at scrummaging, the backs on both sides in turn attacked in splendid formation....it was not until five minutes before the interval that the Scarlets were able to draw first blood.... try....Towards the end of the game Llanelly kicked a goal. Soon after, Llanelly's lead was reduced through Loveluck scoring a try for Mountain Ash."

The following comment was made in the Aberdare Leader about both games above, "Better conditions prevailed at Stradey Park, Llanelli on Monday evening when the Old Firm paid the famous Scarlets a visit. The play throughout was delightfully open, and from a spectator's point of view, was just the goods. Both back divisions were playing a game of giants....The two defeats were not two disgraces and the day of revenge is not far away."

9 October 1922

Mountain Ash 18 Penarth 5
Western Mail

SEASIDERS SWAMPED.

WONDERFUL GOAL - KICKING AT MOUNTAIN ASH.

	G.	T.	Pts.
Mountain Ash	*4	0	18
Penarth	1	0	5

* Penalty.

Saturday's game at Mountain Ash was brimful of thrilling incident. The outstanding feature was R. G. Beynon's phenomenal goal-kicking. His penalty goal from just inside the half-way and the converting of three tries from difficult angles almost created a record. Nothing finer has ever been seen on the Old Firm's enclosure. In addition Beynon gave a really excellent display of fielding. His efforts were loudly applauded by the largest crowd of the season.

A DESERVED WIN.

Mountain Ash well deserved their win. Their backs were superior, and against a less sound defence than that of Penarth the scoring might have been doubled. Gwilym Loveluck scored on two occasions, and Corsi added the other try. Both packs were evenly matched in the scrums, each side securing a fair share of the ball. Penarth got dangerous on a few occasions, and M. Vyvyan, the visitors' captain, made great efforts to break through a number of times. He was the most prominent of the Penarth backs. Penarth's try was quite unexpected, and was scored in a favourable position to be converted.

14 October 1922

Mountain Ash 12 Neath 4

Mount Team: Backs: P.J. Skym, Buller Loveluck, Harry Corsi, Tom Collins, Gwilym Loveluck, Tom Parry, Sid Congdon Capt,
Forwards: G. Williams, P. Brown, Evans, Williams, Ben Teague, Dick Fryer, A. Evans, Oliver Davies.

The Aberdare Leader commented in its report, "....Six points up, the Old Firm played like champions and would not be denied....Some splendid open midfield play followed and a fine bout of passing ended in Gwilym doing the hat-trick. This proved the final score and Neath retired with a surprise defeat of 12pts to 4. Never has the Old Firm more fully deserved victory than on Monday and the huge crowd were delighted. At all points they were the superiors of their visitors. They engineered their chances and besides using hands and feet, they used brains."

Western Mail

OLD FIRM'S LOVELUCK.

THREE GOOD TRIES AGAINST ALL BLACKS.

	G.	T.	Pts.
Mountain Ash	0	4	12
Neath	*1	0	4

* Dropped.

If Mountain Ash continue to play the sparkling Rugby which enabled them to defeat Neath on Monday they will always command large support. The whole team seemed to be imbued with the spirit that the ball must be given plenty of air, and the result was that they won comfortably and always held the upper hand. The outstanding man on the field was Hugh Jones, the Neath full-back, who touch-kicked, tackled, and ran in brilliant style. Parry and Crabtree were prominent early in the first half, but it was only just before the interval that the Mount opened their account with a try by Gwilym Loveluck. Parry was next over with a smart try.

BEWILDERING PLAY.

Then followed a bewildering piece of play which resulted in Gwilym Loveluck scoring again. The home backs passed in the best Welsh fashion, and the fleet right winger rounded off the movement by touching down near the corner flag. He scored another fine try—his third of the match and eleventh of the season—from good passing, and Hugh Jones reduced the lead with a dropped goal. The Cardiff University player had previously caught the eye, and the crowd gave an ovation for his effort. Altogether it was a splendid sporting game, always keen and clean—just the type to draw the crowd.

4 December 1922

Mountain Ash 11 Cardiff 5
Official Opening of the Grandstand at the Rec

Mount Team: Backs: Hugh Jones, Buller Loveluck, Tom Collins, Harry Corsi, P.J. Skym, Tom Parry, Sid Congdon,
Forwards: G. Williams, Oliver Davies, Tom Brown, Jim Fryer, Ben Teague, Jim Beynon, T. Shepherd, J. Allen.

Western Mail

FOOTBALL

AIM OF MOUNTAIN ASH

TO BE IN THE FOREFRONT OF WELSH RUGBY.

By "OBSERVER."

	G.	T.	Pts.
Mountain Ash	1	2	11
Mr. W. R. Shepherd's (Cardiff) XI.	1	0	5

Mountain Ash is striving to get into the forefront of Welsh Rugby, and on Monday the club formally opened its new grandstand. Mr. Tom Williams, M.E., J.P., performed the opening ceremony, and expressed the wish that all exhibitions on this excellently laid-out ground would be characterised by the spirit of sportsmanship.

Mr. R. W. Shepherd, a member of the Cardiff Athletic Club, took a team chosen by himself to play the "Old Firm." A good side was gathered together, stiffened by the presence of Crad. Rees, D. G. Davies, and Jack Grant, and they were able to put up an excellent fight. The "Old Firm" played brilliant football, however, and deservedly ran out victors by three tries, one of which was converted, to a placed goal.

BULLER LOVELUCK'S DAZZLING RUN.

The Cardiff men opened the scoring through Higginson, who made a wonderful break-through in the first five minutes, and gave Horwood an easy journey over the line. A few minutes later Buller Loveluck obtained possession, and after a dazzling run, in which he worked his way towards the post from the touch-line, he was able to reduce the arrears for Mountain Ash. Collins also scored a lovely try for the home team before the interval, and the Mount were leading at half-time by three points. The second half was fairly even, but the "Old Firm's" better-balanced side enabled them to cross again through Skym.

After the match Mr. Shepherd's team were entertained to a very enjoyable dinner and smoking concert, at which the opinion was expressed that Mountain Ash, by reason of their sportsmanship and delightful open play, were fully deserving of fixtures with the Cardiff Club.

<u>Aberdare Leader</u>
<u>The Old Firm in Excelsis</u>

"For the first time in the history of Mountain Ash Rugby Football Club, a grandstand stands now to their credit and the comfort of their supporters. The aim of the Mountain Ash Club for many years has been, not only to be good rugby players, but also a team of first class ruggers…..Just on the spur of the moment, such names as Wyndham Jones, Millar, the Fryers, Frank Mills and the Grants, all crop up as fervent and devoted adherents of rugger. Wherever the Mount team has travelled and whomsoever they have received, they have been respected not only for their clever display but for their clean outfit."

<u>The Grandstand</u>

"This was exemplified in the speech of Mr Tom Williams M.E., J.P., when formally declaring the Grandstand open on Monday afternoon. He hoped that the supporters of the Club would recognize what had been done for them. Mountain Ash footballers and spectators had always shown a true and loyal standard of fair play.

….The opening of the game was rather wild and the Mount men seemed to have lost their heads……to the Cardiff men, who found one of the silly joker's chances, an open field and an easy try. This was just the sort of thing to buck up the Old Firm and when the try was majorised, nothing better could have happened for the homesters. Coming again and again, the Mount men were completely overwhelming. It was obvious that the pressure must bring reward, for Buller took a scoop from Parry, and racing round the posts, opened the scoring for Mountain Ash….and Collins from the scrum scored a lovely try which was nicely converted by Jones (to give Mount an 8-5 lead at half time). (In the second half), a mighty rush was made by Buller after getting a pretty scoop by Parry….when just within a few yards of the line he was touched into touch. It was a miraculous save but a glorious run. A little later the extraordinary pressure by the Mount resulted in Skym crossing the line. This was not converted and the game ended in a glorious win for the Mount by 11-5."

13 January 1923

The Aberdare Leader reported, "After the match between Glamorgan and Monmouth at Cardiff, the WRU Match Committee selected the sides for the Final Trial at Newport on Thursday, 11 January 1923. The Probable Welsh XV will include Tom Brown of Mountain Ash in the forward line and in The Rest, Sid Congdon and Tom Collins at inside and right centre respectively. The reserves for The Rest will include Buller Loveluck of Mountain Ash at left wing."

27 January 1923

<u>Talywain 11 Mountain Ash 0</u>

The Aberdare Leader reported, "The exigencies of International football sadly depleted the ranks of the Old Firm when they paid their visit to Talywain last Saturday. Tom Collins, Syd Congdon and both Lovelucks, the backbone of the team, were all absentees. The wonder is that the score was so comparatively small against the visitors."

3 February 1923

Mountain Ash 13 Bath 3

Mount Team: Backs: J. Simmonds, Buller Loveluck, Tom Collins, Dyke Jones, Gwilym Loveluck, Sid Congdon, Tom Parry,
Forwards: G. Williams, Tom Brown, T. Shepherd, Oliver Davies, Jim Fryer, Lewis, Allen, Ben Teague.

Western Mail

A GREAT VICTORY.
BATH SUBDUED BY THE OLD FIRM.

	G.	T.	Pts.
Mountain Ash	2	1	13
Bath	0	1	3

Mountain Ash rose to the occasion magnificently and played their best game of the season against Bath. Congdon proved his superiority over his opponent Vowles, and brilliant back play resulted in two great tries being scored, one by Congdon and the other by Buller Loveluck. Both were converted, so that the Old Firm enjoyed a clear lead of ten points in the first half. The second half opened sensationally. Instead of replying to the kick, Lewis, Brown, and other forwards opened an attack which Collins and Buller Loveluck followed up with such advantage that the latter scored a fine try. This was the most thrilling incident of the game. Bath succeeded in scoring a try through Woodward seizing an opportunity. For Mountain Ash the three reserve internationals were in their best form. Congdon, apart from being a great player, is a splendid general. Collins and Buller Loveluck are a dangerous flank, and their pretty interpassing was a feature of the match. Parry has seldom done better. The whole pack displayed a cohesion and wholeheartedness that has not been equalled this season.

"Woodlander" reported in the Aberdare Leader, "The Zummerets from Bath, the team that lowered the flying colours of the famous Cross Keys (reigning Welsh champions from 1921/22), were an undoubted attraction to the Rec on Saturday and gained a splendid ovation from the crowd of 5,000 spectators present. Mr Geo. Hall, M.P., kicked off. After 6 minutes, Mount went 5-0 up through a try by Congdon, converted by Oliver Davies. Loveluck scored the second try, again converted by Oliver Davies to give the Old Firm a 10-0 lead at half time. The re-opening of the game (2nd half) was something like a volcanic disturbance. Congdon secured and cleverly dipped the leather into Parry's hands, who smartly cleared through, racing like a greyhound. Everybody thought he was going through on his own, but he unselfishly passed to Tom Collins, who in turn gave to Loveluck, who scored right in the corner. Kicking became rather wild, two lunges finding touch in the Aberdare Road. The game was strenuously fought right to the end and the whistle blew with Mount in the visitors' 25.

Comments

The game, if not the finest ever seen at the Rec, was worthy of the finest position in the annals of the rugger code. Bath team are always to be respected either as visitors or at home. Parry, Congdon and Simmonds were brilliant, and Loveluck and Oliver Davies were magnificent, especially the latter in his unerring judgement for the cross-bar. The forwards were out for business, and as a whole, the pack were a credit to any side. The Old Firm would have beaten any team on Saturday."

The Aberdare Leader also published an article that appeared in a Bath based newspaper about this game. In a column titled, "Play up Bath", the article commented, "many Bath rugby supporters will remember when Mountain Ash were playing here on Boxing Day, 1921, that Vowles broke away in similar circumstances and gave to J. Richardson who scored, and that thus the match was drawn (10-10 in 1921/22). Probably Congdon, who is first reserve as scrum worker for Wales, smiled when he got his own back.....Loveluck, who rejoices in the nickname of "Buller", created great applause by winding up two excellent passing movements with tries. It was one of the best games seen in Wales for some time a well known Welsh referee told me. The ball was always travelling at a rapid rate, there was an abundance of open play, and the Old Firm's backs combined better than any Welsh line Bath have opposed this season." High praise indeed.

10 February 1923

The Aberdare Leader commented about players going North, "Further Union players have gone north. The wonder is, seeing the continued trade depression, the Rugby League clubs have not been more successful, as there are a large number of International class players who have not been able to get into the national team and are looking for pastures new where their abilities will be appreciated."

10 March 1923

Mountain Ash 6 Llanelly 3
Llanelly Beaten: Line Twice Crossed By The Old Firm

Mount Team: Backs: G. Pritchard; Buller Loveluck, P.J. Skym, Dyke Jones, Gwilym Loveluck; Sid Congdon, G. Walters; Forwards: Oliver Davies, Dick Fryer, Jim Fryer, George Allen, J. Williams, Ben Teague, T. Shepperd, C. Brown.

The Aberdare Leader reported, "....the men of Carmarthen from the tinplate town were accorded a grand reception at the Rec on Monday afternoon." The Western Mail reported, "Both sides fielded substitutes.... Collins, George Williams and Police Constable Tom Brown were absent from the home team....There was a large crowd present. Mountain Ash commenced operations and, following a kicking duel, Mountain Ash held the advantage, the first score coming to the Old Firm through Buller Loveluck, who snapped up a chance during some loose play and romped over....Llanelly again became aggressive but clever work by the home vanguard saw the visitors' line in danger and Congdon came within an ace of dropping a goal....The game was now waged near the home line where Mountain Ash was hard pressed. The home custodian was hurt and retired (meaning the Old Firm had to play on with 14 players). Then a fine movement was started by Buller Loveluck, who, when running strongly, passed to Dyke Jones who kicked, and J. Williams, fielding in fine style, romped over for the Old Firm's second try.

Llanelly's Best Form

Following the restart, some interesting play among the visiting three-quarters ended in Tom Williams going over for a try. The home full back then returned. The visitors were producing their best form at this stage and Mountain Ash had an anxious time. However, a fine rush, led by forward Oliver Davies, brought relief for the remainder of the game, play being confined chiefly to the visitors' territory. Dyke Jones and Congdon came very near to scoring."

Tom Collins
Mountain Ash RFC & Wales
Capped v Ireland 1923

Thomas John Collins was born on 14 August 1895 and hailed from Albert Street, Miskin, Mountain Ash, and played for the Old Firm during his entire rugby union career. He started playing for the Club after World War I and made such an impression that he was capped by Wales against Ireland at Lansdowne Road, Dublin on 10 March 1923. This game, though, was not without its problems as several Welsh players refused to travel due to "the Troubles" in Ireland, and their concerns were confirmed, as snipers were seen near the Welsh team's hotel when the team was in Dublin. Collins was one of 6 new caps that day and his elevation to a Welsh International player put the finishing touches to one of the greatest seasons in the Old Firm's history. Shortly after being capped, he turned professional, joining Hull Rugby League Club. He never received his cap from the Welsh Rugby Union during his lifetime due to the hostility shown towards those players who went North. It wasn't until 1975 – 17 years after his passing in 1958, and 52 years after playing for Wales – that his sons, Howard and John, got the WRU to relent on the issue, and received it.

31 March 1923

Mountain Ash 29 Bridgend 0

Mount Team: W. Thomas, Buller Loveluck, Tom Collins*, Emrys Davies, Gwilym Loveluck, Edward Morgan, Tom Parry, Geo. Williams, Tom Brown, Oliver Davies, Dick Fryer, Jim Fryer, Tom Shepherd, Lewis, Ben Teague.

* denotes Welsh International

"Woodlander" reported in the Aberdare Leader, "The famous Bridgend club sent a sadly depleted team to meet the Old Firm at the Rec on Saturday. At the last meeting, when the Mount visited Bridgend, they came away a defeated team and, of course, some leeway had to be made up....one cannot help but congratulate every home forward....they played like one man, they were at or on the ball like cats. Thomas at full back shone very well. Emrys and Oliver Davies were always about when wanted and Collins and Parry worked wonders. It was a field day for the Mount and, but for several tries going unconverted, the score would have been much heavier. Out of 7 tries, only 2 were majorised. That is miskicking with a vengeance." The Western Mail carried the heading, "Bridgend Crash Heavily" and commented, "The score by no means exaggerates the superiority of the Old Firm...."

31 March 1923

Mountain Ash 16 Headingley 3

Mount Team: Backs: W. Thomas, Buller Loveluck, Tom Collins*, Emrys Davies, Gwilym Loveluck, Thomas, Tom Parry; forwards: G. Williams, Oliver Davies, Dick Fryer, Jim Fryer, George Chamberlain, T. Simmonds, Ben Teague, Shepherd.

* denotes Welsh International

Success for Old Firm: Headingley Lose in First Game of Tour

The Western Mail reported, "Headingley opened their Easter tour in South Wales with a match at Mountain Ash on Good Friday, in which the Old Firm beat them soundly. Headingley deserved more scores than their one try for they did their share of pressing, and some of the passing bouts they contributed were delightful. Mountain Ash were, at times, erratic, but on the whole they did well. Thomas was excellent at full back, while Collins, Davies and Parry were the most consistent of the backs." "Woodlander" commented in the Aberdare Leader, "....The visitors were entertained at the Glancynon Hotel in the evening, where the Captain expressed his enjoyment of a fine sporting match."

9 April 1923

Mountain Ash 3 Cross Keys 0
Western Mail

STERN WELSH RUGBY STRUGGLES.

NEWPORT'S CAST-IRON DEFENCE AT CARDIFF.

LLANELLY'S SECOND-HALF SPURT AGAINST SWANSEA.

The biggest surprise of the day was the victory of the "Old Firm" over Cross Keys at Mountain Ash, and Neath also came a heavy and unexpected cropper at Abertillery. This reverse does not augur well for the All Blacks in their game with Newport next Saturday. A disorganised Pontypool team did well to draw with Gloucester at Kingholm, and Aberavon scored freely at the expense of Penarth.

THE DAY'S STAGGERER

CROSS KEYS BEATEN BY MOUNTAIN ASH.

	G.	T.	Pts.
Mountain Ash	0	1	3
Cross Keys	0	0	0

The "Old Firm" secured a surprise victory over the powerful Cross Keys combination, and strangely enough with a weakened pack, George Williams and Lew Lewis being absentees. The lighter vanguard of Mountain Ash were the chief contributors to a splendid triumph. They dominated the play both in the scrums and loose rushes to an extent that was remark-

> able. There were many anxious moments for Cross Keys in the first half, and only stern defence prevented scores on half-a-dozen occasions. Lyons, the custodian, was a tower of strength to them.
>
> **A SPLENDID GENERAL.**
>
> Congdon was a splendid general and the outstanding back on the field. Repeated attacks by the home three-quarters kept the Cross Keys defenders busy, and two forwards were called upon to closely guard the home wingers. The referee was particularly strict on the loose head and four-in-front tactics, for which Cross Keys were many times penalised. It was a hard, keen, and stubbornly-contested game in which the palm goes to the Mountain Ash forwards, who eclipsed any form they have shown this season.

"Woodlander" reported in the Aberdare Leader, "on December 2nd last, the famous Keys (reigning Welsh champions from 1921/22) had a ground record intact and it was thought that the Old Firm, who were then playing very strongly, would put a big cross on the Keys. They did not, but a different tale has to be told today. The meeting at the Rec last Saturday had been looked forward to and a great crowd cheered the Keys when they entered the ground....Towards the close, the game deteriorated into roughness. The whistle blew with roars of applause, for the Old Firm had won by 3pts to nil."

Comments

"There were giants in those days" will certainly be written on the record of this match....The Mount won by sheer merit and Cross Keys were lucky to escape without a good thrashing."

THE OLD FIRM'S PROUD PAST

Mountain Ash Rugby Football Club
"The Old Firm"
Season 1922/23

Back Row L-R: Jim Sage (Trainer), G. Williams, Enoch Watkins (Secretary), C. Brown, Oliver Davies, D. Jones, R. Bassett, Jim Fryer, A. Evans, J. Allen, F. Morgan, Gwilym Loveluck,

Middle Row L-R: W. Llewellyn (Baggage Man), R. Hillman, Jim Beynon, Dick Fryer, Fred Samuel*, Sid Congdon Capt, Tom Collins*, E. Griffiths, H. Evans,

Seated L-R: Harry Corsi, Tom Parry.

* denotes Welsh International

Season 1923/24

Old Firm Win At Pontypool & Swansea, Draw At Llanelly

There were some good wins during the season over Welsh and English opposition. Maesteg, Pontypool, Tredegar, Penarth, Ebbw Vale, Swansea, Bridgwater & Albion, Otley and Newton Abbot, were all beaten. There were two famous away victories. A week after drawing 5-5 against Llanelly at Stradey Park, Pontypool's ground record was taken in October 1923, Mount winning 10-9, and at the end of April 1924, the season ended on a high note with a 9-8 win at Swansea. The Club continued its policy of travelling into England, winning at Falmouth but losing at Camborne on a short tour, and also losing narrowly at Bridgwater and Albion. There were some close defeats against strong opposition and draws against Llanelly, Ebbw Vale and Cross Keys. Overall, the playing record read played 36, won 18, drawn 4, lost 14, with 57+ tries in the 270+ points scored, and 157+ conceded, which gave a win rate of 55.56%, which was pretty good given the strength of the opposition. It was also reported during the season that Mountain Ash Reserves beat Cardiff Extras away, 5-0, which showed the strength of the Old Firm squad. Although "Buller" Loveluck was never named in a Mount XV during the season, he officially left for Hull Rugby League Club in January 1924.

Fixtures 1923/24

Opponents	Date	Venue	Score	Tries	Scorers/Comments
Grange Baptists	22 Sep 1923	Home	27-0	7	Haydn Coopey 4T, Harry Corsi 3T, Sid Congdon 3C.
Maesteg	29 Sep 1923	Home	3-0	1	Lewis T.
Glamorgan Wanderers	6 Oct 1923	Home	8-10	2	Sid Congdon T, C, Lewis T.
Llanelly	6 Oct 1923	Away	5-5	1	T. Bevan T, Sid Congdon C.
Pontypool	13 Oct 1923	Away	10-9	2	Sam Lewis T, DG, Haydn Coopey T.
Abertillery	20 Oct 1923	Away	8-12	2	Haydn Coopey T, C, Harry Corsi T.
Tredegar	27 Oct 1923	Home	16-0	4	Haydn Coopey T, 2C, Ben Teague T, Sid Congdon T, P. J. Skym T.
Cross Keys	3 Nov 1923	Away	4-6	0	Thomas DG.
Bargoed	10 Nov 1923	Home	14-5	3+	T. Shepherd T, C, Jones T, Jim Fryer T, AN Other 3pts.
Ebbw Vale	17 Nov 1923	Away	3-3	0	Morgan P.
Bridgwater & Albion	24 Nov 1923	Home	15-0	5	Ben Teague 2T, James 2T, Coopey T.
Swansea	8 Dec 1923	Home	9-12	3	Haydn Coopey 2T, James T.
Bridgwater & Albion	15 Dec 1923	Away	6-8	2	James 2T.

Opponents	Date	Venue	Score	Tries	Scorers/Comments
Penarth	17 Dec 1923	Home	17-3	5	Sid Congdon 2T, Haydn Coopey 2T, C, Oliver Davies T.
Neath	24 Dec 1923	Away	0-3	0	No scorers.
Crumlin	5 Jan 1924	Away	3-8	0	Sid Congdon P.
Cross Keys	12 Jan 1924	Home	3-3	1	George Morgan T.
Aberaman	2 Feb 1924	Away	5-8	1	C. Rowlands T, Thomas C.
Penylan	16 Feb 1924	Home	19-0	3+	Wat Phillips T, Jim Fryer T, Hall T, P. J. Skym C, AN Other 8 pts.
Ebbw Vale	23 Feb 1924	Home	6-0	2	Jones T, AN Other T.
Treherbert	1 Mar 1924	Home	3-3	1	Davies T.
Treherbert	8 Mar 1924	Away	0-11	0	No scorers.
Camborne	10 Mar 1924	Away	3-7	1	Jones T.
Falmouth	11 Mar 1924	Away	3-0	1	Wallie Jones T.
Crumlin	22 Mar 1924	Home	23-7	4+	Tom Parry 2T, Oliver Davies T, Jones T, Dr Rees DG, AN Other 7 pts.
Pontypridd	29 Mar 1924	Home	3-7	1	Tom Parry T.
Penarth	31 Mar 1924	Away	0-3	0	No scorers.
Aberaman	29 Mar 1924	Home	3-0	1	Watty Jones T.
Tredegar	7 Apr 1924	Away	3-0	1	Dr Rees T.
Pontypool	7 Apr 1924	Home	0-5	0	No scorers.
Glynneath	12 Apr 1924	Away	4-3	0	Morgan DG.
Otley	21 Apr 1924	Home	31-0	Unknown	Scorers unknown.
Swansea	23 Apr 1924	Away	9-8	1	Haydn Coopey T, Phil Hughes DG, Thomas C.
Maesteg	28 Apr 1924	Away	4-8	0	Sid Congdon DG.
Newton Abbot	3 May 1924	Home	Unknown	2+	Mount win. At least 2 tries scored. Phil Hughes DG, T, Morgan T.
Glynneath	Date unknown	Home	Unknown	Unknown	Mount win.

Summary of Playing Record

P	W	D	L	For	Against	Tries Scored	Win Rate %
36	18	4	14	270+	157+	57+	55.56

Match Reports & Publications

29 September 1923

<u>Mountain Ash 3 Maesteg 0</u>

Mount Team: Backs: W. Thomas, Haydn Coopey, Harry Corsi, P. J. Skym, L. Lewis, Tom Parry, Sid Congdon;
Forwards: Oliver Davies, Dick Fryer, Brown, Tom Sheppard, Jim Fryer, Ben Teague, W. Partridge, J. Simmons.

<u>Play Too Keen In Game Won By Mountain Ash</u>

The Western Mail commented in its match report, "The better team undoubtedly won, and the movement that led to the only score of the game was the most brilliant effort of the match....The general play was far too keen to be attractive. It reminded one of the old League games....The game was fiercely contested and needed a strong hand to administer control....". The Aberdare Leader reported, "The game was not very interesting and man-mauling was too frequent....the Mountain Ash forwards showed much superiority. A curious incident was that a few hot words occurred between two of the players, and Mr. Thomas the referee, ordered both off the field, but recalled them shortly afterwards."

6 October 1923

<u>Llanelly 5 Mountain Ash 5</u>
<u>Llanelly Surprised: Mountain Ash Draw At Stradey Park</u>

The Western Mail reported, "Play was bright and exciting almost throughout. Llanelly opened the scoring within ten minutes of the start. Although the Scarlets attacked persistently after this, the backs failed to make much headway for they were well marked by the Old Firm. Mountain Ash demonstrated early in the second half that they meant business and their forwards were very much in evidence. Oliver Davies, after one great rush, made a perfect opening for Tom Bevan to score a good try under the posts, Congdon converting. Play towards the end became very exciting, both sides striving hard for victory. Had the handling on the Llanelly side been a little more accurate, they might have crossed, but, in the final stages, Mountain Ash swept down the field and claimed a try through Bevan, but he was recalled....for the visitors, Oliver Davies, Skym, Bevan and Congdon were frequently prominent."

13 October 1923

Pontypool 9 Mountain Ash 10

Mount Team: Backs: Dan Collins, Haydn Coopey, P. J. Skym, Tom Edwards, Sam Lewis, Sid Congdon Capt, Tom Bevan,
Forwards: P. C. Brown, Oliver Davies, R. Fryer, Jim Fryer, Mog Lloyd, Tom Shepherd, Jack Simmonds, G. Harris.

Western Mail

A BIG SURPRISE.

PONTYPOOL GO DOWN AT HOME TO MOUNTAIN ASH.

	G.	T.	Pts.
Mountain Ash	*1	2	10
Pontypool	†1	2	9

* Dropped.   † Penalty.

It is a very long time since a more exciting game has been seen at Pontypool than that which the "Old Firm" provided on Saturday, when Pontypool were beaten for the second time this season by the odd point. Both times a dropped goal has made all the difference. Mountain Ash were good in all departments—brilliant at times—whereas the home back division seemed to be at sixes and sevens. One could find no fault with the forwards, but the number of times opportunities were lost, mistakes in tactics made, and passes fumbled sorely disappointed their supporters, especially in the first half. But if the Mount cannot be begrudged their win, some of their tactics were far from sporting and the crowd several times voiced resentment. Crossing over with a solid lead of seven points, the visitors sat firmly on their lead, as they were entitled to do. But time after time Collins, at full-back, stepped aside to allow a bouncing ball to roll over his line and then touch down when he had ample time and room to keep the ball in play.

AN EARLY LEAD.

Pontypool scored early through James, who charged the full back's kick, breasted the ball over the line, and reached it first. Thereafter the visitors played like winners, with spirit and polish, and each of the wings, Coopey and Lewis, registered a try in their respective corners after exhilarating passing. Lewis, who was, perhaps, the best man on his side, followed this up with a dropped goal; the opportunity was for which was presented to him by James. The home wing just saved a try by gathering on his own line, but punted right into the hands of the opposing wing. The visitors showed little ambition to increase their advantage after the interval, but gave nothing away in defence. Ford placed a penalty, awarded for obstruction, and Vaisey, with a great dash, put the last touch to a concerted movement in which forwards and backs swept irresistibly up the field by scoring in the extreme corner. For the last ten minutes intense excitement prevailed, but though Pontypool were always within striking distance, there was no gap to be found in the visitors' defence.

"Pontypool's Ground Record Taken"

The Aberdare Leader reported, "On Saturday, Mountain Ash paid their annual visit to Pontypool accompanied by about 300 (or 500, print unclear) supporters....Harry Jones, the fast Pontypool wing, put in a huge fly kick which bounced awkwardly....James followed up at top speed, charged down the return and scored for Ponty in the first 2 minutes of the game. However, every man on the Mount side was playing the game of his life, and from a passing bout among the visitors backs, Skym gave a perfect pass on the half way line to Coopey who beat 5 opponents and scored what was one of the finest tries seen in Welsh football for many a long day. After only 5 minutes from the first score, Congdon got the ball away beautifully and it travelled via Bevan, Skym and Edwards to Sam Lewis to score a glorious try in the corner. Collins, who had opened shakily, had now settled down. He had the misfortune to leave his boots at home and had to put up with a pair two sizes too big, so, under the circumstances, he was doing very well. The Old Firm continued to have much the better of the game and Sam Lewis coolly dropped a magnificent 40 yard goal after a kicking duel. Pontypool opened the 2nd half as if they intended sweeping the Old Firm off the field, but the defence of the Mount boys was excellent. The referee was the subject of a lot of bantering from the Mount supporters for what appeared to be his partiality to Pontypool. He gave them 14 free kicks in 10 minutes. The Pontypool supporters, seeing that their pets never looked like scoring and their ground record slipping away, started to barrack the Mount boys, Sid Congdon in particular suffering at their hands. With only 10 minutes to go and Pontypool only four points behind, excitement was at fever pitch. Pontypool, from a rush in which forwards and backs took part, were awarded a try in the corner, which to say the least, was a very doubtful one as the ball had been passed forward and knocked on in the rush. Such, however, is in the fortunes of the game and with only one point between the teams, excitement was intense. There was some strenuous scrummaging near the Old Firm's line and Jack Simmonds, Tom Bevan, Congdon and Dick Fryer did some heroic defensive work. The Old Firm again worked out of danger and when no-side was called, the play was at half way, thus leaving the Mount boys the proud and deserving conquerors of Pontypool's ground record. Hats off to every member of the side for a magnificent performance. Every man on the Old Firm's side was at the top of his form. Following so closely on the splendid draw achieved at Llanelli the previous Monday, we have ample evidence of what was written in this column after the trials – that we have a better balanced team than either of the two previous seasons. Skipper Congdon should be a proud man these days, and it is only necessary for him to get that coveted Welsh Cap this season for his cup of happiness to be full. Such performances are bound to bring the required increase in gates and it only requires careful attention to training to make the Mount one of the best sides in the country. The Reserves played Cardiff Extras at Cardiff and kept their unbeaten record, winning 5-0."

20 October 1923

Abertillery 12 Mountain Ash 8
A Fine Exhibition
Mountain Ash Beaten But Far From Disgraced

The Western Mail reported, "Abertillery managed to beat Mountain Ash by four points but had the Glamorgan side been the victors, even the most ardent supporter would not have begrudged them success, for it was a fine exhibition of football, neither side attempting to spoil the game, but all 30 players striving their utmost to serve up the attractive. Abertillery enjoyed a 12 point advantage lead at the interval, but had the Old Firm not been so faulty in fielding, the score would not have reached such a total....Mountain Ash played like a different team in the second portion, and Congdon was brilliant despite the fact that Fear at wing and Fisher paid him particularly strict attention. Coopey got over in the corner for the visitors, and then, after a fine individual effort, Corsi scored for Coopey to convert."

24 November 1923

Mountain Ash 15 Bridgwater & Albion 0

Mount Team: Backs: W. Thomas, Haydn Coopey, P. J. Skym, Geo. Morgan, T. James, Dyke Jones, Sid Congdon,
Forwards: Dick Fryer, Oliver Davies, Jim Fryer, P. C. Hall, Tom Sheppard, Ben Teague, Jack Simmonds, C. Scrivens.

Exhilarating Rugby Witnessed At Mountain Ash

The Western Mail reported, "A large crowd at Mountain Ash saw an exhilarating display of rugby. The visitors were a stronger proposition than the score suggests....Mountain Ash were severely handicapped in losing Congdon in the first five minutes of the game." With substitutes not allowed in the 1920s, Mount played the rest of the game with 14 men. "The second half produced thrills galore. It was rugby at its best, forwards and backs playing with abandon....Mountain Ash finished with thirteen men, George Morgan sustaining an injury to his shoulder."

8 December 1923

Mountain Ash 9 Swansea 12

Mount Team: Backs: J. Thomas, Haydn Coopey, P. J. Skym, Dyke Jones, James, Parry, Sid Congdon,
Forwards: Dick Fryer, Oliver Davies, Ben Teague, Jim Fryer, Tom Sheppard, P. C. Hall, P. C. Letts, Jack Simmonds.

Swansea Team: Hodges, Rowe Harding, Smith, T. Lewis, Watkins, D. J. John, W. John, Tom Parker, A. Pasker, J. Michael, Howell John, G. White, H. Rees, W. Williams, E. Thomas.

For information, in the above Swansea XV, Rowe Harding gained 17 Welsh caps between 1923 and 1928, Tom Parker played for Wales 14 times between 1920 and 1923, and Howell John won 8 Welsh caps in 1926 and 1927.

The Aberdare Leader reported, "....Rowe Harding brought a real "All White" team to oppose the Old Firm at the Rec on Monday afternoon. From a tight scrum, Skym secured and passed to Coopey who went over in the corner. The early success added vim to the struggle. Sid Congdon was playing right up to the top of his form, and was a rare puzzle to his opponents....but Coopey again gained possession and went across the centre, right through the All Whites, passing to Skym, who was pushed into touch right on the corner flag. It was a brilliant effort. Mountain Ash were now showing great speed and the visitors had their work cut out to stop them scoring....Harding of Swansea, the clever International, ran from his own 25 to score a lovely try....Great excitement prevailed, when James secured, just a few minutes later, and crossed over in the corner for the Old Firm....Michael ran up and knocked the ball from Dick Fryer and fell on it and scored. The kick was converted to make it 8-6 to Swansea. Play from now on was most exciting and the ball was kept travelling at a terrific pace. Parry passed to Skym who transferred to Coopey, who crossed the line in the corner to make it 9-8 to Mount. Just before time Swansea found the scoreboard, Parker kicking a dropped goal."

Western Mail
An Excellent Game

"Rowe Harding, the Wales and Swansea wing three-quarter, took a strong team to Mountain Ash and an excellent game was witnessed by fully 3,000 spectators....The Mountain Ash pack were having the better of the scrummages, beautiful passing took place among the backs and the Old Firm were rewarded through

Coopey, who scored a great try in the corner. The kick failed. Interesting play followed in which the home backs were again conspicuous, experiencing frequent hard lines in not scoring. Congdon and John were fighting a rare duel at the base of the scrum, the advantage going to Congdon, who was on top form. The visitors, however, were slowly settling down to good work and a brilliant run by Rowe Harding, who was only forced into touch in the nick of time, aroused great enthusiasm. The Old Firm returned to the attack and a beautiful movement by Coopey, who cut through, almost brought another try....the visiting forwards rushed to half way and a great try followed....a perfect pass to Rowe Harding, who, with a dazzling run, scored in a fairly good position. The try was unconverted. Mountain Ash took the lead when Teague, breaking away from a lineout, gave to James, who scored a good try. The second half opened with Mountain Ash attacking, Rowe Harding's great speed, however, saved the situation. The visiting backs brought off some brilliant handling, and with play right on the home line, Michael snapped up a chance and scored, Harding converted. Coopey, who was in splendid form, quickly gave the home team a point lead by scoring a fine try, towards which Skym had done excellent work. The kick failed. In the closing stages, Swansea played grandly and Smith, securing from John, landed a splendid drop goal. Both teams were entertained to dinner at the Glancynon Hotel after the match. Mr Rowe Harding was warmly thanked for bringing such a splendid side to Mountain Ash, and in acknowledging, he congratulated the home team upon its excellent display."

17 December 1923

<u>Mountain Ash 17 Penarth 3</u>

The Western Mail commented in its match report, "Mountain Ash only settled down to serious business at rare intervals. The forwards, however, held the upper hand throughout the game, and had the backs made use of the opportunities given them, the score would have been considerably larger. The outstanding player on the field was Congdon. Both his tries were the result of clever opportunism, and on each occasion, the opposition was baffled. His service from the scrummages was excellent, and when forced to kick, he always gained a great advantage. On present form, he must command serious consideration for International honours."

24 December 1923

<u>Neath 3 Mountain Ash 0</u>
<u>Mountain Ash Almost Snatch Victory</u>

The Western Mail reported, "What might have easily been an exhilarating game on the Gnoll developed into one of the kick and rush variety. This was the result of too much keenness on both sides, especially at half, where the two rivals for International honours, Congdon and Eddie Watkins, were playing. The Mountain Ash forwards were a formidable pack, and heeled oftener than Neath, while their following up was keen, with the result that the game was smothered....Watkins clung to Congdon like a terrier, and the inside half had little chance of sending out clean passes....Congdon was the mainstay of his side as his defensive work was masterly...."

12 January 1924

<u>Mountain Ash 3 Cross Keys 3</u>

Mount Team: W. Thomas, George Morgan, P. J. Skym, Dyke Jones, James, Tom Parry, Sid Congdon, Dick Fryer, Jim Fryer, Oliver Davies, Jack Simmonds, P. C. Lett, P. C. Hall, Ben Teague, Tom Sheppard.

"Woodlander" reported in the Aberdare Leader, "The meeting of the two Lions of South Wales rugby on the Rec last Saturday provided a succession of thrills rarely witnessed. There could be no doubting the popularity of the Keys for they had a rousing reception.....the Mount played very vigorously to get on level terms, Congdon continually outpacing the Keys....the Mount still held their own in the scrums but were visibly tiring from the superior weight of their opponents. Sheer pluck kept them at it....The game was really a battle of forward giants, in which the Fryers, P.C. Lett and Sheppard shone. Parry, after his long illness was remarkably keen and Congdon, of course, was brilliant. Coopey was missed from the back division. It was a game of thrills and the Mount should just have made a win of it."

<u>Western Mail</u>

SCORE REFLEX OF PLAY

CROSS KEYS FIELD A STRONG TEAM AND ONLY DRAW.

	G.	T.	Pts.
Mountain Ash	0	1	3
Cross Keys	0	1	3

A drawn game was a reflex of the play. Mountain Ash did most of the attacking in the first half, especially following Benson's smart try. The Mountain Ash pack played magnificently right up to within a quarter of an hour from the finsh. They did excellently against a much heavier pack both in the scrimmages and the loose. Their pace helped them to great advantage, and had the backs been more thrustful a sufficient lead should have resulted to have merited a win. Congden was as brilliant as ever, and, with the exception of one or two instances, Parry was more like his former self than he has been since his long illness. The movement which led up to George Morgan's try was the tit-bit of the game, Congden, Parry, and Skym contributing largely to it. Both tries, in fact, were splendid efforts, and proved the real capabilities of both sides. Cross Keys forwards, having the advantage in weight, lasted better, and in the closing stages made desperate efforts to win. Steve Morris, Pettiford, and Blakemore were most prominent for Cross Keys, and Oli Davies, P.C. Lett, and Sheppard for Mountain Ash. The full-backs gave a good display. Cross Keys' centres made good use of the touchline with long kicking, but had they given their wings more chances it is quite possible they would have made the difference between a drawn game and a win. It was a great compliment to the "Old Firm" that Cross Keys fielded their strongest possible fifteen. Teams:—

Mountain Ash: W. Thomas; Geo. Morgan, D. Jones, D. Skym, and T. James; T. Parry and S. Congden; R. Fryer, J. Fryer, O. Davies, J. Symmonds, P.C. T. C. Hall, P.C. Lett, B. Teague, and T. Sheppard.

Cross Keys. R. Lyons; T. R. Benson, W. Burnett, O. Hicks, and D. Williams; H. Rowe and F. Reeves; Steve Morris, W. Hicks, L. Richards, W. James, A. Blakemore, W. Millard, S. Parfitt, and E. Pettiford.

21 April 1924

Mountain Ash 31 Otley 0
Western Mail

OTLEY OVERWHELMED

MOUNTAIN ASH GIVE A BRILLIANT DISPLAY.

	G.	T.	Pts.
Mountain Ash	5	3	31
Otley	0	0	0

The "Old Firm" gave a delightful display against Otley on Saturday. The movements were characterised with a cohesion that fairly nonplussed the defence of the visitors, particularly in the second half. Otley were not so decisively beaten as the score suggests. There were periods when they contributed delightful movements. Hall, Pawson, and Rogers were men of great pace, and used it to advantage at times. Some of their movements deserved success. It was a typical holiday game, with any amount of open play. Dr. Rees, Morgan, Congdon, and Coopey were excellent, and contributed much to the splendid display of the "Old Firm." Otley were unfortunate in loosing Thomson, who was injured in the first half. He attempted to resume, but was forced to retire in the second half. Teams:—

Mountain Ash: W. Thomas; G. Morgan, Dr. Rees, H. B. Coopey, and T. Jones; S. Congdon (capt.) and T. Parry; R. Fryer, J. Fryer, O. Davies, C. C. Lett, B. Teague, P. Brown, T. Sheppard, and T. Griffiths.

Otley: C. P. Gilbert; H. P. Rogers, L. B. Pason, R. M. Greston, and J. A. Hall; H. Thomson and T. Currie; T. Trenhon (capt.), V. Broumfit, E. Blacker, H. P. Corrie, C. J. Ellis, T. Hollings, W. Chalcroft, and W. Howton.

Referee: Mr. M. T. Davies (Treforest).

23 April 1924

Swansea 8 Mountain Ash 9
South Wales Daily News

SWANSEA 2-0-8, MOUNTAIN ASH 2-0-9.

Swansea were rather fortunate that their last home fixture of the season, which was played yesterday, did not result in a more decisive defeat. Mountain Ash, their opponents, were their superiors in every phase of the game with the exception of half-back play, S. Congdon and Elvet Rees having a rare tussle at the base of the scrum. The Mountain Ash forwards had a distinct advantage in avoirdupois, and their backs, without being too sure in handling, were much more penetrative than the Swansea men, whose strongest point was their sound defence.

Mountain Ash opened the scoring within five minutes of the start, H. V. COOPEY terminating a good sprint by scoring a try which W. Thomas converted. Subsequent play favoured Swansea, but the home team although exerting themselves, were unable to reduce the lead other than by a dropped goal, which was very coolly kicked by I. JEREMIAH.

Play after the interval was almost always in the Swansea half. The respective defences were so sound when called upon that the additional scores were only secured through clever kicking, G. HUGHES dropping a neat goal for Mountain Ash, and T. EVANS replying for Swansea with a left foot effort. Teams:—

Mountain Ash—W. Thomas; H. V. Coopey, G. Hughes, G. Morgan and Dr. R. E. Rees; S. Congdon and T. Parry; R. Fryer, O. Davies, C. Rees, P.C. Lett, J. Fear, C. Brown, J. Fryer and T. Griffiths.

Swansea—T. Jones; D. Jenkins, T. Evans, Trevor Davies and S. Eddins; E. Rees and I. Jeremiah; E. Thomas, G. White, G. James, I. Morris, J. H. John, Alf Parker, D. Parker, and H. Rees.

Season 1924/25

Good Season For Old Firm Marred By Tragedy

Although the Old Firm undertook another tough fixture list, they finished the season with a very respectable playing record from the 29 known games played of 17 wins, 3 draws, and 8 losses – with the result of the tour game against Stade Francais in Paris unknown – scoring at least 122 points, which included 29+ tries, and conceding 110+, which gave a win rate of 66.07%. Scrum half Sid Congdon, who was trying to win a coveted Welsh cap, had another fine season with his performances mentioned in several Western Mail match reports. Mount made a good start to the season, "Woodlander" reporting in the Aberdare Leader at the start of November 1924, "up to now, the Old Firm has lost one match in 10 and has scored 108 points to 30 against." There had been visits to France in 1921/22 and 1922/23 and the French connection was still very much in existence. The 1975/76 Centenary Season's historical account, "The First 100 Years", and the South Wales Echo's historical account published in January 1958, both stated that in 1925 the Old Firm played at the Stade Francais in Paris. In addition to this, the following was published in the Aberdare Leader in November 1924, "IMPORTANT ANNOUNCEMENT – The principal rugger combination in France, "The Stade Francais", have already promised to visit the Old Firm's ground next season." Exciting as this no doubt was back then, there was no record in the Aberdare Leader of a fixture with Stade in 1925/26 and no details were forthcoming from the French Club when they were contacted in 2014.

The season saw Mount get a prestigious "double" over Cross Keys and there were home wins over Ebbw Vale, Abertillery, Penarth, Bridgend and Glamorgan Wanderers. There was a win at Pontypridd on Boxing Day 1924 and a couple of trips into England which resulted in two wins, at Nuneaton and Birmingham. The season also had two down sides, both of which happened against Welsh champions for the season, Aberavon. The first game, played at the Rec, was marred by crowd disorder and the return at Aberavon in March 1925 tragically saw the accidental death of young Old Firm three-quarter, Percy Hoskins, after a collision during the game. The season was also the last for Mount forward Tom Sheppard. He had played for the Old Firm for at least 18 years, first being named in a Mount team in 1906/07. During that time, he had given the Club sterling service and had become one of the most respected forwards throughout South Wales, being thought unlucky not to have achieved higher representative honours.

Fixtures 1924/25

Opponents	Date	Venue	Score	Tries	Scorers/Comments
Glynneath	20 Sep 1924	Home	6-3	2	Brown T, AN Other T.
Birmingham	Sep/Oct 1924	Away	Unknown	Unknown	Mount win. Scorers unknown.
Ebbw Vale	4 Oct 1924	Home	6-0	2	Dr Rees T, Sid Congdon T.
Pontypool	11 Oct 1924	Away	8-13	2	Dr Rees T, Tom Parry T, AN Other C.
Abertillery	20 Oct 1924	Home	8-0	Unknown	Scorers unknown.
Treherbert	1 Nov 1924	Away	7-5	1	Oliver Davies T, Phil Hughes DG.
Penarth	10 Nov 1924	Home	14-5	3	Dr Rees T, Oliver Davies T, Hoskins T, W. Thomas P, Phil Hughes C.

Opponents	Date	Venue	Score	Tries	Scorers/Comments
Maesteg	22 Nov 1924	Away	3-6	1	Griffiths T.
Nuneaton	29 Nov 1924	Away	3-0	1	Tom Parry T.
Cross Keys	6 Dec 1924	Away	6-3	2	George Chamberlain T, Hughes T.
Aberavon	13 Dec 1924	Home	0-11	0	No scorers.
Penarth	20 Dec 1924	Away	3-9	1	George Morgan T.
Pontypridd	27 Dec 1924	Away	3-0	1	Percy Hoskins T.
Cilfynydd	27 Dec 1924	Away	6-0	2	Sid Congdon T, Tom Parry T.
Maesteg	12 Jan 1925	Home	3-3	1	Hellings T.
Bridgend	19 Jan 1925	Away	3-8	1	Dewi Phillips T.
Pontypool	26 Jan 1925	Home	0-0	0	No scorers.
Aberaman	7 Feb 1925	Home	5-0	1	Match abandoned due to wet weather. Sam Lewis T, George Morgan C.
Aberaman	14 Feb 1925	Away	6-0	1	Percy Hoskins T, George Morgan P.
Glamorgan Wanderers	14 Feb 1925	Home	3-0	1	Hellings T.
Ebbw Vale	16 Feb 1925	Away	0-6	0	No scorers.
Treherbert	23 Feb 1925	Home	3-0	1	Hughes T.
Bridgend	16 Mar 1925	Home	11-3	3	AN Other 3T, C.
Aberavon	23 Mar 1925	Away	0-13	0	No scorers.
Glynneath	13 Apr 1925	Away	0-0	0	No scorers.
Blaenavon	20 Apr 1925	Away	3-17	1	P.C. Lett T.
Cardiff Loudouns	27 Apr 1925	Home	6-5	Unknown	Scorers unknown.
Cross Keys	9 May 1925	Home	6-0	1	Tom Sheppard T, D. Hopkins P.
Stade Francais (France)	Unknown	Away	Unknown	Unknown	Scorers unknown.

Summary of Playing Record

P	W	D	L	Results Unknown	For	Against	Tries Scored	Win Rate %
29	17	3	8	1	122+	110+	29+	66.07

Match Reports & Publications

4 October 1924

<u>Mountain Ash 6 Ebbw Vale 0</u>

Mount Team: R. Hoskins, Dyke Jones, Hughes, Geo. Morgan, Dr Rees, Sid Congdon, Tom Parry, Oliver Davies, Hellings, Dick Fryer, Jim Fryer, Jim Beynon, Daly James, Ben Teague, J. Allen.

The Aberdare Leader reported, "....Many have been the stern tussles that these old rivals have put up....The resumption (of the second half) was somewhat sensational and right from the kick off Dr Rees secured and went over the visitors line like a bird....The Mount halves were watched well, but Congdon tricked the backs eventually and scored a beauty. Thus, though at full strength, the Valians failed to penetrate the Old Firm's defence. Hoskins and Dr Rees were outstanding players, although the Old Firm played altogether with wonderful cohesion and full understanding."

20 October 1924

<u>Mountain Ash 8 Abertillery 0</u>
<u>Western Mail</u>

GOOD PERFORMANCE BY MOUNTAIN ASH.

	G.	T.	Pts.
Mountain Ash	1	1	8
Abertillery	0	0	0

Mountain Ash accomplished a meritorious performance by recording an eight points to nil victory over Abertillery. Both sides displayed a keenness that was maintained throughout. The forwards played a prominent part in what was a keen and exciting game. Abertillery had hard lines on a few occasions. D. Griffiths and Percy Williams were the best of the backs.

Mountain Ash owe their win to the splendid display of the forwards, who were opposed to a fine pack. The home eight secured the ball oftener and were particularly smart with their great rushes. Congdon, however, was the outstanding player on the field, and played probably the finest game of his career. Parry also played well, cutting through the defence on several occasions. Both full backs gave a good exhibition, and saved their respective sides repeatedly.

10 November 1924

<u>Mountain Ash 14 Penarth 5</u>
<u>Mountain Ash in Form</u>
<u>Penarth's Sound Defence Keeps Score Down</u>

The Western Mail reported, "Mountain Ash fully deserved their win....There was more method in their attack and the foundation for victory was laid by their forwards, who enjoyed superiority in the scrums. The home quartette combined splendidly, and had it not been for Penarth's splendid defence, the score would have been much larger. Congdon was again in excellent form and was particularly prominent in opening up the attack. Joe Hellings (Mountain Ash) was the outstanding forward on view….Oli Davies' (Mountain Ash) try was the tit-bit of the match, Phil Hughes and Hoskins playing a great part in the score…."

29 November 1924

<u>Nuneaton 0 Mountain Ash 3</u>

"Woodlander" reported in the Aberdare Leader, "The English premier teams are playing such fine football this season that the second visit to Warwickshire….and to bag another victory, is a meritorious performance. Nuneaton have always been a tough nut to tackle, as witness the game between them and the famous Tigers (Leicester). Both Fryers, Griffiths and W. Thomas were the pick of a grand team."

6 December 1924

<u>Cross Keys 3 Mountain Ash 6</u>

Mount Team: W. Thomas, Hoskins, Pugh, Morgan, Jack Jones, Sid Congdon, Tom Parry, Oliver Davies, Dick Fryer, Jim Fryer, Hellings, George Chamberlain, T. Griffiths, Gilbert, Hughes.

The Aberdare Leader stated, "The matches with the famous Cross Keys are always events of supreme importance in the Old Firm's seasonal engagements. They have always provided "the goods" in the football world and last Saturday's match saw redemption of the promise of a real set-to….At the conclusion of the game, the Mount were swarming the Keys line and they deservedly came out masters 6-3."

13 December 1924

<u>Mountain Ash 0 Aberavon 11</u>

Mount Team: W. Thomas, Dr Rees, George Morgan, Hughes, Hoskins, Sid Congdon, Tom Parry, Oliver Davies, Dick Fryer, Jim Fryer, Joe Hellings, George Chamberlain, Tom Shepherd, P.C. Lett, Ben Teague.

The Aberdare Leader reported, "The visit of the proud "Bravon" team to the Rec on Saturday was an event long looked for. The prowess of the visitors and the consistent good form of the Old Firm promised, as was realised, a great game. Many hopes were raised by the home supporters in consequence of their defeat of Cross Keys, the only team to make the "Bravons" bite the dust this season. There were plenty of startles from the very commencement of the game, the crowd, about 3000 strong, responding to the electricity in the air.

<u>A Regrettable Scene</u>

The electricity had been sparkling and crackling like a galvanic battery and at last the storm broke, Llew Jenkins (who scored Aberavon's first try) and Jim Fryer were seen "having a go". Matters were lively for some time, but surrounded by the teams and the referee ordering both men off, matters quietened down.

<u>Comments</u>

There is no doubt that the little contretemps between Fryer and Jenkins greatly upset the Old Firm and the crowd on the quarry side, much to be blamed for breaking into the enclosure. There have been many scenes before, and the least said soonest mended."

20 December 1924

Penarth 9 Mountain Ash 3

"Woodlander" commented in the Aberdare Leader, "that Mountain Ash rugby team are making for themselves a notoriety with which it can very well dispense is undeniable. That the stigma of having a man ordered off in two successive matches is a bad blot on a hitherto splendid reputation, and that a halt must be called by the management in this malodorous monotony, are also undeniable. It is to be hoped that the matches for the rest of the season will not be marred by such an incident as an attempt to argue with the referee, which occurred on Saturday at Penarth. Few teams have crossed the Mount line three times in one match this season, and nobody can begrudge Penarth that honour."

27 December 1924

Pontypridd 0 Mountain Ash 3
Western Mail

MOUNTAIN ASH WIN ON TIME AGAINST PONTYPRIDD.

	G.	T.	Pts.
Mountain Ash	0	1	3
Pontypridd	0	0	0

Mountain Ash deserved to win at Pontypridd on Boxing Day by a try. Their forward play was of a more skilful character, and they tackled well. In many of their movements they showed more than ordinary initiative. It was a last-minute round of passing by Mountain Ash that enabled Percy Hoskins to romp over with an excellent try. The ground, after the recent rain and the match between the Pontypridd and Cardiff Schoolboys in the morning, was of a very muddy and slippery nature, and the consequence was that the game was not as scientific as one could have wished.

12 January 1925

Mountain Ash 3 Maesteg 3
Maesteg Secure a Division of the Honours

The Western Mail commented, "A draw was hardly a true reflex of the run of play at Mountain Ash as the home side had more of the exchanges....Mountain Ash had decidedly hard lines in the second half, Hellings being literally held up with the ball after forcing himself over the line. Hoskins, Parry and Congdon experienced very hard lines on other occasions....The forwards monopolised the play and in this particular, Mountain Ash were superior. Hellings played a great game, P.C. Tom Brown and Sheppard were always good."

26 January 1925

Mountain Ash 0 Pontypool 0
Western Mail

NO SCORE AT MOUNTAIN ASH.

PONTYPOOL HELD IN A FORWARD STRUGGLE.

	G.	T.	Pts.
Mountain Ash	0	0	0
Pontypool	0	0	0

The conditions at Mountain Ash on Saturday militated against anything like a good display. The forwards bore the brunt of the battle, and in this department the honours rested with Mountain Ash, for whom O. Davies, Chamberlain, Fryer, and Lett were the most prominent. Congdon revelled in the mud, and although his new partner, Phillips, was handicapped he did several smart things. Tom Parry was the outstanding threequarter, and he made the best runs of the game. Dewi Phillips and Sam Lewis had few opportunities to display their prowess, but under better conditions their efforts would undoubtedly have been rewarded.

Pontypool have to thank Ford and McCreith for saving them from defeat. Ford was a great defender, especially in the second half. Pontypool have good forwards in C. Pritchard, Joe Williams, Pike, and Oliver.

The game was strenuously contested, and the forward play was desperately keen. Mountain Ash certainly deserved to score, and the final effort by their backs was the tit-bit of a keenly contested game.

16 February 1925

Ebbw Vale 6 Mountain Ash 0
Snowstorm Stops Game
Mountain Ash Player Collapses at Ebbw Vale

The Western Mail reported, "The meeting of these two sides almost invariably provides a first class attraction at Ebbw Vale but the weather conditions that prevailed on Saturday made good football impossible, and 10 minutes before time the referee applied closure. He struggled through the torrential rain alright, but when a blinding snowstorm swept the ground, it was time to call a halt. Just before the end, Jim Fryer, one of the Mountain Ash forwards, collapsed on the field, apparently in a fit, and medical aid had to be summoned before he was brought round….Thomas, the visitors' full back, played a wonderful game, his defence being very fine."

16 March 1925

Mountain Ash 11 Bridgend 3
Mountain Ash Defeat Bridgend

The Western Mail reported, "The game at Mountain Ash was thoroughly interesting….Mountain Ash were somewhat slow settling down and were 3 points in arrears at the interval. Mountain Ash were seen to great advantage in the second half and crossed the Bridgend line on 3 occasions. Congdon, Parry, George Morgan and Phil Hughes were outstanding players."

Mountain Ash Rugby Football Club
"The Old Firm"
Season 1924/25

The above photograph is reportedly that of the Mount squad that went on tour to France and played Stade Francais in Paris. This information came from a relative of forward George Chamberlain, who stands in the back row as you look, sixth from the left. The captain appears to be second row forward, Oliver Davies, who is holding the ball. A young looking Sid Congdon, who was in the running at this time for a Welsh cap, is sitting in front, on the right, with his legs folded. In the centre of the back row, wearing a suit and tie, is Club Chairman Shad Lewis.

23 March 1925

Aberavon 13 Mountain Ash 0
Western Mail

REMOVED TO HOSPITAL
MOUNTAIN ASH MAN INJURED IN ABERAVON GAME.

MISHAP TO MOUNTAIN ASH PLAYER.

An unfortunate mishap to Hoskins, the Mountain Ash wing, caused a considerable stoppage in the second half, following which he had to be carried from the field in evident pain. Dr. Richards, the medical officer of health, was in the stand at the time and attended Hoskins in the dressing-room, but so serious was his condition that he deemed it advisable to have him removed to hospital after the match. On inquiry on Sunday the *Western Mail* was informed that the injured player would have to be detained for a few days.

The game was sportingly contested all the way through, and Aberavon deserved their win although the exchanges for the most part were scrappy. Jeremy made

28 March 1925

Aberavon v Mountain Ash

The Aberdare Leader reported, "The news of the death of young Hoskins has shocked our district from end to end, for he was not only a promising footballer, but also a boy of genial, lovable character and an exemplary disposition. Few attain that dual position in public life at so early an age and Byron's words "whom the Gods love.....die young" are appropriate in this sad case. Every week our sporting columns portray the casualties and cussedness in our games, but more particularly in the rugby forces. One cannot help but remember several of this season's incidents with the "Old Firm" and especially the home fixture with Aberavon. There were some ugly tints in that flashy fixture. It was openly talked about before last Saturday's match that there would be anything but "if you please" about it. It is deplorable to the deeps, that sport should be so prostituted to passion and special nurseries maintained for getting my own back. No "high-falutin" will restore young Hoskins to life, but a few words may go a long way to restore a calm dispassionate mien, to resurrect the true spirit of sport from the grave where it has unfortunately lain so long."

4 April 1925

Mountain Ash Footballer's Death
Aberdare Leader

"Mr B. Edward Howe, the West Glamorgan Coroner, with the aid of a jury, conducted an inquiry on Thursday last at Port Talbot into the circumstances surrounding the death of Percy Hoskins, aged 20, the Mountain Ash wing three-quarter, who passed away at the Cottage Hospital the previous Thursday following an injury received during the progress of the Aberavon v Mountain Ash game on the 21st of March.

Mr Pryce Jones and Mr Vivian Deer represented the Aberavon Club and Mr David Perkins the Mountain Ash Club.

Evan Williams, the Welsh International centre, who was playing in the match, said the deceased was playing on the left wing. He could not recall the incident which happened immediately before he saw Hoskins stretched out on the ground. He ran to his assistance; he seemed in great pain and ambulance men carried him off. He did not see the deceased handling the ball. There was no roughness. Llew Jenkins, an ex-Welsh International and Aberavon forward, said just before the close the deceased was rendered "hors de combat".

The Coroner: "Do you remember what happened to cause it?"

"No Sir, except that I think he might have gone down to a loose rush."

"You are an experienced footballer, Mr Jenkins. Can you say whether the game was pleasantly contested?"

"Yes Sir, in the very best sporting fashion."

Wm. J. Moon, the referee appointed by the WRU, of Neath, said there was no roughness and he had no occasion to caution or warn any player. Just before the accident, a scrum was formed, the ball came loose and the deceased was sandwiched between two opponents. A moment later he saw the deceased on the ground and stopped the game.

William R. Thomas, Chairman of Aberavon, endorsed what the referee had said about the good spirit.

Edward D. Richards, Secretary of the Mountain Ash Club, who was in charge of the team, described the game as a clean one.

Clem Austin, Treasurer of the Mountain Ash Club, and Thomas J. Shepherd, the Vice Captain of the Mountain Ash team, concurred the latter describing it as a good sporting game.

Dr David Rees, who witnessed the match, examined Hoskins in the dressing room, and came to the conclusion that he had had an internal injury. There was no external bruising and he ordered his removal to hospital. He saw him later in the evening; he was fully conscious and made no mention of the game. He continued to progress, and later Mr Wade, a specialist of Cardiff, saw him and thought his progress good. On Tuesday last he collapsed and was too ill to be operated upon, and died in the evening. The cause of death was internal haemorrhage.

The Coroner: "Had he been kicked you would have expected to have found a bruise?"

"Yes, but there was not a mark on his body. In my opinion, the injury was caused by a pressure."

The Jury returned a verdict of "accidental death"."

9 May 1925

Mountain Ash 6 Cross Keys 0

Mount Team: D. Hopkins, George Morgan, S. Lewis, J. Jeremiah, T.P. Griffiths, Sid Congdon, Phil Hughes, Oliver Davies, Tom Sheppard, Dick Fryer, P.C. Lett, J. Hellings, George Chamberlain, Jack Simmonds, S. Rees.

"Woodlander" reported in the Leader, "Mountain Ash forwards were grand and laid the foundations on which victory was built. Congdon, George Morgan and Hughes were splendid. The Mount have thus the credit of home and away victories over the crack Keys."

Season 1925/26

Old Firm's Fortunes Start To Dip

After four very good seasons, the Old Firm's form slumped, so much so that more games were lost than won. The season was not without some good wins, though – all at home – against Maesteg, Penarth, Abercarn, Treorky, Glamorgan Wanderers and Cross Keys. There was also a scoreless draw at home to Pontypool in the Godfrey Jones Trophy, which was an invitation tournament which included several Monmouthshire Clubs and Mountain Ash. The season also saw close defeats to Ebbw Vale, Cardiff, Cross Keys and Abertillery. There were two games with Aberaman over Easter 1926, one on Good Friday and the return in Mountain Ash on Easter Monday, and a first known game against Llanharan. A trip was also made to Devon to play Newton Abbot, which ended in defeat, the Old Firm having the better of the game until forward Jim Fryer broke his collar bone just before half time, which resulted in playing the entire second half one man short. The known playing record for the season was played 26, won 9, drawn 3 and lost 14, with 175 points scored, which included 38+ tries, and 215 conceded, to give a win rate of 40.39%, which was a far cry from previous seasons. What must not be forgotten, though, is that although it was a disappointing season by the standards the Old Firm had set in the early 1920s and prior to that, the Club's fixture list, season in, season out, was always strong and included both "first" and "second class" opposition. Mount's captain between 1905 and 1909, Wyndham Jones, who played outside half and scored a try in his only Welsh appearance against Ireland in 1905 to help Wales win the Triple Crown, became a Welsh Selector – one of the so-called "Big Five".

Fixtures 1925/26

Opponents	Date	Venue	Score	Tries	Scorers/Comments
Llanharan	12 Sep 1925	Home	10-0	2	Jonah Rees T, Phil Hughes T, George Morgan DG.
Ebbw Vale	26 Sep 1925	Home	0-3	0	No scorers.
Abertillery	28 Sep 1925	Away	3-6	1	Dr Rees T.
Maesteg	10 Oct 1925	Home	11-6	2	Morgan 2T, Sid Congdon C, Phil Hughes P.
Penygraig	17 Oct 1925	Away	0-0	0	No scorers.
Glamorgan Wanderers	24 Oct 1925	Away	3-21	1	Dick Fryer T.
Penarth	31 Oct 1925	Home	6-0	2	Phil Hughes T, Tom James T.
Penylan	7 Nov 1925	Home	34-6	7	Tom Parry 2T, Sam Lewis 2T, George Retter T, James T, Thomas T, Phil Hughes 2C, P, DG, George Morgan C.
Pontypool	14 Nov 1925	Away	4-20	0	Phil Hughes DG.
Ebbw Vale	21 Nov 1925	Away	8-17	1	J. Rees T, Geo. Morgan P, C.
Penarth	30 Nov 1925	Away	0-13	0	No scorers.
Abercarn	14 Dec 1925	Home	6-3	2	W.M. Jones T, George Retter T.
Treorky	21 Dec 1925	Away	0-7	0	No scorers.

Opponents	Date	Venue	Score	Tries	Scorers/Comments
Treorky	9 Jan 1926	Home	9-6	3	Emlyn Griffiths 3T.
Treherbert	16 Jan 1926	Home	6-6	2	Retter T, Geo. Morgan T.
Cross Keys	6 Feb 1926	Away	11-12	3	Morgan T, C, Foote T, AN Other T.
Newton Abbot	15 Feb 1926	Away	4-16	0	Howe DG.
Glamorgan Wanderers	27 Feb 1926	Home	13-12	3	D.J. Thomas T, James C, AN Other 2T, C.
Pontypool	6 Mar 1926	Home	0-0	0	No scorers.
Abertillery	13 Mar 1926	Home	6-7	2	Oliver Davies T, D. Phillips T.
Cross Keys	20 Mar 1926	Home	15-14	3	Phil Hughes T, C, DG, Geo. Morgan T, Rees T.
Treherbert	29 Mar 1926	Away	5-12	Unknown	Scorers unknown.
Aberaman	10 Apr 1926	Away	5-6	1	Parsell T, Phil Hughes C.
Aberaman	10 Apr 1926	Home	13-3	3	Phil Hughes T,C, Thomas T, Parsell T, Morgan C.
Pontypridd	1 May 1926	Home	0-11	0	No scorers.
Cardiff	Unknown	Home	3-8	Unknown	Result printed in the Cardiff v Mountain Ash programme, WRU Cup, 13 December 1972.

Summary of Playing Record

P	W	D	L	For	Against	Tries Scored	Win Rate %
26	9	3	14	175	215	38+	40.39

Match Reports & Publications

5 September 1925

Aberdare Leader reporter, "Woodlander", commented, "....Nothing could testify more for the necessity of keeping up a nursery than the play of those two lads, Harry Mills and Ernie Foote. It is pleasing to record this and the Old Firm's lustre will never dim while such players in the Mount are to be picked up....Although several members of the Mountain Ash Rugby Football Club have left this season, there are plenty of good fish left in the "Rec Sea". George Chamberlain has gone to Birmingham and Willie Thomas, the full back, to Otley, Yorkshire, where he will find Haydn Coopey, who is the Captain of Otley RFC."

12 September 1925

<u>Mountain Ash 10 Llanharan 0</u>

The Aberdare Leader reported, "Mr Wyndham Jones, an old "Old Firm" player was present and was congratulated on all sides on his election to the "Big Seat" in Rugby Football."

26 September 1925

<u>Mountain Ash 0 Ebbw Vale 3</u>

"Woodlander" reported in the Aberdare Leader, "the second stage of the Godfrey Jones Trophy was played at the Rec last Saturday. Drenching rain induced the committee of the Old Firm to postpone the match but at the last moment, when the sun shone, decided to open the gates. The opening exchanges were not very brisk, the water ponds militating against real football."

17 October 1925

<u>Penygraig 0 Mountain Ash 0</u>

"Woodlander" reported in the Aberdare Leader, "....a much weakened Old Firm travelled to Penygraig to renew acquaintances with the Rhondda team, which had been broken for close upon a score of years....The Old Firm conceded a penalty and the homesters full back missed by the breadth of a hayseed. That was the only serious menace to the score sheet."

31 October 1925

<u>Mountain Ash 6 Penarth 0</u>

Mount Team: Sid Congdon, S. Lewis, James, W. Jones, Benger, Ernie Foote, Phil Hughes, Gough Retter, P.C. Lett, White, Harry Mills, P.C. Thomas, Dick Fryer, Jack Simmonds, Joe Hellings.

<u>Mountain Ash Play Well</u>

The Western Mail reported, "Mountain Ash proved on Saturday that they are still a force to be reckoned with. Tom James and Harry Mills filled vacancies at three-quarter and both did well. Congdon, at full back, was a great success and saved his side repeatedly. Ernie Foote, the ex-Schoolboy International, gave a clever display and was more than a match for his opponent. Phil Hughes hit it off splendidly with him and he deserves a further chance. It was at forward that Mountain Ash's superiority was most pronounced. They scrummaged better and secured the ball more often than in any other match this season. P.C. Thomas, Retter, Simmonds and Fryer were the most prominent. The first named is ideally built and should go a long way to securing International honours. The whole pack played splendidly and laid the foundation for victory....There were very few dull moments throughout, the exchanges being always fast and interesting."

9 January 1926

<u>Mountain Ash 9 Treorky 6</u>
<u>Western Mail</u>

MOUNTAIN ASH AVENGED ON TREORKY.

	G.	T.	Pts.
Mountain Ash	0	3	9
Treorky	*1	1	6

* Penalty.

By defeating Treorky at home, Mountain Ash avenged their defeat of a fortnight ago. Emlyn Griffiths played an excellent game and scored all three tries. The Mountain Ash back division enjoyed a great superiority over their opponents. Both set of forwards played a hard game in the open, and there was little to choose between them in this respect, but Mountain Ash had the better of matters in the scrums.

27 February 1926

<u>Mountain Ash 13 Glamorgan Wanderers 12</u>
<u>Glamorgan Wanderers Defeated by a Single Point at Mountain Ash</u>

The Western Mail reported, "This game proved one of the most exciting seen on the Mountain Ash ground for some time, both sides playing with abandon which makes for attractive rugby. No one would wish to see anything finer than the great effort by Howe and Davies which gave Mountain Ash an early lead....The second half produced many pretty incidents, Mountain Ash doing most of the pressing. They were robbed of a certain score owing to obstruction and the referee promptly awarded a penalty try."

6 March 1926

<u>Mountain Ash 0 Pontypool 0</u>
<u>Western Mail</u>

NO SCORE AT MOUNTAIN ASH.

PONTYPOOL FORWARDS INFERIOR TO HOME PACK.

	G.	T.	Pts.
Mountain Ash	0	0	0
Pontypool	0	0	0

The forwards bore the brunt of the fray in the game at Mountain Ash, the home pack giving a splendid account of themselves. They controlled the scrums and secured the ball in the loose more often than Pontypool. They were much faster and by fast following up completely baulked any effort of the visiting backs to develop attacks.

Both sides missed chances to score owing to difficulty in handling the greasy ball. Jonah Rees was the best wing on view and he put in the best runs of the game. James was the best of the Pontypool backs, although Ford was a tower of strength in defence. For Mountain Ash Phil Hughes and George Morgan did a lot of good work, and James, the custodian, was very sound. The closing stages were most exciting.

13 March 1926

<u>Mountain Ash 6 Abertillery 7</u>
<u>Western Mail</u>

HOW ABERTILLERY AVERTED DEFEAT.

PLAYER LEAPS IN THE AIR AND PREVENTS A GOAL.

	G.	T.	Pts.
Abertillery	*1	1	7
Mountain Ash	0	2	6

* Dropped.

Neither team showed anything like their best form in the game at Mountain Ash. Abertillery should have done much better in the first half, when they had the advantage of the high wind, Mountain Ash being handicapped. Seely dropped a clever goal for Abertillery, that being the only score of the uninteresting first half.

The second half, however, reached a high standard. Abertillery increased their lead by a really fine try scored by Cecil. In the closing stages Mountain Ash produced the best play of the match. The backs passed splendidly and Dewi Phillips scored. An unusual incident happened when James took the kick for goal after Oli Davies had scored a try. Will Morris jumped and touched the ball as it went over the bar and saved his side from defeat.

Season 1926/27

Dire Season For Old Firm

If the Old Firm's fortunes had taken a dip in 1925/26, things got much worse in 1926/27. The season was as poor as any the Club had endured. In total, 22 known games were played, 4 won, 1 drawn, and 17 lost, with a mere 86+ points scored, which included only 14+ tries, and 239+ conceded, which gave a win rate of 20.46%. There was hardly a bright spot in the whole season which the Aberdare Leader's rugby reporter, "Woodlander", commented on when not even half the season had elapsed, writing on 4 December 1926, "When writing up the history of the Old Firm for the 1926 season, it will certainly be noted as one of the most disappointing in its history."

The start to the season promised better with two of the first three games won, with the first win, 17-11, opening Aberaman RFC's new ground. Other than a one point win over Penygraig shortly after, the Old Firm had to wait until Boxing Day 1926 for a third win. This was a game against a Mountain Ash County School Old Boys XV. It was a match the Old Firm reportedly won – although no details were available in the Aberdare Leader about it – Mount Secretary Enoch Watkins reportedly winning a £5 bet he had with the County School's caretaker, Jimmy Austin, who organised the Old Boys XV. An idea had been born and exactly a year later, on Boxing Day 1927, the Welsh Academicals RFC was formed. There was a comparatively good result away to Cardiff where the loss was only 15-7, but the 8-5 away defeat to Pontypridd, in a game which was restricted to 20 minutes in each half due to "the Ynysangharad meadow was in a fearful condition, and drenching rain at the time", was a disappointment in that not many games were lost to Ponty back then. Perhaps economic conditions played a part in the Old Firm's poorest season to date. This was the year of the Great Strike, the South Wales coalfield was in decline, unemployment was rising and times were tough, with most Clubs in the valleys in dire straits financially. However, the fact that Mountain Ash RFC survived and battled on, fulfilling its fixtures week in, week out, which some Clubs failed to do due to a lack of funds, should not be underestimated, and in this regard, Club Chairman Shad Lewis reportedly played a big part, but how much exactly, is unknown.

Fixtures 1926/27

Opponents	Date	Venue	Score	Tries	Scorers/Comments
Aberaman	4 Sep 1926	Away	17-11	Unknown	Scorers unknown.
Glamorgan Wanderers	25 Sep 1926	Home	3-11	1	Ernie Foote T.
Penygraig	2 Oct 1926	Home	15-14	2	Jack Price T, Gough Retter T, George Morgan DG, AN Other P, C.
Cardiff	9 Oct 1926	Away	7-15	1	Foote T, Rees DG.
Maesteg	23 Oct 1926	Away	0-31	0	No scorers.
Abercarn	6 Nov 1926	Away	4-18	0	Phil Hughes DG.
Abertillery	8 Nov 1926	Unknown	0-9	0	No scorers.
Treherbert	4 Dec 1926	Away	0-11	0	No scorers.
Glamorgan Wanderers	11 Dec 1926	Away	3-8	1	Jonah Rees T.
Pontypool	18 Dec 1926	Home	5-17	1	Jonah Rees T, Goff Retter C.
Mountain Ash County School Old Boys	26 Dec 1926	Home	Unknown	Unknown	Mount win. Scorers unknown.
Bryncethin	28 Dec 1926	Away	3-6	Unknown	Scorer unknown.
Resolven	8 Jan 1927	Home	9-12	3	E. Griffiths T, Jonah Rees T, AN Other T.

Opponents	Date	Venue	Score	Tries	Scorers/Comments
Pontypool	8 Jan 1927	Away	3-22	1	Scorer unknown.
Treherbert	21 Feb 1927	Home	3-0	1	Gilbert T.
Cardiff 2nd XV	28 Feb 1927	Home	0-0	0	No scorers.
Penygraig	7 Mar 1927	Unsure	0-3	0	No scorers.
Swansea	14 Mar 1927	Away	3-21	1	Jonah Rees T.
Abercarn	26 Mar 1927	Home	3-6	1	Bartlett T.
Pontypridd	9 Apr 1927	Away	5-8	1	Bartlett T, C.
Treorky	18 Apr 1927	Away	3-8	Unknown	Scorer unknown.
Aberaman	14 May 1927	Home	0-8	0	No scorers.

Summary of Playing Record

P	W	D	L	For	Against	Tries Scored	Win Rate %
22	4	1	17	86+	239+	14+	20.46

Match Reports & Publications

9 October 1926

<u>Cardiff 15 Mountain Ash 7</u>

Mount Team: Bennett, James, George Morgan, Dr Griffiths, Em Davies, E. Foote, Phil Hughes, G. Retter, S. Rees, T. Edmunds, J. Simmonds, T. Griffiths, Fryer, Harry Mills, M. Ambrose.

"Woodlander" commented in the Aberdare Leader, "the Old Firm were up against stiff opposition when they visited Cardiff last Saturday there is no denying, but that they would emerge from the contest with real honours was not only unexpected but handsomely deserved….The match revealed some fine attacking form among the Old Firm players….The scrum was much better managed than Cardiff, and on the whole the visitors with a little bit of luck might easily have pulled the game out of the fire. Bennett was decidedly good and fearless at full back, and Rees and Retter, Ernie Foote and Mills deserve special mention."

28 February 1927

<u>Mountain Ash 0 Cardiff 2nd XV 0</u>
<u>Cardiff's Other Team Play Pointless Draw at Mountain Ash</u>

The Western Mail commented, "….the home forwards showed superior powers of endurance and Cardiff were hard pressed in the second half….Mountain Ash penned Cardiff inside their own 25….Congdon was again in good form. On the run of play, Mountain Ash deserved to win."

Mountain Ash Rugby Football Club
"The Old Firm"
Circa 1926/27

Only some of the names of the players and committee members are known in the above photograph and they are as follows.

In the back row, from left to right, the first person is Glyn John (Committee), the second is Billy Llewellyn (Baggage Man), the third is Dai Davies (Committee), the fourth is Dan Horrigan (Trainer), the fifth is Jason Job (Rec Groundsman), and the seventh is Ted Bradwick (Secretary).

In the middle row, seventh from the left is Dick Fryer, and on the far right, wearing an overcoat, is Sid Congdon.

In the front row, the first person sitting is Harry Mills, and the third from the left is Jim Coughlin.

Season 1927/28

Another Disappointing Season For Old Firm

Although this was another mediocre season for the Old Firm, it wasn't helped by games being cancelled due to bad weather, the Aberdare Leader's reporter, "Woodlander", commenting in February 1928, "At long last Mountain Ash were able to commence the second half of their 1927/28 engagements. Probably a record has been set up in rugby union football to suffer the loss of eight matches consecutively in one season owing to bad weather conditions....". Two of these cancellations were the games at Bath on New Year's Eve 1927, which was cancelled due to snow, and at Ebbw Vale in January 1928 which was abandoned early in the second half due to torrential rain and a gale force wind turning the ground into a quagmire. Of the 23 known games played, Mount won 6, drew 5 and lost 12, scoring 133+ points, which included 33+ tries, and conceded 177+, to finish with a win rate of 36.96%. Wins were recorded against Pontypridd, Glamorgan Wanderers, Cross Keys, Cilfynydd and Aberaman. There were also draws with Tredegar twice, and Pontypool, and there was a narrow home loss to Abertillery. The Aberdare Leader stated in an article that "the Club is to compete for the Godfrey Jones Trophy and also the Glamorgan League". This was the first time the Glamorgan League had been mentioned in any report in the 1920s which suggests that this may have been the first season the Old Firm had entered the competition since 1913/14 – when the "double" of Cup and League was won. There was also an interesting article in the Aberdare Leader called, "I Remember", which recalled a Welsh International trial match that took place at Mountain Ash in the late 1890s, with the writer recounting his memories of the day. Following on from beating a Mountain Ash County School Old Boys XV a year earlier, another game was organised for Boxing Day 1927, this time the School XV strengthening their team by including former students from inside and outside the town. This was the official formation of the Welsh Academicals and a game the "Accies" reportedly won, School caretaker Jimmy Austin winning back the £5 he lost to Enoch Watkins the year before. However, just like the game played in 1926/27, no report of the match could be found.

Fixtures 1927/28

Opponents	Date	Venue	Score	Tries	Scorers/Comments
Treorky (L)	10 Sep 1927	Away	3-9	1	AN Other T.
Tredegar	17 Sep 1927	Home	3-3	1	Gwyn Thomas T.
Aberaman (PL)	24 Sep 1927	Away	12-13	1	J. Morgan T, Thompson DG, C, P.
Ebbw Vale	26 Sep 1927	Home	0-5	0	No scorers.
Pontypridd (L)	8 Oct 1927	Away	8-5	2	J. Allen T, P.C. Brown T, Morgan C.
Pontypool	15 Oct 1927	Home	3-3	1	AN Other T.
Penygraig (L)	7 Nov 1927	Away	3-6	1	W. Morgan T.
Glamorgan Wanderers	14 Nov 1927	Away	15-8	3	Thomas 2T, W. Morgan T, Brown 3C.
Crumlin	26 Nov 1927	Home	0-0	0	No scorers.
Pontypool	10 Dec 1927	Away	0-33	0	No scorers.
Aberaman (PL)	10 Dec 1927	Home	11-0	3	Erricker T, Rickards T, Morgan T, P.C. Brown C.
Welsh Academicals	26 Dec 1927	Home	Unknown	Unknown	Mount loss. Scorers unknown.
Blaenavon	21 Jan 1928	Away	0-5	0	No scorers.

Opponents	Date	Venue	Score	Tries	Scorers/Comments
Ebbw Vale	23 Jan 1928	Away	0-3	0	No scorers.
Cross Keys	11 Feb 1928	Home	6-3	2	G. Retter T, Morgan T.
Cilfynydd (PL)	18 Feb 1928	Away	6-5	2	Jack Simmonds 2T.
Tredegar	3 Mar 1928	Away	11-11	3	George Maskell T, Phillips T, Thomas T, Tom James C.
Treherbert (PL)	10 Mar 1928	Away	13-14	3	E. Thomas T, Morgan T, AN Other T, Curley Thomas DG.
Glamorgan Wanderers	19 Mar 1928	Home	12-14	3	Curly Thomas T, G. Retter T, J. Allen T, Harry Mills P.
Blaenavon	7 Apr 1928	Home	0-0	0	No scorers.
Cross Keys	14 Apr 1928	Away	3-23	1	Jenkins T.
Abertillery	14 Apr 1928	Home	0-3	0	No scorers.
Pontardawe	30 Apr 1928	Home	24-11	6	G. Retter 3T, Chas Thompson T, C, P.C. Rickards T, Morgan T, James 2C.

Summary of Matches

P	W	D	L	For	Against	Tries Scored	Win Rate %
23	6	5	12	133+	177+	33+	36.96

Match Reports & Publications

8 October 1927

<u>Pontypridd 5 Mountain Ash 8</u>

Mount Team: T. James, W. Brown, Thompson, J. Morgan, E. Evans, T. Davies, T. Phillips, P.C. Rickards, P.C. Brown, H. Mills, J. Allen, T. Edwards, E. Morgan, T. Evans, Erricker.

"Woodlander" reported in the Aberdare Leader, "the Old Firm had an engagement at Pontypridd on Saturday in the Glamorgan League and they kept it. Strangely enough, the Pontyites, owing to the weather, were unwilling to fulfil the fixture, but after pressure from the visitors, consented to play. The victory for the Mount was well deserved and adds another two valuable League points to their record." The Western Mail commented, "….the visitors it is understood, insisted on claiming two points in the absence of a contest".

26 November 1927

Old "Old Firm"

"An old friend of the Aberdare Leader, Mr Tom Lloyd (Emlyn House), writing in the Swansea Daily Post, recalls some interesting reminiscences of the Old Firm:

I REMEMBER

I remember an International Trial match, similar to the one played at Neath, taking place in a town nestling on the sides of the mountains of Mid Glamorgan. My memory will not provide me with the exact date, but when I state that Strand Jones was one of the players taking part, it will be sufficient as a chronological fact to determine the period. It was the time when Welsh Rugby Football was at the crest of its highest wave, a time when Nicholls, Gabe, Trew, Llewellyn, Morgan, Jones and Owen astonished the world with their brilliant handling and back play, the likes of which has never been seen before. This Trial Match took place at Mountain Ash, on the old field at Newtown – now obliterated by a mountainous coal tip. Mountain Ash and their great rivals, Llwynypia, were then the great sides of the Glamorgan League, and attracted big crowds, so it was no small wonder that on this day a gathering of 10,000 had come to witness the selected players of the Principality take part in the test for promotion to the National side. Outside the ground, there were 6 large barrows of fruit, and in the centre, on a large cart, stood the proprietor of this miniature Covent Garden. Mr Wiltshire, for such was his name, owned also the livery stables, as well as being a familiar character in the town, then a flourishing place. That day he wore, as usual, a large blue sporting necktie, from which shone a golden horseshoe pin. His rotund, red face and large portly figure vibrated to his stentorian voice, as he bellowed forth – accompanied by the lesser six voices of his assistants – "the old firm, the old firm, patronise the old firm!" So impressed was "Old Stager" that to him it remained a symbolical figure, always to be associated with Mountain Ash, in the manner of Britain and John Bull; and in his report of the match he dubbed the Club, which had given Wales a dozen National players, "The Old Firm". By this pseudonym it is to this day known to all football enthusiasts in South Wales." Gwyn Nicholls (Cardiff & Newport) played for Wales between 1896 and 1906, R.T. Gabe (Llanelli & Cardiff) played for Wales between 1901 & 1908 and W. Trew (Swansea) played for Wales between 1900 and 1907. Mount and Llwynypia were the dominant sides in the Glamorgan League when it started in 1894 (as the Rhondda, Aberdare and Merthyr Valleys Cup). There was a Welsh trial match held in Mountain Ash in 1898/99. Whether this was the one being referred to is unknown.

11 February 1928

Mountain Ash 6 Cross Keys 3

Mount Team: Tom James, E. Thomas, Morgan, Thompson, J. Hill, T. Phillips, Curley Thomas, P.C. Rickards, P.C. Brown, Jack Simmonds, Harry Mills, Edwards, Allen, G. Maskell, G. Retter.

"Woodlander" reported in the Aberdare Leader, "At long last Mountain Ash were able to commence the second half of their 1927/28 engagements. Probably a record has been set up in rugby union football to suffer the loss of eight matches consecutively in one season owing to bad weather conditions. On Saturday at the Rec, the conditions were bad enough to declare the match off, but the Old Firm had advertised to play wet or fine." The Western Mail commented, "Mountain Ash played 7 forwards only but it was obvious that they were more than the equal of the 8 visiting forwards….Despite having to contend with a strong opposing wind, the home forwards were now all powerful and severely harassed the visitors' line….From a forward melee near the visitors' 25, Retter broke away to score an unconverted try. Mountain Ash maintained severe pressure upon the visitors' line until the cessation of hostilities."

3 March 1928

<u>Tredegar 11 Mountain Ash 11</u>

Mount Team: Tom James, J. Hill, Thompson, Morgan, Thomas, T. Phillips, Curley Thomas, G. Retter, P.C. Rickards, P.C. Brown, Harry Mills, Jack Simmonds, J. Allen, G. Edwards, G. Maskell.

The Western Mail reported, "After establishing a good lead, the home side absolutely failed to hold their opponents and in the closing stages, Mountain Ash were overwhelmingly the better side and Tredegar were eventually hard pressed to keep the game to a draw."

<u>Mountain Ash Rugby Football Club</u>
<u>"The Old Firm"</u>
<u>Circa 1927/28</u>

Only some of the names in the above photograph are known.

In the back row, left to right, the first person is Jason Job (Rec Groundsman), the third is Billy Llewellyn (Baggage Man), the fourth is scrum half Sid Congdon, the eighth person is Dai Davies (Committee), and on the far right is Dan Horrigan (Trainer).

In the front row, from left to right, the first person sitting is Shad Lewis (Chairman), the sixth is forward Trevor Edwards, and to the right of him is Ted Bradwick (Secretary).

Season 1928/29

Mount Continue To Struggle

This was another disappointing season for the Old Firm with tries and points hard to come by. Although the 1920s had low scores for most games, Mount failed to score a point in 10 of the 30 games played and also conceded more than 20 points on 4 occasions. Both these occurrences had rarely, if ever, happened in the past. Even the Western Mail commented in the 23-6 loss at Cross Keys in March 1929, "Mountain Ash are not the "Old Firm" of previous years....". The season had a few high points, though. There were home wins over Treorchy – which inflicted a first Glamorgan League defeat in February 1929 on the eventual season's champions – Ebbw Vale, Maesteg, Glamorgan Wanderers, Abercarn, Crumlin and Glynneath, and there was a local derby win at Pontypridd and a draw at home. At the end of the season, the playing record read played 30, won 11, drawn 2, lost 17, with 179 points scored, including 34+ tries, and 277 conceded, which converted to a win rate of exactly 40%. Mount's scrum half, Sid Congdon, called time on his career at the end of the season with the disappointment of not having gained a coveted Welsh cap after being reserve on up to 14 occasions. Whereas in today's (2015) game, 8 substitutes are allowed in International rugby, none were allowed in the 1920s whatever the reason for a player leaving the field. Congdon vied for the Welsh scrum half position primarily with Bobby Delahay of Bridgend and Cardiff, who gained 18 caps between 1922 and 1927, but never displaced him in the Welsh XV. There was also a comment in an Aberdare Leader report which referred to the generosity of the Mount Chairman, Mr Shad Lewis, who played a big part in keeping the Club going through the tough economic times of the 1920s, the article about schools rugby in the town finishing with the comment, "One is tempted to say that there would be neither premier nor schoolboy rugby in Mountain Ash were it not for good Shad. May he never fail us."

Fixtures 1928/29

Opponents	Date	Venue	Score	Tries	Scorers/Comments
Pontypool	15 Sep 1928	Away	6-11	2	Rickard T, Allen T.
Aberaman (PL)	18 Sep 1928	Home	9-0	1	Morgan T, Sid Congdon DG, Jack Allen C.
Maesteg	22 Sep 1928	Away	13-28	2	Thomas 2T, Allen P, Price DG.
Pontypridd	29 Sep 1928	Away	9-5	1	Morgan T, Allen 2P.
Cilfynydd (L)	29 Sep 1928	Home	0-3	0	No scorers.
Abercarn	6 Oct 1928	Home	8-3	2	Goff Retter T, Hector Fryer T, Allen C.
Bargoed (L)	8 Oct 1928	Unknown	9-3	3	Morgan 2T, Parcell T.
Crumlin	15 Oct 1928	Home	12-6	4	E. Thomas 2T, P.C. Lett T, Thompson T.
Aberaman (PL)	20 Oct 1928	Away	8-15	2	Goff Retter T, J. Allen P, C.
Cross Keys	22 Oct 1928	Home	0-6	0	No scorers.
Maesteg	29 Oct 1928	Home	9-6	1	Elvet Thomas T, Jack Allen 2P.

Opponents	Date	Venue	Score	Tries	Scorers/Comments
Abertillery	5 Nov 1928	Away	0-13	0	No scorers.
Penygraig (PL)	12 Nov 1928	Home	0-0	0	No scorers.
Glynneath (PL)	24 Nov 1928	Home	15-11	3	Elvet Thomas 3T, Don Price DG, Chas Thompson C.
Blaenavon	8 Dec 1928	Away	0-9	0	No scorers.
Resolven	15 Dec 1928	Home	6-11	Unknown	Scorers unknown.
Pontypool	5 Jan 1929	Home	0-8	0	No scorers.
Resolven	26 Jan 1929	Away	3-23	Unknown	Scorer unknown.
Ebbw Vale	9 Feb 1929	Away	0-10	0	No scorers.
Treorky (L)	16 Feb 1929	Home	13-6	2	Jenkins T, Thomas T, Don Price DG, AN Other P.
Pontypridd	4 Mar 1929	Home	0-0	0	No scorers.
Crumlin	11 Mar 1929	Away	0-6	0	No scorers.
Cross Keys	18 Mar 1929	Away	6-23	1	Elvet Thomas T, Chas Thompson P.
Glamorgan Wanderers	30 Mar 1929	Home	21-13	5	Elvet Thomas 2T, Price T, Burke T, Pike T, Don Price DG, Jack Allen C.
Ebbw Vale	1 Apr 1929	Home	17-0	5	Chas Thompson 4T, Elvet Thomas T, Jack Allen C.
Treherbert (PL)	6 Apr 1929	Away	3-9	0+	Scorer unknown.
Treorky (PL)	6 Apr 1929	Away	3-14	0+	Scorer unknown.
Penarth	20 Apr 1929	Away	3-27	0+	Scorer unknown.
Abertillery	27 Apr 1929	Home	0-5	0	No scorers.
Treherbert (PL)	27 Apr 1929	Unsure	6-3	Unknown	Scorers unknown.

Summary of Matches

P	W	D	L	For	Against	Tries Scored	Win Rate %
30	11	2	17	179	277	34+	40.00

Match Reports & Publications

15 September 1928

Mountain Ash Schoolboys Rugby League

The Aberdare Leader reported, "Yet another dawn of the rugger season and with it the usual hopes and aspirations of both teachers and boys. It is a good adage which says that the success or failure of the premier side reflects itself on that of the schoolboy side. Certain it is that when the Old Firm enjoyed triumphs and prosperity, so did the schoolboys. Well, the last few seasons have proved lean ones, maybe we are on the threshold of the fat ones, at least let's hope so in case not. It is pleasing to note that quite half of the players performing valiantly in the ranks of this year's Mountain Ash side (which is going to prove a jolly good one before the season's end) were taught their rugby in the schools' rugby league. The President for the year was re-elected – an honour – the greatest the League can bestow, richly deserved. He is Mr Shad Lewis, whose generosity and kindness in multi-various ways to the game of rugger are known to only those in the inner circle. One is tempted to say that there would be neither premier nor schoolboy rugby in Mountain Ash were it not for good Shad. May he never fail us."

18 September 1928

<u>Mountain Ash 9 Aberaman 0</u>
<u>Possible Glamorgan League Fixture</u>
<u>Player Ordered Off At Mountain Ash</u>

The Western Mail reported, "Mountain Ash entertained their old rivals in glorious weather on Monday.... The Mountain Ash three-quarters handled in good style but half time arrived with the score-sheet blank.... Mountain Ash worked their way to the Aberaman line where Congdon dropped a great goal. Thompson made a magnificent run for the Old Firm and when hemmed in transferred to Morgan, who scored under the posts, Jack Allen converting. Mountain Ash was now easily the superior team. A few minutes from time a regrettable incident occurred, which ended in Dick Fryer being ordered off, a decision which did not meet with the approval of the crowd."

29 September 1928

<u>Pontypridd 5 Mountain Ash 9</u>

"Woodlander" reported in the Aberdare Leader, "the Old Firm are serving out some feasts of football not only at home but also on foreign fields....The game was one of the best ever witnessed and the struggle was most keen. The Mount's score sheet was opened by Allen....His long range kick was a beauty and was heartily cheered. There was a hard struggle for supremacy....With Mountain Ash 6 and Pontypridd 5, the game became a tussle of rare sport. It was however Allen who again kicked a long range penalty goal and put the game out of doubt."

6 October 1928

"Mr Ted Bradwick, the Secretary of the Old Firm, feels very deeply about the remarks made in last week's Leader by the Aberaman correspondent regarding rough play at Mountain Ash on September 17. He resents the imputation that all the blame should be fixed on Mountain Ash players. As proof of this, four of the Mountain Ash players are still down with injuries, notably Sid Congdon, from that particular match. It has been reported that Aberaman will probably refuse to play Mountain Ash next season. If that is the attitude adopted, the Mountain Ash Club, says the Secretary, will not have the slightest objection."

20 October 1928

<u>Aberaman 15 Mountain Ash 8</u>
<u>Possible Glamorgan League Fixture</u>
<u>Rough Play Between Aberaman and Mountain Ash Teams</u>

The Aberdare Leader's reporter commented, "This match was played before a record crowd on Monday at Aberaman Park. A rough game was naturally expected to follow that of a fortnight ago at Mountain Ash, when one of the Mount forwards was suspended for three months....". The Western Mail reported, "it was the roughest game seen on the park this season....Phil Hughes had to retire half way through the second half with a gash to his head which required stitching....".

29 October 1928

Mountain Ash 9 Maesteg 6

The Western Mail reported, "....Morgan, the Old Firm's right centre, covered three parts of the field in an electrifying run and put Elvet Thomas over....With the scores level, a ding-dong duel ensued, but in the concluding stages, Jack Allen kicked another penalty to give the Old Firm a deserved victory."

24 November 1928

Mountain Ash Schools Rugby League

The Aberdare Leader reported the game versus Cardiff Schools as follows, "....Tommy Evans was soon the favourite of the crowd and well he deserved the honour. He had a topping partner in Manfield on the wing. As has been said in this column before, Manfield makes the greatest use of every chance he gets and he did on Saturday. He ran resolutely and tackled determinedly and if he can improve at his present rate, he is going to be "some player" before the season ends. The last line of defence created a most favourable impression. Young Close, although only a midget, fielded the ball uncannily at times and his initiative was inspiring."

"Manfield" was Les Manfield, who was capped twice at No.8 for Wales in 1939 while playing for Mountain Ash and Otley RFCs. When rugby resumed after the end of World War II, he was capped another 5 times from Cardiff RFC. "Close" is thought to be Peter Close, the father of Mount's hooker of the late 1960s and early 1970s, the late Malcolm Close.

16 February 1929

Mountain Ash 13 Treorchy 6
Glamorgan League
Western Mail

GLAMORGAN LEAGUE.

Treorchy's First Defeat in the Competition.

Mountain Ash *2 2 13
Treorchy .... †2 0   6
*1 dropped, 1 penalty. †2 penalties.

This Glamorgan League encounter at Mountain Ash on Saturday provided a fast and exciting game. Treorchy were early aggressive, and Broughton landed a penalty goal. Mountain Ash went ahead when Thompson kicked a penalty goal and Jenkins scored an unconverted try. The lead was further increased when Price dropped a pretty goal. Late in the second half Broughton, who rendered good service to the visitors, landed another penalty. A minute from time Thompson, breaking through the Treorchy defence, scored a great try underneath the posts.

This was Treorchy's first defeat in the League this season, and it puts Penygraig in a much brighter position, for they have the same number of points and have only played one game more than Treorchy. The League table up to date is as follows:—

	P.	W.	L.	D.	for	agst.	Pts.
Treorchy	10	7	1	2	95	50	16
Penygraig	11	6	1	4	63	52	16
Mountain Ash	8	5	2	1	70	43	11
Glynneath	7	4	1	2	77	51	9
Cilfynydd	8	4	3	1	24	26	9
Aberaman	10	3	6	1	78	76	7
Treherbert	9	2	5	2	29	57	6
Ynysybwl	9	3	6	0	36	72	6
Bargoed	9	0	9	0	20	96	0

1 April 1929

Mountain Ash 17 Ebbw Vale 0
Western Mail

Mountain Ash Succeed.

	G.	T.	Pts.
Mountain Ash	1	4	17
Ebbw Vale	0	0	0

Both sides were poorly represented. Ebbw Vale arriving four men short, and they found substitutes on the field. Mountain Ash kicked off against a powerful wind which severely interfered with play. The home side were early aggressive and after a good run by Thompson, Thomas scored underneath the posts. Allen converting.

In the second half, with the wind behind them, Mountain Ash had matters their own way and Thompson added tries, neither of which was converted.

Sid Congdon
So Near, Yet So Far

Above is a photograph of scrum half Sid Congdon in his prime. He retired at the end of the 1928/29 season. He joined Mountain Ash from Llanelli in 1921/22 and captained the Old Firm for two seasons from 1922 to 1924. He was one of the unluckiest of players, coming tantalisingly close to a Welsh cap, being Welsh reserve on a dozen or so occasions during his career.

Season 1929/30

1920s End In Disappointing Fashion For Old Firm

This was a very poor season for the Old Firm, the second in the last 5 years, with just 5 wins and 3 draws from the 22 known games played. It was also the 5th consecutive season in which more games were lost than won. Whether the Club entered the Glamorgan League is unknown as the competition was never mentioned. The best wins of the season were at Cross Keys and Glamorgan Wanderers. There were draws against Aberaman and Ynysybwl, and narrow losses to Ebbw Vale, Glamorgan Wanderers and Pontypridd. Junior rugby was encouraged in the town, the Old Firm playing a Sid Congdon XV in order to raise funds. Overall though, it was a low key end to the 1920s for the Old Firm, and although they were down, they were far from out, as the early 1930s proved.

Fixtures 1929/30

Opponents	Date	Venue	Score	Tries	Scorers/Comments
Pontypridd Harlequins	14 Sep 1929	Home	21-4	4	Johnny Allen 2T, Thomas T, Thompson T, P.C. Evans P, 3C.
Pontypool	14 Sep 1929	Away	10-25	2	Scorers unknown.
Aberaman	21 Sep 1929	Home	3-3	0	P.C. Evans P.
Ynysybwl	28 Sep 1929	Away	5-5	1	Elvet Thomas T, P.C. Evans C.
Resolven	5 Oct 1929	Home	5-12	1	W. Burke T, P.C. Evans C.
Cilfynydd	14 Oct 1929	Home	3-5	1	P.C. Vaughan T.
Aberaman	26 Oct 1929	Away	6-10	2	Wyndham Jones T, Thompson T.
Resolven	2 Nov 1929	Away	0-6	0	No scorers.
Pontypool	9 Nov 1929	Home	0-11	0	No scorers.
Treorky	18 Nov 1929	Home	0-6	0	No scorers.
Glamorgan Wanderers	2 Dec 1929	Home	7-9	0	Thompson P, Jim Coughlin DG.
Glamorgan Wanderers	23 Dec 1929	Away	9-8	1	Coughlin T, Thompson DG, C.
Ebbw Vale	6 Jan 1930	Home	3-5	0	Thompson P.
Cross Keys	3 Feb 1930	Away	3-0	1	Jones T.
Sid Congdon XV	10 Feb 1930	Home	9-14	3	Elvet Thomas T, Wyndham Jones T, J.H. Williams T.
Penygraig	17 Feb 1930	Home	3-3	1	Evans T.
Kenfig Hill	24 Feb 1930	Away	3-0	1	H. Murphy T.
Pontypridd	8 Mar 1930	Away	0-3	0	No scorers.
Penygraig	17 Mar 1930	Away	3-4	1	Elvet Thomas T.
Crumlin	24 Mar 1930	Home	12-3	3	Elvet Thomas 2T, Jim Coughlin T, Williams P.
Treorky	7 Apr 1930	Away	5-11	1	Elvet Thomas T, P.C. Vaughan C.
Bargoed	12 Apr 1930	Home	8-16	2	Williams T, Thomas T, George C.

Summary of Matches

P	W	D	L	For	Against	Tries Scored	Win Rate %
22	5	3	14	118	163	25	29.55

Match Reports & Publications

21 September 1929

<u>Mountain Ash 3 Aberaman 3</u>

Mount Team: W. Webber, E. Thomas, C. Thompson, Wyndham Jones, Percy Roberts, W. Burland, G. Parker, J. Allen, P.C. Evans, W. Bishop, A. Davies, W. Morgan, W. Close, G. Maskell, J.W. Price.

The Aberdare Leader reported, "The second half was pointless, although owing to the linesman's judgement and the referee's decision, a try obtained by Wyndham Jones was ruled out. There was a rather hostile demonstration by a section of the crowd." Wyndham Jones was probably the son of the Old Firm's outside half of the same name who was capped in 1905.

23 December 1929

<u>Glamorgan Wanderers 8 Mountain Ash 9</u>

Mount Team: Walton, Jones, Thompson, P.C. Tom Parry, Roberts, Murphy, Coughlin, P.C. Lett, P.C. Vaughan, P.C. Evans, P.C. Isaacs, James, Burke, Morgan, Sage.

<u>By One Point</u>

The Western Mail reported, "....there was an abundance of strong running and sound tackling....Mountain Ash were the heavier but the Wanderers had an interval lead of a point...."

3 February 1930

<u>Cross Keys 0 Mountain Ash 3</u>
<u>Western Mail</u>

A REAL SURPRISE.

Mountain Ash's Victory at Cross Keys.

	G.	T.	Pts.
Mountain Ash	0	1	3
Cross Keys	0	0	0

Mountain Ash brought off a real surprise on Saturday by winning at Cross Keys. Conditions were certainly not favourable for a brilliant display of football, but the game proved more than interesting.

The main factor in the home side's defeat was the complete failure of the forwards, who gave a listless display. Their rushes lacked the keenness shown by their opponents, and the Mountain Ash backs had little difficulty in holding up all their attacks. In contrast was the general display of the visitors, who, while failing in the finer phases of the game exhibited a keenness which proved an important asset throughout, and they never failed to turn to advantage every opportunity that afforded itself.

The only try was scored by Jones after a dribble by Thompson.

Mountain Ash Rugby Football Club
"The Old Firm"
Circa 1929/30

Above is the Mount team at the end of the 1920s. Only some of the names in the picture are known. In the back row, second from the left is Ned Bradwick, the Club Secretary, third from the left is Will Close, the author's grandfather, fourth from the left is Dan Horrigan, the club's Trainer, and seventh from the left is forward Trevor Edwards. In the middle row, on the far left, is just-retired scrum half Sid Congdon wearing a cap.

A Selection of the Old Firm's Results 1920/21 to 1929/30

Matches v Pontypridd

Opponents	Season	Venue	Score	P	W	D	L
Pontypridd	1920/21	Home	8-3	1	1	0	0
Pontypridd	1921/22	Away	5-3	2	2	0	0
Pontypridd	1923/24	Home	3-7	3	2	0	1
Pontypridd	1924/25	Away	3-0	4	3	0	1
Pontypridd	1925/26	Home	0-11	5	3	0	2
Pontypridd	1926/27	Away	5-8	6	3	0	3
Pontypridd (L)	1927/28	Away	8-5	7	4	0	3
Pontypridd	1928/29	Away	9-5	8	5	0	3
Pontypridd	1928/29	Home	0-0	9	5	1	3
Pontypridd	1929/30	Away	0-3	10	5	1	4

Matches v Ebbw Vale

Opponents	Season	Venue	Score	P	W	D	L
Ebbw Vale	1920/21	Away	0-3	1	0	0	1
Ebbw Vale	1920/21	Home	3-6	2	0	0	2
Ebbw Vale	1921/22	Away	4-5	3	0	0	3
Ebbw Vale	1921/22	Away	3-10	4	0	0	4
Ebbw Vale	1922/23	Away	3-3	5	0	1	4
Ebbw Vale	1922/23	Home	0-10	6	0	1	5
Ebbw Vale	1923/24	Away	3-3	7	0	2	5
Ebbw Vale	1923/24	Home	6-0	8	1	2	5
Ebbw Vale	1924/25	Home	6-0	9	2	2	5
Ebbw Vale	1924/25	Away	0-6	10	2	2	6
Ebbw Vale	1925/26	Home	0-3	11	2	2	7
Ebbw Vale	1925/26	Away	8-17	12	2	2	8
Ebbw Vale	1927/28	Home	0-5	13	2	2	9
Ebbw Vale	1927/28	Away	0-3	14	2	2	10
Ebbw Vale	1928/29	Away	0-10	15	2	2	11
Ebbw Vale	1928/29	Home	17-0	16	3	2	11
Ebbw Vale	1929/30	Home	3-5	17	3	2	12

Matches v Bridgend

Opponents	Season	Venue	Score	P	W	D	L
Bridgend	1920/21	Away	0-15	1	0	0	1
Bridgend	1920/21	Home	6-5	2	1	0	1
Bridgend	1921/22	Home	3-0	3	2	0	1
Bridgend	1921/22	Away	9-11	4	2	0	2
Bridgend	1922/23	Home	29-0	5	3	0	2
Bridgend	1924/25	Away	3-8	6	3	0	3
Bridgend	1924/25	Home	11-3	7	4	0	3

Matches v Abertillery

Abertillery were Welsh Club Champions in 1929/30

Opponents	Season	Venue	Score	P	W	D	L
Abertillery	1920/21	Away	Mount loss. Score unknown.	1	0	0	1
Abertillery	1921/22	Home	3-9	2	0	0	2
Abertillery	1921/22	Home	0-0	3	0	1	2
Abertillery	1922/23	Away	0-0	4	0	2	2
Abertillery	1922/23	Home	3-3	5	0	3	2
Abertillery	1923/24	Away	8-12	6	0	3	3
Abertillery	1924/25	Home	8-0	7	1	3	3
Abertillery	1925/26	Away	3-6	8	1	3	4
Abertillery	1925/26	Home	6-7	9	1	3	5
Abertillery	1926/27	Unknown	0-9	10	1	3	6
Abertillery	1927/28	Home	0-3	11	1	3	7
Abertillery	1928/29	Away	0-13	12	1	3	8
Abertillery	1928/29	Home	0-5	13	1	3	9

Matches v Penarth

Opponents	Season	Venue	Score	P	W	D	L
Penarth	1920/21	Home	Mount loss. Score unknown.	1	0	0	1
Penarth	1921/22	Away	7-0	2	1	0	1
Penarth	1921/22	Home	9-0	3	2	0	1
Penarth	1922/23	Home	18-5	4	3	0	1
Penarth	1922/23	Home	19-3	5	4	0	1
Penarth	1923/24	Home	17-3	6	5	0	1
Penarth	1923/24	Away	0-3	7	5	0	2
Penarth	1924/25	Home	14-5	8	6	0	2
Penarth	1924/25	Away	3-9	9	6	0	3
Penarth	1925/26	Home	6-0	10	7	0	3
Penarth	1925/26	Away	0-13	11	7	0	4
Penarth	1928/29	Away	3-27	12	7	0	5

Matches v Cardiff

Opponents	Season	Venue	Score	P	W	D	L
Cardiff	1921/22	Home	6-7	1	0	0	1
Cardiff Official opening of the Grandstand at the Rec	1922/23	Home	11-5	2	1	0	1
Cardiff	1925/26	Home	3-8	3	1	0	2
Cardiff	1926/27	Away	7-15	4	1	0	3

Matches v Aberavon

Aberavon were Welsh Club Champions in 1923/24, 1924/25, 1925/26 & 1926/27

Opponents	Season	Venue	Score	P	W	D	L
Aberavon	1921/22	Away	0-9	1	0	0	1
Aberavon	1921/22	Home	7-3	2	1	0	1
Aberavon	1924/25	Home	0-11	3	1	0	2
Aberavon	1924/25	Away	0-13	4	1	0	3

Matches v Treorky

Opponents	Season	Venue	Score	P	W	D	L
Treorky	1921/22	Home	10-3	1	1	0	0
Treorky	1922/23	Home	3-3	2	1	1	0
Treorky	1925/26	Away	0-7	3	1	1	1
Treorky	1925/26	Home	9-6	4	2	1	1
Treorky	1926/27	Away	3-8	5	2	1	2
Treorky (L)	1927/28	Away	3-9	6	2	1	3
Treorky (L)	1928/29	Home	13-6	7	3	1	3
Treorky (PL)	1928/29	Away	3-14	8	3	1	4
Treorky	1929/30	Home	0-6	9	3	1	5
Treorky	1929/30	Away	5-11	10	3	1	6

Matches v Cross Keys

Cross Keys were Welsh Club Champions in 1921/22

Opponents	Season	Venue	Score	P	W	D	L
Cross Keys	1920/21	Home	Mount loss. Score unknown.	1	0	0	1
Cross Keys	1921/22	Away	4-6	2	0	0	2
Cross Keys	1921/22	Home	3-5	3	0	0	3
Cross Keys	1922/23	Away	0-8	4	0	0	4
Cross Keys	1922/23	Home	3-0	5	1	0	4
Cross Keys	1923/24	Away	4-6	6	1	0	5
Cross Keys	1923/24	Home	3-3	7	1	1	5
Cross Keys	1924/25	Away	6-3	8	2	1	5
Cross Keys	1924/25	Home	6-0	9	3	1	5
Cross Keys	1925/26	Away	11-12	10	3	1	6
Cross Keys	1925/26	Home	15-14	11	4	1	6

Opponents	Season	Venue	Score	P	W	D	L
Cross Keys	1927/28	Home	6-3	12	5	1	6
Cross Keys	1927/28	Away	3-23	13	5	1	7
Cross Keys	1928/29	Home	0-6	14	5	1	8
Cross Keys	1928/29	Away	6-23	15	5	1	9
Cross Keys	1929/30	Away	3-0	16	6	1	9

Matches v Maesteg

Opponents	Season	Venue	Score	P	W	D	L
Maesteg	1922/23	Home	6-10	1	0	0	1
Maesteg	1922/23	Away	0-24	2	0	0	2
Maesteg	1923/24	Home	3-0	3	1	0	2
Maesteg	1923/24	Away	4-8	4	1	0	3
Maesteg	1924/25	Away	3-6	5	1	0	4
Maesteg	1924/25	Home	3-3	6	1	1	4
Maesteg	1925/26	Home	11-6	7	2	1	4
Maesteg	1926/27	Away	0-31	8	2	1	5
Maesteg	1928/29	Away	13-28	9	2	1	6
Maesteg	1928/29	Home	9-6	10	3	1	6

Matches v Glamorgan Wanderers

Opponents	Season	Venue	Score	P	W	D	L
Glamorgan Wanderers	1921/22	Home	9-0	1	1	0	0
Glamorgan Wanderers	1922/23	Away	17-5	2	2	0	0
Glamorgan Wanderers	1922/23	Home	22-12	3	3	0	0
Glamorgan Wanderers	1923/24	Home	8-10	4	3	0	1
Glamorgan Wanderers	1924/25	Home	3-0	5	4	0	1
Glamorgan Wanderers	1925/26	Away	3-21	6	4	0	2
Glamorgan Wanderers	1925/26	Home	13-12	7	5	0	2
Glamorgan Wanderers	1926/27	Home	3-11	8	5	0	3
Glamorgan Wanderers	1926/27	Away	3-8	9	5	0	4
Glamorgan Wanderers	1927/28	Away	15-8	10	6	0	4
Glamorgan Wanderers	1927/28	Home	12-14	11	6	0	5
Glamorgan Wanderers	1928/29	Home	21-13	12	7	0	5
Glamorgan Wanderers	1929/30	Home	7-9	13	7	0	6
Glamorgan Wanderers	1929/30	Away	9-8	14	8	0	6

Matches v Llanelly

Llanelly were Welsh Club Champions in 1927/28

Opponents	Season	Venue	Score	P	W	D	L
Llanelly	1922/23	Away	3-6	1	0	0	1
Llanelly	1922/23	Home	6-3	2	1	0	1
Llanelly	1923/24	Away	5-5	3	1	1	1

Matches v Swansea

Opponents	Season	Venue	Score	P	W	D	L
Swansea	1923/24	Home	9-12	1	0	0	1
Swansea	1923/24	Away	9-8	2	1	0	1
Swansea	1926/27	Away	3-21	3	1	0	2

Matches v Pontypool

Pontypool were Welsh Club Champions in 1920/21

Opponents	Season	Venue	Score	P	W	D	L
Pontypool	1922/23	Away	3-8	1	0	0	1
Pontypool	1922/23	Home	0-0	2	0	1	1
Pontypool	1923/24	Away	10-9	3	1	1	1
Pontypool	1923/24	Home	0-5	4	1	1	2
Pontypool	1924/25	Away	8-13	5	1	1	3
Pontypool	1924/25	Home	0-0	6	1	2	3
Pontypool	1925/26	Away	4-20	7	1	2	4
Pontypool	1925/26	Home	0-0	8	1	3	4
Pontypool	1926/27	Home	5-17	9	1	3	5
Pontypool	1926/27	Away	3-22	10	1	3	6
Pontypool	1927/28	Home	3-3	11	1	4	6
Pontypool	1927/28	Away	0-33	12	1	4	7
Pontypool	1928/29	Away	6-11	13	1	4	8
Pontypool	1928/29	Home	0-8	14	1	4	9
Pontypool	1929/30	Away	10-25	15	1	4	10
Pontypool	1929/30	Home	0-11	16	1	4	11

Matches v Neath

Opponents	Season	Venue	Score	P	W	D	L
Neath	1922/23	Home	12-4	1	1	0	0
Neath	1922/23	Away	4-19	2	1	0	1
Neath	1923/24	Away	0-3	3	1	0	2

Matches v Penygraig

Opponents	Season	Venue	Score	P	W	D	L
Penygraig	1925/26	Away	0-0	1	0	1	0
Penygraig	1926/27	Home	15-14	2	1	1	0
Penygraig	1926/27	Unsure	0-3	3	1	1	1
Penygraig (L)	1927/28	Away	3-6	4	1	1	2
Penygraig (PL)	1928/29	Home	0-0	5	1	2	2
Penygraig	1929/30	Home	3-3	6	1	3	2
Penygraig	1929/30	Away	3-4	7	1	3	3

Matches v Tredegar

Opponents	Season	Venue	Score	P	W	D	L
Tredegar	1923/24	Home	16-0	1	1	0	0
Tredegar	1923/24	Away	3-0	2	2	0	0
Tredegar	1927/28	Home	3-3	3	2	1	0
Tredegar	1927/28	Away	11-11	4	2	2	0

Matches v Treherbert

Opponents	Season	Venue	Score	P	W	D	L
Treherbert	1920/21	Home	3-3	1	0	1	0
Treherbert	1923/24	Home	3-3	2	0	2	0
Treherbert	1923/24	Away	0-11	3	0	2	1
Treherbert	1924/25	Away	7-5	4	1	2	1
Treherbert	1924/25	Home	3-0	5	2	2	1
Treherbert	1925/26	Home	6-6	6	2	3	1
Treherbert	1925/26	Away	5-12	7	2	3	2
Treherbert	1926/27	Away	0-11	8	2	3	3
Treherbert	1926/27	Home	3-0	9	3	3	3
Treherbert (PL)	1927/28	Away	13-14	10	3	3	4
Treherbert (PL)	1928/29	Away	3-9	11	3	3	5
Treherbert (PL)	1928/29	Unsure	6-3	12	4	3	5

Matches v Bath

Opponents	Season	Venue	Score	P	W	D	L
Bath	1921/22	Away	10-10	1	0	1	0
Bath	1922/23	Home	13-3	2	1	1	0

Matches v Bridgwater & Albion

Opponents	Season	Venue	Score	P	W	D	L
Bridgwater & Albion	1922/23	Home	24-0	1	1	0	0
Bridgwater & Albion	1923/24	Home	15-0	2	2	0	0
Bridgwater & Albion	1923/24	Away	6-8	3	2	0	1

Matches v Nuneaton

Opponents	Season	Venue	Score	P	W	D	L
Nuneaton	1924/25	Away	3-0	1	1	0	0

Matches v Otley

Opponents	Season	Venue	Score	P	W	D	L
Otley	1921/22	Away	11-0	1	1	0	0
Otley	1921/22	Home	11-0	2	2	0	0
Otley	1923/24	Home	31-0	3	3	0	0

Matches On Tour In France

Opponents	Season	Venue	Score	P	W	D	L	Result Unknown
Périgueux	1921/22	Away	Result & score unknown.	1	0	0	0	1
Brive	1921/22	Away	Result & score unknown.	2	0	0	0	2
Clermont Ferrand	1922/23	Away	Result & score unknown.	3	0	0	0	3
Clermont Ferrand	1922/23	Away	Result & score unknown.	4	0	0	0	4
Stade Francais	1924/25	Away	Result & score unknown.	5	0	0	0	5

There were no known games played against Llwynypia (disbanded), London Welsh, Newport, Leicester, Plymouth and Coventry in the 1920s.

Mountain Ash RFC Players That Went North 1920/21 to 1929/30

A. FELTHAM, Christian name unknown, "went North" in January 1921. Other than this, nothing is known about his career.

CHARLES SAGE, played for Hunslet in the 1920s. In his book "Gone North", Volume 1, Rugby League historian, Robert Gate, lists Sage as one of only 3 Welsh hookers who really made the grade in League. He played for the Welsh Rugby League side twice, both times against England in 1925.

T. EMLYN GWYNNE played Union for Mountain Ash and Swansea. In his two books, "Gone North", Volumes 1 and 2, Robert Gate confirms he joined Hull and made his debut on 10 September 1921. He scored 108 tries in 283 matches played for the Club over 9 seasons. In 1928, while playing for Hull, he played for the Welsh Rugby League team versus England at Cardiff and went on the Great Britain tour of Australia and New Zealand, playing in 2 tests on the wing.

FRED SAMUEL, who was the Old Firm's Welsh International full back, capped in 1922, made his debut for Hull on 11 October 1922 and played for the Club in the Rugby League Cup Final of 1923 against Leeds. He played 20 games for Hull, kicking 2 goals.

TOM COLLINS, Mount's Welsh International centre, capped by Wales once in 1923, joined Hull and played his first game in the professional code on 1 September 1923. He went on to make 153 appearances and scored 52 tries. He remained at Hull for 7 seasons and followed this with 2 seasons at Keighley RFC, who won the Rugby League Championship when he was with them. Due to the hostility to rugby league by the Union governing bodies, Collins never received his International cap in 1923. He passed away in 1958 and it was not until 1975, after pressure from his family that the Welsh Rugby Union relented and forwarded his cap.

W.R. "BULLER" LOVELUCK joined Hull and made his debut on 19 January 1924 where he played 23 games and scored 3 tries. In 1926 he joined the Pontypridd Rugby League team and played in their first match at Taff Vale Park in front of 10,000 fans against the previous season's Challenge Cup finalists, Oldham. In 1926/27, he finished the season as Pontypridd's top try scorer with 10 and played in the Club's last ever rugby league match, coincidentally against Oldham again. The game was lost 14-5, Loveluck scoring the last ever try for the Pontypridd Club.

ERNIE FOOTE made his Hull Rugby League debut in 1926, but other than this, nothing else is known about his rugby league career.

Mountain Ash Rugby Football Club
"The Old Firm"

The 1930s

The Playing Record Of The 1930s

The decade was cut short due to Britain's involvement in the Second World War from September 1939 on. In 7 of the 9 seasons prior to this, more games were won than lost with the seasons 1930/31, 1931/32, 1932/33, 1934/35 and 1938/39 being exceptional. Below are the known seasonal playing records of the 1930s:

Season	P	W	D	L	For	Against	Tries Scored	%
1930/31	26	17	2	7	192+	101+	45+	69.23
1931/32	32	21	2	9	332	187	56+	68.75
1932/33	33	25	2	6	363	120	78+	78.79
1933/34	26	13	4	9	228+	148+	49+	57.69
1934/35	28	22	3	3	386	82	79+	83.93
1935/36	22	9	1	12	143	125	35+	43.18
1936/37	28	15	4	9	168	132	40+	60.71
1937/38	20	7	2	11	84+	194+	14+	40.00
1938/39	44	24	6	14	340	226	81	61.36
1939/40	1	0	0	1	0	8	0	0.00
Total for 1930s	260	153	26	81	2236+	1323+	477+	63.85

The Old Firm's Fixtures In The 1930s

As well as playing the regular Glamorgan League teams which included Treorchy, Pontypridd, Aberaman, Cilfynydd, Ynysybwl and Penygraig, the Old Firm took on Abertillery, Cardiff, Cross Keys, Pontypool, Aberavon, Bridgend and Penarth, which were all Clubs rated "first class" by the media. There were wins over all these as well as victories over Glamorgan Wanderers, Maesteg and Ebbw Vale, who were all regarded as "second class" Clubs at the time, just like Mount. There were also games against English opposition such as Weston-super-Mare, Cinderford and Cheltenham with the Old Firm proving a match for all comers, at home or away, whatever their so-called "class".

Club Captains

Other than forwards Frank Kempson, Jim Cummings and B. Reakes (Christian name unknown), all the other captains of the Old Firm in the 1930s were backs. Centre Haydn Williams started the 1930s by completing his second successive season as captain and was followed by centre Charlie Thompson. In the mid 30s, the brothers Jack and Phil Davies, the first a centre or outside half and the other a scrum half, did the job for a season each, and then three-quarter Fred Rees took over. In 1938/39, which was the last full season before the outbreak of the Second World War, T.D.E., "Tommy", Williams made a great impression in his season of captaincy, scoring over 100 points which included 19 tries.

<u>Captains</u>

1930-1931	Haydn Williams
1931-1932	Charlie Thompson
1932-1933	Frank Kempson
1933-1934	Jim Cummings
1934-1935	Jack R. Davies
1935-1936	Phil Davies
1936-1937	Fred Rees
1937-1938	B. Reakes
1938-1939	Tommy D.E. Williams
1939-1940	Second World War

A Hat-Trick Of Glamorgan League Championships

The Glamorgan League was still the premier tournament for the best valley Clubs and much sought after. The Old Firm were champions for three successive seasons in 1930/31, 1931/32 and 1932/33 but then withdrew from the competition in pursuit of "first class" status, never playing official League rugby again until the Mid District Rugby Union League started in 1982/83. From 1894/95, when the competition started as the Rhondda, Merthyr and Aberdare League, to the end of Mount's involvement after the end of the 1932/33 season, the Old Firm were Glamorgan League champions on 6 occasions – in 1895/96, 1908/09, 1913/14, 1930/31, 1931/32 and 1932/33 – and losing play-off finalists twice, in 1894/95 and 1904/05. A "double" was achieved in 1913/14 when the Glamorgan Times Cup was also won, which was the Glamorgan League's Cup competition.

Welsh Champions Beaten

In 1932/33, the Old Firm beat the reigning Welsh champions of the time, Pontypool, 16-3, at the Rec. This was the second time the Welsh Club champions had been beaten, Cross Keys being the first back in 1922/23.

Unbeaten Matches

There were two unbeaten runs of note in the 1930s. The first was in 1934/35 when the Old Firm won the first 12 games of the season, remaining unbeaten until mid November. This was bettered in 1938/39 when the team remained unbeaten for 18 games, which was comprised of 14 wins and 4 draws, and lasted from the end of October 1938 until the beginning of March 1939. Regrettably though, the exciting potential shown by the 1938/39 team was never realised due to the commencement of the Second World War in September 1939.

International Recognition

No.8 forward, Les Manfield, became the Club's 8th Welsh International in early 1939 when he was capped against Scotland at Cardiff Arms Park, which turned out to be Wales' last home International before the Second World War. He went on to gain his second cap in Ireland shortly afterwards but had to wait until after the War to gain another five caps. He was one of only four Welsh players to be capped before and after the Second World War.

First Mount Player To Represent The Barbarians

Les Manfield added to his two Welsh caps by becoming Mountain Ash RFC's first player to be selected by the Barbarians RFC when he played against Midland Counties in March 1940.

The Club's Officers

Off the field, two long-serving officers resigned in 1937/38 after being in charge since the mid 1920s. Shad Lewis, who had been Club Chairman since 1926/27 and was a great help to the Club in the desperate economic times of the 1920s and 1930s, finished his tenure. Mr William Christopher temporarily took over as Chairman before Arthur Manfield, who was still a player at the time, took over in 1938/39. Ted Bradwick, who had served as Secretary since 1925/26, also resigned in 1937/38. During the next two seasons, with war becoming ever more likely and "call-up" papers being received, the Secretary's job rotated between William Christopher, David Griffiths, Enoch Watkins, Harvey Hall and D. Gwilym Jones until the outbreak of War in September 1939. Little is known about the post holders of Treasurer except for the name of Tom Howells, who held the post from 1937 or so to 1939/40. The only President on record was a Mr E.M. Hann, who was elected to the post in 1935/36.

The End Of 1930s Rugby

With Britain entering the Second World War on 3 September 1939 and the Welsh Rugby Union suspending rugby on 25 September, the last known game played by the Old Firm was an away 8-0 defeat at reigning Glamorgan League champions, Cilfynydd, in September 1939. The last known home game was at the end of the 1938/39 season, which was a 5-3 win over a Llanelly XV. It would not be until September 1946 – 7 long years later – that the Old Firm would officially play again.

The 1930s
Season by Season

Season 1930/31

Glamorgan League Champions

The Old Firm started the 1930s in great style by winning the Glamorgan League Championship, although they had to wait until September of the 1931/32 season to get their hands on the trophy. It was the 4th time Mount had won the competition and the first time they had lifted the Cup since the "double" of 1913/14, although there is some doubt about whether the Club entered the competition after the end of World War I because of the lack of press coverage until 1927/28. After a 3-3 draw after 30 minutes of extra time at Taff Vale Park, Pontypridd, with Treorchy, who were going for a hat-trick of titles, the Old Firm won a hard fought and exciting replay 5-0 in September 1931 in front of a 4,000 crowd at Ynysangharad Park, Pontypridd, to secure the Championship after a total of 3 hours and 10 minutes of play. The win was the culmination of a fine season for the Old Firm which ended with a playing record of played 26, won 17, drawn 2 and lost 7, with 192+ points scored, which included 45+ tries, and 101+ conceded, to return a win rate of 69.23%. There were some excellent wins at the Rec during the season. Ebbw Vale were put to the sword, 26-3, 6 tries were scored in the 18-3 Glamorgan League win over Treorchy, and Pontypool, who were Welsh champions the following season, 1931/32, were defeated 17-6. There were "doubles" over Maesteg, Glamorgan Wanderers, Penarth and Aberdare. The Old Firm were unbeaten at home until the beginning of March 1931 when a Cardiff XV won 9-0 at the Rec. As a matter of interest, Mr Ivor Edwards, who went on to become the Secretary of Mountain Ash RFC from 1966 to 1984, was the Secretary of the Glamorgan League during the season.

Fixtures 1930/31

Opponents	Date	Venue	Score	Tries	Scorers/Comments
Pontypridd Harlequins	13 Sep 1930	Home	6-3	2	Rees Sage T, Thompson T.
Pontypool	20 Sep 1930	Away	0-13	0	No scorers.
Ebbw Vale	4 Oct 1930	Away	0-10	0	No scorers.
Glynneath	18 Oct 1930	Home	13-0	3	Elvet Thomas 2T, J. Rees T, Haydn Williams 2C.
Penarth	20 Oct 1930	Away	11-3	2	Haydn Williams T, P, Elvet Thomas T, Jim Cummings C.
Aberaman (PL)	25 Oct 1930	Away	3-11	0	Alf Parker P.

Opponents	Date	Venue	Score	Tries	Scorers/Comments
Treorchy (PL)	27 Oct 1930	Home	18-3	6	Frank Kempson T, Chas Thompson T, Jim Coughlin T, Hugh Murphy T, J. Rees T, J. Murphy T.
Aberdare	15 Nov 1930	Home	24-0	6	Jim Coughlin 3T, 2C, Elvet Thomas T, C, Haydn Williams T, J.W. Price T.
Glamorgan Wanderers	22 Nov 1930	Away	7-0	1	Elvet Thomas T, Jim Coughlin DG.
Cross Keys	24 Nov 1930	Away	0-0	0	No scorers.
Penygraig (PL)	Unknown	Away	Unknown	Unknown	Mount win.
Maesteg	1 Dec 1930	Home	9-0	3	Elvet Thomas T, Jim Coughlin T, Chas Thompson T.
Aberdare	15 Dec 1930	Away	5-0	1	Elvet Thomas T, Jim Cummings C.
Penygraig (PL)	27 Dec 1930	Home	8-3	1	Elvet Thomas T, Jim Coughlin P, Frank Kempson C.
Weston-super-Mare	27 Dec 1930	Away	11-13	3	Elvet Thomas 2T, Rees Sage T, Jim Cummings C.
Maesteg	29 Dec 1930	Away	7-6	1	Frank Kempson T, Haydn Williams DG.
Cross Keys	Unknown	Unknown	Unknown	Unknown	Mount win.
Penarth	5 Jan 1931	Home	9-6	1	J. Rees T, Ivor James DG, Jim Coughlin C.
Cilfynydd (PL)	31 Jan 1931	Away	3-0	1	Jim Coughlin T.
Glynneath	21 Feb 1931	Away	0-3	0	No scorers.
Glamorgan Wanderers	28 Feb 1931	Home	9-0	2	Hugh Murphy T, Elvet Thomas T, Jim Cummings P.
Cardiff	2 Mar 1931	Home	0-9	0	No scorers.
Treorchy (PL)	9 Mar 1931	Away	3-6	1	Frank Kempson T.
Pontypool	20 Apr 1931	Home	17-6	2	Haydn Williams T, Frank Kempson T, Elvet Thomas P, 2C, Jim Murphy DG.

Opponents	Date	Venue	Score	Tries	Scorers/Comments
Ebbw Vale	27 Apr 1931	Home	26-3	8	Coughlin 3T, Haydn Williams 2T, Tom Burns T, Chas Thompson T, Rees T, Elvet Thomas C.
Treorchy (L) Glamorgan League Play Off	9 May 1931	Pontypridd	3-3	1	Haydn Williams T.

Summary of Playing Record

P	W	D	L	For	Against	Tries Scored	Win Rate %
26	17	2	7	192+	101+	45+	69.23

Match Reports and Publications

27 October 1930

<u>Mountain Ash 18 Treorchy 3</u>
<u>Possible Glamorgan League Fixture</u>
<u>Western Mail</u>

MOUNTAIN ASH BRILLIANT.

	G.	T.	Pts.
Mountain Ash	0	6	18
Treorchy	0	1	3

The "Old Firm" gave a glorious display in accounting for Treorchy. In the first half they kept the visitors on the defensive and put on such heavy pressure that they pierced a good defence four times through J. Murphy, Kempson, Thompson and Coughlin.

On the resumption Treorchy, having the wind behind them, took a hand in the scoring, T. Thomas obtaining a nice try. Their spell of attack was shortlived and Mountain Ash again asserted themselves. H. Murphy added to the score with a spectacular try, and following a stern struggle on the Treorchy 25 J. Rees ran in with a great try.

15 November 1930

<u>Mountain Ash 24 Aberdare 0</u>

Mount Team: Ivor James, Elvet Thomas, Chas Thompson, Haydn Williams, J. Rees, Hugh Murphy, Jim Coughlin, Frank Kempson, T. Sage, Rees Sage, T. Edwards, J. Allen, John Willy Price, Jim Cummings, J. Murphy.

The Aberdare Leader reported, "has the sun of soccer really set in Aberdare? Judging by the enthusiasm shown by Aberdare players and the crowd of supporters they brought with them for the local derby at the Rec on Saturday, there is every indication that this is a fact. Many had said goodbye to the hopes of seeing these teams meet again many years ago, but like politics ever-changing, the wheel of rugby has revolved once again to make this meeting memorable in the minds of enthusiasts of the handling code. It is all for the good of the game and in the Old Firm, who have fought through thick and thin for the past 30 years, they will find new hopes in the efforts of their near neighbours."

1 December 1930

<u>Mountain Ash 9 Maesteg 0</u>
<u>Western Mail</u>

MOUNTAIN ASH WORTHY WINNERS.

	G.	T.	Pts.
Mountain Ash	0	3	9
Maesteg	0	0	0

The "Old Firm," despite the fact that they were a man short for the major portion of the game, were altogether too good for Maesteg, and were worthy winners of a hard game. Back play was at a discount, yet the three tries were scored by the three-quarters, being cleverly gained by Coughlin, Thompson, and Thomas, the latter scoring a really spectacular try. Up to the time of his injury Murphy established a complete mastery over Hughes at the base of the scrum, and so nullified the good work of the Maesteg forwards in the scrummages.

27 December 1930

<u>Weston-super-Mare 13 Mountain Ash 11</u>
<u>Western Mail</u>

WESTON WIN AGAIN.

But Mountain Ash Put Up Plucky Fight.

	G.	T.	Pts.
Weston-super-Mare	2	1	13
Mountain Ash	1	2	11

Weston maintained their unbeaten record against Welsh clubs this season in their home match with Mountain Ash on Boxing Day. The visitors, however, put up a great fight and were winning until within fifteen minutes of the end.

At the interval Mountain Ash were leading, Sage and Thomas having scored two unconverted tries to a try by Skitter and converted by Hobbs.

In the second half Thomas crossed again, Cummings converting. Clayton and Warner scored further tries for Weston, Hobbs converting one. Weston lasted better.

5 January 1931

Mountain Ash 9 Penarth 6
Mountain Ash Succeed in Good Game

The Western Mail reported, "A large attendance was treated to a fine game at Mountain Ash. Penarth opened strongly but were met with a dour defence....the Old Firm took play to the other end where Ivor James dropped a beautiful goal from near halfway....Johnnie Rees, fielding a loose ball, raced through the Penarth defence to score a brilliant try which Coughlin converted. The second half was fought out at a fast pace and both lines were subjected to severe pressure...."

20 April 1931

Glamorgan League Table
End of Season 1930/31

Club	P	W	L	D	For	Against	Pts
Mountain Ash	14	10	2	2	116	37	22
Treorchy	14	11	3	0	100	59	22
Ynysybwl	13	5	7	1	68	89	11
Cilfynydd	13	4	7	2	50	42	10
Kenfig Hill	12	4	6	2	36	51	10
Penygraig	11	4	6	1	48	50	9
Aberaman	10	4	5	1	43	32	9
Bargoed	11	2	8	1	31	116	5

Glamorgan League Rugby
Mountain Ash and Treorchy Tie
Deciding Match To Be Played

The Aberdare Leader reported, "For the second season in succession, due partly to the improved form of Treorchy during the past few weeks, a "final" has to be played to decide the League Championship. The Old Firm won their last League game against Cilfynydd, and Treorchy won their final game with Ynysybwl, after a most exciting and gruelling game. This close finish in the competition has created tremendous enthusiasm in both the Rhondda and Aberdare Valleys, and with favourable conditions, wherever the deciding match is played, a record gate is assured."

20 April 1931

Mountain Ash 17 Pontypool 6
Western Mail

A SURPRISE FOR PONTYPOOL.

AMAZING FINISH BY MOUNTAIN ASH.

	G.	T.	Pts.
Mountain Ash	†4	0	17
Pontypool	*1	1	6

†Penalty and dropped. *Penalty.

The "Old Firm's" victory was gained in a sensational manner, for with about five minutes to go they were three points down, but a whirlwind finish brought them thirteen points, all of which were cleverly earned.

The first half was fairly even, for although the home forwards controlled the scrums, the spoiling tactics of Axford and his two wing forwards severely hampered Murphy when he attempted to put his backs in motion. At the interval the score was six points to three in favour of Pontypool, the scorers being Woolley (penalty goal) and Targett a try for the visitors against Thomas's penalty goal for the home side.

In the second half Murphy soon took the measure of Axford, with the result that the home backs were seen to better advantage. The Pontypool defence had a gruelling time, but held out until near the end, when Murphy, fielding a kick into the open, dropped a penalty goal, which gave the home side the lead. A few minutes later Pontypool developed a strong attack on the left, but a sudden interception by Williams gave him a straight run in for a great try which Elvet Thomas converted. Straight from the kick-off Mountain Ash returned to the attack, and James, the home full-back, securing went all out for the line, and when hemmed in cross-kicked into Kempson's hands for the latter to touch down for a try. Thomas converted with a great kick. There was no time for the game to be restarted, so that within the space of a few minutes, Mountain Ash had changed a deficit into a handsome victory.

The Aberdare Leader reported, "The long looked for match between the Old Firm and Pontypool played at the Rec on Saturday produced one of the finest games ever witnessed on that ground or indeed any other ground in Mountain Ash. The home team were fully aware of the qualities of the visitors from the neighbouring County and so being forewarned is forearmed….from the restart (after half time)….Mountain Ash showed a marked superiority especially in the back division. A nice run by Haydn Williams and a pass to Murphy enabled the latter to drop a lovely goal. With one point up, the Old Firm played like Internationals. They hemmed in the visitors time after time and came within an ace of scoring several times. With ten minutes to go and still holding their lead, Mountain Ash made several desperate bursts. It was Haydn Williams who gave the finest thrill of the afternoon for he ran magnificently for the line and scored a really wonderful try, and Elvet Thomas made no mistake about the extra points. With 2 minutes to go, Ivor James, well up, crossed to Frank Kempson, who scored easily. Again, Elvet Thomas added the extra points. That kick was the last of a remarkable game, and as the referee's whistle blew, cheers resounded all over the field."

Pontypool were Welsh champions the following season, 1931/32.

27 April 1931

<u>Mountain Ash 26 Ebbw Vale 3</u>

The Western Mail reported, "The Old Firm were by far the better side and considering the greasy ball and condition of the field, the home three-quarters handled very well….The Mountain Ash forwards were magnificent…."

<u>Glamorgan League</u>
<u>Mountain Ash and Treorchy to Decide Championship</u>

The Aberdare Leader reported, "The Old Firm once again figure in a deciding game for the Glamorgan League Championship and their opponents are the ex-champions, Treorchy. Mr Ted Bradwick and the Mountain Ash Committee tried for a Saturday match, but failed, and this important event will be played tomorrow, Friday May 1, at Taff Vale Park, Pontypridd, kick off at 6 o'clock. Gough's charabanc leaves at 4:15. The Mount team will be chosen from the following:

Full Back: Ivor James, ¾ Backs: Elvet Thomas, Chas Thompson, Haydn Williams, Johnnie Rees, T.D. Williams, Halves: Hugh Murphy, Jim Coughlin, D. West;

Forwards: Trevor Edwards, Frank Kempson, Jim Cummings, Tom Burns, J. Murphy, Jim Young, Russell Grant, R. Rogers, R. Harris, Tom Sage, Kingdom, N. Ellis."

9 May 1931

<u>Mountain Ash 3 Treorchy 3</u>
<u>(after extra time)</u>
<u>Glamorgan League Championship Play-Off</u>

<u>Herculean Battle But Little Skill</u>
<u>Mountain Ash Lucky to Draw</u>

"G.P." reported in the Aberdare Leader, "Treorchy were unlucky not to defeat Mountain Ash in this match at Taff Vale Park, Pontypridd, on Friday evening last to win the Glamorgan League Championship for the third consecutive year. I imagine a general cry of dissent from the hundreds of Mountain Ash supporters who journeyed to see the game, but viewing the play with the cold eye of an impartial critic, I have no hesitation in saying that Mountain Ash, although they were the faster and more thrustful attacking force behind the scrum, were fortunate to have gained a draw. Poor generalship and lack of staying power (as revealed in the "extra time" play) contributed to the Old Firm's unimpressive display. There was little skilful rugby.

Much of the over vigorousness of the exchanges was due to the rough tactics of some of the Mountain Ash forwards – Cummings especially being guilty of some very unsporting play in the first half – while the referee can be blamed for not exercising a firmer control over the two packs in the early stages. It is a fact that the referee warned members of the Mountain Ash pack on six separate occasions, while he had once to deliver a general lecture to the players. But as unsatisfactory as the play was, we saw a Herculean battle between two powerful and determined XVs. In the first half, the Old Firm, undoubtedly, were the superior force. While Treorchy did a good share of attacking with some hard, loose rushes, the Mountain Ash forwards met them solidly and combined smartly and effectively with their three-quarters in breaking up the Treorchy attacks and swinging play back dangerously to the other end of the field....in the opening stages the Treorchy forwards were able to establish dangerous positions, but time after time the Old Firm centres, Haydn Williams and Thompson, averted danger with some clever passing and kicking....Treorchy continued to occupy Mountain Ash territory for some time....and it seemed that Treorchy must take an early lead. At one time, two or three of the Rhondda forwards had the line at their mercy, but a knock on spoilt the chance. Scrum followed scrum on the Mountain Ash line, and the Treorchy forwards battled fiercely to take the ball over, but Mountain Ash defended stoutly.

Mountain Ash's Score

Then came a revival by Mountain Ash that marked them as the more businesslike and thrustful combination. Thompson and Haydn Williams in turn made two spectacular breakaways, which took play back to midfield, and then Elvet Thomas, the Old Firm's "flyer" on the left wing, made one of those characteristic dashes which almost took him to the Treorchy line. Checked by Evas, the Treorchy custodian, Elvet cross kicked and the ball was fielded by Haydn Williams, who had the line at his mercy and ran over to score in a good position. The kick, however, failed. Subsequently, Mountain Ash was in the ascendancy, their three-quarters working smartly together, and being provided with good chances by the forwards, who threw the ball back judiciously. Treorchy continued to make some dangerous forward rushes, and were awarded a penalty which D.R. James sent only inches under the bar. Half time came with Mountain Ash on top.

In the second half, however, when we expected Mountain Ash to build up gradual superiority on the solid foundation they had laid before the interval, there came a change in the complexion of the game. After about ten minutes, Boxall, the clever Treorchy scrum half, following an injury which kept him outside the touchline for a little time, put Treorchy on level pegging with the best try of the match. Following good kicking by Evans and some hard following up by the forwards, Treorchy won their way into the Mountain Ash 25, and a scrum was ordered in front of the posts about 20 yards out. Treorchy heeled and Boxall got the ball out smartly and broke away on the blind side, only to be called back by the referee. Getting the ball out again, Boxall repeated his manoeuvre, and beautifully selling the dummy to the Mount centres, cork screwed his way through to ground a brilliant try. James failed with the kick.

Following this, Mountain Ash began to fall away and the fast, young Treorchy forwards were given an opportunity of exploiting so effectively their favourite tactics of punting ahead and speedily following up, that Mountain Ash were again forced to defend. There came another period of terrific pressure on the Mount line soon afterwards – the Treorchy pack battling like tigers. Fierce mauls on the Old Firm line looked as if they could have but one ending – a score for Treorchy. But following this good work by the forwards, Treorchy were badly let down by P.C. D. Thomas, who repeatedly fumbled the ball and showed lack of determination, to throw away several chances.

The enterprising Mountain Ash centres, however, again got the ball away, and the Old Firm, a tiring force, now began to play to Elvet Thomas, and the fleet footed left winger provided several thrills by racing like lightning for the line, only to be held up by the safe Treorchy full back, Evas. Mountain Ash rallied a little in the closing stages, but Boxall did some brilliant defensive work which frequently saved the situation for Treorchy.

Extra Time

With no further scoring before "no side", it was decided to play fifteen minutes each way extra time. A fumble in the Treorchy 25 enabled Mountain Ash to take up a dangerous position in the opening few minutes, but afterwards Treorchy, whose younger forwards were sticking the pace much better, did almost all the attacking. There came a real thrill when P.C. D. Thomas broke away unhampered in midfield. Instead of relying on his own speed to beat the Mount full back, Thomas elected to pass to Lewis Rees who dropped the ball, and Treorchy lost an almost certain score. Treorchy forwards were dominating the game with their fast following up and Mountain Ash were hard pressed until a few moments before the change over, when Elvet Thomas again made a couple of dangerous breakaways.

On the resumption, Thomas was again very dangerous with some lightning sprints along the touchline, but he was unable to break through. Play went on with scarcely diminished vigour in spite of the gruelling time the players had had....the Mountain Ash forwards seemed too weary to stand, and extra time ended with the issue still undecided.

Mountain Ash's Mistake

Mountain Ash were without doubt the better combination – if only for their superior thrust behind the scrum, but they made the mistake of playing into Treorchy hands by allowing the exchanges to be confined to the forwards, where Treorchy, younger and in better physical condition, excelled in the lineouts and the fast loose rushes. D.R. James, Treorchy's International hooker, led his forwards splendidly, but was poorly supported in the scrummages which were generally won by the heavier Mount lot. Murphy (Mount), at inside half, came off second best to Boxall, who was the best attacking back on the field, but the Mount man was experienced enough to put sufficient spoiling work in to prevent the nippy Treorchy man from flashing through the Mount defence more than once. The Old Firm three-quarters did excellent work, Williams and Thompson at centre being better than their opponents in attack and defence. Coughlin was also dangerous at times. Cummings, in spite of his roughness, and Kempson, led the forwards with great credit, but the Mount pack fell away badly in the closing stages, and were quite outplayed by the younger and lighter Rhondda men. Mountain Ash did not have loose forwards equal to Lewis Rees and I. Wright, no scrummager equal to D.R. James and no defensive forward equal to Jim Owen, who did brilliant work for Treorchy."

The Glamorgan League Championship for 1930/31 was decided the following season when the Old Firm and Treorchy replayed at Ynysangharad Park, Pontypridd on 26 September 1931. An account of the game is given in Season 1931/32.

Season 1931/32

Old Firm Win Glamorgan League Championship....Twice

The Old Firm, in effect, won the Glamorgan League Championship twice during the 1931/32 season. In September 1931, they beat holders Treorchy, 5-0, in an exciting match at Ynysangharad Park, Pontypridd, in the replay of the 1930/31 play-off, and then won the trophy outright for 1931/32 by topping the table. It was the second successive season Mount had been crowned Glamorgan League champions, a title much sought after by the best valley Clubs or the "hill sides" as some newspapers referred to them. These two victories brought the total number of times the Club had won the Glamorgan League to five.

The Old Firm had a tough start to the season which showed the resilience of the Mount Club. On Saturday, 12 September 1931, the team played at Pontypool. The following Saturday, 19 September, they played at Aberavon, and just two days before the Glamorgan League play-off replay with Treorchy, travelled to Abertillery, all three considered "first class" Clubs. There then followed the League final replay with Treorchy – won 5-0 – and then a day or so after that, there was a game against Aberaman – which was won 21-3 – in the 1931/32 Glamorgan League competition! Although losing the 3 away games just mentioned, 20 were won, 2 drawn and only 6 lost from the following 28 games which was an excellent return. The season saw "doubles" over Ebbw Vale, Aberdare and Cilfynydd. There were also home wins over Aberavon, Abertillery, Pontypridd, Glamorgan Police and Glamorgan Wanderers, a draw at Pontypridd, and a win at Maesteg. The 7-6 win at Ebbw Vale at the end of the season saw the name of a 16 year old three-quarter back in the Mount team, one who went on to play for Wales in the backrow in 1938/39, namely Les Manfield, who also scored the Old Firm's try that day. There were close defeats, both at the Rec, against Maesteg, 3-0, and the Welsh champions for the season, Pontypool, 6-3, the latter game being abandoned in the second half due to the weather when Mount were well in contention. During the season, there were a number of match reports that referred to the strength of the Old Firm's pack. Even though the game at Pontypool – the eventual Welsh champions of the season – was lost 14-3 in September 1931, the Western Mail started its match report by saying, "It was chiefly Pontypool's good form behind the scrum which enabled them to beat Mountain Ash....for the visiting pack was always a match for the home eight", and in the 8-3 loss at Bridgend in November, the Western Mail commented, "....for once in a while, Bridgend's eight found themselves up against a pack who were their masters in the set scrummages, for it was seldom indeed that the ball came out on the Bridgend side." At the end of a second successful season, the playing record read played 32, won 21, drawn 2 and lost 9, with 332 points scored, which included 56+ tries, and 187 conceded, to give a win rate of 68.75%.

Fixtures 1931/32

Opponents	Date	Venue	Score	Tries	Scorers/Comments
Cardiff Cathedrals	12 Sep 1931	Home	36-8	Unknown	Scorers unknown.
Pontypool	12 Sep 1931	Away	3-14	1	Frank Kempson T.
Aberavon	19 Sep 1931	Away	8-30	1	Baverstock T, C, P.
Abertillery	24 Sep 1931	Away	3-15	1	Rees T.
Treorchy (L) Glamorgan League 1930/31 Play Off Replay	26 Sep 1931	Pontypridd	5-0	1	Jim Coughlin T, Jim Cummings C.
Aberaman (L)	28 Sep 1931	Home	21-3	5	Johnny Rees T, Haydn Williams T, Frank Kempson T, Jim Coughlin T, Evan Isaacs T, Jim Cummings 3C.

Opponents	Date	Venue	Score	Tries	Scorers/Comments
Glamorgan Police	10 Oct 1931	Home	17-0	4	Gwyn Thomas 2T, Jim Coughlin T, Murphy T, Jim Cummings P, Gwyn Knight C.
Cross Keys	12 Oct 1931	Away	3-18	0	Gwyn Knight P.
Penygraig (L)	19 Oct 1931	Home	6-5	2	Evan Isaacs T, Haydn Williams T.
Maesteg	26 Oct 1931	Home	0-3	0	No scorers.
Bargoed (PL)	2 Nov 1931	Home	0-0	0	No scorers.
Bridgend	16 Nov 1931	Away	3-8	1	J. Davies T.
Ebbw Vale	28 Nov 1931	Home	18-0	4	Burke 2T, Haydn Williams T, Gwyn Knight T, Burns P, Coughlin P.
Glamorgan Wanderers	21 Dec 1931	Home	9-3	3	Jim Coughlin 2T, Glyn Thomas T.
Bargoed (PL)	28 Dec 1931	Away	16-8	Unknown	Scorers unknown.
Aberdare	28 Dec 1931	Home	16-0	4	Evan Isaac 3T, Price T, Jim Cummings C, Burke C.
Aberdare	9 Jan 1932	Away	10-0	2	G. Thomas 2T, Haydn Williams DG.
Pontypool	18 Jan 1932	Home	3-6	1	Frank Kempson T.
Pontypridd (PL)	25 Jan 1932	Away	13-13	2	Haydn Williams T, Tom Burns T, Jim Cummings P, C, Collins C.
Cross Keys	8 Feb 1932	Home	3-7	0	Jim Cummings P.
Cilfynydd (L)	27 Feb 1932	Home	22-0	4	J.R. Davies 2T, DG, Vernon May T, Haydn Williams T, Jim Cummings 3C.
Glamorgan Wanderers	29 Feb 1932	Unsure	9-0	3	Vernon May 2T, Tom Burns T.
Cilfynydd (L)	12 Mar 1932	Away	3-0	1	J.R. Davies T.
Maesteg	21 Mar 1932	Away	8-5	2	Haydn Williams T, Tom Burns T, Jim Cummings C.
Treorchy (L)	29 Mar 1932	Away	3-12	0+	P.S. Roberts 3pts.
Abertillery	31 Mar 1932	Home	9-8	1	Phil Davies T, Haydn Williams DG, Wilkins C.

Opponents	Date	Venue	Score	Tries	Scorers/Comments
Crumlin	9 Apr 1932	Home	14-6	2	Haydn Williams T, Jim Cummings C, AN Other T, 2P.
Aberavon	19 Apr 1932	Home	18-6	2	J.R. Davies 2T, Haydn Williams DG, Jim Coughlin DG, AN Other 2C.
Cardiff Romilly	25 Apr 1932	Home	34-3	6+	Haydn Williams 3T, Vernon May 2T, Jim Coughlin T, Jim Cummings 3P, 2C, AN Other 3pts.
Ebbw Vale	7 May 1932	Away	7-6	1	Les Manfield T, J.R. Davies DG.
Pontypridd (PL)	3 May 1932	Home	3-0	1	T.M. Williams T.
Kenfig Hill (L)	7 May 1932	Home	9-0	1	Baverstock T, Jim Coughlin DG, Jim Cummings C.

Summary of Playing Record

P	W	D	L	For	Against	Tries Scored	Win Rate %
32	21	2	9	332	187	56+	68.75

Match Reports and Publications

26 September 1931

<u>Mountain Ash 5 Treorchy 0</u>
<u>1930/31 Glamorgan League Play Off Replay</u>

<u>A Dramatic Finish</u>
<u>Mountain Ash Win Glamorgan League Championship</u>

"G.P." reported in the Leader, "A momentary slackening off by Treorchy a few minutes before the final whistle sounded, a sudden bludgeon-like stroke by Mountain Ash and a winning try scored and converted in the last few seconds – that was the supremely dramatic finish in the deciding match for the Championship of the Glamorgan League (for 1930/31) played between Treorchy, the holders, and Mountain Ash, at Ynysangharad Park, Pontypridd, on Friday last before a crowd of nearly 4,000 leather-lunged, uncompromising partisans of both Clubs. This game was a replay, as the teams fought a titanic struggle without a result at Pontypridd at the end of last season, when even thirty minutes of extra time could not bring about a score. But although enthusiasm and excitement still raged in the breasts of the rival players, the earliness of the season and the fact that lungs and muscles were not "toned up", conspired to make the game less thrilling than the first memorable match. Particularly noticeable was the falling away of the young Treorchy forwards in the closing stages – a direct contrast to the first match, when a magnificent rally by the Rhondda octet under the leadership of D.R. James (the International hooker now gone North), in the second half and during extra time, made Mountain Ash lucky to avoid defeat. In this second attempt, however, it was the superior stamina of the Mountain Ash pack, ably led by Frank Kempson, Burns and Cummings, that was the decisive factor in a dramatic victory.

Forwards Dominate

As was to be expected with such an important prize at stake, rugby science was missing – tackling by both teams was lusty and ruthless, the forwards took control of the exchanges, the backs were "smothered" and often the centres put safety first by kicking instead of opening up the game for their wing men. But the lack of skill in the exchanges was compensated for by the wholehearted manner in which the teams settled down to their work. No quarter was asked or given, but one must mention with gratification that the game, under the strict control of Mr. Dai Huddlestone, the old Welsh International, was played in a much better spirit than was the case earlier this year.

....kick charged down by Gwyn Knight, the Mount custodian who followed up very smartly, gave Mountain Ash an early territorial advantage. On top of this, the Old Firm forwards got the better of the first few scrummages, and Coughlin and Murphy, the half backs, gave nice service to their threes. Afterwards, however, the Treorchy pack steadily worked up superiority in scrummaging that made them look far and away the more useful side. Boxall, at scrum half, the hero of the last game, quickly showed his deftness in handling and his elusiveness in avoiding the attentions of Coughlin....

Treorchy's Mistake

There is no doubt that had the Treorchy centres made the best use of their speedy wingers, Ieuan Thomas and Ieuan Lloyd, the holders would have built up a useful lead before the interval which Mountain Ash might have found impossible to take away....although Treorchy's young, fast moving pack made several spirited raids, the Mount tackling was grim and merciless, and with Gwyn Knight making several nice clearances, Treorchy were successfully kept at bay....masterly work of Haydn Evas, the Treorchy full back....He faced the ugly Mountain Ash forward rushes with admirable coolness, fielded the ball beautifully and with only a couple of exceptions sent the ball up field with cleverly placed kicking. Once, he saved an almost certain try. The Mountain Ash forwards were in full cry for an unobstructed line. Evas, running like a deer, beat them to the loose ball, fell on it, got up from amongst three or four attackers and found touch with the coolness and precision of a master.

Anxious Moments

Treorchy opened the second half with a nice passing movement....A lineout, practically on the Mount line, followed by a series of scrums gave Mountain Ash some anxious moments, but gradually, clever work by Coughlin and Murphy, bull dog defence by the forwards, and a timely kick by Gwyn Knight, sent Treorchy back to midfield. There came a change in the tide of play, the first movement being a bold rally up the right touchline by J. Rees, the red headed Mount winger, who had done some valiant tackling during Treorchy's period of ascendency in the first half. Mountain Ash forwards were hot foot after him, and Evas had to bring off another of his clever saves. Soon afterwards, the Old Firm's pack charged the ball up to the line and this time a minor saved the Rhondda men....then Isaac led the Mountain Ash forwards in a vigorous raid, well supported by Kempson, Burns and Co. A penalty awarded to them in midfield saw Knight take an unsuccessful pot at goal.

Battering Ram Attacks

Then we saw a series of battering ram attacks up the right touchline by the Mountain Ash forwards. In spite of some clever obstructive work by Boxall, the smallest player on the field, who had his jersey half ripped off his back, Mountain Ash rammed their way into their opponents' "25" and these onslaughts were usually whistled up with eight or ten players prone – so vigorous was the attack and so devastating the tackling. Time after time the crowd was brought to the point of yelling at a Mountain Ash score, but time after time Treorchy averted disaster a yard or two from the line. All this time, Gwyn Knight stood an impassable barrier between Treorchy and the Mountain Ash "25". He revealed his very best form and again and again sent play back to the Treorchy half with clever kicking. Then a few minutes before no-side, came the long sought lead, Coughlin carved an opening which only needed smart development to provide Jackie Rees with a clear run through. Handling was sluggish, however, and Rees had to barge through a badly placed defence. A couple of the other Old Firm players followed him hot foot and with the ball being punted ahead, Coughlin won the race to touch down – a ragged score but a thrilling finish – amidst a great shout. Cummings sent the leather sailing over the bar to add the extras. There was little between the two teams but Mountain Ash were the superior XV at the period when the best football was played – in the second half – so they can be said just to have merited their triumph." After 3 hours and 10 minutes of rugby against Treorchy, the Old Firm had won their fourth Glamorgan League Championship in total, and their first since 1913/14.

28 November 1931

Mountain Ash 18 Ebbw Vale 0

Old Firm's Fine Win-Ebbw Vale Thrashed

The Aberdare Leader reported, "In spite of the numerous counter attractions in the football world, the meeting at the Rec on Saturday of these old rivals drew a fair crowd....Mountain Ash were now showing marked superiority in the scrum. Owing to the lateness of the start through the visitors' late arrival, the second half was started in almost semi-darkness. This difficulty was also added to by a deluge of rain and the visitors were handicapped by the non appearance of the two injured players. It was not long before the machine like methods of the Old Firm were repaid. Coughlin set the backs in motion and a fine bout of passing ended in Haydn Williams scoring the best try of the match. Just before the end, an electrifying run by Gwyn Knight resulted in his scoring an unconverted try."

18 January 1932

Mountain Ash 3 Pontypool 6

The Weather Won!

Mountain Ash – Pontypool Game Ruined

Pontypool ended the season as Welsh Club champions. The Aberdare Leader reported this match as follows, "Thirty soaked and bedraggled players, probably with comforting visions of steaming, hot baths flickering before them, thankfully heard the referee stop the play twenty minutes before time at the Rec last Saturday – this being the rather tragic end to the long awaited match between the Old Firm and Pontypool – the most attractive team on Mountain Ash's card, perhaps....After the interval, the game became nothing better than a farce, and even then, the most enthusiastic spectator – sheltered as he was in the Stand – could scarcely blame the saturated referee – rain cascading like a miniature Niagara down his forehead – for putting such an early end to it. Pontypool finished up three points in front – an unconverted try and a penalty goal to Mountain Ash's try – but this was against the run of play, for the Old Firm had adapted themselves to the atrocious conditions in much better style than the visitors, and had actually served up really fast, good football in the first twenty minutes when they handled the slippery ball with surprising skill. The home forwards, led by Kempson, Burns and Cummings, were also playing with great fire. Little need be written about the second half, played in a downpour on a real quagmire. The conditions even defeated the Press at times. The writer, perched in the back of the crowded stand was unable to see the far corner of the ground with any clearness, the moisture on the side of the windows giving them a "frosted glass" effect."

Overleaf is another newspaper report of this match.

Western Mail

MATCH ABANDONED.

Rain Interferes at Mountain Ash.

	G.	T.	Pts.
Pontypool	*1	1	6
Mountain Ash	0	1	3

* Penalty.

What would have been a delightful display at Mountain Ash was marred by heavy rain and a driving wind. In the first half the play was of a very even nature, both sides attacking in turn with intervals of midfield play.

Bodger, the Pontypool wing, made a very rapid advance and Gwyn Knight only effected a partial clearance under pressure. Cummings, Burns, and Kempson, however, came to the rescue and led a forward rush which saved the situation. Just before the interval the visiting forwards worked their way to the home line, and in a melée on the line Baynham scored an unconverted try. A minute later the "Old Firm" were penalised in midfield and Baynham landed a truly magnificent goal.

Mountain Ash strongly attacked in the second half, and after a minute or so Edwards was severely harassed and failed to clear. Kempson, dashing up, touched down to score an unconverted try. The "Old Firm" were now definitely superior, but after fifteen minutes of play in the second half the referee brought the game to an end owing to the conditions.

25 January 1932

Pontypridd 13 Mountain Ash 13
Possible Glamorgan League Fixture

HONOURS SHARED.

Plenty of Thrills in Pontypridd Game.

	G.	T.	Pts.
Pontypridd	2	1	13
Mountain Ash	*3	0	13

*One penalty.

The result of Pontypridd's match against Mountain Ash at Ynysangharad Park was in doubt right to the final whistle, and this factor, combined with brisk scoring, provided plenty of excitement.

A penalty goal kicked by Cummings gave Mountain Ash the lead, which the visitors increased when Haydn Williams, smartly following up a forward rush, dashed over to score a fine try which Cummings converted. Pontypridd regained the lead before the interval. Loosemore, following a dribble by Trevor Davies, scored a try which Ossie Jones converted, and Pontypridd's next try was the result of a brilliant dash by Trevor Davies, who broke through and crossed after giving the dummy smartly. Ossie Jones converted.

Half-way through the second half Mountain Ash regained the lead, Burns scoring a try after Johnny Rees had capped a good run with an inward pass to him. Collins converted and placed the home team three points in arrears, but Pontypridd again drew level when Edgar Phillips scored a try after taking advantage of a beautiful opening made by Trevor Davies.

12 March 1932

Cilfynydd 0 Mountain Ash 3
Glamorgan League

Mount Team: Gwyn Knight, G. Thomas, J.R. Davies, Haydn Williams, Butler, Phil Davies, Jim Coughlin, Tom Burns, J. Murphy, Brits, J.W. Price, Jim Cummings, P.C. Baverstock, Ambrose, Roberts.

The Aberdare Leader reported, "A valuable two points were wrested from Cilfynydd in the Glamorgan League encounter….Barring accidents or some other unforeseen circumstances, the outlook is rather rosy for the Old Firm once again becoming champions."

31 March 1932

Mountain Ash 9 Abertillery 8
Western Mail

EXHILARATING PLAY.

"Old Firm" Win by Single Point.

```
                    G.  T.  Pts.
Mountain Ash ....... *2  0   9
Abertillery ........ †2  0   8
     *One dropped.  †One penalty.
```

A game of fluctuating fortunes, the margin of one point in the "Old Firm's" favour accurately reflects the run of play. Throughout play was of a fast and exhilarating nature, both rear divisions being as incisive in attack as they were stubborn in defence.

The "Old Firm" scored first as a result of a surprise attack, Phil Davies scoring a try which Wilkins converted. Abertillery quickly counter-attacked and reached the home 25 line, where Morgan kicked a really magnificent penalty goal for the visitors. The visitors' dashing tactics were rewarded again when Richardson scored a try which Morgan converted.

The "Old Firm" took the lead in the first few minutes of the second half as the result of a splendid dropped goal by Haydn Williams.

19 April 1932

Mountain Ash 18 Aberavon 6
Western Mail

BRIGHT OPEN GAME.

Mountain Ash Deserve Win Over Aberavon.

```
                    G.  T.  Pts.
Mountain Ash ....... *4  0   18
Aberavon ...........  0  2   6
          *Two dropped.
```

In a bright open game, full of sparkling three-quarter movements, the visitors were evidently thrown out of their stride by a rapid ten points lead gained by the "Old Firm" as the result of two brilliant tries scored by J. R. Davies, following good play by Coughlin and Williams. Both tries were converted.

Aberavon shook off their lethargy and indulged in some spectacular movements which were thwarted by the keen tackling of the home backs. The visitors continued the pressure, and were rewarded by scoring two tries through Matthews and Phillips, the latter's try being the result of a brilliant run from the Mountain Ash '25.

The visitors' hopes of victory were dispelled when Hadyn Williams and Coughlin both dropped goals to give the "Old Firm" a well-deserved victory.

7 May 1932

<u>Ebbw Vale 6 Mountain Ash 7</u>

Mount Team: J. Richards, Vernon May, J.R. Davies, Haydn Williams, Les Manfield, Phil Davies, Jim Coughlin, P.C. Baverstock, Frank Kempson, C. Wilkins, Jim Cummings, Jim Murphy, J. Williams, Phil Demery, Joe Burke.

<u>Mountain Ash Defeat Ebbw Vale</u>
<u>A Brilliant Dropped Goal</u>

The Aberdare Leader reported, "The Mountain Ash forwards were extremely lively in the opening stages of this interesting game, Baverstock and Williams being particularly prominent....From the restart after half time, the Mount pressed and it was not long before reward came. Coughlin passed out to his backs and Manfield securing, scored an unconverted try. Something of a sensation was caused when with lightning rapidity, J.R. Davies seized the opportunity and dropped a grand goal." Les Manfield, who went on to play for Wales seven times between 1939 and 1948, would have been 16 ½ when he played in this match.

Mountain Ash Rugby Football Club
"The Old Firm"
Glamorgan League Champions 1930/31 & 1931/32

Unfortunately, the names of everyone in the above photograph are unknown. The ones that are known are as follows.

In the back row, 3rd from the left is committeeman David Davies, and 6th from the left is the Club's trainer, Dan Horrigan. In the row one below, the first person on the left is Jason Job, the Rec Groundsman, and in the middle of the row with his arms folded and his forearm showing is forward Trevor Edwards. At the start of the seated row holding the flag is retired scrum half Sid Congdon, half back Jim Coughlin is holding the ball, and next to him in a suit is Club Chairman Shad Lewis. On the far right with blond hair is livewire forward Jim Cummings with his arms folded. Sitting on the grass on the far right wearing a shirt and tie is Billy Llewellyn, the Club's Baggage Man.

Season 1932/33

Magnificent Season For Old Firm
3rd Successive Glamorgan League Championship

The Old Firm made it a magnificent hat-trick of wins in the Glamorgan League by being crowned champions at the end of the season. Although on the crest of a wave of success, Mount called time on their participation in the tournament, and prior to the 1933/34 season, withdrew from it and never played in the competition again – which run until the start of World War II and briefly afterwards. The reason why the Club finished its involvement seemed to be in the pursuit of "first class" status. Although Mount was playing and beating so-called "first class" opposition, the Club was never regarded by the media as "first class", whatever that meant. There was never any definition or criteria that determined a Club's classification, but being called "first class" was greatly valued. As for the Welsh Rugby Union, officially they saw all Clubs as equal.

The season saw a convincing win over reigning Welsh champions from 1931/32, Pontypool, 16-3 at the Rec, which was the second time the Old Firm had beaten the reigning Welsh champion Club, Cross Keys being the first back in 1922/23. There were "doubles" over Treorchy, Glamorgan Wanderers, Pontypridd and Maesteg, and also wins over Aberavon, Cross Keys, Ebbw Vale and Bridgend, but one of the best wins of the season came in the last game when Cardiff were beaten 7-0 at the Rec, which ended an impressive season in style. The Welsh Academicals was the only Club to beat the Old Firm on the Rec, and that was 8-5 with less than a fortnight of the season left. There were close losses at Aberavon and Pontypool, and a creditable draw at Abertillery, who were 2nd in the Western Mail's unofficial Welsh Club Championship table at the time of the game and finished runners up to Llanelly at the end of the season. It was a magnificent season for the Old Firm. All in all, 33 games were played, 25 won, 2 drawn and 6 lost, with 78+ tries in the total of 363 points scored, and only 120 conceded, to give a win rate of 78.79%. Although it was a season for the Old Firm to savour, it was goodbye to the Glamorgan League forever.

Fixtures 1932/33

Opponents	Date	Venue	Score	Tries	Scorers/Comments
Cardiff Romilly	10 Sep 1932	Home	35-3	8	Jim Lewis 2T, Albert Davies 2T, Phil Davies 2T, Haydn Williams T, 4C, P, Ben James T.
Aberavon	17 Sep 1932	Away	9-14	3	Ben James T, Jim Coughlin T, Gerald Lewis T.
Treorchy (L)	19 Sep 1932	Home	18-3	4	Phil Davies 2T, Frank Kempson 2T, Haydn Williams 2C, Jim Cummings C.
Kenfig Hill (L)	26 Sep 1932	Unknown	15-6	3	J.R. Davies 2T, Gerald Davies T, Haydn Williams DG, Jim Cummings C.
Penarth	3 Oct 1932	Away	3-6	1	Frank Kempson T.
Bargoed (PL)	10 Oct 1932	Home	6-0	0+	AN Other 6pts.
Abertillery	20 Oct 1932	Away	3-3	1	Gerald Lewis T.
Penygraig (PL)	24 Oct 1932	Home	9-7	3	Morgan 2T, Gerald Lewis T.

Opponents	Date	Venue	Score	Tries	Scorers/Comments
Cardiff Athletic	31 Oct 1932	Away	6-3	1	Haydn Williams T, Jim Cummings P.
Pontypool	12 Nov 1932	Home	16-3	1	Gerald Lewis T, Jim Cummings 3P, Phil Davies DG.
Glamorgan Wanderers	14 Nov 1932	Away	11-0	2	J.R. Davies T, Murphy T, Jim Cummings P, C.
Bargoed (L)	21 Nov 1932	Away	3-7	0	Jim Cummings P.
Crumlin	28 Nov 1932	Unknown	5-0	1	Morgan T, Jim Cummings C.
Pontypridd (PL)	5 Dec 1932	Away	11-4	3	J.R. Davies 2T, Haydn Williams T, Jim Cummings C.
Cross Keys	19 Dec 1932	Home	9-0	1	Tom Burns T, W. Morgan DG, Jim Cummings C.
Aberdare	27 Dec 1932	Home	22-5	6	Don Price 2T, Haydn Williams T, W. Morgan T, Gerald Lewis T, Jim Coughlin T, Jim Cummings 2C.
Aberdare	7 Jan 1933	Away	18-0	6	W. Morgan 2T, Haydn Williams 2T, John Willy Price T, J.R. Davies T.
Ebbw Vale	14 Jan 1933	Home	5-0	1	W. Morgan T, Jim Cummings C.
Pontypridd (PL)	23 Jan 1933	Home	10-0	2	Phil Davies T, P.C. Jones T, Jim Coughlin DG.
Aberaman (L)	13 Feb 1933	Home	8-0	2	Haydn Williams T, Frank Kempson T, Jim Cummings C.
Crumlin	6 Mar 1933	Away	5-0	1	Haydn Williams T, Jim Cummings C.
Cross Keys	13 Mar 1933	Away	5-19	1	Phil Davies T, Jim Cummings C.
Cilfynydd (PL)	20 Mar 1933	Home	30-3	6	Gerald Lewis 3T, Frank Kempson T, Gadd T, Morgan T, Haydn Williams DG, Jim Coughlin DG, Jim Cummings 2C.
Aberavon	25 Mar 1933	Home	6-0	1	Jim Cummings T, Ivor Skyrme P.
Pontypool	March 1933	Away	0-3	0	No scorers.

Opponents	Date	Venue	Score	Tries	Scorers/Comments
Maesteg	1 Apr 1933	Home	9-0	1	Edwards T, Skyrme 2P.
Treorchy (L)	8 Apr 1933	Away	11-0	1	B. Smith T, Haydn Williams 2DG.
Maesteg	15 Apr 1933	Away	9-5	2	Frank Kempson T, McLauchlan T, Jim Cummings P.
Welsh Academicals	18 Apr 1933	Home	5-8	1	A. Roberts T, Jim Cummings C.
Glamorgan Wanderers	29 Apr 1933	Home	27-8	7	Gerald Lewis 2T, Frank Kempson 2T, Jim Coughlin T, Haydn Williams T, Maskell T, Jim Cummings 3C.
Aberaman (L)	29 Apr 1933	Away	7-7	1	W. Morgan T, Haydn Williams DG.
Bridgend	1 May 1933	Unsure	20-3	6	Gerald Lewis 2T, J.R. Davies 2T, John Willy Price T, Haydn Williams T, Jim Cummings C.
Cardiff	2 May 1933	Home	7-0	1	Travers T, Haydn Williams DG.

Summary of Playing Record

P	W	D	L	For	Against	Tries Scored	Win Rate %
33	25	2	6	363	120	78+	78.79

Match Reports & Publications

3 September 1932

<u>Glamorgan League Champions</u>
<u>Mountain Ash RFC Presentations</u>
<u>Club's Good Record</u>

The Aberdare Leader reported, "After the Trial Match held by Mountain Ash RFC on Saturday, there was a splendid gathering of friends and supporters of the Old Firm at the Glancynon Hotel, where members of the team who won the Glamorgan League Championship last season were presented with gold medals; and the Cup – already held – was formally handed over. The Chair was taken by Mr Wyndham Jones, one of the Big Five in the Welsh Rugby Union (and former Old Firm outside half who was capped in 1905). Mr W.J. Heare (who was the Western Mail's revered rugby journalist known as "Old Stager") had a splendid reception on rising and at once complimented the team on their additional success....Mountain Ash he added had been playing good football but perhaps not so good as in the old days, and the task before them was to "build up" as in the past, and if he personally could do anything to help in that direction he would be only too delighted.

Players Presented

The following players received medals: Roy West, Tommy D. Williams, Haydn Williams, Jack Davies, Vernon May, Phil Davies, Jim Coughlin, P.C. Baverstock, Tom Burns, John Willy Price, Phil Demery, Bob Roberts, Jim Murphy, Jim Cummings, and Frank Kempson."

18 October 1932

In the run up to the Old Firm's away game at Abertillery, the Western Mail published its unofficial Welsh Club table:

RUGBY WELSH CHAMPIONSHIP

The present placings on the table are:—

	P.	W.	D.	L.	F.	A.	Per c'tage.
Llanelly	7	7	0	0	104	39	100.00
Abertillery	8	7	0	1	89	32	87.50
Cardiff	7	5	2	0	83	16	85.71
Cross Keys	9	7	0	2	106	45	77.77
Swansea	8	5	2	1	148	38	75.00
Neath	9	6	1	2	110	58	72.22
Pontypool	9	6	1	2	106	35	72.22
Aberavon	12	8	1	3	117	56	70.83
Bridgend	11	7	1	3	146	64	68.18
Penarth	6	2	0	4	34	68	33.33
Newport	8	2	1	5	49	54	31.25

20 October 1932

Abertillery 3 Mountain Ash 3

In front of an attendance of 2,500, the Western Mail's rugby reporter, "Old Stager", commented, "Bird, of Abertillery, was the most successful of the backline and had he not been in opposition to a really sturdy and resourceful wing in Gerald Lewis, there is little question that he would have won the game on his own.... Abertillery's backs had few opportunities than the men opposed to them owing to the better scrummaging of the Mountain Ash forwards, and there can be no denying the fact that if the Mountain Ash centres had had....the necessary confidence in themselves to give accurate transfers at all important moments, Abertillery's three years ground record would have been a thing of the past. And yet those Mountain Ash centres, Price and Williams, were splendid when any kicking, tackling or rush stopping had to be done, reinforcing the exceptionally good work which was done by Coughlin, who was the steadying influence whenever difficulties had to be faced....Price, Gadd and Cummings constantly worked well for Mountain Ash in a pack which would "stand up" to many first class packs and not be found wanting."

24 October 1932

Mountain Ash 9 Penygraig 7
Possible Glamorgan League Fixture

In addition to forward Tommy Burns and a Penarth player being sent off after a "bout of fisticuffs" at the end of September, second row forward Frank Kempson followed him less than a month later in this probable Glamorgan League game with Penygraig, the Western Mail reporting, "Over vigorous forward play spoilt the game as a spectacle and culminated in Kempson (Mountain Ash) and Gardiner (Penygraig) being ordered off the field."

12 November 1932

Mountain Ash 16 Pontypool 3

Mount Team: I. Skyrme, W. Morgan, Haydn Williams Capt, R. Davies, Gerald Lewis, P. Davies, Jim Coughlin, A. Davies, J. Cummings, P.C. Gadd, P.C. Travers, J.W. Price, J. Murphy, A. Roberts, P. Demery.

The Giant Killers! Old Firm Trounce Pontypool
Prettier Play, Though Flattered By Score

At the time of this game, Pontypool were reigning Welsh champions. The Aberdare Leader reported, "Mountain Ash gave their supporters, who were many, the biggest thrill of the season by whipping Pontypool at the Rec last Saturday in a game which must have been one of the best seen there for many a day. Everything contributed to make the fixture a success. The weather was ideal, the turf in good condition, and there was a big crowd who fully appreciated the glimpses of really pretty play which Mountain Ash provided in the early stages. It was a difficult game to sum up – Pontypool, who were without three players – in attendance at the Welsh International trial at Neath – were unlucky to lose by such a big margin; indeed had they grasped their opportunities as well as Mountain Ash – or rather Cummings, the goal kicker – they might well have won! But Pontypool never served up the sparkling play Mountain Ash gave us in the first half, when forwards, half backs, three-quarters and full back worked in delightful unison – and one feels that Mountain Ash thoroughly deserved the win because they thrilled us with glimpses of real "copy-book" play and made full use of almost every opportunity that came their way…..Then came the big thrill of the match. Jim Coughlin, at outside half, got back a sweet pass to Haydn Williams, left centre, who made a dash up the middle before serving J.R. Davies, his co-centre. Davies continued the move with an exhilarating burst in which he cleverly drew the defence before sending the leather to Gerald Lewis, the right winger, who simply streaked over in the corner for a try….

Strong Forwards

Good forward play afterwards kept the Old Firm in the ascendency, P.C. Travers and Gadd, Cummings and Albert Davies leading a strong rush into the Pontypool 25 which resulted in the visitors being penalised from a scrum. Cummings sent the ball sailing over the bar.

Pontypool in Pieces

….the visitors gradually seemed revitalised….Indeed, for a long time Pontypool set the pace…..then in a skirmish came a regrettable incident. The unhappy Belcher (of Pontypool) was summarily ordered from the field by Mr Meggins of Pontyclun for trying deliberately to kick an opponent. Then the visitors seemed to fall to pieces like a house of cards. They were penalised in their 25 and the unerring Cummings kicked his third goal, and a minute later, Phil Davies dropped a goal from halfway between the middle and 25 lines. Mount thoroughly deserved the laurels, they were a really smart side."

19 December 1932

<u>Mountain Ash 9 Cross Keys 0</u>
<u>Old Firm's Fire</u>
<u>Cross Keys Outfought in Dour Struggle</u>

The Aberdare Leader reported, "The Mountain Ash pack covered themselves with glory when they outfought and out-lasted the heavier Monmouthshire Club's forwards and paved the way to a surprisingly good win which sent home supporters into an ecstasy of enthusiasm. One would not like to say the Rec crowd were surprised by the result, for Mountain Ash supporters have tremendous faith in their side, but there was no doubt that the play of the homesters was a revelation to many – it was to me, privileged to see the Old Firm only on rare occasions. The forwards, led by Burns, Cummings and Kempson were magnificent. Others in the home XV emerged from the bitter fight with great credit; Ivor Skyrme at full back, defended with great solidarity; W. Morgan on the left wing, contributed more brilliant flashes of attacking play; and Don Price at outside half must have played one of his best games of the season, his defensive work being particularly fine, but it was the tough, dour pack that carved out the hard won passage to victory....The Old Firm undoubtedly have a great XV this season. In addition to possessing a fine pack, they have a back division of great possibilities. Every one of the forwards is a worker, Cummings, Burns, Murphy, Albert Davies and Kempson being outstanding." The Western Mail report of the game was as follows:

WELL BEATEN
Llanelly's Conquerors Have to Bow the Knee

	G.	T.	Pts.
Mountain Ash	*2	0	9
Cross Keys	0	0	0

*One dropped.

Cross Keys were well beaten at Mountain Ash.

Apart from a few moments at the start of the game, when the bustling tactics of their forwards took them to the home line, the visitors did not once appear to be an effective attacking force.

The home forwards soon took the measure of their opponents, and the only three-quarter movements of any note were those initiated by the "Old Firm," the visitors relying more upon the battering-ram methods of their forwards.

The "Old Firm" were penalised twice in succession early in the game, but Thornbury failed to open the score. After Davies had eased the pressure Gerald Lewis picked up and raced ahead, only to be forced into touch a few yards from the Keys' line. Following the line-out Morgan snapped up the ball and dropped a very fine goal.

In the second half the Monmouthshire line was continually menaced by the determined attacks of the home three-quarters, and it was only the good defensive play of Legg which prevented several scores. The "Old Firm's" efforts were eventually rewarded when Burns scored a try, which Cummings converted.

23 January 1933

Mountain Ash 10 Pontypridd 0
Possible Glamorgan League Fixture

OTHER RUGBY GAMES — By "OLD STAGER"

MOUNTAIN ASH RECORD INTACT

Records of one kind or another continue to exist, and there was general rejoicing at Mountain Ash on Saturday at the success over Pontypridd by ten points to nil, as that win enabled the "Old Firm" to continue the possession of a ground record.

A. Davies and J. Murphy, two of the best of the Mountain Ash forwards, were absent, but that made no substantial difference, for play was always of a high standard, with the "Old Firm" generally holding the upper hand. Phil Davies, back again at scrum half for Mountain Ash, materially assisted in developing combined work, and scored one of the tries, P.C. Jones crossing with the other. Coughlin also dropped a goal.

11 February 1933

The Aberdare Leader reported, "Mountain Ash, with Aberaman, are joint leaders of the Glamorgan League. Both sides have obtained maximum points. The Old Firm have met and overcome some of the best sides in Wales in very convincing style, but as Aberaman do not suffer from an inferiority complex, it should be a great game at the Recreation Ground on Saturday." Mount won this game 8-0 with tries by centre Haydn Williams, second row Frank Kempson, and a conversion by backrow forward Jim Cummings.

Aberavon came to town at the end of March, the Aberdare Leader describing them in its early season match report as "Bravon", "the "scalpers" of many football heads in South Wales."

25 March 1933

Mountain Ash 6 Aberavon 0
The Giant Killers Again! Mountain Ash Outplay Aberavon
Great Forwards

G.P.A. reported the match as follows in the Aberdare Leader, "The cry of "wolf, wolf", is spreading further into the well guarded preserve of Welsh first class rugger. Bringing a powerful team to the Rec on Saturday, Aberavon put their feet into very sharp toothed jaws – becoming the latest victims at the ruthless Mountain Ash "destroyer" by a penalty goal and a try to nil.

The score of six points to nil indicates a fairly comfortable victory – but actually it does not do justice to the Old Firm who, more than merely defeating the Seasiders, gave them a rugby lesson. Mountain Ash lasted the course of a fast game much better than their bigger opponents; they were always quicker on the ball, their marking and tackling was more deadly; they were clever enough to checkmate the visitors superiority in the set scrums and the line-outs by dominating the exchanges with fast and resolute loose forward play, and in the second half the three-quarters emphasised the greater sparkle of the home XV by contributing some delightful handling movements which, although they did not lead to a score, infused considerable colour into the battle. In short, the Old Firm made the well represented visitors' side look second-rateish….Cummings, Kempson, Alby Davies and P.C. Travers were leading a virile home pack which was excelling in the loose; pouncing ruthlessly on the Bravonites and dashing attack after attack.

A Deserved Score

No defence could have withstood such a resolute attack, however, and the score the Old Firm richly deserved came quickly. From a lineout the ball drifted towards the posts and in a fierce skirmish, Travers picked up smartly and flung out to Cummings, who gave to W. Cunningham, who dived over for an unconverted try near the flag. Finding themselves sorely harassed by the fast moving Mount forwards, Aberavon tried to use their three-quarters, but standing close up, the home backs nipped each of these movements in the bud with some deadly tackling; and with the Mount forwards following up at tremendous speed and playing with increasing fire, Aberavon were almost continually on the defensive. One expected a change in the tide after the interval, but after Skyrme had placed a remarkable penalty goal from half way, with the sun now set, Mountain Ash now played with increasing intensity and very seldom did the Seasiders look as if they were going to make a fight of it. Indeed, play for most of the second half remained between the half way line and the Aberavon 25 line. Aberavon made a rather desperate rally in the closing stages but, met by a determined defence, they never looked like getting a score, and the end came with the Old Firm worthy winners. I was very impressed by the Old Firm's display. They are a great side. But jubilation at their victories over the "aristocratic" sides must not blind us to some weaknesses. The three-quarters, although they suffered a certain amount from the somewhat erratic play of J.R. Davies at outside half, provided some lively handling bouts; their raids were fast and determined. But there were too many wild passes and consequently muffed chances.

Splendid Full Back

Skyrme at full back was splendid. Very rarely did he fail to take the ball cleanly and he always kicked a great length with fine judgement. He is a big factor in the Old Firm's success. The brothers Davies at half back are good, if not very enterprising….It is the forwards who deserve greatest admiration. Against a heavier pack, they played with tremendous vim….I have never seen loose forwards play to equal it this season. Alby Davies, who played himself almost to a standstill, gave a great display, especially in the second half. Cummings, Kempson and Travers were also great workers and they were splendidly supported by P.C. T. Gadd, the secondary schoolboy Leslie Manfield, G. Murphy and J. Maskell."

29 April 1933

Aberaman 7 Mountain Ash 7
Glamorgan League

"Hush Hush Tactics"

The Aberdare Leader reported, "Despite the brilliance of this season's Mountain Ash side, Aberaman on Monday last, got as near to thrashing them as any side this year, and indeed the visitors may well feel that the luck that was, favoured them, for territorially Aberaman should have won. At least half the game was played in or around the Old Firm's 25….the game took on an "International like" atmosphere, and indeed, the result to the Clubs concerned was of nearly as much importance as any Welsh victory. "Tense" certainly describes the feeling of both Clubs, supporters and players, "secretive" too, for in the getting of the team sheet, I was almost made to swear an oath to "keep mum". Mountain Ash precautions were indeed touching on the borders of a farce, tactics being discussed behind a locked door, or if not a locked door, something nearly as formidable, a forward's back. I was able to sneak in under cover of a broad back, immediately to be glared upon with disfavour and mistrust until stating in a very timid voice my requirements. I was glad to get out. The game was a battle between the forwards….why Mountain Ash chose the same method of play was a mystery particularly as their fine three-quarters were not given anything like a fair chance owing to the forwards not getting the ball back. Aberaman's prospects of the Championship were indeed looking bright when, with only five minutes left, they held the lead 7-4, but there's many a slip….and the one slip they made was enough for W. Morgan to make a great burst to cross right against the corner flag."

1 May 1933

Mountain Ash 20 Bridgend 3
Western Mail

BRIDGEND OVER-RUN

Mountain Ash, the Glamorgan League champions, added to their laurels by over-running Bridgend, and defeating them by twenty points to a penalty goal (kicked by Stan Roberts). J. R. Davies (2), G. Lewis (2), J. W. Price, and Haydn Williams scored the Mountain Ash tries, Cummings converting one.

2 May 1933

Mountain Ash 7 Cardiff 0
Western Mail

"OLD FIRM" WIN

Cardiff Mastered Everywhere Except in Scrums

	G.	T.	Pts.
Mountain Ash	*1	1	7
Cardiff	0	0	0

*Dropped.

Mountain Ash were in fine fettle on Monday and were the masters of Cardiff in all branches of the game, except in the scrummages, where Cardiff held a decided advantage.

Despite this the visitors failed to score, partly owing to the deadly tackling of the "Old Firm," and partly owing to the poor passing and half-hearted running of the three-quarters.

The forwards fought a rare tussle for supremacy, tempers becoming frayed in the process, but in the second half Mountain Ash asserted their superiority and the visitors found it difficult to get out of their own half.

Skyrme put Mountain Ash in a strong attacking position early in the game, and when the ball went loose Haydn Williams dropped a fine goal. Parfitt, Jones, and Winter participated in a beautiful handling movement for Cardiff, but a fine tackle by Rogers ended a very promising movement. R. Davies next attempted to even the score with a dropped goal, but the ball struck the upright. H. Williams and Gerald Lewis next made a dash for the Cardiff line, and when Gerald Lewis was held a yard from the line he sent out to Travers, who scored a try.

6 May 1933

<u>Old Firm's Nerves?</u>
<u>Protest Against Result At Aberaman</u>

The Aberdare Leader reported, "Surely nothing short of a bad attack of nerves would have prompted Mountain Ash to send a protest to the Glamorgan League in connection with their recent encounter with Aberaman, when as reported last week, the Old Firm scored an unconverted try in the last two minutes to make the scores level. A victory at Kenfig Hill would have placed Aberaman jointly at the head of the table with their local rivals. Is it possible, then, that the prospect of playing a "decider" with the team who had failed to beat them by a few minutes was too much for the Old Firm? Under such conditions, rugby immediately ceases to be a sport and becomes mere pot hunting, with that "you must win" spirit predominating, hardly the principle to be instilled into the heads of young recruits to the game. To lose an occasional game is better than the longest string of victories can ever be....The allegation of the Old Firm was that Aberaman included a Treorchy player in their side. The protest was considered at a meeting of the Glamorgan League, held at Pontypridd on Friday last, and was upheld by four votes to three. As a result of the ruling, Mountain Ash take full points, and at the same time the League Championship."

THE OLD FIRM'S PROUD PAST

Mountain Ash Rugby Football Club
"The Old Firm"
Glamorgan League Champions 1932/33
3rd Successive Season Following 1930/31 & 1931/32

Back Row L-R: G. Morris (committee), Phil Davies, Tommy D.E. Williams, Roy West, Bill Roberts, John Willie Price, Haydn Williams, C. Coopey (committee),

One Down from Back Row L-R: Jason Job (Rec Groundsman), Jim Murphy, Tommy Burns, Phil Demery, Frank Kempson, P.C. Baverstock, Les Manfield, Jack Davies, Jim Cummings, H. Rees (committee), George Bradwick (committee),

One Up from Front Row, sitting, L-R: Jack Thomas (committee), John Lavery (committee), Sid Congdon (committee), Fred Evans (committee), Jim Coughlin, Shad Lewis (Chairman), William Christopher (committee), Ned Bradwick (Secretary), G. Edwards (committee), Dan Horrigan (Trainer), Dai Davies (committee),

Front Row L-R: Glyn John (committee), Stan Thomas (Welsh Schools Cap), Billy Llewellyn (committee).

The End Of An Era Of Glamorgan League Rugby
The Old Firm's Record In The Glamorgan League Championship & Cup
Seasons 1894/95 to 1932/33

From the start of the competition in 1894/95, when it was known in that first season only, as the Rhondda, Merthyr and Aberdare Valleys League, the Old Firm won the competition 6 times – 1895/96, 1908/09, 1913/14, 1930/31, 1931/32 & 1932/33.

In 1913/14, the Old Firm won the "double", winning the Glamorgan League Championship and the Glamorgan League's cup competition, which was known as the Glamorgan Times Cup.

Whereas the League Championship competition was played for every season except for the enforced break during the First World War, it seems unlikely the Cup competition was, due to it hardly being mentioned after Mount's win in 1913/14.

The Old Firm finished joint top of the Glamorgan League on two other occasions – 1894/95 and 1904/05 – but lost both play-offs, both of which were played early in the following seasons, which were 1895/96 and 1905/06 respectively.

Due to the complete absence of the mention of the Glamorgan League in any match reports for the Old Firm after the end of the First World War until 1927/28, and bearing in mind that Mount were always in the running for the Championship, or had a big say in who won it, it may well have been the case that the Club never entered the tournament after the War until 1927/28. There is not enough information available at the time of writing to know either way. The decision to withdraw from the Glamorgan League turned out to be an historic one as Mountain Ash RFC did not compete in another official League for 50 years, until the Mid District League was formed in 1982/83.

Season 1933/34

Mount Withdraw From Glamorgan League

Prior to the season starting, the Old Firm withdrew from the Glamorgan League and never played in the competition again. The reason behind this decision seems to have been the pursuit of "first class" status, which was highly sought after. The withdrawal was summed up in two comments made in the Aberdare Leader. The first, in September 1933, said, "Mountain Ash has been putting their house in order to meet the demand of the public for better rugby. They have been, for three seasons, fairly successful and last year proved that they are one of the most formidable sides in Wales." Six months later, in March 1934, the Leader quoted a source close to the Club as saying, "they considered their Club not in the light of Glamorgan League standards but as a combination capable of providing formidable opposition to any side in Wales. Glamorgan League rugby failed to bring out the best in a man and the games often developed into scrambling stampedes."

The season also saw a deterioration in relations between Mount and Aberaman which resulted in no matches being played. The actual reason for this was never made public but, no doubt, it was due to the way the Glamorgan League was decided at the end of the previous season, 1932/33, when Aberaman played an ineligible player against the Old Firm in what was termed a League decider for both Clubs, and which led to a protest being made by Mountain Ash to the Glamorgan League Committee – a protest which was upheld and which helped decide the destination of the Championship. The season saw "doubles" over Abertillery and Aberdare, and home wins over Pontypridd, Maesteg, Cilfynydd, Cardiff Athletic and Ynysybwl. There were also draws at home to Cross Keys and away to Maesteg, and narrow losses at Pontypool, Aberavon and Pontypridd. The season overall did not hit the heady heights of previous ones with a playing record of played 26, won 13, drawn 4 and lost 9, with 228+ points scored, which included 49+ tries, and 148+ points conceded, to give a win rate of 57.69%, which was still a respectable return.

Fixtures 1933/34

Opponents	Date	Venue	Score	Tries	Scorers/Comments
Blaenavon	11 Sep 1933	Home	7-7	1	Frank Kempson T, Haydn Williams DG.
Aberdare	23 Sep 1933	Home	31-0	9	Haydn Williams 3T, Gerald Lewis 2T, Frank Kempson T, Lloyd T, Morgan T, Regan T, J.R. Davies 2C.
Cross Keys	25 Sep 1933	Away	3-23	1	W. Morgan T.
Cardiff Athletic	2 Oct 1933	Home	21-3	4	Evans 2T, Jones T, Maskell T, Skyrme DG, P, C.
Penygraig	9 Oct 1933	Home	0-0	0	No scorers.
Ynysybwl	16 Oct 1933	Away	4-10	0	Haydn Williams DG.
Penygraig	28 Oct 1933	Away	3-9	1	Haydn Williams T.
Pontypridd	30 Oct 1933	Home	12-8	2	Roy West T, John Lloyd T, James 2P.
Maesteg	6 Nov 1933	Home	11-0	3	Frank Kempson T, Haydn Williams T, Curtis T, J.R. Davies C.

Opponents	Date	Venue	Score	Tries	Scorers/Comments
Glamorgan Wanderers	13 Nov 1933	Home	8-10	2	J.R. Davies T, C, John Lloyd T.
Kenfig Hill	20 Nov 1933	Away	8-3	0	Haydn Williams 2DG.
Cross Keys	27 Nov 1933	Home	11-11	2	Frank Kempson T, Curtis T, J.R. Davies P, C.
Cardiff Athletic	9 Dec 1933	Away	0-11	0	No scorers.
Ynysybwl	27 Dec 1933	Home	3-0	Unknown	Scorer not known.
Bargoed	1 Jan 1934	Away	3-0	1	Baverstock T.
Maesteg	8 Jan 1934	Away	3-3	0	Tom Rees P.
Bargoed	15 Jan 1934	Home	26-0	6	Haydn Williams 2T, DG, Frank Kempson T, Phil Davies T, F. Rees T, Curtis T, Tom Rees C, J.R. Davies C.
Glamorgan Wanderers	29 Jan 1934	Away	11-8	3	F. Rees 2T, C, J.R. Davies T.
Pontypool	5 Feb 1934	Home	4-8	0	J.R. Davies DG.
Pontypridd	12 Feb 1934	Away	3-8	1	Frank Kempson T.
Cilfynydd	26 Feb 1934	Home	18-3	4	John Lloyd 2T, J.R. Davies T, P, Haydn Williams T, F. Rees P.
Aberavon	2 Apr 1934	Away	5-9	1	Baverstock T, J.R. Davies C.
Abertillery	16 Apr 1934	Home	14-3	3	John Lloyd 2T, J.R. Davies T, Les Manfield P, C.
Pontypool	28 Apr 1934	Away	3-11	1	F. Rees T.
Aberdare	12 May 1934	Away	16-0	4	John Jones 2T, Noel Ellis T, Baverstock T, Les Manfield C, J.R. Davies C.
Abertillery	Unknown	Away	Unknown	Unknown	Mount win.

Summary of Playing Record

P	W	D	L	For	Against	Tries Scored	Win Rate %
26	13	4	9	228+	148+	49+	57.69

Match Reports & Publications

23 September 1933

<u>Mountain Ash 31 Aberdare 0</u>

The Aberdare Leader reported, "the Aberdare team that took the field when visiting the Old Firm at the Rec last Saturday will need to be thoroughly overhauled before they can hope to even come within measurable distance of a team like Mountain Ash that comprises many seasoned and experienced players. The game of rugby in South Wales is passing through a renaissance period and much of the old post War methods have got to be forgotten. Mountain Ash have been putting their house in order to meet the demand of the public for better rugby. They have been, for three seasons, fairly successful and last year proved that they are one of the most formidable sides in Wales."

2 October 1933

<u>Mountain Ash 21 Cardiff Athletic 3</u>

The Western Mail commented, "Mountain Ash have long clamoured for recognition as a first class side and they advanced their claim by defeating Cardiff Athletic 21-3."

27 November 1933

<u>Mountain Ash 11 Cross Keys 11</u>
<u>Western Mail</u>

ROBBED OF VICTORY IN LAST MINUTE

Cross Keys Held to Draw by "Old Firm"

	G.	T.	Pts.
Mountain Ash	*2	1	11
Cross Keys	1	2	11

*One penalty.

Cross Keys went to Mountain Ash with a reputation for good team-work, of which they gave ample proof in a game in which they were robbed of victory in the very last stages.

The visiting forwards were all-powerful in the scrummages and in the lines-out, but in the loose they were not one whit better than their opponents. Their forceful methods in the loose were more than countered by the deadliness of the "Old Firm's" tackling.

The Keys' threequarters were ever in the picture, R. Davies and S. Mountain, in particular, making some wonderful efforts to score, only to be baulked by a defence which would not crack under the strain.

The home team were well served by Kempson and Travers amongst the forwards, while Haydn Williams was outstanding among the threequarters. He seemed to be ubiquitous in defence and attack, and by his resolute running, tackling and clever scheming proved himself a thorn in the flesh of the Monmouthshire men.

Team-work was not the strong feature in the "Old Firm's" play, yet as individuals they left little to be desired.

A GREAT RALLY

Early in the game Cross Keys were penalised for offside tactics and Mountain Ash took the lead with a penalty goal scored by J. R. Davies. Encouraged by this success, the "Old Firm" redoubled their efforts and Curtis, profiting by Legge's dilatoriness, snapped up the ball and scored a try.

After a brief period of forceful midfield play Hawker opened the score for Cross Keys with a try which Thornbury converted. Just before half-time the visitors took the lead when Bowdler bustled through the defence and sent out to Williams, who scored a doubtful try, the transfer appearing to be forward.

With only two points difference in the score, Cross Keys went out to consolidate their position, which they did when Roberts scored an unconverted try. In the closing stages Mountain Ash made a wonderful rally and from a line-out the home forwards forced their way to the line and Kempson scored a try, J. R. Davies levelling the scores when he converted.

5 February 1934

Mountain Ash 4 Pontypool 8
Western Mail

VICTORY DUE TO FORWARDS

Frayed Tempers at Mountain Ash

	G.	T.	Pts.
Pontypool	1	1	8
Mountain Ash	*1	0	4

* Dropped.

Pontypool owe their victory to their forwards, although in the gaining of it tempers became frayed.

In the scrums Pontypool held the upper hand, and this superiority gave the Monmouthshire three-quarters ample opportunities, but they failed to profit thereby.

The game generally was marred by off-side play, particularly on the part of the Pontypool winging forward. This fact, and the over-vigorous tactics of some of the forwards, put tempers on edge, and play deteriorated, particularly in the closing stages.

While the Pontypool three-quarter line was peculiarly ineffective in attack, they were stubborn defenders and refused to yield under the many onslaughts which were made upon their line. Axford proved a very effective link between the scrum and the three-quarters, and was always a source of potential danger.

FINE OPENINGS

F. Rees and H. Williams were consistently good as centres for the Old Firm, both making some fine openings which deserved to be crowned with success.

After H. Williams had attempted to open the Mountain Ash score with a dropped goal early in the game, the Pontypool forwards came away with a rush, and from a scrum Watkins cut around the blind side and sent Allen over with a try.

After a period of fluctuating play, Pontypool were forced to touch down to save their line. They attempted to take the Old Firm off their guard with a quick drop out, but J. R. Davies caught the ball and dropped a goal.

Forward play became keen after this and remained so to the end of play, both ends being visited with bewildering rapidity. A dashing raid by Phil Davies and J. Lloyd put Pontypool definitely on the defensive, but Axford relieved with a kick upfield, and Atkins dashing up took the ball at his feet the length of the field to score a try.

10 March 1934

Aberaman – Mountain Ash Split!

The Aberdare Leader reported, "What is the mystery underlying and undermining the relationship between Aberaman RFC and their near rivals, Mountain Ash? It is a regrettable fact that the two games arranged between the Clubs for the present season have been abruptly and unconditionally "called off". Moreover, I have it on very reliable authority that Mountain Ash are adamant in their attitude. Exactly what that "attitude" means I do not know. The Aberaman Committee apparently have very much the same feeling toward the Old Firm and the result has been the building up of a very ugly looking barrier. Indeed, the chances of renewing friendly connections between the two either for next season or for many seasons to come, seem to be highly improbable….from a financial standpoint, this state of affairs undoubtedly knocks both Clubs rather badly, for the reason that the games, home and away, invariably attract some of the biggest gates of the season. Why then, kill the goose that lays the golden egg? Surely neither Aberaman or Mountain Ash money coffers are so full that they can apparently afford to turn down this very useful contribution to their yearly takings!"

12 May 1934

<u>Aberdare 0 Mountain Ash 16</u>
<u>Bravo The Old Firm! Fine Win Over "Special" XV At Aberdare</u>

The Aberdare Leader reported, "Aberdare sprang a surprise on Saturday when, for their game with Mountain Ash, they fielded a XV composed with about half a dozen exceptions, of players drawn from the three first class west Wales Clubs, Swansea, Neath and Aberavon, with D.R. Prosser, the Neath Welsh Cap, as their spearhead of the attack. Notable figures in the side were Phil Lloyd (Swansea) full back, Islwyn Davies (Neath) right wing, Banfield (Aberavon) right centre, Glyn Davies (Neath) left centre, D. Evans (Neath) at stand-off and three Neath men in the forwards in addition to Prosser. It was to the glory of the Old Firm that they thoroughly and deservedly whipped this "team of all the talents". It was a grand victory for the Mount, and though an Aberdarian myself, I revelled in seeing them out-class and out-last the homesters by sheer skill, speed and stamina. There is a glamour about the Old Firm. They remain in second class ranks, but they defeat XVs like Pontypool and Aberavon on merit. They play pretty football. Though they were not at full strength on Saturday, they gave a splendid all round display….there is no doubt that Mountain Ash left the field having enhanced their already big reputation. The Old Firm have a grand line of threes. Johnny Jones and Johnny Lloyd are two fast, thrustful wings with plenty of "guts". Rees is a clever and elusive centre and Haydn Williams a reliable partner. The Davies', J.R. and Phil, are effective half backs, and the forwards are a grand pack with Kempson, Manfield, Baverstock and Williams the pick."

Season 1934/35

Old Firm Hit New Heights

If season 1932/33 was magnificent, then this one was even more so, as the Old Firm swept almost all before them. A known playing record of 22 wins, 3 draws and only 3 losses from the 28 games played, with 386 points scored, including 79+ tries, and a mere 82 conceded, to give a win rate of 83.93%, summed it all up. Of the 3 defeats suffered, two were against Aberavon, 11-7 away after a 12 match unbeaten run to start the season, and a first home defeat in the 13-4 loss in April 1935. There was also an 8-0 defeat at Abertillery, who were a tough nut to crack in this era and had showed their strength five years earlier by finishing 1929/30 as Welsh champions. The season saw "doubles" over Pontypridd, Blaenavon – the previous season's Monmouthshire League champions – and Glamorgan Wanderers. There were also home wins over Treorchy, Bargoed, Penygraig, Crumlin, Cross Keys, Abertillery and Ynysybwl. The Old Firm also travelled to Devon just before Christmas 1934, beating Teignmouth 14-0. Unfortunately, the season ended prematurely for the Club in April 1935 after it was suspended from playing for the rest of the season by the WRU for organising a junior rugby competition and playing two matches in the "close season" of 1933/34. The season also saw the passing of former Welsh International Fred Millar, who was the first player to be capped directly from the Club, gaining 7 caps between 1896 and 1901. He passed away in March 1935, aged 65.

Fixtures 1934/35

Opponents	Date	Venue	Score	Tries	Scorers/Comments
Pontypridd League	3 Sep 1934	Home	46-0	Unknown	Scorers unknown.
Ystrad Rhondda	10 Sep 1934	Home	3-0	1	Lloyd T.
Treorchy	17 Sep 1934	Home	14-8	2	Baverstock T, Lloyd T, Haydn Williams DG, Les Manfield 2C.
Aberdare	24 Sep 1934	Home	21-0	5	Haydn Williams T, J.R. Davies T, Frank Kempson T, Phil Davies T, Lloyd T, Baverstock 2C, Les Manfield C.
Bargoed	1 Oct 1934	Home	33-0	7	Haydn Williams 3T, M. Davies T, DG, P.C. Williams T, Frank Kempson T, Les Manfield T, Baverstock 4C.
Blaenavon	8 Oct 1934	Away	5-3	1	Frank Kempson T, Baverstock C.
Pontypridd	15 Oct 1934	Away	6-0	2	John Lloyd T, Frank Kempson T.
Penygraig	22 Oct 1934	Home	20-6	4	Phil Davies T, John Lloyd T, J. Jones T, Mervyn Davies T, F. Rees DG, Baverstock 2C.

Opponents	Date	Venue	Score	Tries	Scorers/Comments
Merthyr	29 Oct 1934	Away	6-0	2	John Lloyd T, C. Davies T.
Crumlin	5 Nov 1934	Home	13-6	3	John Lloyd 2T, Haydn Williams T, Baverstock 2C.
Aberdare	17 Nov 1934	Away	32-3	8	Haydn Williams 3T, P.C. Baverstock T, 4C, John Lloyd T, T. Williams T, F. Rees T, Frank Kempson T.
Glamorgan Wanderers	19 Nov 1934	Home	26-0	6	F. Rees 2T, DG, T.D. Williams 2T, Lloyd T, P.C. Williams T, Baverstock 2C.
Aberavon	26 Nov 1934	Away	7-11	1	T.D. Williams T, Fred Rees DG.
Merthyr	3 Dec 1934	Home	17-0	4	T.D. Williams T, P, Haydn Williams T, Rees T, J. Lloyd T, Baverstock C.
Abertillery	10 Dec 1934	Away	0-8	0	No scorers.
Ynysybwl	17 Dec 1934	Home	15-0	3	John Lloyd T, Mervyn Davies T, T.D. Williams T, Haydn Williams DG, Baverstock C.
Maesteg	24 Dec 1934	Away	3-3	1	Fred Rees T.
Teignmouth	28 Dec 1934	Away	14-0	4	Baverstock T, C, Fred Rees T, Les Manfield T, J. Davies T.
Cross Keys	7 Jan 1935	Home	6-0	2	T.D. Williams 2T.
Ystrad	14 Jan 1935	Away	9-5	3	T. Lloyd 2T, R. Grant T.
Newport United	21 Jan 1935	Away	0-0	0	No scorers.
Blaenavon	28 Jan 1935	Home	28-3	8	Fred Rees 2T, John Jones 2T, T.D. Williams 2T, P.C. Williams 2T, P.C. Baverstock 2C.
Crumlin	11 Feb 1935	Away	0-0	0	No scorers.

Opponents	Date	Venue	Score	Tries	Scorers/Comments
Glamorgan Wanderers	25 Feb 1935	Away	10-0	2	Fred Rees T, J. Lloyd T, P.C. Baverstock 2C.
Pontypridd	18 Mar 1935	Home	20-0	4	T.D. Williams 2T, Fred Rees T, DG, John Jones T, P.C. Baverstock 2C.
Abertillery	25 Mar 1935	Home	8-6	2	Phil Davies T, P.C. Sheedy T, P.C. Baverstock C.
Ynysybwl	2 Apr 1935	Home	20-7	4	Lloyd 2T, P.C. Baverstock T, 2C, Haydn Williams T, J.R. Davies DG.
Aberavon	6 Apr 1935	Home	4-13	0	Jack Davies DG.

Summary of Playing Record

P	W	D	L	For	Against	Tries Scored	Win Rate %
28	22	3	3	386	82	79+	83.93

Match Reports & Publications

15 October 1934

<u>Pontypridd 0 Mountain Ash 6</u>
<u>Western Mail</u>

PONTYPRIDD LOSE RECORD

Rugby records of various kinds are rapidly disappearing. Several of them have been ended during the last week. Among those to meet that fate were Pontypridd's ground record and their record of immunity from defeat.

Mountain Ash, now the most prominent of the Welsh clubs which have escaped defeat, deprived Pontypridd of their records, mainly because the "Old Firm's" forwards insisted upon having matters their own way.

Pontypridd did a tremendous amount of defensive work, but Mountain Ash scored two tries, to which there was no response. Phil Davies made an opening for J. Lloyd to score the first, and the second, by Kempson, came from a movement started by P.C. Williams.

22 October 1934

<u>Mountain Ash 20 Penygraig 6</u>
<u>Western Mail</u>

The Western Mail commented in its match report of this win, "....the Mountain Ash backs did all the scoring for their side and touched brilliance."

17 November 1934

Aberdare 3 Mountain Ash 32

Mount Team: M. Davies, F. Rees, T. D. Williams, H. Williams, J. Lloyd, P. Davies, J. R. Davies, F. Kempson, P. C. Baverstock, P. C. Travers, J. Davies, R. Jeffries, P. C. Williams, R. James, F. Wright.

Old Firm Run Riot

The Aberdare Leader reported, "Aberdare was riddled and shattered almost beyond hope at the Ynys to give the Old Firm their 12th successive win this season and add glory to their undefeated record. Mountain Ash are a jolly good side, even the most sombre looking of Aberdare's supporters would tell you that readily, and a bit enviously….but there was to be no denying Mountain Ash's greater craft and all round superiority. They maintained their best traditions for forward play – a lusty, tireless pack grandly led by Frank Kempson and Baverstock, with several others doing good support work….two of Mountain Ash's tries in the first half were gems of constructive play."

19 November 1934

Mountain Ash 26 Glamorgan Wanderers 0
Western Mail

OTHER RUGBY GAMES   By "Old Stager"
MOUNTAIN ASH STILL WINNING

The Western Mail reported, "The prolonged immunity from defeat of Mountain Ash, and the fact that they are able to defeat a Club of the standing of Glamorgan Wanderers – a Club which has for years been on the fringe of the first class organisations – by a clear 26 points, suggests that the Old Firm ought to be given a chance against some of the strongest Clubs in Wales."

Aberdare Leader
Old Firm First Class! Glamorgan Wanderers Crushed

The Aberdare Leader reported, "Last Saturday's game at the Rec certainly marked an epoch in the history of the Old Firm, for they definitely passed from second raters into the first flight, and those South Wales organisations which have been for too long in the limelight as "first class clubs" will be compelled to sit up and take notice….Glamorgan Wanderers….came, they saw, but they returned vanquished, in fact crushed."

26 November 1934

Aberavon 11 Mountain Ash 7
Western Mail

MOUNTAIN ASH LOSE RECORD
But Make Many Friends at Port Talbot

	G.	T.	Pts.
Aberavon	*2	1	11
Mountain Ash	†1	1	7

*One penalty. †Dropped.
Attendance, 4,000.

The Western Mail reported, "Although Mountain Ash sacrificed their record to Aberavon on Saturday, they played magnificent football and won the wholehearted admiration of the largest crowd of the season. They played with skill and cleverness, and if there was any weakness in their team work it was, perhaps, at forward, where the pack at times showed a lack of initiative against their heavier and faster opponents. It was due to Aberavon's really brilliant forward display that they were able to dictate terms. When the ball got among the Old Firm backs, there was always danger, the brothers Davies at half back making quick and clever contact with a very fine third line in which T.D. Williams was undoubtedly the star. Williams, as a result of a concerted movement, opened the scoring for Mountain Ash in the first five minutes....Jack Thomas equalised with a very fine try which was goaled. Then....Vickery gave Aberavon the lead. In the second half, T.O. James added a penalty, which appeared to make the game safe. That, however, was not so, for Mountain Ash sprung numerous surprises, and when Fred Rees reduced Aberavon's lead to only 4 points with an opportune dropped goal, they contested the issue strenuously right up to the final whistle. As far as Mountain Ash were concerned, it was team work which made their play so virile and attractive."

7 January 1935

Mountain Ash 6 Cross Keys 0

Old Firm Win

The Western Mail reported, "....as the game progressed it became more and more evident that the rapier-like movements of the Old Firm were more likely to bring scores than the heavy battering-ram attacks of the Monmouthshire men....The Old Firm's three-quarters were not at their best....When they did get going, they had the defence spread-eagled...."

25 February 1935

Glamorgan Wanderers 0 Mountain Ash 10

Western Mail

OTHER RUGBY GAMES

By "Old Stager"

MOUNTAIN ASH TOO GOOD FOR WANDERERS

appeared when Tredegar secured tries

The Western Mail reported, "Mountain Ash have been playing such delightful rugby and achieving so many successes this season, that it is difficult to believe a rumour that their game against Glamorgan Wanderers was dull and fierce...."

18 March 1935

Mountain Ash 20 Pontypridd 0

Western Mail

"Old Firm's" Triumph

Pontypridd must have deteriorated to a marked extent in recent weeks. At Mountain Ash they were completely outclassed and beaten by 20 points. T. D. Williams (2), John Jones, and F. Rees scored tries. Baverstock converted two and F. Rees dropped a goal.

23 March 1935

Tragic Death of Mr Fred Miller, Mountain Ash

The Aberdare Leader reported, "With tragic suddenness, one of our old and respected townsmen dropped dead at Abercynon on Monday at the age of 65. Mr Fred Miller (or Millar) of Cardiff Road, Mountain Ash, was employed at Merthyr Vale Colliery in the grain shed. He had been very unwell for two or three months and decided to start work again although advised not to do so. He left Mountain Ash by the 6:10 Taff and arrived at Abercynon. Leaving the train to catch the Merthyr bus at the Navigation Hotel, he collapsed and had died before Dr Thomas arrived on the scene. He had no children. His wife, Catherine, predeceased him some years ago, but of late he had been carefully tended to by an adopted daughter. Mr Miller was an old playing member for Mountain Ash Rugby team and is spoken of as one of the most brilliant forwards that the Old Firm ever had. In proof of this he was capped by the Welsh Rugby Union on no fewer than 7 occasions in 1896, 1900 and 1901. In the latter year, he left for the North, joining the Hull team of the Northern Rugby Union where he remained 4 years. He returned to Mountain Ash where he became a faithful supporter of the Old Firm until last Saturday."

25 March 1935

Mountain Ash 8 Abertillery 6
Western Mail

MORE SNAP IN ATTACK

Where Mountain Ash Beat Abertillery

	G.	T.	Pts.
Mountain Ash	1	1	8
Abertillery	*1	1	6

*Penalty.

Rarely has a game been played to a finish under such heart-breaking weather conditions as prevailed at Mountain Ash. Yet, in spite of a howling wind and a field which was a quagmire, the game abounded in thrilling movements and play generally was of a high standard.

Play did not deteriorate into a forward duel, although the opposing packs strove relentlessly for the mastery in mid-field —a struggle which ended in the "Old Firm" gaining a slight superiority.

Both three-quarter lines attempted to open up the game, but again it was the "Old Firm's" three-quarter line which showed to better advantage. Their movements were swifter and cleaner, and it was this snappiness in attack, coupled with judicious kicking, which gave the "Old Firm" a narrow but well-deserved victory.

Had Abertillery taken advantage of the wind in the second half as cleverly as the "Old Firm" had in the first half a different result might have been recorded. However, they relied upon the battering ram attacks of their forwards —a policy which was doomed to failure owing to the youthful virility of the Mountain Ash pack.

The only score in the first half was a try by Phil Davies following a scrum on the Abertillery line. Neatly side-stepping Rees, he crossed the line, Baverstock converting.

After a period of mid-field forward play in the second half Abertillery attacked strongly and Norster scored a try, but two minutes later Sheedy was awarded a try for obstruction by a visiting forward. Brooks registered a penalty goal for Abertillery in the closing stages.

13 April 1935

<u>Calamity For Old Firm</u>
<u>Suspended For Remainder Of Season</u>

The Aberdare Leader reported, "Last week will certainly go down in history as the Old Firm's "Black Week".... The Welsh Rugby Union suspended Mountain Ash RFC on Thursday for the remainder of the season. The news burst on all Welsh supporters like a bombshell but in Mountain Ash it was a catastrophe. The curious thing is that the officials of the Club know so very little of the actual charges that the Union have levelled against them, and as a matter of fact, I was informed by the Chairman, Mr Shad Lewis, and the Secretary, Mr Edward Bradwick, no official of the Club had been invited to the Union meeting to give them an opportunity of rebutting any charges of breaking the Union's rules. The Union allege the Mountain Ash team played two matches, on August 31 and May 7, during the "close season" of 1934. The Club deny playing any match on August 31, but regarding the other match say it was a charity match for the hospital and the whole of the money received was handed over to the hospital authorities without the deduction of one penny piece. Another charge is that of organising a series of games in the form of a junior tournament. This is also strenuously denied. The junior teams' tournament was organised by the Supporters Club, with which the seniors (the Old Firm) had nothing whatever to do. It is not known at present what action (if any) the Club Officials will take, but the matter is very serious, as there were six matches still to play like Upper Clacton."

THE OLD FIRM'S PROUD PAST

Mountain Ash Rugby Football Club
"The Old Firm"
Season 1934/35

MOUNTAIN ASH RUGBY TEAM

Back Row L-R: Dan Horrigan (Trainer), C. Williams, P.C. Travers, D.T. Jeffries, P.C. Sheedy, Frank Kempson, R. Davies, Ned Bradwick (Secretary),

Middle Row L-R: P.C. Baverstock, Phil Davies, J.R. Davies Capt, J.H. Williams, T. Lloyd, G. Davies,

Front Row L-R: T. Smith, G.I. Davies, Les Manfield, Fred Evans.

The Seasons 1930-1935
Not Quite A "Golden Era" But Still Impressive

The Old Firm had a very impressive first half of the 1930s with a playing record as follows:

Season	P	W	D	L	For	Against	Tries Scored	%
1930/31	26	17	2	7	192+	101+	45+	69.23
1931/32	32	21	2	9	332	187	56+	68.75
1932/33	33	25	2	6	363	120	78+	78.79
1933/34	26	13	4	9	228+	148+	49+	57.69
1934/35	28	22	3	3	386	82	79+	83.93
Total	145	98	13	34	1501+	638+	307+	72.07

There was a hat-trick of Glamorgan League Championships in 1930/31, 1931/32 and 1932/33, a relatively poor season in 1933/34 and then a return to form with a vengeance in 1934/35. Pontypool RFC, who were Welsh champions in 1931/32, were beaten 17-6 in 1930/31, 16-3 in 1932/33, and narrowly won in their Championship season at the Rec, 6-3, after the game was abandoned with 25 minutes left, with the Western Mail stating in its match report, "The Old Firm were now definitely superior, but after 15 minutes of play (in the second half), the referee brought the game to an end owing to the conditions." There were wins over Aberavon, Bridgend, Cardiff, Treorchy, Cross Keys, Penarth, Glamorgan Wanderers, Pontypridd, Abertillery, Maesteg, Ebbw Vale, Penygraig and, of course, Pontypool. With an excellent playing record and trophies to match, the only thing missing was International recognition, and it is this that was the determining factor in not classing these 5 years as the "Third Golden Era".

Season 1935/36

Disappointing Season For Old Firm

After five impressive seasons, the Old Firm's form slumped with the result they lost more games than they won. Ten games were lost in the first half of the season but Mount rallied after the New Year to win 7 from the 9 played. As usual, the season had its high points. There was a "double" over Ebbw Vale, home wins over Glamorgan Wanderers, Penygraig, Blaenavon, Pill Harriers and Penarth, and an away win at Pontypridd. There were close losses at home to Cardiff Athletic, Crumlin and Maesteg, the first two by a point and the latter by 3. The end of season playing record showed 22 games played, 9 won, 1 drawn and 12 lost, with 143 points scored, which included at least 35 tries, and 125 conceded, to give a win rate of 43.18%. In September 1935, Neath requested the transfer of Mount's future International backrow forward, Les Manfield, with the Aberdare Leader reporting, "The news that Neath RFC have applied for the transfer of the young and brilliant forward, Les Manfield, has come as a great shock to Mountain Ash supporters. Manfield, on this form, is the equal of any player in South Wales and is almost certain to be capped before this season ends." Manfield, though, never transferred and continued to play for the Old Firm. At the end of the season, the Club's trainer since rugby resumed after the First World War, Dan Horrigan – surname pronounced "orrigan" – who was a native of Cork in Ireland and had lived and worked in the town for over 30 years, passed away suddenly.

Fixtures 1935/36

Opponents	Date	Venue	Score	Tries	Scorers/Comments
Cross Keys	16 Sep 1935	Away	3-9	1	Fred Rees T.
Treorchy	23 Sep 1935	Away	6-19	1	Evan Isaacs T, P.C. Baverstock P.
Penygraig	30 Sep 1935	Home	21-3	5	Fred Rees 2T, Frank Kempson T, Haydn Williams T, Lewis T, P.C. Baverstock 3C.
Glamorgan Police	12 Oct 1935	Home	12-22	3+	Russ Grant T, Fred Rees T, Williams T, AN Other 3pts.
Glamorgan Wanderers	14 Oct 1935	Away	0-9	0	No scorers.
Pill Harriers	21 Oct 1935	Home	8-0	2	J.R. Davies T, Fred Rees T, Grant C.
Crumlin	28 Oct 1935	Away	3-6	1	E. Oliver T.
Penygraig	4 Nov 1935	Away	3-3	1	Cled Williams T.
Abertillery	11 Nov 1935	Away	3-9	1	Fred Rees T.
Cardiff Athletic	18 Nov 1935	Home	3-4	1	Haydn Williams T.
Maesteg	25 Nov 1935	Away	0-8	0	No scorers.
Penarth	2 Dec 1935	Away	0-6	0	No scorers.
Maesteg	30 Dec 1935	Home	0-3	0	No scorers.
Welsh Collegians	6 Jan 1936	Home	15-4	3	Phil Davies 2T, Fred Rees T, C, J. Lloyd DG.
Pontypridd	13 Jan 1936	Away	3-0	0	Fred Rees P.

Opponents	Date	Venue	Score	Tries	Scorers/Comments
Blaenavon	22 Feb 1936	Home	13-0	3	Fred Rees T, 2C, Mervyn Davies T, Thomas T.
Ebbw Vale	2 Mar 1936	Away	6-0	2	E. Thomas T, M. Lloyd T.
Crumlin	9 Mar 1936	Home	3-4	0	Fred Rees P.
Ebbw Vale	28 Mar 1936	Home	17-0	5	Cled Williams 2T, Haydn Williams 2T, N. Ellis T, Manfield C.
Glamorgan Wanderers	6 Apr 1936	Home	8-0	2	D. Lloyd T, P.C. Williams T, Fred Rees C.
Pill Harriers	20 Apr 1936	Away	5-16	1	Fred Rees T, M. De Lloyd C.
Penarth	21 Apr 1936	Home	11-0	3	Fred Rees T, C, Haydn Williams T, Davies T.

Summary of Playing Record

P	W	D	L	For	Against	Tries Scored	Win Rate %
22	9	1	12	143	125	35+	43.18

Match Reports & Publications

10 August 1935

Old Firm's Annual Meeting
Prospects of Good Season

The Aberdare Leader reported, "The Annual General Meeting of the Mountain Ash RFC was held at the Glancynon Hotel on Thursday when Mr Shad Lewis presided over a good attendance. The Secretary, Mr Edward Bradwick, read the financial statement which was passed as satisfactory, showing a small balance on the right side. Referring to last season, the Secretary spoke in eulogistic terms of the loyalty of the playing members. They had come through a trying season with great credit and had maintained the high reputation that the Club had held for so many years. Certainly they had suffered a setback when the W.R.U. suspended their last six matches, five of them home games. Mr Bradwick continued that most members had forgotten the incident and like good sportsmen were rallying round the Old Firm's "flag". It was his pleasant duty to inform them that all of last year's successful team was available and that the Rec, after its rest of 5 months, was in excellent condition.

The following Officials were elected, President: Mr E.M. Hann; Chairman: Mr Shad Lewis; Vice Chairman: Mr Wyndham Christopher; Treasurer: Mr W. E. Gough; Secretary: Mr Edward Bradwick (for the 10th successive year); Captain: Mr Frank Kempson."

23 September 1935

Treorchy 19 Mountain Ash 6

The Western Mail commented about the Old Firm's loss at Treorchy and Pontypridd's home defeat to Blaina, "Two of the Welsh Clubs which have been on the fringe of first class circles for some years, Mountain Ash and Pontypridd, met with unexpected reverses on Saturday."

11 November 1935

<u>Abertillery 9 Mountain Ash 3</u>

The Western Mail reported, "Mountain Ash certainly had most of the game and yet lost, a result with which no spectator can quarrel....whereas Abertillery were quick to profit by their opponents' errors, they were fortunate in not finding their own being exploited. In the second half Abertillery were almost continuously on the defensive....and again it was good fortune and not good intent that came to their rescue."

2 December 1935

<u>Penarth 6 Mountain Ash 0</u>
<u>Handling Did Not Pay</u>

The Western Mail commented about this game, "Far too often did Mountain Ash endeavour to launch their attacks through passing among the backs only to find the slippery ball beyond their control....It was the losers, however, who possessed the best back on the field in Fred Rees, who made many smart bursts down the centre."

30 December 1935

<u>Mountain Ash 0 Maesteg 3</u>

The Western Mail reported, "Maesteg accomplished the rare feat of winning at Mountain Ash. According to my Mountain Ash correspondent, Maesteg spent three-fourths of the time in magnificent defensive efforts against a superior team...."

13 January 1936

<u>Pontypridd 0 Mountain Ash 3</u>
<u>Western Mail</u>

OTHER RUGBY GAMES   By "Old Stager"

"OLD FIRM" SUBDUE PONTYPRIDD

Mountain Ash have not been doing too well of late, and their victory at Pontypridd, though by the narrow margin of a penalty goal to nil, will, therefore, be welcomed.

Pontypridd's supporters regarded the contest as one of the most unsatisfactory of the season, for Mountain Ash had a sufficiently tight grip to completely subdue Pontypridd—indeed, had it not been for a particularly fine game by Tom Williams, the Pontypridd full-back, Mountain Ash would have won much more easily. Fred Rees kicked the winning goal.

22 February 1936

<u>Mountain Ash 13 Blaenavon 0</u>

The Aberdare Leader reported, "An old Mountain Ash ruggerite informs me it is necessary to go back to 1895 to find a spell of idleness by the Old Firm comparable to this season. In 1895 there were thirteen weeks of continued frost and ten matches had to be cut out. This season, however, has not such a tale of woe to tell, for only 6 matches have been put off or abandoned."

2 March 1936

Ebbw Vale 0 Mountain Ash 6
Stormy Weather

The Western Mail reported, "Ebbw Vale and Mountain Ash had really wintry conditions, play proceeding in heavy rain, sleet and snowstorms. Mountain Ash were fortunate in having those storms at their backs in the opening half in which 2 tries were scored which won the match."

28 March 1936

Mountain Ash 17 Ebbw Vale 0
Old Firm In Form
Ebbw Vale Outclassed

The Aberdare Leader reported, "Mountain Ash certainly surpassed anything they have done this season and indeed the game compared favourably with many of the old hard fought battles of the past. It was brilliant and sparkling throughout, Ebbw Vale were the visitors and played real good football. Vigorous onslaughts at the start by the Old Firm were splendidly repulsed. The Mount's three-quarters were constantly on the move…. Some very fine passing movements were seen by the Old Firm's three-quarters."

21 April 1936

Mountain Ash 11 Penarth 0
Old Firm Win-All Round Improvement Against Penarth

The Western Mail reported, "In what proved to be the Old Firm's best exhibition at Mountain Ash this season, they gained a well-marked victory….The Old Firm showed an all round improvement. The forwards, after a shaky beginning, settled down to control the scrummages, while the handling movements of the three-quarters were delightful. Penarth pinned their faith to steamroller tactics by their forwards, but time and again they were thwarted by their lighter opponents who snatched the ball from their feet and darted away….A magnificent run by Haydn Williams brought the Old Firm their final try."

16 May 1936

Old Firm's Trainer
Sudden Death of Mr D. Horgan

The Aberdare Leader reported, "It was with deep regret that sportsmen in the lower part of the valley heard on Wednesday week of the sudden death of Mr Daniel Horgan, 33 Bailey Street, Miskin. Widespread sympathy goes out to Mrs Horgan and family in their bereavement. "Dan" Horgan……came to Miskin, Mountain Ash 37 years ago from….County Cork, Ireland, and obtained work at the timber yard of the Deep Dyffryn Colliery. He was 56 years of age and was a well known figure in local sporting circles. Himself a keen sportsman, he had been trainer to Mountain Ash R.F.C. for 20+ years and was a member of the committee. Prior to the Mountain Ash v Cross Keys game last week, a tribute to his memory was paid by the teams who observed a two minute silence. The Club will miss the services of a keen official and a steadfast supporter."

Season 1936/37

<u>Mount Return To Winning Ways</u>

After a disappointing 1935/36 season, the Old Firm returned to something like the form of previous seasons. There were "doubles" over Blaenavon, Cilfynydd and Penarth, and home wins over Cardiff Athletic, Glamorgan Wanderers, Cinderford and university teams from London and Cardiff, with Mount forward Les Manfield playing for the latter due to him studying there. The biggest home win of the season came against Pontypridd who were beaten 17-0 in April 1937. The Old Firm won at Ebbw Vale and Pill Harriers, and of the 4 games drawn, 3 were away from home – at Cardiff Athletic, Cinderford and Tredegar – with the home draw being against Ebbw Vale. The heaviest loss of the season – 20-3 – came at Aberavon on Christmas Day 1936. All this added up to an end of season playing record of 15 wins, 4 draws and 9 losses from the 28 known games played, in which 168 points were scored, which included 40+ tries, and 132 conceded, to give a win rate of 60.71%.

Fixtures 1936/37

Opponents	Date	Venue	Score	Tries	Scorers/Comments
Maesteg	7 Sep 1936	Away	0-6	0	No scorers.
Cilfynydd	14 Sept 1936	Home	3-0	1	Haydn Williams T.
Cardiff Athletic	28 Sep 1936	Home	12-11	2	Haydn Williams T, DG, A. Evans T, W. McArthur C.
Abertillery	12 Oct 1936	Away	5-8	1	Crad Davies T, W. McArthur C.
Glamorgan Wanderers	19 Oct 1936	Home	6-3	2	Phil Davies T, Lloyd T.
Blaenavon	26 Oct 1936	Away	3-0	1	AN Other T.
Ebbw Vale	2 Nov 1936	Home	8-8	1	Bailey T, W. McArthur P, C.
Cardiff Athletic	9 Nov 1936	Away	0-0	0	No scorers.
Glamorgan Wanderers	23 Nov 1936	Away	0-11	0	No scorers.
Cilfynydd	30 Nov 1936	Home	0-7	0	No scorers.
Cinderford	7 Dec 1936	Away	0-0	0	No scorers.
Crumlin	21 Dec 1936	Away	0-3	0	No scorers.
Aberavon	28 Dec 1936	Away	3-20	0+	Scorer unknown.
Pontardawe	28 Dec 1936	Home	15-0	4	J. Jones 2T, Phil Davies T, Haydn Williams T, Mervyn Davies P.
Penarth	4 Jan 1937	Away	12-0	4	Roy West 2T, N. Williams T, McArthur T.
Ebbw Vale	18 Jan 1937	Away	5-3	1	E. Lloyd T, T. Smith C.
Cardiff University	25 Jan 1937	Home	8-3	2	C. Davies 2T, McArthur C.
Abercarn	15 Feb 1937	Home	3-8	1	G. Jones T.

Opponents	Date	Venue	Score	Tries	Scorers/Comments
Cilfynydd	22 Feb 1937	Away	5-3	1	Jack Davies T, McArthur C.
Penarth	8 Mar 1937	Home	8-0	2	John Lloyd 2T, McArthur C.
Cinderford	22 Mar 1937	Home	9-0	2	McArthur T, P, Kelly T.
Pill Harriers	27 Mar 1937	Away	8-3	1	Ken Jones T, McArthur P, C.
London University	29 Mar 1937	Home	8-3	2	Percy Jones T, C. Williams T, McArthur C.
Maesteg	30 Mar 1937	Home	0-3	0	No scorers.
Pill Harriers	5 Apr 1937	Home	8-11	2	Haydn Williams T, Percy Jones T, McArthur C.
Pontypridd	12 Apr 1937	Home	17-0	5	L. Evans 4T, Percy Jones T, McArthur C.
Tredegar	19 Apr 1937	Away	3-3	1	Len Jones T.
Blaenavon	26 Apr 1937	Home	19-15	4	G. Jones 3T, C. Williams T, P.C. George P, McArthur 2C.

Summary of Playing Record

P	W	D	L	For	Against	Tries Scored	Win Rate %
28	15	4	9	168	132	40+	60.71

Match Reports & Publications

12 October 1936

Abertillery 8 Mountain Ash 5
Old Firm Spurn Chances at Abertillery

The Western Mail reported, "Abertillery and Mountain Ash ended their match at Abertillery on Saturday in semi-darkness. The kick off was unusually late, no allowance having apparently been made for the cessation of Summer time. As for the game, it was a general strenuous affair….There was much to admire about the play of many individuals….Mountain Ash paid the penalty for misused opportunities by losing the game…. Perhaps the man who had most to complain of in the result was Phil Davies, the Mountain Ash scrum half. Keen, tireless, and efficient, he did more to keep his side on their toes than anyone else. It was a great pity that most of his efforts were negatived because his colleagues failed to play their part with equal proficiency. He was also prominent for some well judged defensive kicking, in which he was well supported by Haydn Williams…."

2 November 1936

<u>Mountain Ash 8 Ebbw Vale 8</u>

The Western Mail reported, "Ebbw Vale deserve credit and encouragement for securing a draw at Mountain Ash."

4 January 1937

<u>Penarth 0 Mountain Ash 12</u>

NOT SUCH A "VETERAN"

West's Big Part in "Old Firm's" Victory

Mount Team: I. Davies, N. Williams, J. Davies, K. Jones, G. Jones, J. Jones, R. West, R. Grant, T. Thomas, E. Lloyd, W. Crockett, A. McArthur, D. Kelly, W. Pritchard, L. Evans.

The Western Mail reported, "By lending Phil Davies, their usual inside half, to Swansea, Mountain Ash were forced to call on the services of Roy West, a veteran as rugby players go, for their match with Penarth on Saturday. West justified his inclusion in every way, for not only was he prominent with clever defensive kicking, but he was largely responsible for the Seasiders' defeat, for besides scoring two fine tries, he had a hand in a third. Play had remained in Penarth's 25 for some time before a scrum was formed, from which the Old Firm heeled. Quick as a flash, West seized the opportunity and darted through for a corner try. His next score came in an identical manner....The difference between the two packs was most marked, for whereas Penarth were the better eight by far in the loose, Mountain Ash demonstrated their superiority in the set scrums."

18 January 1937

<u>Ebbw Vale 3 Mountain Ash 5</u>

The Western Mail reported, "Ebbw Vale maintained their remarkable improvement in form against Mountain Ash, whose victory was restricted."

22 February 1937

<u>Cilfynydd 3 Mountain Ash 5</u>

The Western Mail reported, "Mr George Hall, M.P., was among the record crowd at Cilfynydd when Mountain Ash won the "rubber" by defeating Cilfynydd...."

8 March 1937

Mountain Ash 8 Penarth 0
Western Mail

THEIR TRIES WERE LUCKY

But Mountain Ash Deserved to Beat Penarth

"Inasmuch as Mountain Ash showed a slight superiority and were in control for the greater part of the game, no one can cavil at their victory, even though that victory only came as a result of what must be fairly described as lucky tries. Mountain Ash were superior in three-quarter play and scrummaging....Gwyn Davies and John Lloyd had a perfect understanding at the base of the scrum, and this perfection of understanding enabled the Old Firm to initiate many good movements....In the second half, a blinding snowstorm complicated matters but, strange to say, play improved. After a ding-dong struggle, John Lloyd scored a try for Mountain Ash from a melee near the Penarth line...."

27 March 1937

Pill Harriers 3 Mountain Ash 8
Smart Old Firm
Strong Pill Harriers Side Beaten

The Western Mail commented, "Though they had the assistance of several men who had played for Newport, Pill had to acknowledge defeat at the hands of a smart Mountain Ash side....Mountain Ash played five three-quarters and seven forwards and had the pull behind the scrum where Roy West, their inside half, played storming football. Ken Jones, one of three brothers in the Mountain Ash three-quarters, was another clever back...."

12 April 1937

Mountain Ash 17 Pontypridd 0

The Western Mail reported, "Mountain Ash returned to something like their old form against Pontypridd, who fielded several substitutes and paid the penalty in losing by 17 points."

Season 1937/38

Tumultuous Season For Mount

Although the known playing record was won 7, drawn 2, and lost 11 of the 20 known games played – a disappointing return for the season, but hardly disastrous – the Aberdare Leader's reporter, "The Watchman", wrote quite a number of articles about what he saw as the decline of Mountain Ash RFC and the way the Club was run, with some of his comments about players being quite scathing on times. Although a mediocre season, there were wins against Glamorgan Wanderers, Pontypridd, and the Monmouthshire Clubs of Abercarn, Blaenavon, Crumlin and Pill Harriers, and home draws against Abertillery and Ebbw Vale. There were more losses than usual but the 44-5 defeat at Aberavon struck a raw nerve, especially in the Aberdare Leader where it was reported as the heaviest defeat in the Club's history, which was probably right as the Old Firm had never been a walkover for any "class" of opposition. Defeats on this scale for any Club, let alone Mountain Ash RFC, were virtually unheard of back then, "The Watchman" seeing this record defeat as unacceptable, and commenting in the Aberdare Leader, "is this once famous institution, probably the last in the town forming a link with the past, to pass into oblivion under our very noses? Cannot anything be done to save the situation?" Whether the poor season and all these comments in the Aberdare Leader influenced the decision of the Club Chairman, Shad Lewis, to resign is unknown, but finish he did. He was subsequently made a Life Member of the Club but whether it was done at this time is not known. During his involvement with the Club, he supported the Old Firm financially and helped keep the rugby union flag flying in the town in the dark economic days of the 1920s and 30s, which was a time when many Clubs in South Wales struggled to stay afloat, with some failing to do so. The Club also had a new Secretary to look for as "Ned" Bradwick, who had held the job for 12 years, also resigned in November 1937. With regard to fixtures with Aberaman, which had not been played since 1932/33, "The Watchman" reported in the Aberdare Leader, "matters are on a more friendly basis and I understand that fixtures will be resumed between the Clubs soon."

Fixtures 1937/38

Opponents	Date	Venue	Score	Tries	Scorers/Comments
Pill Harriers	16 Oct 1937	Home	8-5	1	Reed T, W. McArthur P, C.
Pontypridd	23 Oct 1937	Away	5-6	1	Edwin Lloyd T, W. McArthur C.
Penarth	23 Oct 1937	Away	0-16	0	No scorers.
Blaenavon	30 Oct 1937	Home	3-0	1	P.C. George T.
Pontardawe	6 Nov 1937	Away	Unknown	Unknown	Mount win. Scorers unknown.
Glamorgan Wanderers	13 Nov 1937	Away	6-0	1	P.C. George T, W. McArthur P.
University College	20 Nov 1937	Home	0-3	0	No scorers.
Pontypridd	4 Dec 1937	Away	0-4	0	No scorers.
Pontypridd	25 Dec 1937	Home	11-0	1+	Gooding T, P.C. George P, AN Other 5pts.
Abercarn	8 Jan 1938	Home	8-0	2	Percy Jones T, Bowen T, W. McArthur C.
Penarth	19 Feb 1938	Away	3-18	Unknown	Scorer unknown.
Weston-super-Mare	26 Feb 1938	Away	0-28	0	No scorers.
Pill Harriers	5 Mar 1938	Away	0-3	0	No scorers.

Opponents	Date	Venue	Score	Tries	Scorers/Comments
Aberavon	26 Mar 1938	Away	5-44	1	AN Other T, C.
Abertillery	2 Apr 1938	Home	3-3	0	Tom Smith P.
Ebbw Vale	2 Apr 1938	Away	0-26	0	No scorers.
Penarth	16 Apr 1938	Home	6-8	1	Len Jones T, W. McArthur P.
Crumlin	23 Apr 1938	Home	20-19	4	Percy Jones 2T, 2P, Ken Jones 2T, D. Kelly C.
Ebbw Vale	30 Apr 1938	Home	3-3	1	Reg Jones T.
Maesteg	Unknown	Unknown	3-8	Unknown	Scorer unknown.

Summary of Playing Record

P	W	D	L	For	Against	Tries Scored	Win Rate %
20	7	2	11	84+	194+	14+	40.00

Match Reports & Publications

16 October 1937

Mountain Ash 9 Pill Harriers 5

Mount Team: L. Davies, Harvey, Haydn Williams, P.C. George, T. Godwin, L. Reed, J.R. Davies, W. McArthur Capt, D. Glasson, W. Crockett, P.C. L. Jones, P.C. C. Williams, F. Rees, D. Kelly, E. Lloyd.

Old Firm Win But Don't Impress
Veterans Must Be Replaced

"The Watchman" reported in the Aberdare Leader, "....The return of J.R. Davies did not improve matters very much. J.R. has been a grand player, and prior to a severe injury received whilst playing for Cross Keys some years ago, was probably one of the best centres in the country. He and Haydn Williams, a great defensive player, whose crash tackling has never been excelled, even by Claude Davey, are in the veteran stage, and whilst it is with regret they must pass on, place must be found for younger and better players if the Old Firm are to return to their former glory.....A heavier pack, the acquisition of some good backs, and all will go well for the Old Firm as a side, and for the spectators as a body seeking entertainment."

The Aberdare Leader also published the following on the same date as the above match:

Mountain Ash Rugby Decline

Is There Need for Reforms.

Two Points of View.

BY THE SPORTS EDITOR.

THE DECLINE OF MOUNTAIN ASH RUGBY, WITH ITS GREAT TRADITIONS REACHING BACK OVER HALF-A-CENTURY, IS PERHAPS THE OUTSTANDING SUBJECT IN ABERDARE VALLEY SPORTS TALK THESE DAYS.

This season and last the Old Firm's performances have been very poor; "gates" have diminished; indeed, the walls of a great rugby stronghold seem to be crumbling.
WHY?

Old Supporter's Views

"A lifelong follower of Mountain Ash whom I talked with over the weekend gives some stimulating views on the matter and suggests a number of reforms which might lead to old glories being restored. Mountain Ash rugby, he declared, was too much a "one man show". No annual general meeting is held, officers and committee are appointed by one man, who generally dictates to them. He also criticises the present policy of depending on local players, claiming that this has failed everywhere. If such a policy is adopted, why not the formation of a junior rugby league from Mountain Ash to Abercynon to act as a "nursery", which would provide for the future, well trained players who might help to bring back the erstwhile glories of Mountain Ash rugger, he asks. This would be a better policy than to depend on ex-secondary school players, who, though they might have done well in schools football, are not equipped sufficiently with physique, experience, or skill to stand up to the demands of second class Welsh rugby. But this supporter of the Old Firm sees as the only policy of rebuilding the town's great rugger traditions a good XV recruited from all sources, good fixtures, open play and democratic control.

Only Way

It is only by recruiting good, experienced players from all sources that Mountain Ash can again become a great rugger power, that it will be able to field a XV capable of providing worthy opposition to first class clubs like Pontypool, Cross Keys and Aberavon, as it did in the past, he argues. Those famous sides used to come to the Rec knowing they would have to fight to keep their reputations, he added. But those great days have gone. We have lost good fixtures; we have a team that now cannot hold its own in second class games. He paid a tribute to Mr Shad Lewis, Chairman of the Club and owner of the Rec, to whom he declared must go the credit of having kept the game alive in the town for the last few years. But, he went on, speaking for the good of the Old Firm, he felt compelled to say "there is a potential Saturday "gate" of 4,000 for good rugby on the Rec. When will something be done to realise it?"

What Shad Lewis Says

"If they think they can run the Club on better lines, they are welcome to do so", was the prompt reply given to me by Mr Shad Lewis when I interviewed him on Saturday morning, adding that those who desired to handle the Club would, of course, have to pay the rent of the ground. "If they are willing to get together to take control of the team themselves, I will hand it over," he went on. But Mr Lewis' REAL reply was that there was no adequate public support for rugby in Mountain Ash. "There would still be a big, match winning team there if we had support," he said. "But even when we had our invincible XV two years ago the "gates" were small. Four thousand! That's ridiculous. Our best gate then was £20 and the average was £5 or £6 a match. There are chaps on the dole who can afford to pay 1/6 train fare, 1s admittance to see Cardiff City and won't pay 3d to see rugby here! Let the public support our Club and then we can get better players." As it was, the Club had to depend on home talent, and the position was that if the public did not give better support, then the Old Firm would have to carry on with a junior side. As an example of the lack of support given, Mr Lewis revealed that when an appeal had recently been issued to local trades people to help the Club financially, the response had been four guineas, and two guineas of this had come from outside the district! At present it was a big struggle to run the Club, and there was no "democratically elected committee" and no general meeting because there were no members! "Let us have better support and we will be able to get better players," is Mr Lewis' reply.

Fuller Reports in the Leader

As some contribution to assisting in the recovery of Mountain Ash rugby, the Aberdare Leader has arranged for full reports of matches played on the Rec with constructive criticism by our new contributor, "The Watchman", which may create more public interest."

23 October 1937

A week after the above report, in which defeats at Pontypridd, 6-5, and Penarth, 16-0, were suffered, the Aberdare Leader's reporter, "The Watchman", commented, "The fixtures....brought victories to the Old Firm last season. Things were really not too bad then, although, perhaps not quite so good as tradition warranted. The position at present is this: speaking in general terms, Pontypridd have, during the past two or three seasons, supplanted Mountain Ash, as the best second class Club in Wales. Penarth, as stated, are possibly the poorest first class side in Wales. When Mountain Ash satisfactorily achieve and maintain the position of being a better side than these, able once again to give all and sundry good games, with a fair proportion of home and away victories, then and then only will they arrive back on the rugby map, fulfilling past traditions, well supported and well praised."

4 December 1937

<u>Pontypridd 4 Mountain Ash 0</u>

Mount Team: T. Smith, R. Jones, P.C. George, Haydn Williams, T. R. T. Gooding, L. Reed, P. Giles, W. McArthur, D. Kelly, A. Matthews, W. Crockett, F. Rees, D. L. Williams, L. Jones, A. Manfield.

<u>Old Firm at Pontypridd Lose By Dropped Goal in Hard Tussle</u>
<u>Forwards Play Poorly Against Bigger Pack</u>

"The Watchman" reported in the Aberdare Leader, "In past seasons the train for Pontypridd, on the occasion of a visit by the Old Firm, would be packed with supporters. On Saturday, just a bare handful – the majority of whom had direct connection with the team – made the journey. The crowd at Ynysangharad Park was small but enthusiastic, nevertheless, on a somewhat bleak and cold afternoon. One can remember, within the last year or so, a bigger crowd having travelled with the visitors of today than were actually present for this game....What chances the backs had, therefore, came from an occasional loose ball. Even so, Giles did not inspire as an attacking player; his passing is not accurate and he is on the slow side definitely. Strikes me as being a "has-been"....The Pontypridd score came after one particularly hot set-to by both backs, which ended when the referee had to intervene because of a stand-up fight between three or four forwards. Fists were flying like windmills. Clear, crisp punches could be heard all over the ground. I felt really thrilled; it was almost exhilarating. But wait! I am not a boxing commentator, who may be justified in saying it would mean "curtains" for someone if this blow and that had landed a little higher, or perhaps a little lower....Seeing the Old Firm as visitors is a far different experience to seeing them as the home side, and I would like to risk one or two observations.

<u>That Scruffy Look!</u>

The Old Firm are a "scruffy" looking side taking the field. Their colours, black and amber, are interspersed with other colours, particularly where stockings are concerned. This should surely be rectified." He continued, "Any home crowd are prepared for, and look forward to, some fun out of the visiting flag waver. Arguing with the crowd on the part of the touchjudge is to be deprecated at all times....Let them have their fun by not resenting harmless, mostly always, "waggish" criticism."

11 December 1937

Unwarranted Blank Day for Old Firm

"The Watchman" commented in the Aberdare Leader, "Did the torrential rain on Saturday midday provide the Old Firm "manager" or management with the required excuse for arranging an abandonment of the game due to be played at the Rec with the attractive Monmouthshire side, Abertillery? It is difficult to appreciate the action. Rain does not unduly affect the playing pitch at the Rec – in this respect it compares very favourably with the best grounds in the country. Linking up with a number of supporters....all agreed that the ground was in a fit condition to play. One remarked "any excuse to have the game played on a day when a later kick off can be arranged, did the same thing last year. Time someone did something about it." And these sentiments were re-echoed in terms some of which were, indeed, very unprintable. The position of the Old Firm today is indeed a sorry one. In addition to the general low standard of play this season, and it was not a great deal better last season, there have been the "bungling" of an attractive home game against Abercarn, some dissatisfaction amongst players, an open date for next Saturday and only one home game between now and Christmas. All this on top of Saturday's unwarranted cancellation is putting ardent and loyal rugger fans in a pretty beastly state of mind. Must rugby, in a stronghold of more than 50 years standing, pass out for want of ordinary support, support which is fast being lost? Surely something can be done to win the support necessary for the production of the standard known to be attainable. Once again, would the setting up of the Club on a membership basis solve the problems and for the future, ensure all the assistance, moral and financial, required?"

18 December 1937

Should the Old Firm Return to Competitive Rugby?
Suggestion for New Mid Glamorgan League

"The Watchman" commented in the Aberdare Leader, "the plight in which the Old Firm find themselves at the present time is, generally, the sole topic of conversation amongst rugby fans....the suggestion is that in place of the present Glamorgan League, a new "Mid Glamorgan League" should be instituted to comprise such teams as Mountain Ash – pride of place given its historical background – Pontypridd, Maesteg, Treorchy, Cilfynydd, Aberaman, Briton Ferry, Ynysybwl and possibly one or two of the other, shall we say, without disrespect, smaller second class sides. If the Old Firm see a way out of their difficulties through this suggestion, and if they consider their present organisation good enough, would they take the initiative? What do other local Clubs, Aberaman and Ynysybwl, think of the idea? Again, what do readers think of the scheme? Would "sacking the lot" idea and consequent rebuilding bring eventually, first class status?"

25 December 1937

Mountain Ash 11 Pontypridd 0
Magnificent Display By Old Firm-Pontypridd Outplayed In Good Game
Best Pack Fielded This Season

"The Watchman" reported in the Aberdare Leader, "showing vastly improved form and having the assistance of new players, the Old Firm delighted the fairly good crowd assembled at the Rec by inflicting defeat upon their old and near rivals, Pontypridd, in no uncertain manner to the tune of 11-0, this avenging two narrow defeats sustained at Ynysangharad Park earlier in the season. All the forwards took the eye in turn, but special mention must be made of the value of Leslie Manfield to the pack. By far the best pack the Old Firm have turned out this season."

1 January 1938

Matches Against Local Sides

"The Watchman" reported in the Aberdare Leader, "In a recent article, I urged the necessity and importance of including in the Old Firm fixture list the two other local sides, Ynysybwl and Aberaman....if there has been a spot of bother between these Clubs in the past, I'm sure it's a case of making molehills into mountains – please let bygones be bygones. Rugger supporters at the three centres do not want this nonsense. I hope these three Clubs will get together and arrange fixtures for their mutual benefit, for the benefit of rugger loving crowds and essentially for the benefit of the game.....it is asserted that the Glamorgan League still exists and that invitations have been sent regularly to the Old Firm to rejoin, without result."

8 January 1938

<u>Mountain Ash 8 Abercarn 0</u>

"The Watchman" commented in the Aberdare Leader, "Abercarn, Monmouthshire League champions.... found the Old Firm, with only 14 men, just too good for them....Of the forwards, Leslie Manfield was again outstanding and why he fails to get some form of recognition is a mystery. There may be better forwards but there are surely not eight of them in Wales at the present time."

15 January 1938

<u>Idle Days For Old Firm</u>
<u>What Is Wrong?</u>

"The Watchman" wrote the following in the Aberdare Leader, "Have many of the Clubs previously included in the fixture lists refrained from renewing fixtures due to a cessation in the amicable relationships between themselves and the Old Firm? If so, whose is the responsibility? Surely, in ordinary circumstances, Clubs, apart from the big six or seven, would be glad to arrange fixtures regularly with the Old Firm. Things are very definitely going from bad to worse. Again, I am to ask, is this once famous institution, probably the last in the town forming a link with the past, to pass into oblivion under our very noses? Cannot anything be done to save the situation? It has been suggested that the present organisation might try League rugby to attempt to stave off impending disaster, and I for one, amongst many others, rather than see the end of things, would tolerate this class of game. It would, most certainly, create some interest, especially if the side became within reach of honours, a position not beyond the realms of possibility. But, does it appear that of the obvious faults to be found in the present organisation, apparent obstinacy is the greatest? If that is the case, what about the only other method of getting out of the morass, that of complete reorganisation! The Old Firm must be set up on a membership basis, embracing the whole of the community. I have listened to the constant grumbling of the supporters and have listened to suggestions here and there, but when, and how, can some co-ordinated action be taken? This is what those interested should be concerned about if they are to help in staving off what, in present circumstances, must be considered to be the inevitable doom of the Old Firm. Will someone, or some body of persons, take a lead in this matter? Do not leave it too late. Time is precious."

29 January 1938

<u>Old Firm's Future</u>
<u>The Other Point Of View</u>

"The Watchman" reported in the Aberdare Leader, "I had a long and interesting chat with a committee man during the weekend. There is another side of the story and in fairness to all concerned this column is glad to publish the information gleaned as a result of the conversation referred to....difficulties commenced some five or six years ago when industrial depression was becoming increasingly rampant. Influential townspeople, it is asserted, one by one, became disinterested and left the Club, eventually leaving Mr Shad Lewis to carry on alone. This he has done during a most difficult period and at huge personal cost. Whilst every credit must be given to Mr Lewis for piloting the affairs of the Club thus far, I must observe that during the period some steps might have been taken to seek public help – through the medium of a meeting of supporters and townspeople. This, I understand, has on more than one occasion been considered but the prevailing point of view was that it would be almost impossible to get a sufficient number of persons to act as guarantors. My further observation, why not try? It is admitted that a pretty sorry mess of the fixture list has been made this season, and that, in the main, this is the cause of most of the present criticism. The committee, as a whole, cannot be blamed entirely for this, but someone or other has blundered very badly indeed. It is gratifying to learn, in this connection, that the present Secretary, Mr Griffiths, has almost completed next season's fixture list. Good work!"

Early Kick Offs

"The necessity of an early kick off at this part of the season has difficulties....invariably before the majority of would-be supporters leave their places of toil...."gates" are obviously scant. Later starts at the end of the season will, without doubt, bring along increased support. From a playing point of view and having regard to the efforts already made to improve the side, I must say this is deserved. Almost every possible way out of the difficulties have been discussed by the Committee – re-entry into the League, which they are against at the moment; organising a junior side, the arranging of junior competitions, etc, etc. So that, reader, is something you can think out. An expression of views is invited."

12 February 1938

The Aberdare Leader reported, "the Old Firm are due to play Penarth next Saturday but in view of the visit of Gracie Fields, it is rumoured that the game will be played at Penarth, presumably on a guaranteed share of the gate."

26 March 1938

Aberavon 44 Mountain Ash 5
Decline of Old Firm-Defeat at Aberavon by 44pts to 5
Heaviest Defeat For 50 Years!

"The Watchman" commented in the Aberdare Leader, "I did not see the game. Whilst it is not my aim to offer excuses for this heavy defeat, it might be said that for the second successive game the Old Firm back division was completely disorganised. Reviewing past games at Aberavon, I am almost conclusively led to the belief that the ground at Aberavon has never provided the Old Firm with happy hunting. Was it not on that ground, some years ago (see season 1924/25), that the late Percy Hoskins, a most promising local boy, son of a famous one-time Old Firm player, met with an injury from which, most unfortunately and regretfully, he died not many hours after the game? I remember travelling to Aberavon some three seasons ago (see season 1934/35) in the company of a bigger crowd of supporters than we are accustomed to on the Rec these days, in the hope of seeing the Old Firm maintain an undefeated record which they held as a result of the first twelve games. Whether the unlucky 13th game or the unlucky ground was responsible for the Old Firm defeat that transpired, I do not know. On that day, the sides were so well matched that a drawn game would have been a more fitting result (Mount lost 11-7)."

Heaviest Defeat For 50 Years

"In addition to providing the Old Firm with the biggest defeat in more than 50 years association with the game, Saturday's game has provided an idea of the huge disparity between the classes, first and second, in Welsh rugby. Or hasn't it? Pursuing the latter question and reviewing Saturday's games, in which other second class clubs were pitted against first class sides, Pontypridd, away from home, beat Cross Keys and Crumlin at Pontypool, lost in the last minutes of the game by three points....Highly creditable performances on the part of the second class clubs....Aberavon are a good side but in which way does their one sided victory over Mountain Ash reflect itself in relation to the two similar games mentioned? Results do not show Aberavon to be so vastly superior to either Cross Keys or Pontypool. Can it then be that the second class opposition provided Aberavon on Saturday is vastly inferior to that provided Cross Keys and Pontypool? Looking at the position fairly and squarely, I am afraid that is the case. Tragic! The Old Firm, as previously pointed out in these notes, should be, traditionally and by virtue of their past exemplary reputation, the best second class side in Wales. They are not. They should be in a position to knock persistently and confidently at the door leading to first class status, instead of which they are, unfortunately, banging their heads against a brick wall. The continuance of such a policy means heading for disaster and complete elimination from the game. More tragic still! The season started badly, and, I suppose, will end on a similar note. A heavy programme remains, and everyone concerned, player, administrator and supporter, will, I feel sure, be happy when it is completed."

THE OLD FIRM'S PROUD PAST

Mountain Ash Rugby Football Club
"The Old Firm"
Season 1937/38

Back Row L-R: D. Kelly, K. Jones, F. Rees, P. Demery, E. Lloyd, P.C. George, L. Harvey, Ted Bradwick (Secretary),
Middle Row L-R: J. Savage, H. Morgan, W.I. McArthur (Capt), D.P. Williams, L. Reed,
Front Row L-R: W. Crockett, Haydn Williams, P. Godwin.

Season 1938/39

<u>Mount Go 18 Matches Unbeaten</u>
<u>Les Manfield Wins 1st Welsh Cap</u>

The Old Firm well and truly put the trials and tribulations of 1937/38 behind them with a memorable season which included an 18 match unbeaten run – 14 wins and 4 draws – which started on 29 October 1938 and ended on 4 March 1939. During this run, there were "doubles" over Glamorgan Wanderers and Abercarn, wins over Abertillery, Cinderford, Pill Harriers, Aberavon, Maesteg and Glynneath, and draws against Cheltenham, Abertillery, Penarth and Aberavon. The biggest win of the season was against Newbridge by a margin of approximately 30+ points (exact score unknown) and, outside the unbeaten run, there were also wins against Ebbw Vale, Treorchy and, in the last game of the season, at home against a Llanelly XV. When Pontypridd beat the Old Firm at the Rec at the end of the season, "The Watchman" reported in the Aberdare Leader, "Pontypridd won by nine points….created history by winning for the first time ever at Mountain Ash." Having checked this statement, it is incorrect, but not by much. From the known playing records that go back to the 1880s, it was Ponty's third ever win in Mountain Ash, their two known previous wins being 7-3 in 1923/24 and 11-0 in 1925/26. To cap a fine season, backrow forward Les Manfield, who was working as a P.T. instructor in Yorkshire and playing for Otley RFC and the Yorkshire County XV at the time, gained his first Welsh cap in the victory against Scotland in February 1939 in the Four Nations tournament. A month later, he added a second in the win against Ireland in what turned out to be Wales' last International match before the start of the Second World War. Prior to this, and due to his mother's English nationality, Manfield was picked for England's Probable XV versus "The Rest" in a trial match, but turned the offer down. When he gained his 2 caps during the season, he became the last Old Firm player to be directly capped by Wales from Mountain Ash RFC. For most of the 1930s, Wales, England, Ireland and Scotland banned all contact with French Clubs as well as the French International XV due to suspected professionalism in France, and this was probably why no trip across the Channel took place in the 1930s. At the end of the season, "The Watchman" reported in the Aberdare Leader that the Old Firm had played 44 games, won 24, drawn 6, and lost 14, scoring 340 points, including 81 tries, and conceded 226, which converted to a win rate of 61.36%. Mount captain, T.D.E., "Tommy", Williams scored 114 points in total, which included 19 tries, which was quite a feat pre-War considering the low score of most matches. The season also saw scrum half Glyn Davies and forward Dick Pritchard play for the Club, and these were two players who also played for the Old Firm after the end of World War II. Richard, "Dickie", Williams, who was a talented young player at the time, and was from Lyndhurst Street in Caegarw, gained a Welsh Schools Under 14 cap in 1939. He played briefly for the Old Firm during his career in the early War years, before making his mark in Rugby League from the mid 1940s to the mid 50s, when he went on to become a distinguished International player who captained the Great Britain squad on their tour of Australia and New Zealand in 1954.

Fixtures 1938/39

Opposition	Date	Venue	Score	Tries	Scorers/Comments
Ebbw Vale	10 Sep 1938	Home	19-3	3	T.J. Roberts 2T, C. Roberts T, Tommy Williams 2P, 2C.
Ynysybwl	17 Sep 1938	Home	12-11	2	C. Roberts T, T.J. Roberts T, Tommy Williams 2P.
Pontardawe	24 Sep 1938	Away	7-3	1	P.C. Allen T, Cecil Roberts DG.
Ynysybwl	3 Oct 1938	Away	0-8	0	No scorers.
Aberaman	8 Oct 1938	Home	3-5	0+	Scorer unknown.
Penarth	15 Oct 1938	Away	3-6	1	Williams T.

Opposition	Date	Venue	Score	Tries	Scorers/Comments
Treorchy	22 Oct 1938	Home	13-5	2+	Williams T, Davies T, AN Other 7pts.
Blaenavon	29 Oct 1938	Away	9-12	Unknown	Scorers unknown.
Briton Ferry	5 Nov 1938	Home	3-0	1	Game 1 unbeaten T.J. Davies T.
Cheltenham	12 Nov 1938	Away	0-0	0	Game 2 unbeaten No scorers.
Tylorstown	19 Nov 1938	Home	9-0	3	Game 3 unbeaten Glyn Davies T, Cecil Roberts T, D.R. Pritchard T.
Abertillery	26 Nov 1938	Away	11-9	2	Game 4 unbeaten Tommy Williams 2T, P, C.
Briton Ferry	3 Dec 1938	Away	3-0	1	Game 5 unbeaten Glyn Davies T.
Cinderford	10 Dec 1938	Home	22-0	6	Game 6 unbeaten Cecil Roberts 2T, 2C, Crad Davies 2T, T.D.E. Williams T, Glyn Davies T.
Pill Harriers	17 Dec 1938	Away	3-0	1	Game 7 unbeaten Cecil Roberts T.
Abertillery	24 Dec 1938	Home	0-0	0	Game 8 unbeaten No scorers.
Maesteg	28 Dec 1938	Home	6-0	2	Game 9 unbeaten Kelly T, Crad Davies T.
Abercarn	7 Jan 1939	Home	31-6	7+	Game 10 unbeaten Crad Davies 2T, T.J. Roberts T, P, C, Cecil Roberts T, Danny Walters T, T.D.E. Williams T, Kelly T, Williams C, AN Other 3pts.
Aberavon	14 Jan 1939	Home	13-0	3	Game 11 unbeaten Tommy Williams 2T, R.D. Owen T, T.J. Roberts 2C.
Aberavon	21 Jan 1939	Away	6-6	2	Game 12 unbeaten Crad Davies T, Glyn Davies T.
Penarth	28 Jan 1939	Home	0-0	0	Game 13 unbeaten No scorers.

Opposition	Date	Venue	Score	Tries	Scorers/Comments
Glamorgan Wanderers	4 Feb 1939	Away	11-3	3	Game 14 unbeaten Cecil Roberts 2T, C, T.D.E. Williams T.
Glamorgan Wanderers	18 Feb 1939	Home	5-3	1	Game 15 unbeaten Jim Bowen T, T.D.E. Williams C.
Pontardawe	25 Feb 1939	Home	22-0	6	Game 16 unbeaten Cecil Roberts 3T, Crad Davies 2T, Glyn Davies T, T.D.E. Williams 2C.
Abercarn	4 Mar 1939	Away	13-6	3	Game 17 unbeaten T.D.E. Williams T, 2C, Glyn Davies T, Jim Bowen T.
Glynneath	11 Mar 1939	Home	8-3	2	Game 18 unbeaten T.D.E. Williams T, C, Crad Davies T.
Cilfynydd	18 Mar 1939	Away	0-6	0	No scorers.
H.H. Merrett's XV	25 Mar 1939	Home	8-24	2	T.D.E. Williams 2T, C.
Pontypridd	1 Apr 1939	Away	6-9	1	Alwyn Evans T, P.
Ebbw Vale	8 Apr 1939	Away	3-19	1	Morgan T.
Aberaman	15 Apr 1939	Home	13-3	3	T.D.E. Williams T, 2C, Norman Rees T, Cecil Roberts T.
Treorchy	22 Apr 1939	Away	3-6	0	Cecil Roberts P.
Aberaman	22 Apr 1939	Away	3-8	0	T.J. Roberts P.
Pontypridd	29 Apr 1939	Home	0-9	0	No scorers.
Blaenavon	6 May 1939	Home	9-3	1+	Kelly T, George P, AN Other 3pts.
Llanelli XV	6 May 1939	Home	5-3	1	D. Galsworthy T, Cecil Roberts C.
Newbridge	Unknown	Unknown	Unknown	Unknown	Mount win. Scorers unknown.

Summary of Above Playing Record

P	W	D	L	For	Against	Tries Scored	Win Rate %
37	22	4	11	282+	179+	61+	64.87

Summary of Actual Playing Record

P	W	D	L	For	Against	Tries Scored	Win Rate %
44	24	6	14	340	226	81	61.36

Match Reports & Publications

20 August 1938

Boxing Tournament to Aid Old Firm
But Strong Men Stole the Limelight

The Aberdare Leader reported, "....Mountain Ash RFC is to get the proceeds from a Boxing Tournament at the Pavilion, Mountain Ash....in addition, Goff Retter, popular Old Firm and Glamorgan County rugby forward – Wales' strongest man....jolly, genial, rosy cheeked 17 stone boxer, who specialises in driving six inch nails through a three inch plank with his bare hand and picking up two fourteen stone men with one hand, stole the show at Mountain Ash Pavilion on Monday night."

10 September 1938

Mountain Ash 19 Ebbw Vale 3

Mount Team: I. Davies, T. R. T. Gooding, M. Rees, T. J. Roberts, C. Roberts, Reg Jones, T. D. E. Williams Capt, D. Kelly, Les Manfield, R. Pritchard, Frank Rees, A. Hoffland, P. C. Lewis Jones, J. Roderick, W. Crockett.

"The Watchman" reported in the Aberdare Leader, "Long years have elapsed since the Old Firm were greeted with such lusty cheers at the end of a game as on Saturday at the Rec....after a brilliant second half against visiting side, Ebbw Vale....A surprise result? Yes! Local critics, and those in South Wales rugger circles in particular, will sit up and take notice. In this game, the Old Firm met possibly the season's strongest opponents. Their fine performance forecasts a most successful playing season.

Vale's Bright Start

Ebbw Vale started strongly....The home defence was sound....the home forwards, led by the "old guard" of Manfield and Kelly, were responsible for long periods of play in the visitors' territory. After half time, aided by the breeze, the home side attacked strongly....Behind the scrum, Reg Jones and Tommy Williams were beginning to understand one another and with the "threes" finding each other quite nicely, the home side were on top. L.M. Rees....after charging down a kick, tapped the ball over the try line for T.J. Roberts, running strongly, to touch down....The home side went further ahead in a minute or so....Tommy Williams kicked another penalty, which showed the pressure being inflicted by the home forwards at this stage. This was followed by a sensational try – one that will long be remembered....L.M. Rees run strongly from his own line breaking through the Valians' ranks with opponents in hot pursuit. Confronting two or three would-be tacklers, he sent the ball to C. Roberts who scored, amidst tremendous cheers, a magnificent try...."

5 November 1938

Mountain Ash 3 Briton Ferry 0
Season's Worst Game Before Biggest Gate
Players Ordered Off – Unfortunate Scramble

The Aberdare Leader reported, "...forward play became unnecessarily rough, so much so that the hot work going on in mauls could be plainly seen, and unless stopped, would cause some trouble.

Tempers Blaze

Trouble it did cause. In one particularly fierce maul, three or four Briton Ferry forwards could be seen "piling in" to Hoffland, whilst he was on the ground. As if a match had been put to petrol, both packs played up into a bout of open fisticuffs which ended with Hoffland and Briton Ferry forward, Phillips, receiving their marching orders, a most distasteful occurrence which did little to temper the fast becoming impatient crowd....it is many years since Briton Ferry visited the Rec previously. It is to be hoped that more than twice as many years will elapse before they come again. Progress cannot be made when a team such as this is included in the fixture list."

12 November 1938

Cheltenham 0 Mountain Ash 0

Mount Team: Id. Davies, C. Davies, T. D. E. Williams, C. Roberts, D. George, D. Walters, Glyn Davies, B. Reakes, W. Crockett, R. S. Owen, Lewis Jones, N. Ellis, J. Bowen, Roy West, Arthur Manfield.

Old Firm in Thrilling Game at Cheltenham
Missed Chances Deprive Them of Victory

"The Watchman" reported in the Aberdare Leader, "The Old Firm, travelling almost 100 miles into Gloucestershire, met a strong Cheltenham XV, put up a grand display and shared the honours in a fast and thrilling game. But for one or two pieces of real bad luck, the Old Firm might well have assured themselves of victory in the first half....the backs gave a dashing exposition that received laudable praise meritoriously from the large crowd in attendance. A most pleasant journey in gloriously fine weather was broken at Gloucester for lunch before moving on to the Cheltenham Athletic Grounds, venue of the game. In order to support my view of the first half which would indicate the Old Firm's superiority, the following description of the game up to the interval has been extracted from the "Gloucester Echo" of Saturday evening, "….it is obvious that the Old Firm backs are good – really good. Cheltenham, this season, have proved themselves to be a high scoring XV but the Old Firm provided stern opposition, their superiority in this game, being quite definite."

Appreciative Crowd

The Old Firm's performance was highly creditable. Their style of play suited the large crowd and was appreciated. Both sets of backs, swinging the ball about at every opportunity….produced a commendable measure of thrills….the fifty odd supporters who travelled with the side were delighted, even if slightly disappointed, that a perfectly fair try was disallowed.

What They Say About The Old Firm

The official programme of the Cheltenham v Mountain Ash game refers to the Old Firm in the following terms, "Founded in 1876, the Mountain Ash RFC, our visitors today, is the second oldest club in Wales and known in England and Wales as the "Old Firm". Many International players have been supplied to Wales by the Club. A record of which they may well be proud is that every time Wales has won the International Championship, a Mountain Ash player has been in the team. The Club has recently been reorganised and are regaining their former reputation. T.D.E. Williams and R.D. Owen are Secondary Schoolboy Internationals while D. Kelly obtained his cap as a schoolboy. We heartily accord our Welsh visitors a welcome to the Athletic Ground and look forward to another good, open game. The up to date record of the Old Firm is played 13, won 6, drawn 3, lost 4, Points For 89, Points Against 71. Not too bad, really."

26 November 1938

Abertillery 9 Mountain Ash 11
Old Firm Hit the "High Spots"
Win Magnificently at Abertillery-Skipper Williams "bags" All the Points

"The Watchman" reported in the Aberdare Leader, "Their magnificent away win over first class Club, Abertillery, on Saturday, in addition to surprising the critics over a wide area, will undoubtedly mark the Old Firm as a side making rapid progress in a supreme effort to regain former glory. The Old Firm backs gave another of their bright displays, but on this occasion, an equal amount of praise must go to the pack, which stood up manfully and gallantly to the bigger and robust Abertillery forwards in a manner reminiscent of the "good old days." Skipper Williams, leading his side zealously and with inspiration, "bagged" the whole of the points, scoring two tries, converting one from in front of the posts and landing a brilliant penalty goal from forty yards. This lot brings his total for the season to 101 points in fourteen matches. In their two previous home matches, Abertillery drew with Pontypool and beat Newport. They were all out for a treble in this game and fielded a strong side. The Old Firm were also well represented and having consistently enjoyed a good record at Abertillery throughout the ages, went onto the field with confidence and in high spirits. There was a good crowd present. The playing pitch, surrounded by a banked cycling track, a grandstand the whole length of one side, and well made terracing on the opposite side, all set in picturesque grounds, looked to be in fairly good condition....The game had now developed into a game between the brilliant Old Firm backs and the resolute, hard working Abertillery pack....In the second half, the Old Firm forwards came into their own and did not allow the opposing eight as much freedom in the loose. This led to the backs having more of the play, in which some brilliant runs by Glyn Davies, T.D.E. Williams and Crad Davies were a feature....wherever play was, the Old Firm were the attacking side.... towards the end, Abertillery tried hard but could make little headway against a formidable defence. They did reduce the Old Firm's lead in the closing minutes....the game ended with the Old Firm worthy winners by eleven points to nine.

Although only two points divided the sides, the Old Firm, once they settled down, were vastly superior. There was no fluke about the result, which would have reflected itself in the score to a greater extent had conditions been more conducive to handling. That the Old Firm have a fine set of backs has always been conceded....In this game the forwards were in great form, rising to the occasion in a similar manner to that seen in seasons past. Rarely have I seen eight forwards work so hard and to such good purpose. Behind it all however, is a valiant and happy team spirit, with a will to win which is the secret of the Old Firm's progress and success in this game."

Leslie Manfield To Play for England?

"The Watchman" also reported in the same issue, "The selection of Leslie Manfield in the England side versus "The Rest" trial match at Manchester on December 3 will bring about most certainly a revival of the vexed question of qualifications for International matches. It does seem a great pity that Mount born Leslie is likely to be lost to Welsh national rugby through lack of recognition by the "Big Five" of Wales. For a number of years, this stout hearted young forward has proved beyond doubt his claims for recognition, but has been constantly passed over for reasons not known. Maybe it has been due to lack of "big Club" attachment and yet I have heard a Welsh Union member say, "there are not eight better forwards than Manfield." The Welsh Union will surely select Leslie Manfield for the next Welsh trial when they meet on Thursday of this week. That leads to the point as to what the player concerned will do in this matter. As the recognised leader of this season's successful Yorkshire pack, he has every chance of winning an England cap, but he is a Welsh boy and should play for Wales, who have a greater claim to his services from a qualification point of view. Recognition of young Les by the "Big Five" is justifiable, as I have frequently pointed out in my notes. The award of a Welsh cap to him – adding to the Welsh Secondary Schools cap he has already gained – would be fitting reward for his sound play and great service to the "handling code". Finally, would it not be ridiculous to see a Welsh Secondary Schools International player play for England against his native country in a senior International? Absurd? It would seem there is no reason for having agreements regarding birth, residence or any other qualification. The position is interesting, but in common with all valley rugger enthusiasts, I urge the "Big Five" not to lose the services of a really great forward to Wales."

3 December 1938

Briton Ferry 0 Mountain Ash 3

"The Watchman" reported in the Aberdare Leader, "Saturday's game at Briton Ferry was a far worse game, if it was possible to be, than that played between the teams at the Rec four weeks ago, and about which I wrote some uncomplimentary remarks regarding the doubtful tactics employed by the Old Firm's opponents. Unable to adapt themselves to brighter and more open rugby, Briton Ferry have more successfully than any other team I can think of, become the handling code spoilers par excellence....the Mount players, mostly all badly bruised as a result of being man handled, rather fortunately escaped serious injury. How this was managed in one or two frightfully fierce mauls is a miracle. And so ends, what we all hope will be the one black spot in the season's progress, Old Firm officials and committee will say with relief, "thank goodness that is over."

24 December 1938

Mountain Ash 0 Abertillery 0
Old Firm Withstand Great 'Tillery Drive
Exciting Game Ends Pointless-Tragic Failure of Penalty Kick

"The Watchman" reported in the Aberdare Leader, "Abertillery....in a particularly determined effort to avenge a two point defeat inflicted on their ground by the Old Firm a month ago, brought an especially strong XV. With a particularly strong pack of forwards, the visitors exerted heavy pressure in the closing stages but the Old Firm defence held out magnificently. Had Tommy Williams been a little more lucky with a shot at goal from a free kick – it once again, accompanied by groans from the crowd, hit an upright, bringing his total of direct hits of the posts what must be a record, the Old Firm would have won....only one team has scored against the Old Firm in the last eight matches played."

28 December 1938

Mountain Ash 6 Maesteg 0
Western Mail
Grand Struggle Between Fine Packs

"A fine holiday crowd – the best of the season at Mountain Ash – witnessed a grand struggle between two very evenly matched teams. Both packs were magnificent, relentlessly fighting to the end for the mastery, the home pack showing a noticeable improvement in their scrummaging. To their credit, both packs were always trying to get their three-quarters into action.....Manfield, L.J. Williams, Kelly and Bowen were ever in the van with the Mountain Ash pack. Late in the first half, the Old Firm drew first blood, Kelly scoring a try after a vigorous forward attack. Play continued fast and vigorous in the second half, and on at least three occasions, Maesteg were within an ace of scoring, but on each occasion, coolness under pressure saved Mountain Ash. Crad Davies then broke magnificently. He was partially tackled by Thomas a yard from the line but managed to shake off his opponent to score."

7 January 1939

Mountain Ash 31 Abercarn 6
Abercarn Overwhelmed by Old Firm
Strong and Brilliant Back Play Leads To Huge Score

"The Watchman" commented in the Aberdare Leader, "Abercarn were well represented.....but found the Old Firm in brilliant mood. They could not cope with the brilliance of the home backs....Les Manfield, as if in special preparation for next Saturday's final Welsh Trial, had an enjoyable time performing – showing superhuman feats of strength and endurance in the course of play."

14 January 1939

Mountain Ash 13 Aberavon 0
Old Firm Giant Killers
"Wizards" Well Beaten at the Rec-Skipper Williams Two Great Tries

"The Watchman" reported in the Aberdare Leader, "Welsh rugby "Wizards", Aberavon....failing to master the heavy-going conditions, crashed badly against the Old Firm, who played with greater determination than ever, completely outwitting their redoubtable opponents in a hard, gruelling game.

The home forwards were in relentless mood, and although the extra weight of the opposing pack told against them in set scrums towards the end of the game, were constantly in the picture with fast and constructive raids brought about by sound dribbling. The backs, adapting themselves to conditions in which handling was almost impossible, excelled themselves and proved to be faster than the visitors. Of T.D.E. Williams, always at home on a heavy ground, it can be said he played a real skipper's part. In addition to leading inspiringly, he twice ran through the Aberavon defence to score two magnificent tries near the posts. However meritorious the hard won victory of the Old Firm is likely to be regarded, it may well be recorded that it did come about unexpectedly. The marked progress of the local side is being noted throughout the rugger world. To quote an example, Welsh Rugby critic "Old Stager" of the Western Mail, in his preview of Saturday's game wrote, "Appreciating the seriousness of the task confronting them at Mountain Ash, Aberavon have borrowed A.M. Selby from Bridgend to play at inside half. Mountain Ash has not met with defeat in any of their last ten matches and has a back division that many first class clubs are entitled to envy." "The Watchman" continued, "....Aberavon were without two star players who were figuring in the final Welsh trial at Swansea. Les Manfield would have been available for the Old Firm, but he too was playing at Swansea in the trial. The home players excelled, the determination, will to win, and spirit displayed by them was a most pleasing feature. The performance of the Old Firm was the best for many seasons and will do much to help them to the higher status desired by so many. The persistent rain throughout the morning had the dual effect of making the ground wet and heavy and of keeping the attendance down to small proportions, which was disappointing because a record gate had been anticipated.

A Grand Start

Having advantage of the strong wind, the Old Firm were pressing hard, the visitors' defence being called upon to redouble their efforts....T.D.E. Williams' kick at goal from a free kick just inside the visitors' half, bounced off the cross bar on the right side. The Aberavon line was being constantly threatened, Glyn Davies, Cecil Roberts and T.D.E. Williams almost succeeding in getting over after one particularly fine effort. In fact, the home side were almost always on the verge of scoring and the game continued fast and furious. Kelly and J.L. Williams were held up. Mountain Ash did score to achieve an interval lead of eight points....Hard pressed on his own line, the Aberavon centre attempted to clear with a huge kick....This was fielded by R.D. Owen, who had only to run a few yards to ground under the posts, for T.J. Roberts to add the extra points.

Mount Didn't Falter

Speculation was rife during the interval as to whether the home side lead was good enough. The visitors would certainly make the best possible use of the wind and the Old Firm would have to fight hard to keep them out. Aberavon resumed in promising fashion and forced the home side to defend stubbornly.... T.J. Roberts dribbled away from the halfway line and beating T. James, Aberavon's International full back, got the ball over the line but his final kick was too strong and the ball went dead, but it was a good effort.

Aberavon Well Held

The going was hard but the game continued to be exciting....then came a really sensational, individualistic try by T.D.E. Williams. After a set scrum in the visitors' 25, he picked up loose ball and like a flash threaded his way through the opposing team to ground behind the posts. T.J. Roberts goaled and the Old Firm were thirteen points ahead, a thoroughly deserved position to be in. Aberavon backs put in some huge touch-finders, but this was nullified by good work put in by tenacious forwards, ably shepherded by J.L. Williams who had great support from Pritchard, Bowen and Kelly and determined backs, who set their hearts on keeping the opposition out. When the game ended, the home players were given a grand ovation by an enthusiastic crowd, who had been ably and justly rewarded for braving the elements in comparatively good numbers."

21 January 1939

<u>Aberavon 6 Mountain Ash 6</u>
<u>Mudlarks at Aberavon</u>
<u>Old Firm With 14 Men Defy "Wizards"</u>

"The Watchman" reported in the Aberdare Leader, "Following their brilliant win over Aberavon a week ago, the Old Firm were entertained by the "Wizards" on Saturday and in cold, driving rain that persisted throughout the game, almost brought off a "double." The result was a draw of six points apiece, but the Old Firm had played with fourteen men from ten minutes after the start, Jones, who was hooking being carried off with rib injuries. This handicap was partially overcome up to the interval when the Mount boys had a six point lead. But playing against the wind on resuming, they were hard pressed and Aberavon were able to equalise....the ground was in a bad state. Four motor coaches conveyed the Old Firm and supporters to Aberavon. The Old Firm went ahead in sensational style. Early on, the ball had been punted up to T.O. James, the Aberavon full back, who was near the half way line, but was deceived by the bounce. Crad Davies, breaking in grandly, took the ball in full flight and running half the length of the field, pursued but never overtaken, scored a most glorious try near the posts.

It was from some really good inter-passing play between Glyn Davies and W.J. Lloyd that Mountain Ash obtained their second try. The changeover took place without much rest and Aberavon, with the advantage of the strong wind used high punting tactics to put the Old Firm at a disadvantage, forcing them to kick for relief. The home side reduced the arrears through a penalty....The Old Firm were forced to defend but this they did gallantly. Aberavon equalised through a try....In the closing stages, Aberavon strove for the lead but the Old Firm, equally determined, stopped them. Conditions by now were terrible and some of the Old Firm players, with an increasingly strong down-wind and rain driving into them, had as much as they could do to survive the ordeal. As the final whistle sounded, Idwal Davies was on the verge of collapse through exposure and had to be assisted to the changing rooms.

<u>Some Comments</u>

Whilst most games in the western part of the county were curtailed owing to the weather conditions, this game was permitted to continue to the bitter end in the worst ever conditions. The result, a draw, reflects great credit to the Old Firm, who, playing with fourteen men for the major portion of the game, crossed their opponents' line twice, whereas their own line was only once crossed. Well done, Old Firm!"

<u>Rugby Jottings</u>

The Aberdare Leader continued, "The Old Firm's victory over Aberavon last week was recorded as a humiliating experience by "the Wizards". To have been so soundly beaten by a generally recognised second class side goes to prove it is a very thin line that divides the distinction of class in Welsh rugby. Is it not time that an official Championship system was brought into existence? Mountain Ash, a team that once figured on the fixture lists of the leading Welsh rugby clubs, are showing such grand form this season that they would be serious challengers for promotion."

The Aberdare Leader went on, "The first annual Old Firm dance took place on Thursday as arranged and proved to be a huge success from all points of view. The whole atmosphere at the gaily decorated hall was one of jollity and happiness. A band of willing helpers with refreshments, etc. did much to bring about success and the event has very definitely come to stay. There were two hundred and fifty dancers present and financial success is assured."

Did Leslie Manfield Decide Wrongly?

And lastly, the Aberdare Leader reported, "The announcement of the Welsh XV to play against England at Twickenham on Saturday caused stupification amongst Old Firm officials and supporters when it was seen that Les Manfield had not been included in the side. A million to one had come unstuck. In expressing loyalty to the country of his birth by refusing an invitation to play in the England Trial, Les literally threw away an England Cap. Not only in Mountain Ash has extreme disappointment been expressed. I am told that the announcement of the team after the County game, Glamorgan v Monmouthshire, at Neath last Thursday, was not happily received in so far as the selection of Manfield. Well, big Club outlook apparently still remains as an all important factor amongst our legislature. That is a great pity. He is the fittest rugby forward playing today, the most knowledgeable second rank or back row exponent of pack play. Leslie Manfield should have been capped for Wales against England. He is still quite young, a little over twenty two years of age, and it may be of some consolation if I say he will yet obtain a number of Wales caps. He already deserves them. Better luck next time."

4 February 1939

Les Manfield To Play for Wales
Record That is Unequalled

"The Watchman" reported in the Aberdare Leader, "Leslie Manfield, Old Firm and Otley forward, has been selected to play for Wales against Scotland at Cardiff Arms Park on Saturday next. Having forecast this popular and deserving selection in these columns last week, we are indeed happy to join in the many congratulations showered upon him. The selection of Manfield brings him the unique distinction – unequalled as far as I can ascertain – of having played for his native Wales in three separate phases of rugby, i.e. Schoolboy and Senior Internationals. He has also obtained a County cap in Yorkshire, where – at Huddersfield – he is now employed as a Physical Training master. The gaining of so many honours in the game of rugby, if ever, falls to one as young as Les, who is only twenty two years of age, and proves conclusively his undoubted ability. The good wishes of all readers will go with him to Cardiff Arms Park next Saturday and it is hoped his play will justify further reward. The fact that a Mount player is again to appear in a national XV gives me a chance to delve into the records. Les Manfield is the eighth Old Firm player to gain a place in the Welsh XV."

Les Manfield
Mountain Ash, Cardiff & Wales
7 Welsh Caps
1938/39 v Scotland & Ireland
1947/48 v Australia, England, Scotland, France & Ireland

Above is a photograph of the Wales team captained by Wilf Wooller, who sits with the match ball in the middle row, which played Scotland at Cardiff Arms Park on 4 February 1939. The game was the last home Welsh International before the start of the Second World War. A justifiably proud looking Les Manfield won his first Welsh cap in this game and stands in the back row, fourth from the right as you look.

Les Manfield was born on 10 November 1915 in Mountain Ash. He was capped by Welsh Schools at two age groups, first in 1930 and then in 1932. He first played for the Old Firm aged 15 ½ at Aberavon, and went on to be a member of Mount's Glamorgan League Championship teams of the early 1930s. As a student, he played for Cardiff University and also became the Welsh University Colleges Light Heavyweight Boxing champion in 1937. He continued his studies in Yorkshire and played for Otley RFC. It was from here in 1938 that he was selected to play in an England trial, qualifying through his English-born mother. He turned the offer down and shortly afterwards was chosen to play in a Welsh trial, from where he was chosen for his first cap in the game versus Scotland on 4 February 1939. He gained a second cap shortly after, against Ireland, which turned out to be Wales' last match before the 2nd World War broke out and put his International career on hold. During the War years, he served in the Royal Air Force, primarily in Egypt, where he was a navigator of fighter planes, taking part in bombing raids and special operations. In 1942, he and three others survived rough seas and bad weather after their plane ditched into the Mediterranean. In recognition for his War time effort, he was awarded the Distinguished Flying Cross in 1943. During his time in service, he also represented various Armed Forces XVs, and at the end of the War, in 1945/46, he played in 7 uncapped "Victory" Internationals. After the War, he continued to play for the Old Firm and played in Mount's first home game when rugby was resumed in 1946/47. He went on to join Cardiff RFC from where he resumed his International career, gaining 5 more caps in 1947/48 against Australia, England, Scotland, Ireland and

France. During his International career, he was a No.8 in 7 matches for Wales either side of the War and was the last Mount player to be directly capped by Wales. He was also one of only four players to be capped by Wales before and after the Second World War, the other three being Howard Davies (Swansea & Llanelli), Haydn Tanner (Swansea & Cardiff), and Bill Travers (Newport). Judging by his playing career, it seems a fair assumption to make that he would have challenged for a place in a British Lions squad had there been a tour. However, due to the War, the Lions did not tour after 1938 until 1950 when his International career was over. He was made a Life Member of Mountain Ash RFC in 1993/94 and passed away on 2 November 2006 in Mountain Ash, just before his 91st birthday.

18 February 1939

Mountain Ash 5 Glamorgan Wanderers 3
Lucky Win for Old Firm
Weakened Side Disappoint: Goal Kick Decides Issue

"The Watchman" reported in the Aberdare Leader, "....Mountain Ash on the run of the play were indeed lucky to retain their fine record of not having lost one of the last fifteen matches....it is a true fact that forwards of the calibre of J.L. Williams, Desmond Kelly, Wally Hoffland and Jim Bowen could find a place in any Club pack in the country."

18 March 1939

Cilfynydd 6 Mountain Ash 0
Old Firm Defeated by Cilfynydd

The Old Firm's 18 match unbeaten run came to a disappointing end at Cilfynydd, who had been Glamorgan League champions in 1936/37 and 1937/38 and were to complete a hat-trick of titles at the end of this season. "The Watchman" reported in the Aberdare Leader, "I have yet to see a recognised Club side so completely disorganised as that fielded by the Old Firm upon their visit to Cilfynydd on Saturday last. Midweek, and even up until a short while before kick off, officials and committeemen were in a dilemma as to what they could do to fill vacancies caused through injury, illness and other reasons."

22 April 1939

Great Loss to Old Firm

"The Watchman" reported in the Aberdare Leader, "The Old Firm have unfortunately lost their popular and efficient skipper, T.D.E. Williams, who has left the district with a view to obtaining employment. He is an unemployed school teacher. A week ago, Tom accomplished the rare feat in local rugby of scoring more than one hundred points for his side in a season."

6 May 1939

Mountain Ash 5 Llanelli XV 3
Bad Weather Spoils Old Firm's Final Effort
Famous Visitors Attract Poor Gate

The Aberdare Leader reported, "Mr Fred Rees, erstwhile Old Firm player, brought a Llanelli XV to the Rec on May Day. It was hoped the game would have assisted the home side financially, but cloudy and cold weather interspersed with showers kept the gate down. I can say definitely that the Old Firm will be on the wrong side at the wind up and the future which will be discussed later, is one of conjecture....In the closing moments, the Scarlets' backs gave a huge thrill when a concerted movement initiated from a midfield scissors move, just failed to free the wing man, who knocked down the corner flag for touch in-goal. Up to that time, the home backs, having a far better service from the scrum, were slightly superior."

20 May 1939

Old Firm Season Reviewed

"The Watchman" summarised the season in the Aberdare Leader as follows, "The season now ended has been an important one in the annals of Old Firm rugby activities. It may well be regarded in the light of experience gained....that the handling code has a place in the hearts of the townspeople. Not for many years have Old Firm rugby activities been talked about in the town with so great an interest. Not for many years has the support given been so good. In spite of that, it may be said the gates have been up and down and really not good enough. One has to admit that weather conditions have militated against consistently good attendances.....

Winning Side Needed

....It does seem that organisers of rugby clubs must, at all times, field a strong and essentially winning side to ensure adequate support. On the other hand, this almost impossible task cannot be accomplished without adequate support, which calls for a sense of loyalty amongst supporters, even when unforeseen circumstances mean matters are not running smoothly for the organisers.

Playing Record 1938/1939

Venue	P	W	D	L	For	Against
Home	23	17	3	3	245	90
Away	21	7	3	11	95	136
Total	44	24	6	14	340	226

Points For: 81 tries, 27 conversions, 13 penalties, 1 dropped goal = 340.
Points Against: 43 tries, 12 conversions, 19 penalties, 4 dropped goals = 226.

Not a bad record really. Of the fourteen matches lost, only four exceeded an eight point deficit.

Good Performances

Opposition	Venue	Score	Result
Aberavon	Home	13-0	Win
Ebbw Vale	Home	19-3	Win
Abertillery	Away	11-9	Win
Aberavon	Away	6-6	Draw
Penarth	Home	0-0	Draw
Abertillery	Home	0-0	Draw

Add to the above, away wins at Abercarn, Briton Ferry and Pontardawe.

Highest Scores

v Newbridge 32 points, v Abercarn 31, v Cinderford 22, v Pontardawe 22.

There was a sequence of 18 matches without defeat from 29 October-4 March.

Bad Performances

Opposition	Venue	Score	Result
Pontypridd	Home	0-9	Lost
Aberaman	Home	3-5	Lost
Ebbw Vale	Away	3-19	Lost
Mr H.H. Merrett's XV	Home	8-24	Lost

The Players

T.D.E. Williams, the skipper, who unfortunately left the Club at Easter time must have pride of place. He is now, fortunately, in employment in London. He did much during the season to harness the forces of victory for his side and proved to be an excellent leader. He scored 114 points – 19 tries, 18 conversions and 7 penalties. Glyn Davies, star outside half, did not play very regularly. That proved to be a great pity because his twinkling moves always exhilarated the crowd. Cecil Roberts was a fairly prolific scorer and had 77 points to his credit. He gave appearances of being a moody player but was an asset to the side. Crad Davies and T.J. Roberts, the latter player in vacation games only, each had 30 points. T.J. it is hoped, will be a "regular" next season, and as a three-quarter, appears to be the natural successor to T.D.E. Williams. Idwal Davies at full back, was the most regular player. He was the acme of coolness. Of the forwards, first mention goes to Les Manfield, who, although playing a few games only for the side, must be regarded as having done much to help. Desmond Kelly, Wally Hoffland and John L. Williams have been stalwarts throughout the season....J.L. would make a good captain. Jim Bowen has done a great deal to help, whilst Edgar Wilkins, veteran though he is, has proved in recent matches to be a grand hooker. Pritchard and Reakes have also done very well. Club Chairman, Arthur Manfield, has put in excellent work in the pack when called upon.

The Future

Looking ahead, the outlook must be based on two very important facts, finance and fixtures. Whilst it is not possible to discuss the financial position of the Club at the moment, I can say that the season has not been successful from this point of view. Finance is the real basis of RFC functions, and I feel convinced that the correct basis will ensue. The arrangement of fixtures, both from the date and standard points of view, are essential, which have been brought into operation by Secretary Watkins in preparing for next season, and I am able to say that a great improvement has taken place. It is not by any means the ideal fixture card, but great progress has been made in the right direction in preparation for further improvements within the next two or three seasons.

Socially

The main social event of the season – the first annual dance – proved to be a huge success, and as an event it gives every indication of staying.

Conclusion

Although some difficulties still remain – it would not be much of a job without them – I am optimistic enough to believe in the successful future of rugby in the town. Given adequate support by patient, loyal and well meaning supporters, the game will flourish in face of difficulties and counter attractions. My final point – it is up to the townspeople to play their part. Look out for the General Meeting, attend in large numbers, and here's hoping."

Season 1939/40

<u>Rugby Takes Backseat As Events In Europe Dominate</u>
<u>Les Manfield Plays For Barbarians RFC In Disrupted Season</u>

After the optimism which, no doubt, the 1938/39 season had given, the Old Firm never had the chance to carry things on in 1939/40 due to the declaration of war with Germany on 3 September 1939 which took Britain into the Second World War. The WRU followed this by suspending rugby on 25 September. At this time, only one known game had been played, which was an 8-0 loss at 1938/39 Glamorgan League champions, Cilfynydd. Pre-season, the Aberdare Leader reported there were plans to adopt Mountain Ash YMCA as a 2nd XV for the Club and arrangements had been made for a tour to France. None of these plans materialised and although rugby was played in the town in the War years, with the games played when circumstances allowed and usually in aid of the War effort, it wasn't until 1946/47 – 7 long years later – that the Old Firm officially run out again. In March 1940, there was another honour for Mount backrow forward, Les Manfield, when he was picked to play for the Barbarians against Midland Counties at Leicester, scoring 3 points – which may have been a try or a penalty – in the Baa Baas' 34-18 win.

Match Reports & Publications

5 August 1939

<u>The French Tour</u>

"The Watchman" reported in the Aberdare Leader, "As confidently anticipated, the Rugby Union ban on French Rugby clubs has been raised, and after a lapse of some eight or nine seasons, France and Wales will meet again upon the rugby field. Internationally, France will play against the four home countries during the coming season, and Clubs throughout the British Isles are busily engaged in preparing tours to France. The Old Firm are not lacking in this respect. Previous tours have been so successful and the side had become so popular in certain French districts that months ago, when it became almost a certainty that the ban would be lifted, Mr Enoch Watkins soon set machinery in motion and arranged a tentative tour for the forthcoming season. Confirmation of the plan has now been received and the Club will visit France during the Mardi Gras Festival in February. The festival period includes Shrove Tuesday and Ash Wednesday. Two of the games to be played are against Clubs in Périgueux and Brive. A third game at Pau may be arranged, but that will mean a three day extension of the tour. Mountain Ash, as I have previously stated in my notes, have the distinction of being the first British side ever to play in Bayonne and Pau. This was in the season 1911/12. I hope soon to have information regarding the possibility of supporters accompanying the side on its February tour."

12 August 1939

<u>The Old Firm's Second String</u>

"The Watchman" reported in the Aberdare Leader, "The Old Firm have now adopted the Y.M.C.A. R.F.C. as a second string and representatives will be invited upon the Premier side's match committee."

Personal Recollections

The last say on the 1930s is left to the Old Firm's last directly capped player, Wales' No.8 in 1939, Les Manfield. The article below was first published in the Club's Centenary Season's historical publication, "The First 100 Hundred Years", which was published in 1975/76, and as well as giving an insight into the life and times of the 1930s at Mountain Ash RFC, is a fitting way to end this account of the decade.

Black & Amber Memories

Whenever I catch a whiff of wintergreen oil, I am carried back to a small, grubby changing room under the old Grandstand at the Rec. It is Sunday morning and a few of the local members of the Mount team have turned up to have their bruises rubbed out (and their skin rubbed off) by Dan 'Orrigan. Old Dan, with his bristling moustache and his weather-beaten, typically Irish face, spent all the week tossing pit props around at Deep Duffryn Saw Mill, and this kept his hands white and tender for his job as team masseur! We often wondered what was worse – the bumps we got on the field, or the massage treatment afterwards. Then, once the injured had been dealt with, the trestle table was cleared and out came a well thumbed pack of cards and the cribbage board, and the Sunday morning regulars settled down to their game, the inquest on Saturday's game, and the reminiscences of the great days of "Buller" Loveluck, Tom Collins and Sid Congdon, and the rest of those immortals. There was old man Coopey, with his gamy leg, white, flowing hair, moustache and his refined face; "Chason" Job (never "Jason"), the man who looked after the boots and whose wife laundered the jerseys, which were often washed and drying on the old high iron fireguard around the coke stove by Sunday morning; Billy Llewellyn, the little man who was almost the team mascot, was always telling sexy jokes and assisted "Chason" Job with the kit; and Dai "Penny Readings" – so called because he was said to be so mean that in his youth he would never take his girl to the "pictures", but always persuaded her to go to the "penny readings" in the Library.

There were others, too, who filled the air of the little room with the smoke of their pipes as they puffed their way through the great names and the great tries that lived on in their memories. They themselves had, for the most part, been playing members of those teams, but now they just played their cribbage and lived in their memories.

Now I am in their situation; but then I was a young lad, still at the County school. My heroes then were men like Haydn Williams, Jim and Con. Murphy, Jim Cummings and Frank Kempson, the brothers Phil and Jack Davies, and Alby Davies, to name some of them. A great team that could hold its own with anyone and whose great regret was that Cardiff was no longer on their fixture list. They were giants in the Glamorgan League, which they would have undoubtedly won every year if the referees had not invariably been biased against them! And even with that handicap, they sometimes did manage to win. Remember that great final against Treorchy at Pontypridd to decide the League Championship, when Johnny Lloyd and I were dropped because they were afraid we would be killed? We were disgusted with the selection committee – until we watched the battle at Ynysangharad Park! That game ended in a draw, and I never saw the replay the following season because I was away with the Welsh Academicals on tour, I believe. But, they told me that it was mild compared with the first game and I know Mount won.

With discussions ongoing about the pros and cons of Leagues in Rugby Union, it is fitting to point out the local interest which the Glamorgan League aroused. I remember the quarry side of the Rec covered with spectators every time there was a league game, and the roar that greeted any Mount score could be heard all over the valley. Of course, it had its faults for the purist. There were some very doubtful transfer deals which must have transgressed the amateur laws; and the ferocity of the games between leading Clubs had to be seen to be believed. But it was a good, hard school to be trained in. I remember being warned not to go down on the ball at the feet of the opposition; but I also remember Frank Kempson and Jim Cummings standing over me and lashing out at the opposing forwards when I was foolish enough to disobey the warning. Only once do I remember being really scared and that was when I played at Aberavon in the first game on the resumption of fixtures after the Percy Hoskins "accident". In the first lineout, my feet had just left the ground when I was punched in the back and sent sprawling into touch (no penalty was given, of course). I was then about 15 ½ years old and weighed under 11 stone, and the man who had punched me was the dreaded Ned Jenkins, the terror of the Welsh pack at the time. That was one game that I did not go down on the ball. Even the spectators threw clinkers at us from the bank opposite the Stand towards the end of that game, because not all the Mount forwards were innocent schoolboys!

Good old days! And good old memories! But how many more memories lie among the bones of those old heroes who have worn the black and amber jersey on the rugger field of South Wales for "the Old Firm" during its long and glorious history? I, for one, am proud to have worn that jersey, and I thank those old teammates who helped me on the road to a Welsh cap,

Les Manfield

A Selection of the Old Firm's Results 1930/31 to 1939/40

The Western Mail's unofficial Welsh Championship was comprised of the following Clubs: Aberavon, Abertillery, Bridgend, Cardiff, Cross Keys, Llanelli, Neath, Newport, Penarth, Pontypool and Swansea. These were the only ones regarded as "first class". Below is a summary of the Old Firm's known matches against a selection of Clubs.

Matches v Pontypridd

Opponents	Season	Venue	Score	P	W	D	L
Pontypridd (PL)	1931/32	Away	13-13	1	0	1	0
Pontypridd (PL)	1931/32	Home	3-0	2	1	1	0
Pontypridd (PL)	1932/33	Away	11-4	3	2	1	0
Pontypridd (PL)	1932/33	Home	10-0	4	3	1	0
Pontypridd	1933/34	Home	12-8	5	4	1	0
Pontypridd	1933/34	Away	3-8	6	4	1	1
Pontypridd	1934/35	Away	6-0	7	5	1	1
Pontypridd	1934/35	Home	20-0	8	6	1	1
Pontypridd	1935/36	Away	3-0	9	7	1	1
Pontypridd	1936/37	Home	17-0	10	8	1	1
Pontypridd	1937/38	Away	5-6	11	8	1	2
Pontypridd	1937/38	Away	0-4	12	8	1	3
Pontypridd	1937/38	Home	11-0	13	9	1	3
Pontypridd	1938/39	Away	6-9	14	9	1	4
Pontypridd	1938/39	Home	0-9	15	9	1	5

Matches v Aberavon

Opponents	Season	Venue	Score	P	W	D	L
Aberavon	1931/32	Away	8-30	1	0	0	1
Aberavon	1931/32	Home	18-6	2	1	0	1
Aberavon	1932/33	Away	9-14	3	1	0	2
Aberavon	1932/33	Home	6-0	4	2	0	2
Aberavon	1933/34	Away	5-9	5	2	0	3
Aberavon	1934/35	Away	7-11	6	2	0	4
Aberavon	1934/35	Home	4-13	7	2	0	5
Aberavon	1936/37	Away	3-20	8	2	0	6
Aberavon	1937/38	Away	5-44	9	2	0	7
Aberavon	1938/39	Home	13-0	10	3	0	7
Aberavon	1938/39	Away	6-6	11	3	1	7

Matches v Bridgend

Opponents	Season	Venue	Score	P	W	D	L
Bridgend	1931/32	Away	3-8	1	0	0	1
Bridgend	1932/33	Unsure	20-3	2	1	0	1

Matches v Cardiff

Cardiff were Welsh Club Champions in 1936/37, 1937/38 & 1938/39

Opponents	Season	Venue	Score	P	W	D	L
Cardiff	1930/31	Home	0-9	1	0	0	1
Cardiff	1932/33	Home	7-0	2	1	0	1

Matches v Treorchy

Opponents	Season	Venue	Score	P	W	D	L
Treorchy (PL)	1930/31	Home	18-3	1	1	0	0
Treorchy (PL)	1930/31	Away	3-6	2	1	0	1
Treorchy (L) Glamorgan League Play Off	1930/31	Pontypridd	3-3	3	1	1	1
Treorchy (L) Glamorgan League 1930/31 Play Off Replay	1931/32	Pontypridd	5-0	4	2	1	1
Treorchy (L)	1931/32	Away	3-12	5	2	1	2
Treorchy (L)	1932/33	Home	18-3	6	3	1	2
Treorchy (L)	1932/33	Away	11-0	7	4	1	2
Treorchy	1934/35	Home	14-8	8	5	1	2
Treorchy	1935/36	Away	6-19	9	5	1	3
Treorchy	1938/39	Home	13-5	10	6	1	3
Treorchy	1938/39	Away	3-6	11	6	1	4

Matches v Cross Keys

Cross Keys were Welsh Club Champions in 1935/36

Opponents	Season	Venue	Score	P	W	D	L
Cross Keys	1930/31	Away	0-0	1	0	1	0
Cross Keys	1930/31	Unknown	Mount win. Score unknown.	2	1	1	0
Cross Keys	1931/32	Away	3-18	3	1	1	1
Cross Keys	1931/32	Home	3-7	4	1	1	2
Cross Keys	1932/33	Home	9-0	5	2	1	2
Cross Keys	1932/33	Away	5-19	6	2	1	3
Cross Keys	1933/34	Away	3-23	7	2	1	4
Cross Keys	1933/34	Home	11-11	8	2	2	4
Cross Keys	1934/35	Home	6-0	9	3	2	4
Cross Keys	1935/36	Away	3-9	10	3	2	5

Matches v Tredegar

Opponents	Season	Venue	Score	P	W	D	L
Tredegar	1936/37	Away	3-3	1	0	1	0

Matches v Cardiff Athletic

Opponents	Season	Venue	Score	P	W	D	L
Cardiff Athletic	1932/33	Away	6-3	1	1	0	0
Cardiff Athletic	1933/34	Home	21-3	2	2	0	0
Cardiff Athletic	1933/34	Away	0-11	3	2	0	1
Cardiff Athletic	1935/36	Home	3-4	4	2	0	2
Cardiff Athletic	1936/37	Home	12-11	5	3	0	2
Cardiff Athletic	1936/37	Away	0-0	6	3	1	2

Matches v Maesteg

Opponents	Season	Venue	Score	P	W	D	L
Maesteg	1930/31	Home	9-0	1	1	0	0
Maesteg	1930/31	Away	7-6	2	2	0	0
Maesteg	1931/32	Home	0-3	3	2	0	1
Maesteg	1931/32	Away	8-5	4	3	0	1
Maesteg	1932/33	Home	9-0	5	4	0	1
Maesteg	1932/33	Away	9-5	6	5	0	1
Maesteg	1933/34	Home	11-0	7	6	0	1
Maesteg	1933/34	Away	3-3	8	6	1	1
Maesteg	1934/35	Away	3-3	9	6	2	1
Maesteg	1935/36	Away	0-8	10	6	2	2
Maesteg	1935/36	Home	0-3	11	6	2	3
Maesteg	1936/37	Away	0-6	12	6	2	4
Maesteg	1936/37	Home	0-3	13	6	2	5
Maesteg	1937/38	Unknown	3-8	14	6	2	6
Maesteg	1938/39	Home	6-0	15	7	2	6

Matches v Ebbw Vale

Opponents	Season	Venue	Score	P	W	D	L
Ebbw Vale	1930/31	Away	0-10	1	0	0	1
Ebbw Vale	1930/31	Home	26-3	2	1	0	1
Ebbw Vale	1931/32	Home	18-0	3	2	0	1
Ebbw Vale	1931/32	Away	7-6	4	3	0	1
Ebbw Vale	1932/33	Home	5-0	5	4	0	1
Ebbw Vale	1935/36	Away	6-0	6	5	0	1
Ebbw Vale	1935/36	Home	17-0	7	6	0	1
Ebbw Vale	1936/37	Home	8-8	8	6	1	1
Ebbw Vale	1936/37	Away	5-3	9	7	1	1
Ebbw Vale	1937/38	Away	0-26	10	7	1	2
Ebbw Vale	1937/38	Home	3-3	11	7	2	2
Ebbw Vale	1938/39	Home	19-3	12	8	2	2
Ebbw Vale	1938/39	Away	3-19	13	8	2	3

Matches v Pontypool
Pontypool were Welsh Club Champions in 1931/32

Opponents	Season	Venue	Score	P	W	D	L
Pontypool	1930/31	Away	0-13	1	0	0	1
Pontypool	1930/31	Home	17-6	2	1	0	1
Pontypool	1931/32	Away	3-14	3	1	0	2
Pontypool	1931/32	Home	3-6	4	1	0	3
Pontypool	1932/33	Home	16-3	5	2	0	3
Pontypool	1932/33	Away	0-3	6	2	0	4
Pontypool	1933/34	Home	4-8	7	2	0	5
Pontypool	1933/34	Away	3-11	8	2	0	6

Matches v Penarth

Opponents	Season	Venue	Score	P	W	D	L
Penarth	1930/31	Away	11-3	1	1	0	0
Penarth	1930/31	Home	9-6	2	2	0	0
Penarth	1932/33	Away	3-6	3	2	0	1
Penarth	1935/36	Away	0-6	4	2	0	2
Penarth	1935/36	Home	11-0	5	3	0	2
Penarth	1936/37	Away	12-0	6	4	0	2
Penarth	1936/37	Home	8-0	7	5	0	2
Penarth	1937/38	Away	0-16	8	5	0	3
Penarth	1937/38	Away	3-18	9	5	0	4
Penarth	1937/38	Home	6-8	10	5	0	5
Penarth	1938/39	Away	3-6	11	5	0	6
Penarth	1938/39	Home	0-0	12	5	1	6

Matches v Glamorgan Wanderers

Opponents	Season	Venue	Score	P	W	D	L
Glamorgan Wanderers	1930/31	Away	7-0	1	1	0	0
Glamorgan Wanderers	1930/31	Home	9-0	2	2	0	0
Glamorgan Wanderers	1931/32	Home	9-3	3	3	0	0
Glamorgan Wanderers	1931/32	Unsure	9-0	4	4	0	0
Glamorgan Wanderers	1932/33	Away	11-0	5	5	0	0
Glamorgan Wanderers	1932/33	Home	27-8	6	6	0	0
Glamorgan Wanderers	1933/34	Home	8-10	7	6	0	1
Glamorgan Wanderers	1933/34	Away	11-8	8	7	0	1
Glamorgan Wanderers	1934/35	Home	26-0	9	8	0	1
Glamorgan Wanderers	1934/35	Away	10-0	10	9	0	1
Glamorgan Wanderers	1935/36	Away	0-9	11	9	0	2
Glamorgan Wanderers	1935/36	Home	8-0	12	10	0	2
Glamorgan Wanderers	1936/37	Home	6-3	13	11	0	2
Glamorgan Wanderers	1936/37	Away	0-11	14	11	0	3
Glamorgan Wanderers	1937/38	Away	6-0	15	12	0	3
Glamorgan Wanderers	1938/39	Away	11-3	16	13	0	3
Glamorgan Wanderers	1938/39	Home	5-3	17	14	0	3

Matches v Abertillery

Opponents	Season	Venue	Score	P	W	D	L
Abertillery	1931/32	Away	3-15	1	0	0	1
Abertillery	1931/32	Home	9-8	2	1	0	1
Abertillery	1932/33	Away	3-3	3	1	1	1
Abertillery	1933/34	Home	14-3	4	2	1	1
Abertillery	1933/34	Away	Mount win. Score unknown.	5	3	1	1
Abertillery	1934/35	Away	0-8	6	3	1	2
Abertillery	1934/35	Home	8-6	7	4	1	2
Abertillery	1935/36	Away	3-9	8	4	1	3
Abertillery	1936/37	Away	5-8	9	4	1	4
Abertillery	1937/38	Home	3-3	10	4	2	4
Abertillery	1938/39	Away	11-9	11	5	2	4
Abertillery	1938/39	Home	0-0	12	5	3	4

Matches v Llanelly

Opponents	Season	Venue	Score	P	W	D	L
Llanelly XV	1938/39	Home	5-3	1	1	0	0

Matches v Penygraig

Opponents	Season	Venue	Score	P	W	D	L
Penygraig (PL)	1930/31	Away	Mount win. Score unknown.	1	1	0	0
Penygraig (PL)	1930/31	Home	8-3	2	2	0	0
Penygraig (L)	1931/32	Home	6-5	3	3	0	0
Penygraig (PL)	1932/33	Home	9-7	4	4	0	0
Penygraig	1933/34	Home	0-0	5	4	1	0
Penygraig	1933/34	Away	3-9	6	4	1	1
Penygraig	1934/35	Home	20-6	7	5	1	1
Penygraig	1935/36	Home	21-3	8	6	1	1
Penygraig	1935/36	Away	3-3	9	6	2	1

Matches v Cinderford

Opponents	Season	Venue	Score	P	W	D	L
Cinderford	1936/37	Away	0-0	1	0	1	0
Cinderford	1936/37	Home	9-0	2	1	1	0
Cinderford	1938/39	Home	22-0	3	2	1	0

There were no known games played against Llwynypia (disbanded), Neath, Treherbert, Newport, Swansea, London Welsh, Bath, Leicester, Bridgwater & Albion, Plymouth, Coventry and Nuneaton in the 1930s.

Mountain Ash RFC Players That Went North 1930/31 to 1939/40

WYNDHAM JONES, a three-quarter with the Old Firm, joined Keighley Rugby League Club circa 1930. In 1931/32 he was chosen as a member of the Northern Union Rugby League representative team which toured Australia. Keighley refused a record Club fee of £600-£700 for him, such was their desire to build up a better team. Jones had scored no less than 13 tries in the 1931/32 season when Keighley turned down the offer for him.

ALBY DAVIES played as a back five forward for Mountain Ash and last appeared in an Old Firm team in 1932/33. In the Aberdare Leader dated 4 February 1939, the reporter wrote, "went North for a good figure." Other than this, nothing is known about his Rugby League career or which Club(s) he played for.

Mountain Ash Rugby Football Club
"The Old Firm"

Club Records 1875-1940

Playing Record 1875-1940

Decade	P	W	D	L	Results Unknown	For	Against	Tries Scored	Win Rate %
1875-1879	0	0	0	0	0	0	0	0	0
1880s	33	21	6	5	1	Unknown	Unknown	Unknown	75.00
1890s	225	146	26	53	0	2084+	762+	552+	70.67
1900s	288	170	30	88	0	2111+	1123+	540+	64.24
1910s	167	77	23	67	0	726+	796+	104+	52.99
1920s	308	138	36	131	3	2123+	1821+	351+	51.15
1930s	260	153	26	81	0	2236+	1323+	477+	63.85
Total	1281	705	147	425	4	9280+	5825+	2024+	60.96

Glamorgan League Record
Champions 6 times: 1895/96, 1908/09, 1913/14, 1930/31, 1931/32 & 1932/33

Runners-up twice, lost play-off: 1894/95 (in the Rhondda, Merthyr & Aberdare League, which was renamed the Glamorgan League in 1895/96) & 1904/05

Glamorgan Times Cup Winners: 1913/14

Most Seasons 1st XV Captain
Ben Tiley, 12 seasons, 1882/83-1893/94 inc.

Most Tries Scored in a Season by a Player
42 by wing Reuben Carpenter in 1902/03

Most Team Points Scored in a Season
591 in 1921/22

Most Team Tries in a Season
131+ in 1896/97

Most Wins in a Season
37 in 1921/22

Biggest Margin of Victory In a Match
40 in the 40-0 win v Pontypridd in 1901/02

Biggest Winning Margin of Victory Over Selected Clubs

Opposition	Winning Margin	Score	Venue	Season
Treorky	29pts	29-0	H	1896/97
Ebbw Vale	23pts	26-3	H	1930/31
Pontypridd	40pts	40-0	H	1901/02
Aberavon	13pts	13-0	H, H	1906/07 & 1938/39
Bath	14pts	14-0	H	1909/10
Bridgend	39pts	39-0	H	1899/1900
Llwynypia	25pts	25-0	H	1899/1900
Llanelly	8pts	11-3	A	1900/01
Pontypool/Pontymoile	29pts	29-0	H	1900/01
Pontypool only	13pts	16-3	H	1932/33
Neath	15pts	15-0	H	1901/02
Penarth	20pts	20-0	A	1902/03
Maesteg	25pts	25-0	H	1901/02
Leicester	11pts	11-0	H	1896/97
Bridgwater & Albion	24pts	24-0	H	1922/23
Treherbert	16pts	16-0	H	1905/06
Penygraig	22pts	22-0	H	1902/03
Plymouth	30pts	30-0	H	1902/03
Abertillery	11pts	14-3	H	1933/34
London Welsh	21pts	26-5	H	1902/03
Newport	3pts	3-0	H	1906/07
Swansea	1pt	9-8	A	1923/24
Cardiff	7pts	7-0	H	1932/33
Cross Keys	11pts	17-6	H	1911/12
Nuneaton	12pts	12-0	A	1912/13
Glamorgan Wanderers	26pts	26-0	H	1934/35

Seasons With 20+ Games Played In Order of Highest Win Rate

Season	P	W	D	L	Results Unknown	For	Against	Tries Scored	Win Rate %
1895/96	31	26	2	3	0	278+	63+	74+	87.10
1894/95	22	17	3	2	0	226+	39+	58+	84.09
1902/03	28	22	3	3	0	353+	59+	88+	83.93
1934/35	28	22	3	3	0	386	82	79+	83.93
1896/97	37	27	5	5	0	528	84	131+	79.73
1932/33	33	25	2	6	0	363	120	78+	78.79
1921/22	52	37	5	10	0	591	198	26+	75.96
1904/05	27	20	1	6	0	242	80	68	75.93
1899/1900	34	24	3	7	0	351	124	93+	75.00
1930/31	26	17	2	7	0	192+	101+	45+	69.23
1931/32	32	21	2	9	0	332	187	56+	68.75
1924/25	29	17	3	8	1	122+	110+	29+	66.07
1900/01	25	14	5	6	0	182	91	51	66.00
1903/04	24	14	3	7	0	127+	70+	32+	64.58

Season	P	W	D	L	Results Unknown	For	Against	Tries Scored	Win Rate %
1911/12	36	20	6	10	0	188	137	19+	63.89
1901/02	26	16	1	9	0	287	142	77	63.46
1922/23	41	22	5	12	2	325+	192+	69+	62.82
1908/09	33	19	3	11	0	125+	138+	33+	62.12
1938/39	44	24	6	14	0	340	226	81	61.36
1936/37	28	15	4	9	0	168	132	40+	60.71
1905/06	30	16	4	10	0	211	137	60	60.00
1913/14	40	21	6	13	0	179+	229+	31+	60.00
1909/10	36	18	7	11	0	200	160	27+	59.72
1906/07	33	18	3	12	0	196+	106+	52+	59.09
1910/11	39	21	3	15	0	179+	124+	18+	57.69
1933/34	26	13	4	9	0	228+	148+	49+	57.69
1898/99	27	13	4	10	0	197	103	53	55.56
1923/24	36	18	4	14	0	270+	157+	57+	55.56
1897/98	37	20	1	16	0	349	216	95	55.41
1907/08	26	13	0	13	0	188	140	52	50.00
1935/36	22	9	1	12	0	143	125	35+	43.18
1912/13	28	10	4	14	0	131	159	26+	42.86
1920/21	27	9	5	13	0	124+	93+	26+	42.59
1925/26	26	9	3	14	0	175	215	38+	40.39
1928/29	30	11	2	17	0	179	277	34+	40.00
1937/38	20	7	2	11	0	84+	194+	14+	40.00
1927/28	23	6	5	12	0	133+	177+	33+	36.96
1929/30	22	5	3	14	0	118	163	25	29.55
1919/20	24	5	4	15	0	49	147	10+	29.17
1926/27	22	4	1	17	0	86+	239+	14+	20.46

The only seasons not included in the above table are those where the total number of known games played was less than 20. These were the seasons from 1875 to 1893/94 inclusive and 1939/40.

<u>Mountain Ash RFC 2nd XV</u>
Aberdare and Merthyr District League Champions 1908/09

Representative Honours

Welsh Internationals

No.	Name	Year(s)	Club(s)	Caps
1	F.M. "Frank" Mills	1892-1896 inc.	Mountain Ash, Swansea & Cardiff	13
2	W.H. "Fred" Millar	1896, 1900 & 1901	Mountain Ash	7
3	W.T. "Will" Osborne	1902 & 1903	Mountain Ash	6
4	A.W. "Wyndham" Jones	1905	Mountain Ash	1
5	E.J.R. "Dick" Thomas	1906, 1908 & 1909	Mountain Ash	4
6	T.F. "Fred" Samuel	1922	Mountain Ash	3
7	T.J. "Tom" Collins	1923	Mountain Ash	1
8	L. "Les" Manfield	1939	Mountain Ash	2
	Total Welsh Caps 1875-1940			37

Other Playing Honours
Les Manfield, Barbarians RFC, 1940

Results v Selected Clubs
1875–1940

Fixtures v Aberavon

Decade	P	W	D	L
1880s	0	0	0	0
1890s	9	4	1	4
1900s	16	4	3	9
1910s	4	0	1	3
1920s	4	1	0	3
1930s	11	3	1	7
Total for 1875-1940	44	12	6	26

Fixtures v Treorky/Treorchy

Decade	P	W	D	L
1880s	0	0	0	0
1890s	10	7	1	2
1900s	19	9	2	8
1910s	7	1	2	4
1920s	10	3	1	6
1930s	11	6	1	4
Total for 1875-1940	57	26	7	24

Fixtures v Pontypridd

Decade	P	W	D	L
1880s	1	1	0	0
1890s	20	16	0	4
1900s	19	16	1	2
1910s	8	4	3	1
1920s	10	5	1	4
1930s	15	9	1	5
Total for 1875-1940	73	51	6	16

Fixtures v Bridgend

Decade	P	W	D	L
1880s	0	0	0	0
1890s	5	5	0	0
1900s	10	7	0	3
1910s	4	1	2	1
1920s	7	4	0	3
1930s	2	1	0	1
Total for 1875-1940	28	18	2	8

Fixtures v Llwynypia

Decade	P	W	D	L
1880s	1	0	0	1
1890s	17	8	4	5
1900s	11	6	4	1
1910s	8	2	2	4
1920s	0	0	0	0
1930s	0	0	0	0
Total for 1875-1940	37	16	10	11

Fixtures v Ebbw Vale

Decade	P	W	D	L
1880s	0	0	0	0
1890s	6	3	1	2
1900s	3	2	1	0
1910s	1	0	0	1
1920s	17	3	2	12
1930s	13	8	2	3
Total for 1875-1940	40	16	6	18

Fixtures v Llanelly

Decade	P	W	D	L
1880s	0	0	0	0
1890s	2	0	0	2
1900s	8	3	2	3
1910s	3	0	0	3
1920s	3	1	1	1
1930s	1	1	0	0
Total for 1875-1940	17	5	3	9

Fixtures v Pontymoile/Pontypool

Decade	P	W	D	L
1880s	2	2	0	0
1890s	13	7	4	2
1900s	8	4	1	3
1910s	1	0	0	1
1920s	16	1	4	11
1930s	8	2	0	6
Total for 1875-1940	48	16	9	23

Fixtures v Neath

Decade	P	W	D	L
1880s	0	0	0	0
1890s	7	3	2	2
1900s	3	2	0	1
1910s	6	1	1	4
1920s	3	1	0	2
1930s	0	0	0	0
Total for 1875-1940	19	7	3	9

Fixtures v Penarth

Decade	P	W	D	L
1880s	1	0	0	1
1890s	1	0	0	1
1900s	15	9	1	5
1910s	9	4	0	5
1920s	12	7	0	5
1930s	12	5	1	6
Total for 1875-1940	50	25	2	23

Fixtures v Maesteg

Decade	P	W	D	L
1880s	0	0	0	0
1890s	1	1	0	0
1900s	16	9	2	5
1910s	10	5	0	5
1920s	10	3	1	6
1930s	15	7	2	6
Total for 1875-1940	52	25	5	22

Fixtures v Treherbert

Decade	P	W	D	L
1880s	1	0	0	1
1890s	11	7	1	3
1900s	11	6	1	4
1910s	8	5	1	2
1920s	12	4	3	5
1930s	0	0	0	0
Total for 1875-1940	43	22	6	15

Fixtures v Penygraig

Decade	P	W	D	L
1880s	3	1	2	0
1890s	15	5	3	7
1900s	18	8	2	8
1910s	4	2	1	1
1920s	7	1	3	3
1930s	9	6	2	1
Total for 1875-1940	56	23	13	20

Fixtures v Abertillery

Decade	P	W	D	L
1880s	0	0	0	0
1890s	0	0	0	0
1900s	4	1	0	3
1910s	8	1	0	7
1920s	13	1	3	9
1930s	12	5	3	4
Total for 1875-1940	37	8	6	23

Fixtures v London Welsh

Decade	P	W	D	L
1880s	0	0	0	0
1890s	0	0	0	0
1900s	3	3	0	0
1910s	0	0	0	0
1920s	0	0	0	0
1930s	0	0	0	0
Total for 1875-1940	3	3	0	0

Fixtures v Newport

Decade	P	W	D	L
1880s	0	0	0	0
1890s	1	0	0	1
1900s	1	1	0	0
1910s	0	0	0	0
1920s	0	0	0	0
1930s	0	0	0	0
Total for 1875-1940	2	1	0	1

Fixtures v Tredegar

Decade	P	W	D	L
1880s	0	0	0	0
1890s	1	1	0	0
1900s	2	2	0	0
1910s	0	0	0	0
1920s	4	2	2	0
1930s	1	0	1	0
Total for 1875-1940	8	5	3	0

Fixtures v Cardiff

Decade	P	W	D	L
1880s	0	0	0	0
1890s	0	0	0	0
1900s	0	0	0	0
1910s	3	0	0	3
1920s	4	1	0	3
1930s	2	1	0	1
Total for 1875-1940	9	2	0	7

Fixtures v Swansea

Decade	P	W	D	L
1880s	0	0	0	0
1890s	2	0	0	2
1900s	3	0	0	3
1910s	2	0	0	2
1920s	3	1	0	2
1930s	0	0	0	0
Total for 1875-1940	10	1	0	9

Fixtures v Cross Keys

Decade	P	W	D	L
1880s	0	0	0	0
1890s	0	0	0	0
1900s	1	0	0	1
1910s	4	1	0	3
1920s	16	6	1	9
1930s	10	3	2	5
Total for 1875-1940	31	10	3	18

Fixtures v Glamorgan Wanderers

Decade	P	W	D	L
1880s	0	0	0	0
1890s	0	0	0	0
1900s	0	0	0	0
1910s	0	0	0	0
1920s	14	8	0	6
1930s	17	14	0	3
Total for 1875-1940	31	22	0	9

Fixtures v Leicester

Decade	P	W	D	L
1880s	0	0	0	0
1890s	3	1	0	2
1900s	0	0	0	0
1910s	0	0	0	0
1920s	0	0	0	0
1930s	0	0	0	0
Total for 1875-1940	3	1	0	2

Fixtures v Bath

Decade	P	W	D	L
1880s	0	0	0	0
1890s	0	0	0	0
1900s	8	6	1	1
1910s	4	1	1	2
1920s	2	1	1	0
1930s	0	0	0	0
Total for 1875-1940	14	8	3	3

Fixtures v Plymouth

Decade	P	W	D	L
1880s	0	0	0	0
1890s	5	2	0	3
1900s	7	2	0	5
1910s	0	0	0	0
1920s	0	0	0	0
1930s	0	0	0	0
Total for 1875-1940	12	4	0	8

Fixtures v Bridgwater & Albion

Decade	P	W	D	L
1880s	0	0	0	0
1890s	5	3	1	1
1900s	1	1	0	0
1910s	1	0	0	1
1920s	3	2	0	1
1930s	0	0	0	0
Total for 1875-1940	10	6	1	3

Fixtures v Nuneaton

Decade	P	W	D	L
1880s	0	0	0	0
1890s	0	0	0	0
1900s	0	0	0	0
1910s	4	3	0	1
1920s	1	1	0	0
1930s	0	0	0	0
Total for 1875-1940	5	4	0	1

Fixtures v Cinderford

Decade	P	W	D	L
1880s	0	0	0	0
1890s	2	1	0	1
1900s	0	0	0	0
1910s	2	1	0	1
1920s	0	0	0	0
1930s	3	2	1	0
Total for 1875-1940	7	4	1	2

Fixtures v Coventry

Decade	P	W	D	L
1880s	0	0	0	0
1890s	0	0	0	0
1900s	0	0	0	0
1910s	2	0	1	1
1920s	0	0	0	0
1930s	0	0	0	0
Total for 1875-1940	2	0	1	1

Reflections On The Era 1875-1940

What a great era of rugby the years up to 1940 were for Mountain Ash RFC, and what a legacy it bequeathed on all those who followed it.

Of the 1,200+ known games played, nearly 61% of them were won, which was quite a feat over such a long time against strong opposition. Of the forty seasons listed where at least twenty games were played, twenty two had a win rate of 60% or more and only ten were below 50% – six of those being in the 40% range – which was impressive stuff. The Old Firm were a proud team, competitive, and hard to beat throughout, and well capable of mixing it with the best in the good seasons, despite losing some talented players to the paid ranks of the Northern Union on a regular basis.

Pride shone through in those that wore the black and amber jersey and especially in the ultra-competitive Glamorgan League, where the Old Firm were always in the running, winning the Championship six times in total, and the Cup once in the "double" winning season of 1913/14. They were always one of *the* teams a potential champion Club had to beat to have any chance of winning the coveted trophy.

Outside of the League, the mightier the opposition the merrier is the impression Mount XVs gave as they took on Wales' best with relish, as was the case in 1922/23 and 1932/33 when beating the reigning Welsh champions Cross Keys and Pontypool respectively. And they didn't mind playing the best away from home either, at any time of the year, with some visits made to Leicester, Northampton, Bridgwater & Albion, Plymouth, Llanelli, Coventry and Bath over Christmas, which was far from an easy option back then, with the lack of time off from work, the travelling involved and the cost of it; but go they did, and in the cases of Llanelli and Bath, conquered. The Old Firm were attractive visitors back then, their match at Bath on Boxing Day being a regular fixture between 1905 and 1912.

All of Wales' strongest Clubs, be they "first" or "second class", were beaten during this era, including the "big four" of Cardiff, Llanelli, Newport, and Swansea. And not only were they all beaten in Mountain Ash, there were away wins as well except at Cardiff, Aberavon, and Newport, the latter of which the Old Firm never had the chance of playing.

Not many valley teams can say they've beaten a national XV but Mountain Ash RFC did exactly that in 1902/03 when the first touring Canadian national XV was convincingly beaten 28-0. In addition, at the end of the season wing Reuben Carpenter added to the Club's growing reputation when he became the joint highest try scorer in a season in Wales with 42 tries.

On top of all this, there were eight players who played for the Club and were capped by Wales. Seven of these – Fred Millar, Will Osborne, Wyndham Jones, Dick Thomas, Fred Samuel, Tom Collins and Les Manfield – were capped while playing for the Club, and gained 24 caps in total, while Frank Mills, who gained 13, started with the Old Firm and played for a combination of Swansea, Cardiff and Mountain Ash throughout his International career. Millar, Osborne, Wyndham Jones and Dick Thomas were all capped in the "Golden Era" of Welsh rugby and were all part of Welsh XVs which won the Triple Crown, and Thomas, two Grand Slams as well. Fred Samuel was part of the Welsh team that won the Championship in 1922, and Les Manfield was in the Welsh team that finished joint top of the Championship table with England and Ireland in 1939.

All the above contributed to two "Golden Eras" for the Club which covered twenty seasons in all when the Old Firm were up there competing with the best of them.

It shouldn't be forgotten either that it wasn't only on the field of play that Mountain Ash RFC stepped up to the mark. Week in, week out, season after season, come what may, the Club fulfilled its fixtures without fail. This doesn't seem a great achievement nowadays, but back then when some desperate economic times were encountered, some Clubs failed to keep the wolf from their door and had to stop playing. Over the 65 years covered here, the Mount Club was never in a strong financial position, but kept going and maintained its high standard for the most part due to several unsung heroes. What a contribution Messrs Herbert George, Ted McGregor and David Harris, the Chairman, Secretary and Treasurer respectively of the pre-First World War years made to clear the Club's £180 debt before rugby could resume in 1919/20; or the financial support given by Mr Shad Lewis, who was Club Chairman from 1926 to 1937, which helped keep the Club afloat in the tough economic times of the 1920s and 30s.

Not only was the show kept on the road, there were also four visits to France between 1912 and 1925, playing Pau, Bayonne, Clermont, Stade Francais, Périgueux and Brive, and frequent trips were also made into England at Christmas and Easter to play such Clubs as Plymouth, Bath, Bridgwater & Albion, Nuneaton, Coventry, Leicester, and Devonport Albion. And last but not least, a grandstand was built at the Rec in 1922. How all of this was paid for back then when money was tight speaks volumes for the commitment and pride the people involved in running the Club had.

Perhaps the best way to finish this account and of illustrating this great era of rugby is by listing some of the Old Firm's most famous victories during these years:

<u>10 Famous Mount Wins</u>
<u>1875-1940</u>

	Season	Opposition	Venue	Score	Comments
1	1896/97	Leicester	H	11-0	It may have been long ago, but how can a victory over a Club like Leicester Tigers be ignored?
2	1900/01	Llanelly	A	11-3	A win at Llanelly's legendary former ground, Stradey Park, over Christmas 1900 just had to be included.
3	1902/03	Canada	H	28-0	A win over an International XV touring side doesn't happen very often and just had to be included.
4	1905/06	Bath	A	16-13	A win at Bath on Boxing Day 1905! How could that be ignored?
5	1906/07	Newport	H	3-0	A win over a strong Newport team – one of the "big four" Clubs of Welsh rugby – had to be included.
6	1913/14	Neath	H	5-3	The Old Firm finished the season in style, beating the Welsh All Blacks and then Maesteg a week later in the Glamorgan Times Cup Final to record a prestigious "double" of the Glamorgan League and Cup.
7	1922/23	Cardiff	H	11-5	The Old Firm's first ever win over Cardiff in a match that opened the new grandstand at the Rec just had to be included.
8	1922/23	Swansea	A	9-8	This was the first, and to date, the only win over Swansea, which completed victories over all of the "big four" of Welsh rugby.
9	1932/33	Pontypool	H	16-3	As well as a hat-trick of Glamorgan League championships, this convincing win over the reigning Welsh Champions just had to be included.
10	1938/39	Aberavon	H	13-0	Aberavon had always been a tough Club to beat, and this convincing win, the 11th game unbeaten of an 18 match unbeaten run, showed how good the Mount team was.

A "second class" Club Mountain Ash RFC may have been regarded as, but boy, did it have some "first class" moments. Overall, it wasn't bad for a South Wales valleys Club, was it?

Martyn Ham,
Author & Lifelong Mount Fan

Milton Keynes UK
Ingram Content Group UK Ltd.
UKHW050648260924
448821UK00006B/46